THE
CAMBRIDGE EDITION OF
THE LETTERS AND WORKS OF
D. H. LAWRENCE

THE WORKS OF D. H. LAWRENCE

EDITORIAL BOARD

INTRODUCTIONS AND REVIEWS

D. H. LAWRENCE

EDITED BY
N. H. REEVE
AND
JOHN WORTHEN

CAMBRIDGE
UNIVERSITY PRESS

PUBLISHED BY THE PRESS SYNDICATE OF THE UNIVERSITY OF CAMBRIDGE
The Pitt Building, Trumpington Street, Cambridge, United Kingdom

CAMBRIDGE UNIVERSITY PRESS
The Edinburgh Building, Cambridge, CB2 2RU, UK
40 West 20th Street, New York, NY 10011–4211, USA
477 Williamstown Road, Port Melbourne, VIC 3207, Australia
Ruiz de Alarcón 13, 28014 Madrid, Spain
Dock House, The Waterfront, Cape Town 8001, South Africa
http://www.cambridge.org

Printed in the United Kingdom at the University Press, Cambridge

Typeface EhrhardtMT 10/12 pt. *System* LATEX 2ε [TB]

A catalogue record for this book is available from the British Library

Library of Congress Cataloguing in Publication data
Lawrence, D. H. (David Herbert), 1885–1930.
Introductions and reviews / D. H. Lawrence; edited by N. H. Reeve and John Worthen.
p. cm. – (The Cambridge edition of the letters and works of D. H. Lawrence)
Includes bibliographical references and index.
ISBN 0 521 83584 4
1. Literature – History and criticism. 2. Books – Reviews. I. Reeve, N. H.,
1953– II Worthen, John. III. Title
PR6023.A93A6 2004b
809 – dc22 2004049221

ISBN 0 521 83584 4 hardback

CONTENTS

SECTION B INTRODUCTIONS TO TRANSLATIONS

SECTION C REVIEWS

GENERAL EDITOR'S PREFACE

D. H. Lawrence is one of the great writers of the twentieth century – yet the texts of his writings, whether published during his lifetime or since, are, for the most part, textually corrupt. The extent of the corruption is remarkable; it can derive from every stage of composition and publication. We know from study of his MSS that Lawrence was a careful writer, though not rigidly consistent in matters of minor convention. We know also that he revised at every possible stage. Yet he rarely if ever compared one stage with the previous one, and overlooked the errors of typists or copyists. He was forced to accept, as most authors are, the often stringent house-styling of his printers, which overrode his punctuation and even his sentence-structure and paragraphing. He sometimes overlooked plausible printing errors. More important, as a professional author living by his pen, he had to accept, with more or less good will, stringent editing by a publisher's reader in his early days, and at all times the results of his publishers' timidity. So the fear of Grundyish disapproval, or actual legal action, led to bowdlerisation or censorship from the very beginning of his career. Threats of libel suits produced other changes. Sometimes a publisher made more changes than he admitted to Lawrence. On a number of occasions, in dealing with American and British publishers, Lawrence produced texts for both which were not identical. Then there were extraordinary lapses like the occasion when a typist turned over two pages of MS at once, and the result happened to make sense. This whole story can be reconstructed from the introductions to the volumes in this edition; cumulatively they will form a history of Lawrence's writing career.

The Cambridge edition aims to provide texts which are as close as can now be determined to those he would have wished to see printed. They have been established by a rigorous collation of extant manuscripts and typescripts, proofs and early printed versions; they restore the words, sentences, even whole pages omitted or falsified by editors or compositors; they are freed from printing-house conventions which were imposed on Lawrence's style; and interference on the part of frightened publishers has been eliminated. Far from doing violence to the texts Lawrence would have wished to see published, editorial intervention is essential to recover them. Though we have to accept that some cannot now be recovered in their entirety because early states have not survived, we must be glad that so much evidence remains. Paradoxical as it may seem, the outcome of this recension will be texts which differ, often radically and certainly frequently, from those seen by the author himself.

Editors have adopted the principle that the most authoritative form of the text is to be followed, even if this leads sometimes to a 'spoken' or a 'manuscript' rather than a 'printed' style. We have not wanted to strip off one house-styling in order to impose another. Editorial discretion may be allowed in order to regularise Lawrence's sometimes wayward spelling and punctuation in accordance with his most frequent practice in a particular text. A detailed record of these and other decisions on textual matters, together with the evidence on which they are based, will be found in the Textual apparatus which records variant readings in manuscripts, typescripts and proofs and printed variants in forms of the text published in Lawrence's lifetime. We do not record posthumous corruptions, except where first publication was posthumous. Significant MS readings may be found in the occasional Explanatory note.

In each volume, the editor's Introduction relates the contents to Lawrence's life and to his other writings; it gives the history of composition of the text in some detail, for its intrinsic interest, and because this history is essential to the statement of editorial principles followed. It provides an account of publication and reception which will be found to contain a good deal of hith-erto unknown information. Where appropriate, Appendices make available extended draft manuscript readings of significance, or important material, sometimes unpublished, associated with a particular work.

Though Lawrence is a twentieth-century writer and in many respects remains our contemporary, the idiom of his day is not invariably intelligi-ble now, especially to the many readers who are not native speakers of British English. His use of dialect is another difficulty, and further barriers to full understanding are created by now obscure literary, historical, political or other references and allusions. On these occasions Explanatory notes are supplied by the editor; it is assumed that the reader has access to a good general dictionary and that the editor need not gloss words or expressions that may be found in it. Where Lawrence's letters are quoted in editorial matter, the reader should assume that his manuscript alone is the source of eccentricities of phrase or spelling.

ACKNOWLEDGEMENTS

An award of research leave funded by the Arts and Humanities Research Board
made possible the completion of this edition.

We are grateful in particular to the following for their encouragement,
advice and support: Michael Black, James T. Boulton, Andrew Brown and
Lindeth Vasey.

We are also grateful to the staff of Cambridge University Press (especially
to Linda Bree); to Gerald Pollinger; to Anthony Rota; to Emily Balmages,
Madhuri Sudan, Jessica Lemieux and the staff of the Bancroft Library, The
University of California at Berkeley; Carol Turley and the staff of the Library
of the University of California, Los Angeles; Lori Curtis, Gina Minks and the
staff of the Department of Special Collections, McFarlin Library, University
of Tulsa; Tracy Fleischman and the staff of the Harry Ransom Research
Center at the University of Texas at Austin; Ruth Carruth and the staff of
the Beinecke Library at Yale University; Thelma J. Todd and the staff of
the Library of Congress; Nancy Brown Martinez and the staff of the Center
for Southwest Research, General Library, The University of New Mexico;
Dorothy Johnston and the staff of the Department of Manuscripts, University
of Nottingham; Nina Whitcombe and the staff of the Library of the University
of Wales, Swansea; the staff of the Rare Books Room at the University Library,
Cambridge; the staff of the British Library Newspaper Library.

We also wish to thank the following for their particular contributions:
Keith Cushman, David Ellis, Andrew Harrison, Malcolm Jones, Patrick
McGuinness, See-Young Park, Paul Poplawski, Glyn Pursglove, Victoria
Reid, Jonathan Smith, M. Wynn Thomas, John Turner, Geoff Wall, Geoffrey
Ward and Rhys Williams. Peggy Hung helped enormously by checking the
Magnus manuscript. Louise E. Wright saved us from many errors in connec-
tion with the life and times of Maurice Magnus, was unstintingly generous in
sharing her research with us, and provided the text of Appendix IX.

CHRONOLOGY

11 September 1885	Born in Eastwood, Nottinghamshire
September 1898–July 1901	Pupil at Nottingham High School
1902–1908	Pupil teacher; student at University College, Nottingham
7 December 1907	First publication: 'A Prelude', in *Nottinghamshire Guardian*
October 1908	Appointed as teacher at Davidson Road School, Croydon
November 1909	Publishes five poems in *English Review*
3 December 1910	Engagement to Louie Burrows; broken off on 4 February 1912
9 December 1910	Death of his mother, Lydia Lawrence
19 January 1911	*The White Peacock* published in New York (20 January in London)
20 September 1911	Asked by Austin Harrison to write reviews for *English Review*
November 1911	Writes first review, of *Contemporary German Poetry*, for *English Review* (published same month)
19 November 1911	Ill with pneumonia; resigns his teaching post on 28 February 1912
December 1911	Writes reviews of *The Oxford Book of German Verse* and *The Minnesingers*, for *English Review* (published January 1912)
March 1912	Meets Frieda Weekley; they leave for Metz and Germany on 3 May
23 May 1912	*The Trespasser*
September 1912–March 1913	At Gargnano, Lago di Garda, Italy
February 1913	*Love Poems and Others*
by 24 February 1913	Writes review of *Georgian Poetry*, for *Rhythm* (published March)
29 May 1913	*Sons and Lovers*

June–August 1913	In England
by 17 June 1913	Writes 'German Books': review of *Der Tod in Venedig*, by Thomas Mann, for the *Blue Review* (published July)
August–September 1913	In Germany and Switzerland
1 April 1914	*The Widowing of Mrs. Holroyd* (New York)
July 1914–December 1915	In London, Buckinghamshire and Sussex
13 July 1914	Marries Frieda Weekley in London
26 November 1914	*The Prussian Officer and Other Stories*
30 September 1915	*The Rainbow*; suppressed by court order on 13 November
30 December 1915–15 October 1917	In Cornwall
1 June 1916	*Twilight in Italy*
July 1916	*Amores*
October 1917–November 1919	In London, Berkshire and Derbyshire
26 November 1917	*Look! We Have Come Through!*
October 1918	*New Poems*
by 15 September 1919	Writes 'Foreword' to *All Things Are Possible*
November 1919–February 1922	To mainland Italy, then Capri and Sicily
20 November 1919	*Bay*
March 1920	*All Things Are Possible* published by Secker
9 November 1920	*Women in Love* published (expensive and limited edition) in New York by Seltzer (in England by Secker, normal trade edition, on 10 June 1921)
25 November 1920	*The Lost Girl*
February 1921	*Movements in European History*
4 April 1921	Asks Curtis Brown to act as his English agent
10 May 1921	*Psychoanalysis and the Unconscious* (New York)
5 November 1921	Receives invitation from Mabel Dodge Sterne to stay in Taos, New Mexico

by 18 November 1921	Begins writing introduction to *Dregs* (subsequently *Memoirs of the Foreign Legion*), by Maurice Magnus; finishes late January 1922
9 December 1921	*Tortoises* (New York)
12 December 1921	*Sea and Sardinia* (New York)
26 February 1922	Departs from Naples with Frieda for Ceylon, en route to western hemisphere
March 1922	Completes translation of *Mastro-don Gesualdo*, by Giovanni Verga, and writes 'Introductory Note'
13 March 1922	Arrives in Ceylon; leaves for Australia on 24 April
14 April 1922	*Aaron's Rod* (New York)
4 May 1922	Arrives in Perth; in Sydney on 27 May
11 August 1922	Sails from Sydney for San Francisco on the *Tahiti*, via Wellington, Rarotonga and Tahiti
4 September 1922	Lands at San Francisco; reaches Taos 11 September
12 October 1922	Writes review of *Fantazius Mallare*, by Ben Hecht, in the form of a letter to Willard Johnson
23 October 1922	*Fantasia of the Unconscious* (New York)
24 October 1922	*England, My England and Other Stories* (New York)
December 1922	Review of *Fantazius Mallare* published in the *Laughing Horse*, no. 4
1 December 1922	Moves with Frieda to Del Monte Ranch north of Taos
mid December 1922	Receives Stuart Sherman's book *Americans*; completes review by 16 January (published in *The Dial*, May 1923)
late December 1922–early Jan. 1923	Visits of Seltzers and Mountsier at Del Monte Ranch
3 February 1923	Severs connection with Mountsier
25 February 1923	Accepts Secker's terms for publication of *Studies in Classic American Literature* in England

March 1923	*The Ladybird, The Fox, The Captain's Doll* (London)
March–April 1923	Leaves New Mexico and settles in Chapala, Mexico
9 July 1923	Leaves Mexico; arrives in New York on 19 July
22 August 1923	Leaves New York en route to trip through south-western USA and Mexico
27 August 1923	*Studies in Classic American Literature* (final version) published in USA by Seltzer
September 1923	*Kangaroo*
by mid-September 1923	Writes review of *A Second Contemporary Verse Anthology* (published in *New York Evening Post Literary Review*, 29 September)
9 October 1923	*Birds, Beasts and Flowers*
December 1923–March 1924	In England, France and Germany
March 1924–September 1925	In New and Old Mexico
by August 1924	Writes 'Note on Giovanni Verga' for his translation of *Novelle Rusticane* (*Little Novels of Sicily*)
28 August 1924	*The Boy in the Bush* (with Mollie Skinner)
1 September 1924	Writes 'The Bad Side of Books', introduction to *A Bibliography of the Writings of D. H. Lawrence*
10 September 1924	Death of his father, Arthur John Lawrence
1 October 1924	*Memoirs of the Foreign Legion*, by 'M. M.', published by Secker
February 1925	Replaces Seltzer with Alfred A. Knopf as US publisher
March 1925	*Little Novels of Sicily* published by Seltzer
14 May 1925	*St. Mawr together with the Princess*
23 June 1925	*A Bibliography of the Writings of D. H. Lawrence* published by Centaur Books
by mid-October 1925	Writes reviews of *Hadrian the Seventh* and *Saïd the Fisherman*
by 21 November 1925	Writes review of *The Origins of Prohibition*
December 1925	Review of *Hadrian the Seventh* published in *Adelphi*

by 5 January 1928	Writes introduction to *The Mother*
February 1928	*Cavalleria Rusticana* published by Cape
March 1928	*Mastro-don Gesualdo* published by Cape
April 1928	*The Mother* published by Cape
1 May 1928	Completes 'Chaos in Poetry', introduction to *Chariot of the Sun*
24 May 1928	*The Woman Who Rode Away and Other Stories*
June 1928–March 1930	In Switzerland and, principally, in France
Late June 1928	*Lady Chatterley's Lover* privately published (Florence)
by end July 1928	Writes review for *Vogue*, of *The Station, England and the Octopus, Comfortless Memory* and *Ashenden* (published 8 August)
September 1928	*Collected Poems*
by 24 February 1929	Writes introduction to Edward Dahlberg's novel, later given the title *Bottom Dogs*
August 1929	Writes 'Foreword' to *The Story of Doctor Manente*
September 1929	*The Escaped Cock* (Paris)
November 1929	*Bottom Dogs* published by Putnams
November 1929	*The Story of Doctor Manente* published by Orioli
by 7 November 1929	Writes review of *Fallen Leaves*; published in *Everyman*, 23 January 1930
December 1929	'Chaos in Poetry' published in *Echanges*
by 20 January 1930	Writes introduction to *The Grand Inquisitor*
by end February 1930	Writes review of *Art-Nonsense and Other Essays*
2 March 1930	Dies at Vence, Alpes Maritimes, France
July 1930	*The Grand Inquisitor* published by Elkin Mathews and Marrot
October 1933	Review of *Art-Nonsense and Other Essays* published in the *Book Collector's Quarterly*

CUE-TITLES

A. Manuscript locations

NWU	Northwestern University
UCB	University of California at Berkeley
UCLA	University of California at Los Angeles
UN	University of Nottingham
UNM	University of New Mexico
UT	University of Texas at Austin
UTul	University of Tulsa
YU	Yale University

B. Works by Lawrence

(The place of publication, here and throughout, is London unless otherwise stated.)

Apocalypse   D. H. Lawrence. *Apocalypse and the Writings on Revelation*. Ed. Mara Kalnins. Cambridge: Cambridge University Press, 1979.

Hardy   D. H. Lawrence. *Study of Thomas Hardy and Other Essays*. Ed. Bruce Steele. Cambridge: Cambridge University Press, 1985.

Letters, i.   James T. Boulton, ed. *The Letters of D. H. Lawrence*. Volume I. Cambridge: Cambridge University Press, 1979.

Letters, ii.   George J. Zytaruk and James T. Boulton, eds. *The Letters of D. H. Lawrence*. Volume II. Cambridge: Cambridge University Press, 1981.

Letters, iii.   James T. Boulton and Andrew Robertson, eds. *The Letters of D. H. Lawrence*. Volume III. Cambridge: Cambridge University Press, 1984.

Letters, iv.   Warren Roberts, James T. Boulton and Elizabeth Mansfield, eds. *The Letters of D. H. Lawrence*. Volume IV. Cambridge: Cambridge University Press, 1987.

Letters, v.   James T. Boulton and Lindeth Vasey, eds. *The Letters of D. H. Lawrence*. Volume V. Cambridge: Cambridge University Press, 1989.

Letters, vi.	James T. Boulton and Margaret H. Boulton with Gerald M. Lacy, eds. *The Letters of D. H. Lawrence*. Volume VI. Cambridge: Cambridge University Press, 1991.
Letters, vii.	Keith Sagar and James T. Boulton, eds. *The Letters of D. H. Lawrence*. Volume VII. Cambridge: Cambridge University Press, 1993.
Letters, viii.	James T. Boulton, ed. *The Letters of D. H. Lawrence*. Volume VIII. Cambridge: Cambridge University Press, 2001.
MMM	D. H. Lawrence. *Memoir of Maurice Magnus*. Ed. Keith Cushman. Santa Rosa: Black Sparrow Press, 1987.
Phoenix	Edward D. McDonald, ed. *Phoenix: The Posthumous Papers of D. H. Lawrence*. New York: Viking, 1936.
Plays	D. H. Lawrence. *The Plays*. Ed. Hans-Wilhelm Schwarze and John Worthen. Cambridge: Cambridge University Press, 1999.
Poems	D. H. Lawrence. *The Complete Poems*. Ed. Vivian de Sola Pinto and Warren Roberts. 2 vols. Heinemann, 1964.
Reflections	D. H. Lawrence. *Reflections on the Death of a Porcupine and Other Essays*. Ed. Michael Herbert. Cambridge: Cambridge University Press, 1988.
Sketches	D. H. Lawrence. *Sketches of Etruscan Places and Other Italian Essays*. Ed. Simonetta de Filippis. Cambridge: Cambridge University Press, 1992.
Sons and Lovers	D. H. Lawrence. *Sons and Lovers*. Ed. Carl Baron and Helen Baron. Cambridge: Cambridge University Press, 1992.
Studies	D. H. Lawrence. *Studies in Classic American Literature*. Ed. Ezra Greenspan, Lindeth Vasey and John Worthen. Cambridge: Cambridge University Press, 2002.

C.   Other works

Americans	Stuart P. Sherman. *Americans*. New York: Charles Scribner's Sons, 1922.
Anthology	Charles Wharton Stork, ed. *A Second Contemporary Verse Anthology*. New York: E. P. Dutton, 1923.
Art-Nonsense	Eric Gill. *Art-Nonsense and Other Essays*. Cassell Walterson, 1929.

Chariot	Harry Crosby. *Chariot of the Sun*. Paris: Black Sun Press, 1931.
Clissold	H. G. Wells. *The World of William Clissold: A Novel at a New Angle*. Ernest Benn, 1926.
Dying Game	David Ellis. *D. H. Lawrence: Dying Game 1922–1930*. Cambridge: Cambridge University Press, 1998.
Early Years	John Worthen, *D. H. Lawrence: The Early Years 1885–1912*. Cambridge: Cambridge University Press, 1991.
Fallen Leaves	V. V. Rozanov. *Fallen Leaves*. Tr. S. S. Koteliansky. The Mandrake Press, 1929.
Georgian Poetry	Edward Marsh, ed. *Georgian Poetry 1911–12*. The Poetry Bookshop, 1912.
Gifts of Fortune	H. M. Tomlinson. *Gifts of Fortune*. Heinemann, 1926.
Grand Inquisitor	F. M. Dostoevsky, *The Grand Inquisitor*. Tr. S. S. Koteliansky. Elkin Mathews and Marrot, 1930.
Heat	Isa Glenn. *Heat*. New York: Knopf, 1926.
KJB	*The Holy Bible Containing the Old and New Testaments (Authorised King James Version)*
Mémoires	Duc de Lauzun. *Mémoires*. Ed. with intro. by Louis Lacour. Paris, 1858.
Nehls	Edward Nehls, ed. *D. H. Lawrence: A Composite Biography*. 3 vols. Madison: University of Wisconsin Press, 1957–9.
OED2	*The Oxford English Dictionary*. 2nd edn on compact disc. Oxford: Oxford University Press, 1994.
Pedro de Valdivia	R. B. Cunninghame Graham. *Pedro de Valdivia: Conqueror of Chile*. Heinemann, 1926.
Peep Show	Walter Wilkinson. *The Peep Show*. Geoffrey Bles, 1927.
Roberts	Warren Roberts and Paul Poplawski. *A Bibliography of D. H. Lawrence*. 3rd edn. Cambridge: Cambridge University Press, 2001.
Social Basis	Trigant Burrow. *The Social Basis Of Consciousness*. Kegan Paul, 1927.
Solitaria	V. V. Rozanov. *Solitaria and The Apocalypse of Our Times*. Tr. S. S. Koteliansky. Wishart, 1927.

Tedlock E. W. Tedlock, Jr. *The Frieda Lawrence Collection of D. H. Lawrence Manuscripts: A Descriptive Bibliography.* Albuquerque: University of New Mexico Press, 1948.

Triumph to Exile Mark Kinkead-Weekes. *D. H. Lawrence: Triumph to Exile 1912–1922.* Cambridge: Cambridge University Press, 1996

INTRODUCTION

In the case of another writer, a volume such as this might have been a collection of items brought together almost at random: of introductions, reviews and other pieces composed as professional writers normally create them, as part of their everyday practice of earning a living. What makes this collection of Lawrence's work distinctive is that it brings into existence, for the first time, a version of a book which Lawrence himself, less than a year before he died, was asked to put together by the publisher Jonathan Cape.

Cape had for many years been interested in publishing Lawrence. As far back as 1922, he had come close to being the first English publisher of *Studies in Classic American Literature*,[1] and he had been responsible for the publication of three of Lawrence's books in the late 1920s: the first edition of the translation of Verga's *Cavalleria Rusticana* in February 1928, the first English edition of Lawrence's translation of Verga's *Mastro-don Gesualdo* in March 1928, and – rather surprisingly – the first American edition of Lawrence's *Collected Poems* in July 1929. Cape had also taken over the American publication of *Twilight in Italy*. He had first suggested a book of critical work to Lawrence in September 1927, after reading Lawrence's Introduction to *Mastro-don Gesualdo*: 'Reading this introduction makes me wonder whether you will consider assembling in one volume some of your critical studies. I should think you would have enough to make a very attractive volume.'[2] Nothing came of this in 1927, but Cape remained keen to publish whatever of Lawrence's work he could obtain, and in the spring of 1929 he renewed his suggestion. This time, as Lawrence informed his English agent, 'Cape has asked for a book of my literary criticisms and introductory essays, and it would make a good book, and I'll soon have enough' (vii. 218).[3] He was obviously interested in doing it, especially as by that date his strength was barely enough for him to embark on a new book written from scratch. A book compiled from existing materials was

---

[1] *Letters*, iii. 129, 177, 196–8 (*Letters* hereafter usually cited in text and footnotes by volume and page number).

[2] Autograph letter from Jonathan Cape to DHL, 27 September 1927 (UT), p. 1.

[3] DHL's agent was Laurence Pollinger (1898–1976), who at this period worked in the Book Department at Curtis Brown, and who would later represent the Lawrence Estate; see vi. 29 n. 1 and footnote 58 below.

an attractive proposition. Sadly, he did not live to work on it; but it would have been a kind of literary companion to his book of non-literary essays *Assorted Articles*, published posthumously in April 1930 by his usual publisher Martin Secker, from a similar number of previously published magazine pieces.

We cannot now be sure exactly what Lawrence would have included in such a book of critical essays, but its contents would have been very largely drawn from the materials brought together here, along with a few other items.[4] It would have been his second published book of literary criticism, following *Studies in Classic American Literature* of 1923, and some of the critical writing which he did towards the end of his life may well have been undertaken precisely with its compilation in mind. He had, for example, told his agent that he wanted the right to reprint the introduction he had written to Edward Dahlberg's novel *Bottom Dogs* (vii. 218) – obviously one of the items he had ear-marked for the critical book; and in September 1929, while asking his friend Charles Lahr to keep a collection of his articles and stories as they came out, he added – 'Or any *really* interesting criticism too' (vii. 499).[5]

What also makes the collection in this volume unusual is that, although Lawrence was a professional writer, as concerned as any to make his living from his writing, not one of his introductions, forewords and prefaces for the writings of others was written primarily to earn money. Neither were many of his reviews. The greater part of this volume offers a series of insights into Lawrence's very practical way of using his writing to help his friends and acquaintances, and to assist the publication of work in which he himself believed.

Mention should also be made of the fact that Lawrence wrote a surprising number of pieces designed to introduce his own work to the reading public; eighteen in all. These have not been included in this volume, as they belong with the individual works they were written to introduce, and that is where

---

[4] His major critical essay on the novelist John Galsworthy, written in 1927 (see *Hardy* l–liii and 209–20), had been published in the volume *Scrutinies*, ed. Edgell Rickword, as recently as March 1928; DHL might not have been permitted to reprint it himself so soon afterwards. However, he might very well have planned to draw on some or all of the uncollected literary essays he had written in 1925, 'Art and Morality', 'Morality and the Novel', 'Why the Novel Matters' and 'The Novel and the Feelings', only the first two of which had ever reached print, in the *Calendar of Modern Letters*, ii (November 1925), 171–7, and ii (December 1925), 269–74. If he had wanted to go back further still, his 1923 essay 'The Future of the Novel' also remained uncollected (and unpublished in Britain). See *Hardy* xliv–l, 163–8, 171–6, 193–8, 201–5, 151–5. Three other items would have been included in the present volume had they not already appeared in the Cambridge edition of DHL's works: 'Preface to *Black Swans*' (*The Boy in the Bush*, ed. Paul Eggert, Cambridge, 1990, pp. 375–9); 'Introduction to *The Dragon of the Apocalypse* by Frederick Carter' (*Apocalypse* 43–56); and DHL's review of *The Book of Revelation* by Dr. John Oman (*Apocalypse* 39–42).

[5] Charles Lahr (1885–1971), bookseller and publisher, born Germany; see v. 572 n. 1.

they have been (or will be) published. This Introduction will however refer to some of them, where appropriate, in the course of its chronological narrative of the writing of Lawrence's reviews and introductions of other kinds.[6]

The vast majority of the contents of this volume come from the 1920s, with just a handful of reviews dating from before the First World War. There is a long gap in his reviewing between 1913 and 1922, and it is possible that other reviews exist which have not been located or identified – for in the aftermath of the *Rainbow* disaster of November 1915, it is unlikely that any he wrote would have appeared over his own name.[7] But most of Lawrence's writing of this kind was only done when he was able to exert some influence on behalf of those he liked, by writing an introduction or preface for their work, or by reviewing their books himself, and he did not occupy that position until the 1920s. It is also true that, in the last years of his life, writing a brief introduction or review

---

[6] The complete list of such introductions (with their location in the Cambridge edition) is as follows:

Foreword to *Sons and Lovers* 467–73.
Preface to *Touch and Go* (*Plays* 363 8).
'Verse Free and Unfree': Preface to *New Poems* (to appear in *Poems*, ed. Carole Ferrier and Christopher Pollnitz).
Foreword to *Women in Love* (ed. David Farmer, Lindeth Vasey and John Worthen, Cambridge, 1987), pp. 485–6.
Foreword to *Birds, Beasts and Flowers* (by 28 January 1921: see iii. 657 – not extant).
First Foreword to *Aaron's Rod* (by 15 August 1921: see iv. 71 – not extant).
Second Foreword to *Aaron's Rod* (by 22 October 1921: see iv. 104 – not extant).
Foreword to *Fantasia of the Unconscious* (*Psychoanalysis and the Unconscious and Fantasia of the Unconscious*, ed. Bruce Steele, Cambridge, 2004, pp. 51–65).
'Note to *The Crown*' (included in *Reflections* 247–50).
Introductory Note to *Collected Poems* (to appear in *Poems*, ed. Carole Ferrier and Christopher Pollnitz).
Foreword to *Collected Poems* (to appear in *Poems*, ed. Carole Ferrier and Christopher Pollnitz).
'My Skirmish with Jolly Roger' (Introduction to *Lady Chatterley's Lover*, Paris, 1929); extended into 'A Propos of *Lady Chatterley's Lover*' (*Lady Chatterley's Lover*, ed. Michael Squires, Cambridge, 1993, pp. 305–35).
'Introduction to Pictures' (*Late Essays and Articles*, ed. James. T. Boulton, Cambridge, 2004, pp. 168–74).
Introduction to *The Paintings of D. H. Lawrence* (*Late Essays and Articles*, ed. James. T. Boulton, pp. 185–217).
Introduction to *Pansies* (to appear in *Poems*, ed. Carole Ferrier and Christopher Pollnitz).
Foreword to *Pansies* (to appear in *Poems*, ed. Carole Ferrier and Christopher Pollnitz).
Introduction to *Pansies* (Stephensen) (to appear in *Poems*, ed. Carole Ferrier and Christopher Pollnitz).
Section Introductions to *Birds, Beasts and Flowers* (to appear in *Poems*, ed. Carole Ferrier and Christopher Pollnitz).

[7] As late as April 1919, he and Murry (see footnote 10) agreed that DHL's contribution to the *Athenaeum*, 'Whistling of Birds', should appear over the pseudonym 'Grantorto'. His history book for schools, *Movements in European History*, was published in February 1921 by Oxford University Press under the name of Laurence H. Davidson. See *Reflections* xli–xlii and n. 95, and *Movements in European History*, ed. Philip Crumpton (Cambridge, 1989), p. xxiii.

demanded far less of him than (for example) writing a short story, and it is not surprising to find that his last recorded piece of writing should have been a book review (of Eric Gill's *Art-Nonsense and Other Essays*), written while he sat up in bed in the Ad Astra sanatorium in Vence, only a short while before he died. But more than once he proved able, in the last decade of his writing career, to help into print something which, without his advocacy, would have remained unpublished. Not all his friends are represented here, though many will be mentioned in this Introduction, but this volume stands as a testament to the people he wanted to help, and thought especially worth helping.

The piece in every sense the most distinguished in this volume, as well as the longest – although not a work of literary criticism – demonstrates the operation of friendship in two different ways. Lawrence wrote his Introduction to Maurice Magnus's book *Dregs*,[8] as he himself later stated, 'To discharge an obligation I do not admit' (v. 396) – that is, to earn money owing to Magnus's Maltese friend Michael Borg, which Borg had asked Lawrence to help him recover by getting the dead man's surviving writing into print. Lawrence pursued the problems of its publication for almost three years, in what was, eventually, a successful attempt to have Borg repaid, and also to recover the money which he himself had lent to Magnus. But the piece also stands as Lawrence's longest and most compelling piece of writing about another person. Magnus was a man whom he both liked and disliked, but also one who touched him deeply in ways he could not forget. The Introduction was written, and in the end published, not just to pay a man's debts, or even to help Michael Borg, but to commemorate Lawrence's own feelings towards Magnus; it allowed him to write at length about Magnus's character – in some ways so similar to, in others so different from, Lawrence's own.

This volume also offers an insight into Lawrence as translator: a role demonstrating a very intimate kind of relationship with the writing of those he admired. The items in section B are brought together as Lawrence's ways of introducing and preparing his reader for his own translations from the Italian; the very first item in section A shows him introducing a volume of translations from the Russian, translations he had himself corrected throughout as an act of friendship.

1911–1913: Starting a Literary Career

It is perhaps surprising to discover that, in the middle of his enormous productivity in other genres, Lawrence also reviewed at least thirty books in the

---

[8] Posthumously published as *Memoirs of the Foreign Legion* (1924).

course of his writing life.[9] Surprising, since in 1913 he seems to have decided that, in comparison with someone like his friend John Middleton Murry, he was not really a literary critic; in a letter to Murry of 30 August 1913 he remarked: '– I liked your review of those poets. You can do it jolly well. I wish I could' (viii. 7, and n. 1; Murry must have sent him a copy of his review of John Helston, W. H. Davies and Arthur Symons, which would appear in the *Daily News* on 12 November 1913).[10] But back in 1911, at the very start of his literary career, needing all the experience and reputation that he could obtain, Lawrence had been more than happy to review whatever was offered him. Ford Madox Hueffer had been his crucial means of introduction to serious publication in the *English Review* in 1909, and Hueffer had printed poems by him as well as accepting a story for publication.[11] When Hueffer left the magazine in February 1910, Lawrence was one of his significant legacies to his successor as editor, Austin Harrison, and Harrison continued to print Lawrence's poems and short stories.[12] In the course of 1911, Lawrence became increasingly determined to embark on a full-time career as a writer, and it is probably not an accident that, on 20 September 1911, he should have been invited out to dinner by Harrison, followed by a visit to the theatre. Lawrence wrote to his fiancée Louie Burrows about the results of this socialising: 'Harrison is very friendly. He suggests that I do a bit of reviewing for the *English*. I think I shall. He bids me select from the forthcoming books one I should like to review. What shall it be?' (i. 304–5).[13] We do not know if Louie gave him the advice he asked for, or if his question were merely rhetorical, but the almost immediate result of Harrison's offer was Lawrence's review of *Contemporary German Poetry*, an anthology edited and translated by the energetic young German scholar Jethro Bithell; a review which was printed in the November 1911 issue of the *English Review*, and which Lawrence presumably wrote during the previous month. It appeared anonymously, the usual practice of the *English Review*, and is only identifiable today by the coincidence of a remark in a letter which Lawrence wrote to his sister – 'There is a review by me in

---

9 In addition to the books he is known to have reviewed, he expressed interest in reviewing, in August 1923, some Swedish stories (iv. 494), but nothing apparently survives to show whether he did or not. In 1925 he was waiting for a recent volume by Robinson Jeffers to come, with a view to reviewing it for the *New York Herald Tribune Books*, and he also mentioned his interest in doing *Other Provinces* by Carl van Doren (the husband of the *Herald Tribune* books editor, see footnote 88 below), but so far as we know he did neither (v. 358).

10 John Middleton Murry (1889–1957), journalist and critic; see below, pp. xxix–xxx and ii. 31 n. 6.

11 Ford Madox Hueffer, later Ford (1873–1939), novelist, poet and editor; see i. 138 n. 1.

12 Austin Harrison (1873–1928), editor of the *English Review* until 1923; see i. 152 n. 4.

13 Louisa ('Louie') Burrows (1888–1962); see i. 29 n. 3.

the *English* of this month' (i. 324) – and the fact that we know that a book which he mentions at the start of his review (*Contemporary Belgian Poetry*) was in his possession on 10 November (i. 325).[14] But Lawrence had clearly impressed either Harrison or the reviews editor with his capacity to deal with German poetry, and when he had recovered a little from the dangerous illness which struck him down in the second half of November (he had pneumonia and nearly died), he received two more German books for review. On 6 December 1911, while still not allowed to sit up in bed, he wrote to a friend, May Holbrook: 'I am allowed to read. I have got to review a book of German poetry and a book of Minnesinger translations. I like the German poetry, but not the translations' (i. 331).[15] He probably wrote the two reviews while still spending most of his time in bed, which is where he also wrote his story 'The Soiled Rose', perhaps around 23 December (i. 343). The reviews appeared in the January 1912 *English Review*.

There then apparently followed a brief hiatus in his reviewing, until he went abroad at the start of May 1912. Harrison was well aware of Lawrence's need to earn money in any way he could, to support the literary career into which his pneumonia had in effect precipitated him (he never went back to teaching). Presumably thinking that Lawrence was still living in Croydon, Harrison asked to see him on 12 February, 'to know what books I want to review' (i. 365). Lawrence had, however, returned to Eastwood on the 9th, and told his literary mentor, Edward Garnett, 'I'm glad I shan't have to go to him, to have the fount of my eloquence corked up'.[16] At the same time, he asked Garnett, 'But what books *do* I want to review? For the lords sake, tell me', with a hint of desperation which might suggest that he did rather want to keep up his reviewing. It is possible that his decision not to go down to London to see Harrison meant that he was sent nothing for review: certainly, no identifiable reviews by him would appear in the March, April or May numbers of the magazine, although one of his stories had appeared in the February issue.[17] It is also, however, possible that Garnett advised him not to

---

[14] This book had been reviewed in the *English Review*, viii (July 1911), 706–7, and it is remotely possible that DHL was responsible for the review (and so had the book still in his possession). It is, however, much more likely that he only started reviewing following Harrison's invitation in September 1911, and that he had acquired the *Contemporary Belgian Poetry* second-hand in London, or had been loaned (or given) it by Edward Garnett (see footnote 16).

[15] Muriel May Holbrook, née Chambers (1883–1955); see i. 32 n. 2.

[16] Edward Garnett (1868–1937), writer and critic; see Explanatory note to 127:4.

[17] 'Second Best', *English Review*, x (February 1912), 461–9. A review appearing in the March 1912 issue (p. 734) of *Hieronymous Rides*, a novel by Anna Coleman Ladd, is really the only possible candidate as a review by DHL, and there is nothing specific to link DHL with it.

bother with reviewing. Rewriting *Paul Morel* for Heinemann, which was what he had set himself to do in Eastwood that spring, was far more important for his career than reviewing, as well as (potentially) more rewarding financially.

At all events, Lawrence did not return to London until the end of April, when once again he rather ominously reported to Garnett that he would be seeing 'Walter de la Mare, and Harrison, who want to jaw me' (i. 384)[18] – presumably about what he ought to be doing to advance his career as a professional writer. He had actually been in correspondence with Harrison, receiving letters from him on 28 March and 2 and 4 April (i. 377, 381–2), but Harrison had apparently been criticising him for channelling his writing through Edward Garnett, rather than letting the *English Review* have it direct; Garnett may well have offered the *English Review* one or more of the pieces about the coal strike which Lawrence had been writing in Eastwood. Lawrence wrote to Harrison, 'I should be very sorry to think I had lost your favour' (i. 377), but there was clearly now some coolness in Harrison's attitude to him. Lawrence's late April 1912 visit to London was, anyway, the first (and last) he could make to London (or to Harrison) for over a year; on 3 May he left for Germany with Frieda Weekley. Whatever was said at his meeting with Harrison does not seem to have resulted in an offer of more reviewing, or of much space in the magazine for other pieces; the *English Review* accepted just one poem by Lawrence between February 1912 and September 1913.[19] But his reputation as an expert on German poetry survived, and early in 1913 he was asked if he would contribute 'an article on modern German poetry – about 3000 words' (i. 513). He did not feel he could do it – 'I should love doing it myself, if I knew enough about it' (i. 514) – but he passed on the idea to Frieda's sister Else Jaffe (i. 513–14), with several suggestions as to how it might be done. Nevertheless, nothing by her appeared in the *English Review*.

A new contact with literary London, however, made while he was still abroad, led to his writing reviews for a new magazine. At the end of January 1913, Katherine Mansfield[20] obtained his address from Edward Garnett, and wrote asking whether he would let *Rhythm*, the magazine she ran with her partner John Middleton Murry, have a story to print without payment, as they were too poor to pay for it. Lawrence agreed, as an act of kindness to two

---

[18] See Explanatory note to 203:3.
[19] 'Snapdragon', *English Review*, xi (June 1912), 345–8. A sequence of six poems called 'The Schoolmaster' appeared over four issues of the *Saturday Westminster Gazette* instead (11 May, 18 May, 25 May, 1 June). A study of the *English Review* does not suggest that any further reviews by DHL appeared in it: the review of *Contemporary French Poetry* which appeared in the August 1912 issue (pp. 164–5) was almost certainly not written by DHL, and there were no other reviews of German poetry.
[20] See Explanatory note to 371:12.

people who were (as yet) hardly his friends, but on two conditions: first, that they send him a copy of the magazine, which he confessed to never having seen; 'and second, that you let me have something interesting to review for March – German if you like' (i. 508). That, after all, was where his reputation as a reviewer lay, if he had one. Instead, they asked him to review the recently published anthology *Georgian Poetry 1911–12*, edited by Edward Marsh[21] (*Rhythm*'s main financial supporter), who had included one of Lawrence's own poems ('Snapdragon'), and had indeed approached Lawrence directly about using it. Lawrence was aware of the oddity of reviewing a volume in which a poem of his own appeared, and pointed out the fact in the first paragraph of the review. His review appeared, however, in the March issue of *Rhythm*, so he must have set to work very soon; since he almost certainly already had a copy of the book, he may even have started before the review copy arrived from London. He had sent the review to London by 24 February at the latest, when he told a friend 'You should find some of my stuff in March *Rhythm*. It's a daft paper, but the folk seem rather nice' (i. 519). On 5 March he mentioned the idea of sending his review copy of *Georgian Poetry 1911–12* – 'my copy I had from *Rhythm*' – to Arthur McLeod (i. 524).[22]

We know nothing about the circumstances in which he wrote his other review for Mansfield and Murry in the spring of 1913, but it seems probable that they took him up on his offer to review something 'German if you like', and may well have asked him what had recently been published in Germany which might interest English readers. Lawrence and Frieda were back in Germany by the middle of April, living in Irschenhausen near Munich, and he would doubtless have consulted Frieda's sister and brother-in-law Else and Edgar Jaffe (who lived nearby) on the matter. Alternatively, he may simply have been asked to acquire a copy of the recently published novella by Thomas Mann, *Der Tod in Venedig*, and to send *Rhythm* a review of it; almost certainly Else or Edgar would have bought the book. There must, however, be some doubts as to whether Lawrence's German was really good enough at this stage to allow him to read Mann successfully, though he would certainly have been helped by Frieda and Else, and perhaps Edgar. The references to other works by Mann – he quotes *Tonio Kröger*, for example – and to Flaubert show that he had some access to books and material which probably came from the Jaffes. Neither Edgar nor Else can have checked his final draft, however, or

[21] See Explanatory note to 201:2.
[22] Arthur William McLeod (1885–1956), DHL's fellow-teacher and closest friend at Davidson Road School in Croydon; see i. 136 n. 3.

they would have spotted the howler which made both Mann and Aschenbach 'fifty-three' ('drei-und-fünfzig'), while in the novel the character is 'fünf-und-dreissig' (thirty-five): the whole review, indeed, is organised around the belief that Mann himself in 1913 was 'over middle-age' – at the end of the review this becomes 'old' – while 'we are young'. In fact Mann was only thirty-eight, just ten years older than Lawrence.[23] By the time the review was completed, *Rhythm* had collapsed, leaving Murry with debts which he could only settle by selling his house; but, nothing daunted, he and Katherine, helped again by Edward Marsh, started another short-lived periodical, the *Blue Review*, which printed Lawrence's piece in the July number.

That was apparently the end of Lawrence's pre-war reviewing. But even these very earliest reviews show some of the characteristics which marked his later work as a reviewer. He did not, after his first three reviews, review books for either of the two usual reasons: to make money or to acquire the books. Interestingly, not a single copy of a book which we know he reviewed and may have marked up seems to have survived.[24] His reviews for Mansfield and Murry in 1913 were not paid for, and he may very well have borrowed his copy of *Der Tod in Venedig*, while he did not need to review *Georgian Poetry 1911–12* to acquire a copy. His preference was always to review either for particular magazines, or for particular people who wanted him to. We know that he was an omnivorous reader, but he rarely seems to have offered to review books which he had simply picked up, or had read for another reason. In October 1925 he did suggest to the *New York Herald Tribune* that he would like to review *Whom God Hath Sundered* by Oliver Onions – 'I just read it. I'll do that for you, if you wish' (v. 325) – but he was trying to cultivate his connection with the paper at the time. There are many books which we know he read almost as soon as they were published, and which we might well wish that he had reviewed: Lawrence on Virginia Woolf's *The Voyage Out*, for example – which he may well have read before its publication in 1915 (ii. 291) – would have been fascinating, while he read both James Joyce's *Ulysses* and E. M. Forster's *A Passage to India* very soon after they were published (iv. 306, 335, 340, 345, v. 77). But he reviewed none of them; indeed, when Thomas Seltzer (his American publisher)[25] suggested publishing his comments on Joyce (made in a private letter), Lawrence demurred on the grounds that it

---

[23] Andrew Harrison and Richard Hibbit, in 'D. H. Lawrence and Thomas Mann', *Notes and Queries* (December 1996), 443, first pointed out this error; see 207:11, 208:34, 212:9.

[24] He was happy to pass on such copies; see, e.g., his sending his review copy of *The Peep Show* by Walter Wilkinson to his sister Ada on 6 January 1928 (vi. 256).

[25] Thomas Seltzer (1875–1943), journalist and publisher, born Russia; see iii. 390 n. 2.

would not really be fair to Joyce (iv. 355). On the other hand, Lawrence's relationship with literary London was always equivocal, even before the war, and it is not really surprising that he does not appear to have been offered more work as a reviewer.

1918–1921: Post-War

It is appropriate in several ways that the first Introduction in this collection – Lawrence's Foreword to Leo Shestov's *The Apotheosis of Groundlessness*, which was published with the title *All Things are Possible* – should have been so closely linked with his friend S. S. Koteliansky.[26] No fewer than four items in this volume document and illuminate Lawrence's relationship with Kot, as Koteliansky was familiarly known. Lawrence had met him in 1914, just before the outbreak of war, and remained his friend all his life. During the war, Kot had been a loyal supporter, and, although hard pressed himself, had always tried to ensure that Lawrence had money when he most needed it. Lawrence, in turn, did his utmost to promote Kot's career as a translator and expert on Russian writing – and thus his capacity to earn – as soon as he was in a position to do so, at the end of the war. In the case of the philosophical work *The Apotheosis of Groundlessness* by Kot's Ukrainian compatriot Shestov, Kot produced a translation which Lawrence then, to use his own word, 'Englished' (iii. 455); at this stage, Koteliansky's English was picturesque rather than idiomatic.[27] Lawrence refused, however, to allow his own name to appear on the book's title-page as co-translator, and many years later Kot reported to the bookseller Bertram Rota that Lawrence had told him 'it would do damage to his reputation with publishers as a creative writer if he should appear as translator'.[28] Lawrence had actually written to Kot in August 1919 that 'I don't want my name printed as a translator. It won't do for me to appear to dabble in too many things' (iii. 381). But we need be in no doubt that, as is the case with a number of items in this volume, it was Kot's own reputation as a translator (and his ability to earn by his writing, unaided) which Lawrence was really concerned to safeguard, and which dictated such a decision.

[26] Samuel Solomonovich Kotcliansky (1880–1955), translator and editor, born in the Ukraine; see ii. 205 n. 4.

[27] In 1921 Kot rendered a phrase from Ivan Bunin's 'The Gentleman from San Francisco' as 'a little curved peeled-off dog'; after the translation was, as DHL said, 'by me rubbed up into readable English' (iv. 58), the phrase became 'a tiny, cringing, hairless little dog' (see iv. 37 n. 3).

[28] Memorandum by Bertram Rota (1903–66), London bookseller, dated 28 April 1952 (La Z 2/3/1–2, UN). See also vi. 512 n. 1.

On a visit to London at the end of July 1919, Lawrence had stayed with Kot in St John's Wood, and a letter he wrote on 9 August shows that he had already started work rewriting Kot's Shestov translation. Kot appears to have given him his text of Part I, together with section 45 from towards the end of Part II, entitled 'The Russian Spirit', and it seems likely that Lawrence either took it all back to Pangbourne with him or that Kot posted it to him there. He started work not at the beginning of the book but on 'The Russian Spirit', which Koteliansky had presumably drawn to his attention as particularly significant. Lawrence was not, however, especially taken with Shestov: 'I have done a certain amount of the translation – "Apotheosis". I began "Russian Spirit", but either Shestov writes atrociously – I believe he does – or you translate loosely One sentence has nothing to do with the next, so that it seems like jargon . . . he isn't anything wonderful, is he?' (iii. 380). Nonetheless, Lawrence had been helped by Koteliansky throughout the war – he would remark in mid-September that 'I owe you heaven knows how many pounds' (iii. 397) – and he was now determined to assist him. The following day, 10 August 1919, he asked Kot to send him 'Shestov's "Introduction" if possible before – or with Part II. Also will you send me a small Introduction of your own – the facts of Shestov's life and purpose' (iii. 381). This suggests that Lawrence had already formulated the idea of contributing a Foreword to the volume. He was also full of ideas about how the book might be got into print: 'Don't ask the Woolfs – we will make Heinemann or somebody such print the stuff. Also why not print weekly in *The Nation* or *New Statesman*? We must do this' (iii. 381). Since 1917 Leonard and Virginia Woolf had been running the Hogarth Press, but Lawrence was looking for a mainstream publisher to undertake the book, not a small private concern; almost certainly because he distrusted the small press's ability to pay very much.[29] He also suggested that parts of the translation might appear in the *English Review*, while the connection which both he and Kot had with Murry meant that sections of the translation appeared in the magazine of which Murry was now the editor, the *Athenaeum*.[30]

After a while, however, Lawrence became more interested in Shestov. The following week he told Kot, who was worried that he had saddled his friend with an unpleasant chore, that

[29] From his dealings with Cecil Beaumont, DHL had by now some first-hand experience of how ineffective such a publisher might be – and how small the payment and slow the production. See, e.g., iii. 219, 221, 234, 237, 362, 365, 366.

[30] 'The Russian Spirit' (Part II no. 45) was published in the *Athenaeum* (28 November 1919), 1270–1; sections 30, 31, 49, 52, 6, 71, 22, 24 of Part I (in that order) appeared on 2 January 1920, p. 28.

I have done 71. of the Shestov paragraphs – more than half.[31] No, I don't hate doing it – rather like it – only he often irritates me when he will keep on going on about philosophers, and what they do or don't do. One gets sick of the name of philosophers. – But sometimes he blossoms into a kind of pathetic beauty. (iii. 384)

By the end of August – an extremely hot month, so that he did at least some of the translation in the garden at Pangbourne (iii. 521) – Lawrence had finished the job, which finally extended over 157 completely new manuscript pages.[32] He summed up his feelings: 'I do get tired of his tilting with "metaphysics", positivism, Kantian postulates, and so on – but I *like* his "flying in the face of Reason", like a cross hen' (iii. 387). Again he asked Kot, 'Let me have the Preface as soon as possible: also everything you know about Shestov, and I'll write a tiny introduction, and we'll approach the publishers' (iii. 387). On 2 September he offered the Shestov book to the publisher Martin Secker,[33] in spite of the fact that he had not yet written his Introduction, and (significantly) without going through his agent J. B. Pinker.[34]

I have been editing, for a Russian friend of mine, a rather amusing, not very long translation of a book of philosophy by one of the last of the Russians, called Shestov. It is by no means a heavy work – nice and ironical and in snappy paragraphs. Would it be in your line? (iii. 389)

Secker had published Lawrence's *New Poems* in October 1918 and had just produced a 'New Edition re-set' in August 1919. He had also enquired about the possibility of producing Lawrence's *Collected Poems* (iii. 379). He was thus someone who not only liked Lawrence's work, but was keen on publishing it. By Monday 8 September, having heard that Secker was interested in the new project, Lawrence promised to send it to him 'this week' (iii. 391), and did so on Monday 15th, voicing none of his own doubts about the work:

I send you the Shestov: it's really worth doing, and will probably take well with young people. – You can put 'Edited by D. H. Lawrence', or leave it out, as you like. – I find Shestov's 'Preface' long and tedious and unnecessary. You could leave it out if you thought fit, and put in the little 4-page Foreword I enclose. Shestov's Preface is too heavy, to my thinking. (iii. 394)

---

[31] There are 122 paragraphs in Part I and 46 in Part II (of which DHL had already translated no. 45); he was not yet half-way through. He may have been thinking of Part I on its own.

[32] Roberts E11 (UN).

[33] Martin Secker (1882–1978), in the latter part of DHL's career his principal English publisher; see i. 275 n. 1.

[34] James Brand Pinker (1863–1922), literary agent, worked for DHL between 1914 and 1920. See *Plays* l–li, for details of the deteriorating relations between DHL and Pinker in the summer of 1919.

He also, however, told Secker that 'Kot4eliansky wants Shestov's Preface published' (iii. 398) and noted to Koteliansky that 'I thought the Shestov Preface the worst part of the book – don't think Secker will do badly if he omits it. – I wrote a 4-page Foreword' (iii. 397). Unfortunately, when he saw Lawrence's Foreword in the first proofs of the book, in December, Kot was not at all keen on it, and said so. Lawrence replied:

About the Foreword – I will write to Secker, and tell him you strongly wish it omitted – I will send him your letter. As far as I am concerned he can leave it clean out. But I mean what I say in it: and as it would be my signed opinion, I don't see that it matters: not a bit. Secker will no doubt inform you. (iii. 433)

Lawrence forwarded Kot's unhappy letter to Secker, and was equally honest to the publisher: 'I am perfectly willing to have the "Foreword" omitted altogether – my foreword, that is. Let Koteliansky know, will you, what you decide. And please arrange a title page to suit him, will you. Ach, Ach! these little businesses! Every hen is occupied with her own tail-feathers' (iii. 434). Secker decided, however, to retain Lawrence's Foreword; its presence would be signalled on the book's title-page, in spite of Lawrence's suggestion that, after the line announcing 'AUTHORISED TRANSLATION BY S. S. KOTELIANSKY', there was 'No need to figure me, unless you wish – I am quite indifferent' (iii. 437). Secker obviously recognised that Lawrence's name was better known to the reading public than either Koteliansky's or Shestov's, and that it was needed in a prominent position.

The phrase 'authorised translation', however, is curious. The translation would appear in March 1920, and in June 1920 Shestov himself saw it. He at once complained that he had been given no warning of it, even though the translator had known that he was living in Geneva.[35] It would in fact have been extremely difficult to get (or stay) in touch with him, even if Kot had tried; Shestov had left Russia in October 1919 and arrived in Geneva in February 1920. Who gave the 'authorisation' is impossible to say. Shestov had a son living in London, but as he was asked by his father in June 1920 to try and find out more about the translation, it seems unlikely that the son had authorised it. It may be that, since a 1916 Shestov translation which Kot had previously done had also been 'authorised', Koteliansky believed he had acquired the right to be Shestov's official English translator. On the other hand, Lawrence himself may have been responsible for the phrase; it was he who told Secker to put it on the title-page (iii. 437).

---

[35] Nathalie Baranoff-Chestov, *Vie de Léon Chestov*, i. *L'Homme du Souterrain* (Paris, 1991), pp. 224–7.

It was probably such knowledge as Koteliansky did have of the expatriate Russian and Ukrainian community, however, which made him keep worrying that Lawrence's Foreword would damage the book's chances. This eventually provoked Lawrence's comment to him in January 1920: 'Now look here, I think all this about the preface [i.e. Foreword] is perfect nonsense. What I say can't hurt Russian Literature – nor even Shestov: much more likely to *provoke interest*' (iii. 441) – and the Foreword stayed where it was.

Lawrence had done his best to get the book into print in time to play his part in proof correction before he left England in November 1919, but matters had not developed quickly enough. He arranged for Secker to give Kot one set of proofs in London, and for the other set to be posted to him in Italy: 'I will do the *real* proof correcting' (iii. 412). When Lawrence returned his proofs on 20 December, he wrote:

please correct from *my* corrections, Koteliansky will miss a thousand things, particularly German misprints.[36] Let me know if you decide to keep the foreword as it is. – The book is quite long enough . . . I have only corrected misprints, and changed about ¼ doz. words – except one little paragraph, which was wrong.   (iii. 437)

The first proofs, however, still contained 'many errors' (iii. 455).[37] They did not apparently include the 'short notice of Shestov himself', which Lawrence had told the American publisher Huebsch would form part of the revised proof (iii. 455); it did indeed appear on p. [5] of the printed edition.[38] It is not clear who wrote this 'short notice', but it was almost certainly inserted directly into the first proofs either by Koteliansky or by Lawrence, which is why no manuscript survives. As Lawrence seems to have taken care of all such things – he had asked Kot back in August for 'the facts of Shestov's life and purpose' (iii. 381) and for 'everything you know about Shestov' (iii. 387) – it seems probable that he himself wrote this 'Note on Leo Shestov' and it has accordingly been included here.

Although Secker had initially offered a 10 per cent royalty, Koteliansky would have preferred a lump sum, and would have been happy to sell the book outright. Presumably he would then have tried to give Lawrence half of

---

[36] A quotation from Heine appeared on p. 13, for example, and a good many other German sentences and phrases also occurred: e.g. pp. 100, 126–7, 130, 146, 152 and the title-page of Part II.

[37] A set of corrected page proofs (first sixteen pages 'present in two states') was offered for sale at the Parke-Bernet galleries in 1963 (catalogue of 19 February, Item no. 130, pp. 31–2), but is now unlocated.

[38] Benjamin W. Huebsch (1876–1964), New York publisher, who produced an expurgated edition of *The Rainbow* in 1915; see iv. 82 n. 3.

the money, in spite of the fact that Lawrence had told him that 'when it comes to payment, in mere justice my part is one-third. Don't argue this with me. If you are a Shestovian, accept the facts' (iii. 382). All Secker would pay as a lump sum, however, was £20, to which Lawrence retorted, 'Truly, if for all the work we have both done, £20. is the beginning and the end, best have sat still' (iii. 402). In the same letter, and in hopes of making a little more than £20, he proposed reverting to Secker's original offer of 10 per cent royalties; but since only 1,000 copies of the book were printed, selling at 7s 6d, and allowing for review copies not being sold, the maximum he and Kot could have earned from it would be around £35. In spite of Lawrence's continued insistence on only being paid one-third of the profits, Koteliansky was clearly still trying to make him accept half what they earned from the work; in December 1919, for example, when Kot received a cheque for 35s (i.e. £1 15s) from Murry for the extract ('The Russian Spirit') taken by the *Athenaeum*, he told Lawrence that he would be sending him his share: one-half. Again, Lawrence remonstrated with him: 'I beg you, please *do not* send me ½ of the "Russian Spirit" money: if you have any regard for me, don't bother me about this: please do keep it: I so much wish you to make some money.' (iii. 428) He repeated his insistence on 17 December: 'I should be so glad if you would ignore that dividing of Murry's miserable cheque. Are you afraid of me? Don't I owe you fifty times 35/- – per Dio!' (iii. 433). In January 1920 – for once feeling reasonably well-off (he had been sent money by both Huebsch and his other American publisher, Seltzer) – Lawrence himself sent Kot £10 'of the sums I owe you . . . If any trifle accrues from Shestov, you will merely keep it till your ship comes home' (iii. 442). It is hard to escape the conclusion that Lawrence's engagement in the project throughout had been designed to earn Kot money and reputation, and to allow Lawrence to repay some of his own debt to Kot. The latter, however, seems to have had the last word. A cheque arrived from him on 4 May 1920 which almost certainly represented part of Lawrence's share of the book, which had been published the previous month (iii. 512); and although Lawrence burned another cheque from Kot which came on 29 June, on 15 July yet another £5 cheque connected with Shestov arrived, which Lawrence felt he owed it to Koteliansky to accept.

Lawrence had asked Secker for a second set of proofs, to try to tempt an American publisher, and Benjamin Huebsch expressed an immediate interest (iii. 455 n. 2). Lawrence encouraged him: 'if you can see your way to do so, just buy the American rights for a certain sum – no royalties – for Koteliansky's sake' (iii. 466). But Lawrence was now working without an agent for the first time since 1914, and tangles were starting to appear in his dealings with publishers (the situation was made worse by the fact that post to and from Italy was extremely uncertain in the spring of 1920). Having sent Huebsch a copy of the Shestov proofs, and told him about Koteliansky, Lawrence had to follow up his letter with a request that, after all, he do nothing. Secker had told Lawrence in April 1920 that he had himself arranged for American publication of the book with the American firm of Robert McBride and Co., and Lawrence therefore had to extract himself from his dealings with Huebsch.[39] But then – months late – arrived Huebsch's letter of 27 February expressing his willingness to publish the book and offering £50 for it. Lawrence understandably could not resist the chance of getting Koteliansky such a sum. Accordingly he sent Secker a telegram asking him to relinquish the book to Huebsch after all; while for his part – believing that he himself had the rights to the book, having been offered them by the co-translator – Huebsch went ahead and included extracts from the translation in his magazine the *Freeman* on 7 April 1920 (iii. 516). He did not pay for them, naturally, as he believed he was buying the rights to the entire book; nor did he mention the name of Koteliansky as their translator. Secker, however, had no desire to renege on his agreement with McBride, to whom he had sold sheets, and Huebsch's offer of £50 was lost. The American edition of the book came out in April 1920, but sold just as badly as the English one. In spite of Lawrence's attempts to encourage both Secker and Koteliansky – to whom he wrote, respectively, 'He may start later', and 'he will start to sell later' (iii. 559–60) – the book was never reprinted, and it probably never made them any more than the £20 Secker had initially offered. Lawrence asserted in July 1922 that the time was ripe for a reprint – 'It would certainly sell some now' (iv. 275) – and as late as 1929 he was hoping that they could 'rescue Shestov from Secker' (vii. 474, 538) and have the book reprinted by the Mandrake Press. But nothing came of the idea.[40]

---

[39] *Letters*, iii. 508 n. 1, is erroneous in claiming that no American edition ever appeared. Secker subsequently mentioned 'a separate copyright edition appearing in America (McBride)' (La Z 2/3/1–2, UN), and the American edition, printed from Secker's sheets, was published by McBride, New York, in April 1920. It is not listed in Roberts.

[40] The book was eventually reprinted nearly fifty years later, in an edition adopting the Koteliansky/DHL translation – and DHL's Foreword – without any changes (*All Things Are Possible & Penultimate Words and Other Essays*, ed. Bernard Martin, Athens, Ohio University Press, 1977). DHL appears to have helped Koteliansky with another of his projects, a translation of the play *The Green Ring*, by Zinaida Hippius, about which he and Kot first corresponded in 1919 (iii. 421), and which was eventually published by C. W. Daniel (the publisher of *Touch and Go*) in February 1921. A manuscript of an Afterword to this play, in DHL's hand and signed 'transcribed by D. H. Lawrence', is held at UCLA in the collection of Majl Ewing; it is a translation, improved or 'rubbed up' by DHL, of Hippius's own 'Afterword'.

As explained above, this volume does not include the numerous introductions which, over the years, Lawrence wrote for his own work. If, however, we discount the 1913 Foreword to *Sons and Lovers*, which Lawrence was very clear he did not want published – 'I wanted to *write* a foreword, not to have one printed' (i. 510)[41] – then the introductions and forewords he started to write for his own work in August and September 1919 were his first attempts to write such pieces. It is therefore almost certainly correct to see the Shestov piece he wrote at the same time not just as a way of helping Koteliansky, but as part of a new development in his writing. In the course of four weeks during August–September 1919 Lawrence wrote four pieces designed to introduce or comment on work with which he was concerned. The first to be written had been the Preface to his own play *Touch and Go*, which he wrote some time in the first half of August 1919;[42] then came a Preface for the American edition of his *New Poems*, which he wrote towards the end of the same month (iii. 387). He then first offered to write – and on 12 September actually wrote – 'a short Fore-word' (iii. 391) to his novel *Women in Love* for the American publisher Seltzer; and immediately following that he wrote his Foreword to the Shestov book, between 12 and 15 September.

Thereafter he wrote a considerable number of introductions to his own work. For someone who once cheerfully remarked that 'I just wheel out what dump I've got',[43] he spent a surprising amount of time and care suggesting ways in which his own work might be read (or not be read).[44] After the burst of such pieces in the late summer of 1919, Lawrence seems to have written nothing similar for at least two years, but then came another batch. In the middle of August 1921, soon after completing his novel *Aaron's Rod*, he sent his American publisher Thomas Seltzer a 'little Foreword to it, which you print or not, as you like' (iv. 71); the piece was dated 14 August and was about 300 words long. Seltzer did not, however, print it, and the manuscript – sold in 1936 – has vanished, so that we can say nothing more about it.[45] Two months later, Lawrence sent Seltzer another packet of materials including another apparently different Introduction to *Aaron's Rod* (which has also been lost, and which this time we know nothing at all about), the manuscript of *Fantasia of the Unconscious*, and 'an introduction, a reply to some critics of *Psychoanalysis and the Unconscious*'. This he thought might be published separately – 'in some magazine – do as you think well' (iv. 104). It may have been Seltzer who had encouraged this sudden clutch of introductions; he,

---

[41] See *Sons and Lovers* 467–73.   [42] See *Plays* 363–8.
[43] 'Accumulated Mail', *Reflections* 245:15–16.   [44] See footnote 6.
[45] *Aaron's Rod*, ed. Mara Kalnins (Cambridge, 1988), p. xxix and n. 32.

at least, had sent Lawrence the batch of press-cuttings of *Psychoanalysis and the Unconscious* which Lawrence found 'quite amusing' and which made him determine to 'answer them' with his new introduction (iv. 86). And shortly after this, in November 1921, Lawrence embarked on the longest and most significant of all the introductions he ever wrote.

1921–1922: Maurice Magnus

Lawrence had met the American writer and entrepreneur Maurice Magnus the evening he arrived in Florence, Wednesday 19 November 1919, after leaving England for the first time in five and a half years. He saw Magnus – in company with the English writer Norman Douglas[46] – over the next few days, until Magnus left for Rome on Sunday 23 November. Lawrence obviously kept in touch with him by letter, and visited him for two days at the monastery of Montecassino at the beginning of February 1920. It was during that visit (when he also met Magnus's friend, the monk Don Mauro Inguanez) that he first saw the typescript of the book which Magnus was trying to sell. At some stage the typescript had been worked over by Norman Douglas, perhaps in the autumn of 1919. Lawrence himself read it while staying at Montecassino, and after that Magnus had rewritten and retyped 'the *whole* thing' (v. 240), presumably following some of Lawrence's suggestions. It must have been about this new version that Lawrence wrote from Taormina in Sicily to the publisher Stanley Unwin[47] at the start of April 1920:

an MS. on the Foreign Legion – in Algiers and Lyons – by a man who hated it and deserted from it. It isn't *war* experiences – just peace, or rather at home life in the Foreign Legion, rather awful, and very improper. The man who did the book is in a monastery here in Italy – I think in its unliterary way, it's jolly good; straight and simple . . . What he would like is to sell the book right out for a sum down – English rights presumably.   (viii. 30)

Lawrence saw no more of Magnus – though he probably told him that Unwin was interested – until Magnus unexpectedly arrived in Taormina at the end of April, at which point Lawrence sent off the first half of the book to Unwin: 'The second half is finished, and Magnus will no doubt forward it to you himself' (viii. 31). Lawrence's 'Memoir', and the Explanatory notes here supplied spell out the subsequent details of his relationship with Magnus, in Taormina and then (briefly) in Malta in May, down to the start of November

---

[46] See Explanatory note to 11:12.
[47] Sir Stanley Unwin (1884–1968), publisher; founded George Allen and Unwin Ltd in 1914. See iii. 327 n. 2.

1920, when Magnus committed suicide to avoid falling into the hands of the Italian police on a fraud charge (one of his friends in Malta, Walter Salomone, sent Lawrence a long account of what had happened at the end of November).[48]

Norman Douglas was Magnus's literary executor, but Magnus's papers were actually in the hands of Michael Borg, one of Magnus's two most significant Maltese creditors (he had loaned Magnus £55). Borg had acquired Magnus's manuscripts and typescripts for, in effect, £5, by purchasing them after Magnus's death from Carl R. Loop, the American Consul at Valetta; as Louise E. Wright has shown, this was clearly in the hope of being able to sell the rights to these works and so recoup his loss.[49] Borg probably feared that he would never recover any of Magnus's debt if the works went to Douglas, even though the latter wrote to him offering to try to secure publication of the main typescript – *Dregs*. Instead, Borg sent it to Lawrence, in whose company on Malta he had been at least once while Magnus was alive. Borg may also have known that Lawrence had tried to get the book published in 1920, and had then offered advice for its publication. Lawrence felt some involvement in the Magnus tragedy. He had refused to give the money Magnus had asked for when he turned up in Taormina, although he had paid Magnus's hotel bills in Taormina and Syracuse, and had given him money on a number of other occasions; according to Lawrence's own calculation, the debt Magnus owed him came to about £23.[50] Now Magnus was dead, but the main creditor (Michael Borg) was asking for help in getting the book published.

The book had already been seen by – to quote Martin Secker – 'many publishers' (v. 31 n. 2). Unwin had rejected it at the end of May 1920, noting

---

[48] 'True Copy' of a letter from Walter Salomone to DHL, 22 November 1920 (UT). For a full account of the events, see Appendix IX below.

[49] Louise E. Wright, 'Disputed *Dregs*: D. H. Lawrence and the publication of Maurice Magnus' *Memoirs of the Foreign Legion*', *Journal of the D. H. Lawrence Society* (1995–6), 57–73

[50] *Letters*, viii. 49. Wright disputes this figure, and states that DHL was owed only about £6 ('Disputed *Dregs*', p. 64 n. 30). Magnus, however, had received DHL's original £5 from Capri and then 100 L. (£1 5s) and £7 7s from DHL in Taormina, as well as another 100 L. (= £1 5s) in Syracuse, totalling £14 17s. We do not know how much more in addition to this DHL gave him in Taormina for his hotel and daily food – the 'Memoir' records only 'a few pounds' (45:39) plus an extra 100 L. (£1 5s) – but Magnus was at the San Domenico for 7 nights and also ate there some of the time: probably 350 L. plus another 110 L. for food (= £5 15s: with the extra 100 L. the 'few pounds' would probably have been £7). The total DHL had given Magnus thus comes to at least £21 17s, at the exchange rate of 80 L. to the £1 which operated in the first half of 1920. DHL should have been able to recover the £6 17s from *Land and Water*, thus reducing Magnus's debt to £15, but would also have retained his IOU from Magnus 'for the various sums of money he had had' (51:18); it would be odd if the £23 had no basis in fact. When he mentioned the sum of £23 to Douglas, DHL wrote 'some £23 you know' (viii. 49), as if Douglas were also aware of the sum, or at least likely to be sympathetic about it.

'we do not feel that we should be able to obtain a sufficient sale for it to cover the present exorbitant costs of production' (viii. 32 n. 2), and Secker himself had turned it down later in 1920, Magnus apparently having sent it to him from Malta. Seltzer, too, had acquired a copy in September 1920, from Harold Paget, Magnus's literary agent in America, and it was still in his possession in September 1922, neither accepted nor rejected.[51] What Lawrence could do, to help into print what he thought was Magnus's own best piece of writing, was to write an introduction for it. In that way he could ensure that the book would stand as its own memorial to its author, while what it earned would also allow him to pay off two of Magnus's debts: the money owed to Borg, and the money he himself was owed.

Lawrence received a copy of the typescript from Borg some time in the autumn of 1921, perhaps in the middle of November, and apparently began work on an introduction for it at once: he was writing it on 18 November (iv. 127). It seems quite likely that he started with what is now the final section, intending simply to say something about Magnus's experiences in the Foreign Legion. The sentence beginning 'Yesterday arrived the manuscript of the Legion, from Malta' must originally have been written or conceived in mid-November 1921, and may even have been his original starting point (the manuscript marks this section with a horizontal line to denote a break), even though the next sentence – 'It is exactly two years since I read it first in the monastery' – shows that Lawrence was actually writing in January 1922 (although he had in fact gone to Montecassino in February 1920, he remembered it being in 'January').[52] His reference on 5 January 1922 to his Introduction as a 'little prefacing Memoir' (viii. 50) suggests that this first version may well have been quite short.

After about a month of probably intermittent work on this version, Lawrence must have realised that he needed to ensure he had permission to publish the book itself. Norman Douglas was Magnus's literary executor, and Lawrence would not have known the details of how Borg had come to be in possession of the typescript. On 20 December 1921, accordingly, he wrote to Douglas, explaining that he had 'set to write an introduction giving all I knew about M – not unkindly, I hope' (viii. 48), and that he wished to try to sell the Magnus book, including his own introduction, outright to an

---

[51] Secker mistook the year (v. 31 n. 2) – he assumed 1919, not 1920 – but the posting 'from Malta' establishes the date as the summer or early autumn of 1920. See Harold Paget to Thomas Seltzer, 13 September 1920 (NWU), giving Magnus's address as 'Notabile, Malta', and letter from William Harding to Robert Mountsier, 28 September 1922 (NWU): 'We note your remarks re the copy which the publisher Seltzer has in his possession.'

[52] See below, 63:19–20, 20:18.

American publisher for $400 'or more if possible'. He was very clear about what he wanted the money to do:

if you could agree with Michael Borg to let the Malta debts be paid first – about £60, I believe – then out of what remained I could have a bit for my introduction and the money he owes me – some £23 you know – or even if I had just £20 to clear the debt – and you the rest . . . And even if you only got about £20. it is better than a slap in the eye. (viii. 49)

He also offered to stand aside if Douglas wished to undertake the job himself – though Lawrence's tone suggests he thought this unlikely. Douglas would, of course, figure in Lawrence's own introduction, though 'under a disguised name . . . The only vice I give you is that of drinking the best part of a bottle of whiskey' (viii. 49). This shows that at least some of the first part of the introduction had been written. Douglas replied, spiritedly as always, on 26 December:

Damn the Foreign Legion. As literary executor of M (appointed 4 years before his death, and once again later on) and as *co-writer* of that MS, I applied for it to Borg on the 27 April [1921], and also earlier, immediately after M's death, and again, *via* the U.S. Consul in Valletta [Carl Loop]. Couldn't get an answer out of him . . . Latterly, Grant Richards [the English publisher] has applied to me for it. I referred him to Borg, who has answered him back that the MS has gone to the U.S.

. . . Whoever wants it, may ram it up his exhaust-pipe. I have done my best, and if Borg had sent it on to me then, the book would be published by this time, and Borg about £30 or £50 the richer. Some folks are 'ard to please. By all means do what you like with the MS . . . Put me into your introduction – drunk and stark naked, if you like. I am long past caring about such things . . .

Pocket all the cash yourself. Borg seems to be such a fool that he don't deserve any.

Or put yourself into connection with Grant Richards, if you like to have further complications.

I am out of it, and, for *once in my life*, with a clean conscience. (viii. 49–50)

Lawrence prudently kept that letter: it was his only guarantee that the work he was now doing had the approval of the literary executor, and since December 1919 he had been without a literary agent in England to whom he might entrust such a document.[53]

Some time in the second half of January 1922 Lawrence finished the introduction, which had by now grown to almost 25,000 words.[54] He immediately sent it to his American agent Robert Mountsier,[55] to whom he made it clear

---

53 *Triumph to Exile* 547–8.
54 He did, however, send Mountsier some small factual corrections for the last paragraph of the Introduction in a letter of 7 February 1922 (iii. 186); this was probably because he had heard again from Douglas, to whom he had applied for information about Magnus on 5 January (viii. 50).
55 Robert Mountsier (1888–1972), journalist; see iii. 24 n. 4.

from the start that the money which might be earned by *Dregs* was primarily to benefit Michael Borg (he gave Borg's name and address to Mountsier), even though he also hoped that what he had written would repay what Magnus owed him, as well as earn something (of course) for his agent. He also gave Mountsier the address of Norman Douglas, as a possible writer of an introduction for the English market, though he did not mention Douglas's suggestion that he 'pocket all the cash' himself. Lawrence was clear that he intended the introduction and book for the American market: 'I'm not keen on its going to England' (iv. 179).

Thus began the lengthy process of getting the original Magnus MS and Lawrence's introduction published. One initial problem was that Magnus had been fairly explicit about homosexuality in the Foreign Legion, and Lawrence had written about it even more explicitly in his introduction (another reason, almost certainly, why he was not keen on the book going to an English publisher): 'I did such a "Memoir" of Maurice Magnus, to go in front of his horrid *Legion* book', Lawrence told an English friend who had met Magnus in Malta (iv. 191). It was his first use of the title 'Memoir' in his correspondence; it was a title which also appeared on the first page of his introduction, and he regularly used it subsequently. He also warned Mountsier:

Now probably you will refuse to handle this MS at all: think it too impossible. If you do feel like that, please hand it over to Seltzer and I'll have his advice on it.

A publisher can cut anything he thinks absolutely must be cut.

Perhaps you will hate my associating myself with such a book. But I don't care . . . I enclose in the MSS photographs of Magnus and one of the portraits of his mother.   (iv. 179)

A week later he wrote to Mountsier asking that when the book appeared – 'if ever it does' – a copy should be sent to Don Mauro; he also asked that some details should be changed at the end of his introduction.[56] A note in Mountsier's hand, 'Send copy to Don Mauro Inguanez, / Montecassino / Prov. di Caserta', appears in pencil on the verso of the title-page of the 'Memoir' MS, but Mountsier did not alter the penultimate page of MS (p. 57) as requested.[57] He must have had Lawrence's 'Memoir' typed while it was in his possession, and have sent out the typescript while retaining the manuscript himself (he apparently kept it until his death in 1972). A typescript, therefore, would have been the text which went to Seltzer and then subsequently to Martin Secker, who eventually published the 'Memoir' in 1924.

---

[56] See Explanatory note on 72:19 and iv.186.
[57] DHL's proof changes at 72:19 and 72:20 did something to repair the damage; see 'Texts' below.

Despite the fact that, as Lawrence himself later stated, a number of people offered to print the 'Memoir' by itself, as a separate essay, he continued to press for the whole book to be brought out with the 'Memoir'. Almost nothing is known about the typescript of *Dregs*, or about the typed copy of the 'Memoir', and their peregrinations between February 1922 and the end of 1923; all we know for certain is that Seltzer saw both book and 'Memoir'. It is likely that Mountsier made enquiries on behalf of the book and 'Memoir' among magazine editors and publishers, but as Lawrence later stated that 'Seltzer . . . had the MSS for nearly two years' (v. 31) – 'MSS' here meaning 'TSS', as is usual in the period – it is possible that they never left Seltzer's hands after Mountsier passed them on to him, some time in the spring of 1922.

Seltzer was keen on seeing anything which Lawrence wrote, in these years between 1921 and 1924, but clearly drew the line at *Dregs*, no matter how well Lawrence had written his 'Memoir'. Without, obviously, having any intention of publishing them himself, Seltzer retained the copies of both the 'Memoir' and of *Dregs* down to the winter of 1923, when Lawrence asked him to send them to England for Murry (now editor of his own magazine, the *Adelphi*, for which Koteliansky was business manager). He told Seltzer, on 24 December, that 'Murry wants very much to see that *Memoir* of Maurice Magnus – he thinks he would like it very much, as a serial, in the *Adelphi*. Will you please post it to me, with Magnus' own MS [i.e. TS] of the *Foreign Legion*' (iv. 549). It sounds as if Lawrence were hoping to interest Murry in the whole book rather than simply in his own 'Memoir' (although serialisation in the *Adelphi* would have been unlikely in itself to recoup the various debts), and he was certainly concerned to recover the material from Seltzer in order to explore such other publishing opportunities as might arise. Seltzer had *Dregs* retyped (iv. 559) before sending it to Murry at the *Adelphi*; he also had the typescript of Lawrence's 'Memoir' sent directly to Lawrence on 25 January (viii. 88 n.1) and it seems to have arrived at the start of February (iv. 571), when Lawrence let Koteliansky see it. *Dregs* itself only arrived towards the end of March (v. 16 n. 7). If his comments in conversation were consistent with the wording of his letter to Seltzer, Lawrence may well have given both Murry and Kot the impression that he was, after all, willing to allow his 'Memoir' to be published on its own; they certainly appear to have thought so. But in mid-February he wrote to Kot: 'Don't think about doing that Magnus MS. till we have talked it over. I didn't want my memoir to be published apart from Magnus' own *Foreign Legion* book. There doesn't seem any point in it' (iv. 579). By this time, however, he needed to get the Magnus material away from the *Adelphi*, because he had at last found a possible publisher for both the book and his own 'Memoir'. At some point during his stay in England during the winter of

1923–4 he had told Martin Secker (who by now had become his main publisher in England) 'the whole story' of Magnus (v. 31) and of the 'Memoir', and the most likely time for him to have done this was in January 1924, shortly before he went to France and Germany for a month. He was seeing Secker fairly regularly – they probably lunched together on 21 January (iv. 558) – and an otherwise inexplicable reference in one of his letters to Secker from Germany the following month shows that some correspondence had come to him from America which he thought Secker might have: 'it might one day be useful' (iv. 576). This was almost certainly a copy of the Douglas letter of 26 December 1921, sent on from Curtis Brown New York.[58]

Secker had to wait for the copy of *Dregs* to arrive from America, and Lawrence – himself on the point of travelling to New York, and hardly having heard from Seltzer the whole time he had been away – assumed that the type-script still had not been sent: he promised to have it sent straight to Secker, as soon as he arrived in the USA. It was in fact on its way, to Murry at the *Adelphi*, who sent it round to Secker; the latter had by now also acquired a copy (probably Koteliansky's) of Lawrence's own 'Memoir'; and on 24 March Secker wrote to Lawrence that he was accepting both 'Memoir' and *Dregs* for publication. He had turned the book down when Magnus had sent it to him in 1920, but Lawrence felt that it was because Secker now had a particular knowledge of 'all the Florence and Capri part of it' (v. 31) that he changed his mind: 'he knew the people' (iv. 597). Secker himself stated that 'it was chiefly due to Lawrence's telling me the whole story one day that I promised to consider the matter again' (v. 31 n. 2). At all events, he wrote to Lawrence at the end of March 1924:

I shall be very pleased to publish it, with your introduction, during the coming autumn . . . There will have to be a few excisions made in the text, and I would not propose to call the book 'Dregs', but 'Memoirs of the Foreign Legion'. I think that you should share to the extent of 50% in the proceeds, for it is your introduction which gives value to the document and makes the author of it live. (v. 16 n. 7)

Secker also wanted to claim profits from any subsequent American publication of the book, and Lawrence realised that 'there won't be a great sale for the book' in America. As a result, he was himself prepared to take only 'the ten per cent up to 2000' (v. 31) on American sales. Before he even heard from Secker, Lawrence wrote to him in turn:

---

[58] Albert Curtis Brown (1866–1945) founded the international Curtis Brown literary agency in 1916. DHL engaged him as his literary agent in England in April 1921; see iii. 566 n. 1, iii. 700, and *Triumph to Exile* 639–40.

If you do decide to publish, you are free to make what omissions you like, both from my MS and ~~yours~~ Magnus'. Perhaps best change the name all through – to Maurice Gross or Maurice le Grand. And change anybody else's name. – Let me know. (v. 24)

What Secker decided to do, however, was 'to give the right initials with dashes, and to put the author's initials alone, M. M., on the title page. I think this would be very much better than manufacturing a fictitious name, and would help to preserve its appearance of truth' (v. 24 n. 4). As soon as he heard from Secker, Lawrence told his new English agent Curtis Brown the whole story, and asked him to contact Borg in Malta – 'the MSS. I think legally belong to Michael Borg' – to ask him if 50 per cent of the royalties would be acceptable. Lawrence also wrote to Borg himself: 'Now I hope we can settle this weary business . . . I am glad for your sake – because as you know, I only made this effort because of that debt of Magnus' to you' (v. 33). Borg apparently said that he was agreeable to the publication, writing back to Lawrence in what the latter found 'a very friendly way – as he ought' (v. 54). When Secker paid royalties, Borg was paid the Magnus 50 per cent share of the royalty direct, and there is at least one record of what looks like an additional payment (of £19) made to him in December 1925: 'I want him to have the money' (v. 348), Lawrence remarked, although this may have been the result of a confusion between the London and New York offices of Curtis Brown (v. 361).

Lawrence received proofs – but only of his own 'Memoir' – early in July 1924. Secker described what he had done: 'I have only made a few alterations, and one "cut" at the end, where you let yourself go on the subject of M's attitude towards certain things. Also, I have turned Don Martino into Don Bernardo' (v. 70 n. 3). He had probably not realised that 'Don Martino' was already a fictionalised name. Lawrence in his turn made some revisions and posted the proofs back on the 7th: 'hope they haven't been too long travelling' (v. 70). The introduction and book were published on 1 October 1924. When he saw a copy, at the end of September (v. 133), Lawrence's comment on its black binding (with gold lettering) was that it 'looks like a Church hymnal: *Ora pro nobis*' (v. 141). He had already asked for copies to be sent to Michael Borg and to Don Mauro Inguanez.

Seltzer had never been keen on the book for American publication, as his failure to do anything with it in 1920 and then again during 1922–3 had demonstrated. In mid-1923 he had indicated to Lawrence that he would be prepared 'to publish my introduction alone, as an essay, without the *Legion* MS' (v. 240), but once again Lawrence had rejected the idea: 'Anyhow I *don't* think it's any good publishing my essay without the Magnus part' (v. 78). In the event, it was the American publisher Alfred Knopf[59] who was offered the book and 'Memoir' together in 1924. This was a symbolic act, in some ways, as it marked the first connection between Lawrence and Knopf, who would, between 1924 and 1926, take over the publication of Lawrence's work: Seltzer's business was going into a steep decline before collapsing.

The problems Magnus' book had caused would thus seem to have been solved, but were in fact only just starting. Lawrence wondered to Secker in December 1924 what Norman Douglas would think of the book, not knowing that Douglas had already been in touch with Secker. Douglas had in fact told Secker that 'If you expect a 2nd edition, I might also write an introduction (little memoir): say 4000 words.' Secker (not realising, perhaps, what Douglas was suggesting) had replied most invitingly: 'I should be delighted if you could write a supplementary memoir of 4000 words or so, as you suggest. I will include it in the next printing' (v. 184 n. 2). What he did not know was that Douglas was at that very moment in the process of issuing in Florence (and would publish in England in January 1925), the small pamphlet *D. H. Lawrence and Maurice Magnus: A Plea for Better Manners*, which attacked Lawrence and his version of Magnus on a number of fronts. Douglas objected to the presentation of himself in Lawrence's 'Memoir' as mean; he ascribed what he saw as an unfair attack on Magnus to Lawrence's own small-minded resentment at not getting back the money he had lent; and he also criticised Lawrence's own apparent profiteering, not only out of another man's work, but of work which had been left to him (Douglas), as literary executor, to place. Douglas's pamphlet was favourably reviewed in England in a number of places, with one reviewer – H. M. Tomlinson in the *Weekly Westminster* – suggesting how unlikely it would be that 'a popular novelist' (meaning Lawrence) would tell the truth about anything, complimenting Douglas on his pamphlet (a 'rare and lively book'), and challenging Lawrence to 'explain, at least, who appointed him to be the biographer of Maurice Magnus'. Tomlinson at least admitted that he made these charges and challenges without having read Lawrence's own 'Memoir' (v. 242 n. 3).[60]

We do not know when Lawrence first heard about Douglas's attack, but it must have been fairly soon. By 15 April 1925 he was feeling 'so nagged at about Douglas's pamphlet on me and Magnus' that he sent Douglas's letter of 26 December 1921 – which, sensibly, he still kept – back to his New York agent: 'I really think it ought to be printed: though I don't care much. Use your discretion. But please preserve D's letter' (v. 240). The kind of nagging to which he was subject may be gauged by an extant letter of 25 April to which he

---

[59] Alfred A. Knopf (1892–1984) set up his publishing firm in New York in 1915; see iii. 471 n. 1.
[60] See Explanatory note to 287:1.

replied on 21 May (v. 255), by the fact that he certainly knew by 6 April about Tomlinson's review (v. 231), and by a quotation in his essay 'Accumulated Mail' (written on 18 April) from a letter he had recently received from New York: '*in the controversy between you and Norman Douglas*, (I didn't know myself that there *was* a controversy) . . . *I wish you could make it clear how you come to be profiting by a work that is not your own*'.[61] Lawrence explained the situation in his essay 'Accumulated Mail', with a passing reference to Douglas:

As for Douglas, if he could have paid the dead man's debts, he might have 'executed' the dead man's literary works to his heart's content. Why doesn't he do something with the rest of the remains? Was this poor Foreign Legion MS. the only egg in the nest? – Anyhow, let us hope that those particular debts for which this MS. was detained, will now be paid. And R. I. P. – Anyhow I shan't be a rich man on the half profits.[62]

Earlier in the month, in private, he had been a good deal more outspoken:

Norman Douglas is really terrible. He despised Magnus and used him badly: wouldn't give him a *sou*: said most scandalous things of him: and Magnus was very bitter about it . . . Add to this that the facts about Magnus were much worse than I put them – and that the facts about Douglas no man would dare to print – and there we are. (v. 231)

Lawrence wondered whether to take further the idea of publishing the Douglas letter, and later in April offered it to his new American publisher Knopf (who would be including 'Accumulated Mail' in his yearly publication, the *Borzoi*): 'I think it would come very *a propos* in the 1925 Almanach' (v. 244). But in the event he decided not to bother, ascribing his initial idea of publishing the letter to the fact that he had been ill: 'When I was feeling sick, I felt sore. Now I am better, I don't care what Douglas or anybody else says or pamphletises. They can all go their own way to oblivion . . . I think public "controversies" *infra dig.*, anyhow' (v. 256–7). He continued to receive letters about the matter, however (v. 369), probably because the controversy had been further fuelled by Douglas's inclusion of his Florence pamphlet in his book *Experiments*, published in England in October 1925, which was widely reviewed. Martin Secker strongly encouraged Lawrence to write to an English newspaper about it – he suggested the *Times Literary Supplement* – and on 20 November 1925, now back in Europe, Lawrence finally complied:

I enclose a letter for the *Times*, since you want it. For myself, I'm sick of that stuff. – I left the original of Douglas' letter at the ranch – but you will have a copy: or Curtis Brown will. – You know you may not print the Douglas letter entire – it is his property. – Will you go through my letter, and leave out what is best left out, and put in what needs to be put in. Make it all right. Make it shorter. (v. 340)

[61] 'Accumulated Mail', *Reflections* 240:7–8, 14–15.   [62] *Reflections* 240:28–34.

Secker thought that what Lawrence had sent him was 'a very good letter' – it presumably had paraphrases or gaps where authentic quotations from the Douglas letter had to be inserted – and, on 23 November, Secker wrote to Curtis Brown for a copy of the Douglas original. It seems likely that Secker was not only defending Lawrence's interests; he probably hoped for further sales of the Magnus book as a result of a public controversy. It presumably took some time for the necessary quotations from the Douglas letter to be acquired from New York, and it is possible that Lawrence was consulted again about the wording (Secker saw a good deal of him in Spotorno, where Lawrence was now living, during December 1925 and January 1926). The letter was finally published on 20 February 1926, not in the *Times Literary Supplement*, but in the *New Statesman*, which had reviewed *Experiments* on 13 February, referring to Lawrence's 'Memoir' as 'a brilliant but unfair portrait'.

Lawrence's attitude was still that he would rather not have bothered, but that 'One becomes weary of being slandered'. He outlined the facts of the matter, very tellingly quoted some extracts from the Douglas letter, and ended by describing how 'More than one publisher said: "We will publish the Introduction alone, without the Magnus *Memoirs*."' He meant Seltzer, Murry and, probably, Secker originally:

It is probable that I could have sold the Introduction to one of the large popular American magazines, as a 'personal' article. And that would have meant at least a thousand dollars for me. Whereas I shall never see a thousand dollars, by a long chalk, from this *Memoirs* book. Nevertheless, by this time B— will have received in full the money he lent to Magnus. I shall have received as much – as much, perhaps, as I would get in America for a popular short story.

As for Mr. Douglas, he must gather himself haloes where he may. —   (v. 396–7)

We do not know how Douglas responded to this letter, but the breach between him and Lawrence remained open during the twelve months between May 1926 and May 1927 while they were both living in Florence. A form of reconciliation was eventually effected, but from subsequent events it looks as if Douglas, despite his earlier claim to have been 'long past caring about such things', never really forgave Lawrence: for the 'Memoir', for Lawrence's use of him as James Argyle in *Aaron's Rod*, or for the letter in the *New Statesman*.[63]

1922–1923: Sicily to America, and back to Europe

Lawrence had written his Magnus 'Memoir' in Sicily, shortly before leaving for the first part of his journey to America. It was in connection with that

[63] For further details, see *Dying Game* 248, 282, 379–80, 404. Secker took advantage of the publicity to issue a second impression of the book in the summer of 1926.

journey that he also began his first translation from the Italian: *Mastro-don Gesualdo*, by the Sicilian writer Giovanni Verga. Lawrence had begun reading Verga after returning to Taormina in October 1921, having spent the summer away. Verga, he wrote, 'exercises quite a fascination on me, and makes me feel quite sick at the end. But perhaps that is only if one knows Sicily. – Do you know if he is translated into English? . . . It would be fun to do him – his *language* is so fascinating' (iv. 105–6). He asked his old friend Edward Garnett the same question, when he wrote to him in November 1921: Verga, he insisted,

is *extraordinarily* good – peasant – quite modern – Homeric – and it would need someone who could absolutely handle English in the dialect, to translate him. He would be most awfully difficult to translate. That is what tempts me: though it is rather a waste of time, and probably I shall never do it. Though if I dont, I doubt if anyone else will – adequately, at least. (iv. 115)

Some time that autumn – probably before the matter of who else might have done translations had been resolved – he made a start, perhaps to see what the work of translating Verga would actually be like. He had originally planned to save up the job as something to do on the voyage which he knew he would be taking, either to Ceylon (now Sri Lanka) or to America, in 1922: 'to amuse myself on shipboard and so on I shall probably go on with a translation of the Sicilian novel *Mastro-don Gesualdo* . . . It interests me very much, as being one of the genuine emotional extremes of European literature' (iv. 157). At the start of January 1922 he asked Seltzer the same question about whether there were other translations on the market, but by the beginning of February he had already done 'about one-third' (iv. 186) of the work, and by the 8th was 'nearly half-way through', regretting now that he could not finish the job before leaving (the date fixed for departure from Taormina being 20 February). In the intervening days, when he found himself 'on thorns, can't settle' (iv. 191), the translation kept him occupied, and, by the 17th, the first half of the book was with the typist. He told Robert Mountsier, 'I will send you the rest as soon as it's done, with a small foreword on Verga' (iv. 196). After the ship sailed from Naples on the 26th, he settled into a pleasant routine of shipboard life, 'talking small-talk . . . translating *Mastro-don Gesualdo* and having meals' (iv. 208), but he did not finish the work until the end of his first week in Ceylon, which suggests that he cannot have done much of it on board ship.

Ceylon he found hot and uncomfortable, and he was soon saying he did not believe he would ever 'write a line' there: his American friend Earl Brewster commented that 'because of his illness there he did not trust his impressions'.[64]

---

[64] Nehls, ii. 120. Earl Henry Brewster (1878–1957), American painter, and his wife Achsah Barlow Brewster (1878–1945), close friends of DHL from 1921 onwards; see iii. 711 n. 2.

But although he may not have felt able to work imaginatively, he could still continue his translation. Earl Brewster's wife Achsah recalled how Lawrence

sat curled up with a schoolboy's copy-book in his hand, writing away . . . Across the pages of the copy-book his hand moved rhythmically, steadily, unhesitatingly, leaving a trail of exquisite, small writing as legible as print . . . Sometimes Lawrence would stop and consult us about the meaning of a word; considering seriously whatever comments were offered.[65]

On 2 April the second half of the work was posted to Mountsier (iv. 219); the first version of Lawrence's 'Introductory Note' was written at the end of the translation notebook, dated 'Kandy. March 1922' (there is also a typescript of this 'Introductory Note', with some corrections in Lawrence's hand, dated in the same way). When Seltzer published the book in October 1923, this 'Introductory Note' was replaced by a shorter version, probably written about the same time as the first. In Ceylon, Lawrence also started on his next translation, of Verga's *Novelle Rusticane*, and continued it on the next boat journey, south to Australia, 'to keep myself occupied' (iv. 235); but this translation would not be completed or published for another two years.

As soon as he had gone on from Australia and reached America, in September 1922, he met the writer Witter Bynner and the young man then working as his secretary, Willard ('Spud') Johnson.[66] Lawrence and Frieda spent their first night in New Mexico with them, in Santa Fe. Lawrence devoted a certain amount of time during his first three months in Taos to writing the kinds of things which – as a good guest – he was expected to write. He helped Mabel Luhan[67] with a version of the novel of her life, and in addition he wrote a piece about his first experience of the Arizona Indians, another piece about the Bursum Bill and what it would do to the Pueblo Indians,[68] and a third piece, for the magazine *Laughing Horse* which Spud Johnson co-edited: a review of Ben Hecht's notorious recent novel *Fantazius Mallare: A Mysterious Oath* (Chicago, 1922).

Lawrence had probably not written a formal review for some nine years. His responses to new books had been confined to the letters he had written; for example, to the publisher of Cyril Scott's novel *Blind Mice*, which the publisher

[65] Nehls, ii. 123–4.
[66] Harold Witter Bynner (1881–1968), poet, and Willard Johnson (1897–1968), journalist; see iv. 316 nn. 4, 5.
[67] Mabel Dodge Luhan, née Ganson (1879–1962), author and patroness; see iv. 4–5, 100 n. 4.
[68] The Bursum Bill, introduced into Congress in July 1922 by Senator H. O. Bursum of New Mexico, purported to clarify questions of land ownership among the Pueblo Indians, but opponents of the measure, vigorously organised by Mabel Luhan, argued that it would have a deleterious and possibly fatal impact upon native life. See *Dying Game* 64–5.

had sent him in March 1921, and to Evelyn Scott (Cyril Scott's wife) three months later, in June, after he had been sent a recent novel of hers. He realised that his letters were reviews of a kind, telling Scott about the March letter '*You* may do as you like with it' (iii. 692; he had told the publisher that 'This letter is for Mr Scott, not for the public'), and concluding his letter to Evelyn Scott, 'Tell Boney and Liveright they can say I found *The Narrow House* a damned good cure for the love-disease: a cataplasm' (iii. 735).[69] Whenever he admired someone's work, he was happy to help by supplying the kinds of comment a publisher might take from a review to adorn a blurb or an advertisement, although none had so far been used in this way. Now he set out to help Spud Johnson in the obvious way a writer of repute can help a little magazine, sending his review and leaving Johnson free to 'Publish the enclosed or not, as you like' (iv. 321). In the form of a letter to 'Chère Jeunesse', and very critical of the Hecht book – which Lawrence told Seltzer he thought 'silly: not a bit good' (iv. 345) – the review pulled no punches in naming parts of the body not often mentioned in a literary periodical. The editors of the *Laughing Horse* (Johnson and Roy Chanslor) apparently originally decided not to publish the review, as they did not like it – they may well have been among those who saw 'mordant irony' (iv. 331) in the book – and it seems probable that Johnson wrote to Lawrence telling him of their decision, incidentally informing him that Hecht himself had been arrested in Chicago. Lawrence answered:

Don't bother about apologies: one writes when the spirit moves. As for the 'Jeunesse' letter, much best burn it now, it has done all its work – Or best still, give it to Alice Corbin and let her burn it. Her feminine curiosity couldn't bear it otherwise. I'm sorry I couldn't see the mordant irony etc of Mr Hechts book. But heaven, they might put me in prison as they have him. Martyred in such a cause.[70]   (iv. 331)

Either Lawrence's 'frightened retreat' (as Roy Chanslor would later claim this to have been),[71] or – much more likely – the idea of making the review even more outrageous, nevertheless made the editors change their minds

---

[69] Cyril Kay Scott (later Kay-Scott) was the pen-name of the American writer Frederick Creighton Wellman (1881–1953), who had been Dean of the School of Tropical Medicine at Tulane. He eloped to England in 1913 with Elsie Dunn (1893–1963), a Tulane undergraduate; the couple disguised their whereabouts from their vengeful families by adopting the names Cyril Kay Scott and Evelyn Scott. They subsequently lived in Brazil before settling in New York, and were divorced in 1928. The New York firm of Boni and Liveright published Evelyn Scott's first novel, *The Narrow House*, in 1921; see iii. 733 n. 2, and *Triumph to Exile* 863 n. 84. She reviewed *Women in Love* and *The Lost Girl* for *The Dial* in April 1921.

[70] Alice Corbin Henderson (1881–1949), poet and literary editor, was a friend of Bynner and Johnson and lived in Santa Fe.

[71] Witter Bynner recalled Chanslor writing to him, claiming that DHL had sent a 'frantic wire not to publish the review', the telegram ending 'Heavens what a cause to be martyred for!' (Witter Bynner, *Journey with Genius*, Peter Nevill, 1953, p. 11). Although the existence of this

and publish the review in the December 1922 issue of the magazine (no. 4). Chanslor prefaced it in the following way:

D. H. Lawrence the famous English novelist, writes a letter to the readers of The Laughing Horse, reviewing Ben Hecht's new privately printed novel, 'Fantazius Mallare'; and takes the opportunity to give them some sound advice.
(Note: We were advised, at the last moment to leave out words in this letter which might be considered objectionable. We hope that this censorship will in no way destroy the sense of the text.)

Bracketed dashes, (———), were inserted in the place of all 'objectionable' words. In the sentences following, for example, all the underlined words were removed:

Really, Fantasius Mallare might mutilate himself, like a devotee of one of the early Christian sects, and hang his <u>penis</u> on his nose-end and a <u>testicle</u> under each ear, and definitely testify that way that he'd got such appendages, it wouldn't affect me. The word <u>penis</u> or <u>testicle</u> or <u>vagina</u> doesn't shock me. Why should it? Surely I am enough a man to be able to think of my own <u>organs</u> with calm, even with indifference.[72]

The result was in some ways more 'objectionable' than the original wording of the review had been, even though its apparently censored suggestiveness was precisely the opposite of the clarity of thinking and speaking for which Lawrence was arguing. Chanslor later claimed that it was owing to his publishing Lawrence's review that he was expelled from the University of California at Berkeley, but David Ellis comments that

Chanslor's claim . . . appears dubious. More instrumental probably were his decision to use one of the illustrations from *Fantazius Mallare* as the frontispiece to that number of *Laughing Horse*, and the fact that it mainly consisted of attacks on his university's teaching staff and officials.[73]

Lawrence saw the magazine containing his review at the start of January, when Johnson sent him a copy: 'It's a sad horse, a galled horse. I wish you hadn't printed the article – perhaps you wish so too – but since it is done, no matter' (iv. 366–7). Johnson must have asked if Lawrence wanted to write anything else for the magazine, and Lawrence not surprisingly answered: '– No, I don't want to write a word about anything just now' (iv. 367). He would certainly have found the way his review had been treated offensive. But the episode did

---

telegram is accepted by the *Letters* editors (no. 2640; iv. 331 and n. 2), the phrase quoted is arguably a misremembering of the phrase DHL had used in his letter to Johnson (no. 2639): 'Martyred in such a cause.'
[72] See 215: 14–20
[73] *Dying Game* 75; the illustration showed an erect penis.

not, in the long run, affect Lawrence's relationship with Johnson or with the *Laughing Horse*, which continued to print his work from the end of 1923.

Lawrence's next review was for a periodical very different from a 'little magazine' such as the *Laughing Horse*. He had been publishing regularly in the established Chicago literary journal, *The Dial*, since September 1920; it had taken sketches, stories, poems, selections from *Sea and Sardinia* and *Aaron's Rod*, a translation and some essays. Now *The Dial* asked for a book review. The literary critic Stuart P. Sherman[74] (who would review Lawrence's *Studies in Classic American Literature* when it came out in the summer of 1923) had in 1922 published *Americans*, a collection of essays on prominent American figures. Gilbert Seldes (managing editor of *The Dial*),[75] knowing that Lawrence was now in America, and seeing Lawrence's agent Mountsier in New York (iv. 341 n. 1), may well have negotiated with Mountsier for this new kind of writing from his client, and at the start of December Lawrence told Mountsier 'I'll have a shot at the Sherman book when it comes' (iv. 355). With Lawrence just finishing his *Studies in Classic American Literature*, Mountsier may very well have thought that a review of Sherman could do Lawrence's American reputation no harm, especially as three of the writers discussed in *Americans* – Franklin, Hawthorne and Whitman – featured heavily in Lawrence's own book. *Americans* probably arrived at the ranch in mid-December, and by 16 January Lawrence had posted his review to *The Dial* (viii. 59); by 25 February he had received proofs (iv. 398).

He used for his review a version of the style he was currently employing in his own book of criticism: single-sentence paragraphs at times, with abrupt little spurts of ideas and reactions. He was able to develop, in the passages about Franklin and Hawthorne and Whitman, arguments he had already used himself.[76] He was pleased with the chance to do the review, and wrote to Seldes: 'Hope it will amuse you' (iv. 398); it was part of his new, conscious engagement with things American, as he now competed for the first time as a professional writer on the American market.

He engaged with things American in a rather different way in his next review, of *A Second Contemporary Verse Anthology*, a collection of avowedly amateur poetry put together by C. W. Stork, the editor of the fireside magazine *Contemporary Verse*. Lawrence wrote this brusquely sardonic review for

---

74 See Explanatory note to 221–2.
75 Gilbert Vivian Seldes (1893–1970), journalist and editor; see iv. 339 n. 1.
76 He was also able to use some of Sherman's material; two quotations from Sherman's Hawthorne essay found their way into DHL's own essay, while a quotation – 'Henceforth be masterless' – which it has proved impossible to trace elsewhere appears both in Sherman's book and in DHL's review; see *Studies*, Explanatory notes on 15:20, 81:18, 100:8.

the influential *Literary Review* of the *New York Evening Post*, some time in September 1923. The editor of the *Evening Post*, Henry Seidel Canby, had apparently asked him if he could make Stork's collection 'the point of departure' for some kind of 'critique' (iv. 494), and Lawrence thought of his piece more as an 'article for Canby' than as a straight review (iv. 495).[77] He quoted extensively from the anthology without mentioning the name of a single contributor, and Stork's own wish, expressed in his foreword, that 'readers of this book might see in it not merely an assembly of verse, but the spiritual record of an entire people', came under some particularly withering fire. Lawrence found the whole anthology to be a striking demonstration of how 'Our ideas, our emotions, our experiences are all pot-bound': for him the mark of his generation, and even more perniciously so in America, where 'consciousness . . . is absolutely safe inside a solid and ornamental concept of life', than it had been in Europe (see below, 231:1–2, 234:15–16, 33–35).

The only other review Lawrence is known to have written in the 1923–4 period has already been published elsewhere in the Cambridge edition, and is not reproduced here. This was the review of John Oman's *The Book of Revelation*, which Lawrence wrote in Germany in February 1924. It appeared that April in Murry's new periodical, the *Adelphi*, over the signature 'L. H. Davidson' (a version of the pseudonym Lawrence had used for his *Movements in European History* in 1921) – presumably because either Murry or Lawrence himself thought his own name would not be taken seriously as the reviewer of so scholarly a book. The review is reprinted in *Apocalypse and the Writings on Revelation*.[78] Had Lawrence not returned to America in March 1924, he might have reviewed a book by a friend of Rolf Gardiner, who wrote to him from England in the early summer.[79] The book – *Harbottle: A Modern Pilgrim's Progress From This World to That Which Is To Come*, by John Hargrave – sounded promising: 'I would have done a notice . . . but now it is too late. Anyhow I hope the book comes along. It will interest me' (v. 67). But when he did eventually read it, he found it 'poor stuff: snivelling self-pity, exasperatedly smashing a few cheap parlor-ornaments, but leaving the house standing stuffy, suburban, sterile, smug, a nice little upholstered nest of essential cowardice'; and, in reference to Hargrave's self-awarded title of 'White Fox' in the hierarchy of the 'Kibbo Kift' (the 'Woodcraft Kindred' movement he had founded), Lawrence commented: '– White Fox, forsooth! White rat!' (v. 93). If he had written a review, he would probably have said much the same.

---

[77] Henry Seidel Canby (1878–1961), journalist and editor; see iv. 494 n. 3.
[78] See footnote 4.
[79] Rolf Gardiner (1902–71), farmer and forester, pioneer of Land Service Camps for Youth after the First World War; see Nehls, iii. 665–7 n. 60.

1924–1925: Introductions in America

It was while Lawrence was waiting for Secker's proofs of the Magnus 'Memoir' to arrive at the ranch at the start of July 1924 that he was approached by the American bibliographer and academic Edward D. McDonald (v. 63 n. 3), who intended publishing a volume on Lawrence in the Centaur series of Bibliographies of Modern Authors. As an example of the series, McDonald sent him a copy of the recently published bibliography of James Branch Cabell, which contained an introduction by Cabell himself, and McDonald asked whether Lawrence would perhaps not only help him over details of his publishing career, but be willing to write an introduction too. Lawrence answered:

> I'll help as much as I can. But I'm not much good.
> I will write you a little introduction, but tell me what kind of thing you would like me to say. I don't really care a snap about first editions, or whether e's are upside-down or not. So I also have nothing really to say, in that line. Only I don't feel like saying it in as many words as Cabell does: haven't got the style.   (v. 64)

McDonald sent him a preliminary account of the *oeuvre* at the end of July, prompting Lawrence to comment 'The list of books horrifies me by its length' (v. 87), but there was no further mention of the introduction in Lawrence's reply. A month later came a kind of questionnaire from McDonald, for Lawrence to fill in, but again Lawrence made no mention of the introduction. On 1 September 1924, however, he wrote it, the place and circumstances of its writing being recorded in its opening sentence:

> There doesn't seem much excuse for me, sitting under a little cedar tree at the foot of the Rockies, looking at the pale desert disappearing westward, with hummocks of shadow rising in the stillness of the incipient autumn, this morning, the near pine trees perfectly still, the sunflowers and the purple Michaelmas daises moving for the first time, this morning, in an invisible breath of breeze, to be writing an introduction to a bibliography.

Nonetheless, in what was one of Lawrence's first pieces of explicitly autobiographical writing, he took his chance to record memories of the publication of *The White Peacock*, *Sons and Lovers* and *The Rainbow*,[80] while he compared the books he wrote to a flower which 'flowers once, and seeds, and is gone. First editions or forty-first are only the husks of it.' But in a tribute to the careful work of McDonald, he continued: 'Yet if it amuses a man to save the husks of the flowers that opened once for the first time, one can understand that too . . . we see the trophies once more of man's eternal fight with inertia.'

---

[80] See below, 75:1–7, 78:10–17; and *Early Years* 500–3.

He must have spent some days completing the introduction and revising it, for it was not until 10 September that he posted it to McDonald. 'If you think it is in any way unsuitable, tell me, and I'll alter it. I don't mind a bit' (v. 116). Another set of queries came from McDonald before the introduction arrived, and Lawrence again insisted: 'I . . . want you to tell me if it's what you require' (v. 119). It was, however, exactly what McDonald wanted. Lawrence wrote again when McDonald welcomed the arrival of the piece and asked for a title for it (it was at first called simply 'Introduction to Bibliography'): 'Glad the introduction will do . . . Call it "The Bad Side of Books" – or anything else you like!' (v. 132–3). McDonald adopted Lawrence's suggestion, and that was how it was published, in *A Bibliography of the Writings of D. H. Lawrence*, which came out on 23 June 1925 in an edition of 500 ordinary copies and 100 special copies, signed by both compiler and author. David Jester, the junior partner of Harold Mason at the Centaur Book Shop in Philadelphia,[81] about to send Lawrence his copies, remarked: 'I hope you will be pleased with the finished product. Dr McDonald has taken infinite pains and has compiled, I believe, an accurate and interesting bibliography' (v. 241 n. 3). When the copies arrived, Lawrence was delighted, writing to Jester:

They are very nice: almost nicer done than *any* of my own books. I like them very much. As for Dr McDonald, he leaves me speechless, I feel I have lived in such a state of ignorance of my own fate. What labours! I hope to heaven it will be worth it to him . . . I am really pleased with the bibliography. Almost it makes me feel important.   (v. 271)

To McDonald himself he wrote:

The bibliographies came on Saturday evening, and created quite a sensation on the ranch. I like both the books very much indeed: to look at and to touch. And all the work you have put in, into the inside, abashes me. It seems to me wonderfully complete, and *alive*: marvellous to make a bibliography lively. I have got the signed copy No. 2., and it shall be a *Vade Mecum*, quite invaluable to me, who keep so little track of my things.   (v. 271–2)[82]

We do not know what financial arrangements Lawrence reached for writing the introduction, nor for signing the sheets for the limited edition; no relevant correspondence survives.

Back in 1922 he had been concerned to put *Mastro-don Gesualdo* into the world with the appropriate apparatus of an introductory note of his own, a

---

[81] Harold Trump Mason (1893–1983), proprietor of the Centaur Book Shop and founder of the Centaur Press; see v. 176 n. 2.
[82] By 'both the books' DHL meant both the 'ordinary' and the 'special' copies of the Bibliography which Jester had sent him.

list of the novel's characters, and a bibliography of Verga. His second Verga translation, of the story-collection *Novelle Rusticane*, on which he had begun work in April–May 1922, was now in the hands of Seltzer in America and the publisher Basil Blackwell in England.[83] Lawrence at first suggested *Sicilian Novelettes* as a title (v. 20), but by August 1924 the title had been fixed as *Little Novels of Sicily* (v. 92). Extracts had already been printed in Murry's *Adelphi* in the autumn of 1923. Seltzer's advertisement for *Little Novels of Sicily* appeared at the beginning of August 1924, by which time Lawrence clearly felt there was nothing further he needed to do before the book came out, so his brief 'Biographical Note' on Verga had evidently been written some time before that: either when he completed the original manuscript, or when he began thinking about the forthcoming publication at the end of March 1924 (iv. 20). In the Blackwell edition, the last page or so of Lawrence's 'Note' as printed in the Seltzer edition is omitted, and there are a few slight changes to the rest; it is possible that the Blackwell version represents an earlier draft, which Lawrence himself later expanded, but no manuscripts or typescripts survive to clarify this.

His next introduction had already been completed by the time 'The Bad Side of Books' and the *Little Novels of Sicily* were in print. In 1923, he had rewritten his Australian friend Molly Skinner's novel *The Boy in the Bush*: Secker had published it in August 1924.[84] One of the very few things Lawrence wrote while in Oaxaca, apart from *The Plumed Serpent* and the essays later collected in *Mornings in Mexico*, was an introduction to her next novel, *Black Swans*. He had seen it in Australia in 1922, and she had just written a letter to him saying that she would appreciate his writing an introduction for it. He did so on 24 December 1924, and wrote to her about it at the start of January: 'I had your note about an introduction to *Swans*: and I wrote one. But then I decided – and I'm sure I'm right – that you'd be better *without* an introduction by me. Critics would only be dragging me in all over everything again' (v. 190). The introduction was not published with the novel. It was typical of Lawrence both to write one because she asked for it, and then to suggest that she discard it as it would not help her. It has not been included in this volume because it appears in the Cambridge edition of *The Boy in the Bush*.[85]

There is another introductory piece dating from this period which is also in print elsewhere in the Cambridge edition: a brief 'Note' to the small volume

[83] Sir Basil Henry Blackwell (1889–1984), publisher; see v. 247 n. 1.
[84] Mary Louisa ('Molly') Skinner (1878–1955), Australian writer; see iv. 236 n. 1.
[85] See footnote 4.

of Lawrence's essays being put together by Centaur Books, the publishers of McDonald's *Bibliography*.[86] The original intention had been to produce a collection of early essays which McDonald's researches had uncovered, the centrepiece being the six essays of *The Crown*, which Lawrence had written as far back as 1915. He wrote his 'Note' at the start of August 1925, reminiscing as in 'The Bad Side of Books' – and suggesting that he had barely changed the six essays from their 1915 form ('I alter *The Crown* very little. It says what I still believe'), whereas he had in fact made some very considerable alterations.[87]

1925–1926: American Reviews from Europe

On 14 June 1925, Stuart Sherman reviewed Lawrence's *St. Mawr* in the *New York Herald Tribune Books* – of which he was editor – under the provocative title 'Lawrence Cultivates His Beard' (v. 272 n. 2). Lawrence was amused, and wrote to him on 11 July: 'I like to know what you say, because you do care about the deeper implication in a novel. Damn "holiday reading"!' But he also made a suggestion: 'I have thought many times that it would be good to review a novel from the standpoint of what I call morality: what I feel to be essentially moral. Now and then review a book plainly. – I will do it for your paper if you like' (v. 275). The editors of the *Letters* record 'The offer was not taken up' (v. 275 n. 3). But later that year Irita van Doren took over from Sherman at the *New York Herald Tribune Books*, and one of the first things she did was to write to Lawrence, offering to take reviews by him.[88] It seems very likely that Sherman had passed on the suggestion. On 22 September 1925, Lawrence left America for the last time, and on his way through New York before going on board ship he was given a parcel of recent books by his new publisher, Alfred Knopf, while almost simultaneously receiving the letter from Irita van Doren. Loyal to Knopf, he asked Van Doren: 'Will you tell me if you would care for a review of any of these, from me' (v. 301), and listed *The Origins of Prohibition* by John A. Krout, *Saïd the Fisherman* by Marmaduke Pickthall, and *Hadrian the Seventh* by Frederick Baron Corvo – the latter two in Knopf's Blue Jade Library series, which reprinted literary classics. He may well have had no reply before sailing. By mid-October, however, he was sending to Nancy Pearn, who ran the magazine department for Lawrence's London agent Curtis Brown, 'another little review for the *New York Tribune*' (v. 319), showing that he had already done his review of *Hadrian the Seventh* and had now completed that of *Saïd the Fisherman*.

[86] See *Reflections* xxxvi, 249:1–250:10.   [87] *Reflections* 250:9–10; see also xxxvii–xxxviii.
[88] Irita van Doren (1891–1966), editor, wife of Carl (1885–1950), editor and critic, sister-in-law of Mark (1894–1972; see p. lxii below). See also v. 301 n. 2, and Explanatory note to 221:2.

This contact with the *New York Herald Tribune* marked a new development in his career as a reviewer. He had not been well that autumn, and the review format gave him an opportunity to say things directly and interestingly without overtaxing his strength, as creative work still tended to do; he told Van Doren that 'It amuses me, this winter, to leave my own books alone, and go for other men's' (v. 325). He also told Knopf of the pleasure the work had given him – 'I think my two reviews are rather nice' (v. 321), and 'Hope they suit. I liked those two books very much' (v. 320). In the same letter, he mentioned other recent Knopf publications he was willing to review (Stendhal's *The Life of Henri Brulard*, Barbey D'Aurevilly's *Les Diaboliques* and Captain Cook's *Voyages of Discovery*; v. 321), and when he asked Nancy Pearn to send his review of *Hadrian the Seventh* to Van Doren, he added 'if anybody likes to use the review in England, they're welcome' (v. 317). But for unknown reasons this review was not printed by the *New York Herald Tribune*. When Lawrence wrote to Van Doren, he expressed the hope that his reviews were 'more or less what you want. Tell me, will you?' (v. 325). She may have done so; the remarks about Catholicism in the *Hadrian* review may have made it unacceptable. It was however, taken by Murry for the December 1925 number of *Adelphi*, and was the effective cause of Lawrence's break with the magazine. He had been feeling increasingly alienated from Murry, and wrote to him at the end of January 1926 that, although he did not mind 'if you use that criticism' – and a poem –

I can only repeat, I feel it's a betrayal of myself, as a writer of what I mean, to go into the *Adelphi*, so I'd rather stay out . . . So don't look to me any more for help, after that crit., please. I can't go between the yellow covers of the *Adelphi* without taking on a tinge of yellow which is all right in itself, but not my colour for me.[89]   (v. 385)

Items such as the review would have been a 'help', because Murry would not have paid for them. Lawrence was in fact mistaken about which 'crit.' it was; he thought that it was the review of *Saïd the Fisherman* which Murry had used, as is clear when he attempted to explain the situation to Nancy Pearn:

Murry wanted me to give him things, gratis, for the *Adelphi*. I wouldn't mind a bit, if he didn't do such mean little things, and were not, *in what he says*, so very distasteful. After he's used that little crit. on *Saïd the Fisherman* I don't want him to use anything else: he took a poem this month without any consent from me.   (v. 386)

Murry appears to have taken this as permission to use the *Saïd* review as well as the *Hadrian*, and he printed it in *Adelphi* in January 1927. Lawrence's

---

[89] *Adelphi* appeared in yellow wrappers, but DHL may also have meant 'yellow' in the sense of 'cowardly'.

response – if he knew about this – is not recorded, but would probably have been unprintable. Lawrence had written his review of *Saïd the Fisherman* (Marmaduke Pickthall's most successful novel, originally published in 1903) while on his visit to the Midlands; its comment on Saïd going mad in London – 'Yet one is appalled, thinking of Saïd in London. When one does come out of the open sun into the dank dark autumn of London, one almost loses ones reason, as Saïd does'[90] – reflects back directly on Lawrence's own experience in 1925, when he travelled back from New Mexico, and found the climate of London in October 'unbearable' (v. 322).

He sent the *Saïd* review to Nancy Pearn for typing on 20 October. 'Will you be so good as to have it typed, and charged to me, – and send it to New York. Hope it's not a bore' (vi. 319). It appeared, slightly cut down, in the 27 December 1925 issue. His review of the third book, Krout's *The Origins of Prohibition*, was also accepted. This, however, took Lawrence a good deal longer to write. He started work on it in the Midlands (v. 321), continued while back in London (v. 325), and apparently finished it in Spotorno a month later; his opening remarks show that he had found reading the book rather demanding. He sent the manuscript of his review to his agent on 21 November: 'I promised this review ages ago, to the *New-York Herald-Tribune*. Have it typed, and send it in for me, will you please? Pardon the trouble' (v. 341). It appeared on 31 January 1926, but it was to be his last review for the paper. Back in October, Lawrence had told Irita van Doren, 'if anything comes in, that you'd like me to review, send it along', and he offered her a review of a book he had himself just read,[91] but by February the contact had effectively dried up. It may have been that his reviews were regarded as too idiosyncratic and too little focused upon the book market; it may simply have been that the paper was not especially keen on printing reviews, by a Knopf author, of books published by Knopf (the whole thing seeming too much like free advertising for the publisher), and preferred to distribute books for review in its own way.

The circumstances in which his next two reviews were written are not entirely clear. One final result of the connection with Van Doren may have been the publication in the New York *Nation*, in April 1926, of Lawrence's very favourable and enthusiastic review of *In The American Grain*, by William Carlos Williams. Van Doren herself had been literary editor of this magazine before handing over to her brother-in-law Mark in 1924, and she may have still had some influence over what appeared in it; but no relevant correspondence

[90] See below, 248:18–20.
[91] *Whom God Hath Sundered* by Oliver Onions (1925); see above, p. lx.

survives, nor any record of when Lawrence read the book or wrote his review. It was nearly three years since he had last had work printed in the *Nation*, and in October 1923 he had found what he had heard of John Macy's hostile review in it of *Studies in Classic American Literature* sufficiently irksome to remark that he would 'rather be printed in *Vanity Fair* [a popular magazine] than in these old high-brow weak-gutted *Nations*' (iv. 518).[92] It was not the only time that his reviews would appear in magazines of which he appears not to have approved. This particular arrangement may have been organised by Nancy Pearn; in August of the same year (1926) he did suggest to her that 'Perhaps the *Nation* will have' his review of H. G. Wells's *The World of William Clissold* (v. 513), so presumably she knew about the contact, even if she had not herself been responsible for it.

Another piece almost certainly written around this time, but not mentioned by name in any of Lawrence's surviving correspondence, is the review of *Heat*, by Isa Glenn. Isa Glenn, the daughter of a mayor of Atlanta, had studied art in her teens with Whistler in Paris, and subsequently married an American army general, Bayard Schindel, accompanying him on his various postings abroad, to the Philippines, where *Heat* is set, to Cuba, and to South America. Schindel died in 1921, and his widow settled in New York to write; *Heat* was her first novel. Knopf published it in March 1926, and it quickly became a best-seller. A copy was presumably included among the batches of books Knopf was regularly sending to Lawrence, and the latter may have decided to write a speculative rather than a commissioned review of it, in a bid to extend the range of his magazine contacts. It seems highly likely that the review of *Heat* was the third of the 'three little things' he mentioned to Nancy Pearn on 27 June 1926:

Vogue told Richard Aldington to ask me to do them little articles: paying £10. for . . . 1,500 words. I'm not doing anything else, so have written three little things – though they come about 2,000 – and I'll send them along in a day or two, soon as they're typed. And will you offer them to *Vogue* – unless you think any of them quite unsuitable. Then I've another 'possible' story, nearly done. But little articles, if people like 'em, are much the easiest. In America, *Vanity Fair* asked me to do some. But the American *Vogue* might synchronise with the English one. (v. 482)

Two of the articles, as the *Letters* editors' footnote argued, can be identified fairly confidently: 'The Nightingale' and 'Fireworks', both included in the Cambridge edition of *Sketches of Etruscan Places and Other Italian Essays* (the 'nearly done' story was 'The Man Who Loved Islands').[93] The third article,

[92] John Macy (1877–1932), editor and critic; see iv. 477 n. 2.
[93] See *Sketches* lx–lxii.

as the *Letters* editors say, 'is not known'. But the review of *Heat*, roughly 2,000 words long and, given the publication and likely mailing date of the book from Knopf, very probably written around this time, would certainly fit the description in Lawrence's letter. The style of the piece, largely facetious and sardonic, relying heavily on narrative, might well suggest that Lawrence was writing with a more lightweight periodical than usual in mind. One other piece of circumstantial evidence could also support this argument: the review exists in two versions, a manuscript and a typescript.[94] The latter, which has some corrections in Lawrence's hand, appears previously to have been regarded as a copy of the manuscript, but in many respects, especially its first half, is markedly different. Lawrence remarked in the letter to Nancy Pearn that the 'three little things' were to be typed, and it may be significant that when 'The Nightingale' and 'Fireworks' were eventually published (although not in *Vogue*), the periodicals involved appear to have set from typescript versions, both subsequently lost, which were also markedly different from the manuscripts. If the review of *Heat* was the third piece sent to Nancy Pearn, the fact that it was never published in Lawrence's lifetime might explain why the alternative, typescript version has survived along with the manuscript, while the typescripts of the other pieces did not.

This typescript has its final page or pages missing. It was probably made by Lawrence himself, on a machine whose exclamation mark did not work properly – a particularly exasperating problem, one would think, for a piece of writing with so many exclamations in it. The typist tried several expedients with colons, full stops and inverted commas, and one of the marks is written in by hand. This typescript may have been a revision of the manuscript; it includes comments not made in the latter about the peculiar nature of American Romanticism, and extra details of the racial and sexual charge in the novel to which Lawrence was responding. But since one cannot be certain which of the two versions of the review Lawrence hoped to see printed (nor do we know whether the review was sent out and rejected, or thought 'quite unsuitable' by Nancy Pearn), both have been included here.

1925–1926: *Max Havelaar*

In the course of his October 1925 letter to Alfred Knopf about the reviews of *Hadrian* and *Saïd*, Lawrence recommended another book for the Blue Jade Library series, and in the late spring of 1926 he wrote an introduction to

94 Roberts E158a and E158b.

it. In Western Australia in May 1922, he had met a writer named William Siebenhaar, and had been thoroughly bored by the romance in verse and the book of poems he had been presented with: Lawrence threw them into the south Atlantic while en route for Sydney (iv. 251).[95] But Siebenhaar had also shown Lawrence an essay on Eduard Douwes Dekker, the author, under the pseudonym 'Multatuli' – 'I have suffered much' – of the classic Dutch novel *Max Havelaar*. Lawrence read the essay in Sydney, and wrote to Siebenhaar with a very practical suggestion. No one would be interested in the essay while Dekker's book was so completely unknown; but

If you would care to take the trouble of translating say the first fifty pages of *Max Havelaar*, and would send me the MS., I would submit it to the best publishers in New York, and they could arrange then with you for the book. What New York publishes, London will publish. But you should also find out about the *copyright*, and the previous translations. Probably the copyright has run out by now. (iv. 270)

Siebenhaar would have been foolish to refuse such an offer, and in September 1922 – after Lawrence had arrived in New Mexico – the first part of the translation arrived. Siebenhaar himself seems to have been slightly comical, but Lawrence wrote very warmly of the translation: 'perfectly splendid: you seem to me to have caught so well the true spirit of the thing. Really it seems to me a first rate translation' (iv. 309). He asked for a few more chapters 'before forwarding the book to my agent, to put before the publishers' (iv. 309). More arrived in October (iv. 326–7), and Lawrence duly sent it on to Mountsier: 'I enclose also a part of the MS. of a translation of a Dutch classic, *Max Havelaar*, by a writer "Multatuli", about Java – done by a man in West Australia, and I promised him I'd have you show it to publishers. It's a queer work – real genius. Do something with it if you can, will you?' (iv. 329). Mountsier, however, seems to have done nothing. By February 1923 the part-translation was back with Lawrence, and Mountsier was no longer his American agent (Lawrence had broken with him in January). Lawrence now planned to approach Seltzer directly: 'I'll see if I can't make Seltzer print it' (iv. 386). He received the last parts of the work in the late spring and early summer of 1923 (iv. 435, 449) and – with almost the whole book to hand – returned to the idea of writing an introduction himself: 'The worst of my writing an introd. is that I don't know Multatuli's other books' (iv. 449). What seems to have happened is that Siebenhaar then sent him his own long essay, presumably to fill Lawrence in with the details of the rest of Dekker's career. This essay had arrived by October 1923, and Lawrence apparently sent it on

---

[95] William Siebenhaar (1863–1937), Australian writer, born in Holland; see iv. 240 n. 2.

to Seltzer, telling Siebenhaar: 'Yes, I have the essay on *Havelaar* safely kept' (iv. 518) – but it would still be another four years before the book would appear. It is an indication of Lawrence's extraordinary patience with work which he admired – and with a translator whose work he admired too, even though he described the man as 'a bore, but inoffensive' (v. 538) – that he was prepared to go on taking an interest in such a project over so long a period.

Seltzer's business had started to experience serious problems by the spring of 1924, and all Lawrence could tell Siebenhaar in April was that 'I don't forget *Max Havelaar*. But at the moment publishers are in despair, so I am keeping quiet about it' (v. 34). It was not until he himself had a new publisher, in the person of Alfred Knopf, that he could do anything for Siebenhaar, and it was not until he had for review two of the books in Knopf's Blue Jade Library in October 1925 that he realised that the Blue Jade series would be ideal for *Max Havelaar*. He put the idea to Knopf at once, on 20 October 1925: 'Would you care to put into it the Dutch masterpiece – or semi-masterpiece, it's no better than *Hadrian* – *Max Havelaar*. A man I know did a new translation, and asked me to write him an introduction' (v. 320). It took, however, several months to get the translation back from Seltzer – 'I had quite a job', Lawrence remarked (iv. 458) – and into the hands of Knopf, and it was five months before he heard, from Nancy Pearn, that Knopf would be happy to add *Max Havelaar* to the series and to pay Siebenhaar 'the established honorarium of $250'. As Lawrence pointed out to Siebenhaar, 'It's not much, but I don't suppose you could do better, and the Blue Jade books are beautifully produced' (v. 393). 'I naturally took his advice', Siebenhaar later commented.[96] There had been no further mention of an introduction, as they were not usual in the Blue Jade series, until Lawrence heard 'unexpectedly' from Knopf on 1 May 1926 'asking if I'd do the introduction I promised, so long ago, to *Max Havelaar . . .* Knopf wants to keep me to my word' (v. 446). This left Lawrence in some difficulties. The essay on Dekker which Siebenhaar had sent to America was still with Seltzer in New York, and Lawrence no longer had even a text of the book itself. He asked Siebenhaar – fortunately now over in Europe on a lecturing tour – to let him have copies of both, 'to read both once more, before I attempt an introd.' A few days before 13 May he received an MS copy of the book and, without waiting for the essay (Siebenhaar's long-winded explanations of things never really interested him), he went ahead and wrote his introduction, telling Siebenhaar: 'So I shall send the MS. and introduction on to Knopf at once, as he seemed rather urgent' (v. 452). Siebenhaar's own commentary runs:

[96] Nehls, iii. 110.

His [Knopf's] urgency, and the fact that by this time we were again a considerable distance apart, prevented, to our mutual regret, a personal consultation on the subject of this introduction. Lawrence had to do the best he could in the face of the handicap, and he did. One or two things I could have advised him to present differently, but in the main it was a very capable statement.[97]

One has the distinct impression that the last thing Lawrence wanted was a 'personal consultation' with Siebenhaar, and that he did not find the lack of this in any way a handicap.

The introduction was thus written around 10–13 May 1926, and was sent to America. Proofs came from Knopf early in September. Siebenhaar (still in London) went through them, but as Lawrence told him not to bother to send on the proofs of the introduction – 'I'm sure it will be all right' (v. 527) – we can be fairly sure that Lawrence did not see them.

1926: New Outlets

Lawrence's often slightly uneasy relationship with magazine editors was to some extent ameliorated by the emergence of a new periodical in 1925, the *Calendar of Modern Letters*. The editor, Edgell Rickword, printed work by Lawrence in five of the first ten issues, including the very first number, in March 1925.[98] In August 1926, when Lawrence returned to the United Kingdom for two months, it seems that Nancy Pearn either gave him, or suggested he acquire, the new H. G. Wells novel *The World of William Clissold*, and wondered if he might do a review of it. At this stage she had the magazine *T. P.'s and Cassell's Weekly* in mind. Lawrence took the book to Scotland with him (he was there 9–21 August), and sent her the review on the 20th:

probably too peppery for the unctuous *T. P.* – but really true . . . If *T. P.'s* should happen to like the review, then I will do others for them, if they wish. I rather like doing a serious review, for anybody, now and then. Seems to me there is need of a straightforward bit of criticism sometimes. (v. 513–14)

The 'unctuous' magazine did not take it, and there was some urgency, as Lawrence had reviewed only volume I of the book, and volumes II and III would be published in October and November. But the *Calendar* (its new abbreviated title) accepted it, and published the review in October 1926. It contained some of Lawrence's most characteristic statements about fiction: 'So far, anyhow, this work is not a novel, because it contains none of the passionate and emotional reactions which are at the root of all thought, and

---

[97] Nehls, iii. 111.   [98] Edgell Rickword (1898–1982), poet and critic; see v. 601 n. 2.

which must be conveyed in a novel. This book is all chewed-up newspaper, and chewed-up scientific reports, like a mouse's nest.'[99]

While in England, Lawrence and Frieda had re-established contact with some old friends. They had known the novelist and poet Richard Aldington since 1914, and had seen a good deal of him and his mistress Dorothy ('Arabella') Yorke in 1917–18.[100] Almost as soon as Lawrence and Frieda returned to the Villa Mirenda, near Florence, in October 1926, Aldington and Arabella came to stay with them, and while there Aldington suggested that Lawrence might contribute an introduction to the *Memoirs of the Duc de Lauzun*, one of the volumes of translations Aldington was editing for The Broadway Library of Eighteenth Century French Literature. What happened next is slightly mysterious. Fifteen years after the event, Aldington wrote the following account of it:

How did it happen that among [Lawrence's] posthumous works there appears a short essay on the Duc de Lauzun? . . . I arranged with F. S. Flint to translate the duke's memoirs, but for some reason Flint didn't want to write the introduction. I had the book with me on one of the occasions when I stayed with the Lawrences at Scandicci, and I had Lorenzo read the book to see if he cared to write about it. From his breakfast-table homilies on the subject I gathered that he thought Lauzun and the whole French aristocracy and *littérateurs* of that epoch a collection of lice, and that anything he wrote on the subject would say so. I considered this would be an improper introduction to a public which was pretty languid about the French 18th century anyhow; so I said no more about it, and wrote the essay myself. Apparently Lawrence had already written his essay, for it was among the manuscripts of his I went through in Florence in 1930.[101]

There are three statements here that could give rise to confusion. The first is the mention of F. S. Flint (1885–1960), the Imagist poet, critic and translator, a friend of Pound, Eliot and T. E. Hulme. Flint may have been commissioned to make a translation of Lauzun in 1926, and he did translate other volumes for the series,[102] but when the Lauzun volume eventually appeared, in 1928, the translation was by C. K. Scott Moncrieff, famous for his translation of Proust.[103] It is possible that Flint had decided that he wished to do neither

---

99 See below, 283:9–12.
100 Richard Aldington (1892–1962), poet, novelist and biographer, was separated from his wife, Hilda Doolittle, and was living with Dorothy ('Arabella') Yorke; see v. 104 n. 6.
101 Richard Aldington, *Life for Life's Sake* (1941), pp. 280–1.
102 Flint translated both the memoirs of Madame de Pompadour and those of the Duc de Richelieu for the Broadway series. Aldington may have been confusing this latter with the Duc de Lauzun's memoirs.
103 *The Memoirs of the Duc de Lauzun*, translated by C. K. Scott Moncrieff, with notes by G. Rutherford, and an introduction by Richard Aldington, in the Broadway Library of Eighteenth Century French Literature (London: George Routledge and Sons, 1928). DHL met Scott Moncrieff in 1927; see Explanatory note to 95:7.

introduction nor translation; it is also possible that Aldington confused the two men. Secondly, when Aldington writes that he had 'the book' with him, it was not a translation that he had, but the 1858 Paris edition of Lauzun's *Mémoires*, with an introduction and notes by Louis Lacour. This is the book that Lawrence eventually read, and made translations from himself for his second attempt at an introduction. It is highly unlikely that Lawrence ever saw a professional translation, either by Flint or Scott Moncrieff. Thirdly, Aldington writes that Lawrence's 'essay . . . was among the manuscripts', but as Tedlock has shown, this particular manuscript would actually have contained two separate essays, written consecutively on nine leaves torn from the same exercise book. The first essay originally had the title 'The Duc de Lauzun', but this was struck out, most likely when Lawrence began work on the second essay, to which he gave the same title.[104] The first essay was reprinted in *Phoenix* under the title 'The Good Man'; it occupies the first nine pages of the manuscript book, and is immediately followed, for the next seven pages and one line of the otherwise blank eighth, by the second essay, also reprinted in *Phoenix*, with its correct title, 'The Duc de Lauzun'. This second essay, probably because it breaks off in mid-sentence, was wrongly assumed by the editor of *Phoenix* to have been the first to be written.

It seems reasonable to speculate that Lawrence may have written the first essay immediately upon having the proposal put to him, and quite possibly before he had even read the *Mémoires*, or very far in them, since there is no discussion of them in the piece. It seems equally possible that he may, with or without further consultation with Aldington, have realised that this first attempt at an introduction was unlikely to be thought suitable, and so set to work on the quite different second essay. This piece is much more restrained, less opinionated, more sympathetic to Lauzun, and pays extremely close attention to the text: so close that by the time Lawrence abandoned writing after seven manuscript pages, he had only taken his account of the *Mémoires* as far as page 40 or so of a 250-page book. One can be confident that he was making his own translations directly from the 1858 edition, as he translates two of Lacour's footnotes, which are not found in Scott Moncrieff's volume, and which Flint, if he did ever make a translation, would almost certainly not have included either.[105] Aldington's remark, 'Apparently Lawrence had already written his essay', seems to imply, without making clear which essay is being referred to, that one and perhaps both had been done during the five days Aldington spent at Scandicci. It is not clear whether the piece was broken off so abruptly because Lawrence realised it was not going to find any more favour than the first one, or because he intuited from Aldington's silence that the entire plan had been abandoned. Perhaps he himself had grown tired of it. It may simply be that when Aldington left he took his copy of the book with him, making it impossible for Lawrence to continue.

1926–1927: Concentrating on Reviews

Reviewing was now becoming more important for Lawrence. He had not begun a completely new novel between April 1923 and October 1926, he was writing very little poetry, and his output of short stories after coming back from America had also slowed down; but he and his agents were finding that his short essays and reviews were playing a newly significant part in his earnings. *T. P.'s and Cassell's Weekly* had not wanted the Wells review back in August – or possibly Nancy Pearn had known it was no good offering it to them. But in the autumn of 1926 Lawrence wrote another review for which *T. P's* apparently promised a certain sum. They sent him *Gifts of Fortune*, by H. M. Tomlinson (published in October 1926), and Lawrence returned his review to Nancy Pearn on 9 November, remarking: 'If the *T. P.'s* don't want it, they needn't pay for it. And if they want to cut it shorter, they can please themselves.' He apparently made a second version, probably a heavily revised typescript (see 'Texts'), which the magazine printed, and because this text and the manuscript version differ significantly, both have been included here. Lawrence commented to Nancy Pearn: 'I did the review quickly – feel I've been quite nice to Tomlinson.' It had been as recently as April 1925 that Lawrence had found that Tomlinson had sided with Norman Douglas against Lawrence over the Magnus affair, and at that point, Lawrence – thinking of Magnus – had characterised Tomlinson as 'a sort of failure in himself' (v. 231). He had then named Tomlinson as one of the friends of Murry 'who make attacks on me . . . so often I can see Murry's words coming out against me, through people who frequent him. I don't like that kind of friendship' (v. 242). But he let none of these considerations enter his review, which was favourably disposed; he responded both to Tomlinson's delight in the natural world and to his weariness with humanity in general.

His other review printed in January 1927 was not at all favourably disposed. At the end of November 1926, the *Calendar* had sent him R. B. Cunninghame Graham's recent book *Pedro de Valdivia, Conqueror of Chile*, and Lawrence's first reaction – to Edgell Rickword – was 'I'm sure it will interest me, and shall be glad to have a shot at reviewing it. It's nice to say what one thinks' (viii. 99). A couple of days later, to Nancy Pearn, he was a good deal more critical: 'what a tiresome old fool he is, with a good subject! It will be rather fun to throw something at him – he's too complacent over other people's sufferings' (v. 590). The review was in the hands of the *Calendar* by the middle of December, so clearly Lawrence wrote it at once. As for saying 'what one thinks': 'Not only does [Cunninghame Graham] write without imagination, without imaginative insight or sympathy, without colour, and without real feeling, but he seems to pride himself on the fact.'[106] Lawrence may even have felt that he had gone too far; he wrote to Nancy Pearn on 13 December: 'Would you mind asking the Rickword man, of the *Calendar*, if he could please let me have a proof of the Cunninghame Graham book-review, in case he prints it. I'd like to look through it' (v. 601). There is no record of this having happened, but there would certainly have been time for it in the second half of December. A comparison of the corrected typescript with the review as printed reveals, however, that Lawrence made no verbal changes at this stage, and that the magazine had made no cuts either.

No further invitations to review seem to have come from *T. P.'s*,[107] but Rickword continued to ask for work; he may even have responded to Lawrence's request, made at the end of November 1926: 'Do send me a list of titles of books I might do, if it is not troubling you too much' (viii. 99). As the *Calendar* printed his work without cuts or changes, it was natural that he should have gone on writing for it. For his next review, and for the first time in his reviewing career, Lawrence found himself writing about a number of different books at once; in this case, presented with four new American works of fiction, he was able to bring to bear his own particular knowledge of (and attitudes to) America. The books were *Nigger Heaven* by Carl Van Vechten, *Flight* by Walter White, *Manhattan Transfer* by John Dos Passos, and *In Our Time* by the very young Ernest Hemingway. Again, the magazine seems to have sent him the books direct, and when he posted the review to Nancy Pearn, he wrote: 'Do you mind having it typed and giving it them? They can cut it if it's too long: but it's four books' (v. 647). It appeared, uncut, in the *Calendar* for April 1927. He had finished his first revision of *Lady Chatterley's Lover* just before doing his review, and commented that he would now 'have a shot at a few little things. They keep me going best' (v. 647). Given that it was about now that he wrote his 'Scrutiny' of John Galsworthy for the collection *Scrutinies*, edited, like the *Calendar*, by Edgell Rickword, it is possible that a review he wrote of a reprint of Galsworthy's *The Island Pharisees* (the Heinemann edition of 1927) also dates from this period, and was designed for the *Calendar*. But this review was never published, there is no record of it in

---

[106] See below, 300:4–6.
[107] DHL did, however, publish an essay, 'Laura Philippine', there in July 1928 (Roberts 489).

Lawrence's correspondence, and the manuscript (which seems to have been very short – only two pages long) is now unlocated, after being sold at auction in 1943.[108]

Early in April 1927, Koteliansky sent Lawrence a copy of his new translation from the Russian: *Solitaria*, by V. V. Rozanov. Lawrence had not seen Kot on his 1925 visit to London, but Kot had found lodgings for him and Frieda in 1926, and they had spent some time together. Nothing had apparently been said then about this new project. When Lawrence saw the book on 13 April, he commented: 'it looks quite thrilling, and I shall read it as soon as I feel I'm here' (vi. 30); he had only just returned from his travels around the Etruscan sites with Earl Brewster. This particular translation was not in need of an introduction by Lawrence – the volume already included an 'abridged', but still lengthy, account of Rozanov's life by E. Gollerbach, together with other material relating to the author at the end, and a further introductory piece by Koteliansky himself – but nonetheless, by the 27th Lawrence had both read the book and written about it:

I read Rozanov as soon as he came: and wrote a criticism as soon as I'd read him: and send you the criticism so you will know what I think. Do you agree at all?

As for my crit., will you send it on to Curtis Brown – Magazine Dept. They may get someone to print it, though it's an off-chance. But they usually place anything I send. The *Calendar* would print it, but since it's their own publication, I'd rather it went somewhere else. If you know anybody, give it them. If not, no matter.   (vi. 41)

He told Nancy Pearn what he had done:

I did a review of Koteliansky's translation of the Russian *Rozanov*, which Wishart is bringing out. I sent it to K. to see if he liked it – he's evidently showing it to *The Nation*. But probably it will come on to you. Anyhow you'll arrange for it: It might go to America. I don't mind if they leave any bit out, that they want to.   (vi. 52)

She almost certainly arranged for it to appear in the *Calendar* – still the only place which would securely accept Lawrence's work. It was published in the July number, together with another of his reviews.

Whereas the piece on Rozanov, although referred to as a review, was in effect the introduction Lawrence would have written had one been requested, the review he *had* been asked to do, of a book by his next-door-neighbour's brother, was a very different matter. The Wilkinsons, the family who lived at the Villa Poggi near the Lawrences at the Villa Mirenda in Scandicci – 'our only neighbours – five minutes away' (vi. 128) – had many talents, and Walter (the brother of Arthur Gair Wilkinson) had toured south-west England with a

---

[108] See Roberts E177.3.

puppet theatre, though he was now often in Italy. He had written a book about his experiences, *The Peep Show*, due to be published in the spring of 1927, and Lawrence was asked if he could get a review of it printed. He requested a review copy, which had arrived by 9 April. By the end of the month both Lawrence and Frieda had read the book, and a diary entry by Arthur Wilkinson shows what happened next. On Saturday 23 April,

Lawrence was very naughty about W's book & said it ought to sell as a Sunday school prize – but if he reviews it he would do it more harm than good & screwed his face up so wickedly as he said it! He's in a very cross humour just now & we think Mrs L. has put his back up by overenthusiastic enjoyment of the book.

That last suggestion is almost certainly wrong, although Frieda had been known to try and praise work to stop her husband being critical of it.[109] The most obvious reason was that reviewing the book of a non-literary friend (and Lawrence never baulked at telling the truth as he saw it in his reviews, even reviews of friends) was not something to be undertaken lightly: he might indeed do 'more harm than good'. His initial objection to the job was characteristic, and appears, despite his 'wicked' facial expression, not to have given offence. But equally characteristic was the fact that he went ahead with the review anyway. He wrote it, in fact, in two drafts, so it was obviously carefully considered; he posted it on 12 May to Nancy Pearn, 'for *The Calendar*, who asked me for something. Will you give it to Rickwood [*sic*] – he needn't use it if he doesn't want to' (vi. 54). Not to do it had probably seemed to him churlish; and giving it to the *Calendar* guaranteed its acceptance. The review was merciless in its treatment of some aspects of the book, but it was also very clear-headed, and its appearance alongside the review of *Solitaria* in the July *Calendar* was practical help, in spite of the 'wickedness' and criticism.[110] The *Calendar* obviously sent Lawrence proofs, probably in May or June, as he made some small additions to the text at the proof stage.

He did one more book review later that year; but this, again, was a response to a book written by a friend, rather than a response to a magazine wanting his work. He had been corresponding with the American analyst, writer and teacher Trigant Burrow since 1925, and in the summer of 1927 Burrow's book *The Social Basis of Consciousness*, which he had been offering to publishers without success for some years, finally came out. Burrow had a copy sent to Lawrence, which arrived at the Villa Mirenda on 1 August. Lawrence read it

---

[109] John Turner, 'D. H. Lawrence in the Wilkinson Diaries', *D. H. Lawrence Review*, xxx, no. 2, 40, 42; see, e.g., Nehls, i. 266–7.
[110] For further commentary on the episode, and an example of DHL's practical help, see *Dying Game* 363–4.

at once, and wrote Burrow a long letter about it, ending: 'I shall write a review of your book if I can. Probably even then nobody will print it. But it is most in sympathy with me of any book I've read for a long time' (vi. 115). As the Lawrences left the Villa Mirenda on the 4th and Florence on the 4th or 5th, and Lawrence left his review of the book behind in Florence to be sent on to England (probably by his friend the bookseller Guiseppe 'Pino' Orioli,[111] to whose flat they went on the evening of the 4th), it seems likely that he had written the review at once – probably on the 3rd and 4th. He told Nancy Pearn: 'I should be glad if someone printed it – even in America too – because I should like to help the book for him, if I could. But if it's a lot of trouble, don't you bother' (vi. 120). She did, however, manage to place the review in the American journal *The Bookman*, in November 1927.

The reviews which Lawrence wrote between the autumn of 1925 and the summer of 1927 had occupied a surprising amount of his time, but had not brought him regular reviewing work other than at the *Calendar*. He was once again becoming a little anxious about his capacity to earn his living. With the collapse of Seltzer's business in America, he was increasingly having to rely upon his meagre English sales, and on what the magazines would pay him; by the autumn of 1927 he told Curtis Brown: 'without Miss Pearn I might be whistling, simply though we live' (vi. 222). The whole adventure of the publication of *Lady Chatterley's Lover* was, however, just beginning as he wrote that letter, and it saved him from financial disaster. 'Short things' such as reviews turned out not to be so necessary; and he was moreover just developing a new market in short, popular essays for newspapers, eventually collected in *Assorted Articles*, which took less work and paid very much better (they would bring in anything from £10 to £25 each). He would write just three more reviews during the remaining two-and-a-half years of his life, and he reverted to his old habit of writing them for particular reasons and for particular people.

1927–1928: Italian Introductions

In 1927, however, before the publication of *Lady Chatterley's Lover*, he still had to concentrate upon any possible publishing outlet. Early that spring he had been pleased to find that Jonathan Cape was planning to reissue his translation of Verga's *Mastro-don Gesualdo*. Cape had first published this in 1925, after Lawrence's main English publisher, Martin Secker, had turned it down, feeling as he did 'very dubious indeed about its prospects of appeal

[111] Guiseppe ('Pino') Orioli. (1884–1942), bookseller and publisher; see v. 450 n.30.

to the English public. It is only the slight Lawrence interest in his being associated as translator which would carry it' (v. 165 n. 4). Cape on the other hand thought sufficiently well of it to wish to include it in his 'Travellers' Library', a series of cheap reprints, and for this he wanted a new introduction. Sometime before the end of March 1927 he asked Lawrence to write one, and while in Rome between 4 and 6 April Lawrence had talked to a number of people about Verga, including Lauro de Bosis, the translator and playwright, and an unidentified person named Santellana (vi. 40).[112] But back in Florence in mid-April, Lawrence found some difficulty trying to respond to Cape's now urgent request for the introduction: 'The publisher is harrying me for that essay on Verga. Either a publisher is so dilatory, you think he's dead: or in such a hurry, you think he's taken salts' (vi. 40). He had asked his friend Christine Hughes to find for him, if possible, 'material about Giovanni Verga – some sort of *personal* facts – and some decent *Italian* critique', but none had been forthcoming: 'I scour Florence, but Verga had better have been a Hottentot, the Italians would know more about him. I suppose I'll have to invent it out of my own head – povero me! I wish I knew someone who had *known* Verga – he only died five years ago' (vi. 40).[113]

The introduction he eventually wrote exists in three forms. The first two versions contain some factual errors and hypotheses, and were presumably written before he was able to lay his hands on better information about Verga; the third version is the one published in the Cape edition. How he eventually managed to obtain more information is not clear. But it may be no coincidence that he sent his third introduction to Curtis Brown around 9 May, and two days earlier had thanked his mother-in-law for some otherwise unidentified 'notes' she had sent on from Baden-Baden to Orioli's address. It is possible that these 'notes' included a four-page manuscript found among Lawrence's papers, entitled 'Introduction', and beginning 'Verism, naturalism, realism'.[114] This manuscript, not in Lawrence's hand, appears to be a translation of an Italian essay from the early 1920s on the European novel in the nineteenth century, with several comments on Verga; but there is no conclusive evidence either that Lawrence acquired it at this time, or that it influenced the changes he made to his own piece. The two discarded versions of Lawrence's introduction are included here as Appendixes; the first appeared in *Phoenix*, but the second has not been published before.

---

[112] Lauro de Bosis (1901–31); see Explanatory note to 148:15, and vi. 40 n. 3.
[113] The Lawrences had met Christine Hughes in Santa Fe in 1924; she was now living in Rome. See v. 158 n. 1.
[114] Roberts E416.

Lawrence was still not altogether happy with his introduction when he sent it to Curtis Brown, and wrote to Cape:

> let me know if there's anything you'd like altered. If you think there should be a few more *facts*, you could get them from the old introduction, or from the introd. to *Little Novels of Sicily*. – If *Mastro-don* sells in the *Travellers' Library*, I might finish *Cavalleria Rusticana* for you. I did half the translation a year or two ago. (vi. 53)

The 'Travellers' Library' edition of *Mastro-don Gesualdo* was not in fact published until March 1928, so Cape's pressure on Lawrence to write the introduction in the spring of 1927 would seem to have been unnecessary; it had presumably been a result of Cape's trying to publish the book in a particular batch of releases in the 'Travellers' Library' series (it appeared as no. 71). Cape did add 'a few more *facts*' by appending to Lawrence's new introduction a 'Biographical Note', clearly a trenchantly revised form of the biographical note that had appeared in Seltzer's 1923 edition (whose sheets Cape had reproduced for his own 1925 edition). It is possible that Lawrence had made the alterations to this 'Note' at some stage, or it may be that Cape took up the suggestion in Lawrence's letter and revised the piece himself. He also included the 'Bibliography' of Verga and the list of 'Principal Characters' which Lawrence had appended to the Introductory Note in the 1923 edition.

By the end of May 1927, Cape appears to have responded positively to Lawrence's suggestion about his other Verga translation, and on the 27th Lawrence told Secker that he would 'probably be translating *Cavalleria Rusticana* for Jonathan Cape' (vi. 68). He was also hoping to publish the individual stories and sketches separately (vi. 70). His reference to having started 'a year or two ago' cannot be verified from any surviving manuscripts (or correspondence), but he had told Murry in May 1923 that he would be able to send him translations of two of the stories from the volume ('Cavalleria Rusticana' and 'La Lupa') for *Adelphi* (iv. 447) whenever they were wanted, so it would seem likely that he had done the first two of the total of nine translations as early as 1923.[115] Given that Lawrence seems to have regarded translation work as something to while away the time during journeys, either the voyage from Australia to California in August–September 1922 or the trip down to Mexico in the spring of 1923 would have given him the opportunity. He now worked on the remaining translations during the summer and autumn of 1927, in Italy, Austria and Germany, and by 17 September, in Baden-Baden, the book was 'nearly done . . . then I shall do a longish foreword' (vi. 152).

---

[115] Neither story was published in *Adelphi*, but the September 1923 number (pp. 284–97) included DHL's translation of 'The Saint Joseph's Ass' from *Novelle Rusticane* (it appeared as 'The Story of St. Joseph's Ass' in *Little Novels of Sicily* in 1924).

By the 25th, the work was finished: 'now I've only to do the introduction' (vi. 157). He obviously had no problems this time with biographical material, of which there is a good deal in the piece (thus perhaps confirming that it had been the 'notes' from Baden which had assisted him in May), and he sent it off as his Translator's Preface to Curtis Brown for typing on 28 September (vi. 167). He subsequently made considerable changes to the original type-script (see 'Texts'); the volume was published in February 1928.

Cape was clearly happy with the work Lawrence was doing for him, so that when, in the winter of 1927–8, he developed a plan to publish Mary G. Steegman's translation of *The Mother*, by the Sardinian novelist Grazia Deledda, he invited Lawrence to write the introduction. It may have been a fortunate coincidence, but it is more likely that he already knew, from reading *Sea and Sardinia*, of Lawrence's genuine interest in Deledda. Lawrence had recorded how, when he reached Nuoro in January 1921, he was conscious of its being Deledda's home town: 'we slip into the cold high-street of Nuoro. I am thinking that this is the home of Grazia Deledda, the novelist, and I see a barber's shop: De Ledda.'[116] We know almost nothing about the circumstances of the writing of this new introduction, except that Lawrence worked on it either late in December 1927 or early in January 1928; when he sent it in to Curtis Brown on 5 January 1928, he said that 'Jonathan Cape . . . asked me for it' (vi. 254). Lawrence noted at the end of his manuscript that Cape should be charged 6 guineas for it, 'and anything American extra'; the Dial Press brought out an American edition later in 1928. The Deledda introduction, relatively brief though it was, gave Lawrence a chance to discuss Sardinia, and to comment on the problem of translating from the Italian; it was also a further contribution to the good relationship he had built up with Cape. Lawrence would remark in December 1928 that 'he's been very friendly to me' (vii. 66).

The various introductions for Cape which he had been writing over the years, and the good relationship, must have played a considerable part in Cape's decision to suggest, sometime before February 1929, that Lawrence should compile the 'book of [his] literary criticisms and introductory essays' (vii. 218) mentioned at the start of this Introduction. There seems no doubt that Cape envied Martin Secker his control of Lawrence's work in England, and was being ingenious in finding an area where he might be able to publish an original Lawrence title of his own. Lawrence would play down the signif-icance of Cape's offer when Laurence Pollinger of the Curtis Brown agency (where Pollinger was increasingly taking charge of Lawrence's work in book

---

[116] *Sea and Sardinia*, ed. Mara Kalnins (Cambridge, 1997), pp. 131:3–5.

form) enquired about it: Pollinger remained keen on maintaining the link with Secker. Lawrence answered: 'No, I didn't *promise* Cape that book of literary essays. It was he who wrote me about them, and I said it was too soon to talk about it, we could talk when the time came. I suppose you'd want Secker to have it. Anyhow no hurry' (vii. 231–2). It may be true that Lawrence had told Cape that it was 'too soon to talk about it', though that does not completely square with the enthusiastic tone of his first reference to the idea, when he had said that it 'would make a good book, and I'll soon have enough' (vii. 218), suggesting that he may actually have started to plan it. But it is clear that, throughout the spring of 1929, Lawrence was growing increasingly irritated with Secker (especially over the publication of *Pansies*), so that if he had indeed managed to start putting the book together, he might very well have attempted to ensure that it went to Cape and not to Secker.

1928: Harry Crosby and *Chariot of the Sun*

Help for Cape, who was publishing a good deal of his work – and was taking work which other publishers had turned down – was one thing; but another and even stronger kind of responsiveness led Lawrence to write 'Chaos in Poetry', an introduction to Harry Crosby's volume of poetry *Chariot of the Sun*. The expatriate American Crosby, who owned the Black Sun Press in Paris, had 'discovered' Lawrence's work early in 1927 while on holiday in Egypt, and had sent him a copy of *Chariot of the Sun*, which had been published earlier in the year.[117] He also asked if Lawrence would sell him a manuscript, ideally something about the sun, for which he would pay in gold (American $20 pieces). Lawrence responded that Crosby wrote 'real poetry', and, in search of items to sell to him, rewrote his 1925 story 'Sun', phrasing his covering letter in such a way as to allow Crosby to believe that this manuscript was in fact the original form of a previously expurgated story.[118] He was duly paid in gold (five $20 pieces), and the Black Sun Press published the new 'Sun'. Some kind of introduction had evidently already been under discussion between Crosby and Lawrence – perhaps for another of the Black Sun Press books – when in mid-April 1928 Crosby mentioned that he was intending to produce a new edition of *Chariot of the Sun* and had written some new poems for it. Lawrence wrote in reply: 'Send your complete book of poems, and I'll write a little introduction for *it* – about 2000 words do you

---

[117] See Explanatory note to 111:21.
[118] See *The Woman Who Rode Away and Other Stories*, ed. Dieter Mehl and Christa Jansohn (Cambridge, 1995), pp. xxxi–xxxii.

want? I really like the poems. – Send it soon, so I do it before we leave here' (vi. 372). In the event, he set to work straight away, writing an introduction to *Chariot of the Sun* in its original from, without waiting for the new 'complete' book to arrive, and he wrote again to Crosby on 29 April (the date on his manuscript introduction):

I was afraid it might be too late for me to do it here, if I waited. – I am sending you the MS, which please keep, as I have got a type copy. But if you'd like it bound like the other two, send it to me c/o Pino Orioli, 6 Lungarno Corsini, Florence, and I'll have it done. – You can cut this introduction, and do what you like with it, for your book. If there is any part you don't like, omit it. I give you the thing along with the other MSS. (vi. 389)

Lawrence did not actually post this letter until 1 May, as in the meantime the new poems had finally come, but he did not like them so much, and later advised Crosby to leave them out. He now sent Crosby both the manuscript and a typescript of the introduction (see 'Texts'), and in his postscript pointed out that 'the *typescript* is the complete thing' (vi. 390).

Although Crosby's gold had only been worth about £25 – and Lawrence had given Crosby a number of manuscripts, including the re-written version of 'Sun' – his sense of obligation to Crosby was so strong that he effectively offered him the introduction *gratis*: 'If the publishers feel like paying a few dollars, all right. But not you' (vi. 389). He also put to Crosby the idea of having the introduction published separately, as a kind of advertisement for the poems (though that, of course, would in turn generate Lawrence some income):

And let me know if you'd like me to send the Introduction to my agent, to try on the magazines, or if you'd rather not. Probably no-one would print it – if they did, I'd better have the name of your publisher and date of publication of *Chariot*, you are keeping the same title? – are you keeping that engraving about the sun? If not, then strike out that sentence about it, in my introduction. – But if you'd rather the introduction were not printed except in your book, I am perfectly content. Only as a magazine-article it would be a bit of an advertisement for you. (vi. 389)

Around 20 May[119] Lawrence apparently received permission from Crosby to 'try' the piece 'on the magazines'. Crosby also seems to have asked Lawrence to restore the original manuscript ending (its closing phrase had been 'blows

---

[119] It is arguable that the letter to Crosby (4432: vi. 404–5), provisionally dated [21? May 1928], may have been written before the letter to Nancy Pearn (4431: vi. 403–4), dated 21 May 1928, or at least before the postscript to this latter. DHL remarks in his letter to Crosby, 'I'll send it to the agent in London', but in his postscript to Nancy Pearn he writes 'I send you "Chaos in Poetry"', which suggests that the changes to the text of the introduction had been made by this time (it is also the first mention of the new title which he had inserted on his typescript).

us sun-wards'), as Lawrence replied: 'Do entirely as you like with the Introduction, end it where you like. I'll find "sunwards" on my copy, and end it
there. I'll send it to the agent in London' (vi. 404). He could not, however,
find 'sunwards' on his copy, as the word had only appeared on the manuscript
which he had sent Crosby in the first place; Lawrence had rewritten the ending at the first typing stage. Nevertheless, he proceeded to revise the ending
again, very heavily, and altered the title from 'A Book Of Modern Poems' to
'Chaos in Poetry'. It was in this form that he sent the piece to his agent, and in
which it was first published, in the December 1929 issue of *Echanges*. Crosby,
having been prompted by Lawrence to 'end it where you like', arranged, when
preparing his new edition of *Chariot of the Sun* for the press, for Lawrence's
original manuscript ending to be reinstated (see 'Texts').

It should be stressed that, on the one hand, Lawrence was doing his best
to restore a balance of obligation which, as a result of Crosby's generosity,
he felt had been tilted in his own favour (never a comfortable position for
him). On the other, the introduction was by no means uncritical. Like other
pieces Lawrence wrote on behalf of friends, it shows that doing a favour did
not mean being either fawning or apologetic; the introduction remarks that
Crosby's work has no 'outstanding melody or rhythm or image or epithet or
even sense'. Lawrence calls the book 'a sheaf of flimsies', and a recent com-
mentator has pointed out how, to Lawrence, the fact 'that Crosby's poetry
is often technically incompetent and sometimes silly is less important than
its originality'. David Ellis sums up the introduction as 'praise of a highly
qualified kind'.[120] By the time it appeared in print, Crosby was dead: he committed suicide in New York in December 1929.[121] In January 1930 Lawrence
suggested to Crosby's widow, Caresse – who was thinking of publishing the
'Third Series' of Crosby's diaries, those for his final year – that 'if I could write
a suitable foreword, I'd be glad to' (vii. 634); but he did not himself live to do
so.[122] The expanded volume of *Chariot of the Sun* appeared from the Black
Sun Press in 1931, with Lawrence's introduction in the form Crosby had
preferred.

1928–1929: Reviewing for *Vogue*, and introducing himself

Back in 1928, following the first writing of the introduction for Crosby, and
as another kind of favour – this time to the ever-reliable Nancy Pearn, who
had been loyally trying to extend his reviewing market for years – Lawrence

[120] See below, 113:14–15, 111:22; and *Dying Game* 408.   [121] See vii. 600 and n. 2.
[122] *Shadows of the Sun*, First, Second and Third Series (Paris, 1928–30).

took on another review of several books at once. Nancy Pearn had written on 11 July that the popular fashion magazine *Vogue* had requested a review article on four books: *The Station: Athos, Treasures and Men* by Robert Byron, *England and the Octopus* by Clough Williams-Ellis, *Comfortless Memory* by Maurice Baring, and *Ashenden: or The British Agent* by W. Somerset Maugham. Nancy reminded Lawrence that *Vogue* was 'a terribly refined and pleasant journal' (vi. 463 n. 4), and passed on to him a review recently done for *Vogue*, by Humbert Wolfe,[123] of *Etched in Moonlight* by James Stephens, *Keeping Up Appearances* by Rose Macaulay, and *Jazz and Jasper* by William Gerhardi, which had appeared in the issue of 16 May 1928, and which the editor of *Vogue* had sent on for Lawrence to see, as Nancy Pearn subsequently claimed, to give 'an idea of the *form* of their reviews in the sad but possible event of your not being a reader of her priceless publication' (vi. 464 n. 2). Lawrence had remarked in some asperity, when he sent her his review:

But for disappointing you in your efforts on my behalf, I wouldn't have done it – for they were a dull lot of books – except *Athos.*
  Tell them they can cut it down if they want.
  And I could never rise to the fatuous idiocy of Humbert Wolf, whoever he is. Imagine their sending me him as a pattern! Tell them to go to simpering simpleton's hell. (vi. 463–4)

Nancy Pearn tried to take the sting out of the response when she replied, addressing him as 'Dear darling Mr Lawrence', and writing 'You never for a moment really thought anybody meant you to take *Humbert Wolfe* as an example!! It was merely one that came first to hand' (vi. 464 n. 2). When she wrote of the 'form' of *Vogue* book-reviews, she may have had in mind that they appeared under the standard heading 'Turning Over New Leaves', and usually involved the three or four books under review being linked together in some more or less ingenious way. It may also be that the Wolfe review had indeed been sent to give Lawrence an idea of the slightly facetious, man-about-town tone the editor of *Vogue* might – not unreasonably, given some of the newspaper articles Lawrence had been writing – have wished him to adopt. And the fact that the review exists in two different versions reveals that he worked quite hard at writing the kind of piece which he thought would be appropriate (a fragmentary false start of the version he eventually completed also survives). He had begun by writing about the Williams-Ellis book first, and continuing with the Baring and the Maugham, but broke off this draft before he arrived at the Byron. He must have decided that what he wanted to say about Byron would go best at the start of the piece, and would

[123] Humbert Wolfe (1885–1940), poet and critic; see vi. 464 n. 1.

allow him to organise the review around the contrast between the younger and older generation of writers. The final version praised the books by Byron and Williams-Ellis, but laid into Maurice Baring's *Comfortless Memory* as 'a piece of portentous unreality larded with Goethe, Dante, Heine, hopelessly out of date, and about as exciting as stale restaurant cake'; while it described Somerset Maugham's *Ashenden, or The British Agent*, as 'ill-humoured' and 'faked'.[124] A month later he asked Nancy Pearn 'Did *Vogue* print that review? – I'll bet not!' (vi. 516), but it did, very accurately, on 8 August 1928 – although he was not asked to review for *Vogue* again.

What Lawrence could do in another vein, introducing poems, can be seen in the two introductions he wrote to his own poems on 12 May 1928, just twelve days after writing his piece about Crosby. These were the first of a series of introductions to his own work which he wrote between May 1928 and April 1929. He produced essays to go in front of his two-volume *Collected Poems* (for Secker), his volume of *Paintings* (for the Mandrake Press) and his poetry volume *Pansies* (three different versions in all, one used by Secker, one used by Lahr and one only printed in 1988). He also wrote the essay 'My Skirmish with Jolly Roger', designed to go in front of the cheap reprint of his novel *Lady Chatterley's Lover* (for the Paris publication by Edward Titus).[125] All these essays were in different ways polemics; they represent Lawrence being reminiscent, argumentative, provocative and independent-minded, in the manner that was by now perhaps his most recognisable public style. Finally, in August 1929, he heard that his friend the artist Blair Hughes-Stanton wanted to publish an illustrated version of *Birds, Beasts and Flowers*. Lawrence was happy for this to go ahead, and on 30 August he told Hughes-Stanton to contact Curtis Brown: 'T[ell] them, if they like I'll do them a new foreword, on the essential nature of poetry or something like that' (vii. 457).[126] It was put to him instead that he might write a series of hundred-word captions before each of the nine parts into which the volume was divided. He seemed dubious at first about this: 'If I see any point, and can do it, I'll do it, but at present feel perfectly blank before the idea' (vii. 535), but he did eventually comply. These nine pieces hardly count as full introductions, however, and it is unlikely that he would have considered them candidates for any critical book he wanted to compile.

June–July 1928, when Lawrence saw a good deal of his American friends the Brewsters, is also one of a number of possible dates for the fragmentary notes he made for a piece of writing planned by Earl Brewster, on

[124] See below, 342:15–16, 343:19, 13.   [125] See vii. 225 n. 3.
[126] Blair Rowlands Hughes-Stanton (1902–81), painter and engraver; see vi. 411 n. 3.

'The Hand Of Man'. Another possible date would be late summer 1929; Lawrence wrote to Brewster on 13 August in terms similar to those in his pencil manuscript, about Gandhi and the 'fight . . . to survive the machine' (vii. 424), and again on 5 September (vii. 465). Lawrence's 'Notes' are included here as an Appendix, for their intrinsic interest, and as another small example of the practical help with his friends' writing which he was always so willing to offer. It is not clear whether Brewster's article was ever written, nor exactly what it was to be: a piece entitled 'The Hand Of Man', or a review of a book of that name (no plausible candidate has been located).

Another project took up a good deal of his time and energy between the end of 1928 and the end of 1929. Following the considerable success of the venture of publishing *Lady Chatterley's Lover* with Orioli, Lawrence proposed a whole series of books which Orioli could publish; translations into English of 'Italian Renaissance Novelists', in the so-called 'Lungarno Series': the name was, however, apparently only invented in October 1929 (vii. 526–7). Lawrence offered to start the series with his own translation of Grazzini's (Il Lasca's) *The Story of Doctor Manente* (vi. 595). He made the translation in October and November 1928, and, to help the series along, was happy to draft an announcement (sent to Orioli on 1 November) and to suggest details of costing. In January 1929 he also suggested finding someone to write them 'a good essay on "The Italian Novelette" of the Renaissance', to serve as 'a good Introd. to a *series* of stories of which Lasca's could be the first' (vii. 141). It took a long time for *The Story of Doctor Manente* to get into print, however, and it was not until August 1929 that there is evidence of Lawrence's returning corrected proofs to Orioli (vii. 410, 432, 446, 477, 492). By this point he had obviously written his own Foreword to the Lasca text; he may well have done so as early as the middle of November 1928, when he was finishing the translation, or he may have done it in the spring of 1929. Lawrence also took responsibility for the copious explanatory notes, which he completed only at the proof stage (vii. 415–16). At the end of September, he was asking Orioli about 'sending your circular out' (vii. 502); he himself probably drafted this circular, as a 'Prospectus', for it exists in his hand, and is included here in the Appendices.

The series was not, in fact, a success; too many copies of this first title were printed (2,400 rather than the 1,200 copies on the Statement of Limitation in the book), and it was still on sale in 1957. Lawrence also hoped to go on to a second story from Lasca, the so-called 'Second Supper', and started to translate it in July 1929 (vii. 394), but the book itself was never published.

1929–1930: Last Introductions – Dahlberg, Carter, Koteliansky

Lawrence was still to write three introductions for other people's books, and contemplated yet further writing of that kind. Hearing early in 1928 that his old friend Catherine Carswell (whom he had known even longer than he had known Kot) was trying to persuade the Nonesuch Press to put into print the notorious *Merry Muses of Caledonia* selection of verse, which included some poems by Burns (she would later write a Burns biography), he had written to her: 'if you like, I could do a small introductory essay' (vi. 337, 287).[127] A week later he refined the idea: 'an essay on Burns and the *Muses* by you – and *if you like*, a little essay on being bawdy, by me – but this last by no means necessarily' (vi. 291). Nothing, unfortunately, came of this idea. But at the end of the year the young American novelist Edward Dahlberg asked Lawrence if he would be willing to read his first, as yet untitled, novel, to which Lawrence responded: 'I will of course read your MS. if you wish it' (vii. 65).[128] It arrived on 19 December: Lawrence replied 'I will read it and let you know how it strikes me' (vii. 69). He read it in three days and then sent Dahlberg a letter full of critical praise; the letter is reproduced here, as it is in effect a first version of the introduction he would later write:

I have read your MS. At first I didn't like it – the old-fashioned sort of sordid realism done rather in detail. But when it moves to the orphanage it gets into stride and has the myopic vision and exaggerated sensitiveness and exaggerated *insensitiveness* on the other hand, of the sort of substratum, *gamin* life you are dealing with. It seems to me you have hit that layer of American consciousness very well, *got it*: the blindness of it, the extreme sensitiveness over a small, immediately personal field, and then the dumb, slummy unconsciousness to all the rest of the world. I don't know how you carry the book on. As it is, it looks as if it can only continue in the same monotone, the same thing over and over again, even if the scene shifts. But that is the whole point. There are no relationships, no real human connections, therefore no possible development of drama or tragedy or anything like that. The human being is whittled down to a few elementary and almost mechanical reactions. A relationship that amounted to anything would take the book right out of what it is, and put it on another footing, another plane. One feels it would be false, somehow. But that's not for me to say. – The curious street-arab, down-and-out *stoicism*, something very dreary and yet impressive, denuded, like those brown horrid rocks in Central Park, seems to me the real theme. – As far as I can judge, it's a real book, and with a real new note in it. You ought easily to get a publisher, and the thing ought to have a certain success. (vii. 83)

He told Dahlberg that, when approaching publishers, 'you can say I think it's a worth-while book, if you wish' (vii. 84); he gave him the name and address

---

[127] Catherine Roxburgh Carswell (1879–1946), Scottish writer; see ii. 187 n. 5.
[128] Edward Dahlberg (1900–77), American writer; see Explanatory note to 119:2.

of Curtis Brown, in case he needed an agent, and he also offered to write him a letter to a publisher (vii. 112). He was thus reproducing the kindness which he himself had been shown as a young man, when Ford Madox Hueffer had written him a letter in December 1909 to send to a publisher on behalf of *The White Peacock* (viii. 2–3). When Dahlberg's novel was accepted by the London-based publisher Putnams, at the end of January 1929, Dahlberg wrote to Lawrence asking if he would do an introduction for the book. Lawrence, evidently a little surprised, told a correspondent, 'I've said probably. Nothing like asking' (vii. 157). To Dahlberg himself he replied: 'If you'll send me a complete proof of your novel as soon as it is possible, I'll have a shot at doing a short critical foreword, and Putnams can settle with Curtis Brown' (vii. 156–7).

Dahlberg was apparently contrite at having asked the favour of Lawrence so directly, and Lawrence wrote again: 'Don't bother about that introd. to your novel – I don't mind doing it if I have the proof fairly soon' (vii. 160). Proofs of the novel arrived during February and Lawrence sent his agent the introduction on 24 February 1929 (vii. 191). He also wrote to the publisher with some suggestions for titles: 'As you say, it's not an easy novel for the public to take up. But it should have a certain sale. For a title, you might have "Underdogs"' (vii. 192). He thus had some influence on the title finally adopted: *Bottom Dogs*. To his own agent he wrote, significantly, 'I don't want Dahlberg to *possess* that introd. – that is, I want the right to reprint it' (vii. 218). He had his own volume of critical and introductory essays in mind.

In the event, Dahlberg may well have regretted asking Lawrence for the introduction. The £20 which Lawrence was paid for it by Putnam 'has to be subtracted from his royalties', which made Lawrence feel 'a bit mean' (vii. 526). Also, Dahlberg felt 'a bit irritated by my preface' (vii. 272): 'he wrote me from New York, a wee bit spitefully, that my Introduction was doing him harm, Huebsch saying it was a "bad sales" letter – whatever that may mean' (vii. 526). Lawrence advised Dahlberg: 'It's quite simple to suppress it altogether in U.S.A. – make no mention of it, and it doesn't exist. – It won't hurt *English* sales, as Putnam knows, even if it is a bad Sales-Letter in America. – I can't help it, anyhow – I had to write what I felt' (vii. 272).

Helping his old friend Koteliansky was rather more straightforward. Kot's translation of Rozanov's *Solitaria* had come out in 1927, and at the end of 1928, Lawrence was able to help him get another Rozanov translation into print. The Mandrake Press were consulting with Lawrence over various projects (they would publish *The Paintings of D. H. Lawrence* in June 1929), and one of the partners in the Press, the Australian P. R. Stephensen, visited Lawrence in Bandol in December 1928.[129] Lawrence mentioned Kot's translation of another of Rozanov's books – and was able to tell Kot on 21 December that 'they say they will be glad to do *Fallen Leaves*' (vii. 82); he backed this up when he wrote to Stephensen in January 1929 (vii. 147). By August, the project was obviously well under way (vii. 474), and Lawrence was expecting the book to arrive in October 1929 (vii. 539). Stephensen sent it to him on 31 October with a characteristically cheerful and realistic note:

Dear old Kot. is hoping that somebody will read Rozanov. I am completely pessimistic, and don't suppose we shall sell fifty copies . . . I only published FALLEN LEAVES to do Kot. a service because I like him . . . the book will not sell, because *Solitaria* made hardly any headway at all.   (vii. 556 n. 3)

Nevertheless, friends like Stephensen and Lawrence did what they could, and Lawrence wrote a piece about *Fallen Leaves* as soon as his copy arrived. He sent it to Nancy Pearn on 7 November 1929: 'Here is an article on Rozanov's *Fallen Leaves* and I wish you would find somebody to publish it, for the book's sake' (vii. 556). He was not optimistic that it would get into print, telling Charles Lahr two days later, 'don't know if anyone will print it' (vii. 559), and Kot on the 27th: 'probably they'll not be able to place it'. He also told Kot about the book that 'some of it I think really good – the latter half' (vii. 575). Nancy Pearn managed to place the review in the magazine *Everyman* on 23 January 1930; in spite of his modesty, Lawrence's name, by this stage of his career, was almost a guarantee that such a piece would be printed. *Everyman* headed the article with a recent photograph of Lawrence, claimed that Lawrence was '*one of the first English writers to detect [Rozanov's] greatness*', and also inserted a small box in the middle of the first page of the review, containing a comment by Arnold Bennett: '*It is impossible to ignore a piece of critical work by such a penetrating and original critic as Lawrence.*'[130] In such ways, yet again, Koteliansky could be helped. What Lawrence wrote was not essentially different from what he would have put in an introduction: the difference from 1919 was simply that Koteliansky now had something of a reputation – and it had been Lawrence who had helped him to acquire it.

A rather different problem overtook an introduction he wrote at the start of January 1930, where the author of the book for which it was intended felt he could not use it. Lawrence had first read material by Frederick Carter, about the astrological basis of the Book of Revelation, back in 1923, and had kept in touch with him over the years; in August 1929 Carter approached him to ask what he thought of a new idea for using the old material, much of which

---

[129] Percy Reginald Stephensen (1901–65), Australian publisher; see vii. 31 n. 1.
[130] *Everyman*, ii, no. 52 (23 January 1930), 733.

had never been published.[131] Lawrence replied: 'I'm sure we can find a way of printing it complete, even if I have to write a real spangled foreword to it (perhaps you'd refuse to let me)' (vii. 456). When Carter sent him the material, Lawrence told him that 'What I shall have to do is to write a comment on the Apocalypse also, from my point of view – and touching on yours – and try to give some sort of complete idea. Then the public will be able to read you' (vii. 507). He also complained about the introduction to Carter's 1926 book *The Dragon of the Alchemists*, which had been written by the novelist Arthur Machen: 'that was a feeble introd. to your book. He never *read* you' (vii. 519). But rather than writing something which could be published together with Carter's material, either as an introduction or perhaps as the 'joint book' Lawrence mentioned on 1 October 1929 (vii. 509), Lawrence actually wrote something so long that it became his own book *Apocalypse*. He explained this to Carter when the latter visited Bandol in December 1929; the 'introduction' he had been trying to write 'had then attained the dimensions, I believe he said, of twenty to thirty thousand words' (vii. 555 n. 2). Lawrence wrote to him in January 1930: 'It became so long and somehow unsuitable to go in front of your essays. So at last I laid it aside, and have written you now a proper introduction, about 5000 words, I think, which is really quite good and to the point, I feel' (vii. 613).

A fortnight later he told Carter that 'I hope it's what you want. I like it myself, and think of it as an introduction really . . . I shall lay my longer introduction [i.e. *Apocalypse*] by – not try to publish it now' (vii. 622). He may well have felt that it would have been unfair to Carter to compete in the same market. He had also explained what he thought should be done with the 'proper' introduction:

For such an introduction I usually get £20 or £25, but we could arrange that: as outright payment, with right to include the introd. in a book of collected essays later on: which is quite simple, and leaves you free to arrange all terms yourself; the publisher merely paying me the £20. down for his right to use the introd. for, say, a term of two years. (vii. 613)

To his agent, he offered yet another way of using the piece: 'I have told him [Carter], if he finds the publisher, he can pay £20 for the "Introd." But I think he'll have hard work getting anyone to take his book. – This "Introd." might possibly be serialised' (vii. 613–14). And that was exactly what happened. The introduction appeared in the *London Mercury* in July 1930, but although the Mandrake Press advertised the publication of Carter's book together with Lawrence's introduction, the volume never appeared. Carter could not find a

---

[131] Frederick Carter (1883–1967), painter; see iv. 365 n. 3, and *Apocalypse* 3–24.

publisher until 1932, when the book came out as *Dragon of the Apocalypse*, but without Lawrence's introduction; Carter seems to have felt that Lawrence's interpretation cast too strong a shadow over his own thinking to be tolerated within the same covers. Lawrence's introduction has not been included in this volume because it is already in print in the Cambridge edition,[132] but it would clearly have been a candidate for Lawrence's 'book of collected essays later on' (vii. 613).

It was shortly after Carter had left Bandol, on 9 January 1930, that Lawrence embarked on his last literary introduction, one that took him back almost to the beginning of his career. In 1913, as the opening of his piece records, he had first read *The Brothers Karamazov*, and discussed it with Murry, the latter being particularly well-read in Dostoevsky (in 1916 he would publish a full-length critical book on him);[133] while in 1914 he had first met Koteliansky. In 1919, the then almost unknown Koteliansky needed Lawrence's help with his Shestov translation and with active publishing advice, and although by now Koteliansky was a less obscure figure, his new project still needed all the support it could get. He was planning to produce a new translation of the 'Grand Inquisitor' section of Dostoevsky's novel, and was wondering whether Lawrence would write an introduction. Koteliansky was publishing the book himself, and was looking to guard against the risks of the enterprise in as many ways as possible; for this he once more needed Lawrence's help, and Lawrence, even in a dreadful state of health, was willing to give it.

Koteliansky could in fact hardly have chosen a better moment; Lawrence was about to finish working on *Apocalypse*, and had just been writing

about the impossibility of fitting the Christian religion to the State – Send me the *Grand Inquisitor*, and I'll see if I can do an introduction. Tell me how *long* you'd like it. I did about 6,000 words for Carter's Apocalypse book. For the Introd. to Dahlberg's *Bottom Dogs* I got £20 – but that is a bit low. It depends on the publisher and the price of the edition etc. Tell me what the plan is. We can arrange all right . . . Send me your translation.   (vii. 618)

Within a week, he had a copy of the text, and Koteliansky's request for an introduction of 1,000 words (Kot may well have wanted to keep the price of Lawrence's introduction down, in comparison with the £20 Dahlberg had had to pay). Lawrence replied: 'Just a word to say I have the *Inquisitor* and will try to do a nice little introduction – though I shall never be able to squash myself down to a thousand words' (vii. 620). Laurence Pollinger came to stay the same day that Koteliansky's translation of the Dostoevsky piece arrived, Wednesday 15 January, and when Pollinger went back to London on Monday 20 January, he took with him the completed introduction, around 4,000 words

---

[132] See footnote 4.   [133] John Middleton Murry, *Fyodor Dostoevsky* (1916).

long. Lawrence had obviously read the piece and written his introduction in five days – during which time he was also busy correcting the typescript which had become his own *Apocalypse*; he had Pollinger as a visitor, and Frieda's sister Else had also come to stay. The Dostoevsky introduction was almost his last piece of writing; the day that Pollinger returned to England, Dr Andrew Morland told Lawrence that he must stop work and rest completely – a period of enforced rest which ended only when Lawrence went into the Ad Astra sanatorium on 6 February.[134] In contrast with Carter, and although the introduction was four times the length originally stipulated, Kot faithfully included it in the edition of his translation, which was published in July 1930.[135]

1930: Last Review – Gill

Letters apart, the last thing Lawrence probably ever wrote was a book review. Eric Gill's book *Art-Nonsense and Other Essays* had been published in December 1929, and Lawrence acquired a copy early in 1930. Given how little he was able to get about at that stage of his life, it seems unlikely that he should have bought it himself, and a great deal more likely that someone he knew (such as Stephensen) had sent it to him, or that Pollinger or another friend (perhaps Earl or Achsah Brewster) had given it to him, thinking it would interest him. Someone at some stage wrote 'The last thing written by DHL before he died' on the cover of the notebook in which he wrote his review; the source of the information was certainly Frieda Lawrence, who gave the first publisher of the piece a note 'to this effect': 'Lawrence wrote this unfinished review a few days before he died. The book interested him, and he agreed with much in it. Then he got tired of writing and I persuaded him not to go on. It is the last thing he wrote.'[136] On the notebook itself appear the words 'Ad Astra'; it appears likely therefore that Lawrence actually wrote the review while in the Ad Astra sanatorium in Vence, between 6 February and 1 March.[137]

Tedlock speculates that writing the review may have provoked Lawrence to insert, in the middle of the same notebook, the heading 'God and Art',

---

[134] Dr Andrew John Morland (1896–1957); see vii. 575 n. 3.

[135] Koteliansky however – having also quarrelled with Murry – asked DHL if he could leave out the name 'Middleton Murry' on the first page of the introduction. DHL responded 'Yes, you can leave out Murry's name – put Katharine's instead, if you like' (vii. 643). 'Middleton Murry' has been restored in this edition.

[136] *Book Collector's Quarterly*, xii (October–November 1933), 1.

[137] Gill read the review before it was published; he wrote to Frieda (who had probably sent him a copy), on 17 April 1933, that 'I think he is probably right in most of his strictures. I am indeed an inept and amateurish preacher' (Fiona McCarthy, *Eric Gill*, 1999, p. 257). There is a reproduction in McCarthy of Gill's title-page (mentioned by DHL), p. 233.

which looks like the title of an essay he intended to go on to write. But all that exists of it is the title. Again, there are seventeen blank leaves in the notebook between the end of the Gill review and the heading, which suggests that he had some other writing project which he thought might take up such a space (it seems unlikely that he thought the Gill review would go on for that kind of length). But nothing survives of that either. The review is already as long as his previous review, of *Fallen Leaves*, and it seems unlikely that he would have written much more, even if he had been able to. It had to wait for more than three years before being published.[138]

It was characteristic of Lawrence not only to go on writing to the end, but to engage with someone else's thinking in the way he knew best: by writing, by arguing in writing and (most significantly of all) by insisting, as he had always done, that 'Happy, intense absorption in any work, which is to be brought as near to perfection as possible, this is a state of being with God, and the men who have not known it have missed life itself.'[139] His own work as a writer had always been intensely absorbing to him, and it went on being so, right up to a few days before he died.

Texts

1 Introductions

Foreword to All Things Are Possible

Base-text is the 4-page manuscript (MS), held at UN (Roberts E11a), emended slightly from the first published edition, *All Things Are Possible* (Secker, 1920), pp. 7–12 (E1). MS has light interlinear revision. Lawrence made changes at proof stage, but the corrected proofs are unlocated (see above, p. xxxvi and footnote 37).

Note to All Things Are Possible

The Note appears to have been written directly into the proofs of *All Things Are Possible*. The text is printed on p. [5] of the first published edition (Secker, 1920).

Memoir of Maurice Magnus

Base-text is the 59-page manuscript (MS), held at UN (Roberts E233.7), which Lawrence wrote between November 1921 and January 1922. MS is

---

[138] In the *Book Collector's Quarterly*, xii (October–November 1933).
[139] See below, 358:14–17.

emended from some of the substantive changes made to the 'Introduction' to Secker's first edition of *Memoirs of the Foreign Legion* of 1 October 1924, pp. 11–94 (E1). MS was sent to Mountsier in 1922, who had it typed. It shows occasional signs of being marked up for a typist or printer; on pp. 12 and 23 phrases are pencilled through, and on p. 42, a three-line paragraph is marked 'leave out' in pencil, in what appears to be Mountsier's hand. The pencil directions were all followed in E1: see Textual apparatus for 22:29, 35:21 and 58:9. What look like traces of a printer's spike appear in the top left-hand corner of every page, but as the MS was never handled by a printer, it may have been fastened together by Mountsier's typist, by Lawrence himself, or by Mountsier.

The (now missing) typescript derived from MS must have been sent to Thomas Seltzer and would have been passed on to Secker; it was the origin of the text of E1. The typescript had been conscientiously made, but at times its typist clearly misread MS: e.g. an oddly written 'slowly' (MS, p. 21) turned into 'stoutly' (E1, p. 42), 'borne' (MS, p. 27) became 'done' (E1, p. 51), and a very oddly inscribed 'lurking feeling' (MS, p. 43) turned into the much more conventional 'sinking feeling' (E1 p. 78).

Secker gave this typescript copy of the introduction (which of course Lawrence himself had never seen) to the printer (William Brendon and Son, of the Mayflower Press, Plymouth), together with a retyped copy of Magnus's book also provided by Seltzer. On 23 May 1924 Secker wrote to Lawrence that he was 'looking forward very much now to seeing proofs of the Magnus manuscript, and I expect to be posting these to you next week' (v. 38 n. 2). It was not, however, until 17 June 1924 that Secker sent Lawrence proofs of his introduction for correction. Secker had probably already made one large-scale cut, at 63:27–66:18, and marked other changes, along with name changes (see above, p. xlvii), on the missing typescript (no such changes are marked on the surviving manuscript, of course, as it had remained with Mountsier). It is also possible that these changes were made on the first proofs; this might account for the delay between the end of May, when Secker originally expected to send Lawrence proofs, and 17 June, when he actually sent a set. Lawrence's letter and parcel of 2 May to Secker (with proofs of *The Boy in the Bush* in it) had taken exactly three weeks to get from New Mexico to London (v. 38 n. 2). It seems likely therefore that Secker's 17 June letter with the proofs of the introduction would not have arrived in New Mexico before the first week of July; so that when Lawrence wrote on 7 July 1924, 'Here are the revised proofs of the Magnus Introduction – hope they haven't been too long travelling' (v. 70), he had probably spent two or three days at most examining them.

The Secker edition contains, perhaps as a result, relatively few clear examples of authorial textual changes introduced at the proof stage, though it is full of styling and punctuation differences of the kind which (in the first instance) Mountsier's typist, and subsequently Secker and his printer, would have made without consulting the author. Lawrence's new American publisher, Alfred Knopf, published the first American edition of the 'Memoir' and book in 1925 (A1); he must have produced his re-set edition from a copy of E1, as all the readings of E1 are reproduced in it. In 1937 the essay was reprinted as 'The Portrait of M. M.' in the anthology *Woollcott's Second Reader*, named after the critic Alexander Woollcott (A2); the text of the Knopf edition was used. In 1960 the essay was again reprinted in the bi-annual review *the noble savage*, again as 'The Portrait of M. M.' (Per); the text used was that of A2. The essay appeared again in *Phoenix II: Uncollected, Unpublished and Other Prose Works by D. H. Lawrence*, ed. Warren Roberts and Harry T. Moore (1968), pp. 303–61 (E2), with text taken from E1. A1, A2, Per and E2 have not been collated.

Keith Cushman, the editor of *Memoir of Maurice Magnus*, the first book-length edition of the essay, published in 1987 (A3), assumed that MS (or some derivation of it) was the setting copy of E1. He argued that 'most of' the changes in E1 should be attributed to the printer and publisher subjecting the text to 'house-styling' (A3, p. 7). A3 – which has been collated – accordingly ignored not just 'most of', but all the significant textual differences of E1.[140] Variants in E1 such as those at 12:10 (where MS reads 'spruce' but E1 reads 'natty'), 66:23 and 66:31 (where MS reads 'Maurice' but E1 prints 'our hero'), and at 71:12 (where MS reads 'peace' but E1 prints 'Lethe') demonstrate, however, that Lawrence's corrected proofs arrived in time for his changes to influence E1, and that he had been through them from beginning to end. It follows that any of the other substantive changes in E1 may also be Lawrence's, though we must not forget Secker's admission that he too had made 'a few alterations' in E1 as well as the major cut towards the end, whilst errors would also have been made by the original typist. One 'alteration' originating with Secker is, for example, recorded in the Textual apparatus at 13:10: the title of Douglas's novel *They Went* was omitted in E1, presumably as part of an attempt to disguise Douglas's identity. Secker was also responsible for the omission of the names of Douglas and Magnus throughout the text, and for other names being changed or omitted, and other forms of disguise adopted. There are also some suspicious cuts of a few words in Lawrence's denunciation of war towards the end of the essay (at 70:12, 71:5 and 71:7), and of a short

---

[140] A3 also added a few substantive errors to the text, e.g. omitting 'and' at 40:29; 'was' at 36:32; a repeated 'What can I do?' at 44:12; at 69:26 printing 'terrible' rather than 'horrible'; at 72:4 replacing 'highest' with 'higher'; and misreading DHL's 'Liebetrau' for 'Liebetran' at 72:15.

paragraph at 48:7; these are almost certainly Secker cutting what he thought were prolixities.

A3 did not discuss the problem of these changes. It seems likely, however, that some of the changes made in E1 originated in Lawrence's responses to a set of proofs which drew attention to places where changes might be considered. For example: at 12:10, where the word 'spruce' had in MS been used twice in two lines, E1 replaced the second with the characteristically Lawrentian word 'natty'; no-one except Lawrence is likely to have been responsible for exactly that change, even if adjustment at that point may have been suggested by another person. A3 assumed that all such changes were examples of an editor's or printer's 'desire for regularization' (p. 7), but a sequence of small re-writings was perhaps prompted by a series of queries in the proofs about repetitions. For example, at 16:36 a repeated 'damned' was removed, and a stop was also changed to a comma; at 17:34 a repeated 'only' was cut; at 20:1 'bouncy' became 'buoyant' (the word 'bounce' appeared again four lines later); at 22:3 not only was the repetition of 'certain' eliminated but also an addition – 'with it' – was made; at 30:34 the use of the word 'lies' three times in two lines was reduced to two; and at 46:5 the repetition of 'again' in consecutive sentences was removed. At other points, Lawrence's proof correction is suggested by the addition of material in close proximity to a cut being made; e.g. at 36:32 'heathy' was cut while at 26:33 'and seemed' was added. Other examples include the fact that at 59:34 not only does 'as' become 'and' but 'upon' becomes 'on'; and at 72:19–20 'importance, royal' is removed and 'apparently' inserted.

Our policy has therefore been to restore the major cut at 63:27–66:18 made by Secker, and to disregard the various name changes for which he was responsible; to restore the punctuation of MS which either did not survive the typing by Mountsier's typist or was ignored by Secker's printers; and also conservatively to emend MS with the added, omitted or altered substantives of E1 where the latter are arguably the result of Lawrence's own proof correction. This emendation has been limited to cases where the altered language is in some way characteristic of Lawrence, as in the cases of 'natty' and 'our hero', or because the proximity of cuts and additions suggests authorial work, or because what appears to have been a sequence of proof queries about repetitions had been answered. Each case has been judged on its merits. Where, for example, MS (p. 34) has Melenda saying 'It is many years since he has been in Italy' (48:26), the emendation in E1 (p. 64) to 'It is many years that he has been in Italy' might suggest a typist or printer who has failed to appreciate Lawrence's creation of Melenda's slightly unidiomatic English: MS has been preferred. Here, as elsewhere, MS offers us what Lawrence certainly wrote, which is why any emendation of it must be conservative. On the other hand, one emendation in which Lawrence may well have been involved, at 23:18 – where 'He, by the way, was a Maltese, with English as one of his native languages' was changed to 'He spoke English as if it were his native language' (E1, p. 28) – has been judged an attempt to protect the identity of Don Mauro Inguanez at Montecassino, and has not been adopted. Individual cases of particular interest or difficulty have been discussed in the Explanatory notes.

A 'True Copy' is still extant (UT) of the long letter from 'Salonia' about Magnus's death which Lawrence quotes, and which may well have been the copy which Lawrence himself saw; its variants have been recorded in the Textual apparatus (between 59:18 and 62:28).

'The Bad Side Of Books': introduction to A Bibliography of the Writings of D. H. Lawrence

Base-text is the 4-page manuscript (MS), held at UT (Roberts E36a), emended from the revised typescript (TSR), probably made by Dorothy Brett, also held at UT (Roberts E36b). MS, which is dated 'Lobo. 1ˢᵗ September 1924', contains light interlinear revision, and occupies pp. 19–22 of an exercise book, dated 26 August 1924, and signed 'D. H. Lawrence / Kiowa Ranch. / Near *Taos* New Mexico.' This exercise book also contains the manuscripts of the story 'The Princess', the play 'Noah's Flood', and various essays, including 'Hopi Snake Dance' and 'Climbing Down Pisgah'. The introduction was published in *A Bibliography of the Writings of D. H. Lawrence*, ed. Edward D. McDonald (Philadelphia: The Centaur Bookshop, 1925), pp. 9–14 (A1).

A copy of the text of TSR, held at UTul (TCC; Roberts E36c), is accompanied by a typewritten letter, dated 'September 7, 1932' and signed 'C.W.B.T.', recording that the Centaur Book Shop had, prior to the publication of A1, asked the signatory, evidently a lawyer, whether there was anything in Lawrence's 'preface' that 'was objectionable from a legal standpoint'. There was anxiety about Lawrence's references to Mitchell Kennerley's not having paid for the American rights of *Sons and Lovers*. 'C.W.B.T.' 'informed [the Centaur Book Shop] that unless Lawrence was sure of his ground, this statement might be held to be libelous. Apparently Lawrence was telling the truth, as the preface appeared with this statement included and, as far as I know, no denial of it was made by Kennerly [*sic*].' TCC does not appear to have played any part in the transmission of the text to publication, and its variants are not recorded.

Introduction to Max Havelaar

No manuscript or typescript of this piece has survived. Base-text is the first edition of *Max Havelaar*, by 'Multatuli', tr. William Siebenhaar, and published by Alfred Knopf (New York, 1927), pp. v–ix (A1).

Introduction (version 1) to The Memoirs of the Duc de Lauzun

Base-text is the 9-page manuscript (MS), held at UCB (Roberts E106d). The piece was not published in Lawrence's lifetime. There are two identical carbon copies (TCC), one held at UCB (Roberts E106e) and one at UT (Roberts E106f), of a ribbon-copy typescript, now lost, made most probably in 1933 or 1934, when Edward McDonald was preparing items for *Phoenix* (A1). Lawrence's manuscript was untitled; he had originally headed it 'The Duc de Lauzun', but he crossed this heading out, presumably when he started a new essay with the same title on the succeeding pages of the exercise book in which this manuscript was written. TCC's cover-sheet named the piece 'Untitled Article by D. H. Lawrence'. The UT copy of this cover-sheet has some handwritten additions, possibly by McDonald: over the title is written '[The Good Man] –?', and at the left margin there are some scribbled speculations about the date of composition: '1925 / 1924? / Post-war', followed by an illegible phrase. In A1 (750–4) the essay is called 'The Good Man'. For a discussion of the history of this and the following item, see above, pp. lxviii–lxx.

Introduction (version 2) to The Memoirs of the Duc de Lauzun

Base-text is the 8-page manuscript (MS), held at UCB (Roberts E 106a). MS, which immediately follows the manuscript of the preceding item (Roberts E 106d) in an exercise book, is clearly headed 'The Duc de Lauzun'. It is unfinished, and breaks off in mid-sentence at the end of the first line of its final page. It was not published in Lawrence's lifetime. As with the previous item, there are two carbon copies (Roberts E106b, UCB, and E106c, UT) of a missing ribbon-copy typescript (TCC), presumably made for *Phoenix*, where the piece was first published (pp. 745–9; A1).

Introduction to The Mother

Base-text is the 7-page manuscript (MS) held at UCB (Roberts E249.5a). MS has heavy interlinear revision. Lawrence added a note at the end: 'for Jonathan Cape, as by direct arrangement – he to pay six guineas, and anything American extra.' There are very few variations between MS and the introduction as it appeared in the book, *The Mother*, by Grazia Deledda, tr. Mary G. Steegman (Jonathan Cape, 1928), pp. 7–13 (E1). If a setting-copy was made from the manuscript, it has been lost. There are also two identical carbon copies (Roberts E249.5b, UCB, and E249.5c, UT) of a lost ribbon-copy typescript (TCC), most probably made for *Phoenix*.

'Chaos in Poetry': *introduction to* Chariot of the Sun

Base-text is the 9-page manuscript (MS), held at UT (Roberts E65a), signed and dated 'Villa Mirenda, Scandicci, 29th April 1928'. This is emended from the 10-page typescript (TS), also at UT (Roberts E65b), dated 'Scandicci, May 1st, 1928'. Lawrence typed TS himself, revising its text heavily as he went along. At an early stage he also corrected TS lightly, by hand, in ink.

Another, carbon-copy typescript survives (TCCI), held at UCLA as a gift from Majl Ewing, and not listed in the Roberts bibliography; it is also dated 'Scandicci, May 1st 1928'. TCCI is unrevised. It must have been typed from TS, as it incorporates the few corrections Lawrence initially made to TS. It was probably made by an unknown typist in the Florence region (but not on the machine on which Lawrence had typed TS), between 1 and 20 May 1928, to be sent to Harry Crosby as a clean copy of the revised text. Lawrence planned to send MS, together with either the ribbon-copy of TCCI (now missing) or TCCI itself, as 'the complete thing' (vi. 390), to Crosby, on or soon after 1 May.

Around 20 May, Lawrence heard from Crosby (see above, pp. lxxix–lxxx). Lawrence now revised TS yet again, to create TSR, in the course of which he added the title 'Chaos in Poetry', made emendations throughout, and re-wrote the ending. He sent TSR to his agent on 21 May 1928 (vi. 404), and it was in this form that the piece first appeared in print, in *Echanges* (December 1929), 54–62 (Per). In the 1931 Black Sun Press edition of *Chariot of the Sun*, pp. i–xviii (F1), Lawrence's introduction appears in a form close to that of TCCI, with some sentences from MS reinstated.

In addition to these forms of the text, there is extant a carbon copy (TCCII), held at UT (Roberts E65c), of a lost ribbon-copy typescript, presumably made for *Phoenix* 255–62 (A1). The Textual apparatus records the variants of TS, TCCI, TSR, Per, F1, TCCII and A1.

Introduction to Bottom Dogs

Base-text is the 8-page manuscript (MS), held at UCB (Roberts E54a). MS was headed 'Introd. to Edward Dahlberg's novel, for Putnams', and between this and the opening line of the piece is inserted in pencil, in what appears to be Lawrence's hand, 'Bottom Dogs'. This insertion must have been made at a later stage, since at the time of writing no decision had been made as to the novel's title (see above, pp. lxxxiv–lxxxv). MS is signed and dated 'D. H. Lawrence Bandol. 1929'. There are two separate typescripts. One, held at UNM (Roberts E54c), has 'Bottom Dogs by D. H. Lawrence' written in what again appears to be Lawrence's hand, very shakily, across the top of the opening page, and on the same page an error in the typed title, 'SALILBERG', has been hand-corrected to 'DAHLBERG'. This latter hand-correction uses clear capital letters, and it is not possible to be certain who made it. Because of the signature at the beginning, this typescript has been recorded in the Textual apparatus as TCCIR. Subsequent errors have been corrected by overtyping, but there are no further handwritten corrections or additions. TCCIR appears to have been used as a setting-copy by Putnam's, as the text of the introduction as printed in *Bottom Dogs*, by Edward Dahlberg (Putnam's Sons, 1929), pp. vii–xix (E1), reproduces some of the typist's mistakes, e.g. 'first-comer' for 'first-comers', at 119:13, and 'glow' for 'flow', at 121:12. The other typescript, of which there are two copies (Roberts E54b, UCB, and E54d, UT), is a carbon copy (TCCII) of a lost typescript, presumably made for *Phoenix*.

Introduction to The Grand Inquisitor

Base-text is the 14-page manuscript (MS), held at UCB (Roberts E151a). MS was written in a French school exercise book, on the cover of which Lawrence wrote 'Introd to Grand Inquisitor DHL for Kot. [or] Koteliansky or Mrs Henderson' the latter presumably being the typist to whom MS was sent. The heading of the essay itself, 'Introd. to The Grand Inquisitor', has Lawrence's signature underneath. A carbon-copy held at UCB (Roberts E151b) of a lost ribbon-copy typescript (TCCI) appears to have been taken from MS and used as a setting-copy for the book publication, *The Grand Inquisitor*, by F. M. Dostoevsky, tr. S. S. Koteliansky (Paris: Elkin Mathews and Marrot, 1930), pp. iii–xvi (E1); the text of E1 reproduces the typescript's errors throughout. The typescript held at UT (Roberts E151c) is a carbon copy of a lost ribbon-copy typescript (TCCII), presumably made for *Phoenix*.

2 Introductions to translations

Introductory Note to Mastro-don Gesualdo

Base-text is the 6-page manuscript (MS), held at UT (Roberts E231c). The last 3 pages of MS contain a list of the principal characters of the novel and a brief, not entirely accurate, bibliography of Verga, which have not been reproduced here. A typescript (TCC), also held at UT (Roberts E231d), is an unmarked, fairly faithful transcription of MS, presumably used as a setting-copy for the book publication, *Mastro-don Gesualdo*, by Giovanni Verga, tr. D. H. Lawrence (New York: Thomas Seltzer, 1923), pp. v–vii (A1), in which the piece is entitled 'Biographical Note'. MS and TCC replaced an earlier version of the same item, which appears in this volume as Appendix I.

Note on Giovanni Verga, *in* Little Novels of Sicily

No manuscript or typescript of this item survives. The text is taken from the Seltzer edition of *Little Novels of Sicily*, by Giovanni Verga, tr. D. H. Lawrence (New York, 1925), pp. vii–x (A1). E1, the edition published simultaneously by Basil Blackwell (Oxford, 1925), includes a considerably shorter version of the same 'Note', pp. 5–7 (see above, p. lix).

Introduction to Mastro-don Gesualdo

No manuscript or typescript of this item survives. Base-text is the book publication, *Mastro-don Gesualdo*, by Giovanni Verga, tr. D. H. Lawrence (Paris: Jonathan Cape, 1928), pp. v–xx (E1). This version of Lawrence's introduction was the third of his three attempts (see above, p. lxxv). The first two, for which manuscript and typescript materials do survive, are included as Appendices II and III.

Biographical Note to Mastro-don Gesualdo

No manuscript or typescript of this item survives. Base-text is the 1928 Cape edition, pp. xxi–xxii (E1), where the item is appended to the introduction (see above). This 'Biographical Note' is clearly a substantial and terse revision of the 'Introductory Note' which had appeared, as 'Biographical Note', in the Seltzer edition of 1923 which Cape had reprinted in 1925. One cannot be certain that Lawrence himself was responsible for the revision (see above, p. lxxvi).

Translator's Preface to Cavalleria Rusticana

Base-text is derived from the conflation of the first 11 pages of a 23-page typescript, held at UT (Roberts E63c), and an 11-page manuscript, held at UCB (Roberts E63a), hereafter TCCIR. TCCIR begins with an un-numbered contents page, not reproduced here, followed by 12 pages of text. The first 11 pages have a small number of corrections in Lawrence's hand. There are also some other corrections, presumably made by a compositor, and recorded in the Textual apparatus as TCCIC. After the line 'the ugly triumph of the sophisticated greedy' (168:36–7), the remainder of page 11 and the whole of page 12 are crossed through in ink, and at the point where the crossing-through begins, the note 'continue here from MS' is inserted in Lawrence's hand. These 2 cancelled pages of typescript are reproduced as Appendix IV. They were replaced by a new, greatly expanded ending, in the form of the manuscript (E63a), whose pages are numbered 12–21 (2 pages were by mistake numbered 14) to indicate a continuation of the original typescript. At some point this manuscript was typed, fairly accurately, and the resulting typescript added to the existing typed pages, becoming pages 14–22 (there is no typescript page numbered 13). This second part of the typescript has no handwritten revisions. It is recorded in the Textual apparatus as TCCII. The complete, two-part typescript was used as the setting-copy for the book publication, *Cavalleria Rusticana*, by Giovanni Verga, tr. D. H. Lawrence (Paris: Jonathan Cape, 1928), pp. 7–28 (E1).

The Argus Book Shop Catalogue (no. 827, 1943) advertised a typescript of this item, now listed as Roberts E63b, which has not been located. It was advertised as having 28 pages, although this may have been an error for '23', the page length of TCCIR. It is possible that this unlocated item may have been a later typescript, either made by Curtis Brown or prepared for *Phoenix*.

Foreword to The Story of Doctor Manente

Base-text is the 7-page manuscript (Roberts E380a) held at UN (MS), which was written on the back of the galley sheets of an alternative, rejected introduction to the work, written by Edward Hutton. Base-text is emended from the corrected galley sheets (Roberts E380b) held at UCLA (GR), prepared for Orioli and revised in Lawrence's hand. The differences between MS and GR are so considerable as to suggest that there must have been an intermediate version, a typescript or revised manuscript, now lost, used as setting-copy by Orioli's printer. See also Explanatory note to 177:11. The introduction as published, in *The Story of Doctor Manente*, by A. F. Grazzini, tr. D. H. Lawrence (Florence: G. Orioli, 1929), pp. ix–xxiv (O1), does not vary further from the corrected galley sheets, and reproduces the numerous uncorrected typesetting errors. Appendix V reproduces the advertising Prospectus for O1.

3 Reviews

Review of Contemporary German Poetry

No manuscript or typescript survives. Base-text is the first periodical publication, the *English Review*, ix (November 1911), 721–4 (Per1). As with other reviews in that periodical, the piece was unsigned, and it was not until 1969 that it was rediscovered, by Carl Baron, and published in his article 'Two Hitherto Unknown Pieces by D. H. Lawrence', *Encounter*, xxxiii (August 1969), 3–4 (Per2).

Review of The Oxford Book of German Verse

Again, neither manuscript nor typescript survives. Base-text is the first publication, *English Review*, x (January 1912), 373–5 (Per). The piece was reprinted in Armin Arnold, *D. H. Lawrence and German Literature* (Montreal: Mansfield Book Mart, H. Heinemann, 1963), pp. 21–4 (C1).

Review of The Minnesingers

Again, no manuscript or typescript. Base-text is from the same issue of the *English Review* (x, January 1912), 375–6 (Per), as the previous item, which immediately preceded it. It was also reprinted in Arnold, *D. H. Lawrence and German Literature*, pp. 29–31 (C1).

'The Georgian Renaissance': review of Georgian Poetry 1911–12

Base-text is the first periodical publication, *Rhythm (Literary Supplement)*, ii (March 1913), xvii–xx (Per). Neither manuscript nor typescript survives. The piece was reprinted in *Phoenix* 304–7 (A1), but no typescripts associated with that edition have survived either.

'German Books': review of Der Tod in Venedig

As with the other early reviews, there are no surviving manuscripts or typescripts. Base-text is the *Blue Review*, no. III (July 1913), pp. 200–6 (Per). The piece was reprinted in *Phoenix* 308–13 (A1).

Review of Fantazius Mallare: A Mysterious Oath

Base-text is the 3-page manuscript (MS), held at YU. MS takes the form of a letter, dated 'Taos. 12 Oct.', and prefaced 'Dear Johnson / Publish the enclosed or not, as you like. / Greet Bynner from me, and be greeted / D. H. Lawrence' (iv. 321). MS is clearly written; there are no revisions and hardly any crossings-out. The piece was published, with 'objectionable' words omitted, in *Laughing Horse*, no. 4 (December 1922), n.p. (Per), and subsequently, with a different set of omissions, in *The Letters of D. H. Lawrence*, ed. Aldous Huxley (Heinemann, 1932), pp. 556–8 (E1). See above, pp. lii–liv.

Review of Americans

No manuscript of this item survives. Base-text is the 9-page ribbon-copy type-script, hand-revised by Lawrence (TSR), held at YU (Roberts E14.3b). TSR is emended from the galley-proofs (Roberts E14.3a) for *The Dial*, which were also revised by Lawrence (GR). TSR is headed 'MODEL AMERICANS'. In addition to the ink-revisions in Lawrence's hand, there are numerous corrections in pencil, mostly for house-styling purposes and presumably made by a copy-editor. These corrections are recorded in the Textual apparatus as TSC. The piece was first published in *The Dial*, lxxiv (May 1923), 503–10 (Per), and reprinted in *Phoenix* 314–21 (A1).

Roberts erroneously lists E14.3c as a 10-page typescript held at UT; this has not been located.

Review of A Second Contemporary Verse Anthology

No manuscript or typescript of this item has survived. Base-text is the *New York Evening Post Literary Review*, 23 September 1923, pp. 86–7 (Per). The piece was reprinted in *Phoenix* 322–6 (A1).

Review of Hadrian The Seventh

Base-text is *Adelphi*, iii (December 1925), 502–6 (Per). No earlier form of this item appears to have survived. The *Adelphi* text was reprinted in *Phoenix* 327–30 (A1).

Review of Saïd The Fisherman

There are no manuscripts or typescripts of this piece. Base-text is the version printed, with several sizeable cuts, in the *New York Herald Tribune Books*, 27 December 1925, p. 12 (Per1), emended from the second periodical printing, in *Adelphi*, iv (January 1927), 436–40 (Per2). The *Adelphi* text was reprinted in *Phoenix* 351–4 (A1).

Review of The Origins of Prohibition

The text is taken from the 7-page manuscript (MS), held at UT (Roberts E297a). It is written in pencil, and very heavily revised interlinearly. The top of the first page has a note: 'to Miss Pearn – letter at end.' At the end of the review, pp. 7–8 of MS, Lawrence continued with a letter to Nancy Pearn, signed and dated 'Villa Bernarda. Spotorno. Prov. Di Genova / Italy / 21 Novem 1925' (v. 341). He asked in this letter for MS to be typed, but this typescript, if made, has not survived. The piece appeared in the *New York Herald Tribune Books*, 31 January 1926, p. 7 (Per). There are also two carbon copies, Roberts E297b, at UCB, and E297c, at UT (TCC) of a lost ribbon-copy typescript, almost certainly made for *Phoenix*, where the piece was reprinted, 331–3 (A1). On the title-page of the UT copy of TCC, the words 'INTRODUCTION to' have been crossed through by hand, and 'Review of' written instead, possibly by McDonald.

Review of In The American Grain

There are no surviving manuscripts or typescripts of this item. Base-text is 'American Heroes', *The Nation* (New York), vol. 122, no. 3171 (April 1926), 413–14 (Per). It was reprinted in *Phoenix* 334–6 (A1).

Review (manuscript version) of Heat

Base-text is the 8-page manuscript (MS), held at UCB (Roberts E158a). MS is headed simply 'Heat'. It contains some light interlinear revision. It was never published in Lawrence's lifetime, and first appeared in *Phoenix* 337–41 (A1). For the history of this and the following item, see above, pp. lxiii–lxiv.

Review (typescript version) of Heat

Base-text is a 6-page typescript (TCC), held at UCB (Roberts E158b). The typescript is headed 'HEAT / by / D. H. Lawrence.' It would appear to have been typed by Lawrence himself, and has a small number of corrections in his hand. It breaks off in mid-sentence at the end of page 6, and it is clear that one or more succeeding pages are missing. TCC has up to now apparently been accepted as a copy of MS, but it is in fact a significantly different version of the same essay. It is published here for the first time.

Review of The World of William Clissold

Base-text is the *Calendar*, iii (October 1926), 254–7 (Per). There is no surviving material prior to this. The piece was reprinted in *Phoenix* 346–50 (A1).

Review (manuscript version) of Gifts of Fortune

Base-text is the 8-page manuscript (MS), held at UT (Roberts E145a). MS has neither heading nor signature. There is a carbon copy typescript (TCC), also held at UT (Roberts E145b), of a lost ribbon-copy typescript, presumably made for *Phoenix*, where the review was reprinted, 342–5 (A1).

Review (periodical version) of Gifts of Fortune

Base-text is *T. P.'s and Cassell's Weekly*, vii (1 January 1927), 339–40 (Per). It seems probable that the extensive differences between MS (see above) and Per can be explained by Lawrence's having heavily revised a typescript (no longer extant) made from MS (E145a). The revisions may have been made in response to suggestions from the periodical, which may also have made further alterations of its own (see above, p. lxx).

Review of Pedro de Valdivia

Base-text is the 7-page corrected typescript (TS), held at UCB (Roberts E306). TS appears to have been made by Lawrence himself, and contains some light interlinear revision in his hand. It has also been marked by the typesetter for the *Calendar*, where it appeared in iii (January 1927), 322–6 (Per). The first page of the typescript has written on it 'Calendar. 10pt solid. Add <u>Reviews</u> – Pencil corrections', initialled 'CR', and stamped 'THE PETERBOROUGH PRESS, LTD. 21 DEC 1926'. The piece was reprinted in *Phoenix* 355–60 (A1).

Review of Nigger Heaven, etc.

Base-text is the 10-page manuscript (MS), held at UCLA (Roberts E271a). On the first page, which is headed with a list of the four books under review, Lawrence has corrected his own misspelling 'Hemmingway'. The rest of the manuscript has fairly heavy interlinear revision. There are two carbon copies (TCC), one held at UCB (Roberts E271b), the other at UT (Roberts

E271c), of a lost ribbon-copy typescript, probably made for *Phoenix* (A1). The cover-sheet of the UT copy has the titles of the four books added by hand. The piece was first published in the *Calendar*, iv (April 1927), 17–21, 67–73 (Per), and was reprinted in *Phoenix* 361–6.

Review of Solitaria

Base-text is the 10-page manuscript (MS), held at UT (Roberts E368a). MS contains moderate interlinear revision. There is a setting-copy typescript (TS), presumably prepared for the *Calendar* (Per), held at UN (Roberts E368d); it is heavily marked by a copy-editor, but there is no evidence that Lawrence saw it or revised it. It is stamped 'THE PETERBOROUGH PRESS, LTD. 29 JUNE 1927'. There are also two carbon copies (TCC), one held at UCB (Roberts E368b), and one at UT (E368c), of a lost ribbon-copy typescript, presumably prepared by Curtis Brown in the 1930s. The piece was first published in the *Calendar*, iv (July 1927), 164–8, and reprinted in *Phoenix* 367–71 (A1).

Review of The Peep Show

The text is taken from the 10-page setting-copy manuscript (MS), held at UCB (Roberts E307c), emended slightly from the text printed in the *Calendar*, iv (July 1927), 157–61 (Per). There are some small additions and changes in Per which must have been made by Lawrence at proof stage (see above, p. lxxiii): e.g. the addition of the sentence 'But, still, he is not *too* nice' (325:3). All these alterations were inserted into blank spaces in the proofs, and were designed not to interfere with the proofs' lineation. Per was reprinted in *Phoenix* 372–6 (A1). In MS, the word '(over)' has been inserted by another hand at the bottom of each of the odd numbered pages – i.e. the recto pages taken from an exercise book. The first page has '*Calendar*. Add Reviews. / 10 pt solid' added in hand, with THE PETERBOROUGH PRESS, LIMITED / 19 MAY 1927 stamped.

Frances Steloff, of Gotham Book Mart, New York, held 'a number of Lawrence manuscripts' at some time in the early 1930s (*D. H. Lawrence's Manuscripts: The Correspondence of Frieda Lawrence, Jake Zeitlin and Others*, ed. Michael Squires, 1991, p. 153). A ribbon-copy typescript of E307c, located at McFarlin Library, UTul, was made on Gotham Book Mart headed paper, presumably while E307c was in Steloff's possession.

An incomplete early draft of the review (Roberts E307a) is reproduced here as Appendix VI.

Review of The Social Basis Of Consciousness

The text is taken from the 12-page manuscript (MS), held at UT (Roberts E366a). MS contains light interlinear revision. The lengthy transcriptions from the book under review are unusually accurate. The review first appeared in the *Bookman* (New York), 66 (November 1927), 314–17 (Per), under the heading 'A New Theory Of Neuroses'. It was reprinted in *Phoenix* 377–82 (A1). A carbon copy (TCC) survives of a typescript, held at UCB (Roberts E366b), which does not, however, appear to have been the source of A1.

Review of The Station, etc.

The text is taken from the 8-page manuscript (MS), held at UT (Roberts E377.5c). MS is lightly revised. On the final page, the handwriting becomes increasingly compressed, eventually twisting through 90 degrees to run vertically up the right-hand margin of the page, in an effort to cram everything on to one sheet rather than begin a fresh one. There are no surviving typescripts. The piece first appeared in *Vogue*, 8 August 1928, 35, 58 (Per), in a notably more faithful form than was the case with many of the periodical publications of Lawrence's reviews. It was reprinted in *Phoenix* 383–7 (A1).

Two early incomplete draft versions of the review (Roberts E377.5a and E377.5b) are reproduced here as Appendix VII.

Review of Fallen Leaves

The text is taken from the 8-page manuscript (MS), held at UT (Roberts E124a). MS has only light revision. There is a 7-page typescript (TS), held at UCB (Roberts E124b; an incomplete copy of the same item, E124d, is held at UNM). TS appears to have been used as a setting-copy for *Everyman*, 23 January 1930, 733–4 (Per), where the piece first appeared, heavily cut. TS is unlikely to have been produced by Lawrence himself; two mistyped characters have been corrected by hand, but it is not possible to be certain whose. There are also two carbon copies, one held at UCB (Roberts E124c) and one at UT (E124e), of a ribbon-copy typescript (TCC), presumably prepared for *Phoenix* (A1), where the piece was reprinted (388–92). On the cover-sheet of TCC, the typed words 'INTRODUCTION to' have been crossed out, and 'Review of' added instead, in pencil.

Review of Art-Nonsense and Other Essays

The text is taken from the 7-page manuscript (MS), held at UCLA (Roberts E24.5a). MS has Lawrence's signature under the heading, and the publication details of the book under review added at the bottom of the first page. The manuscript is only very lightly revised. There is a carbon copy typescript (TCC), held at UT (Roberts E24.5b). TCC was probably made for Curtis Brown. It shares some of the same errors of transcription as the text in the *Book Collector's Quarterly*, xii (October–November 1933), 1–7 (Per), e.g. 'Catholics to Protestants' for 'Catholics. As protestants' (356:28), 'preamble' for 'grumble' (356:38), 'casual' for 'carnal' (359:4); it is possible that TCC may have been taken from Per, or that Per and TCC misread MS in the same places.

A lost typescript made from MS may have been setting-copy for Per and also the source of the text in *Phoenix* 393–7 (A1). The piece as printed in Per included a headnote, signed as from Frieda Lawrence (see above, p. lxxxix). This note was reproduced when the piece was reprinted in A1, but not in TCC.

The Textual apparatus records the variants in the order MS, Per, TCC, A1.

Appendices

Appendix I. Introductory note (version 1) to Mastro-don Gesualdo

The text is taken from the 6-page manuscript (MS), held at UT (Roberts E231a), with emendations from the typescript (TS), also held at UT (E231b). The piece is the original version of Lawrence's introductory note to his translation of *Mastro-don Gesualdo*, completed in March 1922. MS is written at the end of the fourth translation notebook. There is a fair amount of interlinear revision. TSC appears to have been made from MS; it contains a number of corrections and revisions, some of which may be in Lawrence's hand, but as none of these can be securely attributed, all have been recorded in the Textual apparatus as TSC. This version of the introductory note was replaced for the Seltzer edition of *Mastro-don Gesualdo* by a shorter version (see above, p. lii), and is published here for the first time.

Appendix II. Introduction (version 1) to Mastro-don Gesualdo

The text is taken from the 17-page manuscript (MS), held at UT (Roberts E231e). MS has no autograph title; the words 'N. 11' and 'Introduction to Mastro don Gesualdo – Translation from Verga' have been added at the head of the first page, not in Lawrence's hand. There is some light interlinear revision. There is a 15-page carbon copy (TCC), held at UCB (Roberts E231f), of a lost ribbon-copy typescript, perhaps made for *Phoenix* (A1), 223–31, where the piece was first published.

Appendix III. *Introduction (version 2) to* Mastro-don Gesualdo

This was Lawrence's second attempt at this introduction. The text is taken from a typescript held at UN (Roberts E231g). The piece as published in Cape's 'Travellers' Library' (see above, p. lxxv) was obviously derived from this version, and resembles it closely at many points, but there are also a number of significant differences. This text is published here for the first time.

Appendix IV. *Cancelled pages from 'Translator's Preface to* Cavalleria Rusticana*'*

These are pages 11 and 12 from the original typescript of this piece (Roberts E63c), which Lawrence crossed through and replaced with a manuscript revision (see above, p. xcix). They are published here for the first time.

Appendix V. *Prospectus for* The Story of Doctor Manente

This was a piece of advertising material hand-written by Lawrence. The text is taken from the 4-page manuscript held in the Lazarus collection at UN (La Z 2/8/5; Roberts E380.1). The first page includes a rough ink drawing of the design used on the frontispiece of the book, of an elderly man, presumably a poet, crowned with laurel leaves and naked from the waist up, holding a spade in one hand, and with the other deftly pouring a bucket of water, or perhaps sand, on to the ground. A lion is sitting next to him, and the Duomo in Florence is visible in the background. The third page includes the words 'ORDER FORM. Page 3', and the fourth page (marked 'Page 2') has the opening lines of the piece written again and crossed out.

The same Lazarus collection includes some other manuscript materials associated with *The Story of Doctor Manente* which are not reproduced here. La Z 2/8/1 is two pages of notes in Lawrence's hand, evidently the basis for the footnotes he produced for his translation. La Z 2/8/2 is a 9-page manuscript of the footnotes which were published in Orioli's edition.

Appendix VI. *Incomplete early version of 'Review of* The Peep Show*'*

The text is taken from the 6-page partial manuscript (MS), held at UCB (Roberts E307a). The pages of MS are hand-numbered 3–8; at the top of page 3 is written, in another hand, 'Review of Puppet Show Pages 1 & 2 miss-ing'. The final line of page 8 ends in mid-sentence two-thirds of the way along the penultimate line of the ruled paper. The manuscript has light interlinear revision. There are two carbon copies (TCC), held at UT (Roberts E307b), of a lost ribbon-copy typescript, probably made in the 1930s. The cover-sheet of TCC is hand-marked 'Defective' and 'Incomplete (? published / yes'; the typescript is entitled 'Review of "PUPPET SHOW"', and closes with '(Unfinished)'. The piece is published here for the first time.

Appendix VII. Two incomplete early versions of 'Review of The Station, etc.'

There are two manuscripts, both held at UT (Roberts E377.5a and E377.5b), of early versions of this review. The first is a 4-page manuscript headed 'Review for Vogue / by D. H. Lawrence.', followed by a list of the books under review, with *The Station*, by Robert Byron, listed last (the others appear in the same order as in the published review). This manuscript is lightly revised. It contains no mention of Byron's book. The second manuscript, only one page, was evidently an attempt at a fresh start. It lists the books again, this time with Byron's placed first; it begins writing about it, and breaks off in mid-sentence and mid-line. These fragments have not previously been published.

Appendix VIII. Notes for The Hand Of Man

This is a 2-page manuscript, held at UT, unlisted in Roberts. It is in pencil, and has neither heading nor signature. At the bottom of the second page is written, in ink: 'Only the writing in pencil is by Lawrence / It was done as a suggestion for an article I was attempting to write on The Hand of Man. / E. H. Brewster'. Brewster also wrote a few words in the margin and beneath the conclusion of Lawrence's text: 'enlarge / Russia = tyranny of man / machine'. The piece is published here for the first time.

SECTION A
INTRODUCTIONS

FOREWORD TO *ALL THINGS ARE POSSIBLE, BY LEO SHESTOV*

Foreword.

In his paragraph on The Russian Spirit,* Shestov gives us the real
clue to Russian literature. European culture is a rootless thing in the
Russians. With us, it is our very blood and bones, the very nerve and
root of our psyche. We think in a certain fashion, we feel in a certain   5
fashion, because our whole substance is of this fashion.* Our speech
and feeling are organically inevitable to us.

With the Russians it is different. They have only been inoculated
with the virus* of European culture and ethic. The virus works in
them like a disease. And the inflammation and irritation comes forth   10
as literature. The bubbling and fizzing is almost chemical, not organic.
It is an organism seething as it accepts and masters the strange virus.
What the Russian is struggling with, crying out against, is not life itself:
it is only European culture which has been introduced into his psyche, and which hurts him.* The tragedy is not so much a real soul   15
tragedy, as a surgical one. Russian art, Russian literature after all does
not stand on the same footing as European or Greek or Egyptian art.
It is not spontaneous utterance. It is not the flowering of a race. It is a
surgical outcry, horrifying, or marvellous, lacerating at first: but when
we get used to it, not really so profound, not really ultimate; a little   20
extraneous.

What is valuable is the evidence against European culture, implied
in the novelists, here at last expressed. Since Peter the Great* Russia
has been accepting Europe, and seething Europe down in a curious
process of katabolism.* Russia has been expressing nothing inherently   25
Russian. Russia's modern Christianity even was not Russian. Her genuine christianity, Byzantine and Asiatic, is incomprehensible to us. So
with her true philosophy. What she has actually uttered is her own
unwilling, fantastic reproduction of European truths. What she has
really to utter the coming centuries will hear. For Russia will certainly   30
inherit the future. What we already call the greatness of Russia is only her
pre-natal struggling.

It seems as if she had at last absorbed and overcome the virus of old Europe. Soon her new, healthy body will begin to act in its own reality, imitative no more, protesting no more, crying no more, but full and sound and lusty in itself. Real Russia is born. She will laugh at us before long. Meanwhile she goes through the last stages of reaction against us, kicking away from the old womb of Europe.

In Shestov one of the last kicks is given. True, he seems to be only reactionary and destructive. But he can find a little amusement at last in tweaking the European nose, so he is fairly free. European idealism is anathema. But more than this, it is a little comical. We feel the new independence in his new, half-amused indifference.

He is only tweaking the nose of European idealism. He is preaching nothing: so he protests time and again. He absolutely refutes any imputation of a central idea. He is so afraid lest it should turn out to be another hateful hedge-stake* of an ideal.

"Everything is possible"—this is his really central cry.* It is not nihilism. It is only a shaking free of the human psyche from old bonds. The positive central idea is that the human psyche, or soul, really believes in itself, and in nothing else.

Dress this up in a little comely language and we have a real new ideal, that will last us for a new, long epoch. The human soul itself is the source and well-head of creative activity. In the unconscious human soul the creative prompting issues first into the universe. Open the consciousness to this prompting, away with all your old sluice gates, locks, dams, channels. No ideal on earth is anything more than an obstruction, in the end, to the creative issue of the spontaneous soul. Away with all ideals. Let each individual act spontaneously from the forever incalculable prompting of the creative well-head within him. There is no universal law. Each being is, at his purest, a law unto himself, single, unique, a Godhead, a fountain from the unknown.

This is the ideal which Shestov refuses positively to state, because he is afraid it may prove in the end a trap to catch his own free spirit. So it may. But it is none the less a real, living ideal for the moment, the very salvation. When it becomes ancient, and like the old lion who lay in his cave and whined, devours all its servants,* then it can be despatched. Meanwhile it is a really liberating word.

Shestov's style is puzzling at first. Having found the "ands" and "buts" and "becauses" and "therefores" hampered him, he clips them all off deliberately and even spitefully, so that his thought is like a man with no buttons on his clothes, ludicrously hitching* along all undone. One must be amused, not irritated. Where the armholes were a bit tight, Shestov cuts a slit. It is baffling, but really rather piquant. The real conjunction, the real unification lies in the reader's own amusement, not in the author's unbroken logic.

NOTE

LEO SHESTOV is one of the living Russians.* He is about fifty years old. He was born at Kiev, and studied at the university there. His first book appeared in 1898, since which year he has gradually gained an assured position as one of the best critics and essayists in Russia. A list of his works is as follows:—

1898.   Shakespeare and his Critic, Brandes.
1900.   Good in the Teaching of Dostoevsky and Nietzsche: Philosophy and Preaching.*
1903.   Dostoevsky and Nietzsche: The Philosophy of Tragedy.
1905.   The Apotheosis of Groundlessness (here translated under the title "All Things are Possible").
1908.   Beginnings and Ends.*
1912.   Great Vigils.*

MEMOIR OF MAURICE MAGNUS:
INTRODUCTION TO MEMOIRS OF
THE FOREIGN LEGION

Memoir of Maurice Magnus*

On a dark,* wet, wintry evening in November 1919 I arrived in Florence, having just got back to Italy for the first time since 1914. My wife was in Germany, gone to see her mother, also for the first time since that fatal year 1914.* We were poor—who was going to bother to publish 5
me and to pay for my writings, in 1918 and 1919? I landed in Italy with nine pounds in my pocket and about twelve pounds lying in the bank in London. Nothing more.* My wife, I hoped would arrive in Florence with two or three pounds remaining. We should have to go very softly, if we were to house ourselves in Italy for the winter. But after the desperate 10
weariness of the war, one could not bother.

So I had written to Norman Douglas* to get me a cheap room some-where in Florence, and to leave a note at Cooks. I deposited my bit of luggage at the station, and walked to Cooks in the Via Tornabuoni. Florence was strange to me: seemed grim and dark and rather awful on 15
the cold November evening. There was a note from Douglas, who has never left me in the lurch. I went down the Lungarno* to the address he gave.

I had just passed the end of the Ponte Vecchio, and was watching the first lights of evening and the last light of day on the swollen river as I 20
walked, when I heard Douglas' voice:

"Isn't that Lawrence? Why of course it is, of course it is, beard and all! Well how are you, eh? You got my note? Well now, my dear boy, you just go on to the Cavalotti*—straight ahead, straight ahead—you've got the number. There's a room for you there. We shall be there in half an 25
hour. Oh, let me introduce you to Magnus—"

I had unconsciously seen the two men approaching, Douglas tall and portly, the other man rather short and strutting.* They were both buttoned up in their overcoats, and both had rather curly little hats. But Douglas was decidedly shabby and a gentleman, with his wicked red 30
face and tufted eyebrows. The other man was almost smart, all in grey, and he looked at first sight like an actor-manager, common. There was a touch of down-on-his-luck about him too. He looked at me, buttoned up in my old thick overcoat, and with my beard bushy and raggy because

11

of my horror of entering a strange barber's shop, and he greeted me in
a rather fastidious voice, and a little patronisingly. I forgot to say I was
carrying a small handbag. But I realised at once that I ought, in this little
grey-sparrow man's eyes—he stuck his front out tubbily, like a bird, and
his legs seemed to perch behind him, as a bird's do—I ought to be in
a cab. But I wasn't. He eyed me in that shrewd and rather impertinent
way of the world of actor-managers: cosmopolitan, knocking shabbily
round the world.

He looked a man of about forty, spruce and youngish in his
deportment,* very pink-faced, and very clean, very natty, very alert,
like a sparrow painted to resemble a tom-tit. He was just the kind of
man I had never met: little smart man of the shabby world, very much
on the spot, don't you know.

"How much does it cost?" I asked Douglas, meaning the room.

"Oh my dear fellow, a trifle. Ten francs a day. Third rate, tenth
rate, but not bad at the price. Pension terms of course—everything
included—except wine."

"Oh no, not at all bad for the money," said Magnus. "Well now, shall
we be moving? You want the post-office, Douglas?"—His voice was
precise and a little mincing—and it had an odd high squeak.

"I do," said Douglas.

"Well then come down here—" Magnus turned to a dark little alley.

"Not at all," said Douglas. "We turn down by the bridge."

"This is quicker," said Magnus. He had a twang rather than an accent
in his speech—not definitely American.

He knew all the short cuts of Florence. Afterwards I found that he
knew all the short cuts in all the big towns of Europe.

I went on to the Cavalotti—and waited in an awful plush and gilt
drawing-room—and was given at last a cup of weird muddy brown
slush called tea and a bit of weird brown mush called jam on some bits
of bread.* Then I was taken to my room. It was far off, on the third
floor of the big, ancient, deserted Florentine house. There I had a big
and lonely, stone-comfortless room looking on to the river. Fortunately
it was not very cold inside—and I didn't care. The adventure of being
back in Florence again after the years of war made one indifferent.

After an hour or so someone tapped. It was Douglas coming in with
his grandiose air—now a bit shabby, but still very courtly.

"Why here you are—miles and miles from human habitation! I *told*
her to put you on the second floor, where we are. What does she mean
by it? Ring that bell. Ring it."

"No," said I, "I'm all right here."

"What!" cried Douglas. "In this Spitzbergen!* Where's that bell?"

"Don't ring it," said I, who have a horror of chambermaids and explanations.

"Not ring it! Well you're a man, you are! Come on then. Come on down to my room. Come on. Have you had some tea—filthy muck they call tea here? I never drink it—"

I went down to Douglas' room on the lower floor. It was a littered mass of books and type-writer and papers: Douglas was just finishing his novel *They Went*.* Magnus was resting on the bed, in his shirt sleeves: a tubby, fresh-faced little man in a suit of grey, faced cloth bound at the edges with grey silk braid. He had light-blue eyes, tired underneath, and crisp, curly, dark-brown hair just grey at the temples. But everything was neat and even finicking about his person.

"Sit down! Sit down!" said Douglas, wheeling up a chair. "Have a whisky?"

"Whisky!" said I.

"Twenty-four francs a bottle—and a find at that," moaned Douglas.—I must tell that the exchange was then about forty five Liras to the pound.

"Oh Norman," said Magnus, "I didn't tell you. I was offered a bottle of 1913 Black and White* for twenty eight Lire."

"Did you buy it?"

"No. It's your turn to buy a bottle."

"Twenty-eight francs—my dear fellow!" said Douglas, cocking up his eyebrows. "I shall have to starve myself to do it."

"Oh no you won't, you'll eat here just the same," said Magnus.

"Yes, and I'm starved to death. Starved to death by the muck—the absolute muck they call food here.—I can't face twenty-eight francs, my dear chap—Can't be done, on my honour."

"Well look here, Norman. We'll both buy a bottle. And you can get the one at twenty-two, and I'll buy the one at twenty-eight."

So it always was. Magnus indulged Douglas, and spoilt him in every way. And of course Douglas wasn't grateful. *Au contraire*—!* And Magnus' pale-blue, smallish, round eyes, in his cockatoo-pink face, would harden to indignation occasionally.

The room was dreadful. Douglas never opened the windows: didn't believe in opening windows. He believed that a certain amount of nitrogen—I should say a great amount—is beneficial. The queer smell of a bedroom which is slept in, worked in, lived in, smoked in, and in which men drink their whiskies, was something new to me. But I didn't care. One had got away from the war.

We drank our whiskies before dinner. Magnus was rather yellow under the eyes, and irritable: even his pink fattish face went yellowish.

5 "Look here," said Douglas. "Didn't you say there was a turkey for dinner? What? Have you been to the kitchen to see what they're doing to it?"

"Yes," said Magnus testily. "I forced them to prepare it to roast."

"With chestnuts—stuffed with chestnuts?" said Douglas.

10 "They *said* so," said Magnus.

"Oh but go down and see that they're doing it.—Yes, you've got to keep your eye on them, got to. The most awful howlers if you don't.— You go now and see what they're up to?" Douglas used his most irresistible grand manner.

15 "It's too late,"persisted Magnus, testy.

"It's *never* too late. You just run down and absolutely prevent them from boiling that bird in the old soup-water," said Douglas. "If you need force, fetch me."

Magnus went. He was a great epicure, and knew how things should be
20 cooked. But of course his irruptions into the kitchen roused considerable resentment, and he was getting quaky. However, he went. He came back to say the turkey was being roasted, but without chestnuts.

"What did I tell you! What did I tell you!" cried Douglas. "They *are* absolute ———— ! If you don't hold them by the neck while they peel
25 the chestnuts, they'll stuff the bird with old boots, to save themselves trouble.—Of course you should have gone down sooner, Magnus."

Dinner was always late, so the whiskey was usually two whiskies. Then we went down, and were merry in spite of all things. That is, Douglas *always* grumbled about the food. There was one unfortunate
30 youth who was boots and porter and waiter and all. He brought the big dish to Douglas—and Douglas always poked and pushed among the portions, and grumbled frantically, sotto voce, in Italian to the youth Beppe, getting into a nervous frenzy. Then Magnus called the waiter to himself, picked the nicest bits off the dish and gave them to Douglas,
35 then helped himself.

The food was not good—but with Douglas it was an obsession. With the waiter he was terrible—"Cos'è? Zuppa? Grazie. No, niente per me. No—*No*!—Quest'acqua sporca non bevo io.* I don't drink this dirty water. What—what's that in it—a piece of dish clout? Oh holy Dio I
40 can't eat another thing this evening—"

And he yelled for more bread—bread being war-rations and very limited in supply—so Magnus in nervous distress gave him his piece—and Douglas threw the crumb part on the floor, anywhere, and called for another litre. We always drank heavy dark-red wine at three francs a litre.* Douglas drank two thirds, Magnus drank least. He loved his liquors, and did not care for wine. We were noisy and unabashed at table. The old Danish ladies at the other end of the room, and the rather impecunious young Duca and family not far off were not supposed to understand English. The Italians rather liked the noise, and the young signorina with the high-up yellow hair eyed us with profound interest. On we sailed, gay and noisy, Douglas telling witty anecdotes and grumbling wildly and only half whimsically about the food. We sat on till most people had finished—then went up to more whisky—one more—perhaps in Magnus' room.

When I came down in the morning I was called into Magnus' room. He was like a little pontiff in a blue kimono-shaped dressing gown with a broad border of reddish-purple: the blue was a soft mid-blue, the material a dull silk. So he minced about, in demi-toilette. His room was very clean and neat, and slightly perfumed with essences. On his dressing-table stood many cut glass bottles and silver-topped bottles with essences and pomades and powders, and heaven knows what. A very elegant little prayer-book lay by his bed—and a life of St Benedict.* For Magnus was a Roman Catholic Convert. All he had was expensive and finicking: thick-leather silver-studded suit-cases standing near the wall, trouser-stretcher all nice, hair brushes and clothes-brush with old ivory backs. I wondered over him and his niceties and little pomposities. He was a new bird to me.

For he wasn't at all just the common person he looked. He was queer and sensitive as a woman with Douglas, and patient and fastidious. And yet he *was* common, his very accent was common, and D. despised him.

And Magnus rather despised me because I did not spend money. I paid a third of the wine we drank at dinner, and bought the third bottle of whiskey we had during Magnus' stay. After all, he only stayed three days. But I would not spend for myself. I had no money to spend, since I knew I must live and my wife must live.

"Oh," said Magnus, "why that's the very time to spend money, when you've got none. If you've got none, why try to save it? That's been my philosophy all my life: when you've got no money, you may just as well spend it. If you've got a good deal, that's the time to look after it." Then

he laughed his queer little laugh, rather squeaky.—These were his exact
words.

"Precisely," said Douglas. "Spend when you've nothing to spend, my
boy. Spend *hard* then."

5   "No," said I. "If I can help it, I will never let myself be penniless
while I live—I mistrust the world too much."

"But if you're going to live in fear of the world," said Magnus, "what's
the good of living at all. Might as well die."

I think I give his words almost verbatim. He had a certain impatience
10   of me and of my presence. Yet we had some jolly times—mostly in one
or other of their bedrooms, drinking a whisky and talking. We drank a
bottle a day—I had very little, preferring the wine at lunch and dinner,
which seemed delicious after the war-famine. Douglas would bring up
the remains of the second litre in the evening, to go on with before the
15   coffee came.

I arrived in Florence on the Wednesday or Thursday evening: I think
Thursday.* Magnus was due to leave for Rome on the Saturday. I asked
Douglas who Magnus was. "Oh, you never know what he's at. He was
manager for Isadora Duncan* for a long time—knows all the capitals of
20   Europe: St Petersburg, Moscow, Tiflis, Constantinople, Berlin, Paris—
knows them as you and I know Florence. He's been mostly in that line—
theatrical. Then a journalist. He edited the Roman Review* till the war
killed it. Oh, a many-sided sort of fellow."

"But how do you know him?" said I.

25   "I met him in Capri years and years ago—oh, sixteen years ago—
and clean forgot all about him till somebody came to me one day in
Rome and said: You're Norman Douglas.—*I* didn't know who he was.
But he'd never forgotten me. Seems to be smitten by me, somehow
or other. All the better for me, ha-ha—if he *likes* to run round for
30   me.—My dear fellow, I wouldn't prevent him, if it amuses him—Not
for worlds—"

And that was how it was. Magnus ran Douglas' errands, forced the
other man to go to the tailor, to the dentist, and was almost a guardian
angel to him.

35   "Look here!" cried Douglas. "I *can't* go to that damned tailor. Let
the thing wait,* I can't go."

"Oh yes now look here Norman, if you don't get it done now while
I'm here you'll never get it done. I made the appointment for three
oclock—"

40   "To hell with you! Details! Details! I can't stand it, I tell you."
Douglas chafed and kicked, but went.

"A little fussy fellow," he said. "Oh yes, fussing about like a woman. Fussy, you know, fussy. I *can't stand* these fussy— — —" And Douglas went off into improprieties.

Well, Magnus ran round and arranged Douglas' affairs and settled his little bills, and was so benevolent, and got impatient and nettled at the ungrateful way in which the benevolence was accepted. And Douglas despised him all the time as a little busybody and an inferior. And I there between them just wondered. It seemed to me Magnus would get very irritable and nervous at midday and before dinner, yellow round the eyes, and played out. He wanted his whisky. He was tired after running round on a thousand errands and quests which I never understood. He always took his morning coffee at dawn, and was out to early Mass and pushing his affairs before eight oclock in the morning. But what his affairs were I still do not know. Mass is all I am certain of.

However, it was his birthday on the Sunday,* and Douglas would not let him go. He had once said he would give a dinner for his birthday, and this he was not allowed to forget. It seemed to me Magnus rather wanted to get out of it. But Douglas was determined to have that dinner.*

"You aren't going before you've given us that hare, don't you imagine it my boy. I've got the smell of that hare in my imagination, and I've damned well got to set my teeth in it. —Don't you imagine you're going without having produced that hare."

So poor Magnus, rather a victim, had to consent. We discussed what we should eat. It was decided the hare should have truffles, and a dish of champignons,—and cauliflower—and zabaioni*—and I forget what else. It was to be on Saturday evening. And Magnus would leave on Sunday for Rome.

Early on the Saturday morning he went out, with the first daylight, to the old market, to get the hare and the mushrooms. He went himself— because he was a connoisseur.

On the Saturday afternoon Douglas took me wandering round to buy a birthday present.

"I shall have to buy him something—have to—have to—" he said fretfully. He wanted to spend only about five francs. We trailed over the Ponte Vecchio, looking at the jewellers' booths there. It was before the foreigners had come back, and things were still rather dusty and almost at pre-war prices. But we could see nothing for five francs except the little saint-medals. Douglas wanted to buy one of those. It seemed to me infra dig. So at last going down to the Mercato Nuovo* we saw little bowls of Volterra marble, a natural amber colour,* for four francs.

"Look, buy one of those," I said to Douglas, "and he can put his pins or studs or any trifle in, as he needs."

So we went in and bought one of the little bowls of Volterra marble. Magnus seemed so touched and pleased with the gift.

5   "Thank you a thousand times Norman," he said. "That's charming! That's exactly what I want."

The dinner was quite a success, and, poorly fed as we were at the pension,* we stuffed ourselves tight on the mushrooms and the hare and the zabaioni, and drank ourselves tight with the good red wine
10   which swung in its straw flask in the silver swing on the table. A flask has two and a quarter litres. We were four persons, and we drank almost two flasks. Douglas made the waiter measure the remaining half-litre and take it off the bill. But good, good food, and cost about twelve francs a head the whole dinner.

15   Well, next day was nothing but bags and suitcases in Magnus' room, and the misery of departure with luggage. He went on the midnight train to Rome: first class.

"I always travel first class," he said, "and I always shall, while I can buy the ticket. Why should I go second? It's beastly enough to travel at
20   all."

"My dear fellow I came up third the last time I came from Rome," said Douglas. "Oh, not bad, not bad. Damned fatiguing journey anyhow."

So the little outsider was gone, and I was rather glad. I don't think he liked me. Yet one day he had said to me at table:

25   "How lovely your hair is—such a lovely colour! What do you dye it with?"

I laughed, thinking he was laughing too. But no, he meant it.

"It's got no particular colour at all," I said, "so I couldn't dye it that."

"It's a lovely colour," he said. And I think he didn't believe me, that
30   I didn't dye it. It puzzled me, and it puzzles me still.

But he was gone. Douglas moved into Magnus' room, and asked me to come down to the room he himself was vacating. But I preferred to stay upstairs.

Magnus was a fervent Catholic, taking the religion alas, rather unc-
35   tuously. He had entered the church only a few years before. But he had a bishop for a god-father, and seemed to be very intimate with the upper clergy. He was very pleased and proud because he was a constant guest at the famous old monastery south of Rome.* He talked of becoming a monk: a monk in that aristocratic and well-bred order. But he had
40   not even begun his theological studies: or any studies of any sort. And

Douglas said he only chose the Benedictines because they lived better than any of the others.

But I had said to Magnus that when my wife came, and we moved south, I would like to visit the monastery some time, if I might. "Certainly," he said. "Come when I am there. I shall be there in about a month's time. Do come! Do be sure and come. It's a *wonderful* place— ah, wonderful. It will make a great impression on you. Do come. Do come. And I will tell Don Martino,* who is my *greatest* friend, and who is guest-master, about you. So that if you wish to go when I am not there, write to Don Martino. But do come when I am there."

My wife and I were due to go into the mountains south of Rome, and stay there some months. Then I was to visit the big, noble monastery that stands on a bluff hill like a fortress crowning a great precipice, above the little town and the plain between the mountains. But it was so icy cold and snowy among the mountains, it was unbearable.* We fled south again, to Naples, and to Capri. Passing, I saw the monastery crouching there above, world-famous. But it was impossible to call then.

I wrote and told Magnus of my move. In Capri I had an answer from him. It had a wistful tone—and I don't know what made me think that he was in trouble, in monetary difficulty. But I felt it acutely—a kind of appeal. Yet he said nothing direct. And he wrote from an expensive hotel in Anzio, on the sea near Rome.*

At the moment I had just received twenty pounds unexpected and joyful from America—a gift too.* I hesitated for some time, because I felt unsure. Yet the curious appeal came out of the letter, though nothing was said. And I felt also I owed Magnus that dinner, and I didn't want to owe him anything, since he despised me a little for being careful. So partly out of revenge, perhaps, and partly because I felt the strange wistfulness of him appealing to me, I sent him five pounds, saying perhaps I was mistaken in imagining him very hard up, but if so, he wasn't to be offended.

It is strange to me even now, how I knew he was appealing to me. Because it was all as vague as I say. Yet I felt it so strongly.—He replied: "Your cheque has saved my life. Since I last saw you I have fallen down an abyss. But I will tell you when I see you. I shall be at the monastery in three days. Do come—and come alone."—I have forgotten to say that he was a rabid woman-hater.—This was just after Christmas. I thought his "saved my life" and "fallen down an abyss" was just the American touch of "*very, very*—" I wondered what on earth the abyss could be, and I decided it must be he had lost his money or his hopes. It seemed to

5

10

15

20

25

30

35

40

me that some of his old buoyant assurance came out again in this letter. But he was now very friendly, urging me to come to the monastery, and treating me with a curious little tenderness and protectiveness. He had a queer delicacy of his own, varying with a bounce and a commonness.

5   He was a common little bounder.* And then he had this curious delicacy and tenderness and wistfulness.

I put off going north. I had another letter urging me—and it seemed to me that, rather assuredly, he was expecting more money. Rather cockily, as if he had a right to it. And that made me not want to give him any.

10 Besides, as my wife said, what *right* had I to give away the little money we had, and we there stranded in the south of Italy with no resources if once we were spent up. And I have always been determined *never* to come to my last shilling—if I have to reduce my spending almost to nothingness, I have always been determined to keep a few pounds

15 between me and the world.

I did not send any money. But I wanted to go to the monastery, so wrote and said I would come for two days. I always remember getting up in the black dark of the January morning, and making a little coffee on the spirit lamp, and watching the clock, the big-faced, blue old clock

20 on the campanile in the piazza in Capri, to see I wasn't late. The electric light in the piazza lit up the face of the campanile. And we were then, a stone's throw away, high in the Palazzo Ferraro, opposite the bubbly roof of the little duomo.* Strange dark winter morning, with the open sea beyond the roofs, seen through the side window, and the thin line

25 of the lights of Naples twinkling far, far off.

At ten minutes to six I went down the smelly dark stone stairs of the old palazzo, out into the street. A few people were already hastening up the street to the terrace that looks over the sea to the bay of Naples. It was dark and cold. We slid down in the funicular to the shore, then

30 in little boats were rowed out over the dark sea to the steamer that lay there showing her lights and hooting.

The long three hours* across the sea to Naples, with dawn coming slowly in the east, beyond Ischia, and flushing into lovely colour as our steamer pottered along the peninsula, calling at Massa and Sorrento and

35 Piano. I always loved hanging over the side and watching the people come out in boats from the little places of the shore, that rose steep and beautiful. I love the *movement* of these watery Neapolitan peoples, and the naïve trustful way they clamber in and out the boats, and their softness, and their dark eyes. But when the steamer leaves the peninsula

40 and begins to make away round Vesuvius to Naples, one is already tired, and cold, cold, cold in the wind that comes piercing from the

snow-crests away there along Italy. Cold, and reduced to a kind of stony apathy by the time we come to the mole* in Naples, at ten oclock—or twenty past ten.

We were rather late, and I missed the train. I had to wait till two oclock. And Naples is a hopeless town to spend three hours in. However, time passes. I remember I was calculating in my mind whether they had given me the right change at the ticket-window. They hadn't—and I hadn't counted in time. Thinking of this, I got in the Rome train. I had been there ten minutes when I heard a trumpet blow.

"Is this the Rome train?" I asked my fellow-traveller.

"Si."

"The express?"

"No, it is the slow train."

"It leaves?"

"At ten past two."

I almost jumped through the window. I flew down the platform.

"The diretto!" I cried to a porter.

"Parte! Eccolo là!"* he said, pointing to a big train moving inevitably away.

I flew with wild feet across the various railway lines and seized the end of the train as it travelled. I had caught it. Perhaps if I had missed it fate would have been different.—So I sat still for about three hours. Then I had arrived.

There is a long drive up the hill from the station to the monastery. The driver talked to me. It was evident he bore the monks no good will.

"Formerly," he said, "if you went up to the monastery you got a glass of wine and a plate of maccheroni.* But now they kick you out of the door."

"Do they?" I said. "It is hard to believe."

"They kick you out of the gate," he vociferated.

We twisted up and up the wild hillside, past the old castle of the town, past the last villa, between trees and rocks. We saw no one. The whole hill belongs to the monastery. At last at twilight we turned the corner of the oak-wood and saw the monastery like a huge square fortress-palace of the sixteenth century crowning the near distance. Yes, and there was Magnus just stepping through the huge old gateway and hastening down the slope to where the carriage must stop. He was bare-headed, and walking with his perky, busy little stride, seemed very much at home in the place. He looked up to me with a tender, intimate look as I got down from the carriage. Then he took my hand.

"So *very* glad to see you," he said. "I'm so *pleased* you've come."

And he looked into my eyes with that wistful, watchful tenderness rather like a woman who isn't quite sure of her lover. He had a certain charm in his manner; and an odd pompous touch with it which* at this moment, welcoming his guest at the gate of the vast monastery which reared above us from its buttresses in the rock, was rather becoming. His face was still pink, his eyes pale-blue and sharp, but he looked greyer at the temples.

"Give me your bag," he said. "Yes do—and come along. Don Martino is just at evensong, but he'll be here in a little while.—Well now, tell me all the news."

"Wait," I said. "Lend me five francs to finish paying the driver—he has no change."

"Certainly. Certainly!" he said, giving the five francs.

I had no news,—so asked him his.

"Oh, I have none either," he said. "Very short of money, that of course is *no* news." And he laughed his little laugh. "I'm so glad to be here," he continued. "The peace, and the rhythm of the life is so *beautiful*! I'm sure you'll love it."

We went up the slope under the big, tunnel-like entrance and were in the grassy courtyard, with the arched walk on the far sides, and one or two trees. It was like a grassy cloister, but still busy. Black monks were standing chatting, an old peasant was just driving two sheep from the cloister grass, and an old monk was darting into the little post-office which one recognised by the shield with the national arms over the doorway. From under the far arches came an old peasant carrying a two-handed saw.

And there was Don Martino, a tall monk in a black, well-shaped gown, young, good-looking, gentle, hastening forward with a quick smile. He was about my age, and he wore spectacles,* and his manner seemed fresh and subdued, as if he were still a student. One felt one was at college with one's college mates.

We went up the narrow stair and into the long, old, naked white corridor, high and arched. Don Martino had got the key of my room: two keys, one for the dark antechamber, one for the bedroom. A charming and elegant bedroom, with an engraving of English landscape, and outside the net curtain a balcony looking down on the garden, a narrow strip beneath the walls, and beyond, the clustered buildings of the farm, and the oak woods and arable fields of the hill summit: and beyond again, the gulf where the worlds valley was, and all the mountains that stand in Italy on the plains as if God had just put them down ready made.

The sun had already sunk, the snow on the mountains was full of a rosy glow, the valleys were full of shadow. One heard, far below, the trains shunting, the world clinking in the cold air.

"Isn't it wonderful! Ah, the most wonderful place on earth!" said Magnus. "What now could you wish better than to end your days here? The peace, the beauty, the eternity of it." He paused and sighed. Then he put his hand on Don Martino's arm and smiled at him with that odd, rather wistful smirking tenderness that made him such a quaint creature in my eyes.

"But I'm going to enter the order. You're going to let me be a monk and be one of you, aren't you Don Martino."

"We will see," smiled Don Martino. "When you have begun your studies— —"

"It will take me two years," said Magnus. "I shall have to go to the college in Rome. When I have got the money for the fees— — —" He talked away, like a boy planning himself a new rôle.

"But I'm sure Lawrence would like to drink a cup of tea," said Don Martino. He, by the way, was a Maltese, with English as one of his native languages.* "Shall I tell them to make it in the kitchen, or shall we go to your room."

"Oh, we'll go to my room. How thoughtless of me! Do forgive me, won't you?" said Magnus, laying his hand gently on my arm. "I'm so awfully sorry, you know. But we get so excited and enchanted when we talk of the monastery. But come along, come along, it will be ready in a moment on the spirit lamp."

We went down to the end of the high white naked corridor. Magnus had quite a sumptuous room, with a curtained bed in one part, and under the window his writing desk with papers and photographs, and nearby a sofa and an easy table, making a little sitting room, while the bed and toilet things, pomades and bottles were all in the distance, in the shadow. Night was fallen. From the window one saw the world far below, like a pool the flat plain, a deep pool of darkness with little twinkling lights, and rows and bunches of light that were the railway station.

I drank my tea, Magnus drank a little liqueur, Don Martino in his black winter robe sat and talked with us. At least he did very little talking. But he listened and smiled and put in a word or two as we talked, seated round the table on which stood the green-shaded electric lamp.

The monastery was cold as the tomb. Couched there on the top of its hill, it is not much below the winter snow-line. Now, by the end of January all the summer heat is soaked out of the vast, ponderous stone

(Line numbers in right margin: 5, 10, 15, 20, 25, 30, 35, 40)

walls, and they become masses of coldness cloaking around. There is
no heating apparatus whatsoever—none. Save the fire in the kitchen,
for cooking, nothing. Dead, silent, stone cold everywhere.

At seven we went down to dinner. Capri in the daytime was hot, so
5   I had brought only a thin old dust-coat.* Magnus therefore made me
wear a big coat of his own, a coat made of thick, smooth black cloth,
and lined with black sealskin, and having a collar of silky black sealskin.
I can still remember the feel of the silky fur. It was queer to have him
helping me solicitously into this coat, and buttoning it at the throat for
10   me.

"Yes, it's a beautiful coat. Of course!" he said. "I hope you find it
warm."

"Wonderful," said I. "I feel as warm as a millionaire."

"I'm so glad you do," he laughed.

15   "You don't mind my wearing your grand coat?" I said.

"Of course not! Of course not! It's a pleasure to me if it will keep
you warm. We don't want to *die* of cold in the monastery, do we? That's
one of the mortifications we will do our best to avoid. What? Don't you
think?—Yes, I think this coldness is going almost too far. I had that coat
20   made in New York fifteen years ago. Of course in Italy—" he said It'ly—
"I've never worn it, so it is as good as new. And it's a beautiful coat,
fur and cloth of the very best. *And* the tailor," he laughed a little, self-
approving laugh. He liked to give the impression that he dealt with the
best shops, don't you know, and stayed in the *best* hotels, etc. I grinned
25   inside the coat, detesting best hotels, best shops, and best overcoats. So
off we went, he in his grey overcoat and I in my sealskin millionaire
monster, down the dim corridor to the guests' refectory. It was a bare
room with a long white table. Magnus and I sat at the near end. Further
down was another man, perhaps the father of one of the boy students.
30   There is a college attached to the monastery.

We sat in the icy room, muffled up in our overcoats. A lay-brother with
a bulging forehead and queer, fixed eyes waited on us. He might easily
have come from an old Italian picture: one of the adoring peasants. The
food was abundant—but alas, it had got cold in the long cold transit from
35   the kitchen. And it was roughly cooked, even if it was quite wholesome.
Poor Magnus did not eat much, but nervously nibbled his bread. I could
tell the meals were a trial to him. He could not bear the cold food in that
icy, empty refectory. And his tisickyness* offended the lay-brothers. I
could see that his little pomposities and his "superior" behaviour and
40   his long stay made them have that old monastic grudge against him,

silent but very obstinate and effectual—the same now as six hundred
years ago. We had a decanter of good red wine—but he did not care
for much wine. He was glad to be peeling the cold orange which was
dessert.

After dinner he took me down to see the church, creeping like two   5
thieves down the dimness of the great, prison-cold white corridors,
on the cold flag floors. Stone cold: the monks must have invented the
term.—These monks were at complines.* So we went by our two secret
little selves into the tall dense nearly-darkness of the church. Magnus,
knowing his way about here as in the cities, led me, poor wondering   10
worldling, by the arm through the gulfs of the tomb like place. He
found the electric-light switches inside the church and stealthily made
me a light as we went. We looked at the lily marble of the great floor, at
the pillars, at the Benvenuto Cellini casket,* at the really lovely pillars
and slabs of different coloured marbles, all coloured marbles, yellow and 15
grey and rose and green and lily-white, veined and mottled and splashed:
lovely, lovely stones—And Benvenuto had used pieces of lapis lazuli,
blue as cornflowers. Yes yes, all very rich and wonderful.

We tiptoed about the dark church stealthily, from altar to altar, and
Magnus whispered ecstasies in my ear. Each time we passed before   20
an altar, whether the high altar or the side chapels, he did a wonderful
reverence, which he must have practised for hours, bowing waxily down
and sinking till his one knee touched the pavement, then rising like a
flower that rises and unfolds again, till he had skipped to my side and
was playing cicerone* once more. Always in his grey overcoat, and in   25
whispers: me in the big black overcoat, millionairish. So we crept into
the chancel and examined all the queer fat babies of the choir-stalls,
carved in wood and rolling on their little backs between monk's place
and monk's place—queer things for the chanting monks to have between
them, these shiny, polished, dark-brown fat babies, all different, and all 30
jolly and lusty. We looked at everything in the church—and then at
everything in the ancient room at the side where surplices hang and
monks can wash their hands.

Then we went down to the crypt, where the modern mosaics glow in
wonderful colours, and sometimes in fascinating little fantastic trees and 35
birds. But it was rather like a scene in the theatre, with Magnus for the
wizard and myself a sort of Parsifal* in the New York coat.* He switched
on the lights, the gold mosaic of the vaulting glittered and bowed, the
blue mosaic glowed out, the holy of holies gleamed theatrically, the stiff
mosaic figures posed around us.   40

To tell the truth I was glad to get back to the normal human room and
sit on a sofa huddled in my overcoat, and look at photographs which
Magnus showed me: photographs of everywhere in Europe. Then he
showed me a wonderful photograph of a picture of a lovely lady—
5   asked me what I thought of it, and seemed to expect me to be struck to
bits by the beauty. His almost sanctimonious expectation made me tell
the truth, that I thought it just a bit cheap, trivial. And then he said,
dramatic:
"That's my mother."*
10   It looked so unlike anybody's mother, much less Magnus', that I was
startled. I realised that she was his great stunt, and that I had put my
foot in it. So I just held my tongue. Then I said, for I felt he was going
to be silent forever:
"There are so few portraits, unless by the really great artist, that
15   aren't a bit cheap.—She must have been a beautiful woman."
"Yes, she *was*," he said curtly. And we dropped the subject.
He locked all his drawers *very* carefully, and kept the keys on a chain.
He seemed to give the impression that he had a great many secrets,
perhaps dangerous ones, locked up in the drawers of his writing-table
20   there. And I always wonder what the secrets can be, that are able to be
kept so tight under lock and key.
Don Martino tapped and entered. We all sat round and sipped a
funny liqueur which I didn't like. Magnus lamented that the bottle was
finished. I asked him to order another and let me pay for it. So he said
25   he would tell the postman to bring it up next day from the town. Don
Martino sipped his tiny glass with the rest of us, and he told me, briefly,
his story and—we talked politics till nearly midnight. Then I came out
of the black Overcoat and we went to bed.
In the morning a fat, smiling, nice old lay-brother brought me my
30   water.* It was a sunny day. I looked down on the farm cluster and the
brown fields and the sere oak-woods of the hill-crown, and the rocks
and bushes savagely bordering it round. Beyond, the mountains with
their snow were blue-glistery with sunshine, and seemed quite near, but
across a sort of gulf. All was still and sunny. And the poignant grip of
35   the past, the grandiose, violent past of the Middle Ages, when blood
was strong and unquenched and life was flamboyant with splendours
and horrible miseries, took hold of me till I could hardly bear it. It
was really agony to me to be in the monastery and to see the old farm
and the bullocks slowly working in the fields below, and the black pigs
40   rooting among weeds, and to see a monk sitting on a parapet in the sun,

and an old, old man in skin sandals and white-bunched, swathed legs
come driving an ass slowly to the monastery gate, slowly, with all that
lingering nonchalance and wildness of the Middle Ages, and yet to know
that I was myself, child of the present. It was so strange from Magnus'
window to look down on the plain and see the white road going straight   5
past a mountain that stood like a loaf of sugar, the river meandering in
loops, and the railway with glistening lines making a long black swoop
across the flat and into the hills. To see trains come steaming, with
white smoke flying. To see the station like a little harbour where trucks
like shipping stood anchored in rows in the black bay of railway. To   10
see trains stop in the station and tiny people swarming like flies! To see
all this from the monastery, where the Middle Ages live on in a sort of
agony, like Tithonus, and cannot die,* this was almost a violation to my
soul, made almost a wound.

Immediately after coffee we went down to mass. It was celebrated   15
in a small crypt chapel underground, because that was warmer. The
twenty or so monks sat in their stalls, one monk officiating at the altar.
It was quiet and simple, the monks sang sweetly and well, there was no
organ. It seemed soon to pass by. Magnus and I sat near the door. He
was very devoted and scrupulous in his going up and down. I was an   20
outsider. But it was pleasant—not too sacred. One felt the monks were
very human in their likes and their jealousies. It was rather like a group
of Dons in the dons room at Cambridge,* a cluster of professors in any
college. But during mass they of course just sang their responses. Only
I could tell some watched the officiating monk rather with ridicule—   25
he was one of the ultra-punctilious sort, just like a Don. And some
boomed their responses with a grain of defiance against some brother
monk who had earned dislike. It was human, and more like a university
than anything. We went to mass every morning, but I did not go to
evensong.   30

After Mass Magnus took me round and showed me every stone of the
vast monastery. We went into the Bramante courtyard,* all stone, with
its great well in the centre, and the colonnades of arches going round,
full of sunshine, gay and Renaissance, a little bit ornate but still so jolly
and gay, sunny pale stone waiting for the lively people, with the great   35
flights of pale steps sweeping up to the doors of the church, waiting for
gentlemen in scarlet trunk-hose, slender red legs, and ladies in brocade
gowns, and page-boys with fluffed, golden hair. Splendid, sunny gay
Bramante courtyard of lively stone. But empty. Empty of life. The gay
red-legged gentry dead forever.—And when pilgrimages do come and   40

throng in, it is horrible artisan excursions from the great town, and the sordidness of industrialism.

We climbed the little watch tower that is now an observatory, and saw the vague and unshaven Don Benedetto among all his dust and instruments. Magnus was very familiar and friendly, chattering in his quaint Italian, which was more wrong than any Italian I have ever heard spoken; very familiar and friendly, and a tiny bit deferential to the monks, and yet, and yet—rather patronising. His little pomposity and patronising tone coloured even his deferential yearning to be admitted to the monastery. The monks were rather brief with him. They no doubt have their likes and dislikes greatly intensified by the monastic life.

We stood on the summit of the tower and looked at the world below: the town, the castle, the white roads coming straight as judgment out of the mountains north, from Rome, and piercing into the mountains south, towards Naples, traversing the flat, flat plain. Roads, railway, river, streams, a world in accurate and lively detail, with mountains sticking up abruptly and rockily, as the old painters painted it. I think there is no way of painting Italian landscape except that way—that started with Lorenzetti and ended with the sixteenth century.*

We looked at the ancient cell away under the monastery, where all the sanctity started.* We looked at the big library that belongs to the State, and at the smaller library that belongs still to the abbot. I was tired, cold, and sick among the books and illuminations. I could not bear it any more. I felt I must be outside, in the sun, and see the world below, and the way out.

That evening I said to Magnus:

"And what was the abyss, then?"

"Oh well, you know," he said, "it was a cheque which I made out at Anzio.* There *should* have been money to meet it, in my bank in New York. But it appears the money had never been paid in by the people that owed it me. So there was I in a very nasty hole, an unmet cheque, and no money at all in Italy. I really had to escape here. It is an *absolute* secret that I am here, and it must be, till I can get this business settled. Of course I've written to America about it. But as you see, I'm in a very nasty hole. That five francs I gave you for the driver was the last penny I had in the world: absolutely the last penny. I haven't even anything to buy a cigarette or a stamp." And he laughed chirpily, as if it were a joke. But he didn't really think it a joke. Nor was it a joke.

I had come with only two hundred Lire in my pocket, as I was waiting to change some money at the bank. Of this two hundred I had

one hundred left—or one hundred and twenty five. I should need a
hundred to get home. I could only give Magnus the twenty five, for the
bottle of drink. He was rather crestfallen. But I didn't want to give him
money this time: because he expected it.

However, we talked about his plans—how he was to earn something. He told me what he had written. And I cast over in my mind, where he might get something published in London, wrote a couple of letters on his account, told him where I thought he had best send his material.* There wasn't a great deal of hope, for his smaller journalistic articles seemed to me very self-conscious and poor. He had one about the monastery, which I thought he might sell because of the photographs.

That evening he first showed me the Legion manuscript. He had got it rather raggedly typed out. He had a type-writer, but felt he ought to have somebody to do his typing for him, as he hated it and did it unwillingly. That evening and when I went to bed and when I woke in the morning I read this manuscript. It did not seem very good—vague and diffuse where it shouldn't have been—lacking in sharp detail and definite event. And yet there was something in it that made me want it done properly. So we talked about it, and discussed it carefully, and he unwillingly promised to tackle it again. He was curious, always talking about his work, even always working, but never *properly* doing anything.

We walked out in the afternoon through the woods and across the rocky bit of moorland which covers most of the hill-top. We were going to the ruined convent which lies on the other brow of the monastery hill, abandoned and sad among the rocks and heath and thorny bushes. It was sunny and warm. A barefoot little boy was tending a cow and three goats and a pony, a barefoot little girl had five geese in charge. We came to the convent and looked in. The further part of the courtyard was still entire, the place was a sort of farm, two rooms occupied by a peasant-farmer. We climbed about the ruins. Some creature was crying—crying, crying, crying with a strange, inhuman persistence, leaving off and crying again. We listened and listened—the sharp, poignant crying. Almost it might have been a sharp-voiced baby. We scrambled about, looking. And at last outside a little cave-like place found a blind black puppy crawling miserably on the floor, unable to walk, and crying incessantly. We put it back in the little cave-like shed, and went away. The place was deserted save for the crying puppy.

On the road outside however was a man, a peasant, just drawing up to the arched convent gateway with an ass under a load of brushwood.

He was thin and black and dirty. He took off his hat, and we told him of
the puppy. He said the bitch-mother had gone off with his son with the
sheep. Yes, she had been gone all day. Yes, she would be back at sunset.
No, the puppy had not drunk all day. Yes, the little beast cried, but the
5 mother would come back to him.

They were the old-world peasants still about the monastery, with the
hard, small bony heads and deep-lined faces and utterly blank minds,
crying their speech as crows cry, and living their lives as lizards among
the rocks, blindly going on with the little job in hand, the present
10 moment, cut off from all past and future, and having no idea and no
sustained emotion, only that eternal will-to-live which makes a tortoise
wake up once more in spring, and makes a grasshopper whistle on in the
moonlight nights even of November. Only these peasants don't whistle
much. The whistlers go to America. It is the hard, static, unhoping
15 souls that persist in the old life. And still they stand back, as one passes
them in the corridors of the great monastery, they press themselves back
against the whitewashed walls of the still place, and drop their heads, as
if some mystery were passing by, some God-mystery, the higher beings,
which they must not look closely upon. So also this old peasant—he
20 was not old, but deep-lined like a gnarled bough. He stood with his hat
down in his hands as we spoke to him, and answered the short, hard,
insentient answers, as a tree might speak.

"The monks keep their peasants humble," I said to Magnus.

"Of course!" he said. "Don't you think they are quite right? Don't
25 you think they *should* be humble?" And he bridled like a little turkey
cock on his hind legs.

"Well," I said, "if there's any occasion for humility, I do."

"Don't you think there *is* occasion?" he cried. "If there's one thing
worse than another, it's this *equality* that has come into the world. Do
30 you believe in it yourself?"

"No," I said. "I don't believe in equality. But the problem is, wherein
does superiority lie."

"Oh," chirped Magnus complacently. "It lies in many things. It lies
in birth and in upbringing and so on, but it is chiefly in *mind*. Don't you
35 think? Of course I don't mean that the physical qualities aren't *charming*.
They are, and nobody appreciates them more than I do. Some of the
peasants are *beautiful* creatures, perfectly beautiful. But that passes. And
the mind endures."

I did not answer. Magnus was not a man one talked far with. But I
40 thought to myself, I *could* not accept Magnus' superiority to the peasant.

If I had really to live always under the same roof with either one of them, I would have chosen the peasant. If I had had to choose, I would have chosen the peasant. Not because the peasant was wonderful and stored with mystic qualities. No, I don't give much for the wonderful mystic qualities in peasants. Money is their mystery of mysteries, absolutely.— No, if I chose the peasant it would be for what he *lacked* rather than for what he had. He lacked that complacent mentality that Magnus was so proud of, he lacked all the trivial trash of glib talk and more glib thought, all the conceit of our shallow consciousness. For his mindlessness I would have chosen the peasant: and for his strong blood-presence. Magnus wearied me with his facility and his readiness to rush into speech, and for the exhaustive nature of his presence. As if he had no strong blood in him to sustain him, only this modern parasitic lymph which cries for sympathy all the time.

"Don't you think *yourself* that you are superior to that peasant?" he asked me, rather ironically. He half expected me to say no.

"Yes, I do," I replied. "But I think most middle-class, most so-called educated people are inferior to the peasant. I do that."

"Of course," said Magnus readily. "In their *hypocrisy*—"He was great against hypocrisy—especially the English sort.

"And if I think myself superior to the peasant, it is only that I feel myself like the growing tip, or one of the growing tips of the tree, and him like a piece of the hard, fixed tissue of the branch or trunk. We're part of the same tree: and it's the same sap," said I.

"Why exactly! Exactly!" cried Magnus. "Of course! The Church would teach the same doctrine. We are all one in Christ—but between our souls and our duties there are great differences."

It is terrible to be agreed with, especially by a man like Magnus. All that one says, and means, turns to nothing.*

"Yes," I persisted. "But it seems to me the so-called culture, education—the so-called leaders and leading-classes today are only parasites—like a great flourishing bush of parasitic consciousness flourishing on top of the tree of life, and sapping it. The consciousness of today doesn't rise from the roots. It is just parasitic in the veins of life. And the middle and upper classes are just parasitic upon the body of life which still remains in the lower classes."

"What!" said Magnus acidly. "Do you believe in the democratic lower classes?"

"Not a bit," said I.

"I should think not, indeed!" he cried complacently.

"No, I don't believe the lower classes can *ever* make life whole again, till they *do* become humble, like the old peasants, and yield themselves to real leaders. But not just to great negators like Lloyd George or Lenin or Briand."*

5   "Of course! Of course!" he cried. "What you need is the Church in power again. The Church has a place for everybody."

"You don't think the church belongs to the past?"* I asked.

"Indeed I don't, or I shouldn't be here.—No," he said sententiously, "the Church is eternal. It puts people in their proper place. It puts

10   women down into *their* proper place, which is the first thing to be done— —"

He had a great dislike of women, and was very acid about them. Not because of their sins, but because of their virtues: their economies, their philanthropies, their spiritualities. Oh, how he loathed women. He had

15   been married,* but the marriage had not been a success. He smarted still. Perhaps his wife had despised him, and he had not *quite* been able to defeat her contempt.

So, he loathed women, and wished for a world of men. "They talk about love between men and women," he said. "Why it's all a *fraud*.

20   The woman is just taking all and giving nothing, and feeling sanctified about it. All she tries to do is to thwart a man in whatever he is doing.— No, I have found my life in my *friendships*. Physical relationships are very attractive, of course, and one tries to keep them as decent and all that as one can. But one knows they will pass and be finished. But one's

25   *mental* friendships last for ever."

"With me, on the contrary," said I. "If there is no profound blood-sympathy, I know the mental friendship is trash. If there is real, deep blood response, I will stick to that if I have to betray all the mental sympathies I ever made, or all the lasting spiritual loves I ever

30   felt."

He looked at me, and his face seemed to fall. Round the eyes he was yellow and tired and nervous. He watched me for some time.

"Oh!" he said, in a queer tone, rather cold.—"Well, my experience has been the opposite."

35   We were silent for some time.

"And you," I said, "even if you do manage to do all your studies and enter the monastery, do you think you will be satisfied?"

"If I can be so fortunate, I do really," he said. "Do you doubt it?"

"Yes," I said. "Your nature is worldly, more worldly than mine. Yet I

40   should die if I had to stay up here."

"Why?" he asked, curiously.

"Oh, I don't know. The past, the past. The beautiful, the wonderful past, it seems to prey on my heart, I can't bear it."

He watched me closely.

"Really!" he said slowly.* Do you feel like that?—But don't you think it is a far preferable life up here than down there. Don't you think the past is far preferable to the future, with all this socialismo and these communisti and so on?"

We were seated, in the sunny afternoon, on the wild hill-top high above the world. Across the stretch of pale, dry, standing thistles that peopled the waste ground, and beyond the rocks, was the ruined convent. Rocks rose behind us, the summit. Away on the left were the woods which hid us from the great monastery. This was the mountain top, the last foot-hold of the old world.—Below we could see the plain, the straight white road straight as a thought, and the more flexible black railway with the railway station. There swarmed the ferrovieri like ants. There was democracy, industrialism, socialism, the red flag of the communists and the red white and green tricolor of the fascisti.* That was another world. And how bitter, how barren a world! Barren like the black cinder-track of the railway, with its two steel lines.

And here above, sitting with the little stretch of pale, dry thistles around us, our back to a warm rock, we were in the middle ages. Both worlds were agony to me. But here, on the mountain top was worst. The past, the poignancy of the not-quite-dead past.

"I think one's got to go through with the life down there—get somewhere beyond it. One can't go back," I said to him.

"But do you call the monastery going back?" he said. "I don't. The peace, the eternity, the concern with things that matter. I consider it the happiest fate that could happen to me. Of course it means putting physical things aside. But when you've done that—why, it seems to me perfect."

"No," I said. "You're too worldly."

"But the monastery is worldly too. We're not Trappists.* Why the monastery is one of the centres of the world—one of the most active centres."

"Maybe. But that impersonal activity, with the blood suppressed and going sour—no, it's too late. It is too abstract—political maybe—"

"I'm sorry you think so," he said, rising. "I don't."

"Well," I said. "You'll never be a monk here, Magnus. You see if you are."

"You don't think I shall?" he replied, turning to me. And there was a catch of relief in his voice. Really, the monastic state must have been like going to prison for him.

"You haven't a vocation," I said.

"I may not *seem* to have, but I hope I actually have."

"You haven't."

"Of course, if you're so sure," he laughed, putting his hand on my arm.

He seemed to understand so much, round about the questions that trouble one deepest. But the quick of the question he never felt. He had no real middle, no real centre bit to him. Yet, round and about all the questions, he was so intelligent and sensitive.

We went slowly back. The peaks of those Italian mountains in the sunset, the extinguishing twinkle of the plain away below, as the sun declined and grew yellow; the intensely powerful mediaeval spirit lingering on this wild hill summit, all the wonder of the mediaeval past; and then the huge mossy stones in the wintry wood, that was once a sacred grove; the ancient path through the wood, that led from temple to temple on the hill summit, before Christ was born; and then the great Cyclopean wall* one passes at the bend of the road, built even before the pagan temples; all this overcame me so powerfully this afternoon, that I was almost speechless. That hill-top must have been one of man's intense sacred places for three thousand years. And men die generation after generation, races die, but the new cult finds root in the old sacred place, and the quick spot of earth dies very, very slowly. Yet at last it too dies. But this quick* spot is still not quite dead. The great monastery couchant there, half empty, but also not quite dead. And Magnus and I walking across as the sun set yellow and the cold of the snow came into the air, back home to the monastery! And I feeling as if my heart had once more broken: I don't know why. And he feeling his fear of life, that haunted him, and his fear of his own self and its consequences, that never left him for long. And he seemed to walk close to me, very close. And we had neither of us anything more to say.

Don Martino was looking for us as we came up under the archway, he hatless in the cold evening, his black dress swinging voluminous. There were letters for Magnus. There was a small cheque for him from America,—about fifty dollars—from some newspaper in the Middle West that had printed one of his articles. He had to talk with Don Martino about this.

I decided to go back the next day. I could not stay any longer. Magnus was very disappointed, and begged me to remain. "I thought you would

stay a week at least," he said. "Do stay over Sunday. Oh do!" But I
couldn't, I didn't want to. I could see that his days were a torture to
him—the long, cold days in that vast quiet building, with the strange
and exhausting silence in the air, and the sense of the past preying on
one, and the sense of the silent, suppressed, scheming struggle of life   5
going on still in the sacred place.

It was a cloudy morning. In the green courtyard the big Don Anselmo
had just caught the little Don Lorenzo round the waist and was swinging
him over a bush, like lads before school. The Prior was just hurrying
somewhere, following his long fine nose. He bade me goodbye; pleasant,   10
warm, jolly, with a touch of wistfulness in his deafness. I parted with
real regret from Don Martino.

Magnus was coming with me down the hill—not down the carriage
road, but down the wide old paved path that swoops so wonderfully
from the top of the hill to the bottom. It feels thousands of years old.   15
Magnus was quiet and friendly. We met Don Vincenzo, he who has the
care of the land and crops, coming slowly, slowly uphill in his black
cassock, treading slowly with his great thick boots. He was reading a
little book. He saluted us as we passed. Lower down a strapping girl was
watching three merino sheep among the bushes. One sheep came on its   20
exquisite slender legs to sniff at* me, with that insatiable curiosity of a
pecora. Her nose was silken and elegant as she reached it to sniff at me,
and the yearning, wondering, inquisitive look in her eye that had such
a marvellous oval iris of living gold, pure living gold of her eyes,* made
me realise that the Lamb of God* must have been such a sheep as this.   25

Magnus was miserable at my going. Not so much at my going, as
at being left alone up there. We came to the foot of the hill, on to
the town high-road. So we went into a little cave of a wine-kitchen to
drink a glass of wine. Magnus chatted a little with the young woman.
He chatted with everybody. She eyed us closely—and asked if we were   30
from the monastery. We said we were. She seemed to have a little lurking
antagonism round her nose, at the mention of the monastery. Magnus
paid for the wine—a franc. So we went out on to the highroad, to part.

"Look," I said. "I can only give you twenty Liras, because I shall
need the rest for the journey—"   35

But he wouldn't take them. He looked at me wistfully. Then I went
on down to the station, he turned away uphill. It was market in the town,
and there were clusters of bullocks, and women cooking a little meal at
a brasier under the trees, and goods spread out on the floor, to sell, and
sacks of beans and corn standing open, clustered round the trunks of   40
the mulberry trees, and wagons with their shafts on the ground. The

old peasants in their brown homespun frieze* and skin sandals were
watching for the world.—And then again was the middle ages.

It began to rain, however. Suddenly it began to pour with rain, and
my coat was wet through, and my trouser-legs. The train from Rome
was late—I hoped not very late, or I should miss the boat. She came at
last: and was full, I had to stand in the corridor. Then the man came
to say dinner was served, so I luckily got a place and had my meal too.
Sitting there in the dining-car, among the fat Neapolitans eating their
maccheroni, with the big glass windows steamed opaque and the rain
beating outside, I let myself be carried away, away from the monastery,
away from Magnus, away from everything.

At Naples there was a bit of sunshine again, and I had time to go on
foot to the Immacolatella,* where the little steamer lay. There on the
steamer I sat in a bit of sunshine, and felt that again the world had come
to an end for me, and again my heart was broken. The steamer seemed
to be making its way away from the old world, that had come to another
end in me.

It was after this I decided to go to Sicily. In February, only a few days
after my return from the monastery, I was on the steamer for Palermo,
and at dawn looking out on the wonderful coast of Sicily. Sicily, tall,
forever rising up to her gem-like summits, all golden in dawn, and
always glamorous, always hovering as if inaccessible, and yet so near,
so distinct. Sicily unknown to me, and amethystine glamorous in the
Mediterranean dawn: like the dawn of our day, the wonder-morning of
our epoch.

I had various letters from Magnus. He had told me to go to Girgenti.
But I arrived in Girgenti when there was a strike of sulphur-miners,*
and they threw stones. So I did not want to live in Girgenti. Magnus
hated Taormina—he had been everywhere, tried everywhere, and was
not, I found, in any good odour in most places. He wrote however saying
he hoped I would like it. And later he sent the Legion manuscript. I
thought it was good, and told him so. It was offered to publishers in
London, but rejected.

In early April I went with my wife down to Syracuse* for a few days:
lovely, lovely days, with the purple anemones blowing in the Sicilian
fields, and Adonis-blood red* on the little ledges, and the corn rising
strong and green in the magical, malarial places, and Etna floating now
to northward,* still with her crown of snow. The lovely, lovely journey
from Catania to Syracuse, in spring, winding round the blueness of that
sea, where the tall pink asphodel was dying, and the yellow asphodel like

a lily showing her silk. Lovely, lovely Sicily, the dawn-place, Europe's dawn, with Odysseus* pushing his ship out of the shadows into the blue. Whatever had died for me, Sicily had then not died: dawn-lovely Sicily, and the Ionian sea.

We came back, and the world was lovely: our own house* above the almond trees, and the sea in the cove below, Calabria glimmering like a changing opal away to the left, across the blue, bright straits, and all the great blueness of the lovely dawn-sea in front, where the sun rose with a splendour like trumpets every morning, and me rejoicing like a madness in this dawn, day-dawn, life-dawn, the dawn which is Greece, which is me.

Well, into this lyricism suddenly crept the serpent. It was a lovely morning, still early. I heard a noise on the stairs from the lower terrace, and went to look. Magnus on the stairs, looking up at me with a frightened face.

"Why!" I said. "Is it you?"

"Yes," he replied. "A terrible thing has happened."

He waited on the stairs, and I went down. Rather unwillingly, because I detest terrible things, and the people to whom they happen. So we leaned on the creeper covered rail of the terrace, under festoons of creamy bignonia flowers, and looked at the pale-blue, ethereal sea.

"What terrible thing?" said I.

"When did you get back?" said he.

"Last evening."

"Oh! I came before. The contadini* said they thought you would come yesterday evening. I've been here several days."

"Where are you staying?"

"At San Domenico."

San Domenico being then the most expensive hotel here,* I thought he must have money. But I knew he wanted something of me.

"And are you staying some time?"

He paused a moment, and looked round cautiously.

"Is your wife there?" he asked, sotto voce.

"Yes she's upstairs."

"Is there anyone who can hear?"

"No—only old Grazia down below, and she can't understand anyhow."

"Well," he said, stammering, "let me tell you what's happened. I had to escape from the monastery. —Don Martino had a telephone message from the town below, that the carabinieri were looking for an

Americano—my name—Of course, you can guess how I felt, up there!
Awful!—Well—! I had to fly at a moment's notice. I just put two shirts
in a handbag and went. I slipped down a path—or rather, it isn't a
path—down the back of the hill. Ten minutes after Don Martino had
5   the message I was running down the hill."

"But what did they want you for?" I asked dismayed.

"Well," he faltered. "I told you about that cheque at Anzio, didn't
I? Well it seems the hotel people applied to the police. Anyhow—" he
added hastily— "I couldn't let myself be arrested up there, could I? So
10 awful for the monastery!"

"Did they know then that you were in trouble?" I asked.

"Don Martino knew I had no money," he said. "Of course, he had
to know. Yes—he knew I was in *difficulty*. But of course, he didn't
know—well—*everything*." —He laughed a little, comical laugh over
15 the *everything*, as if he was just a little bit naughtily proud of it: most
ruefully also.

"No," he continued, "that's what I'm most afraid of—that they'll find
out everything at the monastery. Of course it's *dreadful*—the Americano,
been staying there for months, and everything so nice and—well, you
20 know how they are, they imagine every American is a millionaire, if
not a multi-millionaire. And suddenly to be wanted by the police! Of
course it's *dreadful*! Anything rather than a scandal at the monastery—
anything. Oh, how awful it was! I can tell you, in that quarter of an
hour, I sweated blood. Don Martino lent me two hundred Lire of the
25 monastery money—which he'd no business to do. And I escaped down
the back of the hill. I walked to the next station up the line, and took the
next train—the slow train—a few stations up towards Rome. And there
I changed and caught the diretto for Sicily. I came straight to you—.
Of course I was in *agony*: imagine it! I spent most of the time as far as
30 Naples in the lavatory." He laughed his little jerky laugh—

"What class did you travel?"

"Second. All through the night. I arrived more dead than alive, not
having had a meal for two days—only some sandwich stuff I bought on
the platform."

35 "When did you come then?"

"I arrived on Saturday evening. I came out here on Sunday morning,
and they told me you were away. Of course, imagine what it's like! I'm
in torture every minute, in torture, of course. Why just imagine!" And
he laughed his little laugh.

40 "But how much money have you got?"

"Oh—I've just got twenty-five francs and five soldi." He laughed as if it was rather a naughty joke.

"But," I said, "if you've got no money, why do you go to San Domenico? How much do you pay there?"

"Fifty Lire a day. Of course it's *ruinous*—"   5

"But at the Bristol you only pay twenty-five—and at Fichera's only twenty."

"Yes, I know you do," he said. "But I stayed at the Bristol once, and I loathed the place. Such an offensive manager. And I couldn't touch the food at Fichera's."   10

"But who's going to pay for San Domcnico, then?" I asked.

"Well, I thought," he said— "You know all those manuscripts of mine? Well, you think they're some good, don't you? Well, I thought if I made them over to you, and you did what you could with them, and just kept me going till I can get a new start—or till I can get away—"   15

I looked across the sea: the lovely morning-blue sea towards Greece.

"Where do you want to get away to?" I said.

"To Egypt. I know a man in Alexandria who owns the newspapers there. I'm sure if I could get over there he'd give me an editorship or something. And of course money will come. I've written to Taylor, who   20
was my *greatest* friend, in London.* He will send me something—"

"And what else do you expect—?"

"Oh, my article on the monastery was accepted by Land and Water*—
thanks to you and your kindncss, of course. I thought if I might stay very quietly with you, for a time, and write some things I'm wanting to   25
do, and collect a little money—and then get away to Egypt—."

He looked up into my face, as if he were trying all he could on me. First thing I knew was that I could not have him in the house with me: and even if *I* could have borne it, my wife never could.

"You've got a lovely place here, perfectly beautiful," he said. "Of   30
course, if it *had* to be Taormina, you've chosen far the best place here. I like this side so much better than the Etna side. Etna always there and people raving about it gets on my nerves. And a *charming* house, *charming*."

He looked round the loggia and along the other terrace.   35

"Is it all yours?" he said.

"We don't use the ground floor. Come in here."

So we went into the salotta.*

"Oh what a beautiful room," he cried. "But perfectly palatial. Charming! Charming! *Much* the nicest house in Taormina."   40

"No," I said, "as a house it isn't very grand, though I like it for myself.
It's just what I want. And I love the situation.—But I'll go and tell my
wife you are here."

"Will you?" he said, bridling nervously. "Of course I've never met
5   your wife." And he laughed the nervous, naughty, jokey little laugh.

I left him, and ran upstairs to the kitchen. There was my wife,
with wide eyes. She had been listening to catch the conversation. But
Magnus' voice was too hushed.

"Magnus!" said I softly. "The carabinieri wanted to arrest him at the
10 monastery, so he has escaped here, and wants me to be responsible for
him."

"Arrest him what for?"

"Debts, I suppose.—Will you come down and speak to him."

Magnus of course was very charming with my wife. He kissed her
15 hand humbly, in the correct German fashion, and spoke with an air of
reverence that infallibly gets a woman.

"Such a beautiful place you have here," he said, glancing through the
open doors of the room, at the sea beyond. "So clever of you to find it."

"Lawrence found it," said she. "Well, and you are in all kinds of
20 difficulty!"

"Yes, isn't it terrible!" he said, laughing as if it were a joke—rather
a wry joke. "I felt dreadful at the monastery. So dreadful for them, if
there was any sort of scandal. And after I'd been so well received there—
and so much the Signor Americano—Dreadful, don't you think?" He
25 laughed again, like a naughty boy.

We had an engagement to lunch that morning. My wife was dressed,
so I went to get ready. Then we told Magnus we must go out, and he
accompanied us to the village. I gave him just the hundred francs I had
in my pocket, and he said could he come and see me that evening. I
30 asked him to come next morning.

"You're so awfully kind," he said, simpering a little.

But by this time I wasn't feeling kind.

"He's quite nice," said my wife. "But he's rather an impossible little
person. And you'll see, he'll be a nuisance. Whatever do you pick such
35 dreadful people up for?"*

"Nay," I said. "You can't accuse me of picking up dreadful people.
He's the first. And even he isn't dreadful."

The next morning came a letter from Don Martino addressed to me,
but only enclosing a letter to Magnus. So he was using my address. At
40 ten oclock he punctually appeared: slipping in as if to avoid notice. My
wife would not see him, so I took him out on to the terrace again.

"Isn't it beautiful here!" he said. "Oh so beautiful! If only I had my peace of mind. Of course I sweat blood every time anybody comes through the door. You are splendidly private out here."

"Yes," I said. "But Magnus, there isn't a room for you in the house. There isn't a spare room anyway. You'd better think of getting something cheaper in the village."

"But what can I get?" he snapped.

That rather took my breath away. Myself, I had never been near San Domenico hotel. I knew I simply could not afford it.

"What made you go to San Domenico in the first place?" I said. "The most expensive hotel in the place!"

"Oh, I'd stayed there for two months, and they knew me, and I knew they'd ask no questions. I knew they wouldn't ask for a deposit or anything."

"But nobody dreams of asking for a deposit," I said.

"Anyhow I shan't take my meals there. I shall just take coffee in the morning. I've had to eat there so far, because I was starved to death, and had no money to go out.—But I had two meals in that little restaurant yesterday.—Disgusting food."

"And how much did that cost?"

"Oh fourteen francs and fifteen francs, with a quarter of wine—and such a poor meal!"

Now I was annoyed, knowing that I myself should have bought bread and cheese for one franc, and eaten it in my room. But also I realised that the modern creed says, if you sponge, sponge thoroughly: and also that every man has a "right to live," and that if he can manage to live *well*, no matter at whose expense, all credit to him. This is the kind of talk one accepts in one's slipshod moments. Now it was actually tried on me, I didn't like it at all.

"But who's going to pay your bill at San Domenico?" I said.

"I thought you'd advance me the money on those manuscripts."

"It's no good talking about the money on the manuscripts," I said. "I should have to give it you. And as a matter of fact, I've got just sixty pounds in the bank in England, and about fifteen hundred Lire here. My wife and I have got to live on that. We don't spend as much in a week as you spend in three days at San Domenico. It's no good your thinking I can advance money on the manuscripts, I can't. If I was rich, I'd give you money. But I've got no money, and never have had any. Have you nobody you can go to?"

"I'm waiting to hear from Taylor. When I go back into the village, I'll telegraph to him," replied Magnus, a little crestfallen. "Of course I'm

in torture night and day, or I wouldn't appeal to you like this. I know
it's unpleasant for you—" and he put his hand on my arm and looked
up beseechingly. "But what am I to do?"

"You must get out of San Domenico," I said. "That's the first thing."

5   "Yes," he said, a little piqued now. "I know it is. I'm going to ask
Pancrazio Melenda* to let me have a room in his house. He knows
me quite well—he's an awfully nice fellow. He'll do *anything* for me—
anything. I was just going there yesterday afternoon when you were
coming from Timeo. He was out, so I left word with his wife, who is a

10   charming little person. If he has a room to spare, I know he will let me
have it. And he's a *splendid* cook—splendid. By far the nicest food in
Taormina."

"Well," I said. "If you settle with Melenda, I will pay your bill at San
Domenico, but I can't do any more. I simply can't."

15   "But what am I to *do*?" he snapped.

"I don't know," I said. "You must think."

"I came here," he said, "thinking you would help me. What am I to do,
if you won't. I shouldn't have come to Taormina at all, save for you.—
Don't be unkind to me—don't speak so coldly to me—" He put his

20   hand on my arm, and looked up at me with tears swimming in his eyes.
Then he turned aside his face, overcome with tears. I looked away at the
Ionian sea, feeling my blood turn to ice and the sea go black. I loathed
scenes such as this.

"Did you telegraph to Taylor?" I said.

25   "Yes. I have no answer yet. I hope you don't mind—I gave your
address for a reply."

"Oh," I said. "There's a letter for you from Don Martino."

He went pale. I was angry at his having used my address in this
manner.

30   "Nothing further has happened at the monastery," he said. "They
rang up from the questura, from the police station, and Don Martino
answered that the Americano had left for Rome. Of course I did take
the train for Rome. And Don Martino wanted me to go to Rome. He
advised me to do so. I didn't tell him I was here till I had got here.

35   He thought I should have had more resources in Rome, and of course
I should. I should certainly have gone there, if it hadn't been for *you
here*—"

Well, I was getting tired and angry. I would not give him any more
money at the moment. I promised, if he would leave the hotel I would

40   pay his bill, but he must leave it at once. He went off to settle with

Melenda. He asked again if he could come in the afternoon: I said I was
going out.

He came nevertheless while I was out. This time my wife found him
on the stairs. She was for hating him, of course. So she stood immovable
on the top stair, and he stood two stairs lower, and he kissed her hand in
utter humility. And he pleaded with her, and as he looked up to her on
the stairs the tears ran down his face and he trembled with distress. And
her spine crept up and down with distaste and discomfort. But he broke
into a few phrases of touching German, and I know he broke down her
reserve and she promised him all he wanted. This part she would never
confess, though. Only she was shivering with revulsion and excitement
and even a sense of power, when I came home.

That was why Magnus appeared more impertinent than ever, next
morning. He had arranged to go to Melenda's house the following day,
and to pay ten francs a day for his room, his meals extra. So that was
something. He made a long tale about not eating any of his meals in the
hotel now, but pretending he was invited out, and eating in the little
restaurants where the food was so bad. And he had now only fifteen
Lire left in his pocket. But I was cold, and wouldn't give him any more.
I said I would give him money next day, for his bill.

He had now another request, and a new tone.

"Won't you do *one more* thing for me?" he said. "Oh do! Do do this
one thing for me. I want you to go to the monastery and bring away
my important papers and some clothes and my important trinkets. I
have made a list of the things here—and where you'll find them in my
writing-table and in the chest of drawers. I don't think you'll have any
trouble. Don Martino has the keys. He will open everything for you.
And I beg you, *in the name of God*, don't let anybody else see the things.
Not even Don Martino. Don't, whatever you do, let him see the papers
and manuscripts you are bringing. If he sees them, there's an end to me
at the monastery. I can *never* go back there. I am ruined in their eyes for
ever.—As it is—although Don Martino is the best person in the world,
and my dearest friend—still—you know what people are—especially
monks. A little curious, don't you know, a little inquisitive.—Well, let
us hope for the best as far as that goes.—But you will do this for me,
won't you? I shall be so eternally grateful."

Now a journey to the monastery meant a terrible twenty hours in the
train, each way,—all that awful journey through Calabria to Naples and
northwards. It meant mixing myself up in this man's affairs. It meant
appearing as his accomplice at the monastery. It meant travelling with all

his "compromising" papers and his valuables. And all the time, I never knew what mischiefs he had really been up to, and I didn't trust him, not for one single second. He would tell me nothing save that Anzio hotel cheque. I knew that wasn't all, by any means. So I mistrusted him—And with a feeling of utter mistrust goes a feeling of contempt and dislike.— And finally, it would have cost me at least ten pounds sterling, which I simply did not want to spend in waste.

"I don't want to do that," I, said.

"Why not?" he asked, sharp, looking green. He had planned it all out.

"No, I don't want to."

"Oh but I *can't* remain here as I am. I've got no *clothes*—I've got nothing to *wear*. I *must* have my things from the monastery. What can I do? What can I do? I came to you. If it hadn't been for you I should have gone to Rome. I came to you——Oh yes, you *will* go. You *will* go, won't you? You *will* go to the monastery for my things?—" And again he put his hand on my arm, and the tears began to fall from his upturned eyes. I turned my head aside. Never had the Ionian sea looked so sickening to me.

"I don't *want* to," said I.

"But you *will*! You will! You *will* go to the monastery for me, won't you? Everything else is no good if you won't. I've nothing to wear. I haven't got my manuscripts to work on, I can't do the things I am doing. Here I live in a sweat of anxiety. I try to work, and I can't settle. I can't do anything. It's dreadful. I shan't have a minute's peace till I have got those things from the monastery, till I know they can't get at my private papers.—You will do this for me? You will, won't you? Please do! Oh please do!"—And again tears.

And I with my bowels full of bitterness, loathing the thought of that journey there and back, on such an errand. Yet not quite sure that I ought to refuse. And he pleaded and struggled, and tried to bully me with tears and entreaty and reproach, to do his will. And I couldn't quite refuse. But neither could I agree.

At last I said:

"I don't want to go, and I tell you. I won't promise to go. And I won't say that I will not go. I won't say until tomorrow. Tomorrow I will tell you. Don't come to the house. I will be in the Corso at ten oclock."

"I didn't doubt for a minute you would do this for me," he said. "Otherwise I should never have come to Taormina."—As if he had done me an honour in coming to Taormina: and as if *I* had betrayed *him*.

"Well," I said. "If you make these messes you'll have to get out of them yourself. I don't know why you are *in* such a mess."

"Any man may make a mistake," he said sharply, as if correcting me.
"Yes, a *mistake*!" said I. "If it's a question of a mistake."

So once more he went, humbly, beseechingly, and yet, one could not
help but feel, with all that terrible insolence of the humble. It is the
humble, the wistful, the would-be-loving souls today who bully us with
their charity-demanding insolence. They just make up their minds,
these needful sympathetic souls, that one is there to do their will.—
Very good.

I decided in the day I would *not* go. Without reasoning it out, I knew
I *really* didn't want to go: I plainly didn't want it. So I wouldn't go.

The morning came again hot and lovely. I set off to the village. But
there was Magnus watching for me on the path beyond the valley. He
came forward and took my hand warmly, clingingly. I turned back, to
remain in the country. We talked for a minute of his leaving the hotel—
he was going that afternoon, he had asked for his bill.—But he was
waiting for the other answer.

"And I have decided," I said, "I won't go to the monastery."

"You won't." He looked at me. I saw how yellow he was round the
eyes, and yellow under his reddish skin.

"No," I said.

And it was final. He knew it. We went some way in silence. I turned in
at the garden gate. It was a lovely, lovely morning of hot sun. Butterflies
were flapping over the rosemary hedges and over a few little red poppies,
the young vines smelt sweet in flower, very sweet, the corn was tall and
green, and there were still some wild, rose-red gladiolus flowers among
the watery green of the wheat. Magnus had accepted my refusal. I
expected him to be angry. But no, he seemed quieter, wistfuller, and he
seemed almost to love me for having refused him. I stood at a bend in
the path. The sea was heavenly blue, rising up beyond the vines and
olive leaves, lustrous pale lacquer blue as only the Ionian sea can be.
Away at the brook below the women were washing, and one could hear
the chock-chock-chock of linen beaten against the stones. I felt Magnus
there an intolerable weight and like a clot of dirt over everything.

"May I come in?" he said to me.

"No," I said. "Don't come to the house. My wife doesn't want it."

Even that he accepted without any offence, and seemed only to like
me better for it. That was a puzzle to me. I told him I would leave a
letter and a cheque for him at the bank in the Corso that afternoon.

I did so, writing a Cheque for a few pounds, enough to cover his bill
and leave a hundred Lire or so over, and a letter to say I could *not* do
any more, and I didn't want to see him any more.

So, there was an end of it for a moment. Yet I felt him looming in the village, waiting. I had rashly said I would go to tea with him to the villa of one of the Englishmen resident here, whose acquaintance I had not made. Alas, Magnus kept me to the promise.—As I came home, he
5   appealed to me again. He was rather insolent. What good to him, he said, were the few pounds I had given him. He had got a hundred and fifty Lire left. What good was that? I realised it really was *not* a solution, and said nothing. Then he spoke of his plans for getting to Egypt. The fare, he had found out, was thirty five pounds. And where were thirty
10   five pounds coming from? Not from me.

I spent a week avoiding him, wondering what on earth the poor devil was doing, and yet *determined* he should not be a parasite on me. If I could have given him fifty pounds and sent him to Egypt to be a parasite on somebody else, I would have done so. Which is what we call charity.
15   However, I *couldn't.*

My wife chafed, crying: "What have you done! We shall have him on our hands all our life. We can't let him starve. It is degrading, degrading, to have him hanging on to us."

"Yes," I said. "He must starve or work or something. I am not God
20   who is responsible for him."*

Magnus was determined not to lose his status as a gentleman. In a way I sympathised with him. He would never be out at elbows. That is your modern rogue. He will not degenerate outwardly. Certain standards of a gentleman he *would* keep up: he would be well dressed, he would be
25   lavish with borrowed money, he would be as far as possible honorable in his small transactions of daily life. Well, very good. I sympathised with him, to a certain degree. If he could find his own way out, well and good. Myself, I was not his way out.

Ten days passed. It was hot, and I was going about the terrace in
30   pyjamas and a big old straw hat, when suddenly, a Sicilian, handsome, in the prime of life, and in his best black suit, smiling at me and taking off his hat!

And could he speak to me. I threw away my straw hat, and we went into the Salotta. He handed me a note.

35   "Il Signor Magnus mi ha dato questa lettera per Lei!—"* he began, and I knew what was coming. Melenda had been a waiter in good hotels, had saved money, built himself a fine house which he let to foreigners. He was a pleasant fellow, and at his best now, because he was in a rage. I must repeat Magnus' letter from memory—"Dear Lawrence, would you do
40   me another kindness. Land and Water sent a cheque for seven guineas for the article on the Monastery, and Don Martino forwarded this to

me under Melenda's name. But unfortunately he made a mistake, and put Orazio instead of Pancrazio, so the post office would not deliver the letter, and have returned it to the monastery.—This morning Melenda insulted me, and I cannot stay in his house another minute. Will you be so kind as to advance me these seven guineas, and I shall leave Taormina 5 at once, for Malta . . ."

I asked Melenda what had happened, and read him the letter. He was handsome in his rage, lifting his brows and suddenly smiling:

"Ma senta,* signore! Signor Magnus has been in my house for ten days, and lived well, and eaten well, and drunk well, and I have not 10 seen a single penny of his money. I go out in the morning and buy all the things, all he wants, and my wife cooks it, and he is very pleased, very pleased, has never eaten such good food in his life, and everything splendid, splendid. And he never pays a penny. Not a penny. Says he is waiting for money from England, from America, from India. But the 15 money never comes. And I am a poor man, signore, I have a wife and child to keep. I have already spent three hundred Lire for this Signor Magnus, and I never see a penny of it back. And he says the money is coming, it is coming—But when? But how? He never says he has got no money. He says he is expecting. Tomorrow—always tomorrow. It 20 will come tonight, it will come tomorrow. This makes me in a rage. Till at last this morning I said to him I would buy nothing in, and he shouldn't have not so much as a drop of coffee in my house until he paid for it. It displeases me, signore, to say such a thing. I have known Signor Magnus for many years, and he has always had money, and always been 25 pleasant, molto bravo, and also generous with his money. Si, lo so! And my wife, poverina, she cries and says if the man has no money he must eat. But he doesn't *say* he has no money. He says always it is coming, it is coming, today, tomorrow, today, tomorrow. E non viene mai niente. And this enrages me, signore. So I said that to him this morning. And 30 he said he wouldn't stay in my house, and that I had insulted him, and he sends me this letter to you, signore, and says you will send him the money. Ecco come è!"* Between his rage he smiled at me. One thing however I could see: he was not going to lose his money, Magnus or no Magnus. 35

"Is it true that a letter came which the post would not deliver?" I asked him.

"Si signore, è vero.* It came yesterday, addressed to me. And why, signore, why do his letters come addressed in my name. Why? Unless he has done something—?" 40

He looked at me enquiringly. I felt already mixed up in shady affairs.

"Yes," I said, "there is something. But I don't know exactly what. I don't ask, because I don't want to know in these affairs. It is better not to know."

"Già! Già! Molto meglio,* signore. There will be something. There will be something happened that he had to escape from that monastery. And it will be some affair of the police."

He looked at me shrewdly. He did not believe for a moment that I did not know. But as a matter of fact, I knew no more than that Anzio cheque story.

"Yes, I think so," said I. "Money and the police. Probably debts. I don't ask. He is only an acquaintance of mine, not a friend."

"Sure it will be an affair of the police," he said with a grimace. "If not, why does he use my name! Why don't his letters come in his own name?—Do you believe, signore, that he has any money? Do you think this money will come?"

"I'm sure he's *got* no money," I said. "Whether anybody will send him any I don't know."

The man watched me attentively.

"He's got nothing?" he said.

"No. At the present he's got nothing."

Then Pancrazio exploded on the sofa.

"Allora!* Well then! Well then, why does he come to my house, why does he come and take a room in my house, and ask me to buy food, good food as for a gentleman who can pay, and a flask of wine, and everything, if he has no money. If he has no money, why does he come to Taormina? It is many years since he has been in Italy—ten years, fifteen years. And he has no money. Where has he had his money from before? Where?"

"From his writing, I suppose."

"Well then, why doesn't he get money for his writing now? He writes. He writes, he works, he says it is for the big newspapers."

"It is difficult to sell things."

"Heh! Then why doesn't he live on what he made before. He hasn't a soldo. He hasn't a penny—But how! How did he pay his bill at San Domenico?"

"I had to lend him the money for that. He really hadn't a penny."

"You! You! Well then, he has been in Italy all these years. How is it he has nobody that he can ask for a hundred Lire or two. Why does he come to you? Why? Why has he nobody in Rome, in Florence, anywhere?"

"I wonder that myself."

"Siccuro!* He's been all these years here. And why doesn't he speak proper Italian? After all these years, and speaks all upside-down, it isn't Italian, an ugly confusion. Why? Why? He passes for a signore, for a man of education. And he comes to take the bread out of my mouth. And I have got a wife and child, I am a poor man, I have nothing to eat myself if everything goes to a mezzo-signore like him. Nothing! He owes me now three hundred Lire. But he will not leave my house, he will not leave Taormina till he has paid. I will go to the Prefettura, I will go to the questura, to the police. I will not be swindled by such a mezzo signore. What does he want to do? If he has no money, what does he want to do?"

"To go to Egypt where he says he can earn some," I replied briefly. But I was feeling bitter in the mouth. When the man called Magnus a mezzo signore, a half-gentleman, it was so true. And at the same time it was so cruel, and so rude. And Melenda—there I sat in my pyjamas and sandals—probably he would be calling me also a mezzo signore, or a quarto-signore even. He was a Sicilian who feels he is being done out of his money—and that is saying everything.

"To Egypt! And who will pay for him to go? Who will give him money? But he must pay me first. He must pay me first."

"He says," I said, "that in the letter which went back to the monastery there was a cheque for seven pounds—some six hundred Lire—and he asks me to send him this money, and when the letter is returned again I shall have the Cheque that is in it."

Melenda watched me.

"Six hundred Lire—" he said.

"Yes."

"Oh well then. If he *pays* me, he can stay—" he said: he almost added: "till the six hundred is finished." But he left it unspoken.

"But am I going to send the money? Am I sure that what he says is true?"

"I think it is true. I think it is true," said he. "The letter *did* come."

I thought for a while.

"First," I said, "I will write and ask him if it is quite true, and to give me a guarantee."

"Very well," said Melenda.

I wrote to Magnus, saying that if he could assure me that what he said about the seven guineas was quite correct, and if he would give me a note to the editor of Land and Water, saying that the cheque was to be paid to me, I would send the seven guineas.

Melenda was back in another half hour. He brought a note which began:

"Dear Lawrence, I seem to be living in an atmosphere of suspicion. First Melenda this morning, and now you—" Those are the exact opening words. He went on to say that of course his word was true, and he enclosed a note to the editor, saying the seven guineas were to be transferred to me. He asked me please to send the money, as he could not stay another night at Melenda's house, but would leave for Catania,* where, by the sale of some trinkets, he hoped to make some money and to see once more about a passage to Egypt. He had been to Catania once already—travelling *third class!*—but had failed to find any cargo boat that would take him to Alexandria. He would get away now to Malta. His things were being sent down to Syracuse from the monastery.

I wrote and said I hoped he would get safely away, and enclosed the cheque.

"This will be for six hundred Lire," said Melenda.

"Yes," said I.

"Eh, va bene! If he pays the three hundred Lire, he can stop on in my house for thirty Lire a day."

"He says he won't sleep in your house again."

"Ma! Let us see. If he likes to stay. He has always been a bravo signore. I have always liked him quite well. If he wishes to stay and pay me thirty Lire a day—"

The man smiled at me rather greenly.

"I'm afraid he is offended," said I.

"Eh, va bene! Ma senta, signore. When he was here before—you know I have this house of mine to let. And you know the English signorina always goes away in the summer. Oh, very well. Says Magnus, he writes for a newspaper, he owns a newspaper, I don't know what, in Rome.* He will put in an advertisement advertising my villa. And so I shall get somebody to take it. Very well. And he put in the advertisement. He sent me the paper, and I saw it there. But no one came to take my villa. Va bene! But after a year, in the January, that is, came a bill for me for twenty-two Lire to pay for it. Yes, I had to pay the twenty-two Lire, for nothing—for the advertisement which Signor Magnus put in the paper—"

"Bah!" said I.

He shook hands with me, and left.—The next day he came after me in the street and said that Magnus had departed the previous evening for Catania. As a matter of fact the post brought me a note of thanks from

Catania. Magnus was never indecent, and one could never dismiss him just as a scoundrel. He was not. He was one of these modern parasites who just assume their right to live and live well, leaving the payment to anybody who can, will, or must pay. The end is inevitably swindling—*

There came also a letter from Rome, addressed to me. I opened 5
it unthinking. It was for Magnus, from an Italian lawyer, saying that enquiry had been made about the writ against Magnus, and that it was for *qualche affaro di truffa,* some affair of swindling: that the lawyer had seen this, that and the other person, but nothing could be done. He regretted etc. etc.—I forwarded this letter to Magnus at Syracuse, and 10
hoped to God it was ended. Ah, I breathed free now he had gone.

But no. A friend who was with us dearly wanted to go to Malta.*
It is only about eighteen hours journey from Taormina—easier than going to Naples. So our friend invited us to take the trip with her, as her guests. This was rather jolly. I calculated that Magnus, who had been 15
gone a week or so, would easily have got to Malta. I had had a friendly letter from him from Syracuse, thanking me for the one I forwarded, and enclosing an I O U for the various sums of money he had had—

So, on a hot, hot Thursday, we were sitting in the train again running south, the four-and-a-half hours journey to Syracuse. And Magnus 20
dwindled now into the past. If we should see him! But no, it was impossible. After all the wretchedness of that affair we were in holiday spirits.

The train ran into Syracuse station. We sat on, to go the few yards further into the port. A tout* climbed on the foot-board: were we 25
going to Malta?—Well, we couldn't. There was a strike of the steamers, we couldn't go. When would the steamer go?—Who knows! Perhaps tomorrow.

We got down crestfallen. What should we do. There stood the express train about to start off back northwards. We could be home again that 30
evening. But no, it would be too much of a fiasco. We let the train go, and trailed off into the town, to the Grand Hotel,* which is an old Italian place just opposite the port. It is rather a dreary hotel—and many bloodstains of squashed mosquitoes on the bedroom walls.* Ah vile mosquitoes! 35

However, nothing to be done. Syracuse port is fascinating too, a tiny port with the little Sicilian ships having the slanting eyes painted on the prow, to see the way, and a coal boat from Cardiff, and one American and two Scandinavian steamers—no more. But there were two torpedo boats in the harbour, and it was like a festa, a strange, lousy festa. 40

Beautiful the round harbour where the Athenian ships came. And wonderful, beyond, the long sinuous sky-line of the long flat-topped table-land hills which run along the southern coast, so different from the peaky, pointed, bunched effect of many-tipped Sicily in the north.

5 The sun went down behind that lovely, sinuous sky-line, the harbour-water was gold and red, the people promenaded in thick streams under the pomegranate trees and hibiscus trees, Arabs in white burnooses* and fat Turks in red fezzes and black alpaca long-coats strolled also— waiting for the steamer.

10 Next day it was very hot. We went to the consul and the steamer agency. There was real hope that the brute of a steamer might actually sail that night. So we stayed on, and wandered round the town on the island, the old solid town, and sat in the church looking at the grand Greek columns embedded there in the walls.*

15 When I came in to lunch the porter said there was a letter for me. Impossible! said I. But he brought me a note. Yes. Magnus! He was staying at the other hotel along the front. "Dear Lawrence, I saw you this morning all three of you walking down the Via Nazionale, but you would not look at me. I have got my visés and everything ready. The

20 strike of the steam-boats has delayed me here. I am sweating blood. I have a last request to make of you. Can you let me have ninety Lire, to make up what I need for my hotel bill. If I cannot have this I am lost. I hoped to find you at the hotel but the porter said you were out. I am at the Casa Politi,* passing every half hour in agony.

25 If you can be so kind as to stretch your generosity to this last loan, of course I shall be eternally grateful. I can pay you back once I get to Malta—."

Well here was a blow! The worst was that he thought I had cut him—a thing I wouldn't have done. So after luncheon behold me going

30 through the terrific sun of that harbour front of Syracuse, an enormous and powerful sun, to the Casa Politi. The porter recognised me and looked enquiringly. Magnus was out, and I said I would call again at four oclock.

It happened we were in the town eating ices at four, so I didn't get

35 to his hotel till half-past. He was out—gone to look for me. So I left a note saying I had not seen him in the Via Nazionale, that I had called twice, and that I should be in at the Grand Hotel in the evening.

When we came in at seven, Magnus in the hall, sitting the picture of misery and endurance. He took my hand in both his, and bowed to the

40 women, who nodded and went on upstairs. He and I went and sat in the

empty lounge. Then he told me the trials he had had—how his luggage had come, and the station had charged him eighteen Lire a day for deposit—how he had had to wait on at the hotel because of the ship— how he had tried to sell his trinkets, and had today parted with his opal sleevelinks*—so that now he only wanted seventy, not ninety Lire. I gave him a hundred note, and he looked into my eyes, his own eyes swimming with tears, and he said he was sweating blood.

Well, the steamer went that night. She was due to leave at ten. We went on board after dinner. We were going second class: and so, for once, was Magnus. It was only an eight hours crossing, yet, in spite of all the blood he had sweated, he would not go third class. In a way I admired him for sticking to his principles. I should have gone third myself, out of shame of spending somebody else's money. He would not give way to such weakness. He knew that as far as the world goes, you're a first-class gentleman if you have a first-class ticket; if you have a third, no gentleman at all. It behoved him to be a gentleman. I understood his point, but the women were indignant. And I was just rather tired of him and his gentlemanliness.

It amused me very much to lean on the rail of the upper deck and watch the people coming on board—first going into the little customs house with their baggage, then scuffling up the gangway on board. The tall Arabs in their ghostly white woolen robes came carrying their sacks: they were going on to Tripoli. The fat Turk in his fez and long black alpaca coat with white drawers underneath came beaming up to the second class. There was a great row in the customs house: and then, simply running like a beetle with rage, there came on board a little Maltese or Greek fellow, followed by a tall lantern-jawed fellow: both seedy-looking scoundrels suckled in scoundrelism. They raved and nearly threw their arms away into the sea, talking wildly in some weird language with the fat Turk, who listened solemnly, away below on the deck. Then they rushed to somebody else. Of course we were dying with curiosity. Thank heaven I heard men talking in Italian. It appears the two seedy fellows were trying to smuggle silver coin in small sacks and rolls out of the country. They were detected. But they declared they had a right to take it away, as it was foreign specie, English florins and half-crowns, and South American dollars and Spanish money. The customs-officers however detained the lot. The little enraged beetle of a fellow ran back and forth from the ship to the customs, from the customs to the ship, afraid to go without his money, afraid the ship would go without him.

At five minutes to ten, there came Magnus: very smart in his little grey overcoat and grey curly hat, walking very smart and erect and genteel, and followed by a porter with a barrow of luggage. They went into the customs, Magnus in his grey suède gloves passing rapidly and smartly in, like the grandest gentleman on earth, and with his grey suède hands throwing open his luggage for inspection. From on board we could see the interior of the little customs shed.

Yes, he was through. Brisk, smart, superb, like the grandest little gentleman on earth, strutting because he was late, he crossed the bit of flagged pavement and came up the gangway, haughty as you can wish. The carabinieri were lounging by the foot of the gangway, fooling with one another. The little gentleman passed them with his nose in the air, came quickly on board, followed by his porter, and in a moment disappeared. After about five minutes the porter reappeared—a red-haired fellow, I knew him—he even saluted me from below, the brute. But Magnus lay in hiding.

I trembled for him at every unusual stir. There on the quay stood the English consul with his bull-dog, and various elegant young officers with yellow on their uniforms, talking to elegant young Italian ladies in black hats with stiff ospreys and bunchy furs, and gangs of porters and hotel-people and on-lookers. Then came a tramp-tramp-tramp of a squad of soldiers in red fezzes and baggy grey trousers. Instead of coming on board they camped on the quay. I wondered if all these had come for poor Magnus. But apparently not.

So the time passed, till nearly midnight, when one of the elegant young lieutenants began to call the names of the soldiers: and the soldiers answered: and one after another filed on board with their kit. So, they were on board, on their way to Africa.

Now somebody called out—and the visitors began to leave the boat. Barefooted sailors and a boy ran to raise the gangway. The last visitor or official with a bunch of papers stepped off the gangway. People on shore began to wave hankies. The red-fezzed soldiers leaned like so many flower pots over the lower rail. There was a calling of farewells. The ship was fading into the harbour, the people on shore seemed smaller, under the lamp, in the deep night—without one's knowing why.

So, we passed out of the harbour, passed the glittering lights of Ortygia, past the two lighthouses,* into the open Mediterranean. The noise of a ship in the open sea! It was a still night, with stars, only a bit chill. And the ship churned through the water.

Suddenly, like a *revenant*, appeared Magnus near us, leaning on the
rail and looking back at the lights of Syracuse sinking already forlorn
and little on the low darkness. I went to him.

"Well," he said, with his little smirk of a laugh. "Goodbye Italy!"

"Not a sad farewell either," said I.   5

"No my word, not this time," he said. "But what an awful long time
we were starting! A brutta mezz'ora* for me, indeed. Oh, my word, I
begin to breathe free for the first time since I left the monastery! How
awful it's been! But of course, in Malta, I shall be all right. Don Martino
has written to his friends there. They'll have everything ready for me   10
that I want, and I can pay you back the money you so kindly lent me . . ."

We talked for some time, leaning on the inner rail of the upper deck.

"Oh," he said, "there's Commander So-and-so, of the British fleet.
He's stationed in Malta. I made his acquaintance in the hotel. I hope
we're going to be great friends in Malta. I hope I shall have an oppor-   15
tunity to introduce you to him.— — —Well, I suppose you will want
to be joining your ladies. So long, then.—Oh, for tomorrow morning!
I never longed so hard to be in the British Empire—" He laughed, and
strutted away.

In a few minutes we three, leaning on the rail of the second-class   20
upper deck, saw our little friend large as life on the first class deck,
smoking a cigar and chatting in an absolutely first-class-ticket manner with the above-mentioned Commander. He pointed us out to the
Commander, and we felt the first-class passengers were looking across
at us second-class passengers with pleasant interest. The women went   25
behind a canvas heap to laugh, I hid my face under my hat-brim to grin
and watch. Larger than any first-class ticketer leaned our little friend
on the first-class rail, and whiffed at his cigar. So dégagé* and so genteel
he could be. Only I noticed he wilted a little when the officers of the
ship came near.   30

He was still on the first class deck when we went down to sleep.
In the morning I came up soon after dawn. It was a lovely summer
Mediterranean morning, with the sun rising up in a gorgeous golden
rage, and the sea so blue, so fairy blue, as the Mediterranean is in
summer. We were approaching quite near to a rocky, pale-yellow island   35
with some vineyards, rising magical out of the swift, blue sea into the
morning radiance. The rocks were almost as pale as butter, the islands
were like golden shadows loitering in the midst of the Mediterranean,
lonely among all the blue.

Magnus came up to my side.   40

"Isn't it lovely! Isn't it beautiful!" he said. "I love approaching these islands in the early morning."—He had almost recovered his assurance, and the slight pomposity and patronising tone I had first known in him. "In two hours I shall be free! Imagine it! Oh what a beautiful feeling!"—

I looked at him in the morning light. His face was a good deal broken by his last month's experience, older looking, and dragged. Now that the excitement was nearing its end, the tiredness began to tell on him. He was yellowish round the eyes, and the whites of his round, rather impudent blue eyes were discoloured.

Malta was drawing near. We saw the white fringe of the sea upon the yellow rocks, and a white road looping on the yellow rocky hillside. I thought of St Paul, who must have been blown this way, must have struck the island from this side. Then we saw the heaped glitter of the square facets of houses, Valletta, splendid above the Mediterranean, and a tangle of shipping and Dreadnoughts* and watch-towers in the beautiful, locked-in harbour.

We had to go down to have passports examined. The officials sat in the long saloon. It was a horrible squash and squeeze of the first- and second-class passengers. Magnus was a little ahead of me. I saw the American eagle on his passport. Yes, he passed all right. Once more he was free. As he passed away he turned and gave a condescending affable nod to me and to the Commander, who was just behind me.

The ship was lying in Valletta harbour. I saw Magnus, quite superb and brisk now, ordering a porter with his luggage into a boat. The great rocks rose above us, yellow and carved, cut straight by man. On top were all the houses. We got at last into a boat and were rowed ashore. Strange to be on British soil and to hear English. We got a carriage and drove up the steep highroad through the cutting in the rock, up to the town. There, in the big square we had coffee, sitting out of doors. A military band went by, playing splendidly in the bright, hot morning. The Maltese lounged about, and watched. Splendid the band, and the soldiers! One felt the splendour of the British Empire, let the world say what it likes. But alas, as one stayed on even in Malta, one felt the old lion had gone foolish and aimiable. Foolish and aimiable, with the weak aimiability of old age.

We stayed in the Great Britain Hôtel.* Of course one could not be in Valletta for twenty-four hours without meeting Magnus. There he was, in the Strada Reale,* strutting in a smart white duck suit, with a white piqué cravat. But alas, he had no white shoes: they had got lost or stolen. He had to wear black boots with his summer finery.

He was staying in an hotel a little further down our street, and he begged me to call and see him, he begged me to come to lunch. I promised, and went. We went into his bedroom, and he rang for more sodas.

"How wonderful it is to be here!" he said brightly. "Don't you like it immensely? And oh how wonderful to have a whiskey and soda! Well now, say when."

He finished one bottle of Black and White, and opened another. The waiter, a good-looking Maltese fellow, appeared with two syphons. Magnus was very much the signore with him, and at the same time very familiar: as I should imagine a rich Roman of the merchant class might have been with a pet slave. We had quite a nice lunch, and whiskey and soda and a bottle of French wine. And Magnus was the charming and attentive host.

After lunch we talked again of manuscripts and publishers and how he might make money. I wrote one or two letters for him. He was anxious to get something under weigh. And yet the trouble of these arrangements was almost too much for his nerves. His face looked broken and old, but not like an old man, like an old boy, and he was really very irritable.

For my own part I was soon tired of Malta, and would gladly have left after three days. But there was the strike of steamers still,* we had to wait on. Magnus professed to be enjoying himself hugely, making excursions every day, to St. Paul's Bay and to the other islands.* He had also made various friends or acquaintances. Particularly two young men, Maltese, who were friends of Don Martino. He introduced me to these two young men: one Gabriel Mazzaiba and the other Salonia.* They had small businesses down on the wharf. Salonia asked Magnus to go for a drive in a motor-car round the island, and Magnus pressed me to go too. Which I did. And swiftly, on a Saturday afternoon, we dodged about in the car upon that dreadful island: first to some fearful and stony bay, arid, treeless, desert, a bit of stony desert by the sea, with unhappy villas and a sordid, scrap-iron front: then away inland up long and dusty roads, across a bone-dry, bone-bare, hideous landscape. True, there was ripening corn, but this was all of a colour with the dust-yellow, bone-bare island. Malta is all a pale, softish, yellowish rock, just like bathbrick:* this goes into fathomless dust. And the island is stark as a corpse, no trees, no bushes even: a fearful landscape, cultivated, and weary with ages of weariness, and old weary houses here and there.

We went to the old capital* in the centre of the island, and this is interesting. The town stands on a bluff of hill in the middle of the

5

10

15

20

25

30

35

40

dreariness, looking at Valletta in the distance, and the sea. The houses
are all pale yellow, and tall, and silent, as if forsaken. There is a cathedral
too, and a fortress outlook over the sun-blazed, sun-dried, disheartening
island. Then we dashed off to another village and climbed a church-
dome that rises like a tall blister on the plain, with houses round and
corn beyond and dust that has no glamour, stale, weary, like bone-dust,
and thorn hedges sometimes, and some tin-like prickly pears. In the
dusk we came round by St. Pauls Bay, back to Valletta.

I forgot to say that not far from the old city in the centre of the island
there is a sort of little gully where a few trees are carefully nourished
and where the governor has his summer villa.*

The young men were very pleasant, very patriotic for Malta, very
catholic. We talked politics and a thousand things. Magnus was gently
patronising, and seemed, no doubt, to the two Maltese a very elegant
and travelled and wonderful gentleman. They, who had never seen even
a wood, thought how wonderful a forest must be, and Magnus talked to
them of Russia and of Germany.

But I was glad to leave that bone-dry, hideous island. Magnus begged
me to stay longer: but not for worlds! He was establishing himself
securely: was learning the Maltese language, and cultivating a thor-
ough acquaintance with the island. And he was going to establish himself. Mazzaiba was exceedingly kind to him, helping him in every way.
In Rabato, the suburb of the old town*—a quiet, forlorn little, yellow
street—he found him a tiny house of two rooms and a tiny garden. This
would cost five pounds a year. Mazzaiba lent the furniture—and when I
left Magnus was busily skipping back and forth from Rabato to Valletta,
arranging his little home, and very pleased with it. He was also being
very Maltese, and rather anti-British, as is essential, apparently, when
one is not a Britisher and finds oneself in any part of the British empire.
Magnus was very much the *American* gentleman.

Well, I was thankful to be home again and to know that he was
safely shut up in that beastly island. He wrote me letters, saying how he
loved it all, how he would go down to the sea—five or six miles walk—
at dawn, and stay there all day, studying Maltese and writing for the
newspapers. The life was fascinating, the summer was blisteringly hot,
and the Maltese were *most* attractive, especially when they knew you
were not British. Such good-looking fellows too, and do anything you
want. Wouldn't I come and spend a month?—I did not answer—felt
I had had enough. Came a post-card from Magnus: "I haven't had a
letter from you, nor any news at all. I am afraid you are ill, and feel so
anxious. Do write—" But no, I didn't want to write.

During August and September and half October we were away in the north. I forgot my little friend: hoped he was gone out of my life. But I had that fatal lurking feeling that he *hadn't* really gone out of it yet.

In the beginning of November a little letter from Don Martino: did I know that Magnus had committed suicide in Malta? Following that, a scrubby Maltese newspaper, posted by Salonia, with a marked notice: "The suicide of an American Gentleman at Rabato.—Yesterday the American Maurice Magnus, a well-built man in the prime of life, was found dead in his bed in his house at Rabato. By the bedside was a bottle containing poison. The deceased had evidently taken his life by swallowing prussic acid. Mr Magnus had been staying for some months on the island, studying the language and the conditions, with a view to writing a book. It is understood that financial difficulties were the cause of this lamentable event—"

Then Mazzaiba wrote asking me what I knew of Magnus, and saying the latter had borrowed money which he, Mazzaiba, would like to recover. I replied at once, and then received the following letter from Salonia. "Valletta. 20 November 1920. My dear Mr Lawrence, Some time back I mailed you our Daily Malta Chronicle which gave an account of the death of Magnus. I hope you have received same. As the statements therein given were very vague and not quite correct, please accept the latter part of this letter as a more correct version.*

The day before yesterday Mazzaiba received your letter which he gave me to read. As you may suppose we were very much astonished by its general purport. Mazzaiba will be writing to you in a few days, in the meantime I volunteered to give you the details you asked for.

Mazzaiba and I have done all in our power to render Magnus' stay here as easy and pleasant as possible from the time we first met him in your company at the Great Britain Hotel. (This is not correct. They were already quite friendly with Magnus before that motor-drive, when I saw these two Maltese for the first time.)—He lived in an embarassed mood since then and though we helped him as best we could both morally and financially he never confided to us his troubles. To this very day we cannot but look upon his coming here as his stay amongst us, to say the least of the way he left us, as a huge farce wrapped up in mystery, a painful experience unsolicited by either of us and a cause of grief unrequited except by our own personal sense of duty towards a stranger.

Mazzaiba out of mere respect did not tell me of his commitments towards Magnus until about a month ago, and this he did in a most confidential and private manner merely to put me on my guard, thinking,

(margin line numbers: 5, 10, 15, 20, 25, 30, 35, 40)

and rightly too, that Magnus would be falling on me next time for funds; Mazzaiba having already given him about £55 and could not possibly commit himself any further. Of course, we found him all along a perfect gentleman. Naturally, he hated the very idea that we or anybody else in Malta should look upon him in any other light. He never asked directly, though Mazzaiba (later myself) was always quick enough to interpret rightly what he meant and obliged him forthwith.

At this stage, to save the situation, he made up a scheme that the three of us should exploit the commercial possibilities in Morocco. It very nearly materialised, everything was ready, I was to go with him to Morocco, Mazzaiba to take charge of affairs here and to dispose of transactions we initiated there. Fortunately for lack of the necessary funds the idea had to be dropped, and there it ended, thank God, after a great deal of trouble I had in trying to set it well on foot.

Last July, the Police, according to our law, advised him that he was either to find a surety or to deposit a sum of money with them as otherwise at the expiration of his three months stay he would be compelled to leave the place. Money he had none so he asked Mazzaiba to stand as surety. Mazzaiba could not as he was already guarantor for his alien cousins who were here at the time. Mazzaiba (not Magnus) asked me and I complied, thinking that the responsibility was just moral and only exacted as a matter of form.

When, as stated before, Mazzaiba told me that Magnus owed him £55 and that he owed his grocer and others at Notabile (the old town, of which Rabato is the suburb) over £10, I thought I might as well look up my guarantee and see if I was directly responsible for any debts he incurred here. The words of his declaration which I endorsed stated that "I hereby solemnly promise that I will not be a burden to the inhabitants of these islands, etc." and deeming that unpaid debts to be more or less a burden, I decided to withdraw my guarantee, which I did on the 23rd Ult. The reason I gave to the police was that he was outliving his income and that I did not intend to shoulder any financial responsibility in the matter. On the same day I wrote to him up at Notabile saying that for family reasons I was compelled to withdraw his surety. He took my letter in the sense implied and was no way offended at my procedure.

Magnus, in his resourceful way, knowing that he would with great difficulty find another guarantor, wrote at once to the police saying that he understood from Mr Salonia that he (S) had withdrawn his guarantee, but as he (M) would be leaving the Isld. in about three weeks time (still intending to exploit Morocco) he begged the Commissioner to allow him this period of grace, without demanding a new surety. In fact he asked me to find him a cheap passage to Gib.* in an ingoing tramp steamer. The Police did not reply to his letter at all, no doubt they had everything ready and well thought out. He was alarmed in not receiving an acknowledgement, and, knowing full well what he imminently expected at the hands of the Italian police he decided to prepare for the last act of his drama.

We had not seen him for three or four days when he came to Mazzaiba's office on Wednesday 3rd inst. in the forenoon. He stayed there for some time talking on general subjects and looking somewhat more excited than usual. He went up to town alone at noon as Mazzaiba went to Senglea.* I was not with them in the morning, but in the afternoon about 4.30 whilst I was talking to Mazzaiba in his office, Magnus again came in looking very excited, and, being closing time, we went up the three of us to town and there left him in the company of a friend.

On Thursday morning 4th inst. at about 10 a.m. two detectives in plain clothes met him in a street at Notabile. One of them quite casually went up to him and said very civilly that the inspector of Police wished to see him re a guarantee or something, and that he was to go with him to the police station. This was an excuse as the detective had about him a warrant for his arrest for frauding an hotel in Rome, and that he was to be extradicted* at the request of the Authorities in Italy. Magnus replied that as he was with his sandals he would dress up and go with them immediately, and, accompanying him to his house at No. 1. Strada S. Pietro they allowed him to enter. He locked the door behind him leaving them outside.

A few minutes later he opened his bedroom window and dropped a letter addressed to Don Martino which he asked a boy in the street to post for him, and immediately closed the window again. One of the detectives picked up the letter and we do not know to this day if same was posted at all. Some time elapsed and he did not come out. The detectives were by this time very uneasy and as another Police official came up they decided to burst open the door. As the door did not give way they got a ladder and climbed over the roof and there they found Magnus in his bedroom dying from poisoning, outstretched on his bed and a glass of water close by. A priest was immediately called in who had just time to administer Extreme Unction before he died at 11.45 a.m.

At 8.0 a.m. the next day his body was admitted for examination at the Floriana Civil Hospital* and death was certified to be from poisoning

with hydrocyanic acid. His age was given as 44, being buried on his
birthday, (7th Novr.) with R. Catholic Rites at the expense of *His Friends
in Malta*.

Addenda:—Contents of Don Martino's letter:—

5   "I leave it to you and to Gabriel Mazzaiba to arrange my affairs. I cannot live
any longer. Pray for me."

Document found on his writing table:

"In case of my unexpected death inform American consul.
I want to be buried first class, my wife will pay.

10   My little personal belongings to be delivered to my wife (Address—)
My best friend here, Gabriel Mazzaiba, inform him (Address)
My literary executor Norman Douglas (address)
All manuscripts and books for Norman Douglas. I leave my literary property
to Norman Douglas to whom half of the results are to accrue. The other half

15   my debts are to be paid with.
Furniture etc belong to Coleiro, Floriana.
Silver spoons etc. belong to Gabriel Mazzaiba (address)"

The American Consul is in charge of all his personal belongings.
I am sure he will be pleased to give you any further details you may

20   require. By the way, his wife refused to pay his burial expenses but five
of his friends in Malta undertook to give him a decent funeral.* His
mourners were: The Consul, the Vice consul, Mr M., an American
citizen, Gabriel Mazzaiba and myself.

Please convey to Mrs. Lawrence an expression of our sincere esteem

25   and high regard and you kindly accept equally our warmest respects,
whilst soliciting any information you would care to pass on to us regard-
ing the late Magnus. Believe me,

My dear Mr Lawrence etc.—"

(Mrs Magnus refunded the burial expenses through the American

30   consul about two months after her husband's death.)

When I had read this letter the world seemed to stand still for me. I
knew that in my own soul I had said "Yes, he must die if he cannot find
his own way." But for all that, now I *realised* what it must have meant
to the hunted, desperate man: everything seemed to stand still. I could,

35   by giving half my money, have saved his life. I had chosen not to save
his life.

Now, after a year has gone by, I keep to my choice. I still would not
save his life. I respect him for dying when he was cornered. And for this
reason I still feel connected with him: still have this to discharge, to get

his book published, and to give him his place, to present him just as he
was as far as I knew him myself.

The worst thing I have against him, is that he abused the confidence,
the kindness, and the generosity of unsuspecting people like Mazzaiba.
He did not *want* to, perhaps. But he did it. And he leaves Mazzaiba
swindled, distressed, confused, and feeling sold in the best part of himself. What next? What is one to feel towards one's *strangers*, after having
known Magnus?—It is the Judas treachery, to *ask* for sympathy and for
generosity, to take it when given—and then: "sorry, but anybody may
make a mistake!" It is this betraying with a kiss* which makes me still
say: "He should have died sooner." —No, I would not help to keep
him alive, not if I had to choose again. I would let him go over into
death. He shall and should die, and so should all his sort: and so they
will. There are so many kiss-giving Judases. He was not a criminal:* he
was obviously well-intentioned: but a Judas every time, selling the good
feeling he had tried to arouse, and had aroused, for any handful of silver
he could get. A little loving vampire!

Yesterday arrived the manuscript of the Legion, from Malta. It is
exactly two years since I read it first in the monastery. Then I was
moved and rather horrified. Now I am chiefly amused; because in my
mind's eye is the figure of Magnus in the red trousers and the blue coat
with lappets turned up, surging like a little indignant pigeon across the
drill-yards and into the canteen of Bel-Abbès.* He *is* so indignant, so
righteously and morally indignant, and so funny. All the horrors of the
actuality fade before his indignation, his little, tuppenny indignation.

*De mortui nihil nisi verum.** Reading this Algerian part of the MS.
again makes me stone-cold to this pink-faced, self-indulgent, morally-
indignant pigeon. The Legion is dreadful: very well. But Magnus?—
Bah, he is a liar, he is a hypocrite.

To start with, the "vice" which he holds his hands up so horrified
at, in the "girants"*—(one wonders what the actual word is)—he had
it himself. But he *always* paid his lovers: in money. So he gave me to
understand. The Legionnaire lover of a *girant* would carry the youth's
load and do his chores for him. Benissimo!*—See Magnus carrying
anybody else's load, or doing anybody else's chores! Not him. With a
grandiloquent air he would *make a present*—of so many francs.—Oh yes,
he honorably *paid* for whatever love he took, in any city of the world, and
from any individual. Paid in money, mind you.—Was he not an honorable gentleman, to be horrified at the ways of the Legionaries!—Yet,

let me remember, he ran round for Douglas. But that was not love: or at least it was the "higher plane—," the *mental* friendship.

That's the first grudge I have against Monsieur Maurice, reading this book. The liar!—the hypocrite!—him to talk about *girants* and sodomy. When he himself just paid money for his share of love, and *basta*! or else he begged the love and then borrowed money, and again, *basta*! But both love and money he got from uneducated men with warm blood: his inferiors! "I try to keep my physical friendships as decent as I can, and all that. But—!"—Yes indeed, *But*!

They were so terribly *indecent*, the Legionaries. No doubt, dear Maurice. "It doesn't matter *what* you do, it's the *way you do it*!"— That was one of his favorite clap-traps. I quite agree, my dear. It *is* the way you do it. You spy out a comely looking individual, of the "lower classes," you invite him to smokes and drinks—and afterwards you *pay* him—*Alles in Ehren*!*—all nice and in honor, don't you know!—The way you do it!—Oh yes, money will cover multitudes upon multitudes of sins. Charity is a withered fig-leaf in comparison.—Just *look* at the degraded Legionary, carrying the pack of his *girant* and doing his chores for him! Wouldn't twenty francs have been *so* much more decent in every way!—It is nowadays natural to get the answer: "Il mio onore costa a Lei dieci mila Lire."*

You cur, Maurice!—He had a taking kind of winsomeness himself. He came up so winsomely to appeal for affection. He took the affection, and paid back twenty francs. Bargain!—Later, he took the affection, and *borrowed* twenty francs, and cleared out in triumph. And he to sit in judgment on the Legionaries!—"Oh, I always try to keep my physical friendships as *decent* as possible—while they last."—Just so. Filching the blood-warmth from the lower class, and sailing on bland and superior. A very old dodge.*

The little Judas, he betrayed everybody with a kiss: coming up with a kiss of love, and then afterwards clearing out triumphant, having got all he wanted, thank you. Cold as a bit of white mud. But always white and clean, of course. A *gentleman*!! And of course, always liberal while he had anything to give. Lavish indeed. "È stato sempre generoso,"* says Pancrazio.

To my mind he is worse than the poor devils of legionaries. They had their blood-passions and carried them defiantly, flagrantly, to depravity. But Magnus had whitish blood, and a conceit of spiritual uplift, and he kept up appearances: and *filched* his sexual satisfactions, despising them all the time. Oh yes, he didn't forego his dinner and his sex gratifications and his whiskey. And he paid for them all while he could.

To me, the blood-passions are sacred, and sex is sacred: more sacred than mind or spirit or uplift. In the legionaries, even, the recklessness, the blood-recklessness, is sacred. But alas, that which is most sacred in 5 them they wilfully murder and torture to death. So man turns back on himself, when he finds part of his primal self denied. What distresses me in the Legion is not that it is so "shocking," but that I feel there so much genuine creative blood-passion being self-destroyed, like a snake which should turn and start to gnash at itself and destroy itself, because 10 it is imprisoned or tied up by a cord. The sacredness of the passionate blood was admitted in every religion, before this era of spiritual uplift. And now, what have we got by denying it? Magnus! Magni sumus!*

Now we have these "superior" little Magnuses first buying their modicums of passion, like hashish, at ten francs a time: and then not 15 buying, but *filching* the passion and borrowing money on the strength of it. It is a form of vampirism. It is the modern form of vampirism, sucking the blood from hot living individuals into these white-blooded "superior" individuals like Magnus. Let him die and be thrice dead. "My *mental* friendships, of course, are what matter!"—Such baseness, 20 treating the living blood like dirt!

And we shall never alter it, until we can re-instate the great old gods of the passionate communion: Astarte, Cybele, Bel, Dionysos.* It will never be any better till we admit the sacredness, the profound and *primary* sacredness of the passion of the living blood. Not this white, 25 nerve-thrilled, modern excitement which passes for sensuality: that hateful momentary sensationalism which Magnus and the world calls sex. To hell with it as with him. But the dark blood-sacredness in which lives our deepest soul.

It is a grief to me to see the legionaries torturing, defaming, *obscenely* 30 worshipping the blood-passion. Magnus wonders why they would not go in to church. If they had gone in and seen him smirking before the altars they certainly would have knifed him on the stairs or in the lava-tories. Quite right too.—But they themselves—like devils in revolt— they stand in hate outside the church that denies the living blood— 35 the source of their nature: the church that still has power over them, power to deny them. They hate it. And they go mute to the cemetery. And they turn back to their lustful self-destructions. That, to me, is the tragedy. That they turned *themselves* in defiance against themselves. If they could have kept their souls, and honorably stood by the reality 40

which they *knew*, but were not free to believe in—the reality of passionate blood in the deeps of a man—they would have been great. It is not
the *little* angels like Magnus which fall. Little angels can't fall. It is only
biggish and great angels, like Lucifer, which fall.* If only Lucifer would
now *refuse* to admit himself fallen. Truly is he any more fallen than these
horrible pallid spiritual gods of Magnus and the late war?—the hateful
white gods, white-blooded and venomous!

Ah no, a man must keep his soul unfallen, and above all, his belief in
the passionate blood which is the deeps of him. Never this terrible self-
destroying, self-unbelief of reckless lust. Though even reckless lust is
better than petty prostitution which "saves appearances." Yes far better.
But reckless lust is a tragedy.—We must go back, far back. The belief in
the *sacredness* of the deep blood and the deep blood-desire will now alone
save mankind from a Magnus-vampirism and a Magnus-suicide. —
The hateful whitish spiritual blood in the veins of modern people!—
sheer vampire. —The cautiousness of it too! The quiet cunning and
courage based on fear! Magnus had such courage: indeed he had: like a
persistent louse has courage.

Oh Magnus is a prime hypocrite. *How* loudly he rails against the
Boches!* *How* great his enthusiasm for the pure, the spiritual Allied
cause. Just so long as he is in Africa, and it suits his purpose! His scorn
for the German tendencies of the German legionaries: even Count de R.*
secretly leans towards Germany. "Blood is thicker than water," says our
hero glibly. Some blood, thank God. Apparently not his own. For according to all showing he was, by blood, pure German: father and mother:
even Hohenzollern* blood!!! Pure German! Even his speech, his *mother-
tongue*, was German and not English! And then the little mongrel—!

But perhaps something happens to blood when once it has been taken
to America.

And then, once he is in Valbonne,* lo, a change! Where now is sacred
France and the holy Allied Cause! Where is our hero's fervour? It is
worse than Bel-Abbès! Yes indeed, far less human, more hideously cold.
One is driven by very rage to wonder if he was really a spy, a German
spy whom Germany cast off because he was no good.

The little *gentleman*! God damn his white-blooded gentility. The
legionaries must have been gentlemen, that they didn't kick him every
day to the lavatory and back.

"You are a journalist?" said the colonel.

"No, a littérateur,"* said Maurice perkily.

"That is something more?" said the colonel.

Oh, I would have given a lot to have seen it and heard it.—The *littérateur*! Well, I hope this book will establish his fame as such. I hope the editor, if it gets one, won't alter any more of the marvellously staggering sentences and the joyful French mistakes. The littérateur!—the impossible little pigeon!

But the Bel-Abbès part is alive and interesting. It should be read only by those who have the stomach. Ugly, foul—alas, it is no uglier and no fouler than the reality. Magnus himself was near enough to being a scoundrel, thief, forger, etc etc—what lovely strings of names he hurls at them!—to be able to appreciate his company. He himself was such a liar, that he was not taken in. But his conceit as a gentleman *keeping up appearances* gave him a real standpoint from which to see the rest. The book is in its way a real creation. But I would hate it to be published and taken at its face value, with Magnus as a spiritual dove among vultures of lust. Let us first put a pinch of salt on the tail of this dove.—What did *he* do in the way of vice, even in Bel-Abbès? I never chose to ask him.

Yes yes, he sings another note when he is planted right among the sacred Allies, with never a German near. Then the gorgeousness goes out of his indignation. He takes it off with the red trousers. Now he is just a sordid little figure in filthy corduroys. There is no vice to purple his indignation, the little holy liar. There is only sordidness and automatic, passionless, colourless awful mud. When all is said and done, mud, cold, hideous, foul, engulfing mud, up to the waist, this is the final symbol of the Great War—Hear some of the horrified young soldiers. They dare hardly speak of it yet.

The Valbonne part is worse, really, than the Bel-Abbès part. Passionless, barren, utterly, coldly foul and hopeless. The ghastly emptiness, and the slow mud-vortex, the brink of it.

Well, now Magnus has gone himself. Yes, and he would be gone in the common mud and dust himself, if it were not that the blood still beats warm and hurt and kind in some few hearts. Magnus "hinted" at Mazzaiba for money, in Malta, and Mazzaiba gave it to him,* thinking him a man in distress. He thought him a gentleman, and lovable, and in trouble! And Mazzaiba—it isn't his real name, but there he is, real enough—still has this feeling of grief for Magnus. So much so that now he has had the remains taken from the public grave in Malta, and buried in his own, the Mazzaiba grave, so that they shall not be lost. For my part, I would have said that the sooner they mingled with the universal dust, the better.—But one is glad to see a little genuine kindness and gentleness, even if it is wasted on the bones of that selfish little scamp of a Magnus. He despised his "physical friendships"—though he didn't forego them. So why should anyone rescue his physique from the public grave.

5   But there you are—that was his power: to arouse affection and a certain tenderness in the hearts of others, for himself. And on this he traded. One sees the trick working all the way through the Legion book. God knows how much warm kindness, generosity, was showered on him during the course of his forty-odd years. And selfish little scamp, he took
10   it as a greedy boy takes cakes off a dish, quickly, to make the most of his opportunity while it lasted. And the cake once eaten: buona sera! He patted his own little paunch and felt virtuous. Merely physical feeling, you see!—He had a way of saying "physical"—a sort of American way, as if it were spelt "fisacal,"—that made me want to kick him.

15   Not that he was mean, while he was about it. No, he would give very freely: even a little ostentatiously, always feeling that he was being a *liberal gentleman*. Ach, the liberality and the gentility he prided himself on! *Ecco!*—and he gave a large tip, with a little winsome smile. But in his heart of hearts it was always himself he was thinking of, while he did it.
20   Playing his rôle of the gentleman who was awfully *nice* to everybody: so long as they were nice to him, or so long as it served his advantage—Just private charity!

       Well, poor devil, he is dead: which is all the better. He had his points, the courage of his own terrors, quick-wittedness, sensitiveness to certain
25   things in his surroundings. I prefer him, scamp as he is, to the ordinary respectable person. He ran his risks: he *had* to be running risks with the police, apparently. And he poisoned himself rather than fall into their clutches. I like him for that. And I like him for the sharp and quick way he made use of every one of his opportunities to get out of that beastly
30   army. There I admire him: a courageous, isolated little devil, facing his risks, and like a good rat, *determined* not to be trapped. I won't forgive him for trading on the generosity of others, and so dropping poison into the heart of all warm-blooded faith. But I am glad after all that Mazzaiba has rescued his bones from the public grave. I wouldn't have
35   done it myself, because I don't forgive him his "fisacal" impudence and parasitism. But I am glad Mazzaiba has done it. And, for my part, I will put his Legion book before the world if I can. Let him have his place in the world's consciousness.

       Let him have his place let his word be heard. He went through vile
40   experiences: he looked them in the face, braved them through, and kept his manhood in spite of them. For manhood is a strange quality, to be

found in human rats as well as in hot-blooded men. Magnus carried the
human consciousness through circumstances which would have been
too much for me. I would have died rather than be so humiliated, I could
never have borne it. Other men I know went through worse things, in
the war. But then horrors, like pain, are their own anaesthetic. Men   5
lose their normal consciousness, and go through in a sort of delirium.
The bit of Stendhal which Dos Passos quotes in front of *Three Soldiers**
is frighteningly true.—There are certain things which are *so* bitter,
so horrible, that the contemporaries just cannot know them, cannot
contemplate them.—So it is with a great deal of the late war. It was   10
so foul, and humanity in Europe fell suddenly into such ignominy and
inhuman ghastliness, that we shall *never* fully realise what it was. We
just cannot bear it. We haven't the soul-strength to contemplate it.

And yet, humanity can only finally conquer by *realising*. It is human
destiny, since Man fell into consciousness and self-consciousness, that   15
we can only go forward step by step through realisation, full, bitter,
conscious realisation. This is true of all the great terrors and agonies
and anguishes of life: sex, and war, and even crime. When Flaubert
in his story—it is so long since I read it—makes his saint have to
kiss the leper, and naked clasp the leprous awful body against his   20
own,* that is what we must at last do. It is the great command *Know
Thyself.** We've got to *know* what sex is, let the sentimentalists wriggle
as they like. We've got to know the greatest and most shattering human
passions, let the puritans squeal as they like for screens. And we've
got to know humanity's criminal tendency, look straight at humanity's   25
great deeds of crime against the soul. We have to fold this horrible
leper against our naked warmth: because life and the throbbing blood
and the believing soul are greater even than leprosy. Knowledge, true
knowledge, is like vaccination. It prevents the continuing of ghastly
moral disease.   30

And so it is with the war. Humanity in Europe fell horribly into a
hatred of the living soul, in the war. There is no gainsaying it. We all
fell. Let us not try to wriggle out of it. We fell into hideous depravity of
hating the human soul; a purulent small-pox of the spirit we had. It was
shameful, shameful, shameful, in every country and in all of us. Some   35
tried to resist, and some didn't. But we were all drowned in shame. A
purulent small-pox of the vicious spirit, vicious against the deep soul
that pulses in the blood.

We haven't got over it. The small-pox sores are running yet in the
spirit of mankind. And we have got to take this putrid spirit to our bosom.   40
There's nothing else for it. Take the foul rotten spirit of mankind, full of

the running sores of the war, to our bosom, and cleanse it there. Cleanse
it not with blind love: ah no, that won't help. But with bitter and wincing
realisation. We have to take the disease into our consciousness and let it
go through our soul, like some virus. We have got to *realise*. And then
we can surpass.

Magnus went where I could never go. He carried the human consciousness unbroken through circumstances I could not have borne. It
is not heroism to rush on death. It is cowardice to accept a martyrdom
today. That is the feeling one has at the end of Dos Passos' book. To
let oneself be absolutely trapped? Never! I prefer Magnus. He drew
himself out of the thing he loathed, despised, and feared. He fought it,
for his own spirit and liberty. He fought it open-eyed. He went through
it and *realised* it all. That is what very few other men did. They went
through: they were more publicly heroic, they won war-medals. But
the lonely terrified courage of the isolated spirit which grits its teeth
and stares the horrors in the face and *will* not succumb to them, but
fights its way through them, *knowing* that it must surpass them: this is
the rarest courage. And this courage Magnus had: and the man in the
Dos Passos book* didn't *quite* have it. And so, though Magnus poisoned
himself, and I would not wish him *not* to have poisoned himself: though
as far as warm life goes, I don't forgive him; yet, as far as the eternal
and unconquerable spirit of man goes, I am with him through eternity. I
am grateful to him, he beat out for me boundaries of human experience
which I could not have beaten out for myself. The *human* traitor he was.
But he was not traitor to the spirit. In the great spirit of human consciousness he was a hero, little, quaking, and heroic: a strange, quaking
little star.

Even the dead ask only for *justice*: not for praise or exoneration. Who
dares humiliate the dead with excuses for their living?—I hope I may
do Magnus justice; and I hope his restless spirit may be appeased. I
do not try to forgive. The living blood knows no forgiving. Only the
overweening spirit takes on itself to dole out forgiveness. But Justice is
a sacred human right. The overweening spirit pretends to perch above
justice. But I am a man, not a spirit, and men with blood that throbs
and throbs can only live at length by being just, can only die in peace if
they have justice. Forgiveness gives the whimpering dead no rest. Only
deep, true justice.*

There is Magnus' manuscript then, like a map of the lower places of
mankind's activities. There is the war: foul, foul, unutterably foul. As
foul as Magnus says. Let us make up our minds about it.

It is the only help: to realise, *fully*, and then make up our minds. The war was *foul*. As long as I am a man, I say it and assert it. And further I say, as long as I am a man such a war shall never occur again. It shall not, and it shall not. All modern militarism is foul. It shall go. A man I am, and above machines. Modern militarism is machines, and it shall go, for ever, because I have found it vile, vile, too vile ever to experience again.* Cannons shall go, guns shall go, submarines and warships shall go. Never again shall trenches be dug. They *shall* not, for I am a man, and such things are within the power of man, to break and make. I have said it, and as long as blood beats in my veins, I mean it. Blood beats in the veins of many men who mean it as well as I.*

Man perhaps *must* fight. Mars, the great god of war, will be a god forever. Very well. Then if fight you must, fight you shall, but without engines, without machines. Fight if you like, as the Romans fought, with swords and spears, or like the Red Indian, with bows and arrows and knives and war-paint. But never again shall you fight with the foul, base, fearful, monstrous machines of war which man invented for the last war. You shall not. The diabolic mechanisms are man's, and I am a man. Therefore they are mine. And I smash them into oblivion. With every means in my power, *except* the means of these machines, I smash them into oblivion. I am at war! I, a man, am at war!—with these foul machines and contrivances that men have conjured up. Men have conjured them up. I, a man, will conjure them down again. Won't I?—but I will! I am not one man, I am many. I am most.

So much for the war! So much for Magnus' manuscript! Let it be read. It is not *this* that will do harm, but sloppy sentiment and cant. Take the bitterness, and cleanse the blood.

Now would you believe it, that little scamp Magnus spent over a hundred pounds of borrowed money during his four months in Malta, when his expenses, he boasted to me, need not have been more than a pound a week, once he got into the little house in Notabile. That is, he spent at least seventy pounds too much. Heaven knows what he did with it, apart from "guzzling."—And this hundred pounds must be paid back, in Malta. Which it never will be, unless this manuscript pays it back. Pay the gentleman's *last* debts, if no others.

He had to be a gentleman. I didn't realise till after his death. I never suspected him of royal blood. But there you are, you never know where it will crop out. He was the grandson of an emperor. His mother was the illegitimate daughter of the German Kaiser: Douglas says, of the old Kaiser Wilhelm I, Don Martino says, of Kaiser Frederick

Wilhelm, father of the present ex-Kaiser. She was born in Berlin on the
31 October 1845: and her portrait, by Paul, now hangs in a gallery in
Rome. Apparently there had been some injustice against her in Berlin—
for she seems once to have been in the highest society there, and to have
5   attended at court. Perhaps she was discreetly banished by Wilhelm II,
hence Magnus' hatred of that monarch. She lies buried in the Protestant
Cemetery in Rome, where she died in 1912, with the words *Filia Regis*
on her tomb. Magnus adored her, and she him. Part of his failings one
can *certainly* ascribe to the fact that he was an only son, an adored son,
10 in whose veins the mother imagined only royal blood. And she must
have thought him so beautiful, poor thing! Ah well, they are both dead.
Let us be just, and wish them Lethe.*

Magnus himself was born in New York on 7th November 1876: so at
least it says on his passport. He entered the Catholic Church in England,
15 in 1902. His father was a Mr Liebetrau Magnus,* married to the mother
in 1867.

So poor Magnus had Hohenzollern blood in his veins: close kin
to the ex-Kaiser William. Well, that itself excuses him a great deal:
because of the cruel illusion of importance manqué,* which it must have
20 given him.—He never breathed a word of this to me. Yet apparently it
is accepted at the monastery, the great monastery which knows most
European secrets of any political significance. And for myself, I believe it
is true.—And if he was a scamp and a treacherous little devil, he had also
qualities of nerve and breeding undeniable. He faced his way* through
25 that Legion experience: royal nerves dragging themselves through the
sewers, without giving way. But alas for royal blood! Like most other
blood, it has gradually gone white, during our spiritual era. Bunches
of nerves! And whitish, slightly acid blood. And no bowels of deep
compassion and kindliness. Only charity. A little more than kin, and
30 less than kind.*

Also—Maurice! Ich grüsse dich, in der Ewigkeit. Aber hier, im
Herzblut, hast du Gift und Leid nachgelassen*—to use your own
romantic language.

'*THE BAD SIDE OF BOOKS*':
INTRODUCTION TO A BIBLIOGRAPHY OF
THE WRITINGS OF D. H. LAWRENCE,
EDITED BY EDWARD D. McDONALD

There doesn't seem much excuse for me, sitting under a little cedar tree at the foot of the Rockies,* looking at the pale desert disappearing westward, with hummocks of shadow rising in the stillness of incipient autumn, this morning, the near pine trees perfectly still, the sunflowers and the purple michaelmas daisies moving for the first time, this morn- 5 ing, in an invisible breath of breeze, to be writing an introduction to a bibliography.*

Books to me are incorporate things, voices in the air, that do not dis- turb the haze of autumn, and visions that don't blot out the sunflowers. What do I care for first or last editions? I have never read one of my own 10 published works.* To me, no book has a date, no book has a binding.

What do I care if "e" is somewhere upside down, or "g" comes from the wrong fount?* I really don't.

And when I force myself to remember, what pleasure is there in that?* The very first copy of *The White Peacock* that ever was sent out, I put it 15 into my mother's hands when she was dying.* She looked at the outside, and then at the title page, and then at me, with darkening eyes. And though she loved me so much, I think she doubted whether it could be much of a book, since no-one more important than I had written it. Somewhere, in the helpless privacies of her being, she had wistful 20 respect for me.* But for me in the face of the world, not much. This David would never get a stone across at Goliath.* And why try? Let Goliath alone!—Anyway, she was beyond reading my first immortal work. It was put aside, and I never wanted to see it again. She never saw it again. 25

After the funeral, my father* struggled through half a page, and it might as well have been Hottentot.

"And what dun they gi'e thee for that, lad?"

"Fifty pounds,* father."

"Fifty pound!" He was dumbfounded, and looked at me with shrewd 30 eyes, as if I were a swindler. "Fifty pound! An' tha's niver done a day's hard work in thy life."

75

I think, to this day, he looks on me as a sort of cleverish swindler, who gets money for nothing: a sort of Ernest Hooley.* And my sister* says, to my utter amazement: "You *always* were lucky!"

Somehow, it is the actual corpus and substance, the actual paper and rag volume of any of my works, that calls up these personal feelings and memories. It is the miserable tome itself which somehow delivers me to the vulgar mercies of the world. The voice inside is mine forever. But the beastly marketable chunk of a published volume is a bone which every dog presumes to pick with me.*

William Heinemann published *The White Peacock*. I saw him once:* and then I realised what an immense favour he knew he was doing me. As a matter of fact, he treated me quite well.

I remember, at the last minute, when the book was all printed and ready to bind: some even bound: they sent me in great haste a certain page with a marked paragraph. Would I remove this paragraph, as it might be considered "objectionable", and substitute an exactly identical number of obviously harmless words. Hastily I did so. And later, I noticed that the two pages, on one of which was the altered paragraph, were rather loose, not properly bound in to the book.—Only my mother's one copy had the paragraph unchanged.

I have wondered often if Heinemann's just altered the "objectionable" bit in the first little batch of books they sent out, then left the others as first printed. Or whether they changed all but the one copy they sent me ahead.*

It was my first experience of the objectionable. Later, William Heinemann said he thought *Sons and Lovers* one of the dirtiest books he had ever read. He refused to publish it.—I should not have thought the deceased gentleman's reading* had been so circumspectly narrow.

I forget the first appearance of *The Trespasser* and of *Sons and Lovers*.* I always hide the fact of publication from myself as far as possible. One writes, even as at this moment, to some mysterious presence in the air. If that presence were not there, and one thought of even a single solitary actual reader, the paper would remain forever white.

But I always remember how, in a cottage by the sea, in Italy, I rewrote almost entirely that play *The Widowing of Mrs Holroyd*, right on the proofs which Mitchell Kennerley had sent me. And he nobly forbore with me.*

But then he gave me a nasty slap. He published *Sons and Lovers* in America, and one day, joyful, arrived a cheque for twenty pounds.

Twenty pounds in those days was a little fortune: and as it was a windfall, it was handed over to Madame; the first pin-money she had seen. Alas and alack, there was an alteration in the date on the cheque, and the bank would not cash it. It was returned to Mitchell Kennerley: but that was the end of it. He never made it good, and never to this day made any further payment for *Sons and Lovers*. Till this year of grace 1924, America has had that, my most popular book, for nothing*—as far as I am concerned.

Then came the first edition of *The Rainbow*. I'm afraid I set my rainbow in the sky too soon, before, instead of after the deluge. Methuen published that book, and he almost wept before the magistrate, when he was summoned for bringing out a piece of indecent literature. He said he did not know the dirty thing he had been handling, he had not read the work, his reader had misadvised him—and *Peccavi! Peccavi!* wept the now be-knighted gentleman.* Then around me rose such a fussy sort of interest, as when a really scandalous bit of scandal is being whispered about one. In print, my fellow-authors kept scrupulously silent, lest a bit of the tar might stick to them. Later, Arnold Bennett and May Sinclair raised a kindly protest. But John Galsworthy* told me, very calmly and *ex cathedra*, he thought the book a failure as a work of art.—They think as they please. But why not wait till I ask them, before they deliver an opinion to me? Especially as impromptu opinions by elderly authors are apt to damage him who gives as much as him who takes.*

There is no more indecency or impropriety in *The Rainbow* than there is in this autumn morning—I, who say so, ought to know. And when I open my mouth, let no dog bark.*

So much for the first edition of *The Rainbow*. The only copy of any of my books I ever keep is my copy of Methuen's *Rainbow*. Because the American editions have all been mutilated.* And this is almost my favorite among my novels: this, and *Women in Love*.* And I should really be best pleased if it were never re-printed at all, and only those blue, condemned volumes remained extant.

Since *The Rainbow*, one submits to the process of publication as to a necessary evil: as souls are said to submit to the necessary evil of being born into the flesh. The wind bloweth where it listeth.* And one must submit to the processes of one's day. Personally, I have no belief in the vast public. I believe, that only the winnowed few *can* care. But publishers, like thistles, must set innumerable seeds on the wind, knowing most will miscarry.

To the vast public, the autumn morning is only a sort of stage background against which they can best display their own mechanical importance. But to some men still the trees stand up and look around at the daylight, having woven the two ends of darkness together into visible being and presence. And soon, they will let go the two ends of darkness again, and disappear. A flower laughs once, and having had his laugh, chuckles off into seed and is gone. Whence? whither? who knows, who cares? That little laugh of achieved being is all.

So it is with books.* To every man who struggles with his own soul in mystery, a book that is a book flowers once, and seeds, and is gone. First editions or forty-first are only the husks of it.

Yet if it amuses a man to save the husks of the flower that opened once for the first time, one can understand that too. It is like the costumes that men and women used to wear, in their youth, years ago, and which now stand up rather faded in museums. With a jolt they reassemble for us the day-to-day actuality of the bygone people, and we see the trophies once more of man's eternal fight with inertia.

INTRODUCTION TO MAX HAVELAAR,
BY 'MULTATULI'
(EDUARD DOUWES DEKKER)

INTRODUCTION

Max Havelaar* was first published in Holland, nearly seventy years ago,* and it created a *furore*. In Germany it was the book of the moment, even in England it had a liberal vogue. And to this day it remains vaguely in the minds of foreigners as the one Dutch classic.

I say vaguely, because many well-read people know nothing about it. Mr. Bernard Shaw,* for example, confessed that he had never heard of it. Which is curious, considering the esteem in which it was held by men whom we might call the pre-Fabians,* both in England and in America, sixty years ago.

But then *Max Havelaar*, when it appeared, was hailed as a book with a purpose. And the Anglo-Saxon mind loves to hail such books. They are so obviously in the right. The Anglo-Saxon mind also loves to forget completely, in a very short time, any book with a purpose. It is a bore, with its insistency.

So we have forgotten, with our usual completeness, all about *Max Havelaar* and about Multatuli, its author. Even the pseudonym, Multatuli (Latin for: I suffered much, or: I endured much), is to us irritating as it was exciting to our grandfathers. We don't care for poor but noble characters who are aware that they have suffered much. There is too much self-awareness.

On the surface, *Max Havelaar* is a tract or a pamphlet very much in the same line as *Uncle Tom's Cabin*.* Instead of "pity the poor Negro slave" we have "pity the poor oppressed Javanese"; with the same urgent appeal for legislation, for the government to do something about it. Well, the government did something about Negro slaves, and *Uncle Tom's Cabin* fell out of date. The Netherlands government is also said to have done something in Java,* for the poor Javanese, on the strength of Multatuli's book. So that *Max Havelaar* became a back number.

So far so good. If by writing tract-novels you can move governments to improve matters, then write tract-novels by all means. If the government, however, plays up, and does its bit, then the tract-novel has served its purpose, and descends from the stage like a political orator who has made his point.

This is all in the course of nature. And because this is the course of nature, many educated Hollanders to-day become impatient when they hear educated Germans or English or Americans referring to *Max Havelaar* as "the one Dutch classic." So Americans would feel if they heard *Uncle Tom's Cabin* referred to as "the one American classic." *Uncle Tom* is a back number in the English-speaking world, and *Max Havelaar* is, to the Dutch-speaking world, another.

If you ask a Hollander for a *really* good Dutch novelist he refers you to the man who wrote: *Old People and Things That Pass* (Louis Couperus)*—or else to somebody you know nothing about.

As regards the Dutch somebody I know nothing about, I am speechless. But as regards *Old People and Things That Pass*, I still think *Max Havelaar* a far more real book. And since *Old People* etc. is quite a good contemporary novel, one needs to find out why *Max Havelaar* is better.

I have not tried to read *Uncle Tom's Cabin* since I was a boy, and wept. I will try again, when I come across a copy. But I am afraid it will pall. I know I shan't weep.

Then why doesn't *Max Havelaar* pall? Why can one still read every word of it? As far as composition goes, it is the greatest mess possible. How the reviewers of to-day would tear it across and throw it in the w. p. b.!* But the reviewers of to-day, like the clergy, feel that they must justify God to man,* and when they find they can't do it, when the book or the Almighty seems really unjustifiable, in the sight of common men, they apply the w. p. b.

It is surely the mistake of modern criticism, to conceive the public, the man-in-the-street, as the real god, who must be served and flattered by every book that appears, even if it were the Bible. To my thinking, the critic, like a good beadle,* should rap the public on the knuckles and make it attend during divine service. And any good book is divine service.

The critic, having dated *Max Havelaar* a back number, hits him on the head if he dares look up, and says: Down! Revere the awesome modernity of the holy public!

I say: Not at all! The thing in *Max* that the public once loved, the tract, is really a back number. But there is so very little of the tract, actually, and what there is, the author has retracted so comically, as he went, that the reader can grin as he goes.

It was a stroke of cunning journalism on Multatuli's part (Dostoevsky also made such strokes of cunning journalism) to put his book through on its face value as a tract. What Multatuli really wanted was to get his

book over. He wanted to be heard. He wanted to be read. *I want to be
heard. I will be heard!* he vociferates on the last pages. He himself must
have laughed in his sleeve as he vociferated. But the public gaped and
fell for it.

He was the passionate missionary for the poor Javanese! Because he   5
knew missionaries were, and are, listened to! And the Javanese were
a good stick with which to beat the dog. The successful public being
the dog. Which dog he longed to beat! To give it the trouncing of its
life!

He did it, in missionary guise, in *Max Havelaar*. The book isn't really   10
a tract, it is a satire. Multatuli isn't really a preacher, he's a satirical
humourist. Straight on in the life of Jean Paul Richter* the same bitter,
almost mad-dog aversion from humanity that appeared in Jean Paul,
appears again in Multatuli, as it appears in the later Mark Twain.*
Dostoevsky was somewhat the same, but in him the missionary had   15
swallowed the mad dog of revulsion, so that the howls of derision are
all ventriloquistic undertone.

Max Havelaar isn't a tract or a pamphlet, it is a satire. The satire
on the Dutch bourgeois, in Drystubble,* is final. The coffee-broker is
reduced to his ultimate nothingness, in pure humour. It is the reduction   20
of the prosperous business man in America and England to-day, just
the same, essentially the same: and it is a death-stroke.

Similarly, the Java part of the book is a satire on colonial administration, and on government altogether. It is quite direct and straightforward satire, so it is wholesome. Multatuli never quite falls down the   25
fathomless well of his own revulsion, as Dostoevsky did, to become a
lily-mouthed missionary rumbling with ventral howls of derision and
dementia. At his worst, Multatuli is irritatingly sentimental, harping
on pity when he is inspired by hate. Maybe he deceives himself. But
never for long.   30

His sympathy with the Javanese is also genuine enough; there was a
man in him whose bowels of compassion were moved. Whereas a great
nervous genius like Dostoevsky never felt a moment of real physical
sympathy in his life. But with Multatuli, the sympathy for the Javanese
is rather an excuse for hating the Dutch authorities still further. It is   35
the sympathy of a man preoccupied with other feelings.

We see this in the famous idyll of Saïdyah and Adinda,* once the
most beloved and most quoted part of the book. We see how it bored
the author to write it, after the first few pages. He *tells* us it bored
him. It bored him to write sympathetically. He was by nature a satirical   40

humourist, and it was far more exciting for him to be attacking the
Dutch officials than sympathizing with the Javanese.

This is again obvious in his partiality for the old Native Prince, the
Regent. It is obvious that all the *actual* oppression of the poor Javanese
5   came from the Javanese themselves, the native princes. It isn't the Dutch
officials who steal Saïdyah's buffalo: it is the princely Javanese. The
oppression has been going on, Havelaar himself says it, *since the beginning
of time*. Not since the coming of the Dutch. Indeed, it is the oriental
idea that the prince shall oppress his humble subjects. So why blame
10   the Dutch officials so absolutely? Why not take the old native Regent
by the beard?

But no! Multatuli, Max Havelaar, swims with pity for the poor and
oppressed, but only because he hates the powers-that-be so intensely.
He doesn't hate the powers because he loves the oppressed. The boot
15   is on the other leg. The chick of pity comes out of the egg of hate. It is
perhaps always so, with pity. But here we have to distinguish compassion
from pity.

Surely, when Saïdyah sets off into the world, or is defended by the
buffalo, it is compassion Multatuli feels for him, not pity. But the end
20   is pity only.

The bird of hate hatches the chick of pity. The great dynamic force in
Multatuli is as it was, really, in Jean Paul and in Swift and Gogol* and in
Mark Twain, hate, a passionate, honourable hate. It is honourable to hate
Drystubble, and Multatuli hated him. It is honourable to hate cowardly
25   officialdom, and Multatuli hated that. Sometimes, it is even honourable,
and necessary, to hate society, as Swift did, or to hate mankind altogether,
as often Voltaire* did.

For man tends to deteriorate into that which Drystubble was, and
the Governor-General and Slimering,* something hateful, which must
30   be destroyed. Then in comes Multatuli, like Jack and the Beanstalk,* to
fight the giant.

And when Jack fights the giant, he *must* have recourse to a trick.
David thought of a sling and stone.* Multatuli took a sort of missionary
disguise. The gross public accepted the disguise, and David's stone went
35   home. *À la guerre comme à la guerre.**

When there are no more Drystubbles, no more Governor-Generals
or Slimerings, then *Max Havelaar* will be out of date. The book is a
pill rather than a comfit.* The jam of pity was put on to get the pill
down. Our fathers and grandfathers licked the jam off. We can still go
40   on taking the pill, for the social constipation is as bad as ever.

INTRODUCTION (VERSION 1) TO THE MEMOIRS OF THE DUC DE LAUZUN

There is something depressing about French eighteenth-century literature, especially that of the latter half of the century. All those sprightly memoirs and risky stories and sentimental effusions constitute, perhaps, the dreariest body of literature we know, once we do know it. The French are essentially critics of life, rather than creators of life. And when the life itself runs rather thin, as it did in the eighteenth century, and the criticism rattles all the faster, it just leaves one feeling wretched.

England during the eighteenth century was far more alive. The sentimentalism of Sterne* laughs at itself, is full of teasing self-mockery. But French sentimentalism of the same period is wholesale and like stale fish. It is difficult, even if one rises on one's hind legs and feels "superior," like a high-brow in an east-end music-hall,* to be amused by Restif de la Bretonne.* One just sits in amazement, that these clever French can be such stale fish of sentimentalism and prurience.

The Duc de Lauzun* belongs to what one might call the fag-end period. He was born in 1747, and was twenty-seven years old when Louis XV* died. Belonging to the high nobility, and to a family prominent at court, he escapes the crass sentimentalism of the "humbler" writers, but he also escapes what bit of genuine new feeling they had. He is far more manly than a Jean Jacques,* but he is still less of a man in himself.

French eighteenth-century literature is so puzzling to the *emotions*, that one has to try to locate some spot of firm feeling inside oneself, from which one can survey the morass. And since the essential problem of the eighteenth century was the problem of *morality*, since the new homunculus* produced in that period was the *homme de bien*, the "good man", who, of course, included the "man of feeling,"* we have to go inside ourselves and discover what we really feel about the "goodness", or morality, of the eighteenth century.

Because there is no doubt about it, the "good man" of today was produced in the chemical retorts of the brain and emotional centres of people like Rousseau and Diderot.* It took him, this "good man",

87

a hundred years to grow to his full stature. Now, after a century and a
half, we have him in his dotage, and find he was a Robot.*

And there is no doubt about it, it was the writhing of this new
little "good man," the new *homme de bien*, in the human consciousness, which was the essential cause of the French revolution. The new
little homunculus was soon ready to come out of the womb of consciousness on to the stage of life. Once on the stage, he soon grew up,
and soon grew into a kind of Woodrow Wilson* dotage. But be that as it
may, it was the kicking of this new little monster, to get out of the womb
of time,* which caused the collapse of the old show.

The new little monster, the new "good man" was perfectly reasonable,
and perfectly irreligious. Religion knows the great passions. The *homme
de bien*, the good man, performs the Robot trick of isolating himself from
the great passions. For the passion of life he substitutes the reasonable
social virtues. You must be honest in your material dealings, you must
be kind to the poor, and you must have "feelings" for your fellow-man
and for nature: Nature with a capital. There is nothing to *worship*. Such
a thing as worship is nonsense. But you may get a "feeling" out of
anything.

In order to get nice "feelings" out of things, you must of course be
quite "free", you mustn't be interfered with. And to be "free", you must
incur the enmity of no man, you must be "good." And when everybody is
"good" and "free", then we shall all have nice feelings about everything.

This is the gist of the idea of the "good man", chemically evolved
by emotional alchemists such as Rousseau. Like every other homunculus, this little "good man" soon grows into a slight deformity, then
into a monster, then into a grinning vast idiot. This monster produced
our great industrial civilisation, and the huge thing, gone idiot, is now
grinning at us and showing its teeth.

We are all, really, pretty "good." We are all extraordinarily "free."
What other freedom can we imagine, than what we've got? So then, we
ought all to have amazingly nice feelings about everything.

The last phase of the bluff is to pretend that we *do* all have nice
feelings about everything, if we are nice people. It is the last grin of the
huge grinning sentimentalism which the Rousseau-ists invented. But
really, it's getting harder and harder to keep up the grin.

As a matter of fact, far from having nice feelings about everything,
we have nice feelings about practically nothing. We get less and less our
share of nice feelings. More and more we get horrid feelings, which we
have to suppress hard. Or, if we don't admit it, then we must admit

that we get less and less feelings of any sort. Our capacity for feeling
anything is going numb, more and more numb, till we feel we shall soon
reach zero, and pure insanity.

This is the horrid end of the "good man" homunculus.

Now the "good man" is all right as far as he goes. One must be honest   5
in one's dealings, and one does feel kindly towards the poor man—unless
he's one of the objectionable sort. If I turn myself into a swindler, and
am a brute to every beggar, I shall only be a "not-good man" instead
of a "good man." It's just the same species, really. Immorality is no
new ground. There's nothing original in it. Whoever invents morality   10
invents, tacitly, immorality. And the immoral, unconventional people
are only the frayed skirt-tails of the conventional people.

The trouble about the "good man" is that he's only one-hundredth
part of a man. The eighteenth century, like a vile Shylock, carved a
pound of flesh* from the human psyche, conjured with it like a cunning   15
alchemist, set it smirking, called it a "good man"—and lo! we all began
to reduce ourselves to this little monstrosity. What's the matter with us,
is that we are bound up like a China-girl's foot,* that has got to cease
developing and turn into a "lily." We are absolutely tight bound up in
the bandages of a few ideas, and tight shoes are nothing to it.   20

When Oscar Wilde said that it is nonsense to assert that art imitates
nature, because nature always imitates art,* this is absolutely true of
human nature. The thing called "spontaneous human nature" does not
exist, and never did. Human nature is always made to some pattern or
other. The wild Australian aborigines are absolutely bound up tight,   25
tighter than a China-girl's foot, in their few savage conventions. They
are bound up tighter than we are. But the length of the ideal bandage
doesn't matter. Once you begin to feel it pressing, it'll press tighter and
tighter, till either you burst it, or collapse inside it, or go deranged.
And the conventional and ideal and emotional bandage presses as tight   30
upon the free American girl as the equivalent bandage presses upon
the Australian black girl in her tribe. An elephant bandaged up tight,
so that he can only move his eyes, is no better off than a bandaged-
up mouse. Perhaps worse off. The mouse has more chance to nibble a
way out.   35

And this we must finally recognise. No man has "feelings of his own."
The feelings of all men in the civilised world today are practically all
alike. Men *can* only feel the feelings they know how to feel. The feelings
they don't know how to feel, they don't feel. This is true of all men,
and all women, and all children.   40

It is true, children do have lots of unrecognised feelings. But an unrecognised feeling, if it forces itself into any recognition, is only recognised as "nervousness" or "irritability." There are certain feelings we recognise. And as we grow up, every single disturbance in the psyche, or in the soul, is transmitted into one of the recognised feeling patterns, or else left in that margin called "nervousness."

This is our true bondage. This is the agony of our human existence: that we can only feel things in conventional feeling-patterns. Because when these feeling-patterns become inadequate, when they will no longer body forth the workings of the yeasty soul, then we are in torture. It is like a deaf-mute trying to speak. Something is inadequate in the expression-apparatus, and we hear strange howlings. So are we now howling inarticulate, because what is yeastily working in us has no voice and no language. We are like deaf-mutes, or like the China-girl's foot.

Now the eighteenth-century did let out a little extra length of bandage for the bound-up feet. But oh! it was a short length! We soon grew up to its capacity, and the pressure again became intolerable, horrible, unbearable: as it is today.

We compare England today with France of 1780. We sort of half expect revolutions of the same sort. But we have little grounds for the comparison and the expectation. It is true, our feelings are going dead, we have to work hard to get any feeling out of ourselves: which is true of the Louis XV and more so of the Louis XVI* people like the Duc de Lauzun. But at the same time, we know quite well that if all our heads were chopped off, and the working-classes were left to themselves, with a clear field, nothing would have happened, really. Bolshevist Russia,* one feels and feels with bitter regret, is nothing new on the face of the earth. It is only a sort of America. And no matter how many revolutions take place, all we can hope for is different sorts of America. And since America is *chose connue*,* since America is known to us, in our imaginative souls, with dreary finality, what's the odds? America has no new feelings: less even than England: only disruption of old feelings. America is bandaged more tightly even than Europe in the bandages of old ideas and ideals. Her feelings are even more fixed to pattern: or merely devolutionary. Her art-forms are even more life-less.

So what's the point in a revolution. Where's the homunculus? Where is the new baby of a new conception of life? Who feels him kicking in the womb of time?

Nobody! Nobody! Not even the socialists and bolshevists themselves. Not the Buddhists nor the Christian Scientists* nor the scientists, nor the Christians. Nobody! So far, there is no new baby. And therefore, there is no revolution. Because a revolution is really the birth of a new baby, a new idea, a new feeling, a new way of feeling, a new feeling pattern. It is the birth of a new man. "For I will put a new song into your mouth."*

There is no new song. There is no new man. There is no new baby. And therefore, I repeat, there is no revolution.

You who want a revolution, beget and conceive the new baby in your bodies: and not a homunculus Robot like Rousseau's

But you who are afraid of a revolution, realise that there will be no revolution, just as there will be no pangs of parturition if there is no baby to be born.

Instead, however, you may get that which is not revolution. You may, and you will, get a débâcle. *Après moi le Déluge** was premature. The French revolution was only a bit of a brief inundation. The real deluge lies just ahead of us.

There is no choice about it. You can't keep the *status quo*,* because the homunculus-Robot, the "good man", is dead. We killed him rather hastily and with hideous brutality, in the great war that was to save democracy.* He is dead, and you can't keep him from decaying. You can't keep him from decomposition. You can not.

Neither can you expect a revolution, because there is no new baby in the womb of our society. Russia is a collapse, not a revolution.

All that remains, since it's Louis XV's Deluge which is lowering, rather belated: all that remains is to be a Noah, and build an ark.* An ark, an ark, my kingdom for an ark!* An ark of the covenant, into which also the animals shall go in two by two, for there's one more river to cross!*

INTRODUCTION (VERSION 2) TO
THE MEMOIRS OF THE DUC DE LAUZUN

The Duc de Lauzun

The Duc de Lauzun belongs to the fag-end of the French brocade period.* He was born in 1747, was a man of twenty-seven when Louis XV died, and Louis XVI came tinkering to the throne. Belonging to the high nobility, his life was naturally focussed on the court, though one feels he was too good merely to follow the fashions. 5

He wrote his own memoirs,* which rather scrappily cover the first thirty-six years of his life. The result on the reader is one of depression and impatience. You feel how idiotic that French court was: how fulsomely insipid. Thankful you feel, that they all had their heads off 10 at last. They deserved it. Not for their sins. Their sins, on the whole, were no worse than anybody else's. I wouldn't grudge them their sins. But their dressed-up idiocy is beyond human endurance.

There is only one sin in life, and that is the sin against life, the sin of causing inner emptiness and boredom of the spirit. Whoever 15 and whatever makes us inwardly bored and empty-feeling, is vile, the anathema.

And one feels that this was almost deliberately done to the Duc de Lauzun. When I read him, I feel sincerely that the little baby that came from his mother's womb, and killed her in the coming,* was the germ 20 of a real man. And this real man they killed in him, as far as they could, with cold and insect-like persistency, from the moment he was born and his mother, poor young thing of nineteen, died and escaped the scintillating idiocy of her destiny.

No man on earth could have come through such an upbringing as this 25 boy had, without losing the best half of himself on the way, and emerging incalculably impoverished. Abandoned as a baby to the indifference of French servants in a palace, he was, as he says himself, "like all the other children of my age and condition; the finest clothes for going out, at home half-naked and dying of hunger."* And that this was so, we know 30 from other cases. Even a Dauphin* was begrudged clean sheets for his bed, and slept in a tattered night-shirt, while he was a boy. It was no joke to be a child, in that smart period.

To educate the little duke—though when he was a child he was only a little Count—his father chose one of the dead mother's lacqueys.* This lacquey knew how to read and write, and this amount of knowledge he imparted to the young nobleman, who was extremely proud of himself because he could read aloud "more fluently and pleasantly than is ordinarily the case in France."* Another writer of the period says: "there are, perhaps, not more than fifty persons in Paris capable of reading prose aloud."*—So that the boy became "almost necessary" to Madame de Pompadour,* because he could read to her. And sometimes he read to the king, Louis XV. "Our journeys to Versailles became more frequent, and my education consequently more neglected. . . . At the age of twelve I was entered into the Guards regiment . . ."*

What sort of education it was, which was neglected, would be difficult to say. All one can gather from the Duke himself is that, in his bored forlornness, he had read innumerable novels: the false, reekingly sentimental fal-de-lal love-novels of his day. And these, alas, did him a fair amount of harm, judging from the amount of unreal sentiment he poured over his later love affairs.

That a self-critical people like the French should ever have wallowed in such a white sauce of sentimentalism as did those wits of the eighteenth century, is incredible. A mid-Victorian English sentimentalist at his worst is sincere and naïve, compared to a French romanticist of the mid-eighteenth century. One works one's suffocated way through the sticky-sweet mess with repulsion.

So, the poor little nobleman, they began to initiate him into "love" when he was twelve, though he says he was fourteen. "Madame la Duchesse de Grammont showed great friendship for me, and had the intention, I believe, of gradually forming for herself a little lover whom she would have all to herself, without any inconveniences."* Her chambermaid and confidante, Julie, thought to forestall her mistress. She made advances to the boy. "One day she put my hand in her breast, and all my body was afire several hours afterwards; but I wasn't any further ahead."*—His tutor, however, discovered the affair, nipped it in the bud, and Mademoiselle Julie didn't have the honor of "putting him into the world,"* as he called it. He was keenly distressed.

When he was sixteen, his father began to arrange his marriage with Mademoiselle de Boufflers.* The Duchesse de Grammont turned him entirely against the girl, before he set eyes on her. This was another part of his education.

At the age of seventeen, he had a little actress, aged fifteen, for his mistress "and she was still more innocent than I was."* Another little actress lent them her cupboard of a bedroom, but "an enormous spider came to trouble our rendez-vous; we were both mortally afraid of it; neither of us had the courage to kill it. So we chose to separate, promising to meet again in a cleaner place, where there were no such horrid monsters."*

One must say this for the Duc de Lauzun: there is nothing particularly displeasing about his love-affairs, especially during his younger life. He never seems to have made love to a woman unless he really liked her, and truly wanted to touch her: and unless she really liked him, and wanted him to touch her. Which is the essence of morality, as far as love goes.

The Comtesse d'Esparbes* had thoroughly initiated him, or "put him into the world." She had him to read aloud to her as she lay in bed: though even then, he was still so backward that only at the second reading did he really come to the scratch.* He was still seventeen. And then the Countess threw him over, and put him still more definitely into the world. He says of himself at this point, in a note written, of course, twenty years later: "all my childhood I had read many novels, and this reading had such an influence on my character, I feel it still. It has often been to my disadvantage; but if I have tended to exaggerate my own sentiments and my own sensations, at least I owe this to my romantic character, that I have avoided the treacheries and bad dealings with women, from which many honest people are not exempt."*

So that his novels did something for him, if they only saved him from the vulgar brutality of the non-romantic.

He was well in love with Madame de Stainville,* when his father married him at last, at the age of nineteen, to Mademoiselle de Boufflers. The marriage was almost a worse failure than usual. Mlle. de Boufflers, apparently, liked Lauzun no better than he liked her. Madame de Stainville calls her a "disagreeable child."* She did not care for men: seems to have been a model of quiet virtue: perhaps she was a sweet, gentle thing: more likely she was inwardly resentful from the day of her birth. One would gather that she showed even some contempt of Lauzun, and physical repugnance to the married state. They never really lived together.

And this is one of the disgusting sides to the France of that day. Under a reeking sentimentalism lay a brutal, worse than bestial callousness and insensitiveness. Brutality is wholesome, compared with refined callousness, that truly has no feelings at all, only refined selfishnesses.

The Prince de Ligne* gives a sketch of the marriage of a young woman
of the smart nobility of that day.—"They teach a girl not to look a man
in the face, not to reply to him, never to ask how she happened to be
born. Then they bring along two men in black, accompanying a man
5   in embroidered satin. After which they say, to her: Go and spend the
night with this gentleman.—This gentleman, all afire, brutally assumes
his rights, asks nothing, but exacts a great deal; she rises in tears, at
the very least, and he, at least, wet. If they have said a word, it was to
quarrel. Both of them look sulky, and each is disposed to try elsewhere.
10 So marriage begins, under happy auspices. All delicate modesty is gone:
and would modesty prevent this pretty woman from yielding, to a man
she loves, that which has been forced from her by a man she doesn't
love?—But behold the most sacred union of hearts, profaned by parents
and a lawyer."*

15   Did the Duc de Lauzun avoid this sort of beginning? He was really
enamoured of Madame de Stainville, her accepted and devoted lover.
He was violently disposed against his bride: "this disagreeable child."
And perhaps, feeling himself compelled into the marriage-bed with the
"disagreeable child," his bowels of compassion dried up. For he was
20 naturally a compassionate man. Anyhow the marriage was a drastic
failure. And his wife managed somehow, in the first weeks, to sting him
right on the quick. Perhaps on the quick of his vanity. He never quite
got over it.

So he went on, a dandy,* a wit in a moderate way, and above all,
25 a "romantic," extravagant, rather absurd lover. Inside himself, he was
not extravagant and absurd. But he had a good deal of feeling which he
didn't know what on earth to do with, so he turned it into "chivalrous"
extravagance.

This is the real pity. Let a man have as fine and kindly a nature as
30 possible, he'll be able to do nothing with it unless it has some scope.
What scope was there for a decent manly man, in that France rotten
with sentimentalism and dead with cruel callousness? What could he
do? He wasn't great enough to rise clean above his times: no man is.
There was nothing wholesome doing, in the whole of France. Senti-
35 mental romanticism, fag-end encyclopaedic philosophy,* false pietism,
and emptiness. It was as if, under the expiring monarchy, the devil had
thrown everybody into a conspiracy to make life false and to nip straight,
brave feeling in the bud.

Everything then conspired to make a man little. This was the misery
40 of men in those days: they were made to be littler than they really were,

by the niggling corrosion of that "wit", that "esprit" which had no spirit in it, except the petty spirit of destruction. Envy, spite, finding their outlet, as they do today, in cheap humour and smart sayings.

The men had nothing to do with their lives. So they laid their lives at the feet of the women. Or pretended to. When it came to the point, they snatched their lives back again hastily enough. But even then they didn't know what to do with them. So they laid them at the feet of some other woman.

The Duc de Lauzun was one of the French anglophiles of the day: he really admired England,* found something there. And perhaps his most interesting experience was his affair with Lady Sarah Bunbury,* that famous beauty of George III's reign.

She held him off for a long time: part of the game seemed to be*

INTRODUCTION TO THE MOTHER,
BY GRAZIA DELEDDA

Introduction to *The Mother*

Grazia Deledda* is already one of the elder living writers of Italy, and though her work does not take on quite so rapidly as the novels of Fogaz-zaro, or even D'Annunzio,* that peculiarly obscuring nebulousness of the past-which-is-only-just-gone-by, still, the dimness has touched it. It is curious that fifteen or twenty years ago should seem so much more remote than fifty or eighty years ago. But perhaps it is organically necessary to us that our feelings should die, temporarily, towards that strange intermediate period which lies between present actuality and the revived past. We can hardly bear to recall the emotions of twenty or fifteen years ago, hardly at all, whereas we respond again quite vividly to the emotions of Jane Austen or Dickens,* nearer a hundred years ago. There, the past is safely and finally past. The past of fifteen years ago is still yeastily working in us.

It takes a really good writer to make us overcome our repugnance to the just-gone-by emotions. Even D'Annunzio's novels are hardly readable at present: Matilde Serao's* still less so. But we can still read Grazia Deledda, with genuine interest.

The reason is that, though she is not a first-class genius, she belongs to more than just her own day. She does more than reproduce the temporary psychological condition of her period. She has a background, and she deals with something more fundamental than sophisticated feeling. She does not penetrate, as a great genius does, the very sources of human passion and motive. She stays far short of that. But what she does do is to create the passionate complex of a primitive populace.

To do this, one must have an isolated populace: just as Thomas Hardy isolates Wessex.* Grazia Deledda has an island to herself, her own island of Sardinia, that she loves so deeply: especially the more northerly, mountainous part of Sardinia.

Still Sardinia is one of the wildest, remotest parts of Europe, with a strange people and a mysterious past of its own. There is still an old mystery in the air, over the forest slopes of Mount Gennargentu,* as there is over some old Druid places,* the mystery of an unevolved people.

The war, of course, partly gutted Sardinia, as it gutted everywhere. But the island is still a good deal off the map, on the face of the earth.

An island of rigid conventions, the rigid conventions of barbarism, and at the same time, the fierce violence of the instinctive passions. A savage tradition of chastity, with a savage lust of the flesh. A barbaric overlordship of the gentry, with a fierce indomitableness of the servile classes. A lack of public opinion, a lack of belonging to any other part of the world, a lack of mental awakening, which makes inland Sardinia almost as savage as Benin,* and makes Sardinian singing as wonderful and almost as wild as any on earth. It is the human instinct still uncontaminated. The money-sway still did not govern central Sardinia, in the days of Grazia Deledda's books, twenty, a dozen years ago, before the war. Instead there was a savage kind of aristocracy and feudalism, and a rule of ancient instinct, instinct with the definite but indescribable tang of the aboriginal people of the island, not absorbed into the world: instinct often at war with the Italian government; a determined savage individualism often breaking with the law, or driven into brigandage: but human, of the great human mystery.

It is this old Sardinia, at last being brought to heel, which is the real theme of Grazia Deledda's books. She is fascinated by her island and its folks, more than by the problems of the human psyche. And therefore this book, *The Mother*, is perhaps one of the least typical of her novels, one of the most "continental." Because here, she has a definite universal theme: the consecrated priest and the woman. But she keeps on forgetting her theme. She becomes more interested in the death of the old hunter,* in the doings of the boy Antiochus,* in the exorcising of the spirit from the little girl possessed. She is herself somewhat bored by the priest's hesitations; she shows herself suddenly impatient, a pagan sceptical of the virtues of chastity, even in consecrated priests; she is touched, yet annoyed by the pathetic, tiresome old mother who made her son a priest out of ambition, and who simply expires in the terror of a public exposure;* and, in short, she makes a bit of a mess of the book, because she started a problem she didn't quite dare to solve. She shirks the issue atrociously. But neither will the modern spirit solve* the problem by killing off the fierce instincts that made the problem. As for Grazia Deledda, first she started by sympathising with the mother, and then must sympathise savagely with the young woman, and then can't make up her mind. She kills off the old mother in disgust at the old woman's triumph, so leaving the priest and the young woman hanging in space. As a sort of problem-story, it is disappointing. No doubt, if the priest had gone off with the woman, as he first intended, then all the authoress' sympathy *would* have fallen to the old abandoned mother. As it is, the sympathy falls between two stools, and the title *La Madre* is not really justified. The mother turns out *not* to be the heroine.

But the interest of this book lies, not in plot or characterisation, but in the presentation of sheer instinctive life. The love of the priest for the woman is sheer instinctive passion, pure and undefiled by sentiment. As such it is worthy of respect, for in other books on this theme the instinct is swamped and extinguished in sentiment. Here, however, the instinct of direct sex is so strong and so vivid, that only the other blind instinct of mother-obedience, the child-instinct, can overcome it. All the priest's education and christianity are really mere snuff of the candle.* The old, wild instinct of a mother's ambition for her son defeats the other wild instinct of sexual mating. An old woman who has never had any sex life— and it is astonishing, in barbaric half-civilisations, how many people are denied a sex life; she succeeds, by her old barbaric maternal power over her son, in finally killing his sex life too. It is the suicide of semi-barbaric natures under the sway of a dimly-comprehended Christianity, and falsely-conceived ambition.

The old, blind life of instinct, and chiefly frustrated instinct and the rage thereof, as it is seen in the Sardinian hinterland, this is Grazia Deledda's absorption. The desire of the boy Antiochus to be a priest is an instinct: perhaps an instinctive recoil from his mother's grim priapism. The dying man escapes from the village, back to the rocks, instinctively needing to die in the wilds. The feeling of Agnes, the woman who loves the priest, is sheer female instinctive passion, something as in Emily Bronte.* It too has the ferocity of frustrated instinct, and is bare and stark, lacking any of the graces of sentiment. This saves it from "dating" as D'Annunzio's passions date. Sardinia is by no means a land for Romeos and Juliets, nor even Virgins of the Rocks.* It is rather a land of Wuthering Heights.

The book, of course, loses a good deal in translation, as is inevitable. In the mouths of the simple people, Italian is a purely instinctive language, with the rhythm of instinctive rather than mental processes. There are also many instinct-words with meanings never clearly mentally defined. In fact, nothing is brought to real mental clearness, everything goes by in a stream of more or less vague, more or less realised feeling, with a natural mist or glow of sensation over everything, that counts more than the actual words said; and which, alas, it is almost impossible to reproduce in the more cut-and-dried northern languages, where every word has its fixed value and meaning like so much coinage. A language can be killed by over-precision, killed especially as an effective medium for the conveyance of instinctive passion and instinctive emotion. One feels this, reading a translation from the Italian. And though Grazia

5 Deledda is not masterly as Giovanni Verga* is, yet, in Italian at least, she can put us into the mood and rhythm of Sardinia like a true artist, an artist whose work is sound and enduring.

'CHAOS IN POETRY': INTRODUCTION TO CHARIOT OF THE SUN, BY HARRY CROSBY

Chaos in Poetry

Poetry, they say, is a matter of words. And this is just as much true as that pictures are a matter of paint, and frescoes* a matter of water and colour-wash. It is such a long way from being the whole truth, that it is slightly silly if uttered sententiously.

Poetry is a matter of words. Poetry is a stringing together of words into a ripple and jingle and a run of colours. Poetry is an interplay of images. Poetry is the iridescent suggestion of an idea. Poetry is all these things, and still it is something else. Given all these ingredients, you have something very like to poetry, something for which we might borrow the old romantic name of poesy. And poesy, like bric-à-brac, will forever be in fashion. But poetry is still another thing.

The essential quality of poetry is that it makes a new effort of attention, and "discovers" a new world within the known world. Man, and the animals, and the flowers, all live within a strange and forever-surging chaos. The chaos which we have got used to, we call a cosmos. The unspeakable inner chaos of which we are composed we call consciousness, and mind, and even civilisation. But it is, ultimately, chaos, lit up by visions, or not lit up by visions. Just as the rainbow may or may not light up the storm. And like the rainbow, the vision perisheth.*

But man cannot live in chaos. The animals can. To the animal, all is chaos, only there are a few recurring motions and aspects within the surge. And the animal is content. But man is not. Man must wrap himself in a vision, make a house of apparent form and stability, fixity. In his terror of chaos, he begins by putting up an umbrella between himself and the everlasting whirl. Then he paints the under-side of his umbrella like a firmament. Then he parades around, lives and dies under his umbrella. Bequeathed to his descendants, the umbrella becomes a dome, a vault, and men at last begin to feel that something is wrong.

Man fixes some wonderful erection of his own between himself and the wild chaos, and gradually goes bleached and stifled under his parasol. Then comes a poet, enemy of convention, and makes a slit in the umbrella; and lo! the glimpse of chaos is a vision, a window to the sun.

But after a while, getting used to the vision, and not liking the genuine draught from chaos, commonplace man daubs a simulacrum of
the window that opens on to chaos, and patches the umbrella with the
painted patch of the simulacrum. That is, he has got used to the vision,
5   it is part of his house-decoration. So that the umbrella at last looks
like a glowing open firmament, of many aspects. But alas, it is all simulacrum, in innumerable patches. Homer and Keats,* annotated and with
glossary.

This is the history of poetry in our era. Some-one sees Titans* in
10   the wild air of chaos, and the Titan becomes a wall between succeeding
generations and the chaos they should have inherited. The wild sky
moved and sang. Even that became a great umbrella between mankind
and the sky of fresh air; then it became a painted vault, a fresco on a
vaulted roof, under which men bleach and go dissatisfied. Till another
15   poet makes a slit on to the open and windy chaos.

But at last our roof deceives us no more. It is painted plaster, and
all the skill of all the human ages won't take us in. Dante or Leonardo,
Beethoven or Whitman:* lo! it is painted on the plaster of our vault.
Like St. Francis preaching to the birds in Assisi.* Wonderfully like air
20   and birdy space and chaos of many things—partly because the fresco is
faded. But even so, we are glad to get out of that church, and into the
natural chaos.

This is the momentous crisis for mankind, when we have to get back
to chaos. So long as the umbrella serves, and poets make slits in it, and
25   the mass of people can be gradually educated up to the vision in the
slit: which means they patch it over with a patch that looks just like the
vision in the slit: so long as this process can continue, and mankind can
be educated up, and thus built in, so long will a civilisation continue
more or less happily, completing its own painted prison. It is called
30   completing the consciousness.

The joy men had when Wordsworth, for example, made a slit and
saw a primrose!* Till then, men had only seen a primrose dimly, in the
shadow of the umbrella. They saw it through Wordsworth in the full
gleam of chaos. Since then, gradually, we have come to see primavera*
35   nothing but primrose. Which means, we have patched over the slit.

And the greater joy when Shakspeare* made a big rent, and saw
emotional wistful man outside in the chaos, beyond the conventional
idea and painted umbrella of moral images and iron-bound paladins,*
which had been put up in the Middle Ages. But now, alas, the roof of
40   our vault is simply painted dense with Hamlets and Macbeths,* the

side walls too, and the order is fixed and complete. Man can't be any different from his image. Chaos is all shut out.

The umbrella has got so big, the patches and plaster are so tight and hard, it can be slit no more. If it were slit, the rent would no more be a vision, it would only be an outrage. We should dab it over at once, to match the rest.   5

So the umbrella is absolute. And so, the yearning for chaos becomes a nostalgia. And this will go on till some terrific wind blows the umbrella to ribbons, and much of mankind to oblivion. The rest will shiver in the midst of chaos. For chaos is always there, and always will be, no matter how we put up umbrellas of visions.   10

What about the poets, then, at this juncture? They reveal the inward desire of mankind. What do they reveal?—They show the desire for chaos, and the fear of chaos. The desire for chaos is the breath of their poetry. The fear of chaos is in their parade of forms and technique.   15
Poetry is made of words! they say. So they blow bubbles of sound and image, which soon burst with the breath of longing for chaos, which fills them. But the poetasters* can make pretty shiny bubbles for the christmas tree, which never burst, because there is no breath of poetry in them, but they remain till we drop them.   20

What, then, of *Chariot of the Sun?** It is a warlike and bronzey title, for a sheaf of flimsies, almost too flimsy for real bubbles. But incongruity is man's recognition of chaos.

If one had to judge these little poems for their magic of words, as one judges Paul Valérie,* for example, they would look shabby. There   25
is no obvious incantation of sweet noise; only too often, the music of one line deliberately kills the next, breathlessly staccato. There is no particular jewellery of epithet. And no handsome handling of images. Where deliberate imagery is used, it is perhaps a little clumsy. There is no coloured thread of an idea; and no subtle ebbing of a theme into   30
consciousness, no recognisable vision, new gleam of chaos let in to a world of order. There is only a repetition of sun, sun, sun, not really as a glowing symbol, more as a bewilderment and a narcotic. The images in *Sun Rhapsody* shatter one another, line by line. For the sun,

> "it is a forest without trees   35
> it is a lion in a cage of breeze
> it is the roundness of her knees
> great Hercules
> and all the seas
> and our soliloquies"*   40

The rhyme is responsible for a great deal.—The lesser symbols are as confusing: sun-maids who are naiaids* of the water world, hiding in a cave. Only the forest becomes suddenly logical.

> "I am a tree whose roots are tangled in the sun
> All men and women are trees whose roots are tangled in the sun
> Therefore humanity is the forest of the sun."*

What is there then, in this poetry, where there seems to be nothing? For if there is nothing, it is merely nonsense.

And almost, it is nonsense. Sometimes, as in the "verse" beginning: "Sthhe fous on ssu eod",* since I at least can make no head or tail of it, and the mere sound is impossible, and the mere look of it is not inspiring, to me it is just nonsense. But in a world overloaded with shallow "sense", I can bear a page of nonsense, just for a pause.

For the rest, what is there? Take, at random, the poem called *Néant*.

> "Red sunbeams from an autumn sun
> Shall be the strongest wall
> To shield the sunmaids of my soul
> From worlds inimical.
>
> Yet sunflakes falling in the sea
> Beyond the outer shore
> Reduplicate their epitaph
> To kill the conqueror."*

It is a tissue of incongruity, in sound and sense. It means nothing, and it says nothing. And yet it has something to say. It even carries a dim suggestion of that which refuses to be said.

And therein lies the charm. It is a glimpse of chaos not reduced to order. But the chaos *alive*, not the chaos of matter. A glimpse of the living, untamed chaos. For the grand chaos is all alive, and everlasting. From it we draw our breath of life. If we shut ourselves off from it, we stifle.—The animals live with it, so they live in grace. But when man became conscious, and aware of *himself*, his own littleness and puniness in the whirl of the vast chaos of god, he took fright, and began inventing god in his own image.

Now comes the moment when the terrified but inordinately conceited human consciousness must at last submit, and own itself part of the vast and potent living chaos. We must keep true to ourselves. But we must breathe in life from the living and unending chaos. We shall put up more umbrellas. They are a necessity of our consciousness. But never again shall we be able to put up The Absolute Umbrella, either religious or moral or rational or scientific or practical. The vast parasol of our conception of the universe, the cosmos, the firmament of suns and stars and space, this we can roll up like any other green sunshade, and bring it forth again when we want it. But we mustn't imagine it always spread above us. It is no more absolutely there than a green sunshade is absolutely there. It is casually there, only; because it is as much a contrivance and invention of our mind as a green sunshade is.—Likewise the grand conception of god: this already shuts up like a Japanese parasol,* rather clumsily, and is put by for Sundays, or bad weather, or a "serious" mood.

Now we see the charm of *Chariot of the Sun*. It shuts up all the little and big umbrellas of poesy and importance, has no outstanding melody or rhythm or image or epithet or image or even sense. And we feel a certain relief. The sun is very much in evidence, certainly, but it is a bubble reality that always explodes before you can really look at it. And it upsets all the rest of things with its disappearing.

Hence the touch of true poetry in this sun. It bursts all the bubbles and umbrellas of reality, and gives us a breath of the live chaos. We struggle out into the fathomless chaos of things passing and coming, and many suns and different darknesses. There is a bursting of bubbles of reality, and the pang of extinction that is also liberation into the roving, uncaring chaos which is all we shall ever know of God.

To me, there is a breath of poetry, like an uneasy waft of fresh air at dawn, before it is light. There is an acceptance of the limitations of consciousness, and a leaning up against the sun-imbued world of chaos. It is poetry at the moment of inception in the soul, before the germs of the known and the unknown have fused to begin a new body of concepts. And therefore it is useless to quote fragments. They are too nebulous and *not there*. Yet in the whole there is a breath of real poetry, the essential quality of poetry. It makes a new act of attention, and wakes us to a nascent world of inner and outer suns. And it has the poetic faith in the chaotic splendour of suns.

It is poetry of suns which are the core of chaos, suns which are fountains of shadow and pools of light and centres of thought and lions of passion. Since chaos has a core which is itself quintessentially chaotic and fierce with incongruities. That such a sun should have a chariot makes it only more chaotic.

And in the chaotic re-echoing of the soul, wisps of sound curl round
with curious soothing.—"likewise invisible winds
    Drink fire, and all my heart is sun-consoled."*
And a poem such as *Water Lilies** has a lovely suffusion in which the
visual image passes at once into sense of touch, and back again, so that
there is an iridescent confusion of sense impression, sound and touch
and sight all running in to one another, blending into a vagueness which
is a new world, a vagueness and a suffusion which liberates the soul,
and lets a new flame of desire flicker delicately up from the numbed
body.

The suffused fragments are the best, those that are only compre-
hensible with the senses, with vision passing into touch and to sound,
then again touch, and the bursting of the bubble of an image. There
is always sun, but there is also water, most palpably water. Even some
of the suns are wetly so, wet pools that wet us with their touch. Then
loose suns like lions, soft gold lions and white lions half-visible.* Then
again the elusive gleam of the sun of livingness, soft as gold and strange
as the lion's eyes, the livingness that never ceases and never will cease.
In this there is faith, soft, intangible suffused faith that is the breath of
all poetry, part of the breathing of the myriad sun in chaos. Such sun
breathes its way into words, and the words become poetry, by suffusion.
On the part of the poet it is an act of faith, pure attention and purified
receptiveness. And without such faith there is no poetry. There is even
no life. The poetry of conceit is a dead-sea fruit.* The poetry of sunless
chaos is already a bore, the poetry of a regulated cosmos is nothing but
a wire bird-cage. Because in all living poetry the living chaos stirs, sun-
suffused and sun-impulsive, and most subtly chaotic. All true poetry is
most subtly and sensitively chaotic, outlawed. But it is the impulse of
the sun in chaos, not conceit.

        "the Sun in unconcealèd rage
    Glares down across the magic of the world"*

The sun within us, that sways us incalculably.

        "At night
        Swift to the Sun
        Deep imaged in my soul
        But during the long day black lands
        To cross"*

5

10

15

20

25

30

35

And it is faith in the incalculable sun, inner and outer, which keeps us
alive.

> "Sunmaid
> Left by the tide
> I bring you a conch-shell
> That listening to the Sun you may
> Revive"*   5

And there is always the battle of the sun, against the corrosive, acid
vapour of vanity and poisonous conceit, which is the breath of the
world.   10

> "Dark clouds
> Are not so dark
> As our embittered thoughts
> Which carve strange silences within
> The Sun"*   15

That the next "cinquain" may not be poetry at all* is perhaps just as
well, to keep us in mind of the world of conceit outside. It is the expired
breath, with its necessary carbonic acid.* It is the cold shadow across
the sun, and saves us from the strain of the monos,* from homogeneity
and exaltation and forcedness and all-of-a-pieceness, which is the curse   20
of the human consciousness. What does it matter if half the time a poet
fails in his effort at expression! The failures make it real. The act of
attention is not so easy. It is much easier to write poesy. Failure is part
of the living chaos. And the groping reveals the act of attention, which
suddenly passes again into pure expression.   25

> "But I shall not be frightened by a sound
> Of Something moving cautiously around."*

Whims, and fumblings, and effort, and nonsense, and echoes from
other poets, these all go to make up the living chaos of a little book of real
poetry, as well as pure little poems like *Sun-Ghost, To Those Who Return,*   30
*Torse de Jeune Femme au Soleil, Poem for the Feet of Polia.** Through it
all runs the intrinsic naïveté without which no poetry can exist, not
even the most sophisticated. This naïveté is the opening of the soul to
the sun of chaos, and the soul may open like a lily or a tiger-lily or a
dandelion or a deadly-nightshade or a rather paltry chickweed flower,   35
and it will be poetry of its own sort. But open it must. This opening,
and this alone, is the essential act of attention, the essential poetic and
vital act. We may fumble in the act, and a hail-stone may hit us. But it is

in the course of things. In this act, and this alone, we truly *live*: in that
innermost naïve opening of the soul, like a flower, like an animal, like a
coloured snake, it does not matter, to the sun of chaotic livingness.

Now, after a long bout of conceit and self-assurance and flippancy,
the young are waking up to the fact that they are starved of life and of
essential sun, and at last they are being driven, out of sheer starvedness,
to make the act of submission, the act of attention, to open into inner
naïveté, deliberately, and dauntlessly, admit the chaos and the sun of
chaos. This is the new naïveté, chosen, recovered, re-gained. Round
it range the white and golden soft lions of courage and the sun of
dauntlessness, and the whorled ivory horn of the unicorn* is erect and
ruthless, as a weapon of defense. The naïve, open spirit of man will no
longer be a victim, to be put on a cross, nor a beggar, to be scorned
and given a pittance. This time it will be erect and a bright lord, with
a heart open to the wild sun of chaos, but with the yellow lions of the
sun's danger on guard in the eyes.

The new naïveté, erect, and ready, sufficiently sophisticated to wring
the neck of sophistication, will be the new spirit of poetry and the new
spirit of life. Tender, but purring like a leopard that may snarl, it may
be clumsy at first, and make gestures of self-conscious crudity. But it
is a real thing, the real creature of the inside of the soul. And to the
young, it is the essential reality, the liberation into the real self. The
liberation into the wild air of chaos, the being part of the sun. A long
course of merely negative "freedom" reduces the soul and body both
to numbness. They can feel no more and respond no more. Only the
mind remains awake, and suffers keenly from the sense of nullity; to
be young, and to feel you have every "opportunity", every "freedom"
to live, and yet not to be able to live, because the responses have gone
numb in the body and soul, this is the nemesis that is overtaking the
young. It drives them silly.

But there is the other way, back to the sun, to faith in the speckled
leopard of the mixed self.* What is more chaotic than a dappled leopard
trotting through dappled shade! And that is our life, really. Why try to
whitewash ourselves?—or to camouflage ourselves into an artificially
chaotic pattern? All we have to do is to accept the true chaos that we
are, like the jaguar dappled with black suns on gold.

INTRODUCTION TO BOTTOM DOGS,
BY EDWARD DAHLBERG

Introd. to Edward Dahlberg's novel, for Putnams Bottom Dogs*

When we think of America, and of her huge success, we never realise how many failures have gone, and still go to build up that success. It is not till you live in America, and go a little under the surface, that you begin to see how terrible and brutal is the mass of failure that nourishes the roots of the gigantic tree of dollars. And this is especially so in the country, and in the newer parts of the land, particularly out west. There you see how many small ranches have gone broke in despair, before the big ranches scoop them up and profit by all the back-breaking, profitless, grim labour of the pioneer. In the west you can still see the pioneer work of tough, hard first-comers, individuals, and it is astounding to see how often these individuals, pioneer first-comers who fought like devils against their difficulties, have been defeated, broken,* their efforts and their amazing hard work lost, as it were, on the face of the wilderness. But it is these hard-necked failures who really broke the resistance of the stubborn, obstinate country, and made it easier for the second wave of exploiters to come in with money and reap the harvest. The real pioneer in America fought like hell and suffered till the soul was ground out of him: and then, nine times out of ten, failed, was beaten. That is why pioneer literature, which, even from the glimpses one has of it, contains the amazing Odyssey* of the brute fight with savage conditions of the western continent, hardly exists,* and is absolutely unpopular. Americans will not stand for the pioneer stuff, except in small, sentimentalised doses. They know too well the grimness of it, the savage fight and the savage failure which broke the back of the country but also broke something in the human soul. The spirit and the will survived: but something in the soul perished: the softness, the floweriness, the natural tenderness. How could it survive the sheer brutality of the fight with that American wilderness, which is so big, vast, and obdurate?

The savage America was conquered and subdued at the expense of the instinctive and intuitive sympathy of the human soul. The fight was

too brutal. It is a great pity some publisher does not undertake a series of
pioneer records and novels, the genuine unsweetened stuff. The books
exist. But they are shoved down into oblivion by the common will-to-
forget. They show the strange brutality of the struggle, what would
have been called in the old language the breaking of the heart. America
was not colonised and "civilised" until the heart was broken in the
American pioneers. It was a price that was paid. The heart was broken.
But the will, the determination to conquer the land and make it submit
to productivity, this was not broken. The will-to-success and the will-
to-produce became clean and indomitable once the sympathetic heart
was broken.

By the sympathetic heart, we mean that instinctive belief which lies
at the core of the human heart, that people and the universe itself is
ultimately kind. This belief is fundamental, and, in the old language,
is embodied in the doctrine: God is good.—Now given an opposition
too ruthless, a fight too brutal, a betrayal too bitter, this belief breaks
in the heart, and is no more. Then you have either despair, bitterness,
and cynicism: or you have the much braver reaction which says: God is
not good, but the human will is indomitable, it cannot be broken, it will
succeed against all odds. It is not God's business to be good and kind,
that is man's business. God's business is to be indomitable. And man's
business is essentially the same.—

This is, roughly, the American position today, as it was the position
of the Red Indian, when the white man came, and of the Aztec and of
the Peruvian.* As far as we can make out, neither Redskin nor Aztec
nor Inca had any conception of a "good" god. They conceived of implacable, indomitable Powers, which is very different. And that seems to
me the essential American position today. Of course the white American believes that man should behave in a kind and benevolent manner.
But this is a social belief and a social gesture, rather than an individual flow. The flow from the heart, the warmth of fellow-feeling which
has animated Europe and been the best of her humanity, individual,
spontaneous, flowing in thousands of little passionate currents often
conflicting, this seems unable to persist on the American soil. Instead,
you get the social creed of benevolence and uniformity, a mass will, and
an inward individual retraction, an isolation, an amorphous separateness like grains of sand, each grain isolated upon its own will, its own
indomitableness, its own implacability, its own unyielding, yet heaped
together with all the other grains. This makes the American mass the
easiest mass in the world to rouse, to move. And probably, under a long

stress, it would make it the most difficult mass in the world to hold
together.

The deep psychic change which we call the breaking of the heart,
the collapse of the flow of spontaneous warmth between a man and
his fellows, happens of course now all over the world. It seems to have
happened to Russia in one great blow.* It brings a people into a much
more complete social unison, for good or evil. But it throws them apart
in their private, individual emotions. Before, they were like cells in
a complex tissue, alive and functioning diversely in a vast organism
composed of family, clan, village, nation. Now, they are like grains of
sand, friable, heaped together in a vast inorganic democracy.

While the old sympathetic flow continues, there are violent hostilities
between people, but they are not secretly repugnant to one another. Once
the heart is broken, people become repulsive to one another, secretly, and
they develop social benevolence. They smell in each other's nostrils. It
has been said often enough of more primitive or old-world peoples, who
live together in a state of blind mistrust but also of close physical connection with one another, that they have no noses. They are so close, the flow
from body to body is so powerful, that they hardly smell one another, and
hardly are aware at all of offensive human odours that madden the new
civilisations. As it says in this novel: The American senses other people
by their sweat and their kitchens.*—By which he means, their repulsive
effluvia. And this is basically true. Once the blood-sympathy breaks,
and only the nerve-sympathy is left, human beings become secretly
intensely repulsive to one another, physically, and sympathetic only
mentally and spiritually. The secret physical repulsion between people
is responsible for the perfection of American "plumbing", American
sanitation, and American kitchens, utterly white-enamelled and anti-
septic. It is revealed in the awful advertisements such as those about
"halitosis", or bad breath. It is responsible for the American nausea
at coughing, spitting, or any of those things. The American townships
don't mind hideous litter of tin cans and paper and broken rubbish. But
they go crazy at the sight of human excrement.

And it is this repulsion from the physical neighbour that is now
coming up in the consciousness of the great democracies, in England,
America, Germany. The old flow broken, men could enlarge themselves
for a while in transcendentalism, Whitmanish "adhesiveness"* of the
social creature, noble supermen, lifted above the baser functions. For
the last hundred years man has been elevating himself above his "baser
functions" and posing around as a transcendentalist, a superman, a

perfect social being, a spiritual entity. And now, since the war,* the
collapse has come.

Man has no ultimate control of his own consciousness. If his nose
doesn't notice stinks, it just doesn't, and there's the end of it. If his nose
is so sensitive that a stink overpowers him, then again he's helpless. He
can't prevent his senses from transmitting and his mind from registering
what it does register.

And now, man has begun to be overwhelmingly conscious of the
repulsiveness of his neighbour, particularly of the physical repulsiveness. There it is, in James Joyce,* in Aldous Huxley,* in André Gide,
in modern Italian novels like *Parigi**—in all the very modern novels,
the dominant note is the repulsiveness, intimate physical repulsiveness
of human flesh. It is the expression of absolutely genuine experience.
What the young feel intensely, and no longer so secretly, is the extreme
repulsiveness of other people.

It is, perhaps, the inevitable result of the transcendental bodiless
brotherliness and social "adhesiveness" of the last hundred years. People
rose superior to their bodies, and soared along, till they had exhausted
their energy in this performance. The energy once exhausted, they fell,
with a struggling plunge, not down into their bodies again, but into the
cess-pools of the body.

The modern novel, the very modern novel, has passed quite away
from tragedy. An American novel like *Manhattan Transfer** has in it still
the last notes of tragedy, the sheer spirit of suicide. An English novel
like *Point Counter Point** has gone beyond tragedy into exacerbation,
and continuous nervous repulsion. Man is so nervously repulsive to
man, so screamingly, nerve-rackingly repulsive! This novel goes one
further. Man just *smells*, offensively and unbearably, not to be borne.
The human stink!

The inward revulsion of man away from man, which follows on
the collapse of the physical sympathetic flow, has a slowly increasing
momentum, a wider and wider swing. For a long time, the *social* belief
and benevolence of man towards man keeps pace with the secret physical repulsion of man away from man. But ultimately, inevitably, the
one outstrips the other. The benevolence exhausts itself, the repulsion
only deepens. The benevolence is external and extra-individual. But the
revulsion is inward and personal. The one gains over the other. Then
you get a gruesome condition, such as is displayed in this book.

The only motive power left is the sense of revulsion away from people,
the sense of the repulsiveness of the neighbour. It is a condition we are

rapidly coming to—a condition displayed by the intellectuals much
more than by the common people. Wyndham Lewis* gives a display of
the utterly repulsive effect people have on him, but he retreats into the
intellect to make his display. It is a question of manner and manners.
The effect is the same. It is the same exclamation: They stink! My God, 5
they stink!—

And in this process of recoil and revulsion, the affective consciousness
withers with amazing rapidity. Nothing I have ever read has astonished
me more than the "orphanage" chapters of this book.* There I realised
with amazement how rapidly the human psyche can strip itself of its 10
awarenesses and its emotional contacts, and reduce itself to a sub-brutal
condition of simple gross persistence. It is not animality—far from it.
Those boys are much less than animals. They are cold wills functioning
with a minimum of consciousness. The amount that they are *not* aware
of is perhaps the most amazing aspect of their character. They are 15
brutally and deliberately *unaware*. They have no hopes, no desires even.
They have even no will-to-exist, for existence even is too high a term.
They have a strange, stony will-to-persist, that is all. And they persist
by reaction, because they still feel the repulsiveness of each other, of
everything, even of themselves. 20

Of course the author exaggerates. The boy Lorry "always had his
nose in a book"*—and he must have got things out of the books. If he
had taken the intellectual line, like Mr Huxley or Mr Wyndham Lewis,
he would have harped on the intellectual themes, the essential feeling
being the same. But he takes the non-intellectual line, is in revulsion 25
against the intellect too, so we have the stark reduction to a persistent
minimum of the human consciousness. It is a minimum lower than
the savage, lower than the African Bushman.* Because it is a *willed*
minimum, sustained from inside by resistance, brute resistance against
any flow of consciousness except that of the barest, most brutal egois 30
tic self-interest. It is a phenomenon, and pre-eminently an American
phenomenon. But the flow of repulsion, inward physical revulsion of
man away from man, is passing over all the world. It is only perhaps in
America, and in a book such as this, that we see it most starkly revealed.

After the orphanage, the essential theme is repeated over a wider field. 35
The state of revulsion continues. The young Lorry is indomitable. You
can't destroy him. And at the same time, you can't catch him. He will
recoil from everything, and nothing on earth will make him have a
positive feeling, of affection or sympathy or connection. His mother?—
we see her in her decaying repulsiveness. He has a certain loyalty, because 40

she is his sort: it is part of his will-to-persist. But he must turn his back on her with a certain disgust.

The tragedian, like Theodore Dreiser and Sherwood Anderson,* still dramatises his defeat and is in love with himself in his defeated rôle. But the Lorry Goldsmith is in too deep a state of revulsion to dramatise himself. He almost deliberately finds himself repulsive too. And he goes on, just to see if he can hit the world without destroying himself. Hit the world not to destroy it, but to experience in himself how repulsive it is.

Kansas City, Beatrice,-Nebraska, Omaha, Salt Lake City, Portland,-Oregon, Los Angeles,* he finds them all alike, nothing, if not repulsive. He covers the great tracts of prairie, mountain, forest, coast-range, without seeing anything but a certain desert scaliness. His consciousness is resistant, shuts things out, and reduces itself to a minimum.

In the Y. M. C. A.* it is the same. He has his gang. But the last word about them is that they stink, their effluvia is offensive. He goes with women, but the thought of women is inseparable from the thought of sexual disease and infection. He thrills to the repulsiveness of it, in a terrified, perverted way. His associates—which means himself also—read Zarathustra and Spinosa, Darwin and Hegel.* But it is with a strange external, superficial mind that has no connection with the affective and effective self. One last desire he has—to write, to put down his condition in words. His will-to-persist is intellectual also. Beyond this, nothing.

It is a genuine book, as far as it goes, even if it is an objectionable one. It is, in psychic disintegration, a good many stages ahead of *Point Counter Point*. It reveals a condition that not many of us have reached, but towards which the trend of consciousness is taking us, all of us, especially the young. It is, let us hope, a *ne plus ultra*.* The next step is legal insanity, or just crime. The book is perfectly sane: yet two more strides, and it is criminal insanity. The style seems to me excellent, fitting the matter. It is sheer bottom-dog style, the bottom-dog mind expressing itself direct, almost as if it barked. That directness, that unsentimental and non-dramatised thoroughness of setting down the under-dog mind surpasses anything I know. I don't want to read any more books like this. But I am glad to have read this one, just to know what is the last word in repulsive consciousness, consciousness in a state of repulsion. It helps one to understand the world, and saves one the necessity of having to follow out the phenomenon of physical repulsion any further, for the time being.

INTRODUCTION TO THE GRAND
INQUISITOR, *BY F. M. DOSTOEVSKY*

Introd. to The Grand Inquisitor*

It is a strange experience, to examine one's reaction to a book over a period of years. I remember when I first read *The Brothers Karamazov*, in 1913,* how fascinated yet unconvinced it left me. And I remember Middleton Murry* saying to me: "Of course the whole clue to Dosto-evsky is in that Grand Inquisitor story." And I remember saying: "Why? It seems to me just rubbish."—

And it was true. The story seemed to me just a piece of showing-off: a display of cynical-satanical pose which was simply irritating. The cynical-satanical pose always irritated me, and I could see nothing else in that black-a-vised* Grand Inquisitor talking at Jesus at such length. I just felt it was all pose, he didn't really mean what he said, he was just showing-off in blasphemy.

Since then I have read the *Brothers Karamazov* twice, and each time found it more depressing because, alas, more drearily true to life.* At first it had been lurid romance. Now I read the *Inquisitor* once more, and my heart sinks right through my shoes. I still see a trifle of cynical-satanical showing-off. But under that, I hear the final and unanswerable criticism of Christ. And it is a deadly, devastating summing-up, unanswerable because borne out by the long experience of humanity. It is reality versus illusion, and the illusion was Jesus', while time itself retorts with the reality.

If there is any question: Who is the Grand Inquisitor?—then surely we must say it is Ivan* himself. And Ivan is the thinking mind of the human being in rebellion, thinking the whole thing out to the bitter end. As such he is, of course, identical with the Russian revolutionary of the thinking type. He is also, of course, Dostoevsky himself, in his thought-ful, as apart from his passional and inspirational self. Dostoevsky half hated Ivan. Yet after all, Ivan is the greatest of the three brothers, pivotal. The passionate Dmitri* and the inspired Alyosha* are, at last, only offsets to Ivan.

And we cannot doubt that the Inquisitor speaks Dostoevsky's own final opinion about Jesus. The opinion is, baldly, this: Jesus, you are inadequate. Men must correct you.—And Jesus in the end gives

127

the kiss of acquiescence to the Inquisitor, as Alyosha does to Ivan.
The two inspired ones recognise the inadequacy of their inspiration:
the thoughtful one has to accept the responsibility of a complete
adjustment.

5   We may agree with Dostoevsky or not, but we have to admit that his
criticism of Jesus is the final criticism, based on the experience of two
thousand years (he says fifteen hundred)* and on a profound insight
into the nature of mankind. Man can but be true to his own nature.
No inspiration whatsoever will ever get him permanently beyond his
10   limits.

And what are the limits? It is Dostoevsky's first profound question.
What are the limits to the nature, not of Man in the abstract, but of
men, mere men, everyday men?*

The limits are, says the Grand Inquisitor, three. Mankind in the
15   bulk can never be "free," because man on the whole makes three grand
demands on life, and cannot endure unless these demands are satisfied.

1. He demands bread: and not merely as foodstuff, but as a miracle,
   given from the hand of God.
2. He demands mystery, the sense of the miraculous in life.
20   3. He demands somebody to bow down to, and somebody before whom
   all men shall bow down.

These three demands, for miracle, mystery and authority prevent
men forever from being "free." They are man's "weakness." Only a few
men, the elect, are capable of abstaining from the absolute demand for
25   bread, for miracle, mystery, and authority. These are the strong, and
they must be as gods, to be able to be Christians fulfilling all the Christ-
demand. The rest, the millions and millions of men throughout time,
they are as babes or children or geese, they are too weak, "impotent,
vicious, worthless and rebellious"* even to be able to share out the
30   earthly bread, if it is left to them.

This, then, is the Grand Inquisitor's summing up of the nature of
mankind. The inadequacy of Jesus lies in the fact that Christianity is
too difficult for men, the vast mass of men. It could only be realised by
the few "saints" or heroes. For the rest, man is like a horse harnessed
35   to a load he cannot possibly pull. "Hadst Thou respectedest him less,
Thou wouldst have demanded less of him, and that would be nearer to
love, for his burden would be lighter."*

Christianity, then, is the ideal, but it is impossible. It is impossible
because it makes demands greater than the nature of man can bear. And

therefore, to get a livable, working scheme, some of the elect, such as the Grand Inquisitor himself, have turned round to "him", that other great Spirit, Satan, and have established Church and State on "him." For the Grand Inquisitor finds that to be able to live at all, mankind must be loved more tolerantly and more contemptuously than Jesus loved it, loved, for all that, more truly, since it is loved for itself, for what it is, and not for what it ought to be. Jesus loved mankind for what it ought to be, free and limitless. The Grand Inquisitor loves it for what it is, with all its limitations. And he contends his is the kinder love. And yet he says it is Satan. And Satan, he says at the beginning, means annihilation and not-being.*

As always in Dostoevsky, the amazing perspicacity is mixed with ugly perversity. Nothing is pure. His wild love for Jesus is mixed with perverse and poisonous hate of Jesus: his moral hostility to the devil is mixed with secret worship of the devil. Dostoevsky is always perverse, always impure, always an evil thinker and a marvellous seer.

Is it true that mankind demands, and will always demand miracle, mystery and authority? Surely it is true. Today, man gets his sense of the miraculous from science and machinery, radio, aeroplanes, vast ships, zeppelins,* poison gas, artificial silk: these things nourish man's sense of the miraculous as magic did in the past. But now, man is master of the mystery, there are no occult powers. The same with mystery: medicine, biological experiment, strange feats of the psychic people,* spiritualists, Christian scientists*—it is all mystery. And as for authority, Russia destroyed the Tsar to have Lenin* and the present mechanical despotism, Italy has the rationalised despotism of Mussolini,* and England is longing for a despot.*

Dostoevsky's diagnosis of human nature is simple and unanswerable. We have to submit, and agree that men are like that. Even over the question of sharing the bread, we have to agree that man is too weak, or vicious or something, to be able to do it. He has to hand the common bread over to some absolute authority, Tsar or Lenin, to be shared out. And yet the mass of men are *incapable* of looking on bread as a mere means of sustenance, by which man sustains himself for the purpose of true living, true life being the "heavenly bread". It seems a strange thing that men, the mass of men cannot understand that *life* is the great reality, that true living fills us with vivid life, "the heavenly bread," and earthly bread merely supports this. No, men cannot understand, never have understood that simple fact. They cannot see the distinction between bread, or property, money, and vivid life. They think that property and

money are the same thing as vivid life. Only the few, the potential heroes
or the "elect," can see the simple distinction. The mass *cannot* see it,
and will never see it.

Dostoevsky was perhaps the first to realise this devastating truth,
which Christ had not seen. A truth it is, none the less, and once recognised it will change the course of history. All that remains is for the
elect to take charge of the bread—the property, the money—and then
give it back to the masses as if it were really the gift of life. In this way,
mankind might live happily, as the Inquisitor suggests. Otherwise, with
the masses making the terrible mad mistake that money is life, and that
therefore no-one shall control the money, men shall be "free" to get
what they can, we are brought to a condition of competitive insanity
and ultimate suicide.

So far, well and good, Dostoevsky's diagnosis stands. But is it then
to betray Christ and turn over to Satan if the elect should at last realise
that instead of refusing Satan's three offers,* the heroic Christian must
now accept them. Jesus refused the three offers out of pride and fear: he
wanted to be greater than these, and "above" them. But we now realise,
no man, not even Jesus, is really "above" miracle, mystery, and authority.
The one thing that Jesus is truly above, is the confusion between money
and life. Money is not life, says Jesus, therefore you can ignore it and
leave it to the devil.

Money is not life, it is true. But ignoring money and leaving it to the
devil means handing over the great mass of men to the devil: for the
mass of men *cannot* distinguish between money and life. It is hard to
believe: certainly Jesus didn't believe it: and yet, as Dostoevsky and the
Inquisitor point out, it is so.

Well, and what then? Must we therefore go over to the devil? After
all, the whole of Christianity is not contained in the rejection of the
three temptations. The essence of Christianity is a love of mankind. If
a love of mankind entails accepting the bitter limitation of the mass of
men, their inability to distinguish between money and life, then accept
the limitation, and have done with it. Then take over from the devil
the money (or bread), the miracle, and the sword of Caesar, and, for
the love of mankind give back to men the bread, with its wonder, and
give them the miracle, the marvellous, and give them, in a hierarchy,
someone, some men, in higher and higher degrees, to bow down to. Let
them bow down, let them bow down *en masse*, for the mass, who do not
understand the difference between money and life, should always bow
down to the elect, who do.

And is that serving the devil? It is certainly not serving the spirit of annihilation and not-being. It is serving the great wholeness of mankind, and in that respect, it is Christianity. Anyhow it is the service of Almighty God, who made men what they are, limited and unlimited.

Where Dostoevsky is perverse is in his making the old, old wise governor of men a Grand Inquisitor. The recognition of the weakness of men has been a common trait in all great, wise rulers of peoples, from the Pharaohs and Darius* through the great patient Popes of the early Church* right down to the present day. They have known the weakness of men, and felt a certain tenderness. This is the spirit of all great government. But it was not the spirit of the Spanish Inquisition.* The Spanish Inquisition in 1500 was a new-fangled thing, peculiar to Spain, with her curious death-lust and her bullying; and, strictly, a Spanish-political instrument, not Catholic at all, but rabidly national. The Spanish Inquisition actually was diabolic. It could not have produced a Grand Inquisitor who put Dostoevsky's sad questions to Jesus. And the man who put those sad questions to Jesus could not possibly have been a Spanish Inquisitor. He could not possibly have burnt a hundred people in an *auto da fé*.* He would have been too wise and far-seeing.

So that in this respect, Dostoevsky showed his epileptic* and slightly-criminal perversity. The man who feels a certain tenderness for mankind in its weakness or limitation is not therefore diabolic. The man who realises that Jesus asked too much of the mass of men, in asking them to choose between earthly and heavenly bread, and to judge between good and evil, is not therefore satanic. Think how difficult it is to know the difference between good and evil! Why, sometimes it is evil to be good. And how is the ordinary man to understand that? He can't. The extraordinary men have to understand it for him. And is that going over to the devil? Or think of the difficulty in choosing between the earthly and heavenly bread. Lenin, surely a pure soul, rose to great power simply to give men—what? The earthly bread. And what was the result? Not only did they lose the heavenly bread, but even the earthly bread disappeared out of wheat-producing Russia.* It is most strange. And all the Socialists and the generous thinkers of today, what are they striving for? The same: to share out more evenly the earthly bread. Even *they*, who are practising Christians *par excellence*, cannot properly choose between the heavenly and earthly bread. For the poor, they choose the earthly bread: and once more the heavenly bread is lost: and once more, as soon as it is really chosen, the earthly bread begins to

disappear. It is a great mystery. But today, the most passionate believers in Christ believe that all you have to do is to struggle to give earthly bread (good houses, good sanitation etc) to the poor, and that is in itself the heavenly bread. But it isn't. Especially for the poor, it isn't. It is for
5   them the loss of heavenly bread. And the poor are the vast majority. Poor things, how everybody hates them today! For benevolence is a form of hate.

What then is the heavenly bread? Every generation must answer for itself. But the heavenly bread is life, is living. Whatever makes life vivid
10 and delightful is the heavenly bread. And the earthly bread must come as a by-product of the heavenly bread. The vast mass will never understand this. Yet it is the essential truth of Christianity and of life itself. The few will understand. Let them take the responsibility.

Again, the Inquisitor says that it is a weakness in men, that they must
15 have miracle, mystery and authority. But is it? Are they not bound up in our emotions, always and forever, these three elements of miracle, mystery and authority. If Jesus cast aside miracle in the Temptation, still there is miracle again in the Gospels. And if Jesus refused the earthly bread, still he said: "In my Father's house are many mansions."* And
20 for authority: "Why call ye me Lord, Lord, and do not the things which I say?"*

The thing Jesus was trying to do was to supplant physical emotions by moral emotions. So that earthly bread became, in a sense, immoral, as it is to many refined people today. The Inquisitor sees that this is the
25 mistake. The earthly bread must in itself be the miracle, and be bound up with the miracle.

And here, surely, he is right. Since man began to think and to feel vividly, seed-time and harvest have been the two great sacred periods of miracle, re-birth and rejoicing. Easter and harvest-home* are festivals
30 of the earthly bread, and they are festivals which go to the roots of the soul. For it is the earthly bread as a miracle, a yearly miracle. All the old religions saw it: the Catholic still sees it, by the Mediterranean. And this is not weakness. This is *truth*. The rapture of the Easter kiss,* in old Russia, is intimately bound up with the springing of the seed and the
35 first footstep of the new earthly bread. It is the rapture of the Easter kiss which makes the bread worth eating. It is the absence of the Easter kiss which makes the bolshevist* bread barren, dead. They eat dead bread, now.

The earthly bread is leavened with the heavenly bread. The heavenly
40 bread is life, is contact, and is consciousness. In sowing the seed man

has his contact with earth, with sun and rain: and *he must* not break the contact. In the awareness of the springing of the corn he has his ever-renewed consciousness of miracle, wonder, and mystery: the wonder of creation, procreation, and recreation, following the mystery of death and the cold grave. It is the grief of Holy Week* and the delight of Easter Sunday. And man must not, must not lose this supreme state of consciousness out of himself, or he has lost the best part of him. Again the reaping and the harvest are another contact, with earth and sun, a rich touch of the cosmos, a living stream of activity, and then the contact with harvesters, and the joy of harvest home. All this is life, life, it is the heavenly bread which we eat in the course of getting our earthly bread. Work is, or should be, our heavenly bread of activity, contact and consciousness.* All work that is not this, is anathema. True, the work is hard, there is the sweat of the brow. But what of it? In decent proportion, this is life. The sweat of the brow is the heavenly butter.

I think the older Egyptians understood this, in the course of their long and marvellous history. I think that probably, for thousands of years, the masses of the Egyptians were happy, in the hierarchy of the State.

Miracle and mystery run together, they merge. Then there is the third thing, authority. The word is bad: a policeman has authority, and no one bows down to him. The Inquisitor means: "that which men bow down to."* Well, they bowed down to Caesar, and they bowed down to Jesus. They will bow down, first, as the Inquisitor saw, to the one who has the power to control the bread.

The bread, the earthly bread, while it is being reaped and grown, it is life. But once it is harvested and stored, it becomes a commodity, it becomes riches. And then it becomes a danger. For men think, if they only possessed the hoard, they need not work: which means, really, they need not live. And that is the real blasphemy. For while we live we must live, we must not wither or rot inert.

So that ultimately men bow down to the man, or group of men who can and dare take over the hoard, the store of bread, the riches, to distribute it among the people again. The lords, the givers of bread. How profound Dostoevsky is when he says that the people will forget that it is their own bread which is being given back to them.* While they keep their own bread, it is not much better than stone to them*—inert possessions. But given back to them from the great Giver, it is divine once more, it has the quality of miracle to make it taste well in the mouth and in the belly.

Men bow down to the lord of bread, first and foremost. For, by knowing the difference between earthly and heavenly bread, he is able calmly
to distribute the earthly bread, and to give it, for the commonalty, the
heavenly taste which they can never give it. That is why, in a democracy,
5   the earthly bread loses its taste, the salt loses its savour,* and there is no
one to bow down to.

It is not man's weakness that he needs someone to bow down to. It
is his nature, and his strength, for it puts him into touch with far, far
greater life, than if he stood alone. All life bows to the sun. But the sun
10   is very far away to the common man. It needs someone to bring it to
him. It needs a lord: what the Christians call, one of the elect, to bring
the sun to the common man, and put the sun in his heart. The sight
of a true lord, a noble, a nature-hero puts the sun into the heart of the
ordinary man, who is no hero, and therefore cannot know the sun direct.
15   This is one of the real mysteries. As the Inquisitor says, the mystery
of the elect is one of the inexplicable mysteries of Christianity, just as the
lord, the natural lord among men, is one of the inexplicable mysteries
of humanity throughout time. We must accept the mystery, that's all.

But to do so is not diabolic.

20   And Ivan need not have been so tragic and satanic. He had made a
discovery about men, which was due to be made. It was the re-discovery
of a fact which was known universally almost till the end of the
eighteenth century, when the illusion of the perfectibility of men, of
all men, took hold of the imagination of the civilised nations. It was an
25   illusion. And Ivan has to make a re-statement of the old truth, that most
men *cannot* choose between good and evil, because it is so extremely difficult to know which is which, especially in crucial cases: and that most
men *cannot* see the difference between life-values and money-values,
they can only see money-values; even nice simple people who *live* by
30   the life-values, kind and natural, yet can only estimate value in terms of
money.* So let the specially-gifted few make the decision between good
and evil, and establish the life-values against the money-values. And let
the many accept the decision, with gratitude, and bow down to the few,
in the hierarchy. What is there diabolical or satanic in that? Jesus kisses
35   the Inquisitor: Thank you, you are right, wise old man!—Alyosha kisses
Ivan: Thank you, brother, you are right, you take a burden off me!—So
why should Dostoevsky drag in Inquisition and *autos da fé*, and Ivan
wind up so morbidly suicidal? Let them be glad they've found the truth
again.

SECTION B

INTRODUCTIONS TO TRANSLATIONS

INTRODUCTORY NOTE TO MASTRO-DON GESUALDO, BY GIOVANNI VERGA

Introductory Note.

Giovanni Verga was born in the city of Catania, in Sicily, in the year 1840. He died, in the same city, in January 1922. The family, which is of "gentle" blood, belongs to the village of Vizzini, in South Sicily, between Licodia and Syracuse. In this village Verga passed his youth, and here, apparently, is laid the scene of *Mastro-don Gesualdo*.

As a young man* Verga went to apply himself to literature in Florence and in Milan. His earlier novels, like *Eva*, *Tigre Reale*, and *Eros*, were more popular works, dealing with adultery and elegance in the cities.

His best work is Sicilian, blood and salt of Sicily. The first books were sketches:* excepting the very first, *Storia di Una Capinera*, which is a slight volume of pathos in letter form.* The best known of these volumes of sketches and short stories is the one entitled *Cavalleria Rusticana*,* after the first sketch, the one which provides the libretto for Mascagni's opera.*

Verga contemplated writing a series of novels—his Sicilian *Comédie Humaine*;*—about *I Vinti*: the Defeated. In 1881 Treves of Milan* published the first of this series: *I Malavoglia*.* It is a story of the defeat of poor fisherfolk on the sea-coast near Sicily, their defeat in the struggle for existence. Italian critics claim this as the greatest Italian novel, excepting only *I Promessi Sposi*.*

Mastro-don Gesualdo,* the second of the series, appeared in 1888. It deals with the defeat of the ambitious and wealthy peasant, Gesualdo himself.

Verga then began the third of the series: *La Duchessa di Leyra*:* rising in the social scale, to the Sicilian aristocracy. This novel was never finished. *Mastro-don Gesualdo* was Verga's last serious work.

Basing their judgment on the two novels, *I Malavoglia* and *Mastro-don Gesualdo*, together with the books of Sicilian sketches, practically all serious critics in Italy regard Giovanni Verga as the greatest of Italian writers of fiction: always excepting Manzoni.* This judgment is endorsed in most other countries, although D'Annunzio and Fogazzaro and even Papini* are so much better known.

But Verga, at his best, is not easy to read. His poignant southern irony and his elliptical style make him, in spite of his humble themes, too aristocratic a writer for the casual reader.

As far as the literary style goes, Verga wanted it unliterary, close to the spoken language. He wanted to abandon the Italian eloquence of his first books. These are his own words: "I had published several of my first novels. They went well: I was preparing others. One day, I don't know how, there came into my hand a sort of broadside, a halfpenny sheet sufficiently ungrammatical and disconnected, in which a sea-captain succinctly related all the vicissitudes through which his sailing-ship had passed. Seaman's language, short, without an unnecessary phrase. It struck me, and I read it again; it was what I was looking for, without definitely knowing it. Sometimes, you know, just a sign, an indication, is enough. It was a revelation.—"*

This is the style of Mastro-don Gesualdo. The locality is Verga's own southern Sicily. The village of San Giovanni is supposed to be his own village, Vizzini: the same as in the sketches of *Novelle Rusticane*, *Cavalleria Rusticana*, *Vagabondaggio*. The period is the generation before his own. The story opens about the year 1820. The revolution is the premature revolution of 1821.* This is the year of Isabella's birth. The epidemic of cholera is the famous calamity of 1837:* three years before Verga was born. He is writing, then, of the generation of his own father and mother: of people whom he knew, no doubt, as a child.

The title, Mastro-don Gesualdo, is an irony in itself. Mastro, *maestro,** is the form of address used to a workman. A true peasant is *Compare—compère.** A workman, such as a carpenter, a mason, a barber, is *Mastro*. A gentleman is *Don*. *Mastro-don* is therefore *Workman-gentleman.*—But *Don* is applied, half ironically, to footmen, to the sexton, and to such as are in direct attendance on the gentry.

NOTE ON GIOVANNI VERGA, IN LITTLE
NOVELS OF SICILY

Note on Giovanni Verga

Giovanni Verga, the Sicilian novelist and playwright, is surely the greatest writer of Italian fiction, after Manzoni.

Verga was born in Catania, Sicily, in 1840, and died in the same city,
at the age of eighty-two,* in January, 1922. As a young man he left Sicily   5
to work at literature and mingle with society in Florence and Milan, and
these two cities, especially the latter, claim a large share of his mature
years. He came back, however, to his beloved Sicily, to Catania, the
seaport under Etna,* to be once more Sicilian of the Sicilians and spend
his long declining years in his own place.   10

The first period of his literary activity was taken up with "Society"
and elegant love. In this phase he wrote the novels *Eros*, *Eva*, *Tigre Reale*,
Il Marito di Elena,* real Italian novels of love, intrigue and "elegance": a
little tiresome, but with their own depth. His fame, however, rests on his
Sicilian works, the two novels: *I Malavoglia* and *Mastro Don Gesualdo*,   15
and the various volumes of short sketches, *Vita dei Campi (Cavalleria
Rusticana)*, *Novelle Rusticane*, and *Vagabondaggio*, and then the earlier
work *Storia di Una Capinera*, a slight volume of letters between two
school-girls, somewhat sentimental and once very popular.

The libretto of *Cavalleria Rusticana*, the well-known opera, was   20
drawn from the first of the sketches in the volume *Vita dei Campi*.

As a man, Verga never courted popularity, any more than his work
courts popularity. He kept apart from all publicity, proud in his privacy:
so unlike D'Annunzio. Apparently he was never married.

In appearance, he was of medium height, strong and straight, with   25
thick white hair, and proud dark eyes, and a big reddish moustache: a
striking man to look at. The story *Across the Sea*,* playing as it does
between the elegant life of Naples and Messina,* and the wild places
of south-east Sicily, is no doubt autobiographic. The great misty city*
would then be Milan.   30

Most of these sketches are said to be drawn from actual life, from the
village where Verga lived and from which his family originally came.
The landscape will be more or less familiar to any one who has gone in
the train down the east coast of Sicily to Syracuse, past Etna and the

Plains of Catania and the Biviere, the Lake of Lentini,* on to the hills again. And anyone who has once known this land can never be quite free from the nostalgia for it, nor can he fail to fall under the spell of Verga's wonderful creation of it, at some point or other.

5 The stories belong to the period of Verga's youth. The King with the little Queen was King Francis of Naples, son of Bomba.* Francis and his little northern Queen* fled before Garibaldi* in 1860, so the story *So Much For the King** must be dated a few years earlier. And the autobiographical sketch *Across the Sea* must belong to Verga's first 10 manhood, somewhere about 1870. Verga was twenty years old when Garibaldi was in Sicily and the little drama of *Liberty** took place in the Village on Etna.

During the 'fifties and 'sixties, Sicily is said to have been the poorest place in Europe: absolutely penniless. A Sicilian peasant might live 15 through his whole life without ever possessing as much as a dollar, in hard cash. But after 1870 the great drift of Sicilian emigration set in, towards America. Sicilian young men came back from exile rich, according to standards in Sicily. The peasants began to buy their own land, instead of working on the half-profits system.* They had a reserve 20 fund for bad years. And the island in the Mediterranean began to prosper as it prospers still, depending on American resources. Only the gentry decline. The peasantry emigrate almost to a man, and come back as gentry themselves, American gentry.

Novelle Rusticane was first published in Turin, in 1883.

INTRODUCTION TO MASTRO-DON GESUALDO, *BY GIOVANNI VERGA*

INTRODUCTION

Giovanni Verga was born in the year 1840, and he died at the beginning
of 1922, so that he is almost as much of a contemporary as Thomas
Hardy. He seems more remote, because he left off writing many years
before he died. He was a Sicilian from one of the lonely little townships   5
in the south of the island, where his family were provincial gentlefolk.
But he spent a good deal of his youth in Catania, the city on the sea,
under Etna, and then he went to Naples,* the metropolis; for Sicily was
still part of the Bourbon kingdom of Naples.*

As a young man he lived for a time in Milan and Florence, the intel-   10
lectual centres, leading a more or less fashionable life and also practising journalism. A real provincial, he felt that the great world must
be conquered, that it must hold some vital secret. He was apparently a
great beau, and had a series of more or less distinguished love affairs,
like an Alfred de Vigny or a Maupassant.* In his early novels we see   15
him in this phase. *Tigre Reale*,* one of his most popular novels, is the
story of a young Italian's love for a fascinating but very enigmatical
(no longer so enigmatical) Russian countess of great wealth, married,
but living in distinguished isolation alone in Florence. The enigmatical
lady is, however, consumptive, and the end, in Sicily, is truly horrible,   20
in the morbid and deathly tone of some of Matilde Serao's novels.*
The southerners seem to go that way, macabre. Yet in Verga the savage,
manly tone comes through the morbidity, and we feel how he must have
loathed the humiliation of fashionable life and fashionable love affairs.
He kept it up, however, till after forty,* then he retired back to his own   25
Sicily, and shut himself up away from the world. He lived in aristocratic
isolation for almost another forty years,* and died in Catania, almost
forgotten.* He was a rather short, broad-shouldered man with a big red
moustache.

It was after he had left the fashionable world that he wrote his best   30
work. And this is no longer Italian, but Sicilian. In his Italian style, he
manages to get the rhythm of colloquial Sicilian, and Italy no longer
exists. Now Verga turns to the peasants of his boyhood, and it is they
who fill his soul. It is their lives that matter.

There are three books of Sicilian sketches and short stories,* very brilliant, and drenched with the atmosphere of Sicily. They are *Cavalleria
Rusticana*, *Novelle Rusticane*, and *Vagabondaggio*. They open out
another world at once, the southern, sun-beaten island whose every
outline is like pure memory. Then there is a small novel about a girl who
is condemned to a convent: *Storia di una Capinera*.* And finally, there
are the two great novels, *I Malavoglia* and *Mastro-don Gesualdo*. The
sketches in *Cavalleria Rusticana* had already established Verga's fame.
But it was *I Malavoglia* that was hailed as a masterpiece, in Paris as well
as in Italy. It was translated into French by Jose-Maria de Heredia,* and
after that, into English by an American lady.* The English translation,
which weakens the book very much, came out in America in the nineties,
under the title *The House by the Medlar Tree*, and can still be procured.

Speaking, in conversation, the other day about Giovanni Verga, in
Rome,* one of the most brilliant young Italian literary men said: There
is Verga, ah yes! *Some* of his things! But a thing like the *Storia di una
Capinera*, now, that is ridiculous.—And it was so obvious, the young
man thought all Verga a little ridiculous. Because Verga *doesn't* write
about lunatics and maniacs, like Pirandello,* therefore he is ridiculous. It
is the attitude of the smart young. They find Tolstoi ridiculous, George
Eliot* ridiculous, everybody ridiculous who is not "disillusioned."

The *Story of a Blackcap** is indeed sentimental and overloaded with
emotion. But so is Dickens' *Christmas Carol*, or *Silas Marner*.* They do
not therefore become ridiculous.

It is a fault in Verga, partly owing to the way he had lived his life, and
partly owing to the general tendency of all European literature of the
eighteen-sixties and thereabouts, to pour too much emotion, and especially too much pity, over the humble poor. Verga's novel *I Malavoglia*
is really spoilt by this, and by his exaggeration of the tragic fate of his
humble fisher-folk. But then it is characteristic of the southerner, that
when he has an emotion he has it wholesale. And the tragic fate of the
humble poor was the stunt of that day. *Les Misérables** stands as the great
monument to this stunt. The poor have lately gone rather out of favour,
so Hugo stands at a rather low figure,* and Verga hardly exists. But
when we have got over our reaction against the pity-the-poor stunt, we
shall see that there is a good deal of fun in Hugo, and that *I Malavoglia*
is really a very great picture of Sicilian sea-coast life, far more human
and *valid* than Victor Hugo's picture of Paris.

The trouble with the Italians is, they do tend to take over other
people's stunts and exaggerate them. Even when they invent a stunt

of their own, for some mysterious reason it *seems* second-hand. Victor Hugo's pity-the-poor was a real gallic gesture. Verga's pity-the-poor is just a bit too much of a good thing, and it doesn't seem to come *quite* spontaneously from him. He had been inoculated. Or he had reacted.

In his last novel, *Mastro-don Gesualdo*, Verga has slackened off in his   5
pity-the-poor. But he is still a realist, in the grim Flaubertian sense* of the word. A realism which, as every one now knows, has no more to do with reality than romanticism has. Realism is just one of the arbitrary views man takes of man. It sees us all as little ant-like creatures toiling against the odds of circumstance, and doomed to misery. It is a kind of   10
aeroplane view. It became the popular outlook, and so to-day we actually are, millions of us, little ant-like creatures toiling against the odds of circumstance, and doomed to misery; until we take a different view of ourselves. For man always becomes what he passionately thinks he is; since he is capable of becoming almost anything.   15

Mastro-don Gesualdo is a great realistic novel of Sicily, as *Madame Bovary* is a great realistic novel of France. They both suffer from the defects of the realistic method. I think the inherent flaw in *Madame Bovary*—though I hate talking about flaws in great books; but the charge is really against the realistic method—is that individuals like Emma and   20
Charles Bovary* are too insignificant to carry the full weight of Gustave Flaubert's profound sense of tragedy; or, if you will, of tragic futility. Emma and Charles Bovary are two ordinary persons, chosen because they *are* ordinary. But Flaubert is by no means an ordinary person. Yet he insists on pouring his own deep and bitter tragic consciousness   25
into the little skins of the country doctor and his dissatisfied wife. The result is a certain discrepancy, even a certain dishonesty in the attempt to be too honest. By choosing *ordinary* people as the vehicles of an extraordinarily passionate feeling of bitterness, Flaubert loads the dice, and wins by a trick which is sure to be found out against him.   30

Because a great soul like Flaubert's has a pure satisfaction and joy in its own consciousness, even if the consciousness be only of ultimate tragedy or misery. But the very fact of being so marvellously and vividly *aware*, awake, as Flaubert's soul was, is in itself a refutation of the all-is-misery doctrine. Since the human soul has supreme joy in true, vivid   35
consciousness. And Flaubert's soul has this joy. But Emma Bovary's soul does not, poor thing, because she was deliberately chosen because her soul was ordinary. So Flaubert cheats us a little, in his doctrine, if not in his art. And his art is biased by his doctrine as much as any artist's is.   40

The same is true of *Mastro-don Gesualdo*. Gesualdo is a peasant's son, who becomes rich in his own tiny town through his own force and sagacity. He is allowed the old heroic qualities of force and sagacity. Even Emma Bovary has a certain extraordinary female energy of restlessness
5   and unsatisfied desire. So that both Flaubert and Verga allow their heroes something of the hero, after all. The one thing they deny them is the consciousness of heroic effort.

Now Flaubert and Verga alike were aware of their own heroic effort to be truthful, to show things as they are. It was the heroic impulse which
10   made them write their great books. Yet they deny to their protagonists any inkling of the heroic effort. It is in this sense that Emma Bovary and Gesualdo Motta are "ordinary." Ordinary people don't have much sense of heroic effort in life; and by the heroic effort we mean that instinctive fighting for more life to come into being, which is a basic
15   impulse in more men than we like to admit; women too. Or it used to be. The discrediting of the heroic effort has almost extinguished that effort in the young, hence the appalling "flatness" of their lives.* It is the parents' fault. Life without the heroic effort, and without *belief* in the subtle, life-long validity of the heroic impulse, is just stale, flat and
20   unprofitable.* As the great realistic novels will show you.

Gesualdo Motta has the makings of a hero. Verga had to grant him something. I think it is in *Novelle Rusticane* that we find the long sketch or story of the little fat peasant* who has become enormously rich by grinding his labourers and bleeding the Barons. It is a marvellous story,
25   reeling with the hot atmosphere of Sicily, and the ironic fatalism of the Sicilians. And that little fat peasant must have been an actual man whom Verga knew—Verga wasn't good at inventing, he always had to have a core of actuality—and who served as the idea-germ for Gesualdo. But Gesualdo is much more attractive, much nearer the true hero. In fact,
30   with all his energy and sagacity *and* his natural humaneness, we don't see how Gesualdo quite escaped the heroic consciousness. The original little peasant, the prototype, was a mere frog, a grabber and nothing else. He had none of Gesualdo's large humaneness. So that Verga brings Gesualdo much nearer to the hero, yet denies him still any spark of the
35   heroic consciousness, any spark of awareness of a greater impulse within him. Men naturally have this spark, if they are the tiniest bit uncommon. The curious thing is, the moment you deny the spark, it dies, and then the heroic impulse dies with it.

It is probably true that, since the extinction of the pagan gods, the
40   countries of the Mediterranean have never been aware of the heroic impulse in themselves, and so it has died down very low, in them. In

Sicily, even now, and in the remoter Italian villages, there is what we call a low level of life, appalling. Just a squalid, unimaginative, heavy, petty-fogging, grubby sort of existence, without light or flame. It is the absence of the heroic awareness, the heroic hope.

The northerners have got over the death of the old Homeric idea   5
of the hero, by making the hero self-conscious, and a hero by virtue of suffering and awareness of suffering. The Sicilians may have little spasms of this sort of heroic feeling, but it never lasts. It is not natural to them.

The Russians carry us to great lengths of introspective heroism.   10
They escape the non-heroic dilemma of our age by making every man his own introspective hero. The merest scrub of a pickpocket is so phenomenally aware of his own soul, that we are made to bow down before the imaginary coruscations of suffering and sympathy that go on inside him. So is Russian literature.   15

Of course, your soul will coruscate with suffering and sympathy, if you think it does: since the soul is capable of anything, and is no doubt full of unimaginable coruscations which far-off future civilizations will wake up to. So far, we have only lately wakened up to the sympathy-suffering coruscation, so we are full of it. And that is why the Russians   20
are so popular. No matter how much of a shabby little slut you may be, you can learn from Dostoevsky and Tchekov* that you have got the most tender, unique soul on earth, coruscating with sufferings and impossible sympathies. And so you may be most vastly important to yourself, introspectively. Outwardly, you will say: Of course I'm an   25
ordinary person, like everybody else.—But your very saying it will prove that you think the opposite: namely, that everybody on earth is ordinary, *except* yourself.

This is our northern way of heroism, up to date. The Sicilian hasn't yet got there. Perhaps he never will. Certainly he was nowhere near it in   30
Gesualdo Motta's day, the mediaeval Sicilian day of the middle of the last century, before Italy existed, and Sicily was still part of the Bourbon kingdom of Naples, and about as remote as the kingdom of Dahomey.*

The Sicilian has no soul, except that funny little naked man who hops on hot bricks, in purgatory, and howls to be prayed out into paradise;   35
and is in some mysterious way an *alter ego,** my me beyond the grave. This is the catholic soul, and there is nothing to do about it but to pay, and get it prayed into paradise.*

For the rest, in our sense of the word, the Sicilian doesn't have any soul. He can't be introspective, because his consciousness, so to speak,   40
doesn't have any inside to it. He can't look inside himself, because

he is, as it were, solid. When Gesualdo is tormented by mean people, atrociously, all he says is: I've got bitter in my mouth.*—And when he is dying, and has some awful tumour inside, he says: It is all the bitterness I have known, swelled up inside me.*—That is all: a physical

5   fact! Think what even Dmitri Karamazov* would have made of it! And Dmitri Karamazov doesn't go half the lengths of the other Russian soul-twisters. Neither is he half the man Gesualdo is, although he may be much more "interesting," if you like soul-twisters.

In *Mastro-don Gesualdo* you have, in a sense, the same sort of tragedy

10   as in the Russians, yet anything more un-Russian could not be imagined. Un-Russian almost as Homer. But Verga will have gods neither above nor below.

The Sicilians to-day are supposed to be the nearest descendants of the classic Greeks, and the nearest thing to the classic Greeks in life and

15   nature. And perhaps it is true. Like the classic Greeks, the Sicilians have no insides, introspectively speaking. But, alas, outside they have no busy gods. It is their great loss. Because Jesus is to them only a wonder-man who was killed by foreigners and villains, and who will help you to get out of Hell, perhaps.

20   In the true sense of the word, the Sicily of Gesualdo is drearily godless. It needs the bright and busy gods outside. The inside gods, gods who have to be inside a man's soul, are distasteful to people who live in the sun. Once you get to Ceylon,* you see that even Buddha* is purely an outside god, purely objective to the natives. They have no conception

25   of his being inside themselves.

It was the same with the Greeks, it is the same to-day with the Sicilians. They aren't *capable* of introspection and the inner Jesus. They leave it all to us and the Russians.

Save that he has no bright outside gods, Gesualdo is very like an

30   old Greek: the same energy and quickness of response, the same vivid movement, the same ambition and real passion for wealth, the same easy conscience, the same queer openness, without ever really openly committing himself, and the same ancient astuteness. He is prouder, more fearless, more frank, yet more subtle than an Italian; more on his

35   own. He is like a Greek or a traditional Englishman, in the way he just goes ahead by himself. And in that, he is Sicilian, not Italian.

And he is Greek above all, in having no inside, in the Russian sense of the word.

The tragedy is, he has no heroic gods or goddesses to fix his imagi-

40   nation. He has nothing, not even a country. Even his Greek ambitious

desire to come out splendidly, with a final splendid look of the thing
and a splendid final ring of words, turns bitter. The Sicilian aristocracy
was an infinitely more paltry thing than Gesualdo himself.

It is the tragedy of a man who is forced to be ordinary, because all
visions have been taken away from him. It is useless to say he should have   5
had the northern inwardness and the Russianizing outlet. You might as
well say the tall and reckless asphodel* of Magna Graecia* should learn
to be a snowdrop. "I'll learn you to be a toad!"*

But a book exists by virtue of the vividness, the aliveness and powerful
pulsing of its life-portrayal, and not by virtue of the pretty or unpretty   10
things it portrays. *Mastro-don Gesualdo* is a great undying book, one of
the great novels of Europe. If you cannot read it because it is *à terre*,* and
has neither nervous uplift nor nervous hysteria, you condemn yourself.

As a picture of Sicily in the middle of the last century, it is marvellous.
But it is a picture done from the inside. There are no picture-postcard   15
effects. The thing is a heavy, earth-adhering organic whole. There is
nothing showy.

Sicily in the middle of the last century was an incredibly poor, lost,
backward country. Spaniards, Bourbons,* one after the other they had
killed the life in her. The Thousand and Garibaldi* had not risen over   20
the horizon, neither had the great emigration to America begun, nor
the great return, with dollars and a newish outlook. The mass of the
people were poorer even than the poor Irish of the same period, and save
for climate, their conditions were worse. There were some great and
wealthy landlords, dukes and barons still. But they lived in Naples, or   25
in Palermo* at the nearest. In the country, there were no roads at all for
wheeled vehicles, consequently no carts, nothing but donkeys and pack-
mules on the trails, or a sick person in a mule litter, or armed men on
horseback, or men on donkeys. The life was mediaeval as in Russia. But
whereas the Russia of 1850 is a vast flat country with a most picturesque   30
life of nobles and serfs* and soldiers, open and changeful, Sicily is a
most beautiful country, but hilly, steep, shut-off, and abandoned, and
the life is, or was, grimly unpicturesque in its dead monotony. The great
nobles shunned the country, as in Ireland.* And the people were sunk in
bigotry, suspicion, and gloom. The life of the villages and small towns   35
was of an incredible spiteful meanness, as life always is when there is not
enough change and fresh air; and the conditions were sordid, dirty, as
they always are when the human spirits sink below a certain level. It is
not in such places that one looks for passion and colour. The passion and
colour in Verga's stories come in the villages near the east coast, where   40

there is change since Ulysses sailed that way.* Inland, in the isolation, the lid is on, and the intense watchful malice of neighbours is infinitely worse than any police system, infinitely more killing to the soul and the passionate body.

5   The picture is a bitter and depressing one, while ever we stay in the dense and smelly little streets. Verga wrote what he knew and felt. But when we pass from the habitations of sordid man, into the light and marvellous open country, then we feel at once the undying beauty of Sicily and the Greek world, a morning beauty, that has something

10   miraculous in it, of purple anemones and cyclamens, and sumach* and olive-trees, and the place where Persephone* came above-world, bringing back spring.

And we must remember that eight-tenths of the population of Sicily is maritime or agricultural, always has been, and therefore practically

15   the whole day-life of the people passes in the open, in the splendour of the sun and the landscape, and the delicious, elemental aloneness of the old world. This is a great *unconscious* compensation. But what a compensation, after all!—even if you don't know you've got it; as even Verga doesn't quite. But he puts it in, all the same, and you can't read

20   *Mastro-don Gesualdo* without feeling the marvellous glow and glamour of Sicily, and the people throbbing inside the glow and the glamour like motes in a sunbeam. Out of doors, in a world like that, what is misery, after all! The great freshness keeps the men still fresh. It is the women in the dens of houses who deteriorate most.

25   And perhaps it is because the outside world is so lovely, that men in the Greek regions have never become introspective. They have not been driven to *that* form of compensation. With them, life pulses outwards, and the positive reality is outside. There is no turning inwards. So man becomes purely objective. And this is what makes the Greeks so

30   difficult to understand: even Socrates.* We don't understand him. We just translate him into another thing, our own thing. He is so peculiarly *objective* even in his attitude to the soul, that we could never get him if we didn't translate him into something else, and thus "make him our own."

35   And the glorious objectivity of the old Greek world still persists, old and blind now, among the southern Mediterranean peoples. It is this decayed objectivity, not even touched by mediaeval mysticism, which makes a man like Gesualdo so simple, and yet so incomprehensible to us. We are apt to see him as just meaningless, just stupidly and

40   meaninglessly getting rich, merely acquisitive. Yet, at the same time,

we see him so patient with his family, with the tisical Bianca,* with his daughter,* so humane, and yet so desperately enduring. In affairs, he has an unerring instinct, and he is a superb fighter. Yet in life, he seems to do the wrong thing every time. It is as if, in his life, he has no driving motive at all.

He should, of course, by every standard we know, have married Diodata. Bodily, she was the woman he turned to. She bore him sons. Yet he married her to one of his own hired men,* to clear the way for his, Gesualdo's, marriage with the noble but merely pathetic Bianca Trao. And after he was married to Bianca, who was too weak for him, he still went back to Diodata, and paid her husband to accommodate him. And it never occurs to him to have any of this on his conscience. Diodata has his sons in her house, but Gesualdo, who has only one daughter by the frail Bianca, never seems to interest himself in his boys at all. There is the most amazing absence of a certain range of feeling in the man, especially feeling about himself. It is as if he had no inside. And yet we see that he most emphatically has. He has a warm and attractive presence. And he suffers bitterly, bitterly. Yet he blindly brings most of his sufferings on himself, by doing the wrong things to himself.

The idea of living for love is just entirely unknown to him, unknown as if it were a new German invention. So is the idea of living for sex. In that respect, woman is just the female of the species to him, as if he were a horse, that jumps in heat, and forgets. He never really thinks about women. Life means something else to him.

But what? What? It is so hard to see. Does he just want to *get on,** in our sense of the word? No, not even that. He has not the faintest desire to be mayor, or podesta,* or that sort of thing. But he does make a duchess of his daughter. Yes, Mastro-don Gesualdo's daughter is a duchess of very aristocratic rank.

And what then? Gesualdo realizes soon enough that she is not happy. And now he is an elderly, dying man, and the impetuosity of his manhood is sinking, he begins to wonder what he should have done. What was it all about?

What *did* life mean to him, when he was in the impetuous tide of his manhood? What was he unconsciously driving at? Just blindly at nothing? Was that why he put aside Diodata, and brought on himself all that avalanche of spite, by marrying Bianca? Not that his marriage was a failure. Bianca was his wife, and he was unfailingly kind to her, fond of her, her death was bitter to him. Not being under the tyrannical

sway of the idea of "love," he could be fond of his wife, and he could be
fond of Diodata, and he needn't get into a stew about any of them.

But what was he under the sway of? What was he blindly driving
at? We ask, and we realize at last that it was the old Greek impulse
towards splendour and self-enhancement. Not ambition, in our sense of
the word, but something more personal, more individual. That which
swayed Achilles and swayed Pericles and Alcibiades:* the passionate
desire for individual splendour. We now call it vanity. But in the countries of the sun, where the whole outdoors consists in the splendour of
the sun, it is a real thing to men, to try to make themselves splendid and
like suns.

Gesualdo was blindly repeating, in his own confused way, the magnificent old gesture. But ours is not the age for splendour. We have
changed all that.* So Gesualdo's life amounts to nothing. Yet not, as far
as I can see, to any less than the lives of the "humble" Russians. At least
he lived his life. If he thought too little about it, he helps to counter-
balance all those people who think too much. Because he never has any
"profound" talk, he is not less a man than Myshkin* or a Karamazov.
He is possibly not more a man, either. But to me he is less distasteful.
And because his life all ends in a mistake, he is not therefore any more
meaningless than Tolstoy himself. And because he simply has no idea
whatsoever of "salvation," whether his own or anybody else's, he is not
therefore a fool. Any more than Hector* and Achilles were fools; for
neither of them had any idea of salvation.

The last forlorn remnant of the Greeks, blindly but brightly seeking
for splendour and self-enhancement, instead of salvation, and choosing
to surge blindly on, instead of retiring inside himself to twist his soul
into knots, Gesualdo still has a lovable glow in his body, the very reverse
of the cold marsh-gleam of Myshkin. His life ends in a tumour of
bitterness. But it was a life, and I would rather have lived it than the
life of Tolstoy's Pierre,* or the life of any Dostoevskian hero. It was not
Gesualdo's fault that the bright objective gods are dead, killed by envy
and spite. It was not his fault that there was no real splendour left in
our world for him to choose, once he had the means.

BIOGRAPHICAL NOTE TO MASTRO-DON GESUALDO, *BY GIOVANNI VERGA*

BIOGRAPHICAL NOTE.

Giovanni Verga was born in Catania, the sea-coast city of East Sicily, in 1840, and died in the same town in January 1922. The family, however, owned lands at Vizzini, in Southern Sicily, and here Verga spent much of his time, his youth, and again periods in the second half of his life. 5
In or around Vizzini is laid the scene of *Mastro-don Gesualdo*.

As a young man, Verga lived in Milan and Florence, writing novels and doing some journalism. To this period belong *Eva*, *Tigre Reale*, *Eros*, his more vulgarly-popular novels. In 1880 he returned finally to Sicily, and began his best work, when he was forty years old. 10

He contemplated writing a series of novels about *I Vinti* (the Defeated), in the manner of Hugo or Zola. In 1881 Treves of Milan published the first book of this series: *I Malavoglia*. It is a long novel about the "defeat" of a poor fisher family on the sea-coast near Catania. It was hailed as a masterpiece in Italy and Paris. The second 15 novel of the series is *Mastro-don Gesualdo*, rising in the social scale, but still "defeat." It was published in 1888. From that time till his death, apparently, Verga worked in fits at the manuscript of the third novel of the "defeated" series: *La Duchessa di Leyra*. He never finished it, probably because he had lost all sympathy with the aristocracy of his 20 day, and what he wrote of it has never been published.

The more serious Italian critics regard Verga as the best Italian novelist after Manzoni, and *I Malavoglia* as the best Italian novel after *I Promessi Sposi*. The Italians, however, do not read Verga, and the world knows him as the librettist of the rather trivial opera: *Cavalleria Rusti-* 25 *cana*. So much for the world.

Verga wrote Italian, not Sicilian dialect. But he deliberately made his style, "unliterary," trying to give it the impulsive, non-logical, broken rhythm of peasant speech.

The story of *Mastro-don Gesualdo* opens about 1820, twenty years 30 before Verga's own birth. The revolution is the premature revolution of 1821, the year of Isabella's birth. The epidemic of cholera is the famous calamity of 1837, three years before Verga's own birth.

The title *Mastro-don* is an irony in itself. *Mastro*, which is the same as *Maestro*, is addressed to any adult workman or craftsman. A peasant is addressed as *Compare*, the same as the French *Compère*. A gentleman is *Don*. *Mastro-don*, then, is jeering: *Sir-workman!* But *Don* is also applied by the peasants half ironically to footmen, barbers, sexton, anyone who doesn't really work.

TRANSLATOR'S PREFACE TO CAVALLERIA RUSTICANA, BY GIOVANNI VERGA

TRANSLATOR'S PREFACE.

Cavalleria Rusticana is in many ways the most interesting of the Verga books. The volume of short stories under this title* appeared in 1880, when the author was forty years old, and when he had just "retired" from the world.*

The Verga family owned land around Vizzini, a biggish village in southern Sicily; and here, in and around Vizzini, the tragedies of Turiddu and La Lupa and Jeli* take place. But it was only in middle life that the drama of peasant passion really made an impression on Giovanni Verga. His earlier imagination, naturally, went out into the great world.

The family of the future author lived chiefly at Catania, the sea-port of east Sicily, under Etna. And Catania was really Verga's home town, just as Vizzini was his home village.

But as a young man of twenty he already wanted to depart into the bigger world of "the Continent", as the Sicilians called the mainland of Italy. It was the Italy of 1860, the Italy of Garibaldi,* and the new era. Verga seems to have taken little interest in politics. He had no doubt the southern idea of himself as a gentleman and an aristocrat, beyond politics. And he had the ancient southern thirst for show, for lustre, for glory, a desire to figure grandly among the first society of the world. His nature was proud and unmixable. At the same time, he had the southern passionate yearning for tenderness and generosity. And so he ventured into the world, without much money; and, in true southern fashion, he was dazzled. To the end of his days he was dazzled by elegant ladies in elegant equipages: one sees it, amusingly, in all his books.

He was a handsome man, by instinct haughty and reserved: because, partly, he was passionate and emotional, and did not choose to give himself away. A true provincial, he had to try to enter the *beau monde*.* He lived by journalism, more or less: certainly the Vizzini lands would not keep him in affluence. But still, in his comparative poverty, he must enter the *beau monde*.

He did so: and apparently, with a certain success. And for nearly twenty years he lived in Milan, in Florence, in Naples,* writing, and

163

imagining he was fulfilling his thirst for glory by having love-affairs with elegant ladies:* most elegant ladies, as he assures us.

To this period belong the curiously unequal novels of the city world: *Eva, Tigre Reale, Eros.* They are interesting, alive, bitter, somewhat unhealthy, smelling of the seventies and of the Paris of the Goncourts,* and, in some curious way, abortive. The man had not found himself. He was in his wrong element, fooling himself and being fooled by show, in a true Italian fashion.

Then, towards the age of forty, came the recoil, and the *Cavalleria Rusticana* volume is the first book of the recoil. It was a recoil away from the *beau monde* and the "Continent", back to Sicily, to Catania, to the peasants. Verga never married: but he was deeply attached to his own family. He lived in Catania, with his sister.* His brother, or brother-in-law, who had looked after the Vizzini property, was ill. So for the first time in his life Giovanni Verga had to undertake the responsibility for the family estate* and fortune. He had to go to Vizzini and more or less manage the farm-work—at least keep an eye on it. He said he hated the job, that he had no capacity for business, and so on. But we may be sure he managed very well. And certainly from this experience he gained his real fortune, his genuine sympathy with peasant life, instead of his spurious sympathy with elegant ladies. His great books all followed *Cavalleria Rusticana*: and *Mastro-Don Gesualdo* and the *Novelle Rusticane* (Little Novels of Sicily) and most of the sketches have their scenes laid in or around Vizzini.

So that *Cavalleria Rusticana* marks a turning-point in the man's life. Verga still looks back to the city elegance, and makes such a sour face over it, it is really funny. The sketch he calls *Fantasticheria* (Caprice)* and the last story in the book, *Il Come, il Quando, et il Perché* (The How, When, and Wherefore)* both deal with the elegant little lady herself. The sketch *Caprice* we may take as autobiographical—the story not entirely so. But we have enough data to go on.

The elegant little lady is the same, pretty, spoilt, impulsive, emotional, but without passion. The lover, Polidori,* is only half-sketched. But evidently he is a passionate man who *thinks* he can play at love and then is mortified to his very soul because he finds it is only a game. The tone of mortification is amusingly evident both in the sketch and in the story. Verga is profoundly and everlastingly offended with the little lady, with all little ladies, for not taking him absolutely seriously as an amorous male, when all the time he doesn't quite take himself seriously, and doesn't take the little lady seriously at all.

Nevertheless, the moment of sheer roused passion is serious in the man: and apparently not so in the woman. Each time the moment comes, it involves the whole nature of the man and does not involve the whole nature of the woman: she still clings to her social safe-guards. It is the difference between a passionate nature and an emotional nature. But then the man goes out deliberately to make love to the emotional elegant woman who is truly social and not passionate. So he has only himself to blame if his passionate nose is out of joint.

It is most obviously out of joint. His little picture of the elegant little lady jingling her scent-bottle* and gazing in nervous anxiety for the train from Catania which will carry her away from Aci-Trezza* and her too-intense lover, back to her light, gay, secure world on the mainland is one of the most amusingly biting things in the literature of love. How glad she must have been to get away from him! And how bored she must have been by his preaching the virtues of the humble poor, holding them up before her to make her feel small. We may be sure she didn't feel small, only nervous and irritable. For apparently she had no deep warmth or generosity of nature.

So Verga recoiled to the humble poor, as we see in his "Caprice" sketch. Like a southerner, what he did he did wholesale. Floods of savage and tragic pity he poured upon the humble fisher-folk of Aci-Trezza, whether they asked for it or not;—partly to spite the elegant little lady. And this particular flood spreads over the whole of his long novel concerning the fisherfolk of Aci-Trezza: *I Malavoglia*. It is a great novel, in spite of the pity: but always in spite of it.

In *Cavalleria Rusticana*, however, Verga had not yet come to the point of letting loose his pity. He is still too much and too profoundly offended, as a passionate male. He recoils savagely away from the sophistications of the city life of elegant little ladies, to the peasants in their most crude and simple, almost brute-like aspect.

When one reads, one after the other, the stories of Turiddu, La Lupa, Jeli, Brothpot, Rosso Malpelo,* one after the other, stories of crude killing, it seems almost too much, too crude, too violent, too much a question of mere brutes.

As a matter of fact, the judgment is unjust. Turiddu is not a brute: neither is Alfio.* Both are men of sensitive and even honourable nature. Turiddu knows he is wrong, and would even let himself be killed, he says, but for the thought of his old mother. The elegant Maria and her Erminia* are never so sensitive and direct in expressing themselves; nor so frankly warm-hearted.

As for Jeli, who could call him a brute? or Nanni?* or Brothpot? They are perhaps not brutal enough. They are too gentle and forbearing, too delicately naïve. And so grosser natures trespass on them unpardonably; and the revenge flashes out.

5   His contemporaries abused Verga for being a realist of the Zola school.* The charge is unjust. The base of the charge against Zola is that he made his people too often merely physical-functional arrangements, physically and materially functioning without any "higher" nature. The charge against Zola is often justifiable. It is completely justifiable against

10   the earlier D'Annunzio.* In fact, the Italian tends on the one hand to be this creature of physical-functional activity and nothing else, spasmodically sensual and materialist; hence the violent Italian outcry against the portrayal of such creatures, and D'Annunzio's speedy transition to neurotic Virgins of the Rocks* and ultra-refinements.

15   But Verga's people are always people in the purest sense of the word. They are not intellectual, but then neither was Hector nor Ulysses intellectual. Verga, in his recoil, mistrusted everything that smelled of sophistication. He had a passion for the most naïve, the most unsophisticated manifestation of human nature. He was not seeking the brute,

20   the animal man, the so-called cave man. Far from it. He knew already too well that the brute and the cave-man lie quite near under the skin of the ordinary successful man of the world. There you have the predatory cave-man of vulgar imagination, thinly hidden under expensive cloth.

What Verga's soul yearned for was the purely naïve human being, in

25   contrast to the sophisticated. It seems as if Sicily, in some way, under all her amazing forms of sophistication and corruption, still preserves some flower of pure human candour: the same thing that fascinated Theocritus. Theocritus was an Alexandrine courtier,* singing from all his "musk and insolence"* of the pure idyllic Sicilian shepherds. Verga

30   is the Theocritus of the nineteenth century, born among the Sicilian shepherds, and speaking of them in prose more sadly than Theocritus, yet with some of the same eternal Sicilian dawn-freshness in his vision. It is almost bitter to think that Rosso Malpelo must often have looked along the coast and seen the rocks that the Cyclops flung at Ulysses;* and

35   that Jeli must some time or other have looked to the yellow temple-ruins of Girgenti.*

Verga was fascinated, after his mortification in the *beau monde*, by pure naïveté and by the spontaneous passion of life, that spurts beyond all convention or even law. Yet as we read, one after the other, of

40   these betrayed husbands killing the co-respondents, it seems a little

mechanical. Alfio, Jeli, Brothpot, Gramigna* ending their life in prison: it seems a bit futile and hopeless, mechanical again.

The fault is partly Verga's own, the fault of his own obsession. He felt himself in some way deeply mortified, insulted in his ultimate sexual or male self, and he enacted over and over again the drama of revenge. We think to ourselves, ah, how stupid of Alfio, of Jeli, of Brothpot, to have to go killing a man and getting themselves shut up in prison for life, merely because the man had committed adultery with their wives. Was it worth it? Was the wife worth one year of prison, to a man, let alone a lifetime?

We ask the question with our reason, and with our reason we answer No! Not for a moment was any of these women worth it. Nowadays we have learnt more sense, and we let her go her way. So the stories are too old-fashioned.

And again, it was not for love of their wives that Jeli and Alfio and Brothpot killed the other man. It was because people talked. It was because of the fiction of "honour". —We have got beyond all that.

We are so much more reasonable. All our life is so much more reasoned and reasonable. *Nous avons changé tout cela.**

And yet, as the years go by, one wonders if mankind is so radically changed. One wonders whether reason, sweet reason, has really changed us, or merely delayed or diverted our reactions. Are Alfio and Jeli and Gramigna utterly out of date, a thing superseded for ever? Or are they eternal?

Is man a sweet and reasonable creature? Or is he, basically, a passional phenomenon? Is man a phenomenon on the face of the earth, or a rational consciousness? Is human behaviour to be reasonable, throughout the future, reasoned and rational?—or will it always display itself in strange and violent phenomena?

Judging from all experience, past and present, one can only decide that human behaviour is ultimately one of the natural phenomena, beyond all reason. Part of the phenomenon, for the time being, is human reason, the control of reason, and the power of the Word.* But the Word and the reason are themselves only part of the coruscating phenomenon of human existence, they are, so to speak, one rosy shower from the rocket, which gives way almost instantly to the red shower of ruin or the green shower of despair.

Man is a phenomenon on the face of the earth. But the phenomena have their laws. One of the laws of the phenomenon called a human being is that, hurt this being mortally at its sexual root, and it will recoil

ultimately into some form of killing. The recoil may be prompt, or delay
by years or even by generations. But it will come. We may take it as a
law.

We may take it as another law that the very deepest quick of a man's
nature is his own pride and self-respect. The human being, weird phenomenon, may be patient for years and years under insult, insult to
his very quick, his pride in his own natural being. But at last, oh phenomenon, killing will come of it. All bloody revolutions are the result
of the long, slow, accumulated insult to the quick of pride in the mass
of men.

A third law is that the naïve or innocent core in a man is always his
vital core, and infinitely more important than his intellect or his reason.
It is only from his core of unconscious naïveté that the human being is
ultimately a responsible and dependable being. Break this human core
of naïveté—and the evil of the world all the time tries to break it, in Jeli,
in Rosso Malpelo, in Brothpot, in all these Verga characters—and you
get either a violent reaction, or, as is usual nowadays, a merely rational
creature whose core of spontaneous life is dead. Now the rational creature, who is merely rational, by some cruel trick of fate remains rational
only for one or two generations at best. Then he is quite mad. It is one
of the terrible qualities of the reason that it has no life of its own, and
unless continually kept in check or modified by the naïve life in man and
woman, it becomes a purely parasitic and destructive thing. Make any
human being a really rational being, and you have made him a parasitic
and destructive force. Make any people mainly rational in their life, and
their inner activity will be the activity of destruction. The more the
populations of the world become only rational in their consciousness,
the swifter they bring about their destruction pure and simple.

Verga, like every great artist, had sensed this. What he bewails really,
as the tragedy of tragedies, in this book, is the ugly trespass of the
sophisticated greedy ones upon the naïve life of the true human being:
the death of the naïve, pure being—or his lifelong imprisonment—and
the triumph or the killing of the sophisticated greedy ones.

This is the tragedy of tragedies in all time, but particularly in our
epoch: the killing off of the naïve innocent life in all of us, by which
alone we can continue to live, and the ugly triumph of the sophisticated
greedy.

It may be urged that Verga commits the Tolstoyan fallacy, of repu-
diating the educated world and exalting the peasant.* But this is not
the case. Verga was very much the gentleman, exclusively so, to the

end of his days. He did not dream of putting on a peasant's smock, or
following the plough. What Tolstoi somewhat perversely worshipped
in the peasants was poverty itself, and humility, and what Tolstoi somewhat perversely hated was instinctive pride or spontaneous passion.
Tolstoi has a perverse pleasure in making the later Vronsky* abject and   5
pitiable: because Tolstoi so meanly envied the healthy passionate male
in the young Vronsky. Tolstoi cut off his own nose to spite his face.*
He envied the reckless passionate male with a carking envy, because he
must have felt himself in some way wanting in comparison. So he exalts
the peasant: not because the peasant may be a more natural and spon-   10
taneous creature than the city man or the guardsman, but just because
the peasant is poverty-stricken and humble. This is the malice, the envy
of weakness and deformity.

   We know now that the peasant is no better than anybody else, no
better than a prince or a selfish young army officer or a governor or a   15
merchant. In fact, in the mass, the peasant is worse than any of these.
The peasant mass is the ugliest of all human masses, most greedily-
selfish and brutal of all. Which Tolstoi, leaning down from the gold bar
of heaven,* will have had opportunity to observe. If we have to trust to
a *mass*, then better trust the upper or the middle class mass, all masses   20
being odious.

   But Verga by no means exalts the peasants as a class: nor does he
believe in their poverty and their humility. Verga's peasants are certainly
not Christ-like, whatever else they are. They are most normally ugly
and low, the bulk of them. And individuals are sensitive and simple.   25

   Verga turns to the peasants only to seek for a certain something
which, as a healthy artist, he worshipped. Even Tolstoi, as a healthy
artist, worshipped it the same. It was only as a moralist and a personal
being that Tolstoi was perverse. As a true artist, he worshipped, as
Verga did, every manifestation of pure, spontaneous, passionate life,   30
life kindled to vividness. As a perverse moralist with a sense of some
subtle deficiency in himself, Tolstoi tries to insult and to damp out
the vividness of life. Imagine any great artist making the vulgar social
condemnation of Anna and Vronsky figure as divine punishment! Where
now is the society that turned its back on Vronsky and Anna? Where is   35
it? And what is its condemnation worth, today?

   Verga turned to the peasants to find, *in individuals*, the vivid spontaneity of sensitive passionate life, non-moral and non-didactic. He found
it always *defeated*. He found the vulgar and the greedy always destroying the sensitive and the passionate. The vulgar and the greedy are   40

themselves usually peasants: Verga was far too sane to put an aureole*
round the whole class. Still more are the women greedy and egoistic. But even so, Turiddu and Jeli and Rosso Malpelo and Nanni and
Gramigna and Brothpot are not humble. They have no saint-like self-
sacrificial qualities. They are only naïve, passionate, and natural. They
are "defeated" not because there is any glory or sanctification in defeat,
there is no martyrdom about it. They are defeated because they are
too unsuspicious, not sufficiently armed and ready to do battle with
the greedy and the sophisticated. When they do strike, they destroy
themselves too. So the real tragedy is that they are not sufficiently conscious and developed to defend their own naïve sensitiveness against the
inroads of the greedy and the vulgar. The greedy and the vulgar win all
the time: which, alas, is only too true, in Sicily as everywhere else. But
Giovanni Verga certainly doesn't help them, by preaching humility. He
does show them the knife of revenge at their throat.

And these stories, instead of being out-of-date, just because the manners depicted are more or less obsolete, even in Sicily, which is a good
deal Americanised and "cleaned up," as the reformers would say; instead
of being out of date, they are dynamically perhaps the most up-to-date
of stories. The Tchekovian after-influenza effect of inertia and will-
lessness is wearing off, all over Europe.* We realise we've had about
enough of being null. And if Tchekov represents the human being
driven into an extremity of self-consciousness and faintly wriggling
inertia, Verga represents him as waking suddenly from inaction into the
stroke of revenge. We shall see which of the two visions is more deeply
true to life.

Cavalleria Rusticana and *La Lupa* have always been hailed as masterpieces of brevity and gems of literary form. Masterpieces they are, but
one is now a little sceptical of their form. After the enormous diffusiveness of Victor Hugo,* it was perhaps necessary to make the artist more
self-critical and self-effacing. But any wholesale creed in art is dangerous. Hugo's romanticism, which consisted in letting himself go, in an
orgy of effusive self-conceit, was not much worse than the next creed
the French invented for the artist, of self-effacement. Self-effacement
is quite as self-conscious, and perhaps even more conceited than letting oneself go. Maupassant's self-effacement* becomes more blatant
than Hugo's self-effusion. As for the perfection of form achieved—
Merimée achieved the highest, in his dull stories like *Mateo Falcone* and
L'Enlévement de la Redoute.* But they are hopelessly literary, fabricated.

So is most of Maupassant. And if *Madame Bovary* has form, it is a pretty flat form.

But Verga was caught up by the grand idea of self-effacement in art. Anything more confused, more silly, really, than the pages prefacing the excellent story *Gramigna's Lover*,* would be hard to find, from the pen of a great writer. The moment Verga starts talking theories, our interest wilts immediately. The theories were none of his own: just borrowed from the literary smarties of Paris. And poor Verga looks a sad sight in Paris ready-mades. And when he starts putting his theories into practice, and effacing himself, one is far more aware of his interference than when he just goes ahead. Naturally! Because self-effacement is of course self-conscious, and any form of emotional self-consciousness hinders a first-rate artist: though it may help the second-rate.

Therefore in *Cavalleria Rusticana* and in *La Lupa* we are just a bit too much aware of the author and his scissors. He has clipped too much away. The transitions are too abrupt. All is over in a gasp: whereas a story like *La Lupa* covers at least several years of time.

As a matter of fact we need more looseness. We need an apparent formlessness, definite form is mechanical. We need more easy transition from mood to mood and from deed to deed. A great deal of the meaning of life and of art lies in the apparently dull spaces, the pauses, the unimportant passages. They are truly passages, the places of passing over.

So that Verga's deliberate missing-out of transition passages is, it seems to me, often a defect. And for this reason, a story like *La Lupa* loses a great deal of its life. It may be a masterpiece of concision, but it is hardly a masterpiece of narration. It is so short, our acquaintance with Nanni and Maricchia* is so fleeting, we forget them almost at once. *Jeli* makes a far more profound impression, so does *Rosso Malpelo*. These seem to me the finest stories in the book, and among the finest stories ever written. *Rosso Malpelo* is an extreme of the human consciousness subtle and appalling as anything done by the Russians, and at the same time, substantial, not introspective vapour. You will never forget him.

And it needed a deeper genius to write *Rosso Malpelo* than to write *Cavalleria Rusticana* or *La Lupa*. But the literary smarties, being so smart, have always praised the latter two above all others.

This business of missing out transition passages is quite deliberate on Verga's part. It is perhaps most evident in this volume, because it is here that Verga practises it for the first time. It was a new dodge, and he handled it badly. The sliding over of the change from Jeli's boyhood to his young manhood is surely too deliberately confusing!

But Verga had a double motive. First was the Frenchy idea of self-effacement, which, however, didn't go very deep, as Verga was too much of a true southerner to know quite what it meant. But the second motive was more dynamic. It was connected with Verga's whole recoil from the sophisticated world, and it effected a revolution in his style. Instinctively, he had come to hate the tyranny of a persistently logical sequence, or even a persistently chronological sequence. Time and the syllogism both seemed to represent the sophisticated falsehood and a sort of bullying, to him.

He tells us himself* how he came across his new style. "I had published several of my first novels. They went well: I was preparing others. One day, I don't know how, there came into my hands a sort of broadside, a halfpenny sheet sufficiently ungrammatical and disconnected, in which a sea-captain succinctly relates all the vicissitudes through which his sailing-ship has passed. Seaman's language, short, without an unnecessary phrase. It struck me, and I read it again; it was what I was looking for, without definitely knowing it. Sometimes, you know, just a sign, an indication is enough. It is a revelation—"

This passage explains all we need to know about Verga's style, which is perhaps at its most extreme in this volume. He was trying to follow the workings of the unsophisticated mind, and trying to reproduce the pattern.

Now the emotional mind, if we may be allowed to say so, is not logical. It is a psychological fact, that when we are thinking emotionally or passionately, thinking and feeling at the same time, we do not think rationally: and therefore, and therefore, and therefore. Instead, the mind makes curious swoops and circles. It touches the point of pain or interest, then sweeps away again in a cycle, coils round, and approaches again the point of pain or interest. There is a curious spiral rhythm, and the mind approaches again and again the point of interest, repeats itself, goes back, destroys the time sequence entirely, so that time ceases to exist, as the mind stoops to the quarry, then leaves it without striking, soars, hovers, turns, swoops, stoops again, still does not strike, yet is nearer, nearer, reels away again, wheels off into the air, even forgets, quite forgets, yet again turns, bends, circles slowly, swoops and stoops again, until at last there is the closing in, and the clutch of a decision or a resolve.

This activity of the mind is strictly timeless, and against time. After-wards, you can deduce the logical sequence and the time sequence, as historians do from the past. But in the happening, the logical and the time sequence do not exist.

Verga tried to convey this in his style. It gives at first the sense of   5
jumble and incoherence. The beginning of the story "Brothpot" is a good example of this breathless muddle of the peasant mind. When one is used to it, it is amusing, and a new movement in deliberate conscious-ness: though the humorists have used the form before. But at first it may be annoying.—Once he starts definitely narrating, however, Verga   10
drops the "muddled" method, and seeks only to be concise, often too concise, too abrupt in the transition. And in the matter of punctuation he is, perhaps deliberately, a puzzle, aiming at the same muddled swift effect of the emotional mind in its movements. He is doing, as a great artist, what men like James Joyce* do only out of contrariness and desire   15
for a sensation. The emotional mind, however apparently muddled, has its own rhythm, its own commas and colons and full-stops. They are not always as we should expect them, but they are there, indicating that other rhythm.

Everybody knows, of course, that Verga made a dramatised version   20
of *Cavalleria Rusticana*, and that this dramatised version is the libretto of the ever-popular little opera of the same name. So that Mascagni's rather feeble music* has gone to immortalise a man like Verga, whose only *popular* claim to fame is that he wrote the aforesaid libretto.—But that is fame's fault, not Verga's.   25

FOREWORD TO THE STORY OF DOCTOR MANENTE, *BY A. F. GRAZZINI ('IL LASCA')*

FOREWORD

It is rather by accident than design that the *Story of Doctor Manente**
should be the first book to appear in this Lungarno Series.* Yet the
accident is also fortunate, since it would be difficult to find a work
more typical of the times. It is true, Lasca was not a sensitive genius 5
like Boccaccio:* but then the Renaissance was by no means a sensitive
period. Boccaccio was far lovelier than the ordinary, or even than most
extraordinary men of his day. Whereas Lasca is of the day and of the city,
and as such, as a local and temporal writer, he is a typical Florentine.

Again, this famous story is a magnificent account of what is perhaps 10
the best Florentine *beffa*, or *burla** (practical Joke) on record. The work
is a *novella*, a short novel, composed of various parts which fit together
with the greatest skill. In this respect the story is far superior to most
of Boccaccio's long *novelle*, which are full of unnecessary stuff, often
tedious. Here we are kept sharp to essentials, and yet we are given a 15
complete and living atmosphere. Anyone who knows Florence today
can picture the whole thing perfectly, the big complicated *palazzi** with
far-off attics and hidden chambers, the inns of the country where men
sit on benches outside, and drink and talk on into the night, the houses
with the little courtyards at the back, where everybody looks out of the 20
window and knows all about everybody's affairs. The presentation of
the story is masterly, and could hardly be bettered, setting a pattern
for later works. In character, each man is himself. One can see the sly,
frail Lorenzo* playing this rather monstrous joke. One can see Doctor
Manente through and through. The Grand Vicar, so authoritative and 25
easily cowed, what a fine picture of an Italian inquisitor, how different
from the Spanish type!* The people are people, they are Italians and
Florentines, absolutely. There they are, in their own ordinary daylight,
not lifted into the special gleam of poetry, as Boccaccio's people so often
are. And we have to admit, if Boccaccio is more universal, Lasca is more 30
Tuscan.* The Italians are, when you come down to it, peculiarly *terre à
terre*,* right down on the earth. It is part of their wholesome charm. But
the rather fantastic side of their nature sometimes makes them want to
be angels or winged lions or soaring eagles,* and then they are often

ridiculous, though occasionally sublime. But the people itself is of the earth, wholesomely and soundly so, and unless perverted, will remain so. The great artists were wild coruscations which shone and expired. The people remains the people, and wine and spaghetti are their forms of poetry: good forms too. The peasants who bargain every Friday, year in, year out, in the Piazza della Signoria,* where the great white statue of Michelangelo's *David* stands livid,* have *never even heard* of the name *David*. If you say to them: My name is *David*—they say: What?—To them it is no name. Their outward-roaming consciousness has never even roamed so far as to read the name of the statue they almost touch each Friday. Enquiry is not their affair. They are centripetal.

And that is Italian. This soaring people sticks absolutely to the earth, and keeps the strength of the earth. The cities may go mad; they do. But the real Italian people is on the earth, and the cities will never lift them up. The bulk of the Italian people will never be "interested". They are centripetal, and only the little currents near to them matter.

So Doctor Manente! His courage and his force of life under all his trial are wonderful. Think of the howls, laments, prayers, sighs and recriminations the northerner would have raised, under the circumstances. Not so the Doctor! He refuses to take an objective view of his mishaps, he refuses to *think*, but eats and drinks handsomely, sleeps, builds castles in the air, and sings songs, even improvising. We feel, when he comes back into the world, he is still good and fat. Mental torture has not undermined him. He has refused to *think*, and so saved himself the worst suffering. And how can we fail to admire the superb earthly life-courage which this reveals! It is the strength and courage of trees, deep rooted in substance, in substantial earth, and centripetal. So the Italian is, really, *rooted in substance*, not in dreams, ideas, or ideals, but *physically* self-centred, like a tree.

But then the Italian also gets stuck sometimes, in this self-centred physicality of his nature, and occasionally has wild revolts from it. Then you get the sombre curses of Dante, the torments of Michelangelo and Leonardo, the sexless flights of Fra Angelico and Botticelli,* the anguish of the idealists. The Italian at his best doesn't quarrel with substance on behalf of his soul or his spirit. When he does, you see strange results.

Among which are the famous *burle*, or *beffe* of the Renaissance period: the famous and infamous practical jokes. Apparently the Florentines actually did play these cruel jokes on one another, all the time: it was a common sport. It is so even in Boccaccio, though we feel that he was too true a poet really to appreciate the game. Lasca, who was a real Florentine of the town and taverns, was in heaven when there was a good, cruel joke being perpetrated. Lorenzo de' Medici, who writes so touchingly of the violet, did actually play these pranks on his acquaintances—and if this is not a true story, historically it might just as well be so. The portrait of Lorenzo given here is true to life: that even the most gentle modern Italian critics admit. But they deny the story any historical truth; on very insufficient grounds, really. The modern mind, however, dislikes the *beffa*, and would like to think it never really existed. "Of course Lorenzo never *really* played this trick".—But the chances are that he did. And denying the historical truth of every recorded *beffa* does not wipe the *beffa* out of existence. On the contrary, it only leaves us blind to the real Renaissance spirit in Italy.

If every exalted soul who stares at Fra Angelico and Filippo Lippi,* Botticelli and Michelangelo and Piero della Francesca,* were compelled at the same time to study the practical-joke stories which play around the figures of these men and which fill the background of the great artists, then we should have a considerable change in feeling when we visited the Uffizi Gallery.* We might be a little less exalted: we should certainly be more amused and more *on the spot*, instead of floating in the vapour of ecstasised admiration.

The beffa is real, the beffa is earnest, and what in heaven was its goal? We can only understand it, I think, if we remember the true substantial, *à terre à terre* nature of the Italian. This self-centred physical nature can become crude, gross, even bestial and monstrous. We see it in D'Annunzio's peasant stories.* We see it in the act of that Gonzaga of Mantua* (if I remember right) who met his only son walking near the palace, and because the child did not salute with sufficient obsequiousness, kicked the boy ferociously in the groin, so that he died. The two centuries preceding the Renaissance had been full of such ferocity, beastliness. The spirit of Tuscany recoiled against it, and used every weapon of wit and intelligence against the egoistic brute of the preceding ages. And Italy is always having these periods of self-shame and recoil, not always into wit and fine intelligence, often into squeamish silliness.

Indeed the Renaissance itself fizzled out into silly squeamishness, even in Lasca's day.

There seems to be a cycle: a period of brutishness, a conquering of the brutish energy by intelligence, a flowering of the intelligence, then a fizzling down into nervous fuss. The *beffa* belongs to the period when the brute force is conquered by wit and intelligence, but is not extinguished. It is a form of revenge taken by wit on the self-centred physical fellow. The *beffe* are sometimes simply repulsive. But on the whole it is a sport for spurring up the sluggish intelligence, or taming the forward brute. If a man was a bit fat and simple, but especially if he overflowed in physical self-assertion, was importunate, pedantic, hypocritical, ignorant, all infallible signs of self-centred physical egoism, then the wits marked him down as a prey. He was made the victim of some *beffa*. This put the fear of God into him and into his like. He and his lot did not dare to assert themselves, their pedantry or self-importance or ignorance or brutality or hypocrisy so flagrantly. Chastened, they learned better manners. And so civilisation moves on, wit and intelligence taking their revenge on insolent animal spirits, till the animal spirits are cowed, and wit and intelligence become themselves insolent, then feeble, then silly, then null, as we see during the latter half of the sixteenth century, and the first half of the seventeenth, even in Florence and Rome.

Like all other human corrective measures, the *beffa* was often cruelly unjust and degenerated into a mere lust for sporting with a victim. Nimble wits, which had been in suppression during the preceding centuries, now rose up to take a cruel revenge on the somewhat fat and slower-witted citizen.

It is said that the Brunelleschi who built the Cathedral dome in Florence* played the cruel and unjustified *beffa* on the *Fat Carpenter*,* in the well-known story of that name. Here, the Magnificent Lorenzo plays a joke almost as unjustifiable and cruel, on Doctor Manente. All Florence rings with joy over the success of these terrific pieces of horse-play. The gentle Boccaccio tries to record such jokes with gusto. Nobody seems to have pitied the victim. Doctor Manente certainly never pitied himself; there is that to his credit, vastly: when we think how a modern would howl to the world at large. No, they weren't sorry for themselves—they were tough without being hard-boiled. The courage of life is splendid in them. We badly need some of it today, in this self-pitying age when we are so sorry for ourselves that we have to be soothed by art as by candy. Renaissance art has some of its roots in the cruel *beffa*—you can see it even in Botticelli's *Spring*:* it is glaring in Michelangelo. Michelangelo stuck his languishing Adam high on the Sistine ceiling* for safety, for in Florence they'd have played a rare *beffa* on that chap.

So we have the story of Doctor Manente, history alive and kicking, instead of dead and mummified. It should be given to every student of

that great period, the Italian Renaissance—and who is *not* a student of
the period.

Whether the joke was ever played by the Magnificent, we may ask.
Thin-skinned moderns will certainly shudder and say: No! The real
historian will say: It is possible, but hardly probable! The artist will   5
say: It sounds so true, it must be true! Meanwhile someone ought to
annotate Lasca, and verify his allusions where possible.

Lasca means *Roach*, or some little fish like that. It was the nickname of
Anton Francesco Grazzini, who was born in Florence in March, 1504,
just twelve years after the death of Lorenzo the Magnificent, which took   10
place in 1492. Lasca arranged his stories, after the manner of Boccaccio,
in three Suppers,* and the *Story of Doctor Manente* is the only one
we have complete from the Third and Last Supper. The stories of the
Second Supper and those of the First Supper, will occupy two volumes
following on this one,* and in the final volume will be included a study   15
of Lasca, his life and his work.

SECTION C

REVIEWS

REVIEW OF CONTEMPORARY GERMAN POETRY, BY JETHRO BITHELL

This *Contemporary German Poetry** is very much like the recent *Contemporary Belgian Poetry*.* The bulk of the verse is of the passionate or violent kind. This may be largely owing to the author's taste. His own poem,* which dedicates the volume to Richard Dehmel,* contains "Clashing Clouds that Terrorise" and "Feverous Sands of Modern Ache." However, we accept the collection as representative.

It is remarkable how reminiscent of Verhaeren and Iwan Gilkin,* and the like, these poems sound. Either it is owing to the translation, or else the influence of the Belgians on Germany is beyond all proportion. The very subjects of many of these poems could be found in the Belgian book, wearing the same favour.* These poets seem like little brothers of Verhaeren and Albert Mockel* and the rest, young lads excitedly following the lead of their scandalous elders. Baudelaire,* a while back, sent round with a rather red lantern, showing it into dark corners, and saying "Look here!"; considerably startling most folk. Verhaeren comes after with a bull's-eye lantern of whiter, wider ray than Baudelaire's artistic beam, and flashes this into such obscure places—by no means corners—so that they stand out stark and real. He also, in the daylight, makes a hollow of his hand,* and shades his eyes, and sees, deep in the light, the fabric of shadow. These Germans follow like tourists after a guide. They stop at the places Verhaeren stopped at; they excitedly hold out their candle lanterns; they peer under hollowed hands to find the shadow set deep in the light.

This may be the fault of the translator, though it scarcely seems likely. He speaks of "the beautiful translation of the poem 'Grey,'* the work of Miss H. Friederichs":—

GREY.

Gowns of soft grey I now will wear,
Like willow trees all silvery fair;
My lover, he loves grey.
Like clematis, with silky down,
Which lend the dew-sprent hedge a crown;
My lover, he loves grey.

Wrapped in a dream, I watch where slow
Within the fire the wood-sparks glow;
My love, thou art away . . .
The soft grey ashes fall and shift,
5   Through silent spaces smoke clouds drift,
And I too, I love grey.

I think of pearls, where grey lights dream,
Of alders, where the mist-veils gleam:
My love, thou art away . . .
10   Of grey-haired men of high renown,
Whose faded locks were hazel brown,
And I too, I love grey.

The little grey moth turns its flight
Into the room allured by light;
15   My lover, he loves grey.
O, little moth, we are like thee,
We all fly round a light we see
In swamp or Milky Way.

After that, one thinks of Verlaine's "Green."*
20   The Germans in this book are very interesting, not so much for the
intrinsic value of the pieces of poetry here given, as for showing which
way the poetic spirit trends in Germany, where she finds her stuff,
and how she lifts it. Synge* asks for the brutalising of English poetry.
Thomas Hardy and George Meredith* have, to some extent, answered.
25   But in point of brutality the Germans—and they at the heels of the
French and Belgians—are miles ahead of us; or at the back of us, as the
case may be.

With Baudelaire, Verlaine, and Verhaeren, poetry seems to have broken out afresh, like a new crater. These men take life welling out hot
30   and primitive, molten fire, or mud, or smoke, or strange vapour. But at
any rate it comes from the central fire, which feeds all of us with life,
although it is gloved, clotted over and hidden by earth and greenery and
civilisation. And it is this same central well of fire which the Germans
are trying to tap. It is risky, and they lose their heads when they feel
35   the heat. But sometimes one sees the real red jet of it, pure flame and
beautiful; and often, the hot mud—but that is kin. Why do we set our
faces against this tapping of elemental passion? It must, in its first issuing, be awful and perhaps, ugly. But what is more essentially awful and
ugly than Oedipus? And why is sex passion unsuited for handling, if

hate passion, and revenge passion, and horror passion are suitable, as in Agamemnon and Oedipus, and Medea. Hate passion, horror passion, revenge passion no longer move us so violently in life. Love passion, pitching along with it beauty and strange hate and suffering, remains the one living volcano of our souls. And we must be passionate, we are told. Why, then, not take this red fire out of the well, equally with the yellow of horror, and the dark of hate? Intrinsically, Verhaeren is surely nearer the Greek dramatists* than is Swinburne.*

The Germans indeed are sentimental. They always belittle the great theme of passion. In this book, one turns with disgust from Dehmel's "Venus Pandemos."* It is like the lurid tales the teetotallers tell against drink. And one turns with impatience from Peter Hille's "Morn of a Marriage Night."* It is the slop of philosophy muddled and mixed with a half-realised experience: the poet was not able to *imagine* the woman, so he slopped over the suggestion of her with sentimental philosophy. It is not honest, it [is] as bad as jerry work* in labour. But that doesn't say the subject is wrong. And if the work is offensive, we can wash our hands after it. And it does not mean to say that no man shall try to treat a difficult subject because another man has degraded it. Because a subject cannot be degraded. Sex passion is not degraded even now, between priests and beasts. Verhaeren, at his best, is religious in his attitude, honest and religious, when dealing with the "scandalous" subject. Many of the Germans are not; they are sentimental, dishonest. So much the worse for them, not for us.

The translation of these poems is not remarkably good: but good enough, as a rule, to transfer the rhythm and progress of the feeling of each poem. A perfect translator must be a twin of his original author, like in feeling and age, and even in the turn of his expression and the knack of his phrases. It is absurd to think of translating the spirit and form of a whole host of poets. But here, each poem retains its personality, some of its distinct, individual personality, that it had in the original. The translator is best when he has the plain curve of an emotion— preferably dramatic—to convey.

REVIEW OF THE OXFORD BOOK OF GERMAN VERSE, *EDITED BY H. G. FIEDLER*

THE OXFORD BOOK OF GERMAN VERSE*

This book seems to us extraordinarily delightful. From Walther von der Vogelweide* onwards, there are here all the poems in German which we have cherished since School days.* The earlier part of the book seems almost like a breviary.* It is remarkable how near to the heart many of these old German poems lie; almost like the scriptures. We do not question or examine them. Our education seems built on them.

> "Geh aus, mein Herz, und suche Freud,
> In dieser lieben Sommerzeit
> An deines Gottes Gaben . . ."*

Then again, so many of the poems are known to us as music, Beethoven, Schubert, Schumann, Brahms and Wolf,* that the earlier part of the book stands unassailable, beyond question or criticism.

There are very few of the known things that we may complain of missing. Heine's "Thalatta"* is not included—but it is foolish to utter one's personal regrets, when so much of the best is given.

For most of us, German poetry ends with Heine. If we know Mörike* we are exceptional. In this anthology, however, Heine is finished on page 330, while the last poem in the book, by Schaukal,* is on page 532; that is, two hundred pages of 19th century verse. It is a large proportion. And it is this part of the book that, whilst it interests us absorbingly, leaves us in the end undecided and unsatisfied.

Lenau, Keller, Meyer, Storm,* Mörike are almost classics. Over the seven pages of Paul Heyse* we hesitate uncertainly; would we not rather have given more space to Liliencron,* and less to Heyse?—although Liliencron is well represented. But this soldier poet is so straight, so free from the modern artist's hyper-sensitive self-consciousness, that we would have more of him. We wish England had a poet like him, to give grit to our modern verse.

> TOD IN ÄHREN.
> Im Weizenfeld, in Korn und Mohn
> Liegt ein Soldat, unaufgefunden,

Zwei Tage schon, zwei Nächte schon,
Mit schweren Wunden, unverbunden.

Durstüberquält und fieberwild,
Im Todeskampf den Kopf erhoben.
5   Ein letzter Traum, ein letztes Bild,
Sein brechend Auge schlägt nach oben.

Die Sense sirrt im Ährenfeld,
Er sieht sein Dorf im Arbeitsfrieden.
Ade, ade du Heimatwelt—
10   Und beugt das Haupt und ist verschieden.*

The selections from Dehmel* are not so satisfactory. It is not at all certain whether these poems are altogether representative of the author of "Aber die Liebe" and the "Verwandlungen der Venus." Dehmel is a fascinating poet, but he for ever leaves us doubtful in what rank to 15   place him. He is turgid and violent, his music is often harsh, usually discomforting. He seems to lack reserve. It is very difficult to decide upon him. Then suddenly a fragment will win us over:—

NACH EINEM REGEN.
Sieh, der Himmel wird blau;
20   Die Schwalben jagen sich
Wie Fische über den nassen Birken.
Und du willst weinen?

In deiner Seele werden bald
Die blanken Bäume und blauen Vögel
25   Ein goldnes Bild sein.
Und du weinst?

Mit meinem Augen
Seh' ich in deinen
Zwei kleine Sonnen,
30   Und du lächelst.*

Hauptmann* is dramatic and stirring, Bierbaum* sings pleasantly, Max Dauthendey's brief, impersonal sketches* have a peculiar power; one returns to them, and they remain in mind. Hofmannsthal, the symbolist,* has three very interesting poems. There are many other 35   names, some quite new, and one's interest is keenly roused. It is a question, where so many are admitted, why Geiger and Peter Baum and Elsa Lasker-Schüle* have been excluded. But nothing is so easy as to carp at the compiler of an anthology; and no book, for a long time, has given us the pleasure that this has given.

REVIEW OF THE MINNESINGERS,
BY JETHRO BITHELL

THE MINNESINGERS. By JETHRO BITHELL, M.A. Vol. I.—Translations.*

This is a rather large, important-looking volume of translations with a few comparative footnotes, and a brief appendix which is scarcely scholarly, but shows the author has read widely in verse. It is to be followed next autumn by a second volume, a history of Minnesong as compared with the old lyrical poetry of Provence,* Portugal and Italy. This second volume, we are told in the preface, is to be the "pièce de résistance."*

"These translations," we read, "may be regarded as the by-products of a more painful process—the extraction of parallel passages. The two volumes should, by rights, have appeared together, but the translations were easier, and are finished first."*

This considerably damps our ardour. "The translations were easier." It is a phrase that pricks the gay bladder of our enthusiasm.

The book is issued as an independent volume. It is not a scholastic work. It is an anthology, selected at the author's discretion, of translations of the chief of the Minnesong. That is, it is issued to us as a book of poetry. And instead of a book of poetry, we have a book of by-products.

"The translations were easier . . ." As a result, we have a volume of crude, careless English verse which is not often poetry. Nevertheless, the author is so blithe and unconcerned and facile at his task, that the book has a certain charm.

The method of translation, we are told, is the "plaster-cast:" that is, the outward form is strictly preserved. Also the author has striven to be "Sinngetreu" rather than "Wortgetreu;"* to be true to the poet's thought rather than to his phrasing. But it is not so easy to be "Sinngetreu." The earlier Minnesingers especially are so naïve and winsome in the expression of their sentiment, that they are not to be translated off-hand. Take the very first verse in the book, and put it side by side with the original—none of the German originals, by the way, are included in this book:

Dû bist mîn, ich bin dîn:	Mine thou art, thine am I:
Des solt dû gewis sîn.	Deem not that in this I lie.
Dû bist beslozzen	Locked thou art
In mînem herzen:	In my heart;
Verlorn is das slüzzelîn:	Never canst thou thence depart:
Dû muost immer drinne sîn.	For the key is lost, sweetheart.*

The translation may be "Sinngetreu," but it has lost all poetry by the way. Then take the first stanza of Walther von der Vogelweide's well-known "Tantaradei," or "Unter den Linden."*

> "On the heather-lea,
> In the lime-tree bower,
> There of us twain was made the bed:
> There you may see
> Grass-blade and flower
> Sweetly crushed and shed.
> By the forest, in a dale,
> Tantaradei!
> Sweetly sang the nightingale."

The translation certainly seems to have been easy, and in making it the author will have made enemies of all who remember the original.

Nevertheless, this blithe facility and unconcern on the author's part does give the book a certain quality, almost a charm of its own. And as the Minnesong goes on, becomes more narrative, more ballad-like, less delicately lyrical, it is easier to translate. There is solid stuff of narrative and of dramatic emotion, that does not vanish away in being conveyed from one language to another. And these later translations are often made very attractive by the author's irresponsible, artless manner.

In among the Minnesong is a good proportion of Volkslied.* A bookful of courtly, mediaeval love-song soon cloys. The lays of Marie de France* sicken in the end. So the inclusion of coarse, harsh folksong among so much sugar-cream of sentimental love is welcome.

The book is very interesting, in spite of its faults.

'THE GEORGIAN RENAISSANCE': REVIEW OF GEORGIAN POETRY, 1911–12, EDITED BY EDWARD MARSH

THE GEORGIAN RENAISSANCE

"Georgian Poetry"* is an anthology of verse which has been published during the reign of our present king, George V.* It contains one poem of my own,* but this fact will not, I hope, preclude my reviewing the book.   5

This collection is like a big breath taken when we are waking up after a night of oppressive dreams. The nihilists, the intellectual, hopeless people—Ibsen,* Flaubert, Thomas Hardy—represent the dream we are waking from. It was a dream of demolition. Nothing was, but was nothing. Everything was taken from us. And now our lungs are full of   10
new air, and our eyes see it is morning, but we have not forgotten the terror of the night. We dreamed we were falling through space into nothingness, and the anguish of it leaves us rather eager.

But we are awake again, our lungs are full of new air, our eyes of morning. The first song is nearly a cry, fear and the pain of remembrance   15
sharpening away the pure music. And that is this book.

The last years have been years of demolition. Because faith and belief were getting pot-bound,* and the Temple was made a place to barter sacrifices,* therefore faith and belief and the Temple must be broken. This time Art fought the battle, rather than Science or any new religious   20
faction. And Art has been demolishing for us: Nietzsche the Christian Religion as it stood,* Hardy our faith in our own endeavour, Flaubert our belief in love. Now, for us, it is all smashed, we can see the whole again. We were in prison, peeping at the sky through loop-holes. The great prisoners smashed at the loop-holes, for lying to us.* And behold,   25
out of the ruins leaps the whole sky.

It is we who see it and breathe in it for joy. God is there, faith, belief, love, everything. We are drunk with the joy of it, having got away from the fear. In almost every poem in the book comes this note of exultation after fear, the exultation in the vast freedom, the illimitable wealth that   30
we have suddenly got.

> "But send desire often forth to scan
> The immense night that is thy greater soul,"

says Mr. Abercrombie.* His deadly sin is Prudence,* that will not risk
to avail itself of the new freedom. Mr. Bottomley exults to find men
forever building religions which yet can never compass all.

> "Yet the yielding sky
> Invincible vacancy was there discovered."*

Mr. Rupert Brooke sees

> "every glint
> Posture and jest and thought and tint
> Freed from the mask of transiency,
> Triumphant in eternity,
> Immote, immortal"

and this at Afternoon Tea.*
Mr. John Drinkwater sings:

> "We cherish every hour that strays
> Adown the cataract of days:
> We see the clear, untroubled skies,
> We see the glory of the rose—"*

Mr. Wilfrid Wilson Gibson hears the "terror turned to tenderness"
then

> "I watched the mother sing to rest
> The baby snuggling on her breast."*

And to Mr. Masefield:

> "When men count
> Those hours of life that were a bursting fount
> Sparkling the dusty heart with living springs,
> There seems a world, beyond our earthly things,
> Gated by golden moments."*

It is all the same—hope, and religious joy. Nothing is really wrong.
Every new religion is a waste-product from the last, and every religion
stands for us for ever. We love Christianity for what it has brought us,
now that we are no longer on the cross.

  The great liberation gives us an overwhelming sense of joy, joie d'être,
joie de vivre.* This sense of exceeding keen relish and appreciation of
life makes romance. I think I could say every poem in the book is romantic, tinged with a love of the marvellous, a joy of natural things, as if the
poet were a child for the first time on the seashore, finding treasures.

"Best trust the happy moments,"* says Mr. Masefield, who seems nearest to the black dream behind us. There is Mr. W. H. Davies' lovely
joy,* Mr. De La Mare's perfect appreciation of life at still moments,*
Mr. Rupert Brooke's brightness, when he "lived from laugh to
laugh,"* Mr. Edmund Beale Sargant's pure, excited happiness in the
woodland*—it is all the same, keen zest in life found wonderful. In
Mr. Bottomley it is the zest of activity, of hurrying, labouring men, or
the zest of the utter stillness of long snows.* It is a bookful of Romance
that has not quite got clear of the terror of realism.

There is no "Carpe diem"* touch. The joy is sure and fast. It is not
the falling rose, but the rose for ever rising to bud and falling to fruit
that gives us joy. We have faith in the vastness of life's wealth. We are
always rich: rich in buds and in shed blossoms. There is no winter that
we fear. Life is like an orange tree, always in leaf and bud, in blossom
and fruit.

And we ourselves, in each of us, have everything. Somebody said:
"The Georgian Poets are not Love Poets. The influence of Swinburne*
has gone." But I should say the Georgian Poets are just ripening to
be love-poets. Swinburne was no love-poet. What are the Georgian
poets, nearly all, but just bursting into a thick blaze of being. They are
not poets of passion, perhaps, but they are essentially passionate poets.
The time to be impersonal has gone. We start from the joy we have in
being ourselves, and everything must take colour from that joy. It is the
return of the blood, that has been held back, as when the heart's action
is arrested by fear. Now the warmth of blood is in everything, quick,
healthy, passionate blood. I look at my hands as I write and know they are
mine, with red blood running its way, sleuthing out Truth and pursuing
it to eternity, and I am full of awe for this flesh and blood that holds
this pen. Everything that ever was thought and ever will be thought,
lies in this body of mine. This flesh and blood sitting here writing, the
great impersonal flesh and blood, greater than me, which I am proud to
belong to, contains all the future. What is it but the quick of all growth,
the seed of all harvest, this body of mine. And grapes and corn and birds
and rocks and visions, all are in my fingers. I am so full of wonder at
my own miracle of flesh and blood that I could not contain myself, if I
did not remember we are all alive, have all of us living bodies. And that
is a joy greater than any dream of immortality in the spirit, to me. It
reminds me of Rupert Brooke's moment triumphant in its eternality;*
and of Michael Angelo, who is also the moment triumphant in its eternality; just the opposite from Corot,* who is the eternal triumphing over

the moment, at the moment, at the very point of sweeping it into the flow.

Of all love-poets, we are the love-poets. For our religion is loving. To love passionately, but completely, is our one desire.

5   What is "The Hare"* but a complete love-poem, with none of the hackneyed "But a bitter blossom was born"* about it, nor yet the Yeats, "Never give all the heart."* Love is the greatest of all things, no "bitter-blossom" nor such like. It is sex-passion, so separated, in which we do not believe. The "Carmen" and "Tosca"* sort of passion is not

10   interesting any longer, because it can't progress. Its goal and aim is possession, whereas possession in love is only a means to love. And because passion cannot go beyond possession, the passionate heroes and heroines—Tristans and what-not*—must die. We believe in the love that is happy ever after, progressive as life itself.

15   I worship Christ, I worship Jehovah, I worship Pan, I worship Aphrodite.* But I do not worship hands nailed and running with blood upon a cross, nor licentiousness, nor lust. I want them all, all the gods. They are all God. But I must serve in real love. If I take my whole, passionate, spiritual and physical love to the woman who in return loves

20   me, that is how I serve God. And my hymn and my game of joy is my work. All of which I read in the Anthology of Georgian Poetry.

'GERMAN BOOKS': REVIEW OF DER TOD IN VENEDIG, BY THOMAS MANN

GERMAN BOOKS By D. H. LAWRENCE
Thomas Mann

Thomas Mann* is perhaps the most famous of German novelists now writing. He, and his elder brother, Heinrich Mann, with Jakob Wassermann,* are acclaimed the three artists in fiction of present-day Germany.

But Germany is now undergoing that craving for form in fiction, that passionate desire for the mastery of the medium of narrative, that will of the writer to be greater than and undisputed lord over the stuff he writes, which is figured to the world in Gustave Flaubert.

Thomas Mann is over middle age,* and has written three or four books: "Buddenbrooks," a novel of the patrician life of Lubeck; "Tristan," a collection of six "Novellen"; "Königliche Hoheit,"* an unreal Court romance; various stories, and lastly, "Der Tod in Venedig." The author himself is the son of a Lübeck "Patrizier."*

It is as an artist rather than as a story-teller that Germany worships Thomas Mann. And yet it seems to me, this craving for form is the outcome, not of artistic conscience, but of a certain attitude to life. For form is not a personal thing like style. It is impersonal like logic. And just as the school of Alexander Pope* was logical in its expressions, so it seems the school of Flaubert is, as it were, logical in its aesthetic form. "Nothing outside the definite line of the book,"* is a maxim. But can the human mind fix absolutely the definite line of a book, any more than it can fix absolutely any definite line of action for a living being?

Thomas Mann, however, is personal, almost painfully so, in his subject-matter. In "Tonio Kröger," the long "Novelle" at the end of the "Tristan" volume, he paints a detailed portrait of himself as a youth and younger man, a careful analysis. And he expresses at some length the misery of being an artist. "Literature is not a calling, it is a curse."* Then he says to the Russian painter girl: "There is no artist anywhere but longs again, my love, for the common life."* But any young artist might say that. It is because the stress of life in a young man, but particularly in an artist, is very strong, and has as yet found no outlet, so that it rages inside him in "Sturm und Drang."* But the condition is

the same, only more tragic, in the Thomas Mann of fifty-three.* He
has never found any outlet for himself, save his art. He has never given
himself to anything but his art. This is all well and good, if his art
absorbs and satisfies him, as it has done some great men, like Corot.*
5   But then there are the other artists, the more human, like Shakespeare
and Goethe,* who must give themselves to life as well as to art. And if
these were afraid, or despised life, then with their surplus they would
ferment and become rotten. Which is what ails Thomas Mann. He is
physically ailing, no doubt. But his complaint is deeper: it is of the
10   soul.

And out of this soul-ailment, this unbelief, he makes his particular
art, which he describes, in "Tonio Kröger," as "Wählerisch, erlesen,
kostbar, fein, reizbar gegen das Banale, und aufs höchste empfindlich in
Fragen des Taktes und Geschmacks."* He is a disciple, in method, of the
15   Flaubert who wrote: "I worked sixteen hours yesterday, to-day the whole
day, and have at last finished one page."* In writing of the Leitmotiv* and
its influence, he says: "Now this method alone is sufficient to explain
my slowness. It is the result neither of anxiety nor indigence, but of
an overpowering sense of responsibility for the choice of every word,
20   the coining of every phrase . . . a responsibility that longs for perfect
freshness, and which, after two hours' work, prefers not to undertake an
important sentence. For which sentence is important, and which not?
Can one know beforehand whether a sentence, or part of a sentence
may not be called upon to appear again as motiv, peg, symbol, citation
25   or connection? And a sentence which must be heard twice must be
fashioned accordingly. It must—I do not speak of beauty—possess a
certain high level, and symbolic suggestion, which will make it worthy
to sound again in any epic future. So every point becomes a standing
ground, every adjective a decision, and it is clear that such work is not
30   to be produced off-hand."*

This, then, is the method. The man himself was always delicate in
constitution. "The doctors said he was too weak to go to school, and must
work at home."* I quote from Aschenbach, in "Der Tod in Venedig."
"When he fell, at the age of fifty-three, one of his closest observers said
35   of him: "Aschenbach has always lived like this"—and he gripped his
fist hard clenched; "never like this"—and he let his open hand lie easily
on the arm of the chair."*

He forced himself to write, and kept himself to the work. Speaking of
one of his works, he says: "It was pardonable, yea, it showed plainly the
40   victory of his morality, that the uninitiated reader supposed the book to

have come of a solid strength and one long breath; whereas it was the result of small daily efforts and hundreds of single inspirations."*

And he gives the sum of his experience in the belief—"daß beinahe alles Große, was dastehe, als ein Trotzdem dastehe, trotz Kummer und Qual, Armut, Verlassenheit, Körperschwäche, Laster, Leidenschaft und tausend hemmnischen Zustande gekommen sei."* And then comes the final revelation, difficult to translate. He is speaking of life as it is written into his books:

"For endurance of one's fate, grace in suffering, does not only mean passivity, but is an active work, a positive triumph, and the Sebastian figure is the most beautiful symbol, if not of all art, yet of the art in question. If one looked into this portrayed world and saw the elegant self-control that hides from the eyes of the world to the last moment the inner undermining, the biological decay; saw the yellow ugliness which, sensuously at a disadvantage, could blow its choking heat of desire to a pure flame, and even rise to sovereignty in the kingdom of beauty; saw the pale impotence which draws out of the glowing depths of its intellect sufficient strength to subdue a whole vigorous people, bring them to the foot of the Cross, to the feet of impotence; saw the amiable bearing in the empty and severe service of Form, saw the quickly enervating longing and art of the born swindler: if one saw such a fate as this, and all the rest it implied, then one would be forced to doubt whether there were in reality any other heroism than that of weakness. Which heroism, in any case, is more of our time than this?"*

Perhaps it is better to give the story of "Der Tod in Venedig," from which the above is taken, and to whose hero it applies.

Gustav von Aschenbach, a fine, famous author, over fifty years of age, coming to the end of a long walk one afternoon, sees as he is approaching a burying place, near Munich, a man standing between the chimeric figures of the gateway. This man in the gate of the cemetery is almost the motive of the story. By him, Aschenbach is infected with a desire to travel. He examines himself minutely, in a way almost painful in its frankness, and one sees the whole soul of this author of fifty-three. And it seems, the artist has absorbed the man, and yet the man is there, like an exhausted organism on which a parasite has fed itself strong. Then begins a kind of Holbein "Totentanz."* The story is quite natural in appearance, and yet there is the gruesome sense of symbolism throughout. The man near the burying ground has suggested travel—but whither? Aschenbach sets off to a watering place on the Austrian coast of the Adriatic,* seeking some adventure, some passionate adventure, to which his sick soul and unhealthy body have been kindled. But finding himself on the Adriatic, he knows it is not thither that his desire draws him, and he takes ship for Venice. It is all real, and yet with a curious sinister unreality, like decay, the "biological decay." On board there is a man who reminds one of the man in the gateway, though there is no connection. And then, among a crowd of young Poles who are crossing, is a ghastly fellow, whom Aschenbach sees is an old man dressed up as young, who capers unsuspected among the youths, drinks hilariously with them, and falls hideously drunk at last on the deck, reaching to the author, and slobbering about "dem allerliebsten, dem schönsten Liebchen."* Suddenly the upper plate of his false teeth falls on his underlip.

Aschenbach takes a gondola to the Lido,* and again the gondolier reminds one of the man in the cemetery gateway. He is, moreover, one who will make no concession, and, in spite of Aschenbach's demand to be taken back to St. Mark's,* rows him in his black craft to the Lido, talking to himself softly all the while. Then he goes without payment.

The author stays in a fashionable hotel on the Lido. The adventure is coming, there by the pallid sea. As Aschenbach comes down into the hall of the hotel, he sees a beautiful Polish boy of about fourteen, with honey-coloured curls clustering round his pale face, standing with his sisters and their governess.

Aschenbach loves the boy—but almost as a symbol. In him he loves life and youth and beauty, as Hyacinth in the Greek myth.* This, I suppose, is blowing the choking heat to pure flame, and raising it to the kingdom of beauty. He follows the boy, watches him all day long on the beach, fascinated by beauty concrete before him. It is still the Künstler* and his abstraction: but there is also the "yellow ugliness, sensually at a disadvantage," of the elderly man below it all. But the picture of the writer watching the folk on the beach gleams and lives with a curious, gold-phosphorescent light, touched with the brightness of Greek myth, and yet a modern sea-shore with folk on the sands, and a half-threatening, diseased sky.

Aschenbach, watching the boy in the hotel lift, finds him delicate, almost ill, and the thought that he may not live long fills the elderly writer with a sense of peace. It eases him to think the boy should die.

Then the writer suffers from the effect of the Sirocco,* and intends to depart immediately from Venice. But at the station he finds with joy that his luggage has gone wrong, and he goes straight back to the hotel.

There, when he sees Tadzio* again, he knows why he could not leave Venice.

There is a month of hot weather, when Aschenbach follows Tadzio about, and begins to receive a look, loving, from over the lad's shoulder. It is wonderful, the heat, the unwholesomeness, the passion in Venice. One evening comes a street singer, smelling of carbolic acid, and sings beneath the verandah of the hotel. And this time, in gruesome symbolism, it is the man from the burying ground distinctly.

The rumour is, that the black cholera is in Venice. An atmosphere of secret plague hangs over the city of canals and palaces. Aschenbach verifies the report at the English bureau, but cannot bring himself to go away from Tadzio, nor yet to warn the Polish family. The secretly pest-smitten days go by. Aschenbach follows the boy through the stinking streets of the town and loses him. And on the day of the departure of the Polish family, the famous author dies of the plague.

It is absolutely, almost unintentionally, unwholesome. The man is sick, body and soul. He portrays himself as he is, with wonderful skill and art portrays his sickness. And since any genuine portrait is valuable, this book has its place. It portrays one man, one atmosphere, one sick vision. It claims to do no more. And we have to allow it. But we know it is unwholesome—it does not strike me as being morbid for all that, it is too well done—and we give it its place as such.

Thomas Mann seems to me the last sick sufferer from the complaint of Flaubert. The latter stood away from life as from a leprosy. And Thomas Mann, like Flaubert, feels vaguely that he has in him something finer than ever physical life revealed. Physical life is a disordered corruption, against which he can fight with only one weapon, his fine aesthetic sense, his feeling for beauty, for perfection, for a certain fitness which soothes him, and gives him an inner pleasure, however corrupt the stuff of life may be. There he is, after all these years, full of disgusts and loathing of himself as Flaubert was, and Germany is being voiced, or partly so, by him. And so, with real suicidal intention, like Flaubert's, he sits, a last too-sick disciple, reducing himself grain by grain to the statement of his own disgust, patiently, self-destructively, so that his statement at least may be perfect in a world of corruption. But he is so late.

Already I find Thomas Mann, who, as he says, fights so hard against the banal in his work, somewhat banal. His expression may be very fine. But by now what he expresses is stale. I think we have learned our lesson, to be sufficiently aware of the fulsomeness of life. And even while he has a rhythm in style, yet his work has none of the rhythm of a living thing, the rise of a poppy,* then the after uplift of the bud, the shedding of the calyx and the spreading wide of the petals, the falling of the flower and the pride of the seed-head. There is an unexpectedness in this such as does not come from their carefully plotted and arranged developments. Even "Madame Bovary" seems to me dead in respect to the living rhythm of the whole work. While it is there in "Macbeth" like life itself.

But Thomas Mann is old—and we are young. Germany does not feel very young to me.

REVIEW OF FANTAZIUS MALLARE: A
MYSTERIOUS OATH, *BY BEN HECHT*

Taos   12 October 1922
Chère Jeunesse*
Many thanks for sending me the Ben Hecht book. I read it through.
But I'm sorry, it didn't thrill me a bit, neither the pictures nor the
text.* It all seems to me so would-be. Think of the malice, the sheer   5
malice of a Beardsley drawing,* the wit, and the venom of the mockery.
These drawings are so completely without irony, so crass, so strained,
and so would-be. It isn't that they've got anything to reveal, at all.
That man's coition with a tree, for example. There's nothing in it but
the author's attempt to be startling. Whereas if he wanted to be really   10
wicked he'd see that even a tree has its own daimon,* and a man might
lie with the daimon of a tree. Beardsley saw these things. But it takes
imagination.
    The same with the text. Really, Fantasius Malare* might mutilate
himself, like a devotee of one of the early Christian sects, and hang   15
his penis on his nose-end and a testicle under each ear, and definitely
testify that way that he'd got such appendages, it wouldn't affect me.
The word penis or testicle or vagina* doesn't shock me. Why should it?
Surely I am enough a man to be able to think of my own organs with
calm, even with indifference. It isn't the *names* of things that bother   20
me: nor even ideas about them. I don't keep my passions, or reactions,
or even sensations, *in my head*. They stay down where they belong.
And really, Fantasius, with his head full of copulation and committing
mental fornication and sodomy every minute, is just as much a bore as
any other tedious modern individual with a dominant idea. One wants   25
to say: "Ah, dirty little boy, leave yourself alone."
    Which after all isn't prudery. It's just because one has one's own
genuine sexual experiences, and all these fingerings and naughty words
and shocking little drawings only reveal the state of mind of a man who
has *never* had any sincere, vital experience in sex; just as a little boy   30
never has, and can't have had; and so he's itching with a feeble curiosity

215

and self-induced excitement. Which is principally tedious, because it shows a feeble, spunkless sort of state of things.

If Fantasius wasn't a frightened masturbater,* he'd know that sex-contact with another individual meant a whole meeting, a contact between two alien natures, a grim rencontre,* half battle and half delight, always, and a sense of renewal and deeper being afterwards. Fantasius is too feeble and weak-kneed for the fight, he runs away and chews his fingers and tries to look important by posing as mad. Being too much of a wet-leg,* as they say in England, nakedly to enter into the battle and embrace with a woman.

The tragedy is, when you've got sex in your head, instead of down below where it belongs, and when you have to go on feebly copulating through your ears and your nose. It's such a confession of weakness, impotence. Poor Fantasius is sensually, if not technically, impotent, and the book should have for sub-title: "Relaxations for the Impotent."

But there's the trouble: men have most of them got their sex in their heads nowadays, and nowhere else. They start all their deeper reactions in their heads, and work themselves from the top downwards. Which of course brings disgust, because you're only having yourself all the time. No matter what other individual you take as a *machine à plaisir,** you're only taking yourself all the time.

Why can't you *jeunesse* let all the pus of festering sex out of your heads, and try to act from the original centres? The old, dark religions understood. "God enters from below," said the Egyptians. And that's right. Why can't you darken your minds, and know that the great gods pulse in the dark, and enter you as darkness, through the lower gates. Not through the head. Why don't you seek again the unknown and invisible gods who step sometimes into our great arteries, and down the blood-vessels to the phallos, to the vagina, and have strange meetings there? There are different dark gods, different passions; Hermes Ithyphallos* has more than one road. The god of gods is unknowable, unutterable, but all the more terrible: and from the unutterable god step forth the mysteries of our promptings, in different forms: call it Thoth or Hermes, or Bacchus or Horus or Apollo:* different prompt-ings, different mysterious forms. But why don't you leave off your old white festerings in the head, and let the mystery of life come back to you? Why don't you become silent unto yourselves, and wait and be patient in silence, and let a night* fall over your mind and heal you. And then turn again to the dark gods, which are the dark promptings and passion-motions inside you, and have reverence again, and be grateful for life.

Fantasius Malare seems to me such a poor, impoverished, self-conscious specimen. Why should one be self-conscious and impoverished when one is young and the dark gods are at the gate? 5

You'll understand if you want to. Otherwise it's your own affair.

REVIEW OF AMERICANS, BY STUART P. SHERMAN

MODEL AMERICANS

Professor Sherman* once more coaxing American criticism the way it should go.

Like Benjamin Franklin, one of his heroes, he attempts the invention of a creed that shall "satisfy the professors of all religions, and offend none."*

He smites the marauding Mr. Mencken* with a velvet glove, and pierces the obstinate Mr. More* with a reproachful look. Both gentlemen, of course, will purr and feel flattered.

That's how Professor Sherman treats his enemies: buns to his grizzlies.*

Well, Professor Sherman, being a professor, has got to be nice to everybody about everybody. What else does a professor sit in a chair of English for, except to dole out sweets.

Awfully nice, rather cloying. But there, men *are* but children of a later growth.*

So much for the professor's attitude. As for his "message." He steers his little ship of Criticism most obviously between the Scylla of Mr. Mencken and the Charybdis* of Mr. P. E. More. I'm sorry I never heard before of either gentleman: except that I dimly remember having read, in the lounge of a Naples hotel, a bit of an article by a Mr. Mencken, in German, in some German periodical: all amounting to nothing.

But Mr. Mencken is the Scylla of American Criticism, and hence, of American Democracy. There is a verb "to menckenise," and a noun "menckenism." Apparently *to menckenise* is to manufacture jeering little gas-bomb phrases against everything deep and earnest, or high and noble, and to paint the face of corruption with phosphorus, so it shall glow. And a *menckenism* is one of the little stink-gas phrases.

Now the nouveau riche jeune fille of the bourgeoise,* as Professor Sherman puts it; in other words, the profiteers' flappers,* all read Mr. Mencken and swear by him: swear that they don't give a nickel for any GREAT MAN that ever was or will be. GREAT MEN are all a bombastical swindle. So asserts the "nouveau riche jeune fille," on whom,

apparently, American democracy rests. And Mr. Mencken "learnt it her." And Mr. Mencken got it in Germany, where all stink-gas comes and came from,* according to Professor Sherman. And Mr. Mencken does it to poison the noble and great old spirit of American Democracy,
5   which is grandly Anglo-Saxon in origin, but absolutely AMERICAN in fact.

So much for the Scylla of Mr. Mencken. It is the first essay in the book. The Charybdis of Mr. P. E. More is the last essay: to this monster the professor warbles another tune. Mr. More, author of the "Shel-
10   bourne Essays,"* is learned, and steeped in tradition, the very antithesis of the nihilistic stink-gassing Mr. Mencken. But alas, Mr. More is remote: somewhat haughty and supercilious at his study table. And even alasser, with all his learning and remoteness, he hunts out the risky Restoration wits* to hob-nob with on high Parnassus;* Wycherley,*
15   for example; he likes his wits smutty. He even goes and fetches out Aphra Behn* from her disreputable oblivion, to entertain her in public.

And there you have the Charybdis of Mr. More: snobbish, distant, exclusive, disdaining even the hero from the Marne who mends the
20   gas-bracket:* and at the same time absolutely *preferring* the doubtful odour of Wycherley because it is—well, malodorous, says the professor.

Mr. Mencken: GREAT MEN and the GREAT PAST are an addled egg* full of stink-gas.

Mr. P. E. More: GREAT MEN of the GREAT PAST are utterly
25   beyond the *mobile vulgus*.* Let the *mobile vulgus* (in other words, the democratic millions of America) be cynically scoffed at by the gentlemen of the GREAT PAST, especially the naughty ones.

To the Menckenites, Professor Sherman says: Jeer not at the GREAT PAST and at the GREAT DEAD. Heroes are heroes still, they do
30   not go addled, as you would try to make out, nor turn into stink-bombs. TRADITION is honorable still, and will be honorable for ever, though it may be splashed like a futurist picture with the rotten eggs of menckenism.*

To the smaller and more select company of Moreites: Scorn not
35   the horny hand of noble toil;* "—the average man is, like (Mr. More) himself, at heart a mystic, vaguely hungering for a peace that diplomats cannot give, obscurely seeking the permanent amid the transitory; a poor swimmer struggling for a rock amid the flux of waters, a lonely pilgrim longing for the shadow of a mighty rock in a weary land. And

if 'P. E. M.' had a bit more of that natural sympathy of which he is so distrustful, he would have perceived that what more than anything else to-day keeps the average man from lapsing into Yahooism* is the religion of democracy, consisting of a little bundle of general principles which make him respect himself and his neighbor; a bundle of principles   5
kindled in crucial times by an intense emotion, in which his self-interest, his petty vices, and his envy are consumed as with fire; and he sees the common weal as the mighty rock in the shadow of which his little life and personality are to be surrendered, if need be, as things negligible and transitory."*   10

All right, Professor Sherman. All the profiteers, and shovers, and place-grabbers, and bullies, especially bullies, male and female, all that sort of gentry of the late war were, of course, outside the average. The supermen of the occasion.

The Babbitts,* while they were on the make.   15

And as for mighty rocks in weary lands, as far as my experience goes, they have served the pilgrims chiefly as sanitary offices and places in whose shadows men shall leave their offal and tin cans.

But there you have a specimen of Professor Sherman's "style." And the thin ends of his parabola.   20

The great arch is of course the Religion of Democracy, which the Professor italicises. If you want to trace the curve you must follow the course of the essays.

After *Mr. Mencken* and *Tradition* comes *Franklin*. Now Benjamin Franklin is one of the founders of the Religion of Democracy. It was he   25
who invented the creed that should satisfy the professors of all religions, not of universities only, and offend none. With a deity called Providence. Who turns out to be a sort of superlative Mr. Wanamaker,* running the globe as a revolving dry-goods store, according to a profit-and-loss system: the profit counted in plump citizens whose every want is   30
satisfied: like chickens in an absolutely coyote-proof chicken-run.

In spite of this new attempt to make us like Dr. Franklin, the flesh wearies on our bones at the thought of him. The professor hints that the good old gentleman on Quaker Oats* was really an old sinner. If it had been proved to us, we *might* have liked him. As it is, he just wearies   35
the flesh on our bones. *Religion civile*,* indeed.

Emerson. The next essay is called *The Emersonian Liberation*. Well, Emerson* is a great man still: or a great individual. And heroes are heroes still, though their banners may decay, and stink.

It is true that lilies may fester. And virtues likewise. The great VIRTUE of one age has a trick of smelling far worse than weeds* in the next.

It is a sad but undeniable fact.

5   Yet why so sad, fond lover, prithee why so sad?* Why should *Virtue* remain incorruptible, any more than anything else? If stars wax and wane, why should GOODNESS shine forever unchanged? That too makes one tired. Goodness sweals* and gutters, the light of the GOOD goes out with a stink, and lo, somewhere else a new light, a new GOOD.

10   Afterwards, it may be shown that it is eternally the same GOOD. But to us poor mortals at the moment, it emphatically isn't.

And that is the point about Emerson and the *Emersonian Liberation*— save the word! Heroes are heroes still: safely dead. Heroism is always heroism. But the hero who was heroic one century, uplifting the banner

15   of a creed, is followed the next century by a hero heroically ripping that banner to rags. Sic transit veritas mundi.*

Emerson was an Idealist: a believer in "continuous revelation," continuous inrushes of inspirational energy from the Over-soul.* Professor Sherman says: "His message when he leaves us is not, 'Henceforth be

20   masterless,' but, 'Bear thou henceforth the sceptre of thine own control through life and the passion of life.'"*

When Emerson says: "I am surrounded by messengers of God who send me credentials day by day,"* then all right for him. But he cosily forgot that there are many messengers. He knew only a sort of

25   smooth-shaven Gabriel. But as far as we remember, there is Michael* too: and a terrible discrepancy between the credentials of the pair of 'em. Then there are other cherubim with outlandish names, bringing very different messages than those Ralph Waldo got: Israfel, and even Mormon.* And a whole bunch of others. But Emerson had a

30   stone-deaf ear for all except a nicely-aureoled Gabriel *qui n'avait pas de quoi.**

Emerson listened to one sort of message, and one only. To all the rest he was blank. Ashtaroth and Ammon are gods as well,* and hand out their own credentials. But Ralph Waldo wasn't having any. They

35   could never ring *him* up. He was only connected on the Ideal 'phone. "We are all aiming to be idealists," says Emerson, "and covet the society of those who make us so, as the sweet singer, the orator, the ideal painter."*

Well, we're pretty sick of the ideal painters and the uplifting singers.

40   As a matter of fact we have worked the ideal bit of our nature to death, and

we shall go crazy if we can't start working from some other bit. Idealism
now is a sick nerve, and the more you rub on it the worse you feel
afterwards. Your later reactions aren't pretty at all. Like Dostoevsky's
Idiot, and President Wilson* sometimes.

Emerson believes in having the courage to treat all men as equals. It   5
takes some courage *not* to treat them so now.

"Shall I not treat all men as gods?"* he cries.

If you like, Waldo, but we've got to pay for it, when you've made
them *feel* that they're gods. A hundred million American godlets is
rather much for the world to deal with.   10

The fact of the matter is, all those gorgeous inrushes of exaltation
and spiritual energy which made Emerson a great man, now make us
sick. They are with us a drug habit. So when Professor Sherman urges
us in Ralph Waldo's footsteps, he is really driving us nauseously astray.
Which perhaps is hard lines on the Professor, and us, and Emerson. But   15
it wasn't I who started the mills of God a-grinding.*

I like the essay on Emerson. I like Emerson's real courage. I like his
wild and genuine belief in the Over-soul and the inrushes he got from
it. But it is a museum-interest. Or else it is a taste of the old drug to the
old spiritual drug-fiend in me.   20

We've got to have a different sort of sardonic courage. And the sort
of credentials we are due to receive from the god in the shadow would
have been real bones out of hell-broth to Ralph Waldo. Sic transeunt
Dei hominorum.*

So no wonder Professor Sherman sounds a little wistful, and   25
somewhat pathetic, as he begs us to follow Ralph Waldo's trail.

Hawthorne: A Puritan Critic of Puritanism. This essay is concerned
chiefly with an analysis and a praise of *The Scarlet Letter*.* Well, it is
a wonderful book. But why does nobody give little Nathaniel a kick
for his duplicity. Professor Sherman says there is nothing erotic about   30
The Scarlet Letter.* Only neurotic. It wasn't the sensual act itself had
any meaning for Hawthorne. Only the SIN. He knows there's nothing
deadly in the act itself. But if it is FORBIDDEN, immediately it looms
lurid with interest. He is not concerned for a moment with what Hester
and Dimmesdale* really felt. Only with their situation as SINNERS.   35
And SIN looms lurid and thrilling, when after all it is only just a normal sexual passion. This luridness about the book makes one feel like
spitting. It is something worked up: invented in the head and grafted on
to the lower body, like some serpent of supposition under the fig-leaf.*
It depends so much on *coverings*. Suppose you took off the fig-leaf, the   40

serpent isn't there. And so the relish is all two-faced and tiresome. *The Scarlet Letter* is a masterpiece, but in duplicity and half-false excitement.

And when one remembers *The Marble Faun*,* all the parochial prig-gishness and poor-bloodedness of Hawthorne in Italy, one of the most
5   bloodless books ever written, one feels like giving Nathaniel a kick in the seat of his poor little pants and landing him back in New England again. For the rolling, many-godded mediaeval and pagan world was too big a prey for such a ferret.

*Walt Whitman.** Walt is the high priest of the Religion of Democracy.
10 Yet "at the first bewildering contact one wonders whether his urgent touch is of lewdness or divinity,"* says Professor Sherman.

"All I have said concerns you."*—But it doesn't. One ceases to care about so many things. One ceases to respond or to react. And at length other things come up, which Walt and Professor Sherman never
15 knew.

"Whatever else it involves, democracy involves at least one grand salu-tary elementary admission, namely, that the world exists for the benefit and for the improvement of all the decent individuals in it."*—Oh Lord, how long will you submit to this Insurance Policy interpretation of the
20 Universe. How "decent"? Decent in what way? Benefit! Think of the world's existing for people's "benefit and improvement."

So wonderful, says Professor Sherman, the way Whitman identifies himself with everything and everybody: Runaway Slaves and all the rest. But we no longer want to take the whole hullabaloo to our bosom. We
25 no longer want to "identify ourselves" with a lot of other things and other people. It *is* a sort of lewdness. *Noli me tangere*,* you. I don't want you.

Whitman's "you" doesn't get me.

We don't want to be embracing everything any more. Or to be
30 embraced in one of Walt's vast promiscuous armfuls. *Merci, monsieur!**
We've had enough democracy.

Professor Sherman says that if Whitman had lived "at the right place in these years of Proletarian Millenium, he would have been hanged as a reactionary member of the *bourgeoise*."* (Tis n't my spelling.)
35 And he gives Whitman's own words in proof: "The true gravita-tion hold of liberalism in the United States will be a more universal ownership of property, general homesteads, general comforts—a vast, intertwining reticulation of wealth. . . . . She (Democracy) asks for men and women with occupations, well-off, owners of houses and acres, and

with cash in the bank and with some craving for literature too"*—so
that they can buy certain books.

Oh, Walt!

Allons! The road is before us.*

Joaquin Miller: Poetical Conquistador of the West. A long essay with
not much spirit in it, showing that Miller* was a true son of the Wild and
Woolly West, in so far as he was a very good imitator of other people's
poetry (note the Swinburnian bit)* and a rather poor assumer of other
people's played-out poses. A self-conscious little "wild" man, like the
rest of the "wild" men. The Wild West is a pose that pays Zane Grey
today, as it once paid Miller and Bret Harte and Buffalo Bill.*

A Note on Carl Sandburg. That Carl is a super-self-conscious lit-
erairy gent stampeding around with red-ochre blood on his hands and
smeared-on soot darkening his craggy would-be-criminal brow: but
that his heart is as tender as an old tomato.

Andrew Carnegie. That Andy was the most perfect American citizen
Scotland ever produced, and the sweetest example of how beautifully
the *Religion Civile* pays, in hard cash.

Roosevelt and the National Psychology.* Theodore didn't have a spark
of magnanimity in his great personality, says Professor Sherman, what
a pity! And you see where it lands you, when you play at being pro-
German.* You go quite out of fashion.

Evolution of the Adams Family. Perfect Pedigree of the most aristocratic Democratic family. Your aristocracy is played out, my dear
fellows, but don't cry about it, you've always got your Democracy to
fall back on. If you don't like falling back on it of your own free will,
you'll be shoved back on it by the Will of the People.

"Man is the animal that destiny cannot break."*

But the Will of the People can break Man, and the animal man, and
the destined man, all the lot, and grind 'em to democratic powder,
Professor Sherman warns us.

Allons! en-masse is before us.

But when Germany is thoroughly broken, Democracy finally collapses. (My own prophecy.)

An Imaginary Conversation With Mr P. E. More: You've had the gist
of that already.

Well, there is Professor Sherman's dish of cookies which he bids
you eat and have. An awfully sweet book, all about having your cookies
and eating 'em.* The cookies are Tradition, and Heroes, and Great

5

10

15

20

25

30

35

Men, and $350,000,000* in your pocket. And eating 'em is Democracy, Serving Mankind, piously giving most of the $350,000,000 back again. "Oh nobly and heroically get $350,000,000 together," chants Professor Sherman in this litany of having your cookies and eating 'em, "and then piously and munificently give away $349,000,000 again."

P.S. You can't get past Arithmetic.

REVIEW OF A SECOND CONTEMPORARY
VERSE ANTHOLOGY, *EDITED BY*
C. W. STORK

"It is not merely an assembly of verse, but the spiritual record of an entire people."*—This from the wrapper of "A Second Contemporary Verse Anthology."* The spiritual record of an entire people sounds rather impressive. The book as a matter of fact is a collection of pleasant verse, neat and nice and easy as eating candy.

Naturally, any collection of contemporary verse in any country at any time is bound to be more or less a box of candy. Days of Horace,* days of Milton, days of Whitman, it would be pretty much the same, more or less a box of candy. Would it be at the same time the spiritual record of an entire people? Why not? If we had a good representative anthology of the poetry of Whitman's day, and if it contained two poems by Whitman, then it would be a fairly true spiritual record of the American people of that day. As if the whole nation had whispered or chanted its inner experience into the horn of a gramophone.*

And the bulk of the whisperings and murmurings would be candy: sweet nothings, tender trifles, and amusing things. For of such is the bulk of the spiritual experience of any entire people.

The Americans have always been good at "occasional" verse. Sixty years ago they were very good indeed: making their little joke against themselves and their century. To-day there are fewer jokes. There are also fewer footprints on the sands of time. Life is still earnest, but a little less real. And the soul has left off asserting that dust it isn't nor to dust returneth.* The spirit of verse prefers now a "composition salad" of fruits of sensation, in a cooked mayonnaise of sympathy. Odds and ends of feelings smoothed into unison by some prevailing sentiment:

> My face is wet with the rain
> But my heart is warm to the core—*

Or you can call it a box of chocolate candies. Let me offer you a sweet! Candy! Isn't everything candy?

231

> There be none of beauty's daughters
>   With a magic like thee—
> And like music on the waters
>   Is thy sweet voice to me.*

5   Is that candy? Then what about this?

> But you are a girl and run
>   Fresh bathed and warm and sweet,
> After the flying ball
>   On little, sandalled feet.*

10   One of those two fragments is a classic. And one is a scrap from the
contemporary spiritual record.

> The river boat had loitered down its way,
> The ropes were coiled, and business for the day
> Was done—*

15
> Now fades the glimmering landscape on the sight,
> And all the air a solemn stillness holds;
> Save where—*

Two more bits. Do you see any intrinsic difference between them? After
all, the one *means* as much as the other. And what is there in the mere
20   stringing together of words?

For some mysterious reason, there is everything.

> When lilacs last in the dooryard bloomed—*

It is a string of words, but it makes me prick my innermost ear. So
do I prick my ear to: "Fly low, vermilion dragon." But the next line:
25   "With the moon horns,"* makes me lower that same inward ear once
more, in indifference.

There is an element of danger in all new utterance. We prick our ears
like an animal in a wood at a strange sound.

Alas! though there is a modicum of "strange sound" in this con-
30   temporary spiritual record, we are not the animal to prick our ears at
it. Sounds sweetly familiar, linked in a new crochet pattern.* "Christ,
what are patterns for?"* But why invoke Deity? Ask the *Ladies' Home
Journal.** You may know a new utterance by the element of danger in it.
"My heart aches," says Keats,* and you bet it's no joke.

35
> Why do I think of stairways
> With a rush of hurt surprise?*

Heaven knows, my dear, unless you once fell down.

The element of danger. Man is always, all the time and forever on the brink of the unknown. The minute you realize this, you prick your ears in alarm. And the minute any man steps alone, with his whole naked self, emotional and mental, into the everlasting hinterland of consciousness,   5
you hate him and you wonder over him. Why can't he stay cozily playing word-games around the camp fire?

Now it is time to invoke the Deity, who made man an adventurer into the everlasting unknown of consciousness.

The spiritual record of any people is 99 per cent a record of games   10
around a camp fire: word-games and picture-games. But the one per cent is a step into the grisly dark, which is forever dangerous and wonderful. Nothing is wonderful unless it is dangerous. Dangerous to the *status quo* of the soul. And therefore to some degree detestable.

When the contemporary spiritual record warbles away about the won-   15
der of the blue sky and the changing seas, etc., etc., etc., it is all candy. The sky is a blue hand-mirror to the modern poet and he goes on smirking before it. The blue sky of our particular heavens is painfully well known to us all. In fact, it is like the glass bowl to the goldfish, a *ne plus ultra* in which he sees himself as he goes round and round.   20

The actual heavens can suddenly roll up like the heavens of Ezekiel.* That's what happened at the Renaissance. The old heavens shrivelled and men found a new empyrean above them. But they didn't get at it by playing word-games around the camp fire. Somebody has to jump like a desperate clown through the vast blue hoop of the upper air. Or   25
hack a slow way through the dome of crystal.*

Play! Play! Play! All the little playboys and playgirls of the Western world,* playing at goodness, playing at badness, playing at sadness, and playing deafeningly at gladness. Playboys and playgirls of the Western world, harmlessly fulfilling their higher destinies and registering the   30
spiritual record of an entire people. Even playing at death, and play-ing with death. Oh, poetry, you child in a bathing-dress, playing at ball!

You say nature is always nature, the sky is always the sky. But sit still and consider for one moment what sort of nature it was the Romans saw   35
on the face of the earth, and what sort of heavens the mediaevals knew above them, and your sky will begin to crack like glass. The world is what it is, and the chimerical universe of the ancients was always child's play. The camera cannot lie. And the eye of man is nothing but a camera photographing the outer world in color-process.   40

This sounds very well. But the eye of man photographs the chimera of nature, as well as the so-called scientific vision. The eye of man photographs gorgons and chimeras,* as the eye of the spider photographs images unrecognizable to us and the eye of the horse photographs flat

5   ghosts and looming motions. We are at the phase of scientific vision. This phase will pass and this vision will seem as chimerical to our descendants as the mediaeval vision seems to us.

The upshot of it all is that we are pot-bound* in our consciousness. We are like a fish in a glass bowl, swimming round and round and gaping

10   at our own image reflected on the walls of the infinite: the infinite being the glass bowl of our conception of life and the universe. We are prisoners inside our own conception of life and being. We have exhausted the possibilities of the universe, as we know it. All that remains is to telephone to Mars for a new word of advice.

15   Our consciousness is pot-bound. Our ideas, our emotions, our experiences are all pot-bound. For us there is nothing new under the sun.* What there is to know, we know it already, and experience adds little. The girl who is going to fall in love knows all about it beforehand from books and the movies. She knows what she wants and she wants what

20   she knows. Like candy. It is still nice to eat candy, though one has eaten it every day for years. It is still nice to eat candy. But the spiritual record of eating candy is a rather thin noise.

There is nothing new under the sun, once the consciousness becomes pot-bound. And this is what ails all art to-day. But particularly Ameri-

25   can art. The American consciousness is peculiarly pot-bound. It doesn't even have that little hole in the bottom of the pot through which desperate roots straggle. No, the American consciousness is not only potted in a solid and everlasting pot, it is placed moreover in an immovable ornamental vase. A double hide to bind it and a double bond to hide it.

30   European consciousness still has cracks in its vessel and a hole in the bottom of its absoluteness. It still has strange roots of memory groping down to the heart of the world.

But American consciousness is absolutely free of such danglers. It is free from all loopholes and crevices of escape. It is absolutely safe

35   inside a solid and ornamental concept of life. There it is Free! Life is good, and all men are meant to have a good time. Life is good! that is the flower-pot. The ornamental vase is: Having a good time.

So they proceed to have it, even with their woes. The young maiden knows exactly when she falls in love: she knows exactly how she feels

40   when her lover or husband betrays her or when she betrays him: she

knows precisely what it is to be a forsaken wife, an adoring mother, an
erratic grandmother. All at the age of eighteen.

Vive la vie!*

There is nothing new under the sun, but you can have a jolly good
old time all the same with the old things. A nut sundae or a new beau,   5
a baby or an automobile, a divorce or a troublesome appendix: my dear,
that's Life! You've got to get a good time out of it, anyhow, so here goes!

In which attitude there is a certain piquant stoicism. The stoicism of
having a good time. The heroism of enjoying yourself. But, as I say, it
makes rather thin hearing in a spiritual record. *Réchauffés* of *réchauffés*.*   10
Old soup of old bones of life, heated up again for a new consommé.
Nearly always called *printanière*.*

> I know a forest, stilly-deep—*

Mark the poetic novelty of stilly-deep, and then say there is nothing
new under the sun.   15

> My soul-harp never thrills to peaceful tunes;*

I should say so.

> For after all, the thing to do
> Is just to put your heart in song—*

Or in pickle.   20

> I sometimes wish that God were back
>   In this dark world and wide;
> For though some virtues he might lack,
>   He had his pleasant side.*

"Getting on the pleasant side of God, and how to stay there."—Hints   25
by a Student of Life.

> Oh, ho! Now I am masterful!
> Now I am filled with power.
> Now I am brutally myself again
> And my own man.   30

> For I have been among my hills to-day,
> On the scarred dumb rocks standing;*

And it made a man of him . . .
Open confession is good for the soul.
The spiritual record of an entire . . . what?   35

REVIEW OF HADRIAN THE SEVENTH, *BY*
FR. ROLFE (BARON CORVO)

In *Hadrian the Seventh*, Frederick Baron Corvo* falls in, head over heels, in deadly earnest. A man must keep his earnestness nimble, to escape ridicule. The so-called Baron Corvo by no means escapes. He reaches heights, or depths, of sublime ridiculousness.

It doesn't kill the book, however. Neither ridicule nor dead earnest 5
kills it. It is extraordinarily alive, even though it has been buried for twenty years. Up it rises to confront us. And, great test, it does not "date" as do Huysmans's books,* or Wilde's,* or the rest of them. Only a first-rate book escapes its date.

Frederick Rolfe was a fantastic figure of the 'nineties, the 'nineties of 10
the Yellow Book,* Oscar Wilde, Aubrey Beardsley,* Simeon Solomon,* and all the host of the godly. The whole decade is now a little ridiculous, ridiculous decadence as well as ridiculous pietism. They said of Rolfe that he was certainly possessed of a devil. At least his devil is still alive, it hasn't turned into a sort of gollywog,* like the bulk of the 'nineties' 15
devils.

Rolfe was one of the Catholic converts of the period, very intense. But if ever a man was a Protestant in all his being, this one was. The acuteness of his protest drove him, like a crazy serpent, into the bosom* of the Roman Catholic Church. 20

He seems to have been a serpent of serpents in the bosom of all the 'nineties. That in itself endears him to one. The way everyone dropped him with a shudder is almost fascinating.

He died about 1912,* when he was already forgotten: an outcast and in a sense a wastrel. 25

We can well afford to remember him again: he was not nothing, as so many of the estimables were. He was a gentleman of education and culture, pining, for the show's sake, to be a priest. The Church shook him out of her bosom before he could take orders. So he wrote himself Fr. Rolfe. It would do for Frederick, and if you thought it meant Father 30
Rolfe, good old you!

But then his other passion, for mediaeval royalism, overcame him, and he was Baron Corvo when he signed his name. Lord Rook, Lord Raven,* the bird was the same as Fr. Rolfe.

Hadrian the Seventh is, as far as his connection with the Church was concerned, largely an autobiography of Frederick Rolfe. It is the story of a young English convert, George Arthur Rose (Rose for Rolfe), who has had bitter experience with the priests and clergy, and years of frustration and disappointment, till he arrives at about the age of forty, a highly-bred, highly-sensitive, super-aesthetic man, ascetic out of aestheticism, athletic the same, religious the same. He is to himself beautiful, with a slim, clean-muscled grace, much given to cold baths, white-faced with a healthy pallor, and pure, that is sexually chaste, because of his almost morbid repugnance for women. He had no desires to conquer or to purify. Women were physically repulsive to him, and therefore chastity cost him nothing, the Church would be a kind of asylum.

The priests and the clergy, however, turned him down, or dropped him like the proverbial snake in the bosom, and inflamed him against them, so that he was burned through and through with white, cease-less anger. His anger had become so complete as to be pure: it really was demonish. But it was all nervous and imaginative, an imaginative, sublimated hate, of a creature born crippled in its affective organism.

The first part of the book, describing the lonely man in a London lodging, alone save for his little cat, whose feline qualities of aloofness and self-sufficiency he so much admires, fixes the tone at once. And in the whole of literature I know nothing that resembles those amazing chapters, when the Bishop and the Archbishop come to him, and when he is ordained and makes his confession. Then the description of the election of the new Pope, the cardinals shut up in the Vatican, the failure of the Way of Scrutiny and the Way of Access, the fantastic choice, by the Way of Compromise,* of George Arthur Rose, is too extraordinary and daring ever to be forgotten.

From being a rejected aspirant to the priesthood, George Arthur Rose, the man in the London lodging, finds himself suddenly not only consecrated, but elected head of all the Catholic Church. He becomes Pope Hadrian the Seventh.

Then the real fantasy and failure begins. George Arthur Rose, triple-crowned and in the chair of Peter,* is still very much Frederick Rolfe, and perfectly consistent. He is the same man, but now he has it all his own way: a White Pope, pure, scrupulous, chaste, living on two dollars a day, an aesthetic idealist, and, really, a super-Protestant. He has the

British instinct of authority, which is now gloriously gratified. But he
has no inward *power*, power to make true change in the world. Once he
is on the throne of high power, we realize his futility.

He is, like most modern men, especially reformers and idealists,
through and through a protestant. Which means, his life is a changeless   5
fervour of protest. He can't help it. Everything he comes into contact
with he must criticize, with all his nerves, and react from. Fine, subtle,
sensitive, and almost egomaniac, he can accept nothing but the momentary thrill of aesthetic appreciation. His life-flow is like a stream washing
against a false world, and ebbing itself out in a marsh and a hopeless   10
bog.

So it is with George Arthur Rose, become Pope Hadrian the Seventh,
while he is still in a state of pure protest, he is vivid and extraordinary.
But once he is given full opportunity to do as he wishes, and his *raison
d'être** as a Protestant is thereby taken away, he becomes futile, and lapses   15
into the ridiculous.

He can criticize men, exceedingly well: hence his knack of authority.
But the moment he has to build men into a new form, construct something out of men by making a new unity among them, swarming them
upon himself as bees upon a queen, he is ridiculous and powerless, a   20
fraud.

It is extraordinary how *blind* he is, with all his keen insight. He no
more "gets" his cardinals than we get the men on Mars. He can criticize
them, and analyze them, and reject or condone them. But the real old
Adam that is in them, the old male instinct for *power*, this, to him, does   25
not exist.

In actual life, of course, the cardinals would drop a Hadrian down
the oubliette,* in ten minutes, and without any difficulty at all, once he
was inside the Vatican.* And Hadrian would be utterly flabbergasted,
and call it villainy.   30

And what's the good of being Pope, if you've nothing but protest
and aesthetics up your sleeve? Just like the reformers who are excellent,
while fighting Authority. But once authority disappears, they fall into
nothingness. So with Hadrian the Seventh. As Pope, he is a fraud. His
critical insight makes him a politician of the League of Nations sort,* on   35
a vast and curious scale. His mediaevalism makes him a truly comical
royalist. But as a *man*, a real power in the world, he does not exist.

Hadrian unwinding the antimacassar* is a sentimental farce. Hadrian
persecuted to the point of suicide by a blowsy lodging-house keeper* is
a bathetic farce. Hadrian and the Socialist "with gorgonzola teeth"* is   40

puerile beyond words. It is all amazing, that a man with so much insight and fineness, on the one hand, should be so helpless and just purely ridiculous, when it comes to actualities.

He simply has no conception of what it is to be a natural or honestly animal man, with the repose and the power that goes with the honest animal in man. His attempt to appreciate his Cardinal Ragna—probably meant for Rampolla*—is funny. It is as funny as would be an attempt on the part of the late President Wilson to appreciate Hernan Cortes, or even Theodore Roosevelt,* supposing they were put face to face.

The time has come for stripping:* cries Hadrian. Strip then, if there are falsities to throw away. But if you go on and on and on peeling the onion down, you'll be left with blank nothing between your hands, at last.* And this is Hadrian's plight. He is assassinated in the streets of Rome by a Socialist, and dies supported by three Majesties, sublimely absurd. And there is nothing to it. Hadrian has stripped himself and everything else till nothing is left but absurd conceit, expiring in the arms of the Majesties.

*Lord! be to me a Saviour, not a judge!** is Hadrian's prayer: when he is not affectedly praying in Greek. But why should such a white streak of blamelessness as Hadrian need saving so badly? Saved from what? If he has done his best, why mind being judged—at least by Jesus, who in this sense is any man's peer?

The brave man asks for justice: the rabble cries for favours! says some old writer.* Why does Hadrian, in spite of all his protest, go in with the rabble?

It is a problem. The book remains a clear and definite book of our epoch, not to be swept aside. If it is the book of a demon, as the contemporaries said, it is the book of a man-demon, not of a mere poseur. And if some of it is caviare,* at least it came out of the belly of a live fish.

REVIEW OF SAÏD THE FISHERMAN, *BY* MARMADUKE PICKTHALL

Since the days of Lady Hester Stanhope* and her romantic pranks, down to the exploits of Colonel T. E. Lawrence* in the late war, there seems always to have been some more or less fantastic Englishman, or woman, Arabizing among the Arabs. Until we feel we know the desert and the Bedouin* better than we know Wales or our next-door neighbour.

Perhaps there is an instinctive sympathy between the Semite Arab* and the Anglo-Saxon. If so, it must have its root way down in the religious make-up of both peoples. The Arab is intensely a One-God man, and so is the Briton.

But the Briton is mental and critical in his workings, the Arab uncritical and impulsive. In the Arab, the Englishman sees himself with the lid off.

T. E. Lawrence distinguishes two kinds of Englishmen* in the East: the kind that goes native, more or less like Sir Richard Burton,* and takes on native dress, speech, manners, morals, and women; then the other kind, that penetrates to the heart of Arabia, like Charles M. Doughty,* but remains an Englishman in the fullest sense of the word. Doughty, in his rags and misery, his blond beard, his scrupulous honesty, with his Country forever behind him, is indeed the very pith of England, dwelling in the houses of hair.

Marmaduke Pickthall,* I am almost sure, remained an Englishman and a gentleman in the Near East. Only in imagination he goes native. And that thoroughly.

We are supposed to get inside the skin of Saïd the Fisherman, to hunger, fear, lust, enjoy, suffer, and dare as Saïd does, and to see the world through Saïd's big, dark, shining Arab eyes.

It is not easy. It is not easy for a man of one race entirely to identify himself with a man of another race, of different culture and religion. When the book opens, Saïd is a fisherman naked on the coast of Syria, living with his wife Hasneh in a hut by the sands. Saïd is young, strong-bodied, and lusty: Hasneh is beginning to fade.

The first half of the novel is called: The Book of his Luck; the second half: The Book of his Fate. We are to read into the word Fate the old meaning, of revenge of the gods.

Saïd's savings are treacherously stolen by his partner. The poor fish-
5   erman wails, despairs, rouses up, and taking a hint about evil genii,* packs himself and his scraps on an ass, lets Hasneh run behind, and sets off to Damascus.*

The Book of his Luck is a curious mixture of Arabian Nights and mo-dern realism. I think, on the whole, Scheherazade's influence* is stron-
10 gest. The poor fisherman suddenly becomes one of the lusty Sinbad* sort, and his luck is stupendous. At the same time, he is supposed to remain the simple man Saïd, with ordinary human responsibilities.

We are prepared to go gaily on with Saïd, his sudden glory of impu-dence and luck, when straight away we get a hit below the belt.* Saïd,
15 the mere man, abandons the poor, faithful, devoted Hasneh, his wife, in circumstances of utter meanness. We double up, and for the time being completely lose interest in the lucky and lusty fisherman. It takes an incident as sufficiently realistic and as amusing as that of the mission-ary's dressing-gown,* to get us up again. Even then we have cold feet
20 because of the impudent Saïd; he looks vulgar, common. And we resent a little the luck and the glamour of him, the fact that we have to follow him as a hero. A picaresque novel* is all very well, but the one quality demanded of a picaro, to make him more than a common sneak, is a certain reckless generosity.
25 Saïd is reckless enough, but, as shown by Mr. Pickthall, with impu-dence based on meanness, the sort of selfishness that is mongrel, and a bit sneaking. Yet Mr. Pickthall still continues to infuse a certain glamour into him, and to force our sympathy for him.

It is the thing one most resents in a novel: having one's sympathy
30 *forced* by the novelist, towards some character we should never naturally sympathize with.

Saïd is a handsome, strong, lusty scoundrel, impudent, with even a certain dauntlessness. We could get on with him very well indeed, if every now and then we didn't get another blow under the belt, by a
35 demonstration of his cold, gutter-snipe* callousness.

One almost demands revenge on him. The revenge comes, and again we are angry.

The author hasn't treated us fairly. He has identified himself too closely with his hero: he can't see wood for trees. Because, of course,
40 inside the skin of Saïd, Mr. Pickthall is intensely a good, moral English-man, and intensely uneasy.

So with an Englishman's over-scrupulous honesty, he has had to show us his full reactions to Saïd. Marmaduke Pickthall, Englishman, is fascinated by Saïd's lustiness, his reckless, impudent beauty, his immoral, or non-moral nature. We hope it is non-moral. We are shown it is immoral. Marmaduke Pickthall loathes the mean immorality of Saïd, and has to punish him for it, in the Book of his Fate.

All very well, but it's a risky thing to hold the scales for a man whose moral nature is not your own. Mr. Pickthall's moral values are utilitarian and rational: Saïd's are emotional and sensual. The fact that Saïd's moral values are emotional and sensual makes Saïd so lusty and handsome, gives him such glamour for Mr. Pickthall. Mr. Pickthall resents the spell, and brings a charge of immorality. Then the Fates and the Furies* get their turn.

The two charges against Saïd are his abandonment of the poor Hasneh, and his indifference to his faithful friend Selim.

As to Hasneh, she had been his wife for six years and borne him no children, and during these years he had lived utterly poor and vacant. But he was a man of energy. The moment he leaves the sea-shore, he becomes another fellow, wakes up.

The poor lout he was when he lived with Hasneh is transformed. Ca-Ca-Caliban. Get a new mistress, be a new man!* Saïd had no tradition of sexual fidelity. His aim in living—or at least a large part of his aim in living—was sensual gratification; and this was not against his religion. His newly released energy, the new man he was, needed a new mistress, many new mistresses. It was part of his whole tradition. Because all Hasneh's service and devotion did not stimulate his energies, rather deadened them. She was a weight round his neck. And her prostrate devotion, while pathetic, was *not* admirable. It was a dead weight. He needed a subtler mistress.

Here the judgment of Marmaduke Pickthall is a white man's judgment on a dark man. The Englishman sympathizes with the poor abandoned woman at the expense of the energetic man. The sympathy is false. If the woman were alert and kept her end up, she would neither be poor nor abandoned. But it was easier for her to fall at Saïd's feet than to stand on her own.

If you ride a mettlesome horse you mind the bit,* or you'll get thrown. It's a law of nature.

Saïd was mean, in that he did not send some sort of help to Hasneh, when he could. But that is carelessness of a sensual nature, rather than villainy. Out of sight out of mind is true of those who have not much mind: and Saïd had little.

No, our quarrel with him is for being a fool, for not being on the alert: the same quarrel we had with Hasneh. If he had not been a slack fool his Christian wife would not have ruined him so beautifully. And if he had been even a bit wary and cautious, he would not have let himself in for his last adventure.

It is this adventure which sets us quarrelling with Mr. Pickthall and his manipulation of our sympathy. With real but idiotic courage Saïd swims out to an English steamer off Beirut.* He is taken to London: falls into the nightmare of that city: loses his reason for ever, but, a white-haired handsome imbecile, is restored to his faithful ones in Alexandria.*

We would fain think this ghastly vengeance fell on him because of his immorality. But it didn't. Not at all. It was merely because of his foolish, impudent leaping before he'd looked.* He wouldn't realize his own limitations, so he went off the deep end.

It is a summing-up of the Damascus Arab by a sympathetic, yet outraged Englishman. One feels that Mr. Pickthall gave an extra shove to the mills of God.* Perfectly gratuitous!

Yet one is appalled, thinking of Saïd in London. When one does come out of the open sun into the dank dark autumn of London,* one almost loses one's reason, as Saïd does. And then one wonders: can the backward civilizations show us anything half so ghastly and murderous as we show them, and with pride?

REVIEW OF THE ORIGINS OF
PROHIBITION, *BY J. A. KROUT*

The Origins of Prohibition*

This is a book which one may honestly call "an excellent piece of work."
Myself, I feel I have done a more or less excellent piece of work, in having
read it. Because it wearied me a little.

But then, I am not an American, and have never, to my knowledge,   5
had a single relative in the United States. And I am a novelist, not a
scientific historian. All the American names mean nothing to me, and
to this day I don't know where Rhode Island* is. So there are limits to
my sympathy.

Yet I have read the book, and realise it is a sound piece of work: an   10
attempt to convey, dispassionately, the attitude of the American people
to alcoholic drinks, since the early days of the colonies. This is not,
strictly, an enquiry into the *origins* of prohibition. For that, one would
have to go deeper. It is a record of the development of the prohibitionist
feeling: almost, a statistical record. There are copious notes, and an   15
extraordinary bibliography: good scholarship, but on the whole, flat
reading.

One wonders if anything should try to be so angelically dispassion-
ate: anything except an adding-up machine. Reading the chapters about
excise laws, and political campaigns, a deep depression comes over   20
one. There are gleams of warmth and vividness elsewhere. The very
words malmsey, and sack,* and pale sherry, cheer one up a bit. And
the famous cycle* molasses—rum—slaves—molasses—rum—slaves
makes one pause: as does the glimpse of Washington's army getting its
whiskey rations.* As soon as we catch sight of an actual individual, like   25
Dr Rush,* we prick up our ears—but Dr Rush turns out rather boring.
The Washingtonians,* with the Cold Water Army,* and Hawkins and
Gough,* might really have been lively; while to step into the sobbing
literature of teetotalism is a relaxation. But the author is inexorable.
He won't laugh, and he won't let us laugh. He won't get angry, and   30
he prevents our getting angry. He refuses to take an attitude, except
that of impartiality, which is the worst of all attitudes. So he leaves
us depressed, not wanting to hear another word about temperance,

teetotalism, prohibition. We want to relegate the whole business into
the class of "matters indifferent," where John Knox put it.*

We can't, quite: since prohibition has us by the leg. So perhaps it
is as well to read this book, which helps us to come to a decision. For
5   myself—dropping all pretence at impartiality—it makes me regret that
ardent spirits* were ever discovered. Why, oh why, as soon as the New
World waved the sugar-cane, did it start turning molasses into rum?
and as soon as the wheat rose in the colonies, why did it disappear
into whiskey? Apparently, until the time of the Renaissance and the
10   discovery of America, men actually drank no liquors—or very little.
Beer, cider, wine, these had kept the world going, more or less, till
the days of Columbus.* Why did all Europe and America suddenly,
after the Renaissance, demand powerful liquor? Get drunk quick? It is
a mystery, and a tragedy, and part of our evolution.

15   That distilled liquor has been more of a curse than a blessing to
mankind, few surely will deny. It is only the curse of whiskey which
has driven wine and beer into disrepute. Until a few decades ago, even
the temperance societies had nothing to say against beer.—But now it
is the whole hog.

20   In the conclusion, which is cautiously called "A Summary View", the
author finds that Prohibition* in America was inevitable: firstly, because
a self-governing people must be self-responsible.—"Intemperance
might be tolerated in a divine-right monarchy, but in a republic it
endangered the very existence of the state. No popular government
25   could long endure, unless the electorate was persuaded or forced to
follow the straight and narrow path of sobriety."*—"It was ridiculous
to talk of the *will of the sovereign people*, when intoxicated citizens were
taken to the polls—"*

This is confused thinking.* How can the electorate of a popular gov-
30   ernment be *forced* to follow the straight and narrow path? Persuaded,
an electorate may be. But how, and by whom can it be *forced*?

The answer is, by itself: an electorate forcing itself to do a thing it
doesn't want to do, and doesn't intend to do, is indeed making a display
of the sovereign will of the people.

35   But this is the anomaly of popular government. Obviously America
failed to *persuade* herself, or to be persuaded, into the straight and narrow
path of sobriety. So she went one worse, and forced herself.

And this is the dreary, depressing reality. A Republic with a "popular
government" can only exist honorably when the bulk of the individuals
40   choose, of their own free will, to follow the straight and narrow path

necessary to the common good. That is, when every man governs himself, responsibly, from within. Which, say what we may, was the very
germ of the "American idea."

The dreary and depressing fact is that this germ is dying, if not dead.
Temperance reformers decided, after long experience, that America   5
was not to be persuaded. Her citizens could not, or would not control
themselves, with regard to liquor.

Therefore they must be coerced.— By whom? By the electorate itself.
Every man voting prohibition for his neighbour, voted it for himself,
of course. But somewhere he made a mental reservation. He intended,   10
himself, to have his little drink still, if he wanted it. Since he, good
citizen, knew better than to abuse himself.

The cold misery of every man seeking to coerce his neighbour, in the
name of righteousness, creeps out of these pages, and makes depressing
reading.   15

The second reason why prohibition was inevitable—because it is
advantageous to industry—is sound as far as economics go. But how
far do national economics go, even in America, in the ordinary individual. And even then, it is temperance, not prohibition, which is truly
advantageous to industry.   20

One is chilled and depressed. The saloon was bad, and is best abol-
ished. Myself, I believe that. But in prohibition one sees an even worse
thing: a nation, knowing it cannot control itself from the inside, self-
responsibly, each man vindictively votes to coerce his neighbour.

Because surely, seeing the state of things, a great number of the voters   25
voting for prohibition must have reserved for themselves the private
right to a drink, all the same.

A man may vote from his honorable national self: or he may vote
from his vindictive herd self. Which self voted, you will only know by
the smile afterwards.   30

REVIEW OF IN THE AMERICAN GRAIN, BY WILLIAM CARLOS WILLIAMS

American Heroes

Mr. Williams* quotes Poe's distinction between "nationality in letters" and the *local* in literature.* Nationality in letters is deplorable, whereas the *local* is essential. All creative art must rise out of a specific soil and flicker with a spirit of place.

The local, of course, in Mr. Williams's sense, is the very opposite of the parochial, the parish-pump stuff. The local in America is America itself. Not Salem,* or Boston, or Philadelphia, or New York, but that of the American subsoil which spouts up in any of those places into the lives of men.

In these studies of "American" heroes, from Red Eric of Greenland,* and Columbus and Cortes and Montezuma, on to Abraham Lincoln,* Mr. Williams tries to reveal the experience of great men in the Americas since the advent of the whites. History in this book would be a sensuous record of the Americanization of the white men in America, as contrasted with ordinary history, which is a complacent record of the civilization and Europizing (if you can allow the word) of the American continent.

In this record of truly American heroes, then, the author is seeking out not the ideal achievement of great men of the New World but the men themselves, in all the dynamic explosiveness of their energy. This peculiar dynamic energy, this strange yearning and passion and uncanny explosive quality in men derived from Europe, is American, the American element. Seek out *this* American element—Oh Americans!—is the poet's charge.

All America is now going hundred per cent American. But the only hundred per cent American is the Red Indian, and he can only be canonized when he is finally dead. And not even the most American American can transmogrify into an Indian. Whence, then, the hundred per cent?

It is here that Mr. Williams's—and Poe's—distinction between the *national* and the *local* is useful. Most of the hundred per centism is national, and therefore not American at all. The new one hundred per cent literature is all *about* Americans, in the intensest American

257

vernacular. And yet, in vision, in conception, in the very manner, it
still remains ninety nine per cent European. But for "Ulysses" and
Marcel Proust* and a few other beetling high-brows, where would the
modernist* hundred per centers of America have been? Alas, where they
5   are now, save for cutting a few capers.

What then? William Carlos Williams tries to bring into his consciousness America itself, the still-unravished bride of silences.* The great
continent, its bitterness, its brackish quality, its vast glamor, its strange
cruelty. Find this, Americans, and get it into your bones. The powerful,
10 unyielding breath of the Americas, which Columbus sniffed, even in
Europe, and which sent the Conquistadores* mad. National America is
a gruesome sort of fantasy. But the unravished *local* America still waits
vast and virgin as ever, though in process of being murdered.

The author sees the genius of the continent as a woman with exquisite,
15 super-subtle tenderness and recoiling cruelty.* It is a myth-woman who
will demand of men a sensitive awareness, a supreme sensuous delicacy, and at the same time an infinitely tempered resistance, a power of
endurance and of resistance.

To evoke a vision of the essential America is to evoke Americans,
20 bring them into conscious life. To bring a few American citizens into
American consciousness—the consciousness at present being all bas-
tardized European—is to form the nucleus of the new race. To have the
nucleus of a new race is to have a future: and a true aristocracy. It is to
have the germ of an aristocracy in sensitive tenderness and diamond-like
25 resistance.

A man, in America, can only *begin* to be American. After five hundred years there are no *racial* white Americans. They are only national,
woebegone, or strident. After five hundred years more there may be
the developing nucleus of a true American race. If only men, some few,
30 trust the American passion that is in them, and pledge themselves to it.

But the passion is not national. No man who doesn't feel the last
anguish of tragedy—*and beyond that*—will ever know America, or begin,
even at the beginning's beginning, to be American.

There are two ways of being American; and the chief, says Mr.
35 Williams, is by recoiling into individual smallness and insentience, and
gutting the great continent in frenzies of mean fear. It is the Puritan
way. The other is by *touch*; touch America as she is; dare to touch her!
And this is the heroic way.

And this, this sensitive touch upon the unseen America, is to be the
40 really great adventure in the New World. Mr. Williams's book contains

his adventure; and therefore, for me, has a fascination. There are very new and profound glimpses into life: the strength of insulated small-ness in the New Englanders,* the fascination of "being nothing" in the Negroes,* the *spell-bound* quality of men like Columbus, De Soto, Boone.* It is a glimpse of what the vast America *wants men to be*, instead   5 of another strident assertion of what men have made, do make, will make, can make, out of the murdered territories of the New World.

It would be easy enough to rise, in critical superiority, as a critic always feels he must, superior to his author, and find fault. The modernist style is sometimes irritating. Was Tenochtitlan* really so wonderful? (See   10 Adolf Bandelier's "The Golden Man.")* Does not Mr. Williams mistake Poe's agony of *destructive penetration*,* through all the horrible bastard-European alluvium of his 1840 America, for the positive America itself?

But if an author rouses my deeper sympathy he can have as many faults as he likes, I don't care. And if I disagree with him a bit, heaven   15 save me from feeling superior just because I have a chance to snarl. I am only too thankful that Mr. Williams wrote his book.

REVIEW (MANUSCRIPT VERSION) OF HEAT, BY ISA GLENN

Heat.

"Heat" is the title of a novel by an American authoress, Isa Glenn,* a name quite unfamiliar. The cover-notice says "Miss Glenn," but the book is, in the life sense, mature, and seems at least like the work of a married woman. I don't think any married woman would have written *Jane Eyre*, nor either *The Constant Nymph*.* In those books there is a certain naïve attitude to men which would hardly survive a year of married life. But the authoress of "Heat" is not naïve about her men. She is kindly, rather sisterly and motherly, and a trifle contemptuous. Affectionate contempt, coupled with yearning, is the note of her feeling towards the officers in the American army out there in the Philippines,* and to the American fortune-hunting business men. The authoress, or rather, let us say the heroine, Charlotte, is evidently quite a good sport, from the man's point of view. She doesn't let you down. And so the men are quite good sports to her. They like her; and she likes them. But she feels a little contempt for them, amid her liking: and at the same time a yearning after some man who will call her his own. The men, for their part, feel very honorable and kindly towards Miss Charlotte, but they are a little afraid of her. They have to respect her just a bit too much. No man could feel tenderly possessive towards the Statue of Liberty. And Charlotte is, in the way of independence and honesty and thinking for herself, just a bit of a statue of Liberty.

She is not so liberal, though, about the women, the wives of the officers out there in Manila.* They are to her just repellant, even if not repulsive. She sees them with that utter cold antipathy with which women often regard other women—especially when the other women are elderly, physically unattractive, and full of flirtatious grimaces. To a man, there is something strange and disconcerting in the attitude of a woman like Charlotte towards other women, in particular her married seniors. She seems to be able to eye them with such complete cold understanding, that it takes one into quite another world of life. It is how a slim silvery fish in a great tank may eye the shapeless, greyish, gorping fishes that float heavily past her.

263

The story is laid in the Philippines, those islands belonging to the United States far away in the steaming hot Pacific, towards China: islands bought from Spain with good American dollars.* A forlorn, unholily hot, lost remnant of the world belonging, really, to the age of the ichthyosaurus,* not to our day.

To Manila, then, goes Charlotte, to be a school-teacher to the brown native children: a school-teacher, of course, with high missionary fervour. On the same boat, a transport, goes Tom Vernay, young lieutenant in the American army, fresh from the military school of West Point.* There is also a big blond heavy American, Saulsbury, out to make a fortune in cement: modern cement buildings for the Philippines.

This is before the war: twenty years ago, or so. The whole of the first half of the book, at least, is written with the pre-war outlook.* Maybe it was actually written before the war.

Charlotte, of course, loves Tom Vernay. But "loves" can mean so many things. She is thrilled by a certain purity in him, and by his intense, but vague, romantic yearning. He is an American who is "different": he has poetry in him. So Charlotte can feel intensely practical and "wise", hence a little protective and superior. She adores him. But at the same time, she feels a little protectively superior.

And he? At moments he adores her. At moments, he falls within her spell. He always likes her. He always, unconsciously, relies on her: in the background. But! There is also always a but! She is beautiful, with her fine gold hair and her girl's boyish figure. But!

But what, then?

Well, she is not exactly romantic. Going out to be a school-teacher, to "uplift" brown Filipinos! Going out alone, unprotected, so very capable of looking after herself, and looking after him too! Going out with a great idea that natives and niggers are as good as you are, if they are only educated up to your level. We're all alike under the skin, only our education is unequal. So let's level up the education.—That kind of thing!

Yes! It was generous and democratic, and he approved of it in an admiring sort of way. But!

Another but! What is it this time?

This time, it is that his music simply won't play. With the key of her fine democratic spirit she only locks up the flow of his passion tighter, locks it up dead. It needs another key altogether to release the music of his desire.

He is romantic. Manila, shut up tight and tortuous, steaming hot
and smelly within the ponderous Spanish fortifications, fascinates him
with the allure of the haughty and passionate past. Let it steam and
smell! so long as the powerfully sweet flower, the Dama de la Noche,*
also perfumes the nights, and guitars tinkle in unseen patios, and the   5
love-song scrapes and yearns and sinks in the Spanish throat. Romance!
he wants romance.

And as the months pass by, and the heat soaks into his brain, and the
strange reptilian moisture of heat goes through his very bones, he wants
romance more and more.   10

Charlotte, poor thing, in a cheap half-breed lodging house, spending
her days trying to teach insolent brown native children whose heads
are rancid with cocoa-nut oil, and whose nauseating sexual knowingness seems to be born with them, as a substitute for any other kind of
knowledge, does not get so much romance out of it. She is kind to her   15
pupils, she goes to the huts of their parents, and is purely charitable.
For which reason, the lizard-like natives jeer at her with a subtle but
fathomless contempt. She is only the "ticher": she is, to put it orientally,
their servant, their white bond-woman. And as such they treat her, with
infinite subtle disrespect, and that indescribable sexual derision* of the   20
east.

Poor Charlotte doesn't like it at all. A well-born, well-educated American girl, she is accustomed to all the respect in the world. It is *she* who
feels privileged to hold a little contempt for others, not quite as clear
and sure as herself. And now, these dirty little sexual natives give off   25
silent, and sometimes audible mockery at her, because she is kind instead
of bullying, and clean instead of impure. Her sort of sexual cleanness
makes the little brown women scream with derision: to them it is raw,
gawky, incredible incompetence, if not a sort of impotence; the ridiculous female eunuch.   30

And there must be a grain of truth in it: for she cannot keep her
Vernay in her spell. He has fallen wildly romantically in love with a
mysterious Spanish beauty. Romance, this time, laid on with a trowel.
The oldest, haughtiest family on the island,* selling out to retire to
Spain, from under the authority of these dogs of Americans!—a fat,   35
waddling, insolent, black-moustached Spanish mother, with her rasping
Castilian* speech!—and a daughter, ah! a Dolores! small and dusky and
hidden in a mantilla!*—about to be carried off to Spain to be married
to some elderly Spaniard who will throw his hands in the air when he

is excited!—Dolores, who has a fancy for the blue eyes and the white uniform of the American officers!

Tom Vernay has blue eyes and a white uniform, and is tall. One glimpse of the nose-tip of Dolores, from under her mantilla, does what all the intimacy with Charlotte could not do: it starts his music wildly playing. He is enamoured & enamoured of Dolores. Through a little brother,* a meeting is brought about. Then there is the daily clandestine stroll upon the unfrequented wall. In all the heat! Dolores Ayala! Ah heaven of romance! Ah Tom! He feels himself a Don* at last! Don Tomás!

And Charlotte, very much in the background, losing her good looks and the fine brightness of her hair, going thin and raky and bitter in the heat and insult of the islands where already she has sweated for three years, must even now defend Vernay from the officers' wives.

The love affair works up. The Ayalas are about to depart. Tom Vernay must marry Dolores. Against her parents' will, he must marry her clandestinely, in the American church. But he must resign his commission in the army first,* for there will be a great scandal, and he must not expose his country to odium.

So, he resigns his commission. The Ayalas are almost ready to sail. A great buzz goes up among the officers' wives, when the news comes out that Tom Vernay has sent in his resignation. The colonel's wife is giving a dinner party at the Army Club: one of the endless perspiring parties. Charlotte is there, because they want to pump her; otherwise they don't ask her, she is merely the "ticher" of the natives, the school-teacher shrivelling in the heat, becoming an old maid. Vernay is not present.

As the party moves from the table to go to dance, Vernay, white and strained, appears and murmurs to Charlotte that she must come to his room for a moment. Resentfully, she goes. To find—ah, to find the mousey, muffled-up Dolores there, all thrilled with herself for having escaped the family vigilance and arranged a rendezvous.

Tom Vernay, the romantic, is absolutely unequal to the occasion. Dolores, laughing, throws herself on Tom's breast, kissing his mouth. Tom, who has honorable intentions, can't stand it, holds her off and turns her to Charlotte—poor Charlotte! "Listen dear! You must go home tonight with Miss Carson. And tomorrow morning we can get the Chaplain to marry us."—"Why!" cries Dolores. "I can never, never marry you! Didn't you understand?"—"We will talk about that in the morning. Go home now with Miss Carson, like a good girl."*—Dolores, instead of being the "good girl", looks at poor Charlotte. And Dolores refuses to be taken off. "I got here so easily", she laughed. "I can do this wicked thing often and often, before we sail for Spain. I shall have to crawl on my knees to the Stations in penance. But is it not worth it—your eyes are so blue!"*

It isn't what Dolores would say in real Spanish, but the gist is all right. Tom insists that she go home with poor Charlotte, who by no means enjoys this scene in his bedroom at the Club. He gives Dolores to understand that he has resigned his commission in order to marry her: marry her in the morning.

This is too much for Dolores. She loathes being put off. She loathes the other woman, the very school-teacher, dragged in on her. She never intended to marry him, and have heretic babies, and be carted off to the United States. Not she!—But this wicked thing! Ah!—But now, without a uniform, she doesn't intend even to love him. Adios!*

The faithful Charlotte smuggles her out of the club, unseen, as she smuggled herself in. Home goes Dolores. The book, the biggest, romantic part, is finished.

The second part opens some years later. Vernay, his commission gone, has deteriorated rapidly in civilian life, till now he is a mere whiskey lapper, a derelict in smelly clothes, gone native. Charlotte, who has still been teaching school, but far away in a lonely island, returns and determines to find him, to rescue him.

She finds him: but he is beyond rescue. She finds him in a squalid native quarter, down by the ill-smelling river, in a region of broken bottles. He is vague and corrupted, and his reptilian little native wife* is big with his second child. It is enough. The book ends.

Poor Charlotte! There is nothing more to be done.

What was there ever to be done? The kind of attraction he wanted in a woman she hadn't got, and would have despised herself for having. She shuddered at the sexual little beasts of native women, working men up with snaky caresses. Ah yes, she had to admit, poor thing, that these native women had a power, a strange and hideous power over men. But it was a power she would loathe to possess.

And lacking it, she lost her Vernay, and went on being a faded school-teacher.—We can call it the man's fault: the man's imbecility and perversity. But in the long run, a man will succumb to the touch of the woman who, touching him, will start his music playing. And the woman whom he esteems and even cherishes, but who, touching him, leaves him musicless and passionless, he will ultimately abandon. That is, if he gets the chance.

REVIEW (TYPESCRIPT VERSION) OF HEAT, *BY ISA GLENN*

HEAT

"Heat" is the title of a novel by an American authoress, Isa Glenn, whose name seems quite unfamiliar. The cover-notice says "Miss Glenn", though one would have expected at least "Mrs."

No married woman would have written *Jane Eyre*, or, I doubt, *The Constant Nymph*. The men get off too lightly. Whereas the author of *Heat* does not have too many illusions about the male sex, and neither does she rise in old-maidish superiority. She is kindly, rather sisterly and motherly. At the same time, slightly contemptuous. The sisterly-motherly woman, she who flatters her men most by her devoted interest, is always slightly contemptuous of those self-same men, in her ultimate soul. So Miss Glenn; or rather, let us say Charlotte, the heroine of *Heat*.

Charlotte goes out to the Philippines on an American transport, some few years, apparently, before the world war. On board the same boat is Tom Vernay, a young romantic lieutenant in the American army, fresh from the military training school at West Point. Charlotte, of course, falls more or less in love with him; he is "different"; he has poetry in him.

Charlotte is going out to these remote Philippines to be a school-teacher, to teach the little brown natives and make them as good as herself. She has ideals, and she is sane and practical. Whereas Vernay is romantic and "different", he has feelings rather than ideals. If he had been the woman, and she the man, how nice it might all have been!

They are two very true American types. Not all American men care about business, or are slaves to their wives. Not at all! There are plenty of Tom Vernays, romantic and sensuous, living in a world of their own, which is really a world of the past. They are by nature pure, but filled with a heavy, almost dream-like yearning that is essentially voluptuous. They are the romantic Americans, and they have made a good deal of American history. Probably Abraham Lincoln belonged more or less to this type.

They are not Babbitts. Yet you will find them in every Main Street.* Tom Vernay is not vulgar. He is a gentleman, and even an aristocrat, although a loyal citizen of the United States. He does not care about

271

money. He cares too little about it. Neither does he want to change
the world, or to teach it anything whatsoever,* or to improve it in any
respect. In fact, all the things that you expect an American to be, he isn't
at all. Yet he is most truly an American, of a type which has existed from
the beginning of American history, and which has all the time played
a very important part in the development of the new nation. He is the
romantic American, different from any other species in the world, and
not taken sufficiently into account.

The girl, Charlotte, belongs to another and more familiar species.
With her fine gold hair and her delicate complexion, her pure-looking
young face and her slim, boyish, utterly unvoluptuous figure, she is
more or less the usual heroine. But also, she is more. She is no fool, not
in any sense. Nor is she a plaything. Nor is she a mere decoration. She
is brave almost without knowing it, and if we are to respect a pure and
unflinching sense of duty, we must respect it in Charlotte. She really
believes that by educating the world you can make it better. She really
believes that by educating the little Filipinos she can bring them to her
own level. She is willing, anxious to labour for her beliefs. But even
then, she is not fanatical. If experience has got lessons to teach her,
contrary to her beliefs, she will make the great concession, and modify
her beliefs rather than deny her true experience. And you cannot ask
more.

These two true Americans, both of them lovable, in their own way, are
carried out by their destinies to the far-off Philippines. Their destinies
come from within; the move to the Philippines is dictated by the nature
of each of them, though their natures are different. Destiny in the fatal
sense of the word enters in as soon as your nature, reaching out to its
own ends, touches the unknown.

The unknown, in this case, is those Philippines themselves, those
islands payed for to Spain in good dollars; those islands lying sweltering
far away towards China, in the steaming ocean still called the Pacific,
but which is really a sort of nowhere on the face of the earth. A forlorn,
unholily hot, lost remnant of the world belonging, really, to the age of
the ichthyosaurus, not to our day.

Vernay, in Manila, immediately becomes romantic, one might almost
say, to his hearts content; but alas, it is to his hearts disease. The city,
shut up tight in the ponderous Spanish fortifications, he loves with a
heavy helplessness incomprehensible to the ordinary European. To the
ordinary American still more so. The hot, smelly, mildewed, putrid city,
he adores it with a kind of mania. That greenish, over-sweet flower, the

Dama de la Noche, acts on him with strange chemistry, as its perfume
reels on the hot night, and he hears the tinkle of guitars in hidden patios,
and the rasping throat of some Spaniard echoes and sinks with a love-
song. These things act on the American boy as veronal or morphine or
opium* might act. He is quite helpless. The yearning, the helpless nos-   5
talgia for something he will never know, something belonging to a past
which America has never had,* fills him with a swooning consciousness
like an opium dream. He is, strictly, beside himself. And there is no-one
to help him. Because no-one, in the first place, could ever understand,
except one as helpless as himself. And in the second place, he is probably   10
beyond help, anyhow, once having smelt the green, insidious flower.

The girl, Charlotte, would dearly like to help him. She can't. She
herself, poor thing, is having anything but a romantic time; in a cheap
half-breed lodging house, subsisting on a school-teacher's pay, perspiring the night through, and through the day trying to "teach" those awful   15
little brown Filipino children, whose heads are rancid with cocoa-nut
oil, and whose infantile sexual knowingness seems to be born with them,
as a substitute for any other kind of knowledge. Her heart was full of
pure charity. She is gentle to her pupils, she treats them as if they were
like herself; she visits the homes of the parents, in simple charity. And   20
what she gets in return is an ever-increasing disrespect. The lizard-like
natives jeer at her with a subtle but fathomless contempt. The "ticher"!
What is she, the "ticher", but *their* servant! Oh triumph! Their white
servant, their white bond-woman! Glory! They will have some of their
own back.   25

And so they treat her with infinite smiling disrespect, and with that
indescribable lewd sexual suggestiveness of the oriental, more insulting
than anything on earth. To Charlotte, this is tables turned. A pure,
well-educated, intelligent, good-looking American girl of good family,
she is accustomed to being treated as if she were the highest thing   30
on man's earth, and really esteemed as such. It is her privilege to feel
a little contempt of others, not quite such pure products as herself.
Now, however, the low little brown waiter in the restaurant pours a
plate of pink ice-cream into her lap, and then shrugs his shoulders with
unconcern. She is only the "ticher", and a mere female without a man.*   35
She goes to the hut of one of her pupils, and finds the men naked save
for loin-cloths. And they look at her with those filmy black eyes of pure
sexual suggestion and the derision of sexual hate. Her sort of sexual
cleanliness, or her absence of any appearance of sex, makes the little
brown women scream with amused contempt of her. To them, it is   40

like having no female money to spend, a ridiculous pauperism, like the
eunuch's.

It is the more cruel to Charlotte, as she is just losing Tom Vernay
completely. He has been her pal all the time. He has danced with her,
and even at moments he has been in love with her, under her spell. He
has wanted to touch her.

Yet she can't keep him. He likes her. She knows he likes her, and
depends on her; in the background. But he doesn't want her. She can't
keep him in her spell. She can't make his music play in him. She is very
good to him. But she can't start the flow of his sensuous passion. Secretly,
he resents even her goodness to him. And secretly, she despises him for
it. And somewhere he knows it. What man doesn't know, somewhere,
when the woman despises him? And what man forgives it, except the
man who is truly despicable. And not often he.

At the same time, poor Charlotte, she loves him, and needs him to
soothe her and shelter her a bit. She is not so almighty self-sufficient
really, and she knows it. Oh, she knows a great deal. The only thing she
does not admit to herself, is the gnawing mortification she feels, because
she can't start the music of sensuous desire for her, in him. She can't.
And it is for this inadequacy in her, this sort of sexual atrophy, that
the native women despise her so insolently and so completely. A man
like Vernay, any little native woman would know how to start his music,
once she had access to him; and then he would marry easily enough.
Whereas this Charlotte, with all her opportunities—!

Vernay has fallen in love with a little Spanish creature whom he
has had half a glimpse of, in a shop where she came with her puffing,
black-moustached Spanish mother. It is high romance! Dolores, Dolores
Ayala! The oldest family in the islands, conquistadores; now selling out
to retire to Spain from under the rule of the despised Americans, and
to marry the same Dolores to some elderly Spaniard who will throw up
his hands when he talks.

But Dolores has a fancy for the white uniforms and the tall figures
and the blue eyes of the American officers. Vernay has all these. The
nose-tip of Dolores under a mantilla starts his music wildly playing.
A little "Don" brother helps the beginnings of an intrigue. And poor
Charlotte has to know all about it, and screen Vernay from the wives of
his superior officers, ghastly women. Poor Charlotte, losing her good
looks and the fine brightness of her hair, going thin and scrawny in the
heat, teaching native children!

The time goes on, so does the romance. The Ayalas are completing the preparations for departure. Tom must hurry up and marry the little Dolores: marry her against her parents' will, secretly. To do so, in order not to bring odium upon his country, he must first resign his commission in the army.   5

Up goes a buzz from the officers' wives, when Tom Vernay resigns his commission. Why? Why has he done it? Charlotte, who is rarely asked out any more, is invited to dinner at the Army Club, where Tom lives. The Colonel's wife is giving one of the endless perspiring parties among the usual set, to get at the secret.   10

Charlotte is still equal to these ghastly women, though her resistance is waning. Tom Vernay has not been asked to the dinner, naturally. But suddenly, as the party is moving from table to go to dance, he appears before Charlotte and asks her secretly and hurriedly please to come to his room for one moment. Rather coldly and resentfully, she goes.   15

To find—! Why, to find the mousey little Dolores there, all muffled up and thrilled with herself for having escaped the family vigilance. Dolores never even sees Charlotte, but flings herself into the arms of Tom, and starts kissing him. Poor Tom, pitched back upon his honorable citizen-of-the-United-States self, holds off Dolores and turns to Charlotte.   20
"Take her away, Charlotte!"—Poor Charlotte is dumb. *She* has never kissed Vernay. "Listen dear", he says to Dolores, "tonight you must go home with Miss Carson. And tomorrow morning we

REVIEW OF THE WORLD OF WILLIAM CLISSOLD, *BY H. G. WELLS*

*The World of William Clissold** is, we are told, a novel. We are assured
it is a novel, and nothing but a novel. We are not allowed to think of it
even as a "mental autobiography" of Mr. Wells.* It is a novel.

Let us hope so. For, having finished this first volume, nothing but
the hope of finding something in the two volumes yet to appear* will
restrain us from asserting, roundly and flatly, that this is simply not
good enough to be called a novel. If *Tono-Bungay** is a novel, then this
is not one.

We have with us the first volume of *The World of William Clissold*.
The second volume will appear on October 1st, the third on November
1st. We may still hope, then, if we wish to.

This first volume consists of "A Note before the Title-Page", in which
we are forbidden to look on this book as anything but a novel, and especially forbidden to look on it as a *roman à clef*:* which means we mustn't
identify the characters with any living people such as, for instance, Mr.
Winston Churchill or the Countess of Oxford and Asquith;* which
negative command is very easy to obey, since, in this first volume, at
least, there are no created characters at all: it is all words, words, words,
about Socialism and Karl Marx, bankers and cave-men, money and the
superman. One would welcome any old scarecrow of a character on this
dreary, flinty hillside of abstract words.

The next thing is the title page: "The World of William Clissold:
A Novel from a New Angle"*—whatever that pseudo-scientific phrase
may mean.

Then comes *Book I: The Frame of the Picture*. All right, we think! If
we must get the frame first, and the picture later, let's make the best of
the frame.

The frame consists of William Clissold informing us that he is an
elderly gentleman of fifty-nine, and that he is going to tell us all about
himself. He is quite well-off, having made good in business, so that now
he has retired and has bought a house near Cannes,* and is going to
tell us everything, absolutely everything about himself: insisting rather

5

10

15

20

25

30

279

strongly that he is and always has been a somewhat scientific gentleman with an active mind, and that his mental activities have been more important than any other activity in his life. In short, he is not a "mere animal", he is an animal with a ferocious appetite for "ideas", and enor-
5 mous thinking powers.

Again, like a submissive reader, we say: "Very well! proceed!"; and we sit down in front of this mental gentleman. William Clissold immediately begins to tell us what he believes, what he always has believed, and what he hasn't always believed, and what he won't believe, and we
10 feel how superior he is to other people who believe other mere things. He talks about God, is very uneasy because of Roman Catholics—like an Early Victorian—and is naughtily funny about Mr. G.—which can mean either Mr. Gladstone* or Mr. God.

But we bear up. After all, God, or Mr. G., is only the frame for William
15 Clissold. We must put up with a frame of some sort. And God turns out to be Humanity in its nobler or disinterestedly scientific aspect: or the Mind of Men collectively: in short, William Clissold himself, in a home-made halo. Still, after all, it is only a frame. Let us get on to the picture.

20 Mr. Clissold, being somewhat of an amateur at making a self-portrait and framing it, has got bits of the picture stuck on to the frame, and great angular sections of the frame occupying the space where the picture should be. But patience! It is a sort of futuristic* interpenetration, perhaps.

25 The first bit of the story is a little boy at a country house, sitting in a boat and observing the scientific phenomena of refraction and reflection. He also observes some forget-me-nots on the bank, and rather likes the look of them. So, scrambling carefully down through mud and sedges, he clutches a handful of the blue flowers, only to find his legs scratched and
30 showing blood, from the sedges. "Oh! Oh! I cried in profound dismay . . . Still do I remember most vividly my astonishment at the treachery of that golden, flushed, and sapphire-eyed day.—That it should turn on me!"*

This "section" is called "The Treacherous Forget-me-nots". But
35 since, after all, the forget-me-nots had never asked the boy to gather them, wherein lay the treachery?

But they represent poetry. And perhaps William Clissold means to convey that, scrambling after poetry, he scratched his legs, and fell to howling, and called the poetry treacherous.

As for a child thinking that the sapphire-eyed day had turned on him—what a dreary old-boy of a child, if he did! But it is elderly-gentleman psychology, not childish.

The story doesn't get on very fast, and is extremely sketchy. The elderly Mr. Clissold is obviously bored by it himself. Two little boys, their mother and father, move from Bexhill* to a grand country house called Mowbray. In the preface we are assured that Mowbray does not exist on earth, and we can well believe it. After a few years, the father of the two boys, a mushroom city magnate,* fails, is arrested as a swindler, convicted, and swallows potassium cyanide. We have no vital glimpse of him. He never says anything, except "Hello, Sonny!".* And he does ask the police to have some *déjeuner** with him, when he is arrested. The boys are trailed round Belgium by a weeping mother, who also is not created, and with whom they are only bored. The mother marries again: the boys go to the London University: and the story is lost again in a vast grey drizzle of words.

William Clissold, having in *The Frame* written a feeble resumé of Mr. Wells's *God the Invisible King,** proceeds in *The Story, Book II*, to write a much duller resumé of Mr. Wells's *Outline of History.** Cavemen, nomads, patriarchs, tribal Old Men, out they all come again, in the long march of human progress. Mr. Clissold, who holds forth against "systems", cannot help systematizing us all into a gradual and systematic uplift from the ape. There is also a complete *exposé* of Socialism and Karl Marxism and finance, and a denunciation of Communism. There is a little feeble praise of the pure scientist who does physical research in a laboratory, and a great contempt of professors and dons who lurk in holes and study history. Last, and not least, there is a contemptuous sweeping of the temple,* of all financiers, bankers, and money-men: they are all unscientific, untrained semi-idiots monkeying about with things they know nothing of.

And so, rather abruptly, end of Vol. I.

Except, of course, William Clissold has been continually taking a front seat in the picture, aged fifty-nine, in the villa back of Cannes. There is a slim slip of a red-haired Clem, who ruffles the old gentleman's hair.

" 'It's no good!' she said. 'I can't keep away from you to-day.' And she hasn't! She has ruffled my hair, she has also ruffled my mind"*—much more important, of course, to William C.

This is the young Clementina: "She has a mind like one of those water-insects that never get below the surface of anything . . . She

professes an affection for me that is altogether monstrous"—I should
say so—"and she knows no more about my substantial self than the
water-insect knows of the deeps of the pond. . . . She knows as little
about the world".*

5   Poor Clementina, that lean, red-haired slip of a young thing. She is
no more to him than an adoring sort of mosquito. But oh! wouldn't we
like to hear all she *does* know about him, this sexagenarian bore, who says
of her: "the same lean, red-haired Clem, so absurdly insistent that she
idolizes me, and will have no other man but me, invading me whenever
10   she dares, and protecting me", etc.*—

Clementina, really, sounds rather nice. What a pity *she* didn't herself
write *The World of William Clissold*: it would have been a novel, then. But
she wouldn't even look at the framework of that world, says Clissold.
And we don't blame her.

15   What is the elderly gentleman doing with her at all? Is it his "racial
urge",* as he calls it, still going on, rather late in life? We imagine the
dear little bounder saying to her: "You are the mere object of my racial
urge". To which, no doubt, she murmurs in the approved Clissold style:
"My King!"*

20   But it is altogether a poor book: the effusion of a peeved elderly
gentleman who has nothing to grumble at, but who peeves at everything,
from Clem to the High Finance, and from God, or Mr. G., to Russian
Communism. His effective self is disgruntled, his ailment is a peevish,
ashy indifference to *everything*, except himself, himself as centre of
25   the universe. There is not one gleam of sympathy with anything in
all the book, and not one breath of passionate rebellion. Mr. Clissold
is too successful and wealthy to rebel and too hopelessly peeved to
sympathize.

What has got him into such a state of peevishness is a problem: unless
30   it is his insistence on the Universal Mind, which he, of course, exempli-
fies. The emotions are to him irritating aberrations. Yet even he admits
that even thought must be preceded by some obscure physical happenings, some kind of confused sensation or emotion which is the necessary
coarse body of thought and from which thought, living thought, arises
35   or sublimates.

This being so, we wonder that he so insists on the Universal or racial
mind of man, as the only hope or salvation. If the mind is fed from
the obscure sensations, emotions, physical happenings inside us, if the
mind is really no more than an exhalation of these, is it not obvious that
40   without a full and subtle emotional life the mind itself must wither: or

that it must turn itself into an automatic sort of grind-mill, grinding upon itself?

And in that case the superficial Clementina no doubt knows far more about the "deeps of the pond" of Mr. Clissold than that tiresome gentleman knows himself. He grinds on and on at the stale bones of soci-   5
ology, while his actual living goes to pieces, falls into a state of irritable peevishness which makes his "mental autobiography" tiresome. His scale of values is all wrong.

So far, anyhow, this work is not a novel, because it contains none of the passionate and emotional reactions which are at the root of all thought,   10
and which must be conveyed in a novel. This book is all chewed-up newspaper, and chewed-up scientific reports, like a mouse's nest. But perhaps the novel will still come: in Vols. II and III.

For, after all, Mr. Wells is not Mr. Clissold, thank God! And Mr. Wells has given us such brilliant and such very genuine novels that we   15
can only hope the Clissold "angle" will straighten out in Vol. II.

REVIEW (MANUSCRIPT VERSION) OF
GIFTS OF FORTUNE, BY H. M. TOMLINSON

Supplementary note to the text

On several occasions (287:23, 290:8, 290:16, 290:17, 290:18, 290:19, 290:23), DHL began transcribing an extract from *Gifts of Fortune* before breaking off, sometimes adding 'etc.', followed by the relevant page number. These may have been instructions to a typist or printer to continue transcribing the extract until the next natural break. Since it is not entirely clear whether DHL did intend this, only his own writing appears here, with the page numbers of *Gifts of Fortune* omitted. The editor of *Phoenix* followed the same practice.

The periodical version of the review (see below) included several such continuations, and on one occasion (295:32) the transcription begins at a point earlier than that indicated in DHL's manuscript.

"Gifts of Fortune"* is not a travel book. It is not even, as the jacket describes it, a book of travel memories. Travel in this case is a stream of reflections, where images intertwine with dark thoughts and obscure emotion, and the whole flows on turbulent and deep and transitory. It is reflection, thinking back on travel and on life, and in the mirror sense, throwing back snatches of image.

Mr Tomlinson's own title: "Gifts of Fortune. With Some Hints to Those About to Travel," is a little grimly misleading. Those about to travel, in the quite commonplace sense of the word, will find very few encouraging hints in the long essay which occupies a third of this book, and is entitled: Hints to Those About to Travel. The chief hint they would hear would be, perhaps, the sinister suggestion that they had better stay at home.

There are travellers and travellers, as Mr Tomlinson himself makes plain. There are scientific ones, game-shooting ones, Thomas Cook ones,* thrilled ones, and bored ones. And none of these, as such, will find a single "hint," in all the sixty-six hinting pages, which will be of any use to them.

Mr Tomlinson is travelling in retrospect, in soul rather than in the flesh, and his hints are to other souls. To travelling bodies he says little.

The sea tempts one to travel. But what is the nature of the temptation? To what are we tempted? Mr Tomlinson gives us the hint, for his own case. "What draws us to the sea is the light over it." etc.*

There you have the key to this book.—Coasts of illusion! "There are other worlds."* A man who has travelled this world in the flesh travels again, sails once more wilfully along coasts of illusion, and wilfully steers into other worlds. Take then the illusions, accept the gifts of fortune, "that passen as a shadow on the wall."*

"My journeys have all been the fault of books, though Lamb would never have called them that."* Mr Tomlinson is a little weary of books, though he has here written another. A talk with seamen in the forecastle of a ship has meant more to him than any book. So he says. But that is how a man feels, at times. As a matter of fact, from these essays it

5

10

15

20

25

30

287

is obvious that books like Bates' "Amazon", Conrad's "Nigger of the Narcissus", and Melville's "Moby Dick"* have gone deeper into him than any talk with seamen in forecastles of steamers.

How could it be otherwise? Seamen see few coasts of illusion. They see very little of anything. And what is Mr Tomlinson after? What are we all after, if it comes to that? It is our yearning to land on the coasts of illusion, it is our passion for other worlds that carries us on. And with Bates or Conrad or Melville we are already away over the intangible seas. As Mr Tomlinson makes very plain, a P. & O. liner* will only take us from one hotel to another. Which isn't what we set out for, at all. *That* is not crossing seas.

And this is the theme of the Hints to Those. We travel in order to cross seas and land on other coasts. We do not travel in order to go from one hotel to another, and see a few side-shows. We travel, perhaps, with a secret and absurd hope of setting foot on the Hesperides,* of running our boat up a little creek and landing in the Garden of Eden.

This hope is always defeated. There is no Garden of Eden, and the Hesperides never were. Yet, in our very search for them, we touch the coasts of illusion, and come into contact with other worlds.

This world remains the same, wherever we go. Every ship is a money-investment, and must be made to pay. The earth exists to be exploited, and is exploited. Malay head-hunters are now playing football instead of hunting heads. The voice of the gramophone is heard in the deepest jungle.

That is the world of disillusion. Travel, and you'll know it. It is just as well to know it. Our world is a world of disillusion, whether it's Siam or Kamschatka or Athabasca:* the same exploitation, the same mechanical lifelessness.

But travelling through our world of disillusion until we are finally and bitterly disillusioned, we come home at last, after the long voyage, home to the rain and the dismalness of England. And how marvellously well Mr Tomlinson gives the feeling of a ship at the end of the voyage, coming in at night, in the rain, the engines slowed down, then stopped: and in the unspeakable emptiness and blankness of silent engines and rain and nothingness, the passengers wait for the tug, staring out upon utter emptiness, from a ship that has gone suddenly quite dead! It is the end of the voyage of disillusion.

But behold, in the morning, England, England in her own wan sun, her strange, quiet Englishmen so silent and intent and self-resourceful!* It is the coast of illusion, the other world itself.

This is the gist of the Hints to Those About to Travel. You'll never find what you look for. There are no happy lands. But you'll come upon coasts of illusion when you're not expecting them.

Following the Hints come three sketches which are true travel memories, one on the Amazon, one in the Malay States, one in Borneo.* They are old memories, and they gleam with illusion, with the iridescence of illusion and disillusion at once. Far off, we are in the midst of exploitation and mechanical civilisation, just the same. Far off, in the elysium of a beautiful spot in Borneo, the missionary's wife sits and weeps for home, when she sees an outgoing ship. Far off, there is the mad Rajah, whom we turned out,* with all kinds of medals and number-plates on his breast, thinking himself grander than ever, though he is a beggar.

And all the same, far off, there is that other world, or one of those other worlds, that give the lie to those realities we are supposed to accept.*

The rest of the book is all in England. There is a sketch—*Conrad is dead.** And another, an appreciation of *Moby Dick*. But for the rest, it is the cruel disillusion, and then the infinitely soothing illusion of this world of ours.

Mr Tomlinson has at the back of his mind, forever, the grisly vision of his war experience. In itself, this is a horror of disillusion in the world of man. We cannot get away from it, and we have no business to. Man has turned the world into a thing of horror. What we have to do is to face the fact.

And facing it, accept other values and make another world. "We now open a new volume on sport," says Mr Tomlinson, "with an antipathy we never felt for Pawnees,* through the reading of a recent narrative by an American who had been collecting in Africa for an American museum. He confessed he would have felt some remorse when he saw the infant still clinging to the breast of its mother, a gorilla, whom he had just murdered; so he shot the infant without remorse, because he was acting scientifically. As a corpse, the child added to the value of its dead mother—"*

We share Mr Tomlinson's antipathy to such sportsmen and such scientists absolutely. And it is not mere pity on our part for the gorilla. It is an absolute detestation of the *insentience* of armed, bullying men, in face of living, sentient things. Surely the most beastly offence against life is this degenerate insentience. It is not cruelty, exactly, which makes such a sportsman. It is crass insentience, a crass stupidity and deadness of fibre. Such overweening fellows, called men, are barren of the feeling for life. A gorilla is a live thing, with a strange unknown life of its own.

Even to get a glimpse of its weird life, one little gleam of insight, makes our own life so much the wider, more vital. As a dead thing it can only depress us. We *must* have a feeling for life itself.

And this Mr Tomlinson conveys: the strangeness and the beauty of life. Once be disillusioned with the man-made world, and you will see the magic, the beauty, the delicate realness of all the other life. Mr Tomlinson sees it in flashes of great beauty. It comes home to him even in the black moth he caught. "It was quiet making a haze" etc.* He sees the strange terror of the world of insects. "A statue to St George killing a mosquito instead of a dragon would look ridiculous. But it was lucky for the saint he had only a dragon to overcome."*

Life! Life exists: and perhaps men do not truly exist.—"And for a wolf who runs up & down his cage sullenly ignoring our overtures, and behaving as though we do not exist, we begin to feel there is something to be said."*

"And consider the fascination of the octopus!"*

"I heard a farmer" etc.*

"At sunrise today"*

"Perhaps the common notion" etc.*

One gradually gets a new vision of the world, if one goes through the disillusion absolutely. It is a world where all things are alive, and where the life of strange creatures and beings flickers on us and makes [us]* take strange new developments. "But in this estuary" etc.*—And it is exactly so. The earth is a planet, and we are inhabitants of the planet, along with many other strange creatures. Life is a strange planetary phenomenon, all interwoven.

Mr Tomlinson gives us glimpses of a new vision, what we might call the planetary instead of the mundane vision. The glimpses are of extreme beauty, so sensitive to the other life in things. And how grateful we ought to be to a man who sets new visions, new feelings sensitively quivering in us.

REVIEW (PERIODICAL VERSION) OF
GIFTS OF FORTUNE, *BY H. M. TOMLINSON*

"Gifts of Fortune" is not a travel book. It is not even, as the jacket describes it, a book of travel memories. Travel is, in this case, a stream of reflection, where scenes intertwine with thoughts and with unresolved emotions, and the whole flows on disturbed and disturbing. It is reflection, visual, emotional, and mental, thinking back on travel and on life, and feeling it over again, and throwing back, in the mirror sense, snatches of the image.

Mr. H. M. Tomlinson's own title: "Gifts of Fortune. With Some Hints to Those about to Travel" (Heinemann, 8s. 6d.), is a little grimly misleading. Those about to travel, in the quiet commonplace of the world, will find very few encouraging hints in the long essay which occupies a third of his book, and is entitled: "Some Hints, etc." The chief hint they would hear, perhaps, might be the sinister suggestion that they had better stay at home.

There are travellers and travellers, as Mr. Tomlinson makes very plain. Game-shooting ones, scientific ones, Thomas Cook ones, thrilled ones, and bored ones.

Mr. Tomlinson is travelling in retrospect, in spirit rather than in the flesh, and his hints are to other restless spirits. To travellers merely travelling he says little.

The sea itself tempts us to travel. But what is the real nature of the temptation? Mr. Tomlinson gives us the clue for his own case. "What draws us to the sea is the light over it. Try listening, in perfect safety, to combers breaking on a reef on a dark night, and then say whether you enjoy the voice of great waters. I think it must be the wonder of light without bounds which draws us to the docks to overcome the distractions and discomforts of departure. We see there is a wide freedom in the world, after all, if only we had the will to take it. And, unfailingly, we make strange landfalls during an escape, coasts of illusion if you like, and under incredible skies, but sufficient to shake our faith in those realities we had supposed we were obliged to accept. There are other worlds."*

There we have one of the keys of the book. Coasts of illusion! "There are other worlds." A man who has travelled this world in the flesh travels again, sails once more wilfully along the coasts of illusion, and wilfully steers into other worlds. Accept, then, the gifts of fortune "that passen as a shadow on the wall."

"My journeys have all been the fault of books, though Lamb would never have called them that." Mr. Tomlinson is a little weary of books, though he has here written another. A talk with seamen in the forecastle of a ship has meant more to him than any book. So he says. From these essays it is obvious that books like Bates' "Amazon," Conrad's "Nigger of the *Narcissus*," and Melville's "Moby Dick" have gone deeper into him than any talk with seamen in forecastles of steamers.

How could it be otherwise? Seamen don't see much on any coast, illusion or otherwise. Seamen see little of anything. They have too much of the banal world in them. And Mr. Tomlinson is travelling to get away from the banal world. He wants something else. He is yearning to land on the coasts of illusion. It is his passion for other worlds that carries him on. As Mr. Tomlinson makes very plain, a P. and O. steamer will only take us from one hotel to another. Which is not what we are travelling for at all. *That* is not crossing seas.

All of which we learn in the "Hints to Those." We do not travel in order to go from one hotel to another, and perhaps see a few side-shows. We travel to get away from a world we hate, which is the world of man as we have made it. We travel, maybe, with a secret and absurd hope of setting foot on the Hesperides, if only for half an hour: of running our boat up a little creek and landing in a garden of Eden.

No good! There is no garden of Eden on this commercial and predatory earth. The Hesperides never were. Abandon all hope of a quick trip to paradisial places. There aren't any. Accept disillusion, bitter disillusion of the world. And then, maybe, in our voyage of disillusion we may suddenly find ourselves touching at coasts of illusion, and landing in other worlds.

The world is a world of disillusion. Travel, and you'll know it. Worse still if you have been in the war, and have the horror of that always at the back of your mind, you will see that the world of man is ghastly everywhere, but particularly the world of civilized man.

Then take ship and come home. How bitterly well Mr. Tomlinson gives the feeling of a liner at the end of the voyage. It is night when you come in. The engines slow down. It is raining. The engines stop, and it seems as if everything had stopped. Darkness and rain, a ship

suddenly gone dead as a coffin, passengers standing like souls waiting
to be landed in Hades, staring out at nothingness. It is the end of the
voyage of disillusion.

But behold, in the morning, England, our own England, in her strange
pale sunshine, with her Englishmen going about so quietly, as if with a   5
dream upon them! Suddenly it is the coast of illusion. We are landing,
in England, on one of the other worlds.

This is the final hint. The world of man is horrible, and on the face of
the earth you'll never find what you are looking for. But you will come
upon the coast of illusion that you were not looking for, and maybe   10
you'll land in another world that you had not dreamed of.

Mr. Tomlinson has at the back of his mind, for ever, the grisly vision
of his war experience. It colours with horror all his vision of our modern
civilized world. He cannot get away from it, and, reading him, we do
not get away from it. We feel, moreover, he is right; we have no business   15
to be getting away from it. Let us not forget. Man has turned himself
into something that fills us with horror. What we have to do is to accept
the fact, fully.

Mr. Tomlinson, in this book, having faced a great cruelty of disillusion, shows a very lovely sensitiveness to the real living world. Once   20
finally accept disillusion with the man-made world, and the strangeness
and beauty of life, the delicate realness of all other life seems to open
out before you. It is the other-world.

Thus in "Gifts of Fortune" we keep glimpsing all the time into the
other-world of delicate, mysterious life. We see the strange, teeming   25
world of the insects, the one world perhaps more terrifying than our
own. It is not the great beasts that may finally exterminate us. It is
the tiny insects. "A statue to St. George killing a mosquito instead of a
dragon would look ridiculous. But it was lucky for the saint he had only
a dragon to overcome."   30

Yet, in the world of insects there is the same fearsome beauty and
mystery. A black moth has been caught in the net. "I watched the captive
where it quivered, though not in alarm, in a loose fold of the muslin. It
was quiet, making a haze of its wings, at times checking them so that I
could attempt a translation of its golden message. It had a face—rather   35
a large black face, in which those glowing eyes were conspicuous. I
took the cork out of the killing bottle, looked again at the quivering and
fearsome beauty, but put back the cork and shoved the bottle away. It was
impossible. It would have been worse than murder. They who destroy
beauty are damned. I did not want to be damned. That wonderful   40

form, the stillness, and the silence, overcame me. This creature was not mine."*

Exactly! These creatures are never ours. If St. Francis had realized as much about the birds, instead of preaching to them,* we might have been better.

As it is, life hardly exists to us, and perhaps we hardly exist to life. ". . . And for a wolf who runs up and down his cage sullenly ignoring our overtures, and behaving as though we did not exist, we begin to think there is something to be said."*

It is astonishing how we behave, as if there were no life on the face of the earth except our own. "I heard a farmer the other day calling this a bad year. But what did he want? If he had climbed out of his fields to where the young green and gold of the furze was among the purple heather he would have seen that the fount of life was just as good as ever it was."*

So, gradually man moves into a new world, as he makes himself a new vision. It is a world where all things are alive, and the life of other creatures flickers on us and makes us take new developments. It is no longer our city or our suburb, with nothing to look up to but a clock on a tower, or an advertisement sign.

"But in this Estuary I have changed that view of the world for one that is flooded with light. The earth, I can see, is a planet, a vast reflector."

The earth is a planet. We are inhabitants of a planet, along with other uncanny inhabitants. And life is a strange planetary phenomenon, all interwoven.

REVIEW OF PEDRO DE VALDIVIA:
CONQUEROR OF CHILE, *BY R. B.*
CUNNINGHAME GRAHAM

PEDRO DE VALDIVIA—Conqueror of Chile.

This book will have to go on the history shelf; it has no chance among the memoirs or the lives. There is precious little about Valdivia* himself. There is, however, a rather scrappy chronicle of the early days of Chile, a meagre account of its conquest and settlement under Pedro de Valdivia   5

Having read Mr Graham's* preface, we suddenly come upon another title-page, and another title.—"Pedro de Valdivia, Conqueror of Chile. Being a short Account of his Life, together with his Five Letters to Charles V."—So? We are to get Valdivia's own letters! Interminable epistles of a conquistador, we know more or less what to expect. But let   10
us look where they are.

It is a serious-looking book, with 220 large pages, and costing 15/- net. The Short Account we find occupies the first 123 pages, the remaining 94 are occupied by the translation of the five letters. So! Nearly half the book is Valdivia's; Mr Graham only translates him. And we shall have   15
a lot of Your-Sacred-Majestys to listen to, that we may be sure of.

When we have read both the "Short Account" and the Letters, we are left in a state of irritation and disgust. Mr. Cunninghame Graham steals all his hero's gunpowder. He deliberately—or else with the absent-mindedness of mere egoism—picks all the plums out of Val-   20
divia's cake, puts them in his own badly-kneaded dough, and then has the face to serve us up Valdivia whole, with the plums which we have already eaten sitting as large as life in their original position. Of course, all Valdivia's good bits in his own letters read like the shamelessest pla-giarism. Haven't we just read them in Mr Graham's Short Account?   25
Why should we have to read them again? Why does that uninspired old conquistador try to fob them off on us?

Poor Valdivia! That's what it is to be a conquistador and a hero to Mr Graham. He puts himself first, and you are so much wadding to fill out the pages.   30

The Spanish conquistadores, famous for courage and endurance, are by now notorious for insentience and lack of imagination. Even Bernal Diaz,* after a few hundred pages, makes one feel one could yell, he is so doggedly, courageously unimaginative, visionless, really *sightless*:

sightless, that is, with the inner eye of living discernment. Cortés,* strong man as he is, is just as tough and visionless, in *his* letters to His-Most-Sacred-Majesty. And Don Cunninghame, alas, struts feebly in the conquistadorial footsteps. Not only does he write without imagination, without imaginative insight or sympathy, without colour and without real feeling, but he seems to pride himself on the fact. He is being conquistadorial.

We, however, refuse entirely to play the part of poor Indians. We are not frightened of old Dons in caracoling armchairs.* We are not even amused by their pretence of being on horse-back. A horse is a four-legged sensitive animal. What a pity the Indians felt so frightened of it! Anyhow, it is too late now for cavalierly conduct.

Mr Graham's Preface sets the note, in the very first words. It is a note of twaddling impertinence, and it runs through all the work. "Commentators tell us [do they, though?] that most men are savages at heart, and give more admiration to the qualities of courage, patience in hardships, and contempt of death, than they accord to the talents of the artist, man of science, or the statesman. [Funny sort of commentators Mr Graham reads.]

If this is true of men, they say it is doubly true of women, who would rather be roughly loved by a tall fellow of his hands [hands, forsooth!] even though their physical and moral cuticle (sic) suffer some slight abrasion, than inefficiently wooed by a philanthropist. [Ah ladies, you who are inefficiently wooed by philanthropists, is there never a tall fellow of his hands about?]

"This may be so, [continues Mr Graham], and if it is, certainly Pedro de Valdivia was an archetype [!—] of all the elemental qualities nature implants in a man. [He usually had some common Spanish wench for his kept woman, though we are not told concerning her cuticle.]

"Brave to a fault, [chants Mr Graham] patient and enduring to an incredible degree, of hardships under which the bravest might have quailed, [what's a quail got to do with it?] loyal to king and country [Flemish Charles V]* and a stout man-at-arms, he had yet no inconsid-erable talents of administration, talents not so conspicuous today among the Latin race. [dear-dear!]

"Thus—and I take all the above for granted—etc."*

Mr Graham has shown us, not Valdivia, but himself. He lifts a swash-buckling fountain pen, and off he goes. The result is a shoddy, scrappy, and not very sincere piece of work. The conquistadores were damned by their insensitiveness to life, which we call lack of imagination. And they

let a new damnation into the America they conquered. But they couldn't
help it. It was the educational result of Spanish struggle for existence
against the infidel Moors. The conquistadores were good enough instruments, but they were not good enough men for the miserable and melancholy work of conquering a continent. Yet at least they never felt them-   5
selves *too good* for their job, as some of the inky conquerors did even
then, and do still.

Mr Graham does not take Valdivia very seriously. He tells us almost
nothing about him: save that he was born in Estremadura* (who cares!)
and had served in the Italian and German wars,* had distinguished   10
himself in the conquest of Venezuela,* and in 1532 accompanied Pizarro
to Peru. Having thrown these few facts at us, off goes Mr Graham
to the much more alluring, because much better known, story of the
Pizarros,* and we wonder where Valdivia comes in. We proceed with
Pizarro to Peru, and so, apparently, did Valdivia, and we read a little   15
piece of the story even Prescott has already told us.* Then we get a
glimpse of Almagro crossing the Andes* to Chile, and very impressive
little quotations from Spanish writers. After which Valdivia begins to
figure, in some unsubstantial remote regions with Indian names, as a
mere shadow of a coloniser. We never see the country, we never meet   20
the man, we get no feeling of the Indians. There is nothing dramatic, no
Incas, no temples and treasures and tortures, only remote colonisation
going on in a sort of nowhere. Valdivia becomes a trifle more real when
he comes again into Peru, to fight on the loyal side against Gonzalo
Pizarro and old Carvajal,* but this is Peruvian history, with nothing   25
new to it. Valdivia returns to Chile and vague colonising; there are
vague mentions of the Maghellan Straits;* there is a Biobio River,* but
to one who has never been to Chile, it might just as well be Labrador.*
There is a bit of a breath of life in the extracts of Valdivia's own letters.
And there are strings of names of men who are nothing but names, and   30
continual mention of Indians who also remain merely nominal. Till the
very last pages, when we do find out, after he is killed, that Valdivia was
a big man, fat now he is elderly, of a hearty disposition, good-natured
as far as he has enough imagination, and rather common-place save for
his energy as a colonising instrument.   35

It is all thrown down, in bits and scraps, as Mr Graham comes across
it in Garcilaso's book, or in Gómara.* And it is interlarded with Mr
Graham's own comments, of this nature: "Christians seemed to have
deserved their name in those days, for faith and faith alone could have
enabled them to endure such misery, and yet be always ready at the   40

sentinel's alarm to buckle on their swords."* Oh what clichés! Faith in
the proximity of gold, usually!—"Cavalry in those days played the part
now played by aeroplanes,"* says Mr Graham suavely. He himself seems
to have got into an aeroplane, by mistake, instead of on to a conquista-
5   dorial horse, for his misty bird's-eye views are just such confusion.

The method followed, for the most part, seems to be that of sequence
of time. All the events of each year are blown together by Mr Graham's
gustiness, and you can sort them out. At the same time, great patches
of Peruvian history suddenly float up out of nowhere, and at the end,
10   when Valdivia is going to get killed by the Indians, suddenly we are
swept away on a biographical carpet, and forced to follow the life of the
poet Ercilla,* who wrote his Araucana poem about Valdivia's Indians,
but who never came to Chile till Valdivia was dead. After which, we are
given a feeble account of a very striking incident, the death of Valdivia.
15   And there the Short Account dies also, abruptly, and Chile is left to its
fate.

Then follow the five letters. They are moderately interesting, the best,
of course, belonging to Peruvian story, when Valdivia helped the mean
La Gasca* against Gonzalo Pizarro. For the rest, the "loyalty" seems a
20   little overdone, and we are a little tired of the bluff manly style of soldiers
who have not imagination enough to see the things that really matter.
Men of action are usually deadly failures in the long run. Their precious
energy makes them uproot the tree of life, and leave it to wither, and
their stupidity makes them proud of it. Even in Valdivia, and he seems
25   to have been as human as any conquistador, the stone blindness to any
mystery or meaning in the Indians themselves, the utter unawareness of
the fact that they might have a point of view, the abject insensitiveness
to the strange, eerie atmosphere of that America he was proceeding to
exploit and to ruin, puts him at a certain dull level of intelligence which
30   we find rather nauseous. The world has suffered so cruelly from these
automatic men of action. Valdivia was not usually cruel, it appears. But
he cut off the hands and noses of two hundred "rebels",* Indians who
were fighting for their own freedom, and he feels very pleased about it.
It served to cow the others. But imagine deliberately chopping off one
35   slender brown Indian hand after another! Imagine taking a dark-eyed
Indian by the hair, and cutting off his nose! Imagine seeing man after
man, in the prime of life, with his mutilated face streaming blood, and
his wrist-stump a fountain of blood, and tell me if the men of action
don't need absolutely to be held in leash by the intelligent being who
40   *can* see these things as monstrous, root cause of endless monstrosity!

We, who suffer from the bright deeds of the men of action of the past, may well keep an eye on the "tall fellows of their hands" of our own day.

Prescott never went to Mexico nor to Peru, otherwise he would have sung a more scared tune. But Mr Graham is supposed to know his South America. One would never believe it. The one thing he could   5 have done, re-created the landscape of Chile for us, and made us feel those Araucanians* as men of flesh and blood, he never does, not for a single second. He might as well never have left Scotland; better, for perhaps he would not have been so glib about unseen lands. All he can say of the Araucanians today is that they are "as hard-featured a race as   10 any upon earth."*

Mr Graham is trivial and complacent. There is, in reality, a peculiar dread horror about the conquest of America, the story is always dreadful, more or less. Columbus, Pizarro, Cortés, Quesada, de Soto,* the conquistadores seem all like men of doom. Read a man like Adolf   15 Bandelier, who knows the *inside* of his America, read his *Golden Man— El Dorado*—and feel the reverberation within reverberation of horror the conquistadores left behind them.

Then we have Mr Graham as a translator. In the innumerable and sometimes quite fatuous and irritating foot-notes—they are   20 sometimes interesting—our author often gives the original Spanish for the phrase he has translated. And even here he is peculiarly glib and unsatisfactory.—" 'God knows the trouble it cost,' he says pathetically."*—Valdivia is supposed to say this "pathetically". The foot-note gives Valdivia's words: "Un bergantin y el trabajo que costó,   25 Dios lo sabe." "A brigantine, and the work it cost, God knows." Why *trouble* for *trabajo?* And why *pathetically?* Again, the proverb: A Dios rogando, y con la maza dando, is translated: Praying to God, and battering with the mace.*—But why *battering* for *dando*, which means merely *donnant*, and might be rendered *smiting*, or *laying on*, but surely not   30 *battering*! Again, Philip II* is supposed to say to say to Ercilla, who stammered so much as to be unintelligible: *Habladme por escrito, Don Alonso!* Which is: *Say it to me in writing, Don Alonso!*—Mr Graham, however, translates it: *Write to me, Don Alonso!*—These things are trifles, but they show the peculiar laziness or insensitiveness to language   35 which is so great a vice in a translator.

The motto of the book* is:

> "El mas seguro don de la fortuna
> Es no lo haber tenido vez alguna."*

Mr Graham puts it: "The best of fortune's gifts is never to have had good luck at all."—Well, Ercilla may have meant this. The literal sense of the Spanish, anybody can make out: "The most sure gift of fortune, is not to have had it not once."—Whether one would be justified in changing the "fortuna" of the first line into "good luck" in the second, is a point we must leave to Mr Graham. Anyhow, he seems to have blest his own book in this equivocal fashion.

REVIEW OF NIGGER HEAVEN, *BY CARL VAN VECHTEN,* FLIGHT, *BY WALTER WHITE,* MANHATTAN TRANSFER, *BY JOHN DOS PASSOS, AND* IN OUR TIME, *BY ERNEST HEMINGWAY*

Nigger Heaven is one of the negro names for Harlem,* that dismal region of hard stone streets way up Seventh Avenue beyond One hundred and twenty-fifth Street, where the population is all coloured, though not much of it is real black. In the daytime, at least, the place aches with dismalness and a loose-end sort of squalor, the stone of the streets seeming particularly dead and stony, obscenely stony.

Mr Van Vechten's book* is a nigger book, and not much of a one. It opens and closes with nigger cabaret scenes in feeble imitation of Cocteau or Morand,* second-hand attempts to be wildly lurid, with background effects of black and vermilion velvet. The middle is a lot of stuffing about high-brow niggers, the heroine being one of the old-fashioned school-teacherish sort, this time an assistant in a public library; and she has only one picture in her room, a reproduction of the Monna Lisa,* and on her shelves only books by James Branch Cabell, Anatole France,* Jean Cocteau etc; in short, the literature of disillusion. This is to show how refined she is. She is just as refined as any other "idealistic" young heroine who earns her living, and we have to be reminded continually that she is golden brown.

Round this heroine goes on a fair amount of "race" talk, nigger self-consciousness which, if it didn't happen to mention that it was black, would be taken for merely another sort of self-conscious grouch. There is a love-affair—a rather palish brown—which might go into any feeble American novel whatsoever. And the whole coloured thing is peculiarly colourless, a second-hand dish barely warmed up.

The author seems to feel this, so he throws in a highly-spiced nigger in a tartan suit, who lives off women—rather in the distance—and two perfect red peppers of nigger millionairesses who swim in seas of champagne and have lovers and fling them away and sniff drugs; in short, altogether the usual old bones of hot stuff, warmed up with all the fervour the author can command—which isn't much.

It is a fake book by an author who lingers in nigger cabarets hoping to heaven to pick up something to write about and make a sensation—and, of course, money.

307

Flight is another nigger book; much more respectable, but not much more important. The author, we are told, is himself a negro.* If we weren't told, we should never know. But there is rather a call for coloured stuff, hence we had better be informed, when we're getting it.

5   The first part of *Flight* is interesting—the removal of Creoles,* just creamy-coloured old French-negro mixture—from the Creole quarter of New Orleans to the negro quarter of Atlanta.* This is real, as far as life goes, and external reality: except that to me, the Creole quarter of New Orleans is dead and lugubrious as a Jews Burying Ground, instead
10   of highly romantic. But the first part of *Flight* is good negro *data*.

The culture of Mr White's Creoles is much more acceptable than that of Mr Van Vechten's Harlem Golden-browns. If it is only skin-deep, that is quite enough, since the pigmentation of the skin seems to be the only difference between the negro and the white man. If
15   there be such a thing as a negro soul, then that of the Creole is very very French-American, and that of the Harlemite is very very Yankee-American. In fact, there seems no blackness about it at all. Reading negro books, or books about negroes written from the negro standpoint, it is absolutely impossible to discover that the nigger is any blacker inside
20   than we are. He's an absolute white man, save for the colour of his skin: which, in many cases, is also just as white as a Mediterranean white man's.

It is rather disappointing. One likes to cherish illusions about the race soul, the eternal negroid soul, black and glistening and touched with awfulness and with mystery. One is not allowed. The nigger is a white
25   man through and through. He even sees himself as white men see him, blacker than he ought to be. And his soul is an Edison gramophone* on which one puts the current records: which is what the white man's soul is, just the same, a gramophone grinding over the old records.

30   New York is the melting pot which melts even the nigger. The future population of this melting pot will be a pale greyish-brown in colour, and its psychology will be that of Mr White or Byron Kasson,* which is the psychology of a shrewd mixture of English, Irish, German, Jewish, and Negro. These are the grand ingredients of the melting-pot, and the
35   amalgam, or alloy, whatever you call it, will be a fine mixture of all of them—Unless the melting-pot gets upset.

Apparently there is only one *feeling* about the negro, wherein he differs from the white man, according to Mr White; and this is the feeling of warmth and humanness. But *we* don't feel even that. More
40   mercurial, but not by any means warmer or more human, the nigger

seems to be: even in nigger books.—And he sees in himself a talent for
life which the white man has lost. But remembering glimpses of Harlem
and Louisiana, and the down-at-heel greyness of the colourless negro
ambiente,* myself I don't feel even that.

But the one thing the negro *knows* he can do, is sing and dance. He 5
knows it, because the white man has pointed it out to him so often.
There again, however, disappointment! About one nigger in a thousand
amounts to anything in song or dance: the rest are just as songful and
limber as the rest of Americans.

Mimi, the pale-biscuit heroine of *Flight* neither sings nor dances. She 10
is rather cultured and makes smart dresses and passes over as white,
then marries a well-to-do white American, but leaves him because he is
not "live" enough, and goes back to Harlem.—It is just what Nordic*
wives do, just how they feel about their husbands. And if they don't
go to Harlem, they go somewhere else. And then they come back. As 15
Mimi will do. Three months of Nigger Heaven will have her fed up,
and back she'll be over the white line, settling again in the Washington
Square region,* and being "of French extraction." Nothing is more
monotonous than these removals.

All these books might as well be called *Flight*. They give one the 20
impression of swarms of grasshoppers hopping big hops, and buzzing
occasionally on the wing, all from nowhere to nowhere, all over the
place. What's the point of all this flight, when they start from nowhere
and alight on nowhere? For the Nigger heaven is as sure a nowhere as
anywhere else. 25

*Manhattan Transfer** is still a greater ravel of flights from nowhere
to nowhere. But at least the author knows it, and gets a kind of tragic
significance into the fact. John Dos Passos is a far better writer than Mr
Van Vechten or Mr White, and his book is a far more real and serious
thing. To me, it is the best modern book about New York that I have 30
read. It is an endless series of glimpses of people in the vast scuffle
of Manhattan Island, as they turn up again and again and again, in a
confusion that has no obvious rhythm, but wherein at last we recognise
the systole-diastole* of success and failure, the end being all failure,
from the point of view of life; and then another flight towards another 35
nowhere.

If you set a blank record revolving to receive all the sounds, and a
film-camera going to photograph all the motions of a scattered group of
individuals, at the points where they meet and touch in New York,
you would more or less get Mr Dos Passos' method. It is a rush 40

of disconnected scenes and scraps, a breathless confusion of isolated
moments in a group of lives, pouring on through the years, from almost
every part of New York. But the order of time is more or less kept.
For half a page you are on the Lackawanna ferry-boat*—or one of
5   the ferry-boats—in the year 1900 or somewhere there—the next page
you are in the Brevoort* a year later—two pages ahead it is Central
Park,* you don't know when—then the wharves—way up Hoboken—
down Greenwich Village—the Algonquin Hotel*—somebody's apartment! And it seems to be different people, a different girl every time.
10   The scenes whirl past like snowflakes—Broadway* at night—whizz!
gone!—a quick-lunch counter! gone! a house on Riverside Drive,* the
Palisades,* night,—gone! But gradually you get to know the faces. It is
like a movie picture with an intricacy of different stories and no close-
ups and no writing in between. Mr Dos Passos leaves out the writing in
15   between.

But if you are content to be confused, at length you realise that
the confusion is genuine, not affected; it is life, not a pose. The book
becomes, what life is, a stream of different things and different faces
rushing along in the consciousness, with no apparent direction save that
20   of time, from past to present, from youth to age, from birth to death, and
no apparent goal at all. But what makes the rush so swift, one gradually
realises, is the wild, strange frenzy for success: egoistic, individualistic
success.

This very complex film, of course, does not pretend to film *all* New
25   York. Journalists, actors and actresses, dancers, unscrupulous lawyers,
prostitutes, Jews, out-of-works, politicians, Labour agents—that kind
of gang. It is on the whole a gang, though we do touch respectability on
Riverside Drive now and then. But it is a gang, the vast loose gang of
strivers and winners and losers which seems to be the very pep of New
30   York, the city itself an inordinately vast gang.

At first it seems too warm, too passionate. One thinks: this is much
too healthily lusty for the present New York.—Then we realise we are
away before the war, when the place was steaming and alive. There is
sex, fierce, ranting, sex, real New York: sex as the prime stimulant to
35   business success. One realises what a lot of financial success has been
due to the reckless speeding-up of the sex dynamo. Get hold of the right
woman, get absolutely rushed out of yourself loving her up, and you'll
be able to rush a success in the city. Only, both to the man and woman,
the sex must be the stimulant to success; otherwise it stimulates towards

suicide, as it does with the one character whom the author loves, and
who was "truly male."*

The war comes, and the whole rhythm collapses. The war ends. There
are the same people. Some have got success, some haven't. But success
and failure alike are left irritable and inert. True, everybody is older,   5
and the fire is dying down into spasmodic irritability. But in all the city
the fire is dying down. The stimulant is played out, and you have the
accumulating irritable restlessness of New York of today. The old thrill
has gone, out of socialism as out of business, out of art as out of love, and
the city rushes on ever faster, with more maddening irritation, knowing   10
the apple is a Dead Sea shiner.*

At the end of the book, the man who was a little boy* at the beginning
of the book, and now is a failure of perhaps something under forty,
crosses on the ferry from Twenty-third street, and walks away into the
gruesome ugliness of the New Jersey side. He is making another flight   15
into nowhere, to land upon nothingness.

' "Say, will you give me a lift?" he asks the red-haired man at the
wheel. (of a furniture van)

"How fur ye goin'?"

"I dunno . . . Pretty far."   20

'The End.'

He might just as well have said "nowhere!"

In Our Time is the last of the four American books, and Mr
Hemingway* has accepted the goal. He keeps on making flights, but
he has no illusion about landing anywhere. He knows it will be nowhere   25
every time.

In Our Time calls itself a book of stories, but it isn't that. It is a
series of successive sketches from a man's life, and makes a fragmentary
novel. The first scenes, by one of the big Lakes in America—probably
Superior*—are the best; when Nick is a boy. Then come fragments of   30
war—on the Italian front. Then a soldier back home very late, in the
little town way west in Oklahoma. Then a young American and wife in
post-war Europe: a long sketch about an American jockey in Milan and
Paris: then Nick is back again in the Lake Superior region, getting off
the train at a burnt-out town, and tramping across the empty country to   35
camp by a trout-stream. Trout is the one passion life has left him—and
this won't last long.

It is a short book: and it does not pretend to be about one man. But
it is. It is as much as we need know of the man's life. The sketches

are short, sharp, vivid, and most of them excellent. (The "Mottoes"*
in front seem a little affected.)—And these few sketches are enough to
create the man and all his history: we need know no more.

Nick is a type one meets in the more wild and woolly regions of
the United States. He is the remains of the lone trapper and cowboy.
Nowadays he is educated, and through with everything. It is a state
of *conscious*, accepted indifference to everything except freedom from
work and the moment's interest. Mr Hemingway does it extremely well.
Nothing matters. Everything happens. One wants to keep oneself loose.
Avoid one thing only: getting connected up. Don't get connected up.
If you get held by anything, break it. Don't be held. Break it, and get
away. Don't get away with the idea of getting somewhere else. Just get
away, for the sake of getting away. Beat it!—"Well, boy, I guess I'll beat
it."* Ah, the pleasure in saying that!

Mr Hemingway's sketches, for this reason, are excellent: so short,
like striking a match, lighting a brief sensational cigarette, and it's over.
His young love affair ends as one throws a cigarette end away. "It isn't
fun any more."—"Everything's gone to hell inside me."*

It is really honest. And it explains a great deal of sentimentality. When
a thing has gone to hell inside you, your sentimentalism tries to pretend
it hasn't. But Mr Hemingway is through with the sentimentalism. "It
isn't fun anymore. I guess I'll beat it."

And he beats it, to somewhere else. In the end he'll be a sort of
tramp, endlessly moving on for the sake of moving away from where he
is. This is a negative goal, and Mr Hemingway is really good, because
he's perfectly straight about it. He is like Krebs, in that devastating
Oklahoma sketch:* he doesn't love anybody, and it nauseates him to
have to pretend he does. He doesn't even *want* to love anybody; he
doesn't want to go anywhere, he doesn't want to do anything. He wants
just to lounge around and maintain a healthy state of nothingness inside
himself, and an attitude of negation to everything outside himself. And
why shouldn't he, since that is exactly and sincerely what he feels? If he
really *doesn't* care, then why should he care? Anyhow he doesn't.

REVIEW OF SOLITARIA, *BY V. V. ROZANOV*

Solitaria by *V. V. Rozanov.*

We are told on the wrapper of this book that Prince Mirsky* considered
Rozanov* "one of the greatest Russians of modern times . . . Rozanov
is the greatest revelation of the Russian mind yet to be shown to the
West."

We become diffident, confronted with these superlatives. And when
we have read E. Gollerbach's long Critico–biographical Study,* 43
pp., we are more suspicious still, in spite of the occasionally profound
and striking quotations from *Solitaria* and from the same author's *Fallen
Leaves*. But there we are, we've got another of these morbidly introspective Russians, morbidly wallowing in adoration of Jesus, then getting
up and spitting in his beard, or in his back hair, at least; characters
such as Dostoevsky has familiarised us with, and of whom we are tired.
Of these self-divided, gamin-religious Russians, who are so absorbedly
concerned with their own dirty linen and their own pie-bald souls, we
have had a little more than enough. The contradictions in them are not
so very mysterious, or edifying, after all. They have a spurting, *gamin*
hatred of civilisation, of Europe, of Christianity, of governments, and
of everything else, in their moments of energy; and in their inevitable
relapses into weakness, they make the inevitable recantation, they whine,
they humiliate themselves, they seek unspeakable humiliation for themselves, and call it Christlike, and then with the left hand commit some
dirty little crime or meanness, and call it the mysterious complexity of
the human soul. It's all masturbation, half-baked, and one gets tired of
it. One gets tired of being told that Dostoevsky's *Legend of the Grand
Inquisitor* "is the most profound declaration which ever was made about
man and life—"* As far as I'm concerned, in proportion as a man gets
more profoundly and personally interested in himself, so does my interest in him wane. The more Dostoevsky gets worked up about the tragic
nature of the human soul, the more I lose interest. I have read the *Grand
Inquisitor* three times, and never can remember what it's really about.
This I make as a confession, not as a vaunt. It always seems to me, as
the Germans say, *mehr Schrei wie Wert.**

5

10

15

20

25

30

And in Rozanov one fears one has got a pup out of the Dostoevsky kennel. *Solitaria* is a sort of philosophical work, about 100 pp., of a kind not uncommon in Russia, consisting in fragmentary jottings of thoughts which occurred to the author, mostly during the years 1910 and 1911, apparently, and scribbled down where they came, in a cab, in the train, in the W. C., on the sole of a bathing slipper. But the thought that came in a cab might just as well have come in the w. c. or "examining my coins,"* so what's the odds! If Rozanov wanted to give the physical context to the thought, he'd have to create the scene. "In a cab" or "examining my coins" means nothing.

Then we get a whole lot of bits, some of them interesting, some not; many of them to be classified under the heading of: to jesus or not to jesus! if we may profanely parody Hamlet's: to be or not to be.*—But it is the Russians' own parody.—Then you get a lot of self-conscious personal bits: "The only *masculine* thing about you – – is your trousers:"* which was said to Rozanov by a girl; though, as it isn't particularly true, there was no point in his repeating it. However, he has that "self-probing" nature we have become acquainted with.—"Teaching is form, and I am formless. In teaching there must be order and a system, and I am systemless and even disorderly. There is duty—and to me any duty at the bottom of my heart always seemed comical, and on any duty, at the bottom of my heart, I always wanted to play a trick (except tragic duty) . . ."*

Here we have the pup of the Dostoevsky kennel, a so-called nihilist: in reality, a Mary Mary quite contrary.* It is largely tiresome contrariness, even if it is spontaneous and not self-induced.

And of course, in Mary Mary quite contrary we have the ever-recurrent whimper: I want to be good! I *am* good! Oh, I am *so* good, I'm better than anybody! I love Jesus and all the saints, and above all, the blessed Virgin! Oh, how I love purity!—and so forth. Then they give a loud *crepitus ventris,* as a punctuation.

Dostoevsky has accustomed us to it, and we are hard boiled. Poor Voltaire, if he recanted, he only recanted once,* when his strength had left him, and he was neither here nor there. But these Russians are forever on their death-beds, and neither here nor there.

Rozanov's talk about "lovely faces and dear souls" of children,* and "for two years I have been 'in Easter', 'in the pealing of bells,' truly 'arrayed in white rayment' ",* just makes one feel more hard boiled than ever. It's a cold egg.*

Yet, in Solitaria, there are occasional profound things. "I am not such a scoundrel yet as to think about morals."*—"Try to crucify the sun, and you will see which is God—"* and many others. But to me, self-conscious personal revelations, touched with the gutter-snipe and the actor, are not very interesting. One has lived too long.

So that I come to the end of Gollerbach's "Critico-Biographical Study" sick of the self-fingering sort of sloppiness, and I have very much the same feeling at the end of *Solitaria*, though occasionally Rozanov hits the nail on the head and makes it jump.

Then come twenty pages extracted from Rozanov's *Apocalypse of Our Times*,* and at once, the style changes, at once you have a real thing to deal with. The *Apocalypse* must be a far more important book than *Solitaria*, and we wish to heaven we had been given it instead. Now at last we see Rozanov as a real thinker, and "the greatest revelation of the Russian mind yet to be shown to the West."

Rozanov had a real man in him, and it is true, what he says of himself, that he did not feel in himself that touch of the criminal which Dostoevsky felt in *himself*.* Rozanov was not a criminal. Somewhere, he was integral, and brave, and a seer, a true one, not a *gamin*. We see it all in his *Apocalypse*. He is not really a Dostoevskian. That's only his Russianitis.

The book is an attack on Christianity, and as far as we are given to see, there is no canting or recanting in it. It is passionate, and suddenly valid. It is not jibing or criticism or pulling to pieces. It is a real passion. Rozanov has more or less recovered the genuine pagan vision, the phallic vision, and with these eyes he looks, in amazement and consternation, on the mess of Christianity.

For the first time, we get what we have got from no Russian, neither Tolstoy nor Dostoevsky nor any of them, a real, positive view on life. It is as if the pagan Russian had wakened up in Rozanov, a kind of Rip Van Winkle,* and was just staggering at what he saw. His background is the vast old pagan background, the phallic. And in front of this, the tortured complexity of Christian civilisation—what else can we call it—is a kind of phantasmagoria to him.

He is the first Russian, as far as I am concerned, who has ever said anything to me. And his vision is full of passion, vivid, valid. He is the first to see that immortality is in the vividness of life, not in the loss of life. The butterfly becomes a whole revelation to him: and to us.

When Rozanov is wholly awake, and a new man, a risen man, the living and resurrected pagan, then he is a great man and a great seer,

and perhaps, as he says himself, the first Russian to emerge. Speaking of
Tolstoy and Leontiev* and Dostoevsky, Rozanov says: "I speak straight
out what they dared not even suspect. I speak because after all I am
more of a thinker than they. That is all.—But the problem (in the
5   case of Leontiev and Dostoevsky) is and was about anti-Christianity,
about the victory over the very essence of Christianity, over that terrible
avitalism. Whereas from him, from the phallus everything flows.—"*

When Rozanov is in this mood, and in this vision, he is not dual, nor
divided against himself. He is one complete thing. His vision and his
10   passion is positive, non-tragical.

Then again he starts to Russianise, and he comes in two. When he
becomes aware of himself, and personal, he is often ridiculous, sometimes pathetic, sometimes a bore, and almost always "dual." Oh, how
they love to be dual, and divided against themselves, these Dostoevskian
15   Russians! It is as good as a pose: always a Mary Mary quite contrary
business.—"The great horror of the human soul consists in this, that
while thinking of the Madonna it at the same time does not cease thinking of Sodom and of its sins; and the still greater horror is that even in
the very midst of Sodom it does not forget the Madonna, it yearns for
20   Sodom and the Madonna, and this at one and the same time, without
any discord."*

The answer to that, is that Sodom and Madonna-ism are two halves of
the same movement, the mere tick-tack* of lust and asceticism, pietism
and pornography. If you're not pious, you won't be pornographical,
25   and vice versa. If there are no saints there'll be no sinners. If there were
no ascetics, there'd be no lewd people. If you divide the human psyche
into two halves, one half will be white, the other black. It's the division
itself which is pernicious. The swing to one extreme causes the swing
to the other. The swing towards Immaculate Madonna-ism* inevitably
30   causes the swing back to the whore of prostitution, then back again to
the Madonna, and so *ad infinitum*.* But you can't blame the *soul* for this.
All you have to blame is the craven, cretin human intelligence, which is
always seeking to get away from its own centre.

But Rozanov, when he isn't russianising, is the first Russian really to
35   see it, and to recover, if unstably, the old human wholeness.

So that this book is extremely interesting, and really important. We
get impatient with the russianising. And yet, with Gollerbach's Introduction and the letters at the end, we do get to know all we want to
know about Rozanov, personally. It is not of vast importance, what he
40   was personally. If he behaved perversely, he was never, like Dostoevsky,

inwardly perverse, and when he says he was not "born rightly",* he is only yelping like a Dostoevsky pup.

It is the voice of the new man in him, not the Dostoevsky whelp, that means something. And it means a great deal. We shall wait for a full translation of *The Apocalypse of Our Times*, and of *Oriental Motifs*;*   5
Rozanov matters, for the future.

REVIEW OF THE PEEP SHOW, BY WALTER WILKINSON

When I was a budding author, just before the war, I used to hear Ford Hueffer asserting that every man could write *one* novel, and hinting that he ought to be encouraged to do it. The novel, of course, would probably be only a human document.* Nevertheless, it would be worth while, since every life is a life.

There was a subtle distinction drawn, in those halcyon days of talk "about" things, between literature and the human document. The latter was the real thing, mind you, but it wasn't art. The former was art, you must know, but—but—it wasn't the raw beefsteak of life, it was the dubious steak-and-kidney pie. Now you must choose: the raw beefsteak of life, or the suspicious steak and kidney pie of the public restaurant of art.

Perhaps that state of mind and that delicate stomach for art has passed away. To me, literary talk was always like a rattle that literary men spun to draw attention to themselves. But *The Peep Show* reminds me of the old jargon. They would have called it "a charming human document," and have descanted on the naïve niceness of the unsophisticated author.* It used to seem so delightful, to the latter-day *littérateur*, to discover a book that was not written by a writer. "Oh, he's not a writer, you know! That's what *makes* it so delightful!"

The Peep Show is a simple and unpretentious account of a young man who made his own puppets and went round for a few weeks in Somerset and Devon, two or three years ago,* in the holiday season, giving puppet shows. It wasn't just Punch and Judy, because the showman, though not exactly a high-brow, was neither exactly a low-brow. He believed in the simple life: which means, nuts, vegetables, no meat, tents, fresh air, nature, and niceness. Now this puppet showman was *naturally* vegetarian, and *naturally* nice, with the vices *naturally* left out: a nice, modern young fellow, who had enjoyed William Morris' "News from Nowhere"* immensely, as a boy. One might say, a grandson of the William Morris stock, but a much plainer, more unpretentious fellow than his cultural forbears. And really "of the people." And really penniless.

But he is not a high-brow: has hardly heard of Dostoevsky,* much less read him: and the "works of William Shakspeare, in one volume," which accompanied the puppet show for the first week, is just a standing joke to the showman. As if anybody ever *did* read Shakspeare, actually! That's the farce of it. Bill Shakspeare! "Where's the works of the immortal William?—Say, are you sitting on Big Bill in one vol.?"*

The author has very little to do with culture, whether in the big sense or the little.* But he is a simple lifer.* And as a simple lifer he sets out, with much trepidation, to make his living by showing his "reformed" puppets: not so brutal, beery and beefy, as Punch:* more suitable to the young, in every way. Still, they actually *are* charming puppets.

The book is an absolutely simple and unaffected account of the two-months' or six-weeks' tour, from the Cotswolds down through Ilfra-combe to Bideford, then back, inland, by Taunton and Wells. It was mostly a one-man show: the author trundled his "sticks" before him, on a pair of old bath-chair wheels.*

And curiously, the record of those six weeks makes a book. Call it a human document, call it literature, I don't know the difference. The style is, in a sense, amateur: yet the whole attempt was amateur, that whole Morris aspect of life is amateur. And therefore the style is perfect: even, in the long run, poignant. The very banalities at last have the effect of the *mot juste*.*—"It is an exquisite pleasure to find oneself so suddenly in the sweet morning air, to tumble out of bed, to clamber over a stone wall and scramble across some rushy dunes down to the untrodden seashore, there to take one's bath in the lively breakers."*

That is exactly how the cleverest youth writes, in an essay on the sea-side, at night-school. There is an inevitability about its banality, the "exquisite pleasure", the "sweet morning air", to "tumble out of bed"—which in actuality was carefully crawling out of a sleeping sack—; the "clamber over a stone wall", the "scramble across some rushy (sic) dunes" to the "untrodden shore", the "bath" in the "lively breakers": it is almost a masterpiece of clichés. It is the way thousands and thousands of the cleverest of the "ordinary" young fellows write, who have had just a touch more than our "ordinary" education, and who have a certain limpidity of character, and not much of the old Adam* in them. It is what the "ordinary" young man, who is "really nice", does write. You have to have something vicious in you, to be a creative writer. It is the something vicious, old-adamish, incompatible to the "ordinary" world, inside a man, which gives an edge to his awareness, and makes it impossible for him to talk of a "bath" in "lively breakers."

The puppet showman has not got this something vicious, so his perceptions lack fine edge. He can't help being "nice." And niceness is negative only too often. But, still, he is not *too* nice.

So the book is a book. It is not insipid. It is not banal. All takes place in the banal world: nature is banal, all the people are banal, save perhaps the very last "nobber":* and all the philosophy is banal. And yet it is all *just*.—"If I were a philosopher expounding a new theory of living, inventing a new 'ism', I should call myself a holidayist, for it seems to me that the one thing the world needs to put it right is a holiday. There is no doubt whatever about the sort of life nice people want to lead. Whenever they get the chance, what do they do but go away to the country or the seaside, take off their collars and ties and have a good time playing at childish games and contriving to eat some simple (sic) food very happily without all the encumbrances of chairs and tables. This world might be quite a nice place if only simple people would be content to be simple and be proud of it; if only they would turn their backs on these pompous politicians and ridiculous Captains of Industry who, when you come to examine them, turn out to be very stupid, ignorant people, who are simply suffering from an unhappy mania of greediness; who are possessed with perverse and horrible devils which make them stick up smoky factories in glorious Alpine valleys; or spoil some simple country by digging up and exploiting its decently buried mineral resources; or whose moral philosophy is so patently upside down when they attempt to persuade us that quarrelling, and fighting, and wars, or that these ridiculous accumulations of wealth are the most important, instead of the most undesirable things in life. If only simple people would ignore them and behave always in the jolly way they do on a seashore what a nice world we might have to live in.

Luckily Nature has a way with her, and we may rest assured that this wretched machine age will be over in a few years' time. It has grown up as quickly as a mushroom, and like a mushroom it has no stability. It will die.—"*

But this is just "philosophy," and by the way. It is the apotheosis of ordinariness. The narrative part of the book is the succinct revelation of ordinariness, as seen from the puppet showman's point of view. And owing to the true limpidity and vicelessness of the author, ordinariness becomes almost vivid.

The book is a book. It is not something to laugh at. It is so curiously *true*. And it has therefore its own touch of realisation of the tragedy of human futility: the futility even of ordinariness. It contains the ordinary

man's queer little bitter disappointment in life, because life, the life of
people, is more ordinary than even he had imagined. The puppet showman is a bit of a pure idealist, in a fairly ordinary sense. He *really* doesn't
want money. He *really* is not greedy. He *really* is shy of trespassing on
5 anybody. He *really* is nice. He starts out by being too nice.

What is his experience? He struggles and labours, and is lucky if he
can make five shillings in a day's work. When it rains, when there's no
crowd, when it's Sunday, when the police won't allow you to show, when
the local authorities won't allow you to pitch the sticks—then there is
10 nothing doing. Result—about fifteen-shillings a week earnings. That is
all the great and noble public will pay, for a puppet show. And you can
live on it.

It is enough to embitter any man, to see people gape at a show, then
melt away when the hat comes round.* Not even a penny that they're
15 not *forced* to pay. Even on their holidays. Yet they give shillings to go in
the dirty cinema.*

The puppet showman, however, refuses to be embittered. He remembers those who do pay, and pay heartily: sixpence the maximum. People are on the whole "nice" to him. Myself, I should want to spit on
20 such niceness.* The showman, however, accepts it. He is cheery by
determination.—When I was a boy among the miners, the question that
would have been flung at the puppet showman would have been: "Lad,
wheer 'st keep thy ba's?"* For his unfailing forbearance and meekness!
It is admirable—but—. Anyhow, what's the good of it? They just trod
25 on him, all the same: all those masses of ordinary people more vulgar
than he was; because there is a difference between vulgarity and ordinariness. Vulgarity is low and greedy. The puppet-showman is never
that. He is at least pure, in the ordinary sense of the word: never greedy
nor base.

30 And if he is not embittered, the puppet-showman is bitterly disappointed and chagrined. No, he has to decide that the world is not
altogether a nice place to show puppets in. People are "nice", but by
Jove, they are tight.* They don't want puppets. They don't want anything but chars-a-bancs* and cinemas, girlies and curlies and togs* and
35 a drink. Callous, vulgar, less than human the ordinary world looks, full
of "nice" people, as one reads this book. And that holiday region of
Ilfracombe and Bideford, those country lanes of Devonshire reeling
with char-a-bancs and blurting blind dust and motor-horns, or mud
and motor-horns, all August:* that is hell! England my England!* Who

would be a holidayist? Oh, people are "nice"! But you've got to be vulgar, as well as ordinary, if you're going to stand them.

To me, a book like *The Peep Show* reveals England better than twenty novels by clever young ladies and gentlemen. Be absolutely decent in the ordinary sense of the word, be a "holidayist" and a firm believer   5 in niceness; and then set out into the world of all those nice people, putting yourself more or less at their mercy. Put yourself at the mercy of the nice holidaymaking crowd. Then come home, absolutely refusing to have your tail between your legs, but—"singing songs in praise of camping and tramping and the stirring life we jolly showmen lead."*   10 Because absolutely nobody has been *really* nasty to you. They've all been quite nice. Oh, quite! Even though you *are* out of pocket on the trip.

All the reader can say, at the end of this songful cheerful book is: God save me from the nice ordinary people, and from ever having to make a   15 living out of them. God save me from being "nice."

REVIEW OF THE SOCIAL BASIS OF CONSCIOUSNESS, *BY TRIGANT BURROW*

The Social Basis of Consciousness by
Trigant Burrow

Dr Trigant Burrow* is well known as an independent psychoanalyst
through the essays and addresses he has published in pamphlet form
from time to time. These have invariably shown the spark of origi-   5
nal thought and discovery. The gist of all these essays now fuses into
this important book, the latest addition to the International Library of
Psychology, Philosophy and Scientific Method.*

Dr Burrow is that rare thing among psychiatrists, a humanly honest
man. Not that practitioners are usually dishonest. They are intellectu-   10
ally honest, professionally honest, all that. But that other simple thing,
human honesty, does not enter in, because it is primarily subjective;
and subjective honesty, which means that a man is honest about his
own inward experience, is perhaps the rarest thing, especially among
professionals. Chiefly, of course, because men, and especially men with   15
a theory, don't know anything about their own inward experiences.

Here Dr Burrow is a rare and shining example. He set out, years ago, as
an enthusiastic psychoanalyst and follower of Freud, working according
to the Freudian method, in America. And gradually, the sense that
something was wrong, vitally wrong, in the theory and in the practice   20
of psychoanalysis both, invaded him. Like any truly honest man, he
turned and asked himself what it was that was wrong, with himself, with
his methods, and with the theory according to which he was working?

This book is the answer, a book for every man interested in the human
consciousness to read carefully. Because Dr Burrow's conclusions, sin-   25
cere, almost naïve in their startled emotion, are far-reaching, and vital.

First, in his criticism of the Freudian method, Dr Burrow found, in
his clinical experience, that he was always applying a *theory*.* Patients
came to be analysed, and the analyst was there to examine with open
mind. But the mind could not be open, because the patient's neurosis,   30
all the patient's experience *had* to be fitted to the Freudian theory of the
inevitable incest-motive.*

And gradually Dr Burrow realised that to fit life every time to a theory
is in itself a mechanistic process, a process of unconscious repression,

a process of image substitution. All theory that has to be applied to life proves at last just another of these unconscious images which the repressed psyche uses as a substitute for life, and against which the psychoanalyst is fighting. The analyst wants to break all this image
5   business, so that life can flow freely. But it is useless to try to do so by replacing in the unconscious another image—this time, the image, the fixed motive of the incest-complex.

Theory as theory is all right. But the moment you apply it to *life*, especially to the subjective life, the theory becomes mechanistic, a
10 substitute for life, a factor in the vicious unconscious. So that while the Freudian theory of the unconscious and of the incest motive is valuable as a *description* of our psychological condition, the moment you begin to *apply* it, and make it master of the living situation, you have begun to substitute one mechanistic or unconscious illusion for
15 another.

In short, the analyst is just as much fixed in his vicious unconscious as is his neurotic patient, and the will to apply a mechanical incest-theory to every neurotic experience is just as sure an evidence of neurosis, in Freud or in the practitioner, as any psychologist could ask.
20 So much for the criticism of the psychoanalytic method.

If then, Dr Burrow asks himself, it is not sex-repression which is at the root of the neurosis of modern life, what is it? For certainly, according to his finding, sex-repression is not the root of the evil.

The question is a big one, and can have no single answer. A single
25 answer would only be another "theory." But Dr Burrow has struggled through years of mortified experience to come to some conclusion, nearer the mark. And his finding is surely much deeper and more vital, and also, much less spectacular than Freud's.

The real trouble lies in the inward sense of "separateness," which
30 dominates every man. At a certain point in his evolution, man became cognitively conscious: he bit the apple:* he began to know. Up till that time his consciousness flowed unaware, as in the animals. Suddenly, his consciousness split.

—"It would appear that in his separativeness man has inadvertently
35 fallen a victim to the developmental exigencies of his own consciousness. Captivated by the phylogenetically new and unwonted spectacle of his own image, it would seem he has been irresistibly arrested before the mirror of his own likeness and that in the present self-conscious phase of his mental evolution he is still standing spell-bound before it. That
40 such is the case with man is not remarkable. For the appearance of the

phenomenon of consciousness marked a complete severance from all
that was his past. Here was broken the chain of evolutionary events
whose links extended back through the nebulous aeons of our remotest
ancestry, and in the first moment of his consciousness man stood, for
the first time, *alone*. It was in this moment that he was 'created,' as the   5
legend runs, 'in the image and likeness of God.' For breaking with the
teleological traditions of his agelong biology, man now became suddenly
aware."—*

Consciousness is self-consciousness. —"That is, consciousness in its
inception entails the fallacy of *a self as over against other selves*."—*   10

Suddenly aware of himself, and of other selves over against him, man
is a prey to the division inside himself. Helplessly he must strive for
more consciousness, which means, also, a more intensified aloneness, or
individuality; and at the same time he has a horror of his own aloneness,
and a blind, dim yearning for the old togetherness of the far past, what   15
Dr Burrow calls the preconscious state.*

What man really wants, according to Dr Burrow, is a sense of togetherness with his fellow men, which shall balance the secret but overmas-
tering sense of separateness and aloneness which now dominates him.
And therefore, instead of the Freudian method of personal analysis, in   20
which the personality of the patient is pitted against the personality of
the analyst in the old struggle for dominancy, Dr Burrow would substitute a method of group analysis, wherein the reactions were distributed
over a group of people, and the intensely personal element eliminated
as far as possible. For it is only in the intangible reaction of several   25
people, or many people together, on one another, that you can really get
the loosening and breaking of the me-and-you tension and contest, the
inevitable contest of two individualities brought into connection. What
must be broken is the ego-centric absolute of the individual. We are all
such hopeless little absolutes to ourselves. And if we are sensitive, it   30
hurts us, and we complain, we are called neurotic. If we are complacent,
we enjoy our own petty absolutism, though we hide it and pretend to
be quite meek and humble. But in secret, we are absolute and perfect
to ourselves, and nobody could be better than we are. And this is called
being normal.   35

Perhaps the most interesting part of Dr Burrow's book is his examination of normality. As soon as man became aware of himself, he made
a picture of himself. Then he began to live according to the picture.
Mankind at large made a picture of itself, and every man had to con-
form to the picture, the ideal.   40

This is the great image or idol which dominates our civilisation, and which we worship with mad blindness. The idolatry of self. Consciousness should be a flow from within outwards. The organic necessity of the human being should flow into spontaneous action and spontaneous awareness, consciousness.

But the moment man became aware of himself he made a picture of himself, and began to live from the picture: that is, from without inwards. This is truly the reversal of life. And this is how we live. We spend all our time over the picture. All our education is but the elaborating of the picture. "A good little girl"—"a brave boy"—"a noble woman"— "a strong man"—"a productive society"—"a progressive humanity"— it is all the picture. It is all living from the outside to the inside. It is all the death of spontaneity. It is all, strictly, automatic. It is all the vicious unconscious which Freud postulated.

If we could once get into our heads—or if we once dare admit to one another—that we are *not* the picture, and the picture is not what we are, then we might lay a new hold on life. For the picture is really the death, and certainly the neurosis of us all. We have to live from the outside in, idolatrously. And the picture of ourselves, the picture of humanity which has been elaborated through some thousands of years, and which we are still adding-to, is just a huge idol. It is not real. It is a horrible compulsion set over us.

Individuals rebel, and these are the neurotics, who show some sign of health.* The mass, the great mass goes on worshipping the idol, and behaving according to the picture: and this is the normal. Freud tried to force his patients back to the normal, and almost succeeded in shocking them into submission, with the incest-bogey. But the bogey is nothing compared to the actual idol.

As a matter of fact, the mass is more neurotic than the individual patient. This is Dr Burrow's finding. The mass, the normals, never live a life of their own. They cannot. They live entirely according to the picture. And according to the picture, each one is a little absolute unto himself, there is none better than he. Each lives for his own self-interest. The "normal" activity is to push your own interest with every atom of energy you can command. It is "normal" to get on,* to get ahead, at whatever cost. The man who does disinterested work is abnormal. Every Johnny must look out for himself: that is normal. Luckily for the world, there still is a minority of individuals who do disinterested work, and are made use of by the "normals." But the number is rapidly decreasing.

And then, the normals betray their utter abnormality in a crisis like the late war.* There, there indeed the uneasy individual can look into the abysmal insanity of the normal masses. The same holds good of the bolshevist hysteria of today:* it is hysteria, incipient social insanity. And the last great insanity of all, which is going to tear our civilisation to pieces, the insanity of class hatred, is almost entirely a "normal" thing, and a "social" thing. It is a state of fear, of ghastly collective fear. And it is absolutely a mark of the normal. To say that class hatred *need not exist* is to show abnormality. And yet it is true. Between man and man, class hatred hardly exists. It is an insanity of the mass, rather than of the individual.

But it is part of the picture. The picture says it is horrible to be poor, and splendid to be rich, and in spite of all individual experience to the contrary, we accept the terms of the picture, and thereby accept class war as inevitable.

Humanity, society has a picture of itself, and lives accordingly. The individual likewise has a private picture of himself, which fits into the big picture. In this picture he is a little absolute, and nobody could be better than he is. He must look after his own self-interest. And if he is a man, he must be very male. If she is a woman, she must be very female.*

Even sex, today, is only part of the picture. Men and women alike, when they are being sexual, are only acting up. They are living according to the picture. If there is any dynamic, it is that of self-interest. The man "seeketh his own" in sex, and the woman seeketh her own: in the bad, egoistic sense in which St Paul used the words. That is, the man seeks himself, the woman seeks herself, always, and inevitably. It is inevitable, when you live according to the picture, that you seek only yourself in sex. Because the picture is your own image of yourself: your *idea* of yourself. If you are quite normal, you don't have any true self, which "seeketh not her own, is not puffed up."* The true self, in sex, would seek a *meeting*, would seek to meet the other. This would be the true flow: what Dr Burrow calls the "societal consciousness,"* and what I would call the human consciousness, in contrast to the social, or image consciousness.

But today, all is image consciousness. Sex does not exist, there is only sexuality.* And sexuality is merely a greedy, blind self-seeking. Self-seeking is the real motive of sexuality. And therefore, since the thing sought is the same, the self, the mode of seeking is not very important. Heterosexual, homosexual, narcistic, normal or incest, it is all the same thing. It is just sexuality, not sex. It is one of the universal forms of self-seeking.* Every man, every woman just seeks his own self, her own self, in the sexual experience. It is the picture over again, whether in sexuality or self-sacrifice, greed or charity, the same thing, the self, the image, the idol: the image of me, and no me!

5   The true self is not aware that it is a self. A bird as it sings sings itself. But not according to a picture. It has no idea of itself.

And this is what the analyst must try to do: to liberate his patient from his own image, from his horror of his own isolation and the horror of the "stoppage" of his real vital flow. To do it, it is no use rousing
10   sex bogeys. A man is not neurasthenic or neurotic because he loves his mother. If he desires his mother, it is because he is neurotic, and the desire is merely a symptom. The cause of the neurosis is further to seek.

And the cure? For myself, I believe Dr Burrow is right: the cure would consist in bringing about a state of honesty and a certain trust among a
15   *group* of people, or many people—if possible, all the people in the world. For it is only when we can get a man to fall back into his true relation to other men, and to women, that we can give him an opportunity to be himself. So long as men are inwardly dominated by their own isolation, their own absoluteness, which after all is but a picture or an idea, nothing
20   is possible but insanity more or less pronounced. Men must get back into *touch*. And to do so they must forfeit the vanity and the *noli me tangere** of their own absoluteness: also they must utterly break the present great picture of a normal humanity: shatter that mirror in which we all live grimacing: and fall again into true relatedness.

25   I have tried more or less to give a *résumé* of Dr Burrow's book. I feel there is a certain impertinence in giving these résumés. But not more than in the affectation of "criticising" and being superior. And it is a book one should read and assimilate, for it helps a man in his own inward life.

REVIEW FOR VOGUE, *OF* THE STATION:
ATHOS, TREASURES AND MEN, *BY ROBERT
BYRON*, ENGLAND AND THE OCTOPUS, *BY
CLOUGH WILLIAMS-ELLIS*, COMFORTLESS
MEMORY, *BY MAURICE BARING, AND*
ASHENDEN, OR THE BRITISH AGENT, *BY
W. SOMERSET MAUGHAM*

Review for Vogue

Athos* is an old place, and Mr Byron* is a young man. The combination
for once is really happy. We can imagine ourselves being very bored by
a book on ancient Mount Athos and its ancient monasteries with their
ancient rule. Luckily Mr Byron belongs to the younger generation, even   5
younger than the Sitwells,* who have shown him the way to be young.
Therefore he is not more than becomingly impressed with ancientness.
He never gapes in front if it. He settles on it like a butterfly, tastes it, is
perfectly honest about the taste, and flutters on. And it is charming.

We confess that we find this youthful revelation of ancient Athos   10
charming. It is all in the butterfly manner. But the butterfly, airy creature, is by no means a fool. And its interest is wide. It is amusing to watch
a spangled beauty settle on the rose, then on a spat-out cherry-stone,
then, with a quiver of sunny attention, upon a bit of horse-droppings in
the road. The butterfly tries them all, with equal concern. It is neither   15
shocked nor surprised, though sometimes, if thwarted, it is a little exas-
perated. But it is still a butterfly, graceful, charming, and ephemeral.
And, of course, the butterfly on its careless, flapping wings is just as
immortal as some hooting and utterly-learned owl. Which is to say, we
are thankful Mr Byron is no more learned and serious than he is, and   20
his description of Athos is far more vitally convincing than that, for
example, of some heavy Gregorovius.*

The four young men set out from England with a purpose. The
author wants to come into closer contact with the monks and monasteries, which he has already visited; and to write a book about it. He   25
definitely sets out with the intention of writing a book about it. He
has no false shame. David, the archaeologist, wants to photograph the
Byzantine frescoes in the monastery buildings. Mark chases and catches
insects. And Reinecker looks at art and old pots.* They are four young
gentlemen with the echoes of Oxford still in their ears, light and frivolous   30
as butterflies, but with an underneath tenacity of purpose and almost a
grim determination to *do something*.

The butterfly and the Sitwellian manner need not deceive us. These
young gentlemen are not simply gay. They are grimly in earnest, to

get something done. They are not young sports amusing themselves. They are young earnests making their mark. They are stoics rather than frivolous, and epicurean truly in the deeper sense, of undergoing suffering in order to achieve a higher pleasure.

5   For the monasteries of Mount Athos are no paradise. The food which made the four young men shudder makes us shudder. The vermin in the beds are lurid.* The obstinacy and grudging malice of some of the monks, whose one pleasure seems to have been in thwarting and frustrating the innocent desires of the four young men, make our blood
10   boil too. We know exactly what sewage is like, spattering down from above on to leaves and rocks. And the tortures of heat and fatigue are very real indeed.

It is as if the four young men expected to be tormented at every hand's turn. Which is just as well, for tormented they were. Monks
15   apparently have a special gift of tormenting people: though of course some of the monks were charming. But it is chiefly out of the torments of the young butterflies, always humorously and gallantly told, that we get our picture of Athos, its monasteries and its monks. And we are left with no desire at all to visit the holy mountain, unless we could go
20   disembodied, in such state that no flea could bite us, and no stale fish could turn our stomachs.

Then, disembodied, we should like to go and see the unique place, the lovely views, the strange old buildings, the unattractive monks, the paintings, mosaics, frescoes of that isolated little Byzantine world.

25   For everything artistic is there purely Byzantine. Byzantine is to Mr Byron what Baroque is to the Sitwells.* That is to say, he has a real feeling for it, and finds in it a real kinship with his own war-generation mood. Also, it is his own special elegant stone to sling at the philistine world.*

30   Perhaps, in a long book like this, the unfailing humoresque of the style becomes a little tiring. Perhaps a page or two here and there of honest-to-God simplicity might enhance the high light of the author's facetious impressionism.—But then the book might have been undertaken by some honest-to-God professor, and we so infinitely prefer Mr Byron.

35   When we leave Mr Byron we leave the younger generation for the elder: at least as far as style and manner goes. Mr Williams-Ellis* has chosen a thankless subject: *England and the Octopus*: the Octopus being the millions of little streets of mean little houses that are getting England in their grip, and devouring her. It is a depressing theme, and the author
40   rubs it in. We see them all, those millions of beastly little red houses

spreading like an eruption over the face of rural England.—Look! Look! says Mr Williams-Ellis, till we want to shout: Oh shut up! What's the good of our looking! We've looked and got depressed too often. Now leave us alone.

But Mr Williams-Ellis is honestly in earnest and has an honest sense of responsibility. This is the difference between the attitude of the younger and the older generations. The younger generation can't take anything very seriously, and refuses to feel responsible for humanity. The younger generation says in effect: I didn't make the world. I'm not responsible. All I can do is to make my own little mark, and depart.—But the elder generation still feels responsible for all humanity.

And Mr Williams-Ellis feels splendidly responsible for poor old England: the face of her, at least. As he says: You can be put in prison for uttering a few mere swear-words to a policeman, but you can disfigure the loveliest features of the English countryside, and probably be called a public benefactor.*—And he wants to alter all that.

And he's quite right. His little book is excellent: sincere, honest, even passionate, the well-written, humorous book of a man who knows what he's writing about. Everybody ought to read it, whether we know all about it beforehand or not. Because in a question like this, of the utter and hopeless disfigurement of the English countryside by modern industrial encroachment,* the point is not whether we can do anything about it or not, all in a hurry. The point is, that we should all become acutely conscious of what is happening, and of what has happened; and as soon as we are really awake to this, we can begin to arrange things differently.

Mr Williams-Ellis makes us conscious. He wakes up our eye to our own immediate surroundings. He makes us able to look intelligently at the place we live in, at our own street, our own post-office or pub or bank or petrol pump-station. And when we begin to look around us critically and intelligently, it is fun. It is great fun. It is like analysing a bad picture and seeing how it could be turned into a good picture.

Mr Williams-Ellis' six questions* which should be asked of every building ought to be printed on a card and distributed to every individual in the nation. Because, as a nation, it is our intuitive faculty for seeing beauty and ugliness which is lying dead in us. As a nation we are dying of ugliness.

Let us open our eyes, or let Mr Williams-Ellis open them for us, to houses, streets, railways, railings, paint, trees, roofs, petrol-pumps, advertisements, tea-shops, factory-chimneys, let us open our eyes and see them as they are, beautiful or ugly, mean and despicable, or grandiose, or pleasant. People who live in mean, despicable surroundings become mean and despicable. The chief thing is to become properly conscious of our environment.

5   But if some of the elder generation really take things seriously, some others only pretend. And this *pretending* to take things seriously is a vice, a real vice, and the young know it.

Mr Baring's book* *Comfortless Memory* is, thank heaven, only a little book, but it is sheer pretence of taking seriously things which its own
10   author can never for a moment consider serious. That is, it is faked seriousness, which is utterly boring. I don't know when Mr Baring wrote this slight novel. But he ought to have published it at least twenty years ago, when faked seriousness was more in the vogue. Mr Byron, the young author, says that progress is the appreciation of Reality. Mr
15   Baring, the elderly author, offers us a piece of portentous unreality larded with Goethe, Dante, Heine,* hopelessly out of date, and about as exciting as stale restaurant cake.

A dull, stuffy elderly author makes faked love to a bewitching but slightly damaged lady who has "lived" with a man she wasn't mar-
20   ried to!! She is an enigmatic lady: very! For she falls in love, violently, virginally, deeply, passionately and exclusively, with the comfortably-married, stuffy elderly author. The stuffy elderly author himself tells us so, much to his own satisfaction. And the lovely, alluring, enigmatic, experienced lady actually expires, in her riding-habit, out of sheer love
25   for the comfortably-married elderly author. The elderly author assures us of it. If it were not quite so stale it would be funny.

Mr Somerset Maugham* is even more depressing. His Mr Ashenden is also an elderly author, who becomes an agent in the British Secret Service during the war. An agent in the Secret Service is a sort of spy.
30   Spying is a dirty business, and Secret Service altogether is a world of under-dogs, a world in which the meanest passions are given play.

And this is Mr Maugham's, or at least Mr Ashenden's world. Mr Ashenden is an elderly author, so he takes life seriously, and takes his fellow-men seriously, with a seriousness already a little out-of-date.
35   He has a sense of responsibility towards humanity. It would be much better if he hadn't. For Mr Ashenden's sense of responsibility oddly enough is inverted. He is almost passionately concerned with proving that all men and all women are either dirty dogs or imbeciles. If they are clever men or clever women, they are crooks, spies, police-agents,
40   and tricksters, "making good," living in the best hotels because they

know that in a humble hotel they'll be utterly déclassé,* and showing off their base cleverness, and being dirty dogs, from Ashenden himself, and his mighty clever Colonel, and the distinguished diplomat, down to the mean French porters.

If, on the other hand, you get a decent, straight individual, especially an individual capable of feeling love for another, then you are made to see that such a person is a despicable fool, encompassing his own destruction. So the American dies for his dirty washing, the Hindu dies for a blowsy woman who wants her wrist-watch back, the Greek merchant is murdered by mistake,* and so on. It is better to be a live dirty dog than a dead lion,* says Mr Ashenden. Perhaps it is, to Mr Ashenden.

But these stories, being "serious," are faked. Mr Maugham is a splendid observer. He can bring before us persons and places most excellently. But as soon as the excellently-observed characters have to move, it is a fake. Mr Maugham gives them a humorous shove or two. We find they are nothing but puppets, instruments of the author's pet prejudice. The author's pet prejudice being "humour", it would be hard to find a bunch of more ill-humoured stories, in which the humour has gone more rancid.

REVIEW OF FALLEN LEAVES, BY V. V. ROZANOV

Fallen Leaves. by *V. V. Rozanov*

Rozanov is now acquiring something of a European reputation. There is a translation in French, and one promised in German, and the advanced young writers in Paris and Berlin talk of him as one of the true lights. Perhaps *Solitaria* is more popular than *Fallen Leaves*:* but then, perhaps it is a little more sensational. *Fallen Leaves* is not sensational: it is on the whole quiet and sad, and truly Russian. 5

The book was written, apparently, round about 1912: and the author died a few years later.* So that, from the western point of view, Rozanov seems like the last of the Russians. Post-revolution Russians are something different. 10

Rozanov is the last of the Russians, after Tchekov. It is the true Russian voice, become very plaintive now. Artzybashev, Gorki, Merejkovsky* are his contemporaries, but they are all three a little bit off the tradition. But Rozanov is right on it. His first wife had been Dostoevsky's mistress:* and somehow his literary spirit showed the same kind of connection: a Dostoevskian flicker that steadied and became a legal and orthodox light; yet always, of course, suspect. For Rozanov had been a real and perverse liar before he reformed and became a pious, yet suspected conservative. Perhaps he was a liar to the end: who knows? Yet *Solitaria* and *Fallen Leaves* are not lies, not so much lies as many more esteemed books. 15 20

The *Fallen Leaves* are just fragments of thought jotted down anywhere and anyhow. As to the importance of the where or how, perhaps it *is* important to keep throwing the reader out into the world, by means of the: At night: At work: In the tram: In the W. C.—which is sometimes printed after the reflections. Perhaps, to avoid any appearance of systematisation, or even of philosophic abstraction, these little *addenda* are useful. Anyhow it is Russian, and deliberate, done with the intention of keeping the reader—or Rozanov himself, in contact with the *moment*, the actual time and place. Rozanov says that with *Solitaria* he introduced a new *tone* into literature, the tone of manuscript, a manuscript being unique and personal, coming from the individual alone direct to the reader. And "the secret, (bordering on madness) that I am talking to 25 30

347

myself: so constantly and attentively and *passionately*, that apart from this I practically hear nothing"*—this is the secret of his newness, and of his book.

The description is just: and fortunately, on the whole Rozanov talks sincerely to himself, he really does, on the whole, refrain from performing in front of himself. Of course he is self-conscious: he knows it and accepts it and tries to make it a stark-naked self-consciousness, between himself and himself as between himself and God. "Lord, preserve in me that chastity of the writer: not to look in the glass."* From a professional liar, it is a true and sincere prayer. "I am coquetting like a girl before the whole world; hence my constant agitation." "A writer must suppress the writer in himself (authorship, literariness)."*

He is constantly expressing his hatred of literature, as if it poisoned life for him, as if he felt he did not live, he was only *literary*. "The *most happy* moments of life I remember were those when I saw (heard) people in a state of happiness. Stakha and A. P. P-va, 'My Friend's' story of her first love and marriage (the culminating point of my life). From this I conclude that I was born a contemplator, not an actor. I came into the world in order to *see*, and not to *accomplish*."* There is his trouble, that he felt he was always looking on at life, rather than partaking in it. And he felt this as a humiliation: and in his earlier days, it had made him act up, as the Americans say. He had acted up as if he were a real actor on life's stage. But it was too theatrical: his "lying", his "evil" were too much acted up. A liar and an evil bird he no doubt was, because the lies and the acting up to evil, whether they are "pose" or spontaneous, have a vile effect. But he never got any real satisfaction even out of that. He never felt he had really been evil. He had only acted up, like all the Stavrogins* or Ivan Karamazovs of Dostoevsky. Always acting up, trying to *act* feelings because you haven't really got any. That was the condition of the Russians at the end: even Tchekov. Being terribly emotional, terribly full of feeling, terribly good and pathetic or terribly evil and shocking, just to *make* yourself have feelings, when you have none. This was very Russian—and is very modern. A great deal of the world is like it today.

Rozanov left off "acting up" and became quiet and decent, except, perhaps, for little bouts of hysteria, when he would be perfectly vicious towards a friend, or make a small splash of "sin." As far as a man who *has* no real fount of emotion can love, he loved his second wife, "My Friend."* He tried very, very hard to love her, and no doubt he succeeded. But there was always the taint of pity, and she, poor thing, must have been terribly emotionally overwrought, as a woman is with an emotional husband who has no real virile emotion or compassion, only "pity." "European civilisation will perish through compassion,"* he says: but then goes on to say, profoundly, that it is not compassion but pseudo-compassion, with an element of perversity in it. This is very Dostoevskian: and this pseudo-compassion tainted even Rozanov's love for his wife. There is somewhere an element of mockery. And oh, how Rozanov himself would have liked to escape it, and just to feel simple affection. But he couldn't. " 'Today' was completely absent in Dostoevsky,"* he writes. Which is a very succinct way of saying that Dostoevsky never had any immediate feelings, only "projected" ones, which are bound to destroy the immediate object, the actual "today," the very body which is "today." So poor Rozanov saw his wife dying under his eyes with a paralysis, due to a disease of the brain. She was his "today", and he could not help, somewhere, jeering at her. But he suffered, and suffered deeply. At the end, one feels his suffering *was* real: his grief over his wife *was* real. So he had gained that much reality: he really grieved for her, and that was love. It was a great achievement, after all: for the most difficult thing in the world is to achieve real feeling, especially real sympathy, when the sympathetic centres seem, from the very start, as in Rozanov, dead. But Rozanov knew his own nullity, and tried very hard to come through to real honest feeling. And in his measure, he succeeded. After all the Dostoevskian hideous "impurity" he did achieve a certain final purity, or genuineness, or true individuality, towards the end. Even at the beginning of *Fallen Leaves* he is often sentimental and false, repulsive.

And one cannot help feeling a compassion for the Russians of the old régime. They were such healthy barbarians in Peter the Great's time.* Then the whole accumulation of Western ideas, ideals and inventions was poured in a mass into their hot and undeveloped consciousness, and worked like wild yeast. It produced a century of literature, from Pushkin* to Rozanov, and then the wild working of this foreign leaven had ruined, for the time being, the very constitution of the Russian psyche. It was as if they had taken too violent a drug, or been injected with too strong a vaccine. The affective and effective centres collapsed, the control went all wrong, the energy died down in a rush, the nation fell, for the time being completely ruined. Too sudden civilisation always kills. It kills the South Sea Islanders:* it killed the Russians, more slowly, and perhaps even more effectually. Once the idea and the ideal become too strong for the spontaneous emotion in the individual, the civilising influence ceases to be civilising and becomes very harmful, like powerful drugs which ruin the balance and destroy the control of the organism.

Rozanov knew this well. What he says about revolution and democracy leaves nothing to be said. And what he says of "officialdom" is equally final. I believe Tolstoi would be absolutely amazed if he could come back and see the Russia of today. I believe Rozanov would feel no surprise. He knew the inevitability of it. His attitude to the Jews is extraordinary,* and shows uncanny penetration. And his sort of "conservatism," which would be Fascism today, was only a hopeless attempt to draw back from the way things were going.

But the disaster was inside himself already, there was no drawing back. Extraordinary is his note on his "dreaminess." "At times I am aware of something monstrous in myself. And that monstrous thing is my dreaminess. Then nothing can penetrate the circle traced by it.

I am all stone.
And a stone is a monster.
For one must love and be aflame.

From that dreaminess have come all my misfortunes in life (my former work in the Civil Service), the mistake of my whole proceedings (only when 'out of myself' was I attentive to My Friend—[his wife]—and her pains), and also my sins.

In my dreaminess I could do nothing.
And on the other hand I could do anything ('sin').

Afterwards I was sorry: but it was too late. Dreaminess has devoured me, and everything round me."—*

There is the clue to the whole man's life: this "dreaminess" when he is like stone, insentient, and can do nothing yet can do "anything." Over this dreaminess he has no control, nor over the stoniness. But what seemed to him dreaminess and stoniness seemed to others, from his actions, vicious malice and depravity. So that's that. It is one way of being damned.

And there we have the last word of the Russian, before the great débâcle. Anyone who understands in the least Rozanov's state of soul, in which, apparently he was born, born with this awful insentient stoniness somewhere in him, must sympathise deeply with his real suffering and his real struggle to get back a positive self, a feeling self: to overcome the "dreaminess", to dissolve the stone. How much, and how little he succeeded we may judge from this book: and from his harping on the beauty of procreation and fecundity: and from his strange and self-revealing statements concerning Weininger.* Rozanov is modern, terribly modern. And if he does not put the fear of God into us, he puts a real fear of destiny, or of doom: and of "civilisation" which does not come from within, but which is poured over the mind, by "education."*

5

REVIEW OF ART-NONSENSE AND OTHER ESSAYS, *BY ERIC GILL*

Eric Gill's "Art Nonsense."

"Art Nonsense and Other Essays,"* reads the title of this expensive, handsomely printed book. Instinctively the eye reads: "Art Nonsense and Other Nonsense," especially as the letter O in Mr Gill's type* rolls so large and important, in comparison with the other vowels.   5

But it isn't really fair. "Art Nonsense" is the last essay in the book, and not the most interesting. It is the little essays at the beginning that cut most ice. Then in one goes, with a plunge.

Let us say all the bad things first. Mr Gill is not a born writer: he is a crude and crass amateur. Still less is he a born thinker, in the   10
reasoning and argumentative sense of the word. He is again a crude and crass amateur: crass is the only word: maddening, like a tiresome uneducated workman arguing in a pub.—*argefying** would describe it better—and banging his fist. Even, from his argument, one would have to conclude that Mr Gill is not a born artist. A born craftsman, rather.   15
He deliberately takes up the craftsman's point of view, argues about it like a craftsman, like a man in a pub., and really has a craftsman's dislike of the fine arts. He has, *au fond*,* the man-in-a-pub's *moral* mistrust of art, though he tries to get over it.

So that there is not really much about art in this book. There is   20
what Mr Gill feels and thinks as a craftsman, shall we say as a medi-aeval craftsman? We start off with a two-page Apology: bad. Then comes an essay on *Slavery and Freedom* (1918), followed by *Essential Perfection* (1918), *A Grammar of Industry* (1919), *Westminster Cathedral* (1920), *Dress* (1920), *Songs without Clothes* (1921), *Of Things Necessary*   25
and Unnecessary (1921), *Quae ex Veritate et Bono* (1921), on to the last essay, the twenty-fourth on *Art Nonsense*, written in 1929. The dates are interesting: the titles are interesting. What is "Essential Perfection"? and what are "Songs without Clothes"? and why these tags of Latin? and what is a *Grammar of Industry*?, since industry has nothing to do   30
with words. So much of it is jargon, like a workman in a pub.

So much of it is jargon. Take the blurb on the wrapper, which is extracted from Mr Gill's *Apology*. "Two primary ideas run through all the essays of this book: that 'art is simply the well making of what needs making' and that 'art is collaboration with God in creating.'—"*

Could anything, I ask you, be worse? 'Art is *simply* the well making of what needs making.' There's a sentence for you! So simple! Imagine
5　　that a song like *Sally in our Alley**—which is art—should be "simply the well making of what needs making." Or that it should be "collaboration with God in creating." What a nasty, conceited, American sort of phrase! And how one dislikes this modern hobnobbing with God, or giving Him the go-by.*

10　　But if one once begins to quarrel with Mr Gill, one will never leave off. His trick of saying, over and over: "Upon the contrary," instead of "on the contrary": his trick of firing off phrases, as in the essay on *Essential Perfection*, which opens: "God is Love. That is not to say merely that God is loving or lovable, but that he *is* Love. In this, Love is an absolute
15　　not a relative term. The Love of God is man's Essential Perfection. The Essential Perfection of man is not in his physical functions—the proper material exercise of his organs—but in his worship of God, and the worship of God is perfect in Charity—"* all of which means really nothing: even his trick of printing a line under a word, for emphasis,
20　　instead of using italics—an untidy proceeding; if he doesn't like italics, why not space wider, in the continental fashion;*—all this is most irritating. Irritating like an uneducated workman in a pub. holding forth and showing off, making a great noise with a lot of clichés, and saying nothing at all.

25　　Then we learn that Mr Gill is a Roman Catholic: surely a convert. And we know these new English Catholics. They are the last words in Protest. They are Protestants protesting against Protestantism, and so becoming Catholics. As protestants, they have protested against every absolute. As Catholics, therefore, they will swallow all the old abso-
30　　lutes whole, swallow the pill without looking at it, and call that Faith. The big pill being God, and little pills being terms like Charity and Chastity and Obedience and Humility. Swallow them whole, and you are a good Catholic, lick at them and see what they taste like, and you are a queasy Protestant. Mr Gill is a Catholic, so he uses terms like
35　　*Holy Church* and *a good R. C.* quite easily at first; but as the years go by, more rarely. The mere function of swallowing things whole becomes tedious.

That is a long grumble, and perhaps an unkind one. But Mr Gill is so bad at the mere craft of language, that he sets a real writer's nerves
40　　on edge all the time.

Now for the good side of the book. Mr Gill is primarily a craftsman, a workman, and he has looked into his own soul deeply to know what he feels about work. And he has seen a truth which, in my opinion, is a great truth, an invaluable truth for humanity, and a truth of which Mr Gill is almost the discoverer. The gist of it lies in the first two paragraphs 5 of the first essay, Slavery and Freedom.

"That state is a state of Slavery in which a man does what he likes to do in his spare time and in his working time that which is required of him. This state can only exist when what a man likes to do is to please himself. 10

That state is a state of Freedom in which a man does what he likes to do in his working time and in his spare time that which is required of him. This state can only exist when what a man likes to do is to please God."—*

It seems to me there is more in those two paragraphs than in all Karl 15 Marx or Professor Whitehead* or a dozen other philosophers rolled together. True, we have to swallow whole the phrase "to please God," but when we think of a man happily working away in concentration on the job he is doing, if it is only soldering a kettle,* then we know what living state it refers to. "To please God" in this sense only means happily 20 doing one's best at the job in hand, and being livingly absorbed in an activity which makes one in touch with—with the heart of all things; call it God. It is a state which any man or woman achieves when busy and concentrated on a job which calls forth real skill and attention, or devotion. It is a state of absorption into the creative spirit, which is God. 25

Here then is a great truth which Mr Gill has found in his living experience, and which he flings in the teeth of modern industrialism. Under present conditions, it is useless to utter such truth: and that is why none of the clever blighters do utter it. But it is only the truth that is useless which really matters. 30

"The test of a man's freedom is his responsibility as a workman. Freedom is not incompatible with discipline, it is only incompatible with irresponsibility. He who is free is responsible for his work. He who is not responsible for his work is not free."

"There is nothing to be said for freedom except that it is the Will of 35 God.

The Service of God is perfect freedom."*

Here again, the "service of God" is only that condition in which we feel ourselves most truly alive and vital, and the "will of God" is the inrush of pure life to which we gladly yield ourselves. 40

It all depends what you make of the word God. To most of us today it is a fetish-word, dead, yet useful for invocation. It is not a question of Jesus. It is a question of God, Almighty God. We have to square ourselves with the very words. And to do so, we must rid them of their maddening moral import, and give them back—Almighty God—the old vital meaning, Strength and glory and honour and might and beauty and wisdom. These are the continual attributes of Almighty God, in the far past. And the same today, the god who enters us and imbues us with his strength and glory and might and honour and beauty and wisdom, this is a god we are eager to worship. And this is the god of the craftsman who makes things well, so that the presence of the god enters into the thing made. The workman making a pair of shoes with happy absorption in skill is imbued with the god of strength and honour and beauty, undeniable. Happy, intense absorption in any work, which is to be brought as near to perfection as possible, this is a state of being with God, and the men who have not known it have missed life itself.*

This is what Mr Gill means, I take it, and it is an enormously important truth. It is a truth on which a true civilisation might be established. But first, you must give men back their belief in God, & then their free responsibility in work. For belief, Mr Gill turns to the Catholic Church. Well, it is a great institution, and we all like to feel romantic about it. But the Catholic Church needs to be born again, quite as badly as the Protestant. I cannot feel there is much more belief in God in Naples or Barcelona, than there is in Liverpool or Leeds.* Yet they are truly Catholic cities. No, the Catholic Church has fallen into the same disaster as the Protestant: of preaching a *moral* God, instead of Almighty God, the God of strength and glory and might and wisdom: a "good" God, instead of a vital and magnificent God. And we no longer any of us *really* believe in an exclusively "good" God. The Catholic Church in the cities is as dead as the Protestant church. Only in the country, among peasants, where the old ritual of the seasons lives on in its beauty, is there still some living, instinctive "faith" in the God of life.

Mr Gill has two main themes: "work done well", and "beauty," or rather "Beauty." He is almost always good, simple and profound, truly a prophet, when he is speaking of work done well. And he is nearly always tiresome about Beauty. Why oh why will people keep on trying to define words like Art and Beauty and God, words which represent deep emotional states in us, and are therefore incapable of definition.

Why bother about it? "Beauty is absolute, loveliness is relative,"* says
Mr Gill. Yes yes, but really, what does it matter? Beauty is beauty,
loveliness is loveliness, and if Mr Gill thinks that Beauty ought really
to have a subtly moral character, while loveliness is merely carnal,
or equivalent for prettiness—well, why not? But other people don't   5
care.

APPENDICES

APPENDIX I

INTRODUCTORY NOTE (VERSION 1) TO MASTRO-DON GESUALDO, BY GIOVANNI VERGA

Introductory Note.

Giovanni Verga was born in Catania, in Sicily, on the 31st August 1840. He died, also in Catania, in January 1922. The family belongs originally to the village of Vizzini, in south-east Sicily, and apparently in this little town is laid the scene of Mastro-don Gesualdo.

Verga left Sicily as a young man to work at literature in Florence and Milan—a southerner, a provincial, he was inevitably fascinated by elegance and luxury and costly love. But his heart was always in Sicily. So his work is divided between his two selves. Much of his early work, like the three novels *Eva*, *Tigre Reale*, and *Eros*, deal with the expensive love-passion theme. It is interesting to compare these romances with those of D'Annunzio or Fogazzaro or Matilde Serao. Verga has always such a bitter moral sanity at the bottom of his soul.

But the real man is Sicilian, Sicilian of the open country. The first book that obtained popularity was *Storia di una Capinera*, a slight volume of letters from a school-girl to her friend, telling how she is carried off to the slopes of Etna when cholera is raging in Catania, then how she is brought back and enters the convent, to die there raving. It is sentimental, maybe, and unbalanced, but certainly a classic.

Capinera appeared in Milan in 1871. It was followed by *Eva*, 1873, *Tigre Reale*, 1873, *Nedda*, a Sicilian sketch, 1874, *Eros*, 1875. In 1880, in Milan, appeared the volume of short sketches *Vita dei Campi*: the first sketch being the well-known *Cavalleria Rusticana*, which story was dramatised later to form the libretto of the popular opera. *Vita dei Campi* is pure Sicilian, salt of the Sicilian earth, and contains marvellous novelettes such as *La Lupa*, *Jeli il Pastore*, *Rosso Malpelo*, *L'Amante di Gramigna*.

In 1881 Treves of Milan published *I Malavoglia*, the novel which Italian critics consider the greatest of Verga's works. It is the story of humble fisher-folk on the east coast of Sicily, just north of Catania: a book that stands alone in European literature. If for my own part I prefer *Mastro-don Gesualdo*, it is because bitterness appeals to me more than pity.

Il Marito di Elena, 1881, returns to the complicated love-interest. But the *Novelle Rusticane*, published in 1883, are once more Sicilian and marvellous: surely the best "little novels" in all European literature. I have never read anything so straight from the blood.

5   *Mastro-don Gesualdo* appeared in 1888, and was Verga's last serious work. He had planned to write a series of novels about *I Vinti*: The Vanquished. The series began with *I Malavoglia*, the really poor. It continued with *Mastro-don Gesualdo*, which is the history of the rich peasant and the rural *noblesse*. And for years Italy awaited the appearance

10 of the third volume of the series: *La Duchessa di Leyra*. But apparently Verga could never finish The Duchess. She was to be "elegant" once more, and he could not get on with her.

    The title *Mastro-don Gesualdo* is an irony in itself. In Sicily titles are still subtle. The ordinary peasants call each other *Compare*, like the

15 French *compère*, and *Comare*, *commère*. A workman is called *Mastro*, master. Anyone in the rank of gentleman is *Don*. But nowadays almost any respectable peasant woman, if she has a bit of property, is called *Donna*. And the house-servants of the gentry, and church-servants get the title *Don*, by a kind of reflected glory.

20   So that Mastro-don Gesualdo means Workman-gentleman Gesualdo. It is the history of a laborer who has amassed a fortune: which nobody forgives him. The story opens somewhere about 1818 or 1820, at the time when the restored Bourbons are again ruling the Two Sicilies, after the English interference under Nelson.* We know that Ciolla was put

25 into prison in the riots of 1821, some months before Isabella was born; the cholera came in 1837; and Don Gesualdo's house was threatened in the serious, but futile rebellion of 1848. Don Gesualdo himself in 48 was already in his last illness—so we may presume he died about 1850. Even when Garibaldi was in Sicily there was no highroad from Palermo

30 to Messina. Travelling inland was performed either on horseback or in a litter, a sort of big sedan-chair* with a mule in front and a mule behind. In this way ladies traversed the wild and stony tracks of the island.

    As far as the style of the writing goes, Verga deliberately wanted it to be unliterary, loose, casual, hap-hazard. He wanted to change from

35 his first style, the style of *Tigre Reale* and *Eros*, and hit another mode. These are his own words: "I had published several of my first novels. They went well: I was preparing others. One day, I don't know how, there came into my hand a sort of *broadside*, a document sufficiently ungrammatical and disconnected, in which a sea-captain succinctly

40 related all the vicissitudes through which his sailing-ship had passed.

Seaman's language, short, without an unnecessary phrase. It struck me, and I read it again; it was what I was looking for without definitely knowing. Sometimes, you know, just a sign, an indication is enough. It was a revelation—"*

So that the magic of Verga's prose depends chiefly on this style which   5
is no style. I have tried to keep the tang of it. I make no pretensions to a perfect knowledge of Italian. Almost certainly there are plenty of mistakes in my translation. But if only I have kept the bitter taste and irony and the sardonic fall of the rhythm, in some measure, it is all I care.   10

Verga stands along with Tolstoi and Balzac and Dickens, one of the greatest European novelists: undoubtedly the greatest Italian, after Manzoni. He is not popular even in Italy. But greater he is than any of the popular ones.

Mastro-don Gesualdo was published in New York, in English trans-   15
lation, somewhere about 1892. Apparently this translation is long forgotten. Verga says to an interviewer:

"Listen to this. *I Malavoglia*, translated by an American, (Mary A. Craig), was issued also in England and sold fairly well. A London publisher proposed to me a new translation and offered me either a sum   20
down or a percentage on sales. Seeing the good success of the previous edition, I accepted the percentage . . . And I got practically nothing. I was amazed: first it sold so well . . . But anyhow if those were the real sales, the publisher could not carry on, and I myself offered to dissolve the similar contract which bound him for *Mastro-don Gesualdo*. But he   25
wouldn't hear of it, and *Mastro-don Gesualdo* was translated—And the percentage always the same—"*

It is an old story.—But if this will help Giovanni Verga to his true standing in front of mankind, here goes—

APPENDIX II

INTRODUCTION (VERSION 1) TO MASTRO-DON GESUALDO, *BY GIOVANNI VERGA*

It seems curious that modern Italian literature has made so little impression on the European consciousness. A hundred years ago, when Manzoni's *I Promessi Sposi* came out, it met with European applause. Along with Sir Walter Scott and Byron,* Manzoni stood for "Romance", to all Europe. Yet where is Manzoni now, even compared to Scott and   5
Byron? Actually, I mean. Nominally, *I Promessi Sposi* is a classic; in fact, it is usually considered *the* classic Italian novel. It is set in all "literature courses." But who reads it? Even in Italy, who reads it? And yet, to my thinking, it is one of the best and most interesting novels ever written: surely a greater book than *Ivanhoe* or *Paul et Virginie* or *Werther*.* Why   10
then does nobody read it? Why is it found boring? When I gave a good English translation to the late Katharine Mansfield,* she said, to my astonishment: I couldn't read it. Too long and boring.

It is the same with Giovanni Verga. After Manzoni, he is Italy's accepted greatest novelist. Yet nobody takes any notice of him. He is,   15
as far as anybody knows his name, just the man who wrote the libretto to *Cavalleria Rusticana*. Whereas, as a matter of fact, Verga's story *Cavalleria Rusticana* is as much superior to Leoncavallo's* rather cheap music as wine is superior to sugar-water. Verga is one of the greatest masters of the short story. In the volume, *Novelle Rusticane*, and in   20
the volume entitled *Cavalleria Rusticana* are some of the best short stories ever written. They are sometimes as short and as poignant as Tchekov. I prefer them to Tchekov. Yet nobody reads them. They are "too depressing." They don't depress me half as much as Tchekov does. I don't understand the popular taste.   25

Verga wrote a number of novels, of different sorts: very different. He was born about 1850, and died, I believe, at the beginning of 1921. So he is a modern. At the same time, he is a classic. And at the same time, again, he is old-fashioned.

The earlier novels are rather of the French type of the seventies—   30
Octave Feuillet, with a touch of Gyp.* There is the depressing story of the Sicilian young man who made a Neapolitan marriage, and on the last page gives his wife a much-belated slap across the face.* There is

371

the gruesome book, *Tigre Reale*, of the Russian countess—or princess, whatever it is—who comes to Florence and gets fallen in love with by the young Sicilian, with all the subsequent horrid affair: the weird woman dying of consumption, the man weirdly infatuated, in the suicidal South-Italian fashion.* It is a bit in the manner of Matilde Serao. And though unpleasant, it is impressive.

Verga himself was a Sicilian, from one of the lonely agricultural villages in the south of the island. He was a gentleman—but not a rich one, presumably: with some means. As a young man, he went to Naples, then he worked at journalism in Milan and Florence. And finally he retired to Catania, to an exclusive, aristocratic old age. He was a shortish, broad man with a big red moustache. He never married.

His fame rests on his two long Sicilian novels, *I Malavoglia* and *Mastro-don Gesualdo*, also on the books of short pieces, *Cavalleria Rusticana*, *Novelle Rusticane*, and *Vagabondaggio*. These are all placed in Sicily, as is the short novel, *Storia di una Capinera*. Of this last little book, one of the leading literary young Italians in Rome said to me the other day: Ah yes, Verga! *Some* of his things! But a thing like *Storia di una Capinera*, now, is ridiculous.

But why? It is rather sentimental, maybe. But it is no more sentimental than *Tess*.* And the sentimentality seems to me to belong to the Sicilian characters in the book, it is true to type, quite as much so as the sentimentality of a book like Dickens' *Christmas Carol*, or George Eliot's *Silas Marner*, both of which works are "ridiculous", if you like, without thereby being wiped out of existence.

The trouble with Verga, as with all Italians, is that he never seems quite to know where he is. When one reads Manzoni, one wonders if he is not more "gothic", or Germanic, than Italian. And Verga, in the same way, seems to have a borrowed outlook on life: but this time, borrowed from the French. With D'Annunzio the same, it is hard to believe he is really being himself. He gives one the impression of "acting up." Pirandello goes on with the game today. The Italians are always that way: always acting up to somebody else's vision of life. Men like Hardy, Meredith, Dickens, they are just as sentimental and false as the Italians, in their own way. It only happens to be our own brand of falseness and sentimentality.

And yet, perhaps, one can't help feeling that Hardy, Meredith, Dickens, and Maupassant and even people like the Goncourts and Paul Bourget,* false in part though they be, are still looking on life with their own eyes. Whereas the Italians give one the impression that they are

always borrowing somebody else's eyes to see with, and then letting
loose a lot of emotion into a borrowed vision.

This is the trouble with Verga. But on the other hand, everything he
does has a weird quality of Verga in it, quite distinct and like nothing
else. And yet, perhaps the gross vision of the man is not quite his own.
All his movements are his own. But his main motive is borrowed.

This is the unsatisfactory part about all Italian literature, as far as I
know it.

The main motive, the gross vision of all the nineteenth century literature is what we may call the emotional-democratic vision or motive.
It seems to me that since 1860, or even 1830, the Italians have always
borrowed their ideals of democracy from the northern nations, and
poured great emotion into them, without ever being really grafted by
them. Some of the most wonderful martyrs for democracy have been
Neapolitan men of birth and breeding. But none the less, it seems a
mistake: an attempt to live by somebody else's lights.

Verga's first Sicilian novel, *I Malavoglia*, is of this sort. It was considered his greatest work. It is a great book. But it is *parti pris.** It is
onesided. And therefore, it dates. There is too much, too much of the
tragic fate of the poor, in it. There is a sort of wallowing in tragedy: the
tragedy of the humble. It belongs to a date when the "humble" were
almost the most fashionable thing. And the Malavoglia family are most
humbly humble. Sicilians of the sea-coast, fishers, small traders—their
humble tragedy is so piled on, it becomes almost disastrous. The book
was published in America under the title of *The House by the Medlar
Tree*, and can still be obtained. It is a great book, a great picture of poor
life in Sicily, on the coast just north of Catania. But it is rather overdone
on the pitiful side. Like the woe-begone pictures by Bastien Lepage!*
Nevertheless, it is essentially a true picture, and different from anything
else in literature. In most books of the period—even in *Madame Bovary*,
to say nothing of Balzac's earlier *Lys dans la Vallée*—one has to take off
about twenty per-cent of the tragedy. One does it in Dickens, and one
does it in Hawthorne, one does it all the time, with the great writers.
Then why not with Verga? Just knock off about twenty per-cent of the
tragedy in *I Malavoglia*, and see what a great book remains. Most books
that live, live in spite of the author's laying it on thick. Think of *Wuthering Heights*. It is quite as impossible to an Italian as ever *I Malavoglia* is
to us. But it is a great book.

The trouble with realism—and Verga was a realist—is that the writer,
when he is a truly exceptional man like Flaubert or like Verga, tries to

read his own sense of tragedy into people much smaller than himself.
I think it is a final criticism against *Madame Bovary*, that people such
as Emma Bovary and her husband Charles simply are too insignificant
to carry the full weight of Gustave Flaubert's sense of tragedy. Emma
5   and Charles Bovary are a couple of little people. Gustave Flaubert is
not a little person. But, because he is a realist and does not believe in
"heroes", Flaubert insists on pouring his own deep and bitter tragic
consciousness into the little skins of the country doctor and his uneasy
wife. The result is a discrepancy. Madame Bovary is a great book and
10 a very wonderful picture of life. But we cannot help resenting the fact
that the great tragic soul of Gustave Flaubert is, so to speak, given only
the rather commonplace bodies of Emma and Charles Bovary. There's
a misfit. And to get over the misfit, you have to let in all sorts of seams
of pity. Seams of pity, which won't be hidden.
15   The great tragic soul of Shakspeare borrows the bodies of Kings
and princes, not out of snobbism, but out of natural affinity. You can't
put a great soul into a commonplace person. Commonplace persons
have commonplace souls. Not all the noble sympathy of Flaubert or
Verga for Bovarys and Malavoglias can prevent the said Bovarys and
20 Malavoglias from being commonplace persons. They were deliberately
chosen because they *were* commonplace, and not heroic. The authors
insisted on the treasure of the humble.* But they had to lend the humble
by far the best part of their own treasure, before the said humble could
show any treasure at all.
25   So, if *I Malavoglia* dates, so does *Madame Bovary*. They belong to the
emotional-democratic, treasure-of-the-humble period of the nineteenth
century. This period is just rather out of fashion. We still feel the impact
of the treasure-of-the-humble too much. When the emotion will have
quite gone out of us, we can accept *Madame Bovary* and *I Malavoglia*
30 in the same free spirit, with the same detachment as that in which we
accept Dickens or Richardson.*
     Mastro-don Gesualdo, however, is not nearly so much treasure-of-the-
humble as *I Malavoglia*. Here, Verga is not dealing with the disaster of
poverty, and calling it tragedy. On the contrary, he is a little bored by
35 poverty. He must have a hero who wins out, and makes his pile, and
then succumbs under the pile.
     Mastro-don Gesualdo started life as a barefoot peasant brat, not a
don at all. He becomes very rich. But all he gets of it is a great tumour
of bitterness inside, which kills him.
40   Verga must have known, in actual life, the prototype of Gesualdo. We
see him in the marvellous realistic story in Cavalleria Rusticana,* of a fat

little peasant who has become enormously rich, grinding his laborers, and now is diseased and must die. This little fellow is quite unheroic. He has the indomitable greedy will, but nothing else of Gesualdo's rather attractive character.

Gesualdo is attractive, and in a sense, heroic. But still he is not allowed to emerge in the old heroic sense, with swagger and nobility and head-and-shoulders taller than anything else. He is allowed to have exceptional qualities, and above all, exceptional force. But these things do not make a hero of a man. A hero must be a hero by grace of God, and must have an inkling of the same. Even the old Paladin heroes* had a great idea of themselves as exemplars, and Hamlet had the same. "O cursèd spite that ever I was born to set it right."* Hamlet didn't succeed in setting anything right, but he felt that way. And so all heroes must feel.

But Gesualdo, and Jude,* and Emma Bovary are not allowed to feel any of these feelings. As far as *destiny* goes, they felt no more than anybody else. And this is because they belong to the realistic world.

Gesualdo is just an ordinary man with extraordinary energy. That, of course, is the intention. But he is a Sicilian. And here lies the difficulty. Because the realistic-democratic age has dodged the dilemma of having no heroes by having every man his own hero. This is reached by what we call subjective intensity, and in this subjectively-intense every-man-his-own-hero business the Russians have carried us to the greatest lengths. The merest scrub of a pickpocket is so phenomenally aware of his own soul, that we are made to bow down before the imaginary coruscations that go on inside him. That is almost the whole of Russian literature: the phenomenal coruscations of the souls of quite commonplace people.

Of course, your soul will coruscate if you think it does. That's why the Russians are so popular. No matter how much of a shabby animal you may be, you can learn from Dostoevsky and Tchekov etc how to have the most tender, unique, coruscating soul on earth. And so you may be most vastly important to yourself. Which is the private aim of all men. The hero had it openly. The commonplace person has it inside himself, though outwardly he says: Of course I'm no better than anybody else!—His very asserting it shows he doesn't think it for a second. Every character in Dostoevsky or Tchekov thinks himself *inwardly* a nonsuch, absolutely unique.

And here you get the blank opposite, in the Sicilians. The Sicilians simply don't have any subjective idea of themselves, or any souls. Except, of course, that funny little *alter ego* of a soul which can be prayed out of purgatory into paradise, and is just as objective as possible.

The Sicilian, in our sense of the word, doesn't have any soul. He just hasn't got our sort of subjective consciousness, the soulful idea of himself. Souls, to him, are little naked people uncomfortably hopping on hot bricks, and being allowed at last to go up to a garden where there is music and flowers and sanctimonious society, Paradise. Jesus is a man who was crucified by a lot of foreigners and villains, and who can help you against the villainous lot nowadays: as well as against witches and the rest.

The self-tortured Jesus, the self-tortured Hamlet, simply does not exist.—Why should a man torture himself? Gesualdo would ask in amazement. Aren't there scoundrels enough in the world to torture him?

Of course, I am speaking of the Sicilians of Verga's day, fifty and sixty years ago, before the great emigration to America, and the great return, with dollars and bits of self-aware souls: at least politically self-aware.

So that in *Mastro-don Gesualdo* you have the very antithesis of what you get in *The Brothers Karamazov*. Anything more un-Russian than Verga it would be hard to imagine: save Homer. Yet Verga has the same sort of pity as the Russians. And, with the Russians, he is a realist. He won't have heroes, nor appeals to gods above nor below.

The Sicilians of today are supposed to be the nearest thing to the classic Greeks that is left to us: that is, they are the nearest descendants on earth. In Greece today there are no Greeks. The nearest thing is the Sicilian, the eastern and south-eastern Sicilian.

And if you come to think of it, Gesualdo Motta might really be a Greek in modern setting: except that he is not intellectual. But then many Greeks were not. And he has the energy, the quickness, the vividness of the Greek, the same vivid passion for wealth, the same ambition, the same lack of scruples, the same queer openness, without ever really openly committing himself. He is not a bit furtive, like an Italian. He is astute instead, far too astute and Greek to let himself be led by the nose. Yet he has a certain frankness, far more than an Italian. And far less fear than an Italian. His boldness and his queer sort of daring are Sicilian rather than Italian, so is his independent manliness.

He is Greek above all in not having any soul or any lofty ideals. The Greeks were far more bent on making an audacious, splendid impression than on fulfilling some noble purpose. They loved the splendid look of a thing, the splendid ring of words. Even tragedy was to them a grand gesture, rather than something to mope over. Peak and pine* they would not, and unless some Fury* pursued them to punish them for their sins, they cared not a straw for sins: their own or anyone else's.

As for being burdened with souls, they were not such fools.

But alas, ours is the day of soul, when soul pays, and when having a soul is as important to the young as solitaire* to a valetudinarian. If you don't have feelings about your soul, what sort of person can you be?

And Gesualdo didn't have feelings about his soul. He was remorse-   5
lessly and relentlessly objective, like all people that belong to the sun. In the sun, men are objective, in the mist and snow, subjective. Subjectivity is largely a question of the thickness of your overcoat.

When you get to Ceylon, you realise that, to the swarthy Singhalese, even Buddhism is a purely objective affair. And we have managed to   10
spiritualise it to such a subjective pitch.

Then you have the setting to the hero. The south-Sicilian setting to *Mastro-don Gesualdo* is perhaps nearer to the true mediaeval than anything else in modern literature, even barring the Sardinian medi-aevalism of Grazia Deledda. You have the Sicily of the Bourbons, the   15
Sicily of the Kingdom of Naples. The island is incredibly poor and incredibly backward. There are practically no roads for wheeled vehi-cles, and consequently, no wheeled vehicles, neither carts nor carriages, outside the towns. Everything is packed on asses or mules, man travels on horseback or on foot, or, if sick, in a mule litter. The land is held by   20
the great landowners, the peasants are almost serfs. It is as wild, as poor, and in the ducal houses of Palermo, even as splendid and ostentatious as Russia.

Yet how different from Russia! Instead of the wild openness of the north, you have the shut-in, guarded watchfulness of the old Mediter-   25
ranean. For centuries, the people of the Mediterranean have lived on their guard, intensely on their guard, on the watch, wary, always wary, and holding aloof. So it is even today, in the villages: aloof, holding aloof, each individual inwardly holding aloof from the other; and this in spite of the returned "Americans".   30

How utterly different it is from Russia, where the people are always— in the books—expanding to one another, and pouring out tea and their souls to one another all night long. In Sicily, by nightfall, nearly every man is barricaded inside his own house. Save in the hot summer, when night is more or less turned into day.   35

It all seems, to some people, dark and squalid and brutal and bor-ing. There is no soul, no enlightenment at all. There is not one single enlightened person. If there had been, he would have departed long ago. He could not have stayed.

And for people who seek enlightenment, oh how boring! But if you   40
have any physical feeling for life, apart from nervous feelings such as

the Russians have, nerves, nerves—if you have any appreciation for the southern way of life, then what a strange, deep fascination there is in *Mastro-don Gesualdo*! Perhaps the deepest nostalgia I have ever felt has been for Sicily, reading Verga. Not for England or anywhere else—for Sicily, the beautiful, that which goes deepest into the blood. It is so clear, so beautiful, so like the physical beauty of the Greek.

Yet the lives of the people all seem so squalid, so pottering, so despicable: like a crawling of beetles. And then, the moment you get outside the grey and squalid walls of the village, how wonderful in the sun, with the land lying apart. And isolated, the people too have some of the old Greek singleness, carelessness, dauntlessness. It is only when they bunch together as citizens that they are squalid. In the countryside they are portentous and subtle, like the wanderers in the Odyssey. And their relations are all curious and immediate, objective. They are so little aware of themselves, and so much aware of their own effects.

It all depends what you are looking for. Gesualdo's life-long love-affair with Diodata is, according to our ideas, quite impossible. He puts no value on sentiment at all: or almost none: again a real Greek. Yet there is a strange forlorn beauty in it, impersonal, a bit like Rachel or Rebecca.* It is of the old, old world, when man is aware of his own belongings, acutely, but only very dimly aware of his own feelings. And feelings you are not aware of, you don't have.

Gesualdo seems so potent, so full of potency. Yet nothing emerges, and he never says anything. It is the very reverse of the Russian, who talks and talks, out of impotence.

And you have a wretched, realistic kind of tragedy for the end. And you feel, perhaps the book was all about nothing, and Gesualdo wasn't worth the labour of Verga.

But that is because we are spiritual snobs, and think, because a man can fume with: To be or not to be,—therefore he is a person to be taken account of. Poor Gesualdo had never heard of: To be or not to be, and he wouldn't have taken any notice if he had. He lived blindly, with the impetuosity of blood and muscles, sagacity and will, and he never woke up to himself. Whether he would have been any the better for waking up to himself, who knows!

APPENDIX III

INTRODUCTION (VERSION 2) TO MASTRO-DON GESUALDO, BY GIOVANNI VERGA

INTRODUCTION

Giovanni Verga was born about 1850, and died at the beginning of 1921, so that he is practically of the same age as Thomas Hardy. He seems more remote, because he left off writing many years before he died. Yet his work bears some parallel to Hardy's. The earlier novels have the sort of desperate, perfervid half-reality which belongs to Hardy's "A Pair of Blue Eyes" or "Desperate Remedies".* Verga, however, was much more influenced by the French, in his early days, than ever Hardy was. And he was utterly unlike Hardy in that he was a beau and man-of-the-world and lover of women until middle age almost, when he retired to Sicily to write his serious work, and hide himself from all his former associates. So that his last novel, *Mastro-don Gesualdo*, like Hardy's last novel *Jude* (really the last)* is his best. Also, Verga creates the primitive life of rural Sicily as Hardy creates Wessex.—But it is better to let the comparison stop there.

Verga was a Sicilian, from one of the lonely agricultural townships in the south of the Island. He was a gentleman, though perhaps not exactly rich. As a young man, he went to Naples, then he did some journalism and lived the more-or-less fashionable life in Milan and Florence, a little like Maupassant. Then he was in Naples again. And finally he retired to Catania, in Sicily, and lived an exclusive, aristocratic life there until his death, almost forgotten by the world. But he was naturally exclusive, and had had enough of the world, preferred to be alone. He was a shortish, broad-shouldered man with a big red moustache. He never married.

Towards the end of his career, Verga wrote two long novels of Sicily, *I Malavoglia* and *Mastro-don Gesualdo*. These novels had been presaged by books of stories and country sketches, all about Sicily: *Cavalleria Rusticana*, *Novelle Rusticane*, and *Vagabondaggio*. The sketches had already made him famous. *I Malavoglia* was hailed as a masterpiece, in Paris as well as in Italy.

Another earlier little Sicilian story is the *Storia di una Capinera*. When Verga was mentioned the other day among some of the leading young literary men in Rome, one exclaimed: Ah Verga, yes! *Some of* his things! But the *Storia di una Capinera*, now, is ridiculous.

It reveals the atttitude of the clever young men. The *Story of a Black-cap* is sentimental, no doubt, and overloaded with pity. But not more
5 so than *A Christmas Carol*, or George Eliot's *Silas Marner*. And neither of these works is ridiculous. Nor is Verga's little book. It has more atmosphere than all the post-war Italian novels put together. But young people are so clever. They say: Oh Cromwell! Why he had a wart on his face!*—And they think they have said something.

10 Verga's novel *I Malavoglia* is really spoilt by excessive pity for the poor, and exaggeration of their tragic fate. But that was the stunt of the age; *Les Misérables* stands as the great monument to the stunt. Whereas the poor are now just out of fashion, so Hugo is quoted at a very low figure.* Verga hardly exists. Yet when we have got over our
15 reaction against the pity-the-poor stunt, we shall see that *I Malavoglia* contains a far more intimate and revealing picture of the life of the seacoast Sicilians, than Hugo's book does of the Parisians. Verga's novel was published, in a translation which weakens the book very much, in America in the nineties. The translation, entitled *The House by the*
20 *Medlar Tree*, can still be obtained.

The trouble with the Italians is, that they do tend to take over other people's stunts and exaggerate them. Hugo's pity-the-poor was a real French gesture of his own. Verga's pity-the-poor is not quite natural to him. But it belonged to the European emotion of the moment.

25 In his last novel, *Mastro-don Gesualdo*, Verga has slackened off in his pity-the-poor. But he is still a realist, in the Flaubert meaning of the word. Realism, as everybody now knows, has no more to do with reality than romanticism has. Realism is just one arbitrary view of man. It sees man as a little, ant-like creature toiling against the odds of circumstance,
30 and doomed to misery. It became the popular outlook, and so we have today millions of little ant-like creatures toiling against the odds of circumstance, and doomed to misery, until they take a different view of themselves. For man always becomes what he passionately thinks he is; since he is capable of becoming almost anything.

35 *Mastro-don Gesualdo* is a great realistic novel of Sicily, as *Madame Bovary* is a great realistic novel of France. They both suffer from one of the defects of the realistic method. I think the inherent flaw in *Madame Bovary*—though I hate talking about flaws in great books; but the charge is really against the realistic method—is that individ-
40 uals like Emma and Charles Bovary are too insignificant to carry the

full weight of Gustave Flaubert's profound sense of tragedy; or, if you will, of tragic futility. Emma and Charles Bovary are two ordinary persons, chosen because they *are* ordinary. But Flaubert is by no means an ordinary person. Yet he insists on pouring his own deep and bitter tragic consciousness into the little skins of the country doctor and his dissatisfied wife. The result is a certain discrepancy, even a certain dishonesty in the attempt to be too honest. By choosing *ordinary* people as the vehicles of an extraordinarily passionate feeling of bitterness, Flaubert loads the dice, and wins by a trick which is sure to be found out against him.

Because a great soul like Flaubert's has a pure satisfaction and joy in its own consciousness, even if the consciousness be only of ultimate tragedy or misery. But the very fact of being so marvellously and vividly *aware*, awake, as Flaubert's soul was, is in itself a refutation of the all-is-misery doctrine. Since the human soul has supreme joy in true, vivid consciousness. And Flaubert's soul has this joy. But Emma Bovary's soul does not, poor thing, because she was deliberately chosen because her soul was ordinary. So Flaubert cheats us a little, in his doctrine, if not in his art. And his art is biased by his doctrine as much as any artist's is.

The same is true of *Mastro-don Gesualdo*. Gesualdo is a peasant's son, who becomes rich in his own tiny town through his own force and sagacity. He is allowed the old heroic qualities of force and sagacity. Even Emma Bovary has a certain extraordinary female energy of restlessness and unsatisfied desire. So that both Flaubert and Verga allow their heroes something of the hero, after all. The one thing they deny them is the consciousness of heroic effort.

Now Flaubert and Verga alike were aware of their own heroic effort to be truthful, to show things as they are. It was the heroic impulse which made them write their great books. Yet they deny to their protagonists any inkling of the heroic effort. It is in this sense that Emma Bovary and Gesualdo Motta are "ordinary." Ordinary people don't have much sense of heroic effort in life; and by the heroic effort we mean that instinctive fighting for more life to come into being, which is a basic impulse in more men than we like to admit; women too. Or it used to be. The discrediting of the heroic effort has almost extinguished that effort in the young, hence the appalling "flatness" of their lives. It is the parent's fault. Life without the heroic effort, and without *belief* in the subtle, life-long validity of the heroic impulse, is just stale, flat and unprofitable. As the great realistic novels will show you.

Gesualdo Motta has the makings of a hero. Verga had to grant him
something. I think it is in *Cavalleria Rusticana* that we find the long
sketch or story of the little fat peasant who has become enormously
rich by grinding his laborers and bleeding the Barons. It is a marvellous story, reeling with the hot atmosphere of Sicily, and the ironic
fatalism of the Sicilians. And that little fat peasant must have been
an actual man whom Verga knew—Verga wasn't good at inventing,
he always had to have a core of actuality—and who served as the idea-
germ for Gesualdo. But Gesualdo is much more attractive, much nearer
the true hero. In fact, with all his energy and sagacity *and* his natural humaneness, we don't see how Gesualdo quite escaped the heroic
consciousness. The original little peasant, the prototype, was a mere
frog, a grabber and nothing else. He had none of Gesualdo's large
humaneness. So that Verga brings Gesualdo much nearer to the hero,
yet denies him still any spark of the heroic consciousness, any spark
of awareness of a greater impulse within him. Men naturally have this
spark, if they are the tiniest bit uncommon. The curious thing is, the
moment you deny the spark, it dies, and then the heroic impulse dies
with it.

It is probably true that, since the extinction of the pagan gods, the
countries of the Mediterranean have never been aware of the heroic
impulse in themselves, and so it has died down very low, in them. In
Sicily, even now, and in the remoter Italian villages, there is what we
call a low level of life, appalling. Just a squalid, unimaginative, heavy,
petty-fogging, grubby sort of existence, without light or flame. It is the
absence of the heroic awareness, the heroic hope.

The northerners have got over the death of the old Homeric idea
of the hero, by making the hero self-conscious, and a hero by virtue
of suffering and awareness of suffering. The Sicilians may have little
spasms of this sort of heroic feeling, but it never lasts. It is not natural
to them.

The Russians carry us to great lengths of introspective heroism.
They escape the non-heroic dilemma of our age by making every man
his own introspective hero. The merest scrub of a pickpocket is so
phenomenally aware of his own soul, that we are made to bow down
before the imaginary coruscations of suffering and sympathy that go on
inside him. So is Russian literature.

Of course, your soul will coruscate with suffering and sympathy, if you
think it does: since no doubt it is always performing that coruscation,
amid many others undiscovered and therefore affectively non-existent.

The soul is doing endless things we are not aware of. But we have wakened to the sympathy-suffering coruscation. And that is why the Russians are so popular. No matter how much of a shabby little slut you may be, you can learn from Dostoevsky and Tchekov that you have got the most tender, unique soul on earth, coruscating with sufferings and impossible sympathies. And so you may be most vastly important to yourself, introspectively. Outwardly, you will say: Of course I'm an ordinary person, like everybody else.—But your very saying it will prove that you think the opposite: namely, that everybody on earth is ordinary, *except* yourself.

This is our northern way of heroism, up to date. The Sicilian hasn't yet got there. Perhaps he never will. Certainly he was nowhere near it in Gesualdo Motta's day, the mediaeval Sicilian day of the middle of the last century, before Italy existed, and Sicily still was part of the Bourbon kingdom of Naples, and about as remote as the kingdom of Dahomey.

The Sicilian has no soul, except that funny little naked man who hops on hot bricks, in purgatory, and howls to be prayed out into paradise; and is in some mysterious way my *alter ego*, my me beyond the grave. This is the catholic soul, and there is nothing to do about it but to pay, and get it prayed into paradise.

For the rest, in our sense of the word, the Sicilian doesn't have any soul. He can't be introspective, because his consciousness, so to speak, doesn't have any inside to it. He can't look inside himself, because he is, as it were, solid. When Gesualdo is tormented by mean people, atrociously, all he says is: I've got bitter in my mouth.—And when he is dying, and has some awful tumour inside, he says: It is all the bitterness I have known, swelled up inside me.—That is all: a physical fact! Think what even Dmitri Karamazov would have made of it! And Dmitri Karamazov doesn't go half the lengths of the other soul-twisters. Neither is he half the man Gesualdo is, although he may be so much more "interesting," if you like soul-twisters.

In *Mastro-don Gesualdo* you have, in a sense, the same sort of tragedy as in the Russians, yet anything more unRussian could not be imagined. UnRussian almost as Homer. But Verga will have gods neither above nor below.

The Sicilians today are supposed to be the nearest descendants of the classic Greeks, and the nearest thing to the classic Greeks in life and nature. And perhaps it is true. Like the classic Greeks, the Sicilians have no insides, introspectively speaking. But alas, outside they have no busy gods. It is their great loss. Because Jesus is to them only a wonder-man

who was killed by foreigners and villains, and who will help you to get
out of Hell, perhaps.

In the true sense of the word, the Sicily of Gesualdo is drearily godless.
It needs the bright and busy gods outside. The inside gods, gods who
5   have to be inside a man's soul, are distasteful to people who live in the
sun. Once you get to Ceylon, you see that even Buddha is purely an
outside god, purely objective to the natives. They have no conception
of his being inside themselves.

It was the same with the Greeks, it is the same today with the Sicilians.
10   They aren't *capable* of introspection and the inner Jesus. They leave it
all to us and the Russians.

Save that he has no bright outside gods, Gesualdo is very like an
old Greek: the same energy and quickness of response, the same vivid
movement, the same ambition and real passion for wealth, the same
15   easy conscience, the same queer openness, without ever really openly
committing himself, and the same ancient astuteness. He is prouder,
more fearless, more frank, yet more subtle than an Italian; more on his
own. He is like a Greek or a traditional Englishman, in the way he just
goes ahead by himself. And in that, he is Sicilian, not Italian.

20   And he is Greek above all, in having no inside, in the Russian sense
of the word.

The tragedy is, he has no heroic gods or goddesses to fix his imagination. He has nothing, not even a country. Even his Greek ambitious
desire to come out splendidly, with a final splendid look of the thing
25   and a splendid final ring of words, turns bitter. The Sicilian aristocracy
was an infinitely more paltry thing than Gesualdo himself.

It is the tragedy of a man who is forced to be ordinary, because all
visions have been taken away from him. It is useless to say he should have
had the northern inwardness and the Russianising outlet. You might as
30   well say the tall and reckless asphodel of Magna Graecia should learn
to be a snowdrop. "I'll learn you to be a toad!"

But a book exists by virtue of the vividness, the aliveness and powerful
pulsing of its life-portrayal, and not by virtue of the pretty or unpretty
things it portrays. *Mastro-don Gesualdo* is a great undying book, one of
35   the great novels of Europe. If you cannot read it because it is *à terre*, and
has neither nervous uplift nor nervous hysteria, you condemn yourself.

As a picture of Sicily in the middle of the last century, it is marvellous.
But it is a picture done from the inside. There are no picture-postcard
effects. The thing is a heavy, earth-adhering organic whole. There is
40   nothing showy.

Sicily in the middle of the last century was an incredibly poor, lost,
backward country. Spaniards, Bourbons, one after the other they had
killed the life in her. The Thousand and Garibaldi had not risen over
the horizon, neither had the great emigration to America begun, nor
the great return, with dollars and a newish outlook. The mass of the   5
people were poorer even than the poor Irish of the same period, and save
for climate, their conditions were worse. There were some great and
wealthy landlords, dukes and barons still. But they lived in Naples, or
in Palermo at the nearest. In the country, there were no roads at all for
wheeled vehicles, consequently no carts, nothing but donkeys and pack–   10
mules on the trails, or a sick person in a mule litter, or armed men on
horseback, or men on donkeys. The life was mediaeval as in Russia. But
whereas the Russia of 1850 is a vast flat country with a most picturesque
life of nobles and serfs and soldiers, open and changeful, Sicily is a
most beautiful country, but hilly, steep, shut-off, and abandoned, and   15
the life is, or was grimly unpicturesque in its dead monotony. The great
nobles shunned the country, as in Ireland. And the people were sunk in
bigotry, suspicion, and gloom. The life of the villages and small towns
was of an incredible spiteful meanness, as life always is when there is not
enough change and fresh air; and the conditions were sordid, dirty, as   20
they always are, when the human spirits sink below a certain level. It is
not in such places that one looks for passion and colour. The passion and
colour in Verga's stories come in the villages near the east coast, where
there is change since Ulysses sailed that way. Inland, in the isolation,
the lid is on, and the intense watchful malice of neighbours is infinitely 25
worse than any police system, infinitely more killing to the soul and the
passionate body.

The picture is a bitter and depressing one, while ever we stay in
the dense and smelly little streets. Verga wrote what he knew and felt.
But when we pass from the habitations of sordid man, into the light   30
and marvellous open country, then you feel at once the undying beauty
of Sicily and the Greek world, a morning beauty, that has something
miraculous in it, of purple anemones and cyclamens, and sumach and
olive trees, and the place where Persephone came above-world, bringing
back spring.   35

And we must remember that eight-tenths of the population of Sicily
is agricultural, always was, and so practically the whole day-life of the
people passes in the open, in the splendour of the sun and the landscape,
and the elemental aloneness of the old world. This is a great *unconscious*
compensation. But it is great compensation all the same, even if you   40

don't know you've got it. Even Verga doesn't realise all it means. But he puts it in, all the same, and you can't read *Mastro-don Gesualdo* without feeling the marvellous glow and glamour of Sicily, and the people throbbing in it like motes in a sunbeam. A compensation!

5 And perhaps it is because the outside world is so lovely, that men in the Greek regions never became introspective. Man pulses outwards, not inwards. The positive, vital beauty is around, outside, not inward. So man becomes purely objective. This is what makes it difficult to understand the Greeks, even Socrates. We never understand him. We
10 just translate him into another thing, our own thing. He is so peculiarly *objective* even in his attitude to the soul, that we could never get him if we didn't translate him into something else, and thus "make him our own".

And it is the old, decayed objectivity in the Sicilians which makes
15 their feelings so difficult for us to understand and to respect. Gesualdo of course should have married Diodata, by all our standards. If he loved anybody, he loved her. He had children by her. He consorted with her all his life, without any qualm of conscience. He paid for her.

But, as far as conscious love went, it didn't exist for him. Neither did
20 it exist for anybody else in his world. It is almost a German invention, and has not yet reached so far south. Young gentlemen might have their passions, and ride their mistresses as they rode their horses, with that kind of love. Nothing was ever supposed to come of it, unless it was some unfortunate bastard. But when men married, they married for
25 something more important than sex. They married for "interest", in the widest sense of the word: for pride, and honour, and dignity, and distinction above other men. Even the peasant demands *some* wealth and increase with a wife.

So with Gesualdo. In the ancient world, woman was to man just
30 the female of the species. But the man was to the woman not only the male of the species, but the potential god of the house, and destiny in person. What was sacred was the outer aspect of the man: man as creator, procreator, master, provider, and enlarger of life. The private, personal, *inward* man was not known to exist. And when woman entered into the
35 life of man, as his fecund spouse, she contributed to and shared in his glory and enlargement. For this reason Helen was fetched back from Troy: not for herself, not for her personal charms, but because she was an integral part of the splendour of "King" Menelaus.*

So Gesualdo marries the pitiful, if noble Bianca Trao, for splendour.
40 It was all a man could seek in life: splendour! just as all he can seek out

of doors is the sun, the fountain of splendour in the universe. But alas, ours is not the age for splendour, even for a rich peasant.

But we need not say that Gesualdo is "stupid" or "meaningless", and the book is "all about nothing". If Gesualdo was repeating the old Mediterranean gesture of seeking for splendour, even without knowing it, and in a world from which all splendour save the sun's has been wiped out, still he was not meaningless any more than Achilles is meaningless. It is only that we have lost, or destroyed, the old meanings.

APPENDIX IV

CANCELLED PAGES FROM 'TRANSLATOR'S PREFACE TO CAVALLERIA RUSTICANA'

This volume of stories, instead of being out of date, is rapidly becoming the most modern of works: for mankind is working very close to the position of Jeli, Rosso Malpelo, Brothpot and the rest.

As far as literary quality goes, the two stories *Cavalleria Rusticana* and *La Lupa*, which have always been hailed as literary gems of brevity and 5 perfect form, seem to one now rather overdone in their concision. The scissors of the author are too evident, paring them down into 'form'. One needs more looseness, and more easy transition from mood to mood and deed to deed. A great deal of the meaning of life lies in the apparently blank spaces, the unimportant passages. They are truly passages, the 10 places of passing over.

So that *Jeli* and *Rosso Malpelo* are far more satisfactory, in the long run, than *Cavalleria Rusticana* or *La Lupa*. They leave a far deeper and more lasting impression, even if they do not excite so much admiration from the literary smarties of the age. *Rosso Malpelo* is one of the most 15 extraordinary stories in the world, and needs a far greater genius to write it than does *Cavalleria Rusticana*. But of course the literary smarties are more nearly capable of writing, and so of appreciating, the latter.

As for Verga's style, it is often a trial. Perhaps partly in harmony with his recoil against the sophisticated world, he recoiled against a 20 sophisticatedly "logical" style. He deliberately just chucked it down, and left the reader, and the translator, to make the best of it. It was his mood. But he wrote in good Italian, not in dialect. It is only in the matter of sequence and connection that he rebels. He has none of the new tricks. He just felt he couldn't be bothered with all the in-between 25 sentences, so he left them out: or, perhaps, occasionally, he crossed them out.

Everybody knows that Verga made a small drama from his story *Cavalleria Rusticana*—it means *Rustic Chivalry*—and that Leoncavallo set this dramatised version to music: whence the ever-popular little 30 opera whose libretto, alas, is Verga's chief claim to fame. But that is fame's fault, not Verga's.

393

APPENDIX V
PROSPECTUS FOR THE STORY OF DOCTOR MANENTE

The Lungarno Series of translations from Italian Poets and Novelists of the 15th & 16th Centuries

The Lungarno Series proposes to be a series of translations from the most typical and interesting Italian authors of the Renaissance, especially Tuscan, such as Lasca, Lorenzo de' Medici, Macchiavelli, Piovano Arlotta, Sirmini, Fortini, Sachetti, Poggio, Piccolomini, Alberti, Puliziani, Michelangelo, Gelli, Doni* and others.

The translations will be made by well known English authors, Norman Douglas, Edward Hutton,* Aldous Huxley, R. Scott Moncrieff,* Richard Aldington, D. H. Lawrence, and will contain copious notes, and where possible or useful, also maps and wood-cuts.

The series is intended not only for connoisseurs and collectors, but also for students and colleges wishing to have original books of the period.

The Second Volume* will contain a comedy and a story by Nicolo Machiavelli, translated by Aldous Huxley, and will be ready in December.

The STORY OF DOCTOR MANENTE being the TENTH and LAST STORY from the SUPPERS OF A. F. GRAZZINI called Il LASCA. Translation and introduction by D. H. LAWRENCE.

TWELVE HUNDRED COPIES OF THIS EDITION HAVE BEEN PRINTED, of which two hundred signed copies on Bindu handmade paper, and one thousand copies on Lombardy ruled paper.

Price two pounds or 10 dollars per signed copy

one pound or five dollars per copy, unsigned.

Ready October 10th

APPENDIX VI

INCOMPLETE EARLY VERSION OF 'REVIEW OF THE PEEP SHOW'

but not essentially living" artist, valid any more?

Take *The Peep Show*, for example. In the old jargon, it would have been a "charming human document," fresh from the "contact with true everyday life," but not quite "lifted into the realm of art." There would have been a patting of the peep-showman on the back, because he was so unsophisticated and "ordinary," and not a "damned author" after all, but the real stuff of life: the man in the street.—"Oh yes, he's not a *writer*, you know! That's what makes his book so delightful." This was more or less the old attitude to W. H. Davies.* The trouble is, where is the "life" in these books, and in these admirable "ordinary" people, the men in the street?

The Peep Show is a simple and unpretentious account of a young man who hated the "mechanical and industrial world" and didn't want to live in it, so made his own puppets, and invented his own patter, and set off into the world—that is, into Somerset and Devon—and tried to make a living by giving little puppet shows, Punch and Judy shows with better-brought-up Punches and Judys—to people in villages and on the August sea-sands. The puppet-showman was more or less an amateur: the trip lasted only six weeks or two months: and it took place, perhaps, a couple of summers ago. The book is a plain account, giving the amounts of spendings and takings, records of all the hardships and pleasures of camping in a little four-by-six tent,* pushing the "sticks" and the puppets and all the outfit up steep hills and down steep dales, on a pair of old bath-chair wheels, wearily getting into villages and chasing the policeman for permission to give a show, struggling with farmers for permission to pitch the scrap of tent, meeting with endless "ordinary" people, trippers, cottagers, ice-cream-men, boatmen, ladies of title, highbrows, and roundabouts-men,* and children; being soaked in rain, smothered in dust and petrol by char-a-bancs and motor cars, chivvied, welcomed, snubbed, and given pennies. It is a plain account of ordinary people, unvarnished save for occasional "nature" spots, and absolutely true. That is, the puppet-showman has given his experience absolutely truly, according to his own consciousness. That is the value of the book: the peculiar candour. That is the charm. It is the simple narrative of an ordinary person.

The puppet-showman, of course, is not quite ordinary, or he would never have made puppets. But the desire to get away from the industrial world is pretty common. It is only that men don't ordinarily hit on the puppet as a means of escape. And apparently they are wise.

The showman is, first and foremost, a simple-lifer. But he is not a high-brow; he comes, like myself, from the lower classes. Unlike myself, however, he accepted William Morris' world as valid, and still holds to it. "News from Nowhere," as he tells us, fixed his imagination and his creed. He is a simple lifer: vegetarian, "bread steaks," camping out, Nature, and niceness. But no high-falute.* The simple-life thing is instinctive in him. With the death of the old Adam in us, bread steaks become our instinctive desire, and by instinct, the smell of frying pork becomes "the stench of burning pig-corpse."

But it is necessary to realise that the puppet-showman has no high-brow aloofness. He is not booky: books are very little in his line, and R. M. Ballantyne, whose world is so very simple, is a happy discovery to him. The "works of William Shakspeare, in one volume," which accompanied the puppet show for the first week, is a standing joke to the showman. As if anybody ever *did* read Shakspeare! That's just the joke! Bill Shakspeare!—"Where's the works of the immortal William?—Say, are you sitting on Big Bill in one vol.?"

The showman doesn't want *not* to be ordinary. The ordinary people are the slap-bang thing, all the rest is toffee. But you've got to be "nice." Even Punch and Judy are too crude for our day. Must be brought forward a few years. Not so beefy and beery, you know. Nicer!

Nevertheless, the Peep Show puppets *are* charming, and the puppet showman has a real gift with them.

So you start on this trip of "nice" ordinariness; and start, characteristically, in a sort of free life colony up in the Cotswolds. Not that the free-lifers are extraordinary. They have most of them settled down, after some years, into real ordinariness. But nice, you know. They don't approve of the industrial world, and they wear sandals. But they never were "extraordinary." They were always the ordinary, just being unordinary.

Leaving the free-lifers, the puppet-showman sets out, not without trepidation, into the harsh world where people are quite nice, you know, but not simple enough. But still, the showman has a simple-life companion with him for the first week, so it's not so bad. In fact, it's great fun. It's most awfully jolly, to wake up in a tent and not in some stuffy room—etc.

However, the companion must depart, the showman must proceed alone. He is really rather shy, and not tough enough for a vagabond. A vagabond must be a liar of sorts, and the showman is limpidly truthful. A vagabond must be a sort of Ishmael,* with his hand stealthily clenched against society. Whereas the puppet-showman believes in a "reformed" society. If we would only all be simple, and not mercenary, and really "nice."

The puppet-showman is peculiarly nice. It is perhaps unusual that the "old Adam" is left so completely out of him. But perhaps it is now *ordinary* to have very little of the old Adam in you. Perhaps that is what makes ordinariness. Perhaps that is why the world is getting more and more ordinary. The old Adam is being more and more blanked out.

It is the peculiar limpidity in the puppet-showman's character that makes his book a real book. It is a simple record of six weeks or so. It is, in a sense, amateur, with all the simple-life amateurism. At the same time, it is so veracious, it is poignant. The whole thing is ordinary almost to banality. Yet the limpidity of character of the showman makes even the banality real. The very banalities of style have at last the effect of the *mot juste*. Take any sample of "nature" appreciation—remembering that a simple-lifer is an incurable optimist—and count the clichés.

—"It is an exquisite pleasure to find oneself so suddenly in the sweet morning air, to tumble out of bed

APPENDIX VII

TWO INCOMPLETE EARLY VERSIONS OF 'REVIEW OF THE STATION, ETC.'

(Version 1)

Review for Vogue

There's a difference between a sad book and a depressing book. If you say of a book: Oh, but it's so sad!—then many people will rush to read it. But if you say: It's such depressing reading!—they will hold off. 5

Three of these books are distinctly depressing. England is in the clutch of an octopus. The octopus is the millions of streets and rows of mean little houses which spread over the face of the land and devour the country. This phenomenon has depressed most of us quite acutely, 10 without Mr Clough Williams-Ellis' little book rubbing it in.

Yet after all we say Bravo! to the book. The author knows he's got a depressing and thankless subject. He knows we want to say: Oh do shut up! What can anybody do about it?— He knows perfectly well we can do as good as nothing about it. He is almost in despair himself. Yet 15 he quite rightly feels that despair is a cardinal sin,* and he tackles the octopus. He is not long-winded. He makes us listen. And in the end we feel the man is right, and we ought to listen, and everybody ought to listen.

We can't, in five minutes, do anything to prevent England being 20 swallowed up entirely by beastly little pink houses and blasphemous bungalows. But we can be made fully aware that something's *got* to be done about it. And we can be given an inkling of *what* can be done. And then, as soon as enough people are brought to this state of awareness, something *will* be done: and Mr Williams-Ellis' book will have 25 helped.

It is an alive, interesting book. The six questions that should be asked of every building ought to be printed on a card and learnt by heart by every person in England over the age of fourteen. I imagine men, women, youths and maidens, with question-cards in their hands, 30 standing in front of the family residence or the local post-office or the nearest garage and sternly demanding of the edifice:

1. Are you practical—etc?
2. Are you soundly and honestly built, etc?
3. If you are new, are you going to look (a) shabby or (b) still raw, in ten years time—etc?
4. Are you beautiful, or at any rate to me, or if not, did you seem so to those who built you, and if so, why? (devastating question!)
5. Do you express some sort of an idea—are you, for instance, notably restful or vigorous, emphatically horizontal or vertical, demure or gay, refined or robust, light or dark, feminine or masculine? In short, have you character, and if so, of what kind?
6. Are you a good neighbour?—do you love the Georgian inn next door, or the Regency chemist's shop opposite, or the pollarded* lime trees, or the adjoining church and elm-grove, as yourself? Do you do-as-you-would-be-done-by? —etc.*

If we have got to become conscious, let us become conscious of beauty or ugliness in our immediate surroundings. Let us tackle Advertisements, trees, paint, petrol pumps, railings, railways, all the endless superimposed features in the landscape, and ask them what they're doing there, and how they are behaving themselves? Let us be bold little heroes in the wake of the doughty Mr Williams-Ellis, and at least look the octopus in the face.

So we cheer up from our first depression, and gird the armour of intelligence on. Then we turn to *Comfortless Memory* and are slowly and helplessly dragged back into depression. I don't know when Mr Maurice Baring wrote this book, but he certainly should have printed it not less than twenty years ago. It dates most drearily in the nineties, and is about as exciting as stale cake. The hero tells his feeble tale in the first person: he is an elderly author, married, with some reputation, but of an infinite stuffy dulness. There were lots of authors like that in the nineties, even if there aren't today. Pretending, as a trick, to make love to a demi-monde* lady, in order to save a young artist and his ART from her clutches, this stuffy-elderly author causes the wonderful and elusive-pimpernel* "smirched" lady to fall, if you please, purely, deeply, and passionately in love with him: the one pure love of a deep and passionate nature. And all the time he is only pretending love for her—or thinks he's only pretending—he's not quite sure—in fact—! Well, when the rare lady, after doing tableaux vivants,

ye gods!, of Orpheus and Eurydice*—she was Orpheus in the tableau
vivant—goes and expires, in her riding-habit, out of sheer love for
the elderly, stuffy author, we cease to be depressed and are faintly
amused.

But in this matter of depression Mr Somerset Maugham is the worst   5
offender. He would even be a humorist at it. His hero, a certain Mr
Ashenden, also a somewhat elderly author of the I! I! I! variety of stuffi-
ness, becomes an agent in the secret service during the war, is stationed
in Geneva,* and has a series of—not adventures—but encounters with
spies and diplomats and such-like. The book is not a novel, but a series   10
of secret-service episodes.

Mr Maugham is an excellent observer. He can show us most
admirably what his people looked like, and what they probably were
like. He can put them in their environment excellently. He can create
the atmosphere of hotels and railway stations and steam-boats and trains   15
to a nicety—and the people in them. So far he is an artist. But there he
ends.

His figures won't move. They don't move. As soon as any movement
takes place, it is Mr Maugham shoving his characters about. When they
come to act, we just don't believe it. We don't believe that the little   20
painted old lady* barked *England*! on her death-bed, and then no more.
We don't believe in the Hairless Mexican* at all! We don't believe the fat
Englishman in Lucerne* was a spy, no fool would have employed him.
We don't believe the dog howled. We don't believe the Hindoo poisoned
himself, we don't believe the woman asked for the wrist-watch back,   25
we don't believe the American* died for his dirty linen—Just as Queen
Victoria was not amused,* we are not convinced. It is all too much Mr
Maugham.

It is Mr Maugham's little personal joke. Mr Maugham is a humorist,
and he funnily wants to convince us that all people are either clever   30
gutter-snipes, like his Mr Ashenden and his Colonel and his genteel
diplomat (connected with the best families in England), very smart
guttersnipes with completely base emotions, who daren't stay in any
but the best hotels, for fear of looking what they are; or else they are all
comically good people who simply make fools of themselves, like the   35
American who died for his dirty washing. If Mr Maugham portrays
real emotion (this was love, if ever there was love!) he has to make it
not only grotesque but squalid, like the Italian woman who asked for

the wrist-watch (which she never did; and even if she did, who knows, it was probably the only thing she had in the world to raise money on, poor thing.)

On the top of it all, we are asked to find it funny. And we don't. We don't find base well-connected guttersnipes funny, and we don't find unfortunate people funny. We don't find Mr Maugham funny. We find him depressingly ill-humoured, instead of humorous.

(Version 2)

Athos is an old place, and Mr Byron is a young man, so the combination works very well, we get an entertaining book where we might have had a stodgy one. The younger generation, the war generation, has a charming butterfly manner, and an engaging honesty. It avoids, at all cost, being heavy. It is not out for anything in particular, has no axe to grind. Axe? what is an axe? It is not prepared to be enthusiastic. Like a butterfly, it is settle and gone again. And like a butterfly, 5

APPENDIX VIII

NOTES FOR THE HAND OF MAN

I went out of the busy street where the traffic rushed, through the doors of the museum, and into a sudden stillness, a peace. Almost before I could grasp what had happened, I felt the eternal quiet of the Buddha statues around me.

Yet still I went forward, pushed by the wave of restlessness, and came 5 into the rooms where were many objects from the East, representing the arts and crafts of Asia and the Pacific. And here the stillness of Buddha changed to a new vibration of life, so that almost I could smell sandal wood and the champak flower.* Life itself came from the things in the room which eastern hands had held so close and fashioned so carefully 10 and tenderly, life had been put into fabrics and carvings of wood, and life emanated subtly out of them again, like a perfume, like a soft glow, warm and strangely thrilling after the iron streets of the Western city.

There was a canoe
objects   15
memories
—
life is put into an object & the object lives
—

all we possess is life—life must flow—making things in the passion 20
of life—weaving, carving, building—this is the flow of life, life flows
into the object—& life *flows out again* to the beholder—so that whoever
makes anything with real interest, puts life into it,* and makes it a
little fountain of life for the next comer. Therefore a ghandi weaver* is
transmitting life to others—& that is the great charity.   25
—

Western restlessness & quick wearying comes from the fact that western machine-made objects are dead, & *give nothing* out. So western
fashions change so rapidly etc

APPENDIX IX

'THE DEATH OF MAURICE MAGNUS' BY LOUISE E. WRIGHT

'The Death of Maurice Magnus'

In his Introduction to Maurice Magnus's *Memoirs of the Foreign Legion*, D. H. Lawrence presents two accounts of Magnus's death on 4 November 1920. The first of these derives from the *Daily Malta Chronicle*; the second from a letter written on 20 November 1920 by Walter Salomone. A friend and business associate of Michael Borg, Salomone wished to amplify and correct the information contained in the newspaper article. Neither of these accounts, however, provides an entirely accurate picture of Magnus's suicide or of the events surrounding it.

Lawrence recalls that Salomone sent him a copy of the *Daily Malta Chronicle*, in which an article beginning 'The suicide of an American gentleman at Rabato' presented the details of Magnus's death. The article would seem to have appeared on 5 November 1920, for it states that the discovery of Magnus's body took place the day before. In fact, the only report of Magnus's death which the *Chronicle* published appears in the edition of 6 November 1920, as the final item in a column headed 'Local News'.[1] More informative than the account which Lawrence quotes, it also covers the inquest, held 'yesterday afternoon . . . in the mortuary of the Central Civil Hospital, Notre Dame Gate, Floriana', the hospital which Salomone referred to as 'the Floriana Civil Hospital'. The article gives the cause of death as 'poisoning', but does not mention the kind of poison that Magnus used, which Salomone correctly identified as 'hydrocyanic acid'. The reference to 'prussic acid' (a familiar name for hydrocyanic acid) in Lawrence's account, together with other discrepancies between that account and the one in the *Daily Malta Chronicle*, suggests that Lawrence did not have the newspaper in front of him while he was working on his Introduction, and was quoting from memory.

Writing to Lawrence, Walter Salomone not only got many facts wrong, but made several questionable assumptions. He misquoted the

---

[1] 'Local News', *Daily Malta Chronicle*, 6 November 1920, p. 7. I am extremely grateful to all those individuals who assisted in my research, particularly M. Camilleri, J. Caruana, and Mieke Ijzermans.

documents which Magnus left behind at the time of his death, and suggested that there were two, rather than three, of them. He supplied only an incomplete text of Magnus's letter to Don Mauro Inguanez, and conflated Magnus's letter to Carl R. Loop, the American consul in Malta, with another document headed 'In case of my death'. Salomone condensed the events of the morning of 4 November, reducing a series of comings and goings between Magnus's house and the police station to a single scene. The depositions of the police officers involved, and the report of the magistrate's inquiry, tell a much more complicated story.

Early on the morning of 4 November 1920, Sergeant Francesco Cassar and Constable Paolo Cutajar travelled from Valletta to Rabato, a suburb of Notabile, on the western side of the island. At the police station, Cassar presented a warrant for Magnus's arrest to Carmelo Agius, the inspector for the district, and Agius despatched Constable Salvatore Galea to summon Magnus to the station. Galea arrived at Magnus's house, 1 Strada San Pietro, at 9.30 a.m., and informed Magnus that Agius wished to speak with him. Magnus replied that he needed to bathe and would be along within the hour, so Galea returned to the station. At approximately ten to eleven, Magnus, wearing sandals and dressed in a white suit, entered the police station and asked what Agius wanted. Unwilling to alarm him, Agius replied that, because Magnus's guarantee had been withdrawn, he would have to go to Valletta with Cassar. When Magnus asked to be allowed to return home to change his clothes, Agius agreed; but he also ordered Cutajar and Constable Carmelo Micallef, both dressed in plain clothes, to keep Magnus under surveillance.[2]

The policemen followed him home, saw him enter, and, taking up positions in front of the house where they could not be seen, kept watch. About twenty minutes later they heard an upstairs window opening. Magnus called to a boy in the street to mail the letter which he tossed to him along with a coin for running the errand. Micallef confiscated the letter, which was addressed to Don Mauro Inguanez. Then Micallef heard something which sounded like a pistol shot, and, believing that Magnus had killed himself, decided to return to the police station while Cutajar remained behind.[3] Micallef reached the station at about 11.30,

[2] Statement of Francesco Cassar, 4 Nov. 1920; statement of Salvatore Galea, 5 Nov. 1920, Inquest Held by Crown Advocate on 6 November re Suicide of M. Magnus, National Archives of Malta. This file will subsequently be referred to as Inquest.
[3] Statements of Carmelo Micallef and Paolo Cutajar, 5 Nov. 1920, Inquest. Magnus evidently intended the coin for the boy as the letter had three penny stamps affixed.

and he, Agius and Cassar immediately set out for 1 Strada San Pietro, Agius ordering the others to break down the door should Magnus offer any resistance.

Cassar read the letter to Don Mauro on the way, and informed Agius of its contents. Magnus had written:

Nov. 4, 1920

Dear Don Mauro:
    I leave to you & Michael Borg to settle my affairs.
    I can't live any longer.
    Pray for me[.]

                Yours
                Dickie.

I appoint Norman Douglas chez Mme. Rola 4 Rue St. Charles Mentone Alpes Maritimes, France my literary executor.

All my letters (personal) & photographs are for Madame Inga Moellerberg 11 Rue Chalet Malakoff Paris[.][4]

When the police reached Magnus's address, they knocked and called out, receiving no response, they tried in vain to open the door. Micallef and Cutajar gained entry from a neighbouring house, but when they went upstairs they found the door of the hall leading to the bedroom bolted. Micallef broke the hall window, and made his way to the bedroom, accompanied by Cutajar, with Cassar and Agius following.

Magnus, at the point of death, was lying on the bed with his teeth clenched. The police called to him, but he did not respond. On a chair by the bed, they saw a glass with liquid in it, a container of white powder they assumed to be poison, and a bottle of water. On his person they found a wallet containing almost thirteen shillings. The police sent for a priest and a doctor and, while they waited, tried unsuccessfully to induce vomiting. One of the two priests who answered the summons, Paolo

---

[4] Magnus to Inguanez, 4 Nov. 1920, Inquest. Inga Moellerberg was Magnus's niece. Magnus's copyright holder has not been identified. Loop refused to acknowledge the documents Magnus left behind as legally binding. Instead of turning Magnus's books and manuscripts over to Douglas, he sold them, along with Magnus's other belongings, to Borg. Magnus's wife Lucy relinquished all claim to her husband's property. See Louise E. Wright, 'Disputed *Dregs*: D. H. Lawrence and the Publication of Maurice Magnus's *Memoirs of the Foreign Legion*', *Journal of the D. H. Lawrence Society* (1996), pp. 58–9. Magnus used the nickname Dickie with his closest friends: I have discovered another instance of it in a note to Isadora Duncan, 30 July 1916, on 'Penelope Sikelianos Duncan to Magnus, 24 July 1916', The Irma Duncan Collection of Isadora Duncan Materials, Jerome Robins Dance Division, New York Public Library for the Performing Arts.

Vassallo, administered the sacrament of Extreme Unction. Magnus died at 11.45 a.m., just as the doctor arrived.[5]

By permitting Magnus to return home, Agius had unwittingly afforded him the opportunity to take his own life. On hearing what sounded like a pistol shot, Micallef had concluded that Magnus had committed suicide, but instead of attempting to enter the house, he had returned to the police station. He is unlikely to have shared his fears with his superiors, since if he had, Agius would not have issued orders to break down the door should Magnus offer resistance. Even after Cassar read Magnus's letter to Don Mauro, the police seem not to have responded to the urgency of the situation, for they attempted to force entry only after calling and knocking in vain. Given the nature of hydrocyanic acid, the police could have done little to save Magnus's life, but had they arrived earlier Magnus might have been comforted by the presence of the priest. The wording of Cassar's statement suggests that Magnus may not have received Extreme Unction until after he was dead.

What is also clear from this account is that the police proceeded very cautiously. They had a warrant for Magnus's arrest, but they did not use it. Instead, they summoned him to the police station, waited for him to arrive, and permitted him to leave. The police did not disclose the real reason for the trip to Valletta so as not to alarm him; they told him it was concerning his guarantee. It is quite possible that the police behaved as they did because, contrary to what Salomone believed, Magnus's arrest and extradition were by no means certain.

In July 1920 Salomone had agreed to act as Magnus's guarantor in Malta. On 23 October, fearful that he would be held responsible for the debts Magnus had incurred, Salomone withdrew his guarantee. He advised Magnus of this the same day, whereupon Magnus immediately wrote to the police requesting permission to remain on the island for an additional three weeks. Salomone told Lawrence that the police made no reply 'at all' to Magnus's letter, and he attributed this silence to the fact that the police 'had everything ready and well thought out' for Magnus's arrest. Such was not the case.

It seems doubtful that Magnus had heard nothing from the police, as he had a friend on the force: Carmelo Micallef, the constable who thought he heard a pistol shot, admitted at the magistrate's enquiry

---

[5] Statements of Cassar, Micallef, and Agius, 4 Nov. 1920, Inquest.

that he had known Magnus for some time.[6] Magnus had borrowed a
Maltese dictionary from him, and early in October thought of entrust-
ing Micallef with the keys to his house. To Norman Douglas, Magnus
described Micallef as 'an architect and a very decent person'.[7] He did not
mention that Micallef was a police officer, an omission rather indicating Magnus's priorities than his ignorance of the fact. One of the things
about the Maltese that impressed Magnus was that everyone, regard-
less of occupation or walk in life, pursued the arts: the island's premier guitarist was a butcher; the foremost playwright a schoolteacher.[8]
Micallef's artistic pursuits mattered more to Magnus than the way he
earned his living. But as a police officer Micallef could have provided
information, if only unofficially.

Of further significance is Magnus's behaviour on 3 November, the
day before he died. According to Salomone, Magnus paid two visits to
Michael Borg, who thought he seemed unusually excited. On one of
these visits, Magnus signed an IOU for the fifty-five pounds he owed
Borg.[9] Salomone implied in his letter to Lawrence that Magnus had
borrowed the money in small increments over a period of time rather
than as a lump sum; furthermore, Borg had not provided any new funds
for about two weeks. The timing of the IOU suggests that Magnus—
and perhaps Borg as well—knew that something of consequence was
about to occur.

If, however, the police did remain completely silent, this need not
imply that they had 'everything ready' for Magnus's capture. Magnus
wrote to the police on 23 October, and not until 29 October did the
Italian consul general request his arrest and extradition. Documentation
included with the request indicated that two complaints had been sworn
against Magnus for passing bad cheques, one by Leone Colleoni of the
Excelsior Hotel in Rome, and the other by Amadeo Brocco of the Hotel
Vittoria in Anzio. On 2 November the commissioner of police asked for
a warrant, and the next day the lieutenant-governor's office determined
that, *prima facie*, the documentation provided by the Italian consulate

---

[6] Statement of Micallef, 4 Nov. 1920, Inquest.

[7] Magnus, 'In case of my death . . .' 4 Nov. 1920, Inquest; Magnus to Douglas, 2 Oct.
1920, The Norman Douglas Collection, Beinecke Rare Book and Manuscript Library
(YU).

[8] Magnus to Douglas, ibid.

[9] Michael Borg, receipt, 4 April 1921, *records of the Foreign Service Posts of the Department
of State*, Consulate Valletta, Malta: Correspondence re death of Maurice Magnus, class
330, RG 84, National Archives at College Park. This file is subsequently referred to as
RG 84.

justified the issuing of a warrant—although the final say rested with the court of magistrates. Accordingly, the governor's office issued a warrant authorising the police

to apprehend the said Maurizio Magnus for the purpose of his being surrendered to a proper person in order to be conveyed to the Kingdom of Italy, if, on the proceedings which you are hereby enjoined to institute, there will appear to be sufficient grounds for such surrender under the provisions of the ordinances cited.[10]

A warrant for Magnus's arrest, therefore, did not exist until the day before he committed suicide. Moreover, this warrant merely 'enjoined' the police to conduct an investigation in order to determine whether there were 'sufficient grounds' for Magnus's extradition. This would seem to explain why an arrest warrant was not served, and why the police proceeded so circumspectly. In all likelihood, Cassar had come to Rabato on the morning of 4 November simply to escort Magnus to Valletta for questioning.

Salomone also maintained that Magnus, having heard nothing from the police, became 'alarmed', and 'decided to prepare for the last act of his drama'. For at least a year, Magnus had considered suicide as a possible solution to his problems. In *Alone*, Douglas records a conversation in which Magnus confided 'I may be taking that little sleeping-draught of mine any one of these days'.[11] On 9 May 1920, while waiting in Taormina for funds to arrive so that he could leave Italy, Magnus advised Douglas 'If anything happens in the meantime—you know what I mean—look for my grave here in the foreigners' cemetery'.[12] After Magnus's death, Constable Galea discovered a second vial of poison on the chest of drawers in the bedroom.[13] But despite these indications of Magnus's readiness to end his life, little evidence exists to support Salomone's conclusion. On the contrary, Magnus's behaviour between 23 October

[10] Consul General for Italy to Lieutenant Governor of Malta, 29 October 1920; Colleoni to Royal Prosecutor, Rome, 13 March 1920; Brocco, verbal statement of complaint lodged against Maurice Magnus, 1 April 1920; Lord Plumer (governor of Malta) to Harry William Morrey Bamford (commissioner of police), 3 Nov 1920; CSG 01 5775/Consular/1920, National Archives of Malta. This file is subsequently referred to as Arrest.

[11] Norman Douglas, *Alone* (New York: McBride, 1923), p. 135. Although this encounter between Douglas and Magnus is difficult to date, it may have been in the autumn of 1919; Douglas's diary indicates that he was in Rome between the 21st and 25th October (Norman Douglas Collection, Yale University). The same collection includes a letter of 26 Nov. 1919 in which Magnus declares his intent to leave his 'literary material and letters' to Douglas, suggesting that his state of mind may have been similar to that which Douglas records.

[12] Magnus to Douglas, 9 May 1920 (YU).   [13] Statement of Galea.

and 4 November suggests that he was exploring less drastic ways of ending his difficulties.

Early in November, Magnus wrote to Irene M. Ashby Macfadyen, the woman whose letter to the *Spectator* Douglas reprinted in *D. H. Lawrence and Maurice Magnus: A Plea for Better Manners*. According to Macfadyen, Magnus sounded much his usual self and seemed in good spirits.[14] To other correspondents, however, Magnus revealed something of his financial difficulties. In August, C. W. Daniel had accepted three of his translations of works by Leonid Andreev, *To the Stars*, *His Excellency the Governor*, and *And it Came to Pass that the King was Dead*. Magnus had accepted the terms offered—a 10 per cent royalty on the first 2,000 copies and 15 per cent thereafter—but asked for an advance; he received an acknowledgement by postcard dated 1 September but, despite sending another letter, heard nothing more. Explaining the situation in a letter to Douglas Goldring on 31 October, Magnus admitted that he was 'up against it', and indicated that he would 'be most grateful' should Goldring be able to solve 'the mystery'.[15]

Magnus also asked several friends for money. The fact that their cabled replies arrived only after his death suggests that Magnus, lacking the means to send his requests by telegram, had depended on the weekly mail-boat between Malta and Syracuse. His niece, Inga Moellerberg, cabled twenty pounds, and someone named Harry Withers instructed Magnus to get in touch with him in Honolulu. Ivan Lavretsky, employed at the US Consulate in Frankfurt-am-Main, who had worked with Magnus at the European Literary Bureau and the *Roman Review*, replied that he could do nothing before December.[16] From New York came a fourth telegram containing the single word 'yes'. The sender, whose name is not legible, was most likely Mitchell Kennerley, who had known

---

[14] Macfadyen to Loop, 1 March 1921, 1 April 1921, RG 84; Norman Douglas, *D. H. Lawrence and Maurice Magnus: A Plea for Better Manners* (privately printed, 1924), pp. 27–30. One of the mysteries surrounding Magnus's death involves Macfadyen's insistence that his last letter to her was dated 7 November 1920. She sent a tracing of the date and the words 'My birthday', which Magnus had added, to Loop on 25 April 1921 (RG 84).

[15] Magnus to Goldring, 31 October 1920, quoted in Douglas Goldring, *The Nineteen Twenties: A General Survey and Some Personal Memories* (London: Nicholson and Watson, 1945), p. 208. Although Magnus mentioned only two Andreev works in his letter to Goldring, C. W. Daniel's records show that the firm had accepted three, all of which were published in 1921. Lawrence knew the novelist, playwright and editor Douglas Goldring (1887–1960), well, particularly in connection with the People's Theatre; see *Letters*, iii. 371.

[16] The telegrams are held in the file RG 84; see also Magnus to Douglas, 2 October 1920 (YU).

Magnus for almost twenty years and who had vouched for his loyalty and patriotism during the war. Found among Magnus's papers was a notice dated 27 August 1920 requiring 'Mitchell Kennely' to deposit three hundred dollars at the Hanover National Bank, New York, in order to cover a night draft drawn by 'Maurice Lyons'. The notice serves as an indication that Magnus knew he could count on Kennerley for financial help.[17] Magnus's correspondence, then, reveals that, far from resigning himself to suicide, he was endeavouring to raise enough cash either to post bond himself, or, more likely, to get himself off the island.

Magnus also thought to solve his problems, according to Salomone, by devising a scheme whereby he, Borg, and Salomone would 'exploit the commercial possibilities in Morocco'. Although Salomone invested a good deal of time and energy in the project, which he presented to Lawrence as Magnus's brainchild, he felt relieved when it fell through owing to a lack of funds. His implication is clear: the project would have proved costly to Borg and himself. Magnus's letters to Douglas, however, present the venture in a different light. Far from being the instigator, Magnus seems to have been acting for the two Maltese. 'There is some talk here of sending me on a mission to Morocco for a month,' he wrote in early October, 'but I am not sure yet'. At about this time, Douglas considered visiting Malta, but then decided against it. Magnus responded as follows:

Now . . . I can safely go to Morocco. When your letter came that you might come here I regretted having said 'yes' to the people here about Morocco. After all what the hell is the use of life unless one is happy—or comparatively so. Well nothing awaits me in Morocco except a few desirable Arabs.

Only at the end of the month, when Magnus was especially strapped for cash and had no one to guarantee his stay in Malta, did he express much

---

[17] [Kennerley?] to Magnus, telegram, 10 Nov. 1920, RG 84; Charles B. Dillingham to Nicholas Biddle, memorandum, 20 June 1918, War Department General and Special Staffs, Personal Name File for Maurice Magnus, file PF 10118, RG 165, National Archives, Washington, D.C.; William E. Cable Jr. to Kennerley, bank notice, 27 Aug. 1920, RG 84. For Mitchell Kennerley, see Explanatory notes to *The Bad Side of Books*, 76:38 and 77:7.

What Magnus did with the three hundred dollars remains a mystery. His letters to Douglas (18 July 1920, 2 Oct. 1920), as well as one from Borg to Douglas dated 4 December 1920 (YU) reveal that Magnus lived very frugally. His need for such a large sum suggests that he was trying to satisfy creditors, although the possibility that he was being blackmailed, perhaps by the 'vile creature' who informed the police of his whereabouts (Douglas, *A Plea for Better Manners*, pp. 35–6), cannot be dismissed out of hand.

concern about the project. Noting that it was 'off again', he lamented: 'Good God—what next. Everything seems to go wrong with me of late—and not a helping hand from anywhere'.[18]

By the morning of 4 November, when Constable Galea summoned Magnus to the police station, the much needed financial help had not arrived. Magnus probably understood the summons in connection with his request to extend his stay in Malta. But he must have admitted to himself the possibility of deportation to Italy and its consequences— capture, trial and imprisonment—even if he did not suspect extradition. Unable to face that possibility, he almost certainly wrote one of the three documents left behind at his death before setting out for the police station. Unlike the letter to Don Mauro, which reveals Magnus's decision to take his own life, this one begins 'In case of my death'. It continues:

advise American Consul Valletta and the American Consul please bury me first class   the expenses will be paid by my wife Mrs. Lucy Magnus c/o Mrs. Vernon Rosewarren Mawnan (MAWNAN) near Falmouth Cornwall England. My best friend here: Michael Borg 34 Fuori la Mina Valletta advise him. My literary executor Norman Douglas Chez Mlle Rola 4 Rue St. Charles Mentone France Alpes Maritimes. The Kodak and the dishes & silver belong to Michael Borg. The lamps, furniture & linen to Coleros Floriana. The Maltese dictionary to Carmello Micaleff 161 Via Boschetto, Rabato. All manuscripts & books for Norman Douglas.[19]

After making these provisions, Magnus walked to the police station, where Agius informed him he would have to go to Valletta with Cassar. In all likelihood, it was this that pushed Magnus over the edge. Having already decided that death was preferable to an Italian jail, he must have perceived the trip to Valletta as an indication that the authorities had caught up with him at last. Permitted to return home, he wrote the letter to Don Mauro, as well as one to Carl R. Loop, the American consul, labelling the envelope 'My will.' The letter reads as follows:

I leave my property to Norman Douglas to whom half of the results are to accrue—the other half my debts are to be paid with.
My little personal belongings are to go to my wife Mrs. Lucy Magnus, Mawnan, near Falmouth, Cornwall, England.

Maurice Magnus
Notabile Nov. 4, 1920.

[18] Magnus to Douglas, 2, 13, 28 Oct. 1920 (YU).
[19] Magnus, 'In case of my death', 4 Nov. 1920, Inquest.

Magnus added Douglas's address to the bottom of the letter.[20] His preparations completed, he mixed hydrogen cyanide with water, swallowed it and lay down on his bed to die.

It is, of course, possible that the Maltese authorities might have decided against his arrest and extradition. Even if they had sent him to Italy, opportunities for escape might have presented themselves. Magnus had escaped before: from the Foreign Legion, from Monte Cassino, from Sicily. At the end of September, however, he had disclosed to Douglas: 'I haven't any energy left to get up and go chasing madly through the world . . . I am tired. I want to be quiet & sit still and just go on writing in my own little way.' On 13 October he observed that unless one were 'happy—or comparatively so', life was useless.[21] Magnus waited until what must have seemed to him the last minute and then, believing that life could no longer afford him the little he asked, committed suicide.

The funeral took place, as Salomone noted, on what would have been Magnus's 44th birthday, 7 November 1920. Following the celebration of Roman Catholic funeral rites, the body was buried at Addolorata Cemetery, Paola. Maltese law required that one year later it be shipped from the island or transferred to a private grave; otherwise it would be consigned to a general one.[22] Lucy Magnus lacked the means to have the body moved to the Protestant Cemetery at Rome, where Maurice had wanted to be buried with his mother. So it was that Michael Borg, after a brief delay, had the remains interred in his family's private grave.[23] The Italian government, although advised of Magnus's suicide, refused to let him rest in peace; on 5 November 1921, the Tribunal at Rome charged him with 'swindling committed in December 1919', and on 7 March 1923 the Court of Appeals in Rome sentenced him to 'three years' solitary confinement and a fine of 4000 lire'.[24]

[20] Magnus to Loop, 4 Nov. 1920, Inquest.
[21] Magnus to Douglas, 23 Sept., 13 Oct. 1920 (YU).
[22] Report of the Death of an American Citizen, enclosed with Loop to Secretary of State, 8 Nov. 1920, General Records of the Department of State, decimal file 1910–29, file 349b.113/6, RG 59, National Archives, Washington, D.C. The decimal file is subsequently referred to as RG 59.
[23] Lucy Magnus to Loop, 24 Nov. 1920, RG 84; Loop to Secretary of State, 13 Jan. 1922, file 349b.113/11, RG 59.
[24] Lieutenant Governor of Malta to Consul General for Italy, 10 Nov. 1920, Arrest; List of Americans Tried and Condemned by Italian Courts, enclosed with John Ball Osborne to Secretary of State, 26 May 1925, file 092.65/546, RG 59.

EXPLANATORY NOTES

EXPLANATORY NOTES

Foreword to *All Things Are Possible*

5:2 paragraph on The Russian Spirit, Part II, no. 45 (E1, pp. 233–42). DHL's account of the relationship between European and Russian culture is, however, very different from Shestov's, which contrasts the youth and innocence of Russian writers with the deceit-ridden decadence of Europeans. Shestov would certainly not agree that Russian writing lacks profundity or is 'a little extraneous' (5:20–1).

5:6 substance is of this fashion. Replacing 'composition is homogeneous' in MS (p. 1).

5:9 inoculated with the virus The principle of inoculating against infection by introducing into the body material drawn from similar infections has been known since the eighteenth century, although the equivalent principle of viral inoculation was not properly understood until the late nineteenth century.

5:15 European culture . . . which hurts him. 'To us in Russia, civilisation came suddenly, whilst we were still savages . . . We quickly submitted. In a short time we were swallowing in enormous doses those poisons which Europe had been gradually accustoming herself to . . . A Russian had only to catch a whiff of European atmosphere, and his head began to swim' (Leo Shestov, *All Things Are Possible*, tr. S. S. Koteliansky, Secker, 1920, p. 39).

5:23 Peter the Great Peter I (1672–1725), Tsar of Russia, encouraged Western assistance in modernising his country.

5:25 katabolism Usually 'catabolism'; the process of change whereby complex organic compounds break down into simpler ones.

6:15 hedge-stake A firm stake of wood driven into the ground so that thinner branches can be laid sideways around it to create a hedge; hence something dependable or immovable.

6:16 "Everything is possible" . . . central cry. See Part II, no. 45: 'Until the contrary is proved, we need to think that only one assertion has or can have any objective reality: *that nothing on earth is impossible*' (*All Things Are Possible*, p. 241).

6:35 the old lion . . . devours all its servants, In 'The Sick Lion', one of the fables of Aesop (Greek fabulist of *c.* 6th century BC), an old and infirm lion, unable to hunt for food, stays in his cave and proceeds to eat all the animals who come to offer him assistance, until the last visitor, a fox, realises what is happening and refuses to enter.

7:1 hitching Replacing 'hopping' in MS (p. 4).

Note to *All Things Are Possible*

8:2 LEO SHESTOV . . . living Russians. Leo or Lev Shestov (1866–1938), Ukrainian-Jewish philosopher, was born at Kiev; he was fifty-four when the translation of *All Things Are Possible* was published.

8:8 1900. Good in the . . . Preaching. The title of this work is *Dobro v uchenii gr. Tolstogo i Fr. Nitsshe* ('The Idea of the Good in the Teaching of Tolstoy and Nietzsche').

8:12 1908. Beginnings and Ends. *Nachala i kontsy* ('Beginnings and Endings') was published in English in 1916 as *Anton Chekhov and Other Essays* (in the USA as *Penultimate Words and Other Essays*).

8:13 1912. Great Vigils. *Velikie kanuny* was published in 1910.

Memoir of Maurice Magnus

11:1 *Memoir of Maurice Magnus* Martin Secker presumably suppressed DHL's title when he gave the title *Memoirs of the Foreign Legion* to the book containing both DHL's introduction and the text of *Dregs* by Charles Maurice Liebetrau Magnus (1876–1920), American writer, theatrical agent and journalist. DHL recreated Magnus as 'Mr May' in *The Lost Girl* (1920), written March–May 1920; see *The Lost Girl*, ed. John Worthen (Cambridge, 1981), 85:27 and Explanatory note.

11:2 On a dark, The original opening – deleted in MS (p. 1) – ran 'First let me give an exact account of my experience with Magnus. One dark,'.

11:5 November 1919 . . . 1914. DHL arrived in Florence on Wednesday 19 November 1919, 'coming from Spezia' (deleted in MS, p. 1); he had left Italy on 10 June 1914. Frieda Lawrence had been to see her mother Anna von Richthofen (1851–1930) in Baden-Baden: 'I arrive in Baden, so glad to see my sisters and my mother, but, oh, so many, many dead that had been our life and our youth. A sad, different Germany' (Frieda Lawrence, *"Not I, But the Wind . . ."*, Santa Fe: Rydal Press, 1934, p. 116). She arrived in Florence on 3 December 1919 (*Letters*, iii. 427).

11:8 Nothing more. This is incompatible with the fact that on 29 November 1919 DHL told his friend S. S. Koteliansky 'I have changed altogether £40 of my money – and got Lira 2000 for it' (*Letters*, iii. 425), unless he had unexpectedly received some money (e.g. royalties).

11:12 Norman Douglas Novelist and essayist (1868–1952), born Scotland, met Maurice Magnus in Capri in 1910 (not 'sixteen years ago' – 16:25; see Mark Holloway, *Norman Douglas*, 1967, pp. 177, 246). He met DHL in London *c.* 1913 while working for the *English Review*. In December 1916 he was arrested and charged with indecent assault on a boy of sixteen. Before the court case could be heard, on 2 January 1917, Douglas left England and never returned; he lived in Florence from September 1919 to the summer of 1937.

11:17 Cooks . . . Via Tornabuoni . . . the Lungarno Thos. Cook & Son, famous and pioneering travel agency, 10 Via Tornabuoni, Florence. DHL regularly used their offices abroad as *poste restante* (see *Letters*, iii. 418, 585–7, etc.) . . . Streets running beside the river Arno in Florence: from the Via Tornabuoni, DHL would have walked along the Lungarno Acciaiola to the Ponte Vecchio (11:19) and from there along the Lungarno Gen. Diaz to the Piazza Mentana.

11:24 **the Cavalotti** A recreation of the Pensione Balestri, 5 Piazza Mentana, where Douglas had been staying since September and where in 1919 DHL had a 'room over the river' (*Letters*, iii. 422: see also 12:33). During the first five days of his stay he referred to the pension as 'Balestra' (*Letters*, iii. 418–20). In E1 the name is changed to 'Cavelotti' (p. 13); it is unclear why. In *Aaron's Rod*, DHL recreated it as the Pensione Nardini (see *Aaron's Rod*, ed. Mara Kalnins, Cambridge, 1988, 206:32–207:32); this was the actual name of the pension (at 7, Piazza del Duomo) where Douglas was living in 1921. The Balestri had charged 5–7 lire a day in 1911 and was one of the cheapest pensions, but by 1919 was charging 10 fr. (the equivalent of 10 lire) a day (12:15) for full board, with 10 fr. a week more for heat, light and washing – 'about 85 francs a week, including *everything*, save wine' £1 16s 3d at the contemporary rate of exchange ('50 Lira for £1' – *Letters*, iii.424).

11:28 **strutting.** DHL originally wrote 'mincing' (MS, p. 1), a word he uses at 12:20 and (as 'minced') at 15:18.

12:10 **deportment,** In MS DHL first wrote 'stout appearance', then 'get-up', finally 'deportment' (p. 2)

12:31 **tea . . . jam . . . bread.** Cf. Aaron's experience at his pension in *Aaron's Rod*: 'drinking a peculiar brown herb-brew which tasted like nothing else on earth, and eating two thick bits of darkish bread smeared with a brown smear which hoped it was jam, but hoped in vain' (*Aaron's Rod*, ed. Kalnins, 209:12–15).

13:2 **Spitzbergen!** An archetype of coldness and inhospitality, from the archipelago in the Arctic Ocean (named after the sharply pointed mountains which cover it).

13:10 **novel *They Went*.** Published by Martin Secker in September 1920. E1 (p. 14) omitted the title, presumably so as not to identify Douglas with what it printed as 'D——'.

13:22 **1913 Black and White** I.e. whisky made by Buchanans of Glasgow. DHL does not make the modern 'trade' distinction between Scotch 'whisky' and Irish 'whiskey', but uses the words interchangeably (see 13:16–17, 15:34, etc.).

13:34 *Au contraire*—! On the contrary—! (French).

14:38 **"Cos'è? . . . bevo io.** 'What's this? Soup. No thanks. No, none for me. No—*No*!—I don't drink this filthy water' (Italian).

15:5 **wine at three francs a litre.** Cf. DHL to S. S. Koteliansky, 29 November 1919: 'One moves lightly – and then there is wine. It is 3 francs a litre: but with the exchange at 50, still possible' (*Letters*, iii. 425).

15:22 **St Benedict.** Founder (at Montecassino in 529) of the Benedictine order of monks, d. AD 543 (see note on 28:21).

16:17 **Wednesday . . . Thursday.** In fact on the evening of Wednesday 19 November 1919: see *Letters*, iii. 417–18.

16:19 **Isadora Duncan** American dancer and teacher (1878–1927); in MS (p. 6) DHL first wrote 'Isidora' and then corrected it to 'Isadora'. In 1905 Magnus had been business manager of Gordon Craig (1872–1966), the English theatre director and designer, while Craig was having an affair with Duncan; Magnus helped to manage her business at various times. See Louise E. Wright, 'Touring Russia with Isadora: Maurice Magnus' Account', *Dance Chronicle*, xxiii, no. 3 (2000), 233–61.

16:22 **Tiflis . . . the Roman Review** I.e. Tbilisi, capital of Georgia . . . Weekly sixteen-page newspaper of Italian politics, finance, literature, drama, art and archaeology, edited by Magnus; it ran for only twenty-one issues, starting on 2 June 1914 and ending on 4 November.

16:36 **damned tailor. Let the thing wait,** In MS (p. 6) DHL originally wrote 'damned tailor. Let the damned thing wait.' He subsequently deleted the second 'damned', then reinstated it. It seems most likely that, in proof, he was asked about the repetition of 'damned', and took the opportunity to delete it yet again and to insert the comma in place of the full stop in E1 (p. 19).

17:15 **his birthday on the Sunday,** I.e. Sunday 23 November; however, at 72:13 DHL reports that Magnus was born on 7 November 1876.

17:18 **that dinner.** Deleted in MS (p. 7) is 'a fine first-class dinner at Zamboni's' (in the Piazza d'Azeglio).

17:25 **zabaioni** Common British and American spelling of the Italian 'zabaglione', a light foamy dessert of egg yolks, sugar and Marsala wine.

17:39 **infra dig . . . Mercato Nuovo** Beneath one's dignity: DHL would, for example, remark in 1925 that 'public "controversies"' of the kind he found himself having with Norman Douglas over the Magnus essay were '*infra dig.*, anyhow' (*Letters*, v. 256–7) . . . the New Market.

17:40 **Volterra marble, a natural amber colour,** Actually coloured alabaster, as DHL later saw in Volterra, 90 km s.w. of Florence: 'It is nearly as transparent as alum, and nearly as soft. They peel it down as if it were soap, and tint it pink or amber or blue, and turn it into all those things one does not want . . . vases, bowls with doves on the rim, or vine-leaves around, and similar curios' (*Sketches* 162:40–163:5).

18:8 **poorly fed as we were at the pension,** Not the impression of the Balestri DHL gave to Rosalind Baynes on 28 November: 'the food is good and plenty' (*Letters*, iii. 424).

18:38 **famous old monastery south of Rome.** I.e. Montecassino, the Benedictine abbey where Magnus had been visiting since at least 1917.

19:8 **Don Martino,** DHL's recreation of Don Mauro Inguanez (1887–1955), the Maltese Benedictine monk (ordained 1911) who was archivist–librarian at Montecassino from 1912.

19:15 **it was unbearable.** DHL and Frieda spent only *c.* 15–22 December 1919 in Picinisco, in the Abruzzi mountains (see *Letters*, iii. 431–7), having originally planned to spend the winter there.

19:22 **Anzio . . . near Rome.** Coastal resort and port, 50 km s. of Rome. The *Roman Review* (see note on 16:22) occasionally printed an advertisement for the Victoria Hotel, Anzio, '1½ hours from Rome' (see note on 28:29).

19:24 **twenty pounds . . . from America . . . a gift too.** It has been suggested that the money came from the American poet Amy Lowell (1874–1925), whom DHL had known since 1914 (*MMM* 149). However, according to a deletion in MS, it resulted from the 'kindness of some unknown Americans with whom I was personally unacquainted' (p. 9). DHL's American publisher B. W. Huebsch had sent him 'an unexpected £25' on 4 January 1920, a gift (of $100) from the American writers Louis Untermeyer (1885–1977) and Jean Starr Untermeyer (1886–1970), and a Dutch-American businessman Emile Tas; and Huebsch later confirmed that this was the money DHL 'turned over to M M' (*Letters*, iii. 445 and n. 1).

20:5 **bounder.** I.e. distinguished by vulgar or improper manners or behaviour; hence an outsider to decent or middle-class people.

20:23 **in the Palazzo Ferraro . . . the little duomo.** Cf. DHL and Frieda in Capri in 1919, their apartment 'at the top of this old palazzo . . . we can touch the queer bubbly Duomo, almost' (*Letters*, iii. 442).

20:32 **The long three hours** The reading of MS (p. 10); E1 adjusted to 'It was three long hours' (p. 24). The sentence was originally without a verb, which might have occasioned a publisher to introduce the change; there is no evidence of DHL making any other proof changes nearby.

21:2 **the mole** Steamships from Palermo (see note on 36:13) passed various jetties, including the Molo San Vincenzo, on their way in to dock in Naples.

21:18 **diretto! . . . "Parte! Eccolo là!"** The direct (express) train . . . 'It's leaving! There, look!' (Italian).

21:27 **maccheroni.** DHL uses the modern Italian word; 'macaroni' came into the English language in the late sixteenth century, as a version of the earlier Italian word 'maccaroni'.

22:3 **manner; and an odd pompous touch with it which** DHL had written in MS 'He had a certain charm in his manner, a certain odd ~~signoral~~ pompous touch which' (p. 11). The insertion 'with it' is unlikely to have been made by anyone except DHL; the proofs may well have been marked to draw attention to the fact that the sentence used 'certain' twice. Deleting the second, DHL arguably inserted 'with it' and also changed the comma after 'manner' to a semi-colon. At some point, however, 'which' was also deleted; DHL may have mistakenly removed it, or the typist of MS or compositor may have done so. This edition accepts what DHL probably did in proof, while restoring what was inadvertently cut.

22:29 **and he wore spectacles,** Before MS was typed, some small alterations were made in pencil, almost certainly by Robert Mountsier; he crossed out this phrase (p. 12). The Textual apparatus records similar interpolations in MS at 35:21 and 58:9: all have been restored.

23:19 **He, by . . . native languages.** Changed – presumably in proof – to 'He spoke English as if it were his native language' (E1, p. 28). It is hard to see why this change should have been made except as an attempt to protect the identity of Don Mauro Inguanez. Secker may have asked DHL if this is what he wanted, so that the resulting text may possibly be DHL's own. As, however, the identity no longer needs protection, the reading of MS (p. 13) has been preferred.

24:5 **dust-coat.** According to *OED2*, a coat 'worn to keep off the dust'; but DHL must simply mean a light coat.

24:38 **tisickyness** DHL's coinage from 'tis[s]ickiness' and 'tis[s]icky', common and dialect forms of 'phthisis' and 'phthisic', the adjective with the transferred meaning of 'delicate, squeamish' and (in Nottinghamshire dialect) 'dainty, particularly about food'. 'Tisical' can also mean 'consumptive': see note to 155:1.

25:8 **complines.** In Catholic ritual, the last service of the day, completing the services of the canonical hours. E1 (p. 31) altered to 'Compline', but DHL's form is perfectly acceptable: 'In recent times, the plural *complines*, after the Fr. and L. and analogous to *matins*, has come in' (*OED2*).

25:16 **the Benvenuto Cellini casket,** Cellini was a Florentine sculptor, silversmith and goldsmith (1500–71). It is possible that work of his existed at Montecassino, but the marbles there were mostly dated from the rebuilding of the church between 1637 and 1727.

25:25 **cicerone** One who guides and conducts sightseers (Italian).

25:37 **Magnus for the wizard and myself a sort of Parsifal** In Act II of *Parsifal* (1882) by Richard Wagner (1813–83), the evil magician Klingsor attempts to gain power over Parsifal and curses him, so that he will wander hopelessly in search of the castle of Monsalvat, to which he wishes to return.

25:37 **But it . . . York coat.** Replacing the original reading of MS: 'But I hated the famous figures, their self-conscious pietism and their theatrical sanctity' (p. 15).

26:9 **my mother."** Hedwig Rosamunde Magnus, née Liebetrau (born in Berlin, 31 October 1845, died 1912), illegitimate daughter of Kaiser Friedrich III of Germany (1831–88); her tombstone (stone 2350, Zona Terza) in the Protestant Cemetery in Rome records 'Figlia Regis' ('daughter of a king'). She married Charles Ferdinand Magnus in 1867. According to DHL, 'Her portrait by *Paul* is in the *Doria* gallery in Rome' (*Letters*, iv. 186). A photograph (made in Malta) of the portrait survives (UN) but the original is not in the Doria Pamphilis gallery in Rome; the artist was perhaps Georges Hermann René Paul (known as Hermann-Paul) (1864–1940), French illustrator, print-maker and painter.

26:30 **brought me my water.** In houses without running water, water for washing etc., would be brought to the room in a jug.

27:13 **like Tithonus, and cannot die,** In Greek legend, Tithonus was beloved by Aurora, goddess of the dawn; Zeus gave him eternal life but not eternal youth. He grew old and infirm and was turned into a grasshopper. DHL probably knew the poem (composed 1833, published 1860) by Tennyson (1809–92).

27:23 **the dons room at Cambridge,** DHL visited Bertrand Russell at Trinity College, Cambridge, 6–8 March 1915; he dined in hall on the Saturday night, and was doubtless taken to the Senior Common Room after dinner.

27:32 **Bramante courtyard,** The great High Renaissance architect Donato Bramante (?1444–1514) never worked at Montecassino; the only architect of reputation to do so (and only on a single funerary chapel) was Antonio da Sangallo the younger (1484–1546), who had collaborated with Bramante.

28:19   **Lorenzetti ... sixteenth century.**   DHL's knowledge of Pietro Lorenzetti (who worked in Siena *c.* 1306–50) derived in part from his copying of the picture *La Tebaide* (often attributed to Lorenzetti in the early twentieth century) in the Uffizi gallery. See *Letters*, iii. 622 n. 2, and 'Making Pictures' (*Late Essays and Articles*, ed. James T. Boulton, Cambridge, 2004, 231:10).

28:21   **the ancient cell ... where all the sanctity started.**   St Benedict was said to have had his cell near the low passage through the rock which was the original entrance to the monastery; it was restored and decorated in the nineteenth century.

28:29   **a cheque which I made out at Anzio.**   For the Victoria Hotel (see note on 19:22).

29:8   **a couple of letters ... send his material.**   One such letter was probably to the publisher C. W. Daniel, who would (in May 1920) be bringing out DHL's play *Touch and Go* as no. 2 in his series Plays for a People's Theatre. In the course of 1921, Daniel published three of Magnus's translations of the Russian writer Leonid Andreev (*And it Came to Pass that the King was Dead, His Excellency the Governor*, and the drama *To the Stars* as no. 10 of Plays for a People's Theatre). See note on 39:23 for the piece 'about the monastery' (29:10–11).

31:29   **to nothing.**   Substituted in MS (p. 19) for 'rotten.'

32:4   **Lloyd George or Lenin or Briand."**   Premiers of Britain, Russia and France when DHL was writing – David Lloyd-George (1863–1945), British prime minister 1916–22: 'a clever little Welsh *rat*, absolutely dead at the core, sterile, barren, mechanical' (*Letters*, iii 48); Vladimir Ilyich Lenin (1870 1924), first premier of the Soviet Union (1917–24); Aristide Briand (1862–1932), French prime minister eleven times, including 1921–2 (see *Letters*, iv. 133).

32:7   **belongs to the past?"**   Revised in MS (p. 20) from 'is also parasitic?"'

32:15   **He had been married,**   Magnus had married Lucy Seraphine Ardoine Bramley-Moore (1869 1949) on 10 July 1913, but the marriage did not last. See, too note on 62:21.

33:5   **slowly.**   E1 (p. 42) reads 'stoutly', but this is unlikely to be a change by DHL in proof; the word is extremely easy to misread in MS (p. 21), the 'w' looking like a 'u' with an odd upright tail which could be read as a cross-less 't'. The original typist was probably responsible for the change.

33:18   **ferrovieri ... fascisti.**   Railway workers ... fascists (Italian).

33:33   **Trappists.**   Monks of the branch of the Cistercian order observing the reformed rule established in 1664 by De Rancé, abbot of La Trappe, in Normandy. The rule notoriously insisted on the observation of long periods of silence.

34:20   **great Cyclopean wall**   Masonry comprised of very large and irregular stones, commonly found in Greece and Italy, and supposed to be the work of a gigantic Thracian race called Cyclopes (from their King Cyclops); Baedeker's *Southern Italy* (Leipzig, 1930) points out how, on the way up to the monastery, 'At the last bend, to the W. of the summit, on the left, is a piece of cyclopean wall' (p. 18).

34:26   **quick**   Living, alive.

35:21   **sniff at**   MS (p. 23) deletes 'sniff at' and inserts 'smell of' in pencil, an alteration presumably made by Robert Mountsier, who must have noticed the repetition of the words in the next line. E1 (p. 44) printed 'smell of', presumably the reading of the missing setting-copy typescript.

35:24   **her eye . . . living gold of her eyes,**   The slight oddity of the reading of MS (p. 23) probably led Secker to cut everything except 'her eyes' (E1, p. 44).

35:25   **the Lamb of God**   I.e. Jesus (see John i. 29, Revelation xxii. i, etc.).

36:1   **frieze**   A kind of coarse woollen cloth, with a nap usually only on one side.

36:13   **Naples . . . Immacolatella,**   Steamships between Naples and Palermo left from the *Immacolatella nuova*, only fifteen minutes' walk from the main railway station.

36:27   **Girgenti . . . sulphur-miners,**   The old name of Agrigento, on the s.w. coast of Sicily; DHL had visited it on 27 February while looking for a house in Sicily (see *Triumph to Exile* 569). The area was responsible for one-sixth of the entire Sicilian trade in sulphur.

36:34   **I went with my wife down to Syracuse**   DHL originally wrote 'my' and then altered it to 'we', adding 'went down to Syracuse', before substituting 'I went with my wife' in place of 'we', which he now deleted. Robert Mountsier added a pencil comma after 'wife' (MS, p. 24), leaving the text reading 'I went with my wife, went down to Syracuse'. E1 overcame the awkwardness by printing 'I went with my wife to Syracuse' (p. 47). This may have been DHL's correction in proof, but is more likely to be have been Secker's regularisation of the text. This edition has made the smallest possible alteration: when DHL deleted 'we' he probably meant to delete 'we went'. The Lawrences were away from Taormina in Syracuse (95 km s. of Taormina) and Randazzo (30 km w. of Taormina) from *c.* Saturday 24 April until the evening of Tuesday 27 April; Magnus probably arrived in Taormina on the 24th (38:36).

36:36   **Adonis-blood red**   The blood spilled by the dying Adonis (a beautiful youth in Greek myth, loved by the goddess Aphrodite but killed by a wild boar) was in one version of the myth reputed to have stained the anemones. DHL described them again in *The Lost Girl*, ed. John Worthen (Cambridge, 1981), 36:11, and at length in 'Flowery Tuscany', *Sketches* 232:28–233:5; see also that volume's Explanatory note on 232:29.

36:38   **Etna floating now to northward,**   The reading of MS (p. 24). DHL may have altered this in proof, as E1 reads 'Etna flowing now to the northward,' (p. 47); it is also possible that 'flowing' was a typist's error – the 'a' of 'floating' in MS is not joined up, and might have been read as a 'w' – and the inserted 'the' may have been an attempt by someone to smooth out the phrase. MS has not been emended. Mount Etna (3,323 m), in e. Sicily, is the highest volcano in Europe.

37:2   **Odysseus**   One of the foremost of the Greek heroes at the siege of Troy (Roman name Ulysses). His return to his kingdom of Ithaca was fraught with dangers and adventures.

37:5   **Ionian sea . . . our own house**   Between Italy, Sicily and Greece; cf. 'I love the Ionian sea. It is open like a great blue opening in front of us' (*Letters*, iv. 97) and 45:29–30 below . . . the Fontana Vecchia, outside the city of Taormina to the n.e.: 'a nice big house, with fine rooms and a handy kitchen – set in a big garden . . . on a steep slope at some distance above the sea – looking East' (*Letters*, iii. 488).

37:25   **contadini**   Peasants (Italian).

37:29   **San Domenico . . . the most expensive hotel here,**   Baedeker's *Southern Italy* shows that the Grand-Hotel San Domenico, in the old Dominican convent, was indeed the most expensive hotel in Taormina; more expensive than, for example, the Hotel Bristol (39:6), the Hotel Fichera (39:6) or the Hotel Timeo (42:9), where DHL has his 'engagement to lunch' (40:26).

39:21   **a man in Alexandria . . . Taylor, who was my *greatest* friend, in London.** Neither is identifiable.

39:23   **article . . . accepted by Land and Water**   It appeared as 'Holy Week at Montecassino' in the London magazine *Land and Water* on 29 April 1920, pp. 14–15. DHL had asked Francis Brett Young (*Letters*, viii. 124–5) on 8 March 1920 for the 'name and address of *Land and Water* man, *please*, for Magnus' (*Letters*, iii. 480).

39:38   **salotta.**   E1 (p. 51) emended here and at 46:34 to the correct Italian, 'salotto' (sitting-room). DHL may have confused the word with 'sala' (room), as in a letter to the original owner of the house, Marie Hubrecht, 18 April 1920: 'We have painted the shelves in our "Salotta" bright green' (*Letters*, iii. 506).

40:35   **pick such dreadful people up for?"**   The reading of MS (p. 28); E1's 'pick up such dreadful people for?' (p. 52) is more likely to be a regularising typist, compositor or publisher than DHL.

42:6   **Pancrazio Melenda**   Of the fifteen occurrences of the name in MS, the first four appear as 'Melenga', the remainder as 'Melenda': the latter has been editorially adopted (E1 chose to adopt 'Melenga'). The man's real name was 'Cipolla' (which DHL wrote but then deleted in MS, p. 29). 'Pancrazio' was a common name in Taormina: the church of San Pancrazio (patron saint of Taormina) lay beside the road to the Lawrences' house (see note on 37:5).

46:20   **I am not God who is responsible for him."**   Cf. 'Let the God that created him be responsible for his death . . .' ('Man and Bat', *Poems* 346).

46:35   **mi ha dato questa lettera per Lei!—"**   'has given me this letter for you!—' (Italian).

47:9   **"Ma senta,** 'But listen, (Italian).

47:33   **Si, lo so! [47:26] . . . poverina . . . E non viene mai niente . . . Ecco come è!"**   Yes, that's how it is . . . poor thing . . . but nothing ever comes . . . and that's how it is!' (Italian).

47:38   **Si signore, è vero.**   Yes sir, it's true (Italian).

48:4   **"Già! Già! Molto meglio,**   'Right! Right! Much better,' (Italian).

48:22   **"Allora!**   'Well then! (Italian).

49:1   **"Siccuro!**   'Exactly! (Italian).

50:8   **Catania,**   Major seaport town on the e. coast of Sicily, 45 km s. of Taormina, with a direct rail link.

50:29   **he owns a newspaper . . . in Rome.**   In 1914, Magnus had edited (but not owned) the *Roman Review* (see note on 16:22). No advertisement for any Sicilian lodgings ever appeared in it, only for the hotel in Anzio which would later accuse Magnus of failing to pay his bill (see notes on 19:22 and 28:29).

51:4   **parasites who . . . inevitably swindling—**   Substituted in MS (p. 36) for 'creatures who make mistakes.'

51:8   *qualche affaro di truffa*,   Some affair of swindling, (Italian).

51:12   **A friend . . . to Malta.**   Mary Cannan (1867–1950) . . . the party left Taormina on Monday 17th – not 'Thursday' (51:19) – hoping to cross to Malta that day, spend 18th–20th there and get back to Taormina on Friday 21st. Because of the strike, they did not get to Malta until Wednesday 19th, and did not get back to Taormina until the evening of Thursday 27th.

51:25   **A tout**   One who solicits custom, for hotels, etc. ('ticket tout' dates only from the mid twentieth century).

51:32   **Grand Hotel,**   I.e. the Grand Hôtel in the Piazza Mazzini, Syracuse, with thirty-four beds, right on the harbour on the n.w. of the 'Island'.

51:34   **many bloodstains . . . on the bedroom walls.**   Cf. DHL'S poem 'The Mosquito' (*Poems* 332–4) which is given the place of origin '*Siracusa*'.

52:7   **burnooses**   'A mantle or cloak with a hood, an upper garment extensively worn by Arabs and Moors' (*OED2*); more commonly 'burnouses', but DHL's spelling was in use as late as 1975.

52:14   **on the island . . . Greek columns . . . in the walls.**   The old city of Syracuse is on an island called Ortygia (see 54:38) separated from the mainland by a narrow channel; there was a lighthouse at the southern tip of the island . . . The Cathedral is built on the site (and includes many of the remains) of a Greek temple known as the Temple of Minerva; nineteen of the old columns are visible, 8 m high and 2 m thick.

52:24   **Casa Politi,**   I.e. the Hotel des Etrangers Casa Politi in the Via Nizza; not 'the other hotel along the front' – the Grand Hôtel – but also with a sea view, and almost as expensive.

53:5   **sleevelinks**   Predating the modern equivalent 'cufflinks'.

54:38   **Ortygia, past the two lighthouses,**   See note on 52:14.

55:7   **brutta mezz'ora**   Nasty half hour (Italian).

55:28   **dégagé**   At ease, unconstrained (French).

56:15   **Dreadnoughts**   *Dreadnought* was the name of the first of a new class of heavy British battleships launched on 18 February 1906, which provoked Germany and other maritime powers into building similar ships. The name quickly became applied to any large battleship.

56:36   **Great Britain Hôtel.**   Where DHL and party stayed in May 1920, at 67 Strada Mezzodi; Magnus stayed 'a little further down our street' (57:1) at the Hotel Osborne, 50 Strada Mezzodi.

56:38   **Strada Reale,**   According to Baedeker's *Southern Italy*, 'extending from St Elmo to the Porta Reale, a distance of more than ½ M., is the principal street' (p. 392).

57:21   **the strike of steamers still,**   Cf. DHL, 20 and 24 May 1920: 'there's an Italian steamer-strike, so we don't know when we shall get back', 'We came here for two days – kept here for eight by the Sicilian steamer strike' (*Letters*, iii. 529, 531).

57:23   **St. Paul's Bay . . . the other islands.**   St Paul was shipwrecked on the n. coast of Malta in AD 61, 9 km n. of Città Vecchia (see note on 57:39) . . . i.e. Gozo and Comino, n.w. of Malta.

57:26   **Gabriel Mazzaiba . . . Salonia.**   DHL's names for Michael Borg (the real name 'Borg' mistakenly used twice in MS, p. 44), and Walter Salomone. DHL spelled the name 'Mazzaibba' three times (MS, pp. 41–2) before settling on the name and spelling this edition has adopted.

57:36   **bathbrick:**   Properly 'Bath-brick', 'a preparation of calcareous earth moulded in form of a brick, made at Bridgwater; used for cleaning polished metal' (*OED2*).

57:39   **the old capital**   I.e. Città Vecchia or La Notabile, 13 km w. of Valletta, with the Cathedral of St Paul.

58:11   **I forgot . . . a few trees . . . summer villa.**   The paragraph was omittted from E1 because of the pencil note 'leave out' almost certainly made by Robert Mountsier in MS (p. 42), which influenced the typist of the missing setting-copy typescript. DHL probably refers to the 'luxuriantly wooded gorge of *Macluba*, 120 ft deep' (Baedeker, *Southern Italy*, p. 395).

58:23   **Rabato, the suburb of the old town**   Rabato is just to the w. of Città Vecchia; from his house at 1, Strada S. Pietro, Magnus could take a 'five or six miles walk' (58:33) to the s.w. Maltese coast.

59:22   **a more correct version.**   Still not entirely correct; see Appendix IX ('The Death of Maurice Magnus') for a full account.

61:2   **Gib.**   I.e. Gibraltar.

61:12   **Senglea.**   Suburb of Valletta, on a peninsula protruding into the Great Harbour, where Michael Borg lived, and coincidentally the place of birth of Don Mauro Inguanez. DHL's 'Senglea' in MS (p. 45), with the first 'e' compressed into a single loop, was read as 'Singlea' both by the original typist (thus getting into E1, p. 82) and by A3 (p. 90).

61:23   **extradicted**   Salomone's amalgamation of 'extradited' ('surrendered to another country or state a person accused or convicted of a crime committed there') with 'indicted' ('to have a charge brought against someone . . . since 1600 written *indict*, though the spoken word remains *indite*' – *OED2*).

61:40   **Floriana Civil Hospital**   The hospital in Floriana, the western suburb of Valletta, location of the main railway station.

62:21   **his wife refused . . . a decent funeral.**   Magnus's wife (see note on 32:15) later refunded the expenses (see 62:29–30). Magnus was buried in the Borg plot of Addolorata Cemetery (see Appendix IX).

63:10   **the Judas treachery . . . betraying with a kiss**   Cf. Matthew xxvi. 47–9, Mark xiv. 43–5, etc.

63:14   **not a criminal:**   DHL originally wrote 'no criminal' in MS (p. 47); he altered it to 'perhaps not quite criminal' before settling on the final reading.

63:24   **Bel-Abbès.**   Now Sidi Bel Abbes, walled city situated in the n.w. of Algeria, 75 km from the Mediterranean Sea; the headquarters of the Foreign Legion, and the principal setting for chaps. 2–19 of Magnus's book. Magnus described the 'disgust and loathing' he felt for 'the awful depravity, beastliness, and filth' there (E1, pp. 255–6).

63:27 *De mortui nihil nisi verum.* About the dead, nothing except the truth. (Latin): DHL's version of a translation of the Greek philosopher Chilon (7th century BC) concluding 'nisi bene' – 'except the good'.

63:32 **"girants"** DHL is right to wonder about the 'actual word': Magnus must have heard 'girond', French slang (first recorded 1872) for a passive male homosexual.

63:35 **Benissimo!** Very good! (Italian).

64:15 *Alles in Ehren!* Everything honourable! (German).

64:21 **"Il mio onore costa a Lei dieci mila Lire."** 'My honour costs you ten thousand Lire.' (Italian).

64:29 **Just so . . . old dodge.** Replacing the original reading of MS (p. 49): 'Just prostitution, keeping up appearances.'

64:34 **"È stato sempre generoso,"** 'He's always been generous,' (Italian).

65:13 **Magnus! Magni sumus!** Magnus [or 'Big']! We are big! (Latin).

65:23 **Astarte, Cybele, Bel, Dionysos.** Astarte, Cybele and Bel were all versions of the Great Mother, the great female principle: Astarte a Semitic goddess, sometimes called the Syrian goddess, 'latterly of lunar nature' (Sir Edward B. Tylor, *Primitive Culture*, 1903, ii. 301, which DHL read in April 1916 – *Letters*, ii. 593); Cybele the Phrygian goddess of fruitfulness; Bel a Phoenician Sun goddess. Dionysos was the Greek god of wine and fruitfulness (counterpart of the Roman god Bacchus); see *Letters*, ii. 517 and n. 2.

66:4 **angels, like Lucifer, which fall.** Traditionally, Lucifer was one of the angels whom God ejected from heaven: 'How art thou fallen from heaven, O Lucifer, son of the morning' (Isaiah xiv. 12).

66:20 *Boches!* Germans!

66:22 **Count de R.** Count Louis de Renneville; descendant of the sixteenth-century noble family.

66:26 **Hohenzollern** German noble family which provided rulers of Brandenburg and Prussia; the last kings of Prussia (1871–1918) were also emperors of Germany, including Kaiser Friedrich III (see note on 26:9).

66:30 **Valbonne,** Small French town in Provence, 10 km from Cannes, where Magnus was sent after his time in Algeria. He described how his hatred of 'the awful depravity, beastliness, and filth' of Bel-Abbès 'turned here into horror' (E1, pp. 255–6).

66:39 **"littérateur,"** 'Literary man', often used pejoratively (see e.g. 323:14, 18).

67:33 **Yes yes, [67:18] . . . it to him,** Replacing the original reading of MS:

> As for myself – why do I write this memoir? – Why? – Because Magnus's book should have its place in the world. We *must* square ourselves with things as they are. And if we don't want to we must be made to. The white-livered sanctified Magnusites of this world can throw mud if they like.
>
> Secondly I want Mazzaiba to be paid back, and he will never be paid back unless this book pays him. Magnus was a cur to borrow from the poor fellow who wanted to marry and hadn't really enough money or prospects to marry on: but who lent these fifty or sixty pounds to that pink-faced pigeon of a love-Judas, because he wished to help him. (pp. 52–3)

69:7 Stendhal . . . Dos Passos . . . *Three Soldiers* The quotation runs: '*Les contemporains qui souffrent de certaines choses ne peuvent s'en souvenir qu'avec une horreur qui paralyse tout autre plaisir, même celui de lire un conte*' ('Contemporaries who suffer from certain things can only remember them with a horror which paralyses all other pleasure, even that of reading a story'). The source is the first paragraph of chap. XXVII of *Le Rouge et le Noir* (1831) by Henri Beyle [Stendhal] (1783–1842). DHL wrote 'Los' for 'Dos' three times in MS, pp. 54–5; he made the same error in his letter to Mountsier of 26 January 1922 which accompanied the MS of the *Memoir* to America (*Letters*, iv. 178 and n. 3). He seems to have read the book (1919) by John Dos Passos (1896–1970) by December 1921, when he sent 'an American novel I thought amusing' (*Letters*, iv. 151) to Catherine Carswell (see note on 309:26).

69:20 Flaubert . . . his own, See 'La Légende de Saint Julien l'Hospitalier' (1877) by Gustave Flaubert (1821–80), in which Julien is asked by a leper: '"Take off your clothes, because I need the warmth of your body! . . . Come close, warm me! Not with your hands! no! your whole body." Julien spread himself out completely on him, mouth to mouth, stomach to stomach'. See *Studies* 158:7, 160:1.

69:21 *Know Thyself.* Motto, inscribed on the temple of Apollo at Delphi, and attributed by Plato (*Protagoras* 343) to the Seven Wise Men; Juvenal (*Satires* xi. 27) cites it as coming from heaven. See too 'The Proper Study' and 'On Being a Man', *Reflections* 169–70 and 217.

70:19 man in the Dos Passos book I.e. John Andrews, who goes through dreadful experiences, and deserts from the American army, but is captured by the military police on the book's last page.

70:37 I do not try [70:31] . . . true justice. Replacing the original reading of MS: 'Who am I to forgive? Only gods can forgive. But justice is a sacred human right. Gods are above justice. But men can only live by being just, and justice alone is peace in death – not forgiveness' (p. 56).

71:7 is machines . . . experience again. Replacing the original reading of MS: 'shall go, for ever, like some unthinkable disease which we have brought about' (p. 56).

71:11 power of man . . . well as I. Replacing the original reading of MS: 'jurisdiction of man. I have said it. Say it then, you also, who are a man' (p. 56).

72:12 Lethe. From Greek mythology: the river in the underworld that caused forgetfulness in those who drank its waters. The word is evidence that DHL was able to correct the memoir's proofs before publication (see Introduction, pp. xci–xcii); 'peace' was the reading of MS (p. 58).

72:15 Mr Liebetrau Magnus, DHL misunderstood Magnus's complex family tree; see note on 26:9.

72:19 importance manqué, E1 reads 'importance *manqué*' (p. 93) while MS reads 'importance, royal importance manqué' (p. 58). A possible case of Secker cutting prolixity, as elsewhere (see, e.g., Textual apparatus at 71:5 and 71:7); but given that DHL was undoubtedly at work in the proofs nearby (at the proof stage he altered 'peace' to 'Lethe' at 72:12 and at 72:20 he added 'apparently') it seems probable that he was responsible for the verbal change here, though not for the italics.

72:24 He faced his way Before DHL expanded it, the original ending of MS was:

He faced his way through that Legion experience: royal blood dragging itself through the sewers, without being quenched.

Ich grüsse dich, Maurice! In der Ewigkeit.

D. H. Lawrence   (p. 58)

72:30   **A little more than kin, and less than kind.**   *Hamlet* I. ii. 65.

72:32   **Also—Maurice! . . . Leid nachgelassen**   Well then – Maurice! I salute you, in eternity. But here, in the heart's depths, you have left a legacy of poison and grief (German: native-speakers would probably say 'hinterlassen' rather than 'nachgelassen').

'The Bad Side of Books': introduction to *A Bibliography of the Writings of D. H. Lawrence*

75:2   **at the foot of the Rockies,**   The Lawrences had moved up to the Kiowa ranch on Lobo mountain at the start of May 1924; 'a little ranch, 120 acres, at the foot of the mountains, mostly pine trees. It's pretty wild . . .' (*Letters*, iv. 38).

75:7   **a bibliography.**   See Introduction, pp. lvii–lviii.

75:11   **never read one of my own published works.**   In Mexico during the winter of 1924–5 DHL would read *The White Peacock*; he told the journalist Kyle Crichton in the summer of 1925 that 'It seemed strange and far off and as if written by somebody else' (Nehls, ii. 414).

75:13   **fount?**   Up to the middle of the twentieth century, an alternative spelling of 'font'.

75:14   **what pleasure is there in that?**   Revised in MS (p. 1) from 'what is there but bitterness!'

75:16   *The White Peacock* **. . . she was dying.**   DHL's first novel had been published by William Heinemann (1863–1920) on 19 January 1911; an advance copy, which DHL had been 'day by day anxious to receive' (*Letters*, i. 181), arrived on 2 December 1910 in Eastwood, where he was helping to nurse Lydia Lawrence (1851–1910) in her last illness. She did not read it, and died on 9 December; her funeral took place on 12 December. See *Early Years* 143, 271.

75:21   **Somewhere, in . . . respect for me.**   Revised in MS (p. 1) from 'Privately, she had considerable respect for me.'

75:22   **This David . . . at Goliath.**   See 1 Samuel xvii. 4–58; metaphorically, never successfully attack the large and threatening enemy.

75:29   **my father**   Arthur John Lawrence (1847–1924).

86:2   **Fifty pounds,**   For *The White Peacock* Heinemann paid DHL royalties (15 per cent of the published price of 6s). The sum of £50 represents the advance DHL was promised on publication, £15 of which in fact he received early, in September 1910 (*Letters*, i. 177n.).

76:2   **Ernest Hooley**   Ernest Terah Hooley (1859–1947), born in Sneinton, Nottingham, notorious stockbroker and financier, had been bankrupted in 1898. Convicted and sentenced to three years' penal servitude for fraud in 1922, he had been released from Parkhurst prison on 18 July 1924 (DHL may well have heard of this). In 1925 Hooley published his *Confessions*; see too *The Hooley Book; the Amazing Financier* (1904).

76:2 **my sister** Possibly Emily Una (1882–1962), but more likely Lettice Ada (1887–1948); see *Letters*, i. 27 n. 3 and 36 n. 1.

76:9 **a bone . . . to pick with me** To have a bone to pick with someone is to have a disagreement or dispute; a bone of contention.

76:10 **saw him once:** At their meeting on 19 January 1910, Heinemann had 'read me his readers crits' of *The White Peacock* (*Letters*, i. 152).

76:24 **at the last minute [76:13] . . . the paragraph unchanged . . . sent me ahead.** DHL's account is not entirely accurate. As well as rewriting the 'marked paragraph' on p. 230, he made changes to another sentence on the same page, as well as to a sentence on p. 227. Heinemann was unable to effect changes in copies already bound, so that a number of copies survive with both cancelled pages intact, not just the 'one copy' DHL gave to his mother (see Roberts 6). Some of the January 1911 copies and all of the March 1911 reprint of the book, however, have the revised pages integral with the signature, and all subsequent reprints by Duckworth and Secker contain the revised text. See *The White Peacock*, ed. Andrew Robertson (Cambridge, 1983), pp. xxxiv–xxxv.

76:28 *Sons and Lovers* **. . . he refused to publish it . . . deceased gentleman's reading** Heinemann (who had died in 1920) turned the novel down on 1 July 1912, writing to DHL: 'its want of reticence makes it unfit, I fear, altogether for publication in England as things are . . . a book far less outspoken would certainly be damned' (*Letters*, i. 421 n. 4). See also next note.

76:30 **the first appearance of** *The Trespasser* **and of** *Sons and Lovers.* *The Trespasser* was published on 23 May 1912 and *Sons and Lovers* on 29 May 1913, both by Duckworth. DHL was abroad on both occasions. See *The Trespasser*, ed. Elizabeth Mansfield (Cambridge, 1981), pp. 22–3, and *Sons and Lovers* lix–lx.

76:38 **in Italy, I re-wrote . . . forbore with me.** DHL misremembers. He revised the MS of the play in Germany during August 1913 and sent it to Kennerley, but was shocked to find, after moving to Fiascherino in Italy, that Kennerley had already had the play set up in type from an unrevised typescript. DHL now realised that he had 'caused trouble by coming in so late with my revision of the play' (*Letters*, ii. 72). He received proofs in Fiascherino on 4 October, briefly 'wrestled with them' (*Letters*, ii. 79–80) in an attempt to recreate the text of his revised MS, then gave up and waited for his MS revisions to be inserted into the proofs in America. What Kennerley was 'noble' enough to tolerate was an author sending in a heavily revised text after his unrevised text had already been set up in type. See *Plays* xxxix–xli. Mitchell Kennerley (1878–1950), American publisher and editor, became DHL's publisher in the USA with *The Trespasser* in 1912.

77:7 **a cheque for twenty pounds [76:40] . . . for nothing** It is impossible now to be absolutely sure of the justice (or more likely the injustice) of this charge. In the autumn of 1913, Kennerley promised a cheque for £25 'on acc. of *Sons and Lovers*' (*Letters*, ii. 99). It is not known if this ever arrived, but in April 1914 DHL did record receiving '£35 from Kennerley' (*Letters*, ii. 165; see also n. 1). In spite of the comment in the footnote, this sum may well have included money for DHL's play *The Widowing of Mrs. Holroyd* (published by Kennerley on 1 April 1914). There was, however, a cheque for £10 for *Sons and Lovers* (*Letters*, ii. 190) sent early in 1914 which a London bank refused to cash and which DHL had to return to Kennerley (*Letters*, ii. 174), and which may never have been made good: this cheque is most likely to be the one DHL remembered. His relations with Kennerley became increasingly strained; by January 1917 he was complaining that Kennerley 'has swindled me unscrupulously', and was repeating the tale of the bad cheque (*Letters*, iii. 74). See also 'Texts' above.

77:15   **the first edition of *The Rainbow* [77:9] . . . the deluge . . . *Peccavi*! . . . the now be-knighted gentleman.**   *The Rainbow* – its English edition actually bound not in 'blue' (88:21) but dark green: DHL may have possessed a Colonial edition acquired in Australia in 1922 (see Frieda Lawrence, *"Not I, But the Wind . . ."*, p. 113) – was published on 30 September 1915, and prosecuted at Bow Street Magistrate's Court on 13 November. Its publisher Methuen did not defend it and a spokesman commented: 'no doubt the firm acted unwisely in not scrutinising the book again more carefully, and they regretted having published it' (*The Times*, 15 November 1915, p. 3). See *The Rainbow*, ed. Mark Kinkead-Weekes (Cambridge, 1989), pp. xlviii–l . . . Cf. Genesis ix. 11–17 . . . 'I have sinned!' (Latin) . . . Algernon Methuen (who did not himself appear in court) was knighted in 1916 (n.b. the pun on 'benighted').

77:19   **Arnold Bennett and May Sinclair . . . John Galsworthy**   Arnold Bennett (1867–1931), novelist and journalist, referred to *The Rainbow* as a 'beautiful and maligned novel' in December 1915; the novelist May Sinclair (1863–1942) apparently wrote a letter saying 'that the suppression of the book was a crime, the murder of a beautiful thing'. DHL and Galsworthy (1867–1933) met on 16 November 1917 (*Triumph to Exile* 413–14), which may have been the occasion for the remark, and, in 1915, Galsworthy had described the book as 'aesthetically detestable' (see *The Rainbow*, ed. Kinkead-Weekes, pp. lxxiii–xxxiv).

77:26   **him who gives as much as him who takes.**   Cf. Portia's speech on mercy in *The Merchant of Venice*, IV. i. 183–4: 'It is twice blest, / It blesseth him that gives and him that takes'.

77:27   **let no dog bark.**   *The Merchant of Venice*, I. i. 93–4: 'I am Sir Oracle, / And when I ope my lips, let no dog bark'.

77:30   **all been mutilated.**   DHL noted in December 1915 some of the excisions in the American edition published by Benjamin Huebsch in 1916: 'they make me sad and angry' (*Letters*, ii. 480). See also *The Rainbow*, ed. Kinkead-Weekes, pp. xliv n. 34 and lvii.

77:31   **my novels . . . *Women in Love*.**   Revised in MS (p. 4) from 'my books' . . . *Women in Love* was published in 1920 by Seltzer and 1921 by Secker; see *Women in Love*, ed. David Farmer, Lindeth Vasey and John Worthen (Cambridge, 1987).

77:36   **the wind bloweth where it listeth.**   John iii. 8.

78:9   **books.**   Revised in MS (p. 4) from 'real books'.

Introduction to *Max Havelaar*

81:2 *Max Havelaar* A novel by Eduard Douwes Dekker (1820–87), who used the pseudonym 'Multatuli' (see 81:18). Dekker was born in Amsterdam, and worked for the Dutch East Indian Civil Service from 1838 to 1856. *Max Havelaar, or the Coffee Auctions of the Dutch Trading Company*, based on the events that led Dekker to resign his post as Assistant Resident in Lebak, in western Java, was written in 1859. Dekker spent much of the rest of his life campaigning for political reform in the Dutch colonies. He was admired by Freud, who quoted from him in 'The Sexual Enlightenment of Children' (1907).

81:3 **nearly seventy years ago,** The novel was first published in 1860.

81:7 **Mr. Bernard Shaw,** George Bernard Shaw (1856–1950), Irish writer and dramatist, was the author of the *Fabian Manifesto* (1884).

81:9 **whom we might call the pre-Fabians,** Social and political reformers who worked before the founding of the Fabian Society in 1884. The Fabians themselves were a group of prominent intellectuals of the Left who advocated gradual reform rather than revolutionary action. Apart from Shaw, the leading members of the Society were Thomas Davidson and Beatrice and Sidney Webb.

81:23 *Uncle Tom's Cabin.* A novel by the American author Harriet Beecher Stowe (1811–96), published in 1852. It became an immediate best-seller and caused an upsurge of popular feeling against slavery in the United States.

81:28 **The Netherlands government . . . in Java,** *Max Havelaar* is generally felt to have influenced subsequent developments in Dutch colonial policy, and in particular to have hastened the abolition, from 1862 onwards, of the system whereby the government prescribed centrally the kind and quantity of crops to be grown on the colonial plantations.

82:10 *Old People and Things that Pass* **(Louis Couperus)** Louis Marie Couperus (1863–1923), Dutch novelist, was born in The Hague, and spent his boyhood in the East Indies. His first successful novel was *Eline Vere* (1889; published in English translation 1892). *Van oude menschen, de dingen die voorbijgaan* (1906) was translated, by Alexander Teixeira de Mattos, as *Old People and the Things that Pass* (1919, reprinted 1923).

82:21 **w. p. b.!** Waste paper basket.

82:22 **justify God to man,** *Paradise Lost*, by John Milton (1608–74), Book I, l. 25 ('And justifie the wayes of God to men').

82:28 **a good beadle,** A beadle was a parish constable, appointed by the vestry to keep order during church services.

83:12 **Jean Paul Richter** Jean Paul Friedrich Richter (1763–1825), usually known as Jean Paul, German novelist, born in Bavaria. His work was introduced into England by Thomas Carlyle (1795–1881) who translated *Flegeljahre* (1805) as *Wild Oats*, and whose own *Sartor Resartus* (1833) owes much to Jean Paul's influence. Jean Paul's fragment of *Autobiography* would not of itself lend much support to the view presented here, but DHL may have had in mind the work known as *Flower, Fruit, and Thorn Pieces*, a longer title for the novel *Siebenkäs* (1817), which he had asked Catherine Carswell to send him in November 1916 (*Letters*, iii. 38), and in which the hero's desire for freedom from bourgeois restraints is so extreme that he eventually fakes his own death. In one of his 'dream poems' of 1800, *Die wunderbare Gesellschaft in der Neujahrsnacht* (*The Marvellous Company at New Year's Eve*), Jean Paul remarks on 'the bitter time when humanity was found in no hearts but in those of dogs' (translation by Dorothea Berger).

83:14 **the later Mark Twain.** Mark Twain was the pseudonym of Samuel Langhorne Clemens (1835–1910), American writer, author of *The Adventures of Huckleberry Finn* (1884). The late misanthropic works that DHL alludes to include *The Man That Corrupted Hadleyburg* (1900), *What Is Man* (first published anonymously in 1906), and, in particular, *The Mysterious Stranger* (1916).

83:19 **Drystubble,** The character Droogstoppel, a complacent and insensitive Dutch bourgeois, is the self-betraying narrator of large sections of the novel.

83:37 **the famous idyll of Saïdyah and Adinda,** Chapter 17 of *Max Havelaar* tells the story of Saïdyah, a Javanese peasant forced to leave his village by poverty, mainly caused by the persistent thefts, by local native chiefs, of the buffaloes which were the family's only means of subsistence. After three years' work as a servant in Batavia (now Jakarta), Saïdyah returns to keep his pledge to his betrothed Adinda, to find that she and the rest of her family have been driven by a similar impoverishment to take part in a rebellious uprising, and have been massacred by Dutch soldiers. The story was printed, in a translation by Baron Nahuys, in vol. XX (9493–9505) of the *International Library of Famous Literature*, an anthology edited by Richard Garnett, published in 1900, which DHL's brother Ernest had bought, and which, according to Jessie Chambers, was much treasured in the Lawrence household (*Early Years* 111).

84:22 **Swift . . . Gogol** Jonathan Swift (1667–1745), Irish writer and satirist, born in Dublin, where, in 1713, he was installed as Dean of St Patrick's Cathedral. Among his most celebrated satirical works are *Gulliver's Travels* (1726), whose concluding chapter, 'A Voyage to the Country of the Houyhnhnms', was long regarded as the last word in misanthropy, and *A Modest Proposal for Preventing the Children of poor People in Ireland from being a burden to their Parents or Country* (1729) . . . Nikolai Vasilievich Gogol (1809–52), Russian writer and dramatist, born in the Ukraine, author of the satirical comedy *The Government Inspector* (1836) and the novel *Dead Souls* (1842).

84:27 **Voltaire** Pseudonym of François Marie Arouet (1694–1778), French author, freethinker and opponent of orthodox Catholicism, one of the leading figures in the French Enlightenment. He was born in Paris, and lived on the fringes of various European courts, including the English, which he visited in the late 1720s. His most famous works are the satirical novel *Candide* (1759) and the *Dictionnaire philosophique* (1764).

84:29 **the Governor-General and Slimering,** In the novel these characters are respectively Havelaar's overall and immediate superiors, who, through a combination of *realpolitik*, adherence to official procedure, and moral cowardice, fail to back him up when he accuses the native Regent of corruption and complicity in murder.

84:30 **Jack and the Beanstalk,** A folk tale with variant forms, common to many European countries. In the English version, Jack sells his mother's cow in exchange for some magic beans, which his mother angrily throws into the garden. The next day a beanstalk has grown, reaching into the clouds. Jack climbs to the top, steals gold (in some versions a goose which lays golden eggs) from the giant who lives there, and manages to escape back to earth and chop down the beanstalk before the giant can capture him.

84:33 **David thought of a sling and stone.** 1 Samuel xvii. 49. The shepherd-boy David rescued the kingdom of Israel from the Philistines by killing the Philistine champion Goliath with a stone thrown from a sling.

84:35 *À la guerre comme à la guerre.* In war as in war (French), i.e. forget niceties and act as the situation demands.

84:38 **a comfit.** A sweet or bonbon, usually a piece of fruit, or a nut such as an almond, with a sugar coating.

Introduction (version 1) to *The Memoirs of the Duc de Lauzun*

87:10 **Sterne** Laurence Sterne (1713–68), Irish-born novelist, author of *The Life and Opinions of Tristram Shandy* (1759–67) and *A Sentimental Journey through France and Italy* (1768).

87:13 **an east-end music-hall,** Music halls were popular variety theatres. The East End is a predominantly working-class area of London.

87:14 **Restif de la Bretonne.** Nicolas Edmé (1734–1806), known as Restif de la Bretonne, French writer. He produced more than 250 novels and stories, the most famous of which appeared in the collection *Les Contemporains, ou Aventures des plus jolies femmes de l'âge présent* (*Contemporaries, or the adventures of the prettiest women of the present age*), 1780–5.

87:16 **The Duc de Lauzun** Armand Louis de Gontaut, Duc de Lauzun, later Duc de Biron (1747–94), belonged to one of the oldest families of the French nobility. His *Memoirs*, written in 1783–4, give a frank account of his amorous exploits, his military adventures, and the courtly intrigues in which he was involved during the first thirty-five years of his life. He subsequently fell out of favour at the court of Louis XVI, and became instead a supporter of the Duc d'Orléans, joining the National Assembly in 1789 as an enthusiast for the Revolution. In 1791 he was given command of the Army of the North, and thereafter styled himself Biron, Citizen General of the Army. His failure to deal with the situation in the Vendée in a manner satisfactory to the Tribunal led to his arrest and eventual execution on New Year's Day, 1794.

87:18 **Louis XV** King of France from 1715 to 1774.

87:21 **Jean Jacques,** Jean-Jacques Rousseau (1712–78), born in Geneva, the leading figure in pre-Romantic literature and thought; he believed that society corrupted man's natural goodness. His best-known works are *La Nouvelle Héloise* (1761), *Le Contrat social* (1762) and the *Confessions* (written 1764–70).

87:26 **homunculus** From the diminutive of Latin 'homo' (man); hence 'little man', or 'mannikin'.

87:27 **the *homme de bien* . . . "man of feeling,"** The editor of *Phoenix*, Edward D. McDonald, gave this essay the title 'The Good Man' (750–54). DHL had originally headed his manuscript 'The Duc de Lauzun', but crossed this out and left the piece untitled (see Introduction, p. xcv). The eighteenth-century idea of the 'good man' or 'man of feeling' was largely derived from classical praise of the happy life of the farmer, in Virgil's *Georgics*, ii. 458ff., and the opening of Horace's second Epode ('Beatus ille...' – 'Happy the man ...'). This tradition had undergone several mutations in the seventeenth and early eighteenth centuries, with the pleasures of sensibility coming to take precedence over the Stoic and mystic elements in the classical sources, and by the time of *The Man Of Feeling* (1771), a novel by Henry Mackenzie (1745–1831), 'feeling' had almost become synonymous with sentimentality. See Maren-Sofie Rostvig, *The Happy Man: Studies in the Metamorphoses of a Classical Ideal* (2nd edition, Oslo, 1971).

87:32 **Diderot.** Denis Diderot (1713–84), writer and philosopher, editor of the *Encyclopédie* (1751–72), was one of the leading figures of the French Enlightenment. His other works include *Jacques le fataliste et son mâitre* (1771–3).

88:2 **a Robot.** This word was still fairly new in 1926. It was derived from the Czech 'robota', meaning forced labour, and was first used in Karel Capek's 1921 play *R.U.R.* (*Rossum's Universal Robots*).

88:8 **Woodrow Wilson** DHL made numerous derogatory references to Wilson (1856–1924), who was President of the USA from 1912 to 1921, and the chief instigator of the League of Nations; e.g. 'Woodrow Wilson ... never had the right smell' ('Blessed Are The Powerful', *Reflections* 328:15); 'The charlatan and the witch and the fakir can summon up a lot of energy just for their own ends ... a fakir-like energized charlatanry, consciously self-energised. I believe Henry Ford and President Wilson were that way' (*Letters*, vi. 132).

88:10 **the womb of time,** *Othello*, I. iii. 369: 'There are many events in the womb of time, which will be delivered.'

89:15 **like a vile Shylock, carved a pound of flesh** In Shakespeare's *The Merchant of Venice*, the Jewish moneylender Shylock demands a pound of the merchant Antonio's flesh as security against a loan, but in the event the flesh is never actually carved off.

89:18 **a China-girl's foot,** In China, from at least the tenth until well into the twentieth century, tiny feet in women were objects of erotic fetishism, and the feet of small girls were bound up in tight cloths to stunt their growth.

89:22 **Oscar Wilde said ... imitates art,** 'Life imitates art far more than Art imitates life ... It follows, as a corollary from this, that external Nature also imitates Art. The only effects she can show us are effects that we have already seen through poetry or in paintings.' From 'The Decay of Lying', in *Intentions* (1891), by Oscar Wilde (1854–1900), Irish writer, dramatist and wit.

90:24 **Louis XVI** King of France from 1774 to 1793. He was executed during the Revolution, together with his wife Marie Antoinette.

90:28 **Bolshevist Russia,** The Bolsheviks, led by Lenin (see note to 32:4), had overthrown the monarchy and taken control of Russia in the revolution of 1917. By 1926, when DHL was writing, Lenin had been dead for two years and Joseph Stalin (1879–1953) was gradually increasing his grip on power.

90:31 *chose connue,* 'Thing known' (French). The more usual French saying is 'chose perdue, chose connue', whose rough meaning would be 'if you lose something, everyone will know you had it'.

91:2   **Christian Scientists**   A religious movement founded in America in 1879, by Mary Baker Eddy. Its key doctrine is the belief in spiritual healing.

91:7   **"For I will put a new song into your mouth."**   Psalms, xl. 3 ['And he hath put . . . in my mouth'].

91:16   *Après moi le Déluge*   'After me, the Flood' (French). A remark sometimes attributed to Louis XV, and sometimes, as 'Après nous, . . .', to his mistress Madame de Pompadour (see below, note to 96:9), in both cases supposedly foreseeing the French Revolution.

91:19   *status quo,*   'The position existing'; 'as things are' (Latin).

91:22   **the great war that was to save democracy.**   Woodrow Wilson (see note to 88:8) declared to the United States Congress, on 2 April 1917, that the war his country was entering was intended 'to make the world safe for democracy'.

91:27   **be a Noah, and build an ark.**   Having resolved to destroy the world with a great flood, God commanded Noah to build an ark to float upon the waters, saying: 'with thee will I establish my covenant; and thou shalt come into the ark, thou, and thy sons, and thy wife, and thy sons' wives with thee. And of every living thing of all flesh, two of every sort shalt thou bring into the ark' (Genesis vi. 18–19).

91:28   **An ark, an ark   ark!**   In Shakespeare's *Richard III*, King Richard, on the battlefield of Bosworth, cries out 'A horse, a horse, my kingdom for a horse!' (V. iv. 7).

91:30   **there's one more river to cross!**   From a traditional African-American spiritual:

> Old Noah once he built the Ark
> There's one more river to cross.
> And patched it up with hickory bark
> There's one more river to cross.
> One more river, and that's the river of Jordan,
> One more river
> There's one more river to cross.

Introduction (version 2) to *The Memoirs of the Duc de Lauzun*

95:3   **brocade period.**   Brocade is a cloth, often of gold or silver, woven with a raised flowery pattern. The style was characteristic of French furnishings of the mid eighteenth century.

95:7   **his own memoirs,**   See note to 87:16. Although Richard Aldington claimed that F. S. Flint was to do the translation, the Broadway Library of XVIII Century French Literature, for which Aldington was the general editor, eventually published a translation by C. K. Scott Moncrieff, with an introduction by Aldington himself, and notes by G. Rutherford. See Introduction, pp. lxviii–lxx. DHL probably never saw Scott Moncrieff's translation, which is interesting to compare with his own, made from the 1858 Paris edition of Lauzun's *Mémoires*, with introduction and notes by Louis Lacour. DHL knew Scott Moncrieff (1889–1930), famous for his translation of

Proust, in Florence; he wrote to Aldington, on 18 November 1927, 'He has a nice side to him – but really an obscene mind like a lavatory' (*Letters*, vi. 220).

95:20   **killed her in the coming,**   Lauzun's mother, Antoinette-Eustachie Crozat du Châtel (1729–47), died in childbirth at the age of eighteen (not 'nineteen', 95:23).

95:30   **"like all the other . . . dying of hunger."**   As with succeeding extracts, DHL is translating directly from Lauzun: 'J'étais d'ailleurs comme tous les enfants de mon âge et de ma sorte: les plus jolis habits pour sortir, nu et mourant de faim à la maison' (*Mémoires* 4). Scott Moncrieff rendered it thus: 'I was, moreover, like all the boys of my age and condition: the most becoming clothes for out of doors, rags and starvation at home.'

95:31   **Dauphin**   The title given to the eldest son of the king of France.

96:2   **his father chose one of the dead mother's lacqueys.**   Lauzun's father was Charles-Armand-Antoine de Gontaut (1708 – *c*. 1796); the 'lacquey' chosen as tutor was a M. Roch.

96:6   **"more fluently and pleasantly . . . in France."**   'Plus couramment et plus agréablement qu'on ne fait ordinairement en France' (*Mémoires* 6). Scott Moncrieff has 'more fluently and agreeably than is customary in France.'

96:8   **Another writer of the period . . . reading prose aloud."**   DHL is here translating one of Lacour's footnotes to Lauzun: 'Le passage suivant d'un petit ouvrage écrit a peu près à la même époque que ces Mémoires vient donner du poids à l'affirmation de Lauzun: "Toute espèce de talent est rare. Croirait-on qu'il n'y a peut-être pas à Paris cinquante personnes capables de lire haute un ouvrage en prose?"' (*Mémoires* 6). The passage is taken from an anonymous memoir of 1782. Neither this nor the subsequent footnote (see note to 98:14) appears in Scott Moncrieff's translation.

96:9   **"almost necessary" to Madame de Pompadour,**   'presque nécessaire à' (*Mémoires* 6); Scott Moncrieff gives 'almost indispensable'. Jeanne Antoinette Poisson (1721–64), Marquise de Pompadour, was one of Louis XV's mistresses. She had great influence over Court appointments and French foreign and domestic policy.

96:13   **"Our journeys to Versailles . . . into the Guards regiment . . ."**   'Nos voyages à Versailles en devinrent plus fréquents, et mon éducation plus négligée . . . On me fit entrer à douze ans le régiment des Gardes' (*Mémoires* 6); (' . . . all the more frequent . . . placed in the Regiment of Guards' (Scott Moncrieff)). Versailles was the seat of the French Court.

96:30   **"Madame la Duchesse de Grammont . . . without any inconveniences."**   'Madame la duchesse de Gramont me prit dans la plus grande amitié, dans l'intention, je crois, de se former tout doucement un petit amant, qui fût bien à elle et sans inconvénient' (*Mémoires* 10); ('Madame la Duchesse de Gramont was as friendly as could be, with the intention, I dare say, of quietly furnishing herself with a young lover, who should be entirely hers and without risk to herself' (Scott Moncrieff)). The Duchesse de Gramont (1730–94) was formerly Béatrix de Choiseul-Stainville.

96:34   **"One day she put . . . any further ahead."**   'elle me mit un jour la main sur sa gorge; tout mon corps brûlait encore plusieurs heures après, mais je n'en étais pas plus avancé' (*Mémoires* 11); ('one day she placed my hand upon her bosom, all my body was still aflame hours afterwards; but I was no farther advanced' (Scott Moncrieff)).

96:36 **"putting him into the world,"** 'être mis dans le monde' (*Mémoires* 11); ('initiated into the ways of the world' (Scott Moncrieff)).

96:38 **his marriage with Mademoiselle de Boufflers.** Lauzun was married to the fourteen-year-old Amélie de Boufflers (1751–94), grand-daughter of the Maréchal de Luxembourg, in February 1766. In her notes to the Broadway Library edition Miss G. Rutherford comments of Mademoiselle de Boufflers that 'in her youth her excellent upbringing had the effect of making her almost completely silent' (*Memoirs of the Duc de Lauzun*, p. 231).

97:2 **"and she . . . than I was."** 'encore plus innocent que moi' (*Mémoires* 12); ('even more innocent than myself' (Scott Moncrieff)).

97:7 **"an enormous spider . . . horrid monsters."** 'Une énorme araignée vint troubler notre rendez-vous; nous la craignions tous deux mortellement; nous n'eûmes ni l'un ni l'autre le courage de la tuer. Nous prîmes le parti de nous séparer, en nous promettant de nous voir dans un lieu plus propre, et où il n'y aurait pas de monstres aussi effrayants' (*Mémoires* 13); ('An enormous spider appeared to interrupt our dalliance: we were both of us in mortal terror; neither of us could summon up courage to kill it. Instead, we parted, promising each other that we would meet again in a more commodious place, where there would be no such terrifying monsters' (Scott Moncrieff)).

97:13 **The Comtesse d'Esparbes** The correct spelling is d'Esparbès. She was a cousin of Madame de Pompadour.

97:16 **come to the scratch.** The scratch was originally a chalk line drawn on the floor of a prize-fighting ring to show the boxers where they should stand at the start of a bout; colloquially, to perform in the manner desired or expected.

97:24 **"all my childhood . . . not exempt."** 'On m'avait laissé lire beaucoup de romans pendant toute mon enfance, et cette lecture a tellement influé sur mon caractère, et j'en ressens encore les effets. Ils ont été souvent à mon désavantage; mais si je me suis exagéré mes propres sentiments et mes propres sensations, je dois au moins à mon caractère romanesque un éloignement pour les perfidies et les mauvais procédés avec les femmes, dont beaucoup de gens honnêtes ne sont pas exempts' (*Mémoires* 15); ('I had been allowed to read endless novels throughout my boyhood, and this reading had so strong an influence upon my character that I am still conscious of its effects. They have often proved to my disadvantage; but if I have exaggerated my own sentiments and my own sensations, I am at least indebted to my romantic nature for an abhorrence of the treachery and dishonourable conduct towards women, from which many men of honour are not exempt' (Scott Moncrieff)).

97:27 **Madame de Stainville,** Formerly Thomasse-Thérèse de Clermont d'Amboise, married, at the age of fourteen, to the Comte de Stainville.

97:31 **a "disagreeable child."** 'la maussade enfant' (*Mémoires* 17); ('the moping child' (Scott Moncrieff)).

98:1 **The Prince de Ligne** Charles Joseph von Ligne (1735–1814), Austrian soldier and diplomat, born in Brussels. His memoirs, entitled *Mélanges littéraires, militaires* *et sentimentales* (*Literary, military and sentimental miscellanies*) were published between 1795 and 1811.

98:14 **"They teach a girl [98:2] . . . parents and a lawyer."** This passage, from the *Pensées diverses* of the Prince de Ligne, is given in a footnote by Lacour, to page 12 of the *Mémoires*:

> On apprend à une fille à ne pas regarder un homme en face, à ne pas lui répondre, à ne jamais demander comment elle est venue au monde. Arrivent deux hommes noirs avec un homme brodé sur toutes les tailles. On lui dit: Allez passer la nuit avec ce monsieur! Ce monsieur, tout en feu, brutalement fait valoir ses droits, ne demande rien, mais exige beaucoup. Elle se lève en pleurs, tout au moins, et lui, tout en eau. S'ils se sont dit un mot, c'est pour quereller. Ils ont mauvais visage tous les deux et sont déjà portés à se prendre en guignon. Le mariage commence toujours ainsi sous d'heureux auspices. Toute la pudeur est déjà partie. Est-ce la pudeur qui peut empêcher cette jolie femme d'accorder par goût à celui qu'elle aime ce qu'elle a accordé par devoir à celui qu'elle n'aime pas? Et voilà l'engagement le plus sacré des coeurs, profané par des parents et un notaire.

This footnote does not appear in the Broadway Library edition. An intriguingly bowdlerised version of the passage, with the account of the morning-after feelings omitted, can be found in Katherine Prescott Wormeley's 1899 translation of the *Memoirs and Letters of the Prince de Ligne*, vol. II, p. 314.

98:24 **a dandy,** A man preoccupied with fashionable appearance; a fop.

98:35 **encyclopaedic philosophy,** The rationalist philosophy of the *Encyclopédie* of Diderot (see note to 87:32).

99:10 **he really admired England,** Lauzun travelled to England in 1767, primarily to advance his affair with Lady Sarah Bunbury (see next note), and again in 1772 and 1777. Apart from attending race meetings, and winning trophies with his horses, he spent most of his time in England in pursuit of women, including one of the great loves of his life, the Princess Isabelle Czartoryska (1746–1835), by whom Lauzun was thought to have had a son. Miss Rutherford notes of the Princess that 'scandal did not allow all her numerous children the same paternity' (*Memoirs of the Duc de Lauzun*, p. 238). Lauzun had no scruples about using his social contacts in London to gather information for the French Court about English political affairs at the time of the American Revolution, and even contemplated a scheme to lead an invasion force which planned a landing at Portsmouth. In May 1780 he sailed with his regiment to America to join Washington's forces fighting against the British. There is little evidence in the *Mémoires* as to Lauzun's more general opinions of England and the English.

99:11 **Lady Sarah Bunbury,** Formerly Lady Sarah Lennox, daughter of the Duke of Richmond, she was born in 1745. She married Thomas Bunbury in 1762, had numerous notorious affairs, was divorced in 1776, and eventually married the Hon. George Napier in 1781. She died in 1826. Lauzun was her lover for several months in 1767.

99:13 **seemed to be** The manuscript breaks off at this point.

Introduction to *The Mother*

103:2 **Grazia Deledda** Italian novelist (1871–1936). She was born in Nuoro, Sardinia, and published her first stories while still in her teens. After her marriage, in 1897, she lived mainly in Rome, while continuing to set the majority of her writings in Sardinia. She wrote over fifty books, novels, stories, poetry and plays; her most successful works were the novels *Elias Portolu* (1903), and *Cenere* (1904, the first of her works to be translated into English, as *Ashes*, in 1910). She was awarded the Nobel Prize for Literature in 1926 (not 1927, as stated on Cape's title-page), only a year or so before DHL's piece was written, although he makes no mention of this. While his comments about 'her period' and her being an 'elder' among Italy's writers make her sound rather superannuated, she was in fact only fourteen years older than he was, and the novel in question, *La madre* (*The Mother*) had appeared as recently as 1920. DHL had recommended her work to Koteliansky in a letter of 1 December 1916 (*Letters*, iii. 43), and when he and Frieda visited Nuoro in 1921 he was struck by the sight of a butcher's shop bearing the name De Ledda. See *Sea and Sardinia*, ed. Mara Kalnins (Cambridge, 1997), 131:4.

103:4 **Fogazzaro, or even D'Annunzio,** Antonio Fogazzaro (1842–1911), novelist and poet, of pronounced but unorthodox Catholicism; his best-known novels were *Piccolo mondo antica* (1896), and *Il Santo* (in English translation, *The Saint*, 1906) . . . Gabriele D'Annunzio (1863–1938), poet, playwright and novelist. Much of his early work was written in a form of Zola-esque realism, but later he produced morbidly decadent *fin de siècle* pieces such as the novel *Il fuoco* (1900) and the play *Le Martyre de Saint Sébastien* (1911). By the time of DHL's introduction to *The Mother*, D'Annunzio was better known as a maverick and eccentric political figure than as a serious writer; having flown sorties over Austrian positions in the First World War, when he was already well into his fifties, in 1919 he led a detachment of disaffected troops to occupy the town of Fiume, in what is now Croatia, which he believed should have been ceded to Italy in the post-war settlement. He set himself up as 'Regent' in a Renaissance palace, installed exotic furnishings, arranged mock battles to keep his soldiers from boredom, and eventually, once it was clear that his dream of becoming President of Italy was not going to be realised, surrendered to government forces in December 1920. 'Two compartments away we hear soldiers singing, martial still though bruised with fatigue, the D'Annunzio-bragging songs of Fiume' (*Sea and Sardinia*, ed. Kalnins, 173:18–20). D'Annunzio subsequently became one of Mussolini's most prominent supporters. One of his best-known novels was *Le vergini delle rocce* (*The Virgins of the Rocks*, 1895), a languid, part-Symbolist, part-Wagnerian romance of aristocratic decline. Writing to Stuart Sherman on 11 July 1925, DHL said he 'didn't care for' the comparison drawn between him and D'Annunzio in Sherman's article 'Lawrence Cultivates His Beard' (see note to 221:2): 'D'Annunzio is a sensationalist, nearly always in bad taste, as in that rolling over the edge' (*Letters*, v. 276).

103:12 **Jane Austen or Dickens** Jane Austen (1775–1817), English novelist. Her novels include *Pride and Prejudice* (1813) and *Emma* (1816) . . . Charles Dickens (1812–70), English novelist, born at Portsmouth. The most famous writer of the Victorian period, his works include *David Copperfield* (1849–50), *Little Dorrit* (1855–7) and *Great Expectations* (1860–1).

103:17 **Matilde Serao's** Matilde Serao (1856–1927), novelist and journalist, of mixed Greek–Italian parentage, lived mostly in Naples. She wrote many novels, including *La Conquista di Roma* (1885) and *La Ballerina* (1898). DHL asked Kot to obtain one of her books for him in December 1916 (*Letters*, iii. 43).

103:27 **Thomas Hardy isolates Wessex.** 'Wessex', the name of the old West Saxon kingdom in s.w. England, was the name Thomas Hardy (1840–1928) gave to the region where his novels and stories were set; it covered his home county of Dorset and parts of the neighbouring counties of Hampshire, Wiltshire, Somerset and Devon.

103:32 **Mount Gennargentu,** A range of mountains in central Sardinia, the highest of which is La Marmora (1,834 m).

103:33 **old Druid places,** Cf. DHL's experiences in Cornwall, mediated through the fictional character Richard Lovat Somers: 'And then the Cornish night would gradually come down upon the dark, shaggy moors, that were like the fur of some beast, and upon the pale-grey granite masses, so ancient and Druidical, suggesting blood-sacrifice . . . The spirit of the ancient, pre-christian world, which lingers still in the truly Celtic places, he could feel it invade him in the savage dusk' (*Kangaroo*, ed. Bruce Steele, Cambridge, 1994, 237:25–33).

104:9 **Benin,** A country in West Africa. Although DHL uses it almost as a by-word for backwardness, the ancient kingdom of Benin had a highly developed culture. From the sixteenth century onwards many of its rulers co-operated enthusiastically with the Portuguese slave traders.

104:26 **the death of the old hunter,** Most of chap. 8 of *The Mother* is devoted to this episode (pp. 132–44).

104:26 **the doings of the boy Antiochus,** A discussion of Antiochus's desire to become a priest, a desire causing Paul to reflect gloomily upon his own life, occupies the greater part of chap. 10.

104:32 **the pathetic, tiresome old mother . . . terror of a public exposure;** At the climax of *The Mother* (chap. 14, pp. 210–24), the priest, Paul, is celebrating Mass, waiting for the moment when his lover, Agnes, with whom he has refused to go away, will carry out her threat to denounce him in public. She finally decides not to do so, but at the back of the church, Paul's mother, who has also known of the threat, has been unable to stand the tension, and is found lying dead.

104:34 **spirit solve** At this point MS reads 'But neither will the modern spirit will solve the problem' (p. 4). DHL overlooked the erasing of the second 'will' necessitated by his having added 'neither will' interlinearly. The reading of E1 (p. 10) has been adopted.

105:12 **mere snuff of the candle.** The remains of the burnt candle-wick, hard and black.

105:27 **Emily Bronte.** Emily Brontë (1818–48), author of *Wuthering Heights* (1847).

105:30 **Virgins of the Rocks.** A play on the title of one of D'Annunzio's novels (see note to 103:4). *The Virgin of the Rocks* is also the title of a painting by Leonardo da Vinci (1452–1519), in the National Gallery.

106:5 **Giovanni Verga** Italian writer, born Catania, Sicily, 1840, and died there in 1922. DHL first mentions reading Verga in a letter to Koteliansky of 15 December 1916: 'We have read the *Cavalleria Rusticana*: a veritable blood-pudding of *passion*! It is not at all good' (*Letters*, iii. 53). By 24 October 1921 he tells Catherine Carswell that Verga 'exercises quite a fascination on me' (*Letters*, iv. 105), and on 10 November of the same year, in a letter to Edward Garnett, he says Verga 'is *extraordinarily* good' (*Letters*, iv. 115). He subsequently translated three of Verga's works, *Mastro-don Gesualdo*, *Novelle rusticane* and *Cavalleria Rusticana*. See Introduction, pp. li–lii, lix, lxxvi–lxxvii, and notes to 139:7, etc.

'Chaos in Poetry': introduction to *Chariot of the Sun*

109:3 **frescoes** Paintings made on walls, especially church interiors, when the plaster is not quite dry, so the colours sink in and become more durable. From Italian 'fresco' (fresh).

109:20 **the vision perisheth.** Cf. Proverbs xxix, 18: 'Where there is no vision, the people perish.'

110:7 **Homer and Keats,** Homer (*c.* 800 BC), Greek epic poet, author of *The Iliad* and *The Odyssey*; John Keats (1795–1821), English Romantic poet.

110:9 **Titans** In Greek mythology, the twelve children of the Sky and the Earth, defeated by Zeus in the struggle for mastery of the universe.

110:18 **Dante or Leonardo, Beethoven or Whitman:** Dante Alighieri (1265–1321), Italian poet, author of the *Divine Comedy*; Leonardo da Vinci (1452–1519), Italian artist and scientist; Ludwig van Beethoven (1770–1827), German composer; Walt Whitman (1819–92), American poet, one of the most important literary figures for DHL: see especially his essay on Whitman in *Studies* 148–61.

110:19 **St. Francis preaching to the birds in Assisi.** St Francis of Assisi (1181–1226), founder of the Franciscan order, saw all natural things as living praises of God. The story of his preaching to the birds, a favourite subject of Renaissance painting, was recounted in *The Little Flowers of Saint Francis*, which were translated in 1906 by W. Heywood; cf. *Reflections* 346:20n.

110:32 **Wordsworth . . . saw a primrose!** William Wordsworth (1770–1850), English Romantic poet, made many allusions to primroses; the best-known is in his poem *Peter Bell* (1819), ll. 258–60: 'A primrose by a river's brim / A yellow primrose was to him, / And it was nothing more.'

110:34 **primavera** Spring (Spanish).

110:36 **Shakspeare** DHL often used this spelling in preference to 'Shakespeare'.

110:38 **iron-bound paladins,** Medieval knights in armour.

110:40 **Hamlets and Macbeths,** The tragic heroes of Shakespeare's plays *Hamlet* (*c.* 1600) and *Macbeth* (1606).

110:18 **poetasters** Writers of feeble or worthless verse; not real poets.

111:21 *Chariot of the Sun*? A collection of poems first published in 1927, by Harry (Henry Grew) Crosby (1898–1929), poet and publisher, born in Boston. He was a nephew and godchild of the banker J. Pierpoint Morgan. After the First World War, having been decorated for bravery as a volunteer ambulance driver in France, Crosby took a post in the Paris branch of Morgan's bank, rowing himself to work down the Seine each morning in a red felucca. He married, in 1922, a divorcée, Mary Phelps Peabody, whom he rechristened 'Caresse'. He resigned from the bank the following year, and he and his wife pursued a decadent existence, gambling, travelling, sun-worshipping and opium-smoking. In 1927 they established the Black Sun Press, which would publish DHL's *The Escaped Cock* (1929), James Joyce's *Tales Told by Shem and Shaun* (1929), and Hart Crane's *The Bridge* (1930), among other notable works. Crosby had become an enthusiast for DHL's work in 1927, and the following March he asked to buy some manuscripts and offered five gold pieces for them (see Introduction, p. lxxviii). DHL and Frieda stayed with the Crosbys in Paris in the spring of 1929, by which time Crosby's admiration for DHL had cooled (see *Dying Game* 477). In July 1929 Crosby met Josephine Rotch in Venice; she became his mistress, and on 10 December that year he shot her and himself in a New York hotel in what was presumed to be a suicide pact. *Chariot of the Sun* first appeared from a private Paris press, 'At The Sign of the Sundial', in 1928, and an expanded edition was published posthumously by the Black Sun Press in 1931, with DHL's introduction and a note by Caresse.

111:25 **Paul Valérie,** Paul Valéry (1871–1945), French poet and critic, author of *La Jeune Parque* (1917) and *Le Cimitière marin* (1920). He shared with the Symbolists the belief that poetry should be closely allied to music.

111:40 *Sun Rhapsody* [111:34] . . . **our soliloquies"**   *Chariot of the Sun* 12. DHL quotes ll. 7–12.

112:2 **naiaids**   DHL's spelling. Naiads, in Greek mythology, were water-spirits or nymphs.

112:6 **"I am a tree . . . forest of the sun."**   'Q.E.D.', *Chariot of the Sun* 38, quoted in its entirety.

112:10 **the "verse" beginning: "Sthhe fous on ssu eod",**   *Chariot of the Sun* 68. This is the last piece in the volume. It continues as follows:

> Ethueeu touud on ssu eod
> Htetouetdu tds foett
> Fhtdeueeue on ssu eod
>
> Ioes ehtnotee ihue sthe
>
> Odudee noh usuhdtse
> Tdso ssu husioes
> On eod

112:23 *Néant.* [112:14] . . . **the conqueror."**   *Chariot of the Sun* 25, quoted in its entirety ['inimical' . . . 'conqueror'].

113:11 **a Japanese parasol,**   A brightly coloured paper parasol with wooden struts lying on the outside, not the inside, of the paper, so that when folded the parasol closes tightly (usually not 'rather clumsily' 113:11), to resemble a tapered walking-stick, with the paper invisible.

114:3 **"likewise invisible . . . sun-consoled."**   'Quatrains to the Sun', *Chariot of the Sun* 4, ll. 11–12 ['Likewise . . .'].

114:4   *Water Lilies*   'Water-Lilies', *Chariot of the Sun* 3. The poem reads as follows:

> Unwedded from the world, I stray through trees
> To where a pool lies mirrored in the Sun
> A disk of polished gold that I have won
> With labours not unknown to Hercules.
>
> Slender they bathe, all naked as a breeze,
> Their nipples hollow and their hair undone,
> While from their widespread thighs cool ripples run
> To rock the water-lilies round their knees.
>
> Nymphs of the fountain, naiads innocent,
> Frail sunbeams who have passed between my arms
> So beautiful in your imprisonment,
> Fill now my soul with symbols of delight:
> Soft voices and soft fingers and soft charms
> And the curving of a darkness into light.

114:15   **like lions, soft gold lions and white lions half-visible.**   The only lions mentioned in the actual collection are in the poem 'Unanswered': 'red lions roar / To guard the Sun I gave my youth to find' (*Chariot of the Sun* 32, ll. 11–12).

114:23   **dead-sea fruit.**   In legend, the fruit growing on trees around the Dead Sea appeared beautiful but tasted of ashes; hence, a disappointment, an empty promise.

114:30   **"the Sun in . . . the world"**   'Quatrains to the Sun', *Chariot of the Sun* 5, ll. 14–15.

114:36   **"At night . . . To cross"**   'Unhurtful Opposites', from 'Cinquains to the Sun', *Chariot of the Sun* 7, quoted in its entirety.

115:7   **"Sunmaid . . . Revive"**   'Ensablée', from 'Cinquains to the Sun', *Chariot of the Sun* 8, quoted in its entirety.

115:15   **"Dark clouds . . . The Sun"**   'Caliginous', from 'Cinquains to the Sun', *Chariot of the Sun* 9, quoted in its entirety.

115:16   **the next "cinquain" may not be poetry at all**   A cinquain is a verse stanza of five lines; from the French 'cinq' (five). The next in Crosby's sequence, after 'Caliginous', is 'Creation':

> The sun
> A ring of gold
> Which God has thrust upon
> The naked finger of the tree
> Of life

DHL may of course have meant whichever cinquain came 'next' after an enjoyable one; there are sixteen in the sequence.

115:18   **carbonic acid.**   Carbon dioxide dissolved in water.

115:19   **the monos,**   From the Greek 'mono' (single); hence the One, the singleness.

115:27   **"But I shall . . . cautiously around."**   'Meditation Under The Sun', *Chariot of the Sun* 22, ll. 13–14.

115:31   *Sun-Ghost . . . Feet of Polia.*   These poems are on pages 27, 28, 47 and 60 respectively:

Sun-Ghost

The sun that leaves the body
Is naked as the pool
Through whose forgotten beauty
It passes sorrowful
Among the frightened naiads
Who tremble in their cave
To see a sun-ghost weeping
Like eyes within a grave

To Those Who Return

Among the fountains in the sun
          Once you were nude for me
Believing thus to lure my heart
          Into idolatry

You did not see the sunbow nymph
          Miraculous through spray
Whose interweaving limbs were thoughts
          To lead me far astray

Nor I the sun-shaped faun who sprang
          From pedestal of stone
To colonnade himself in you
          Unguarded and alone

But now enclosed by suns we come
          Restrengthened by our shame
By slow approaches into Sun
          Never to part again

Torse de Jeune Femme au Soleil

her nombril is the center of the sun
she is the whiteness of the snow on snow
and I am glad she has no head
nor any color purple green or red
but only ivory of the snow on snow

her breasts are marble suns at break of day
and I am glad she has no arms
to shield the rounded coldness of her charms

Poem for the Feet of Polia

they have walked through the gateways
          of my eyes

they have climbed the mountains
    of my body
they have marched across the desert
    of my heart
they have forded the rivers
    of my mind
they have penetrated into the dark forest
    of my soul

if I were a cannibal I might devour them
if I were Pilate I might crucify them
if I were a sorcerer I might make them vanish away
if I were Neptune I might drown them
if I were a robber I might steal them

but I am a bridge to the sun
bridge leading away from a world of pain
bridge leading away from a night of sin
bridge over the abyss of doubt
bridge for the feet of Polia to the Sun

116:11   **lions of courage... ivory horn of the unicorn**   In his essay 'The Crown', DHL used the nursery-rhyme 'The lion and the unicorn were fighting for the crown', to illustrate his argument, already developed in 'Study of Thomas Hardy' and *Twilight in Italy*, that life is constituted by the eternal contention of opposing forces: 'the unicorn of virtue and virgin spontaneity' and 'the lion of power and splendour' ('The Crown', *Reflections* 253:3–6 and Explanatory note, 259:27–30).

116:32   **the speckled leopard of the mixed self.**   There may be an obscure allusion here to the cult of Bacchus, in which the leopard was a sacred animal; cf. DHL's description of the Tomb of the Leopards in *Sketches* 49:14.

Introduction to *Bottom Dogs*

119:2   **Edward Dahlberg's novel ... Bottom Dogs**   Edward Dahlberg (1900–77) was born in Boston, grew up in Kansas City, and lived at the Jewish Orphans' Asylum in Cleveland, Ohio, between 1912 and 1917. The travels around the west of the USA described in *Bottom Dogs* took place in 1919–20. *Bottom Dogs* (1929) was his first novel; later works include *From Flushing to Calvary* (1932), and *Those Who Perish* (1934), written after a trip to Nazi Germany. In 1964 he published an autobiography, *Because I Was Flesh*, a reworking of the characters and events of *Bottom Dogs*. For DHL's influence on the choice of title, see Introduction, p. lxxxv. DHL tended not to share the standard English sympathy with the underdog: 'Ah no, let us defend ourselves from the bottom dog, with its mean growl and its yellow teeth' (*The Plumed Serpent*, ed. L. D. Clark, Cambridge, 1987, 81:14–15).

119:14   **pioneer first-comers ... defeated, broken,**   DHL included a portrait of such 'first-comers' in *St. Mawr*: a couple from New England in the 1860s who attempted to build a ranch in New Mexico (the ranch Lou Carrington and her mother eventually move to), but who were 'defeated by the "dragon"', by 'the strange rapacity of savage life'; *St. Mawr and Other Stories*, ed. Brian Finney (Cambridge, 1983), 151:6, 150:40. Cf. also DHL's letter to his niece Margaret King of 31 August 1924 about the ranch at Del Monte (*Letters*, v. 110–12).

119:22   **Odyssey**   The title of Homer's epic poem; colloquially, a prolonged and difficult journey through the unknown, full of hardships and strange encounters.

119:23   **pioneer literature . . . hardly exists,**   DHL may have come across a few published works offering a gloomier, or at least more realistic, portrait of pioneer life: for example Mark Twain's 'The Californian's Tale' (1893), with its glimpses of 'defeated and disappointed families', or some passages in Twain's *Roughing It* (1872), or Mary Austin's *The Land Of Little Rain* (1903). By the late 1930s and 1940s, more frequent examples of the kind of literature DHL would have found interesting were beginning to appear, notably Martha L. Smith's *Going to God's Country* (1941), a memoir of settler hardships in the 1890s, and Wallace Stegner's Canadian frontier novel *The Big Rock Candy Mountain* (1938).

120:25   **Aztec . . . Peruvian.**   The Aztecs were the native inhabitants of ancient Mexico; their Peruvian equivalents were the Incas.

121:6   **one great blow.**   I.e., the 1917 revolution.

121:22   **The American senses . . . their kitchens.**   The central character of *Bottom Dogs*, Lorry Goldsmith, 'got at things thru his nose, the way the American estimates other peoples, always through their sweats and kitchens' (*Bottom Dogs*, 1929, p. 187).

121:37   **Whitmanish "adhesiveness"**   In the Preface to *Calamus* (1876), Whitman wrote of 'that fervid comradeship, (the adhesive love, at least rivaling the amative love)'. Cf. *Kangaroo*, ed. Steele, 197:25 and note.

122:1   **since the war,**   I.e., the First World War.

122:10   **in James Joyce,**   DHL made numerous, mostly negative comments on Joyce (1882–1941), parts of whose *Ulysses* he read in its year of publication, 1922: e.g., writing to Thomas Seltzer, on 28 November 1922: '*Ulysses* wearied me: so like a schoolmaster with dirt and stuff in his head: sometimes good, though: but too mental' (*Letters*, iv. 345).

122:10   **Aldous Huxley,**   English novelist and essayist (1894–1963), a close friend of DHL since 1926; they had first met in 1915. Huxley's novels of the 1920s include *Antic Hay* (1923) and *Point Counter Point* (1928), in which the character Mark Rampion is a fictional portrait of DHL. In a letter to Huxley of 28 October 1928, DHL wrote 'I have read *Point Counter Point* with a heart sinking through my boot-soles and a rising admiration. I do think you've shown the truth, perhaps the last truth, about you and your generation, with really fine courage' (*Letters*, vi. 600).

122:11   **André Gide . . . Parigi**   André Gide (1869–1951), French novelist, author of *Les Faux-monnayeurs* (*The Counterfeiters*, 1925) and *La porte étroite* (*Strait is the Gate*, 1909) . . . *Parigi*, a novel, published in 1925, by Lorenzo Viani (1882–1936), partly written in Tuscan dialect. DHL had recently been asked if he would like to translate it; he wrote to Spencer Curtis Brown, the son of his agent Curtis Brown, on 6 January 1928, 'I doubt if I could face the unending squalor of Viani's *Parigi*. It would depress me so, I should never get through with it' (*Letters*, vi. 257).

122:23   *Manhattan Transfer*   Novel by John Dos Passos (1896–1970) which DHL had reviewed in 1927; see note to 309:26.

122:25   *Point Counter Point*   See note to 122:10.

123:2   **Wyndham Lewis**   Percy Wyndham Lewis (1884–1957), novelist, critic and painter, founder of the Vorticist movement. DHL mentions having met him in July 1914 (*Letters*, ii. 193).

123:9   **"orphanage" chapters of this book.**   Chaps. 3–6 of *Bottom Dogs*, 'The Newcumber', 'Herman Mush Tate', 'Bonehead-Star-Wolfe', and 'Cedar Avenue Nites', are set in the orphanage in Cleveland, Ohio, where Lorry is sent to live by his mother's new lover.

123:22   **Lorry "always had his nose in a book"**   'he liked it when his mother used to say, "he's always got his nose in a book"' (*Bottom Dogs*, p. 198).

123:28   **African Bushman**   Around the time of the writing of the Introduction to *Bottom Dogs*, Brewster Ghiselin records that DHL 'spoke of some translations of stories by Bushmen that he had once read, in which the qualities of things seemed to be in continual change' (Nehls, iii. 296). The stories were in a collection edited by Lucy C. Lloyd, *Specimens of Bushman Folklore* (1911), which DHL borrowed from Jan Juta in August 1920; see *Triumph to Exile* 857 and *Studies* Explanatory notes on 291:8 and 346:15.

124:3   **Theodore Dreiser . . . Sherwood Anderson,**   Theodore Dreiser (1871–1945), novelist, born in Indiana. He established social realism at the forefront of American literature, with his novels *Sister Carrie* (1900) and *An American Tragedy* (1925) . . . Sherwood Anderson (1876–1941), born in Ohio, brought Dreiser-esque realism closer to Modernism; his volume of stories *Winesburg, Ohio* (1919) had much influence on Hemingway and Faulkner. DHL read it in December 1919, and wrote to Benjamin Huebsch: 'gruesome it is . . . like a nightmare one can hardly recall distinctly' (*Letters*, iii. 426).

124:11   **Kansas City, Beatrice,-Nebraska, Omaha, Salt Lake City, Portland,-Oregon, Los Angeles,**   In Chap. 10, 'Ridin' the Blinds', Lorry stops briefly in or passes through all these cities, and San Francisco also, while jumping rides on trains. He ends up in Los Angeles and stays at the YMCA.

124:15   **In the Y. M. C. A.**   Every city in the USA and most of the world had, and still has, a hostel and social centre run by the Young Men's Christian Association, an organisation founded in London in 1844.

124:20   **Zarathustra and Spinosa, Darwin and Hegel.**   *Thus Spake Zarathustra*, by Friedrich Nietzsche (1844–1900); Baruch Spinoza (1632–77), Dutch philosopher, author of the *Ethics*; Charles Darwin (1809–82), naturalist and scientist, author of *The Origin of Species* (1859); Georg Wilhelm Friedrich Hegel (1770–1831), German philosopher. Lorry and his associates in the YMCA do read *Zarathustra* (*Bottom Dogs*, p. 248), and there is talk of 'spinozistic dualism' (p. 260), but Darwin is not mentioned; neither is Hegel. There are, however, discussions of Emerson, Epictetus, Tolstoy, Schopenhauer and Spengler.

124:28   *ne plus ultra.*   'Nothing further beyond' (Latin); the greatest possible extent; cf. 'Beyond this, nothing' (124:23).

Introduction to *The Grand Inquisitor*

127:1 **The Grand Inquisitor** Koteliansky's translation was of the close of chap. IV and the whole of chap. V of Book V of *The Brothers Karamazov*, which, as he notes, was first published in *Russky vestnik* (1879–80).

127:4 **in 1913,** The first English translation of *The Brothers Karamazov*, made by Constance Garnett (1862–1946), appeared in 1912. DHL, who knew Constance and her husband Edward Garnett (1868–1936) very well, presumably read the book shortly afterwards, although he does not mention it by name in his comments on Dostoevsky in correspondence with Edward Garnett around that time. He wrote to Lady Ottoline Morrell asking to borrow a copy of *The Brothers Karamazov* on 8 April 1915 (*Letters*, ii. 315).

127:5 **Middleton Murry** Murry's *Fyodor Dostoevsky* appeared in August 1916, one of the publisher Martin Secker's 'Series of Critical Studies'. The *Phoenix* text of DHL's introduction to *The Grand Inquisitor* carries the footnote: 'Before this preface was published in *The Grand Inquisitor* the name of Katherine Mansfield was substituted for that of Middleton Murry.' See Introduction, p. lxxxix n. 135, and *Phoenix* 283.

127:11 **black-a-vised** Of dark complexion.

127:15 **each time . . . drearily true to life.** In *Kangaroo*, Kangaroo argues along similar lines to the Grand Inquisitor, as DHL discusses them here: ' "I should try to establish my state of Australia as a kind of Church, with the profound reverence for life, for life's deepest urges, as the motive power. Dostoevsky suggests this: and I believe it can be done" ' (*Kangaroo*, ed. Steele, 112:10–13 and note. On the other hand, see the review of Rozanov's *Solitaria*, written in 1927, 315:25–33.

127:24 **Ivan** Ivan Karamazov, the second of the three brothers, who tells the story of the Grand Inquisitor to his younger brother Alyosha.

127:30 **Dmitri** The eldest brother, wrongly accused of murdering their father.

127:30 **Alyosha** The youngest brother, a follower of the monk Zossima.

128:7 **(he says fifteen hundred)** *Grand Inquisitor* 3. Dostoevsky says 'fifteen hundred' because Ivan's story is set in the sixteenth century.

128:13 **everyday men?** At this point in MS (p. 3) DHL deleted the following: 'The limits are, that not one in a hundred men is capable of the sustained heroism necessary to the real christian life. Not one man in a hundred is strong enough. Not one man in a hundred has the strength which makes him "chosen", makes him "elect", makes him, in short, a christian.'

128:29 **"impotent, vicious, worthless and rebellious"** *Grand Inquisitor* 15.

128:37 **"Hadst Thou . . . would be lighter."** *Grand Inquisitor* 21 [' . . . respected . . .'].

129:11 **And Satan . . . annihilation and not-being.** *Grand Inquisitor* 12 ['the spirit of self-annihilation and non-being'].

129:20 **zeppelins,** German airships, used for bombing England during the First World War, named after their designer, Count Ferdinand von Zeppelin (1838–1917). Cf. 'And then Zeppelin raids: the awful noise and the excitement . . . there, in the sky like some god vision, a Zeppelin, and the searchlights catching it, so that it gleamed like a manifestation in the heavens' (*Kangaroo*, ed. Steele, 216:1–5).

129:23　**strange feats of the psychic people,**　Interest in spiritualism and the performances of mediums had greatly increased during and after the First World War, encouraged by the enthusiasm of famous writers such as Sir Arthur Conan Doyle, whose *The New Revelation* appeared in 1918. Cf. DHL's discussion of spiritualism and psychic effects in 'Hawthorne's *Blithedale Romance*' (*Studies* 102–3).

129:24　**Christian scientists**　See note to 91:2.

129:25　**Russia destroyed the Tsar to have Lenin**　Lenin (see note to 32:4), the leader of the Bolsheviks, took control of Russia after the Revolution of 1917, which overthrew the last Tsar, Nicholas II. Nicholas and his family were put under house arrest, and executed the following year

129:26　**Mussolini,**　Benito Mussolini (1883–1945) became dictator of Italy in 1922.

129:27　**England is longing for a despot.**　By 1930, when DHL was writing, Oswald Mosley (1896–1980) had not yet offered himself as a potential 'despot' – his New Party was founded in 1931 and his British Union of Fascists in 1932 – but he was already a well-known and charismatic political figure, and it is possible that DHL may have had him in mind. Mosley (mis-spelt 'Moseley' in DHL's letters) was mentioned as a potential Parliamentary intermediary on DHL's behalf during the debate about the seizure of the manuscripts of *Pansies*, in February 1929, but in the event he did not speak. See *Letters*, vii. 161–3.

130:16　**Satan's three offers,**　Matthew iv. 1–10. In the wilderness, the devil challenges Christ three times: firstly to turn stones into bread; secondly, to prove himself immortal by throwing himself down from a height; thirdly, to receive 'all the kingdoms of the world, and the glory of them' in return for bowing down to Satan. Christ refuses the three temptations.

131:8　**the Pharaohs and Darius**　The Pharaohs were the rulers of ancient Egypt; Darius the Great, King of Persia, reigned 522–486 BC.

131:9　**the great patient Popes of the early Church**　DHL probably had in mind such figures as Gregory the Great (reigned 590–604), Gregory VII (reigned 1073–85), and Innocent III (1198–1216); see *Movements in European History*, ed. Philip Crumpton (Cambridge, 1987), 119, 126–7.

131:11　**the Spanish Inquisition**　The Inquisition had originally been established in 1231 by Pope Gregory IX in an attempt to combat the spread of heresy. Inquisitors could investigate anyone on the merest rumour, and the accused were not permitted to challenge their accusers. Torture was sometimes used to extract confessions. The Spanish Inquisition, established by Pope Sixtus IV in 1478, was a late reinvigoration of a procedure that had effectively lapsed; under the direction of Tomàs de Torquemada (1420–98), prosecutions rapidly multiplied, and more than 2,000 accused persons were executed.

131:19　**burnt a hundred people in an *auto da fé*.**　*Auto-da-fé* (Portuguese) means 'act of faith', and usually referred to the burning of a heretic by order of the Inquisition. In the story, the Grand Inquisitor had ordered the burning of 100 heretics in Seville the day before Christ's appearance (*Grand Inquisitor* 6).

131:21   **epileptic**   Dostoevsky suffered from epilepsy, a condition he gave to some of the most prominent characters in his novels, including Prince Myshkin in *The Idiot* (1868). In the first version of his essay on Nathaniel Hawthorne, DHL wrote that Dimmesdale, in Hawthorne's *The Scarlet Letter*, 'has an almost imbecile, epileptic impulse to defile the religious reality he exists in. In Dimmesdale at this period lies the whole clue to Dostoevsky' (*Studies* 254:16).

131:34   **even the earthly bread disappeared out of wheat-producing Russia.**
In the early 1920s Russia suffered widespread famine, largely as a result of the enforced collectivisation of agriculture.

132:19   **"In my Father's house are many mansions."** John xiv. 2.

132:21   **"Why call ye me . . . which I say?"**   Luke vi. 46 ['And why . . .'].

132:29   **harvest-home**   The harvest festival, traditionally celebrated in churches, although not officially part of the Christian calendar.

132:33   **The rapture of the Easter kiss,**   The ancient custom in Russia was for neighbours to exchange red-painted eggs on the eve of Easter Sunday, accompanied by the Easter or Resurrection kiss.

132:37   **bolshevist**   See note to 129:25.

133:5   **Holy Week**   In the Christian calendar, the week beginning on Palm Sunday and leading up to Easter Day.

133:13   **Work is, or should be . . . consciousness.**   Cf. DHL's review of *Art-Nonsense and Other Essays*, written a fortnight or so later (e.g. 358:14–17).

133:23   **"that which men bow down to."**   'There is no anxiety more unceasing, and more tormenting to man, than, when free, to find, as soon as possible, someone to whom to bow' (*Grand Inquisitor* 16).

133:36   **when he says . . . back to them.**   'Getting loaves from us, they will, of course, see clearly that we are taking their own loaves, produced by their own hands, from them in order to distribute them among themselves . . . but verily they will be more pleased with accepting the bread from our hands, than with the bread itself! For too well will they remember that, formerly, without us, the very loaves produced by them turned into mere stones in their hands; but when they came back to us, the very stones turned in their hands into loaves' (*Grand Inquisitor* 25–6).

133:37   **it is not much better than stone to them**   Cf. Matthew vii. 9: 'Or what man is there of you, whom if his son ask bread, will he give him a stone?' See also Luke xi. 11.

134:5   **the salt loses its savour,**   Matthew v. 13; Luke xiv. 34.

134:31   **even nice simple people . . . of money.**   DHL may have had members of his own family in mind here. After his sister Emily had visited him in Switzerland in August 1928, he wrote to Aldous Huxley: 'How I *hate* the attitude of ordinary people to life. How I loathe ordinariness! How from my soul I abhor nice simple people, with their eternal price list' (*Letters*, vi. 542).

Introductory Note to *Mastro-don Gesualdo*

139:7   **As a young man**   Verga left Sicily for Florence in 1865, aged twenty-five, and moved to Milan in 1872. The novels of this early period include *Una peccatrice* (1866), *Eva* (1873) *Tigre Reale* (1873) and *Eros* (1875).

139:11   **The first books were sketches:**   Verga's first 'Sicilian' work in his later style was the short novel *Nedda* (1874), followed in 1880 by the stories of *Vita dei Campi*.

139:12   *Storia di una Capinera* . . . **in letter form.**   A novel published in 1871.

139:13   *Cavalleria Rusticana,*   An alternative title for the volume *Vita dei Campi*.

139:15   **Mascagni's opera.**   The opera *Cavalleria Rusticana*, by Pietro Mascagni (1867–1945), was first performed in 1890. It was one of the first examples of the Italian *verismo* style, and, being a short piece, is often paired in performance with another famous *verismo* opera, *I Pagliacci*, by Ruggiero Leoncavallo (1858–1919). DHL on one occasion confused the two composers (see note to 371:18).

139:17   *Comédie Humaine*;   The collective title of the series of novels – more than eighty of them – by the French novelist Honoré de Balzac (1799–1850). Verga originally intended to write five novels for the series *I Vinti*.

139:17   **Treves of Milan**   Emilio Treves, Verga's friend and publisher.

139:18   *I Malavoglia.*   This was the first of Verga's novels to be published in English, in New York in 1890, as *The House by the Medlar Tree*. The translator was Mary A. Craig, and the edition included a foreword by William Dean Howells. The translation was published in London by J. R. Osgood the following year.

139:21   *I Promessi Sposi.*   In English, *The Betrothed* (1825–7), a novel by Alessandro Manzoni (1785–1873).

139:22   *Mastro-don Gesualdo,*   DHL completed his translation of this novel in Ceylon in March 1922. See Introduction, pp. li–lii.

139:25   *La Duchessa di Leyra*:   Verga worked intermittently at this novel from 1897 to 1899 before apparently abandoning it, leaving only the two opening chapters and notes for more. The Duchess of Leyra was Isabella Trao, the supposed daughter of Gesualdo in the previous novel. In a letter to his translator in 1899 Verga complained of his difficulty in finding the right voice for aristocratic characters and conversation.

139:31   **Manzoni.**   See note to 139:21.

139:33   **D'Annunzio and Fogazzaro . . . Papini**   For D'Annunzio and Fogazzaro, see note to 103:4 . . . Giovanni Papini (1881–1956) was better-known as a philosopher and critic than as a writer of fiction; his most famous work was *The Life of Christ* (1921).

140:14   **These are his own words** [140:6] . . . **a revelation.—"**   This appears to be DHL's own translation of some comments by Verga which first appeared in *La Tribuna* of Rome, 2 February 1911, in an article entitled 'Interviste siciliane: Giovanni Verga', by Riccardo Artuffo: 'Avevo pubblicato qualcuno dei miei primi romanzi. Andavano; ne preparavo degli altri. Un giorno non so come, mi capita fra mano una specie di giornale di bordo, un manoscritto discretamente sgrammaticato e asintattico, in cui un capitano raccontava succintamente di certe peripezie, superate dal suo veliero. Da marinaio, senza una frase più del necessario, breve. Mi colpì e lo rilessi: era cio ch'io cercavo, senza darmene conto distintamente. Alle volte, Lei sa, basta un segno, un punto. Fu un fascio di luce.' Benedetto Croce, in his journal *La Critica* (Bari), 12 January 1916, retold this story in a manner suggesting it to be well known by this time: 'E il Verga, questo puro artista, affatto antilitterario, conobbi di persona alcuni anni dopo in Catania, e udii da lui come gli sorgesse nell'animo l'ideale di un nuovo stile nel leggere cioè lo sgrammatico rapporto di un capitano di lungo corso intorno a una sua fortuna di mare' ('And I met Verga, this pure artist, completely anti-literary, a few years later in Catania, and heard from him how the idea of a new style had come to him while reading a ship's captain's ungrammatical account of what had happened on a sea voyage'). Verga himself, however, appears to have disowned the story; see Gino Raya, ed., *Lettere a Dina* (Rome, 1962), p. 263.

DHL quoted the passage from Artuffo's interview three times; in the two versions of this Introductory Note, and in the 'Translator's Preface to *Cavalleria Rusticana*'. His translation is reasonably accurate, except for 'giornale di bordo', which means a ship's logbook, but for which he gives 'a broadside, a halfpenny sheet'.

140:20 **the premature revolution of 1821.** There had been a rebellion in Sicily in 1820, and the following year the Austrians ordered Ferdinand I of Naples to crush it and annul the new constitution which he had granted.

140:21 **the famous calamity of 1837:** 'The mother saw her at last when she left her college in 1837, when the first rumours of cholera began to spread already in Palermo' (*Mastro-don Gesualdo*, New York, 1923, p. 283).

140:24 *maestro,* Master (Italian).

140:26 *compère,* Companion (French).

Note on Giovanni Verga, in *Little Novels of Sicily*

143:5 **eighty-two,** Verga was eighty-one when he died. DHL wrote to Robert Mountsier, on 7 February 1922, 'Poor old Verga went and died exactly as I was going to see him in Catania' (*Letters*, iv. 186).

143:9 **the seaport under Etna,** Catania, lying at the foot of Etna (see note to 36:38), has several times been severely damaged by eruptions and earthquakes.

143:13 *Eros, Eva, Tigre Reale, Il Marito di Elena,* See note to 139:7. *Il Marito di Elena* is a later work, published in 1882.

143:27 *Across the Sea,* 'Di là del mare', the last in the collection *Novelle Rusticane*. DHL's translation of this story was first published separately in the November 1923 number of *Adelphi*.

143:28 **Messina,** City at the north-easternmost point of Sicily, opposite the mainland. It was destroyed by an earthquake in 1908 and completely rebuilt.

143:29 **The great misty city** In his translation DHL calls it 'the immense misty and gloomy city' (*Little Novels of Sicily*, New York, 1925, p. 224).

144:1 **Syracuse . . . the Plains of Catania and the Biviere, the Lake of Lentini,** Syracuse, Siracusa, founded in 734 BC, was one of the oldest Greek settlements in Sicily; the old city was built on an island. The Plain of Catania, stretching to the

s. of the city, was in Greek mythology the habitation of the cannibalistic Lestrygonians. 'Biviere' – which Blackwell seems to have assumed should have been 'Riviere' (see Textual apparatus) – is another word for 'lake'; the Lake of Lentini, at the southern end of the Catanian plain, is usually called the 'Biviere of Lentini'.

144:6 **King Francis of Naples, son of Bomba.** Francis II (1836–94) was the son of Ferdinand II, who was known as 'Ré Bomba' ('The Bomb King'), after ordering a bombardment of Sicilian towns during the revolution of 1848; see also *Movements in European History*, ed. Crumpton, 229:5 and Explanatory note. Francis II became King of Naples in 1859. He abandoned Naples in the face of Garibaldi's advance in 1860, and the Bourbon kingdom was overthrown.

144:7 **his little northern Queen** Maria Sophia, wife of Francis II. The King and Queen in the story 'So Much for the King' would actually have been Ferdinand II, 'Bomba' (reigned 1830–59), and his wife Maria Theresa, daughter of the Archduke of Austria.

144:7 **Garibaldi** Giuseppe Garibaldi (1807–82), Italian patriot and army commander, born in Nice. He fought as a guerilla leader in South America and returned to Italy to fight in the revolution of 1848. In 1860 he formed an army of 1,000 volunteers and invaded Sicily, defeating Francis II. In 1861 he handed over his conquests to the new King of a united Italy, Victor Emmanuel.

144:8 *So Much For the King* 'Cos' è il re'. A stricter translation would be 'What the King is like'.

144:11 *Liberty* This story was based upon a peasants' revolt at Bronte, n.w. of Catania, in 1860.

144:19 **the half-profits system.** Sicilian peasant life was based upon contracts by which the produce and profits of a piece of land were divided between the owner and the tenant farmer on an agreed basis, not necessarily equally.

Introduction to *Mastro-don Gesualdo*

147:8 **he went to Naples,** Verga does not appear ever to have left Sicily before 1865, when he first went to Florence. He may have visited Naples, but never lived there. He made extended visits to Florence, settling there in 1869, before moving to Milan in 1872.

147:9 **the Bourbon kingdom of Naples.** The kingdom was overthrown in 1860 (see note to 144:6)

147:15 **Alfred de Vigny . . . Maupassant.** Alfred, Comte de Vigny (1797–1863), French Romantic poet and novelist, born at Loches; author of *Cinq-Mars* (1826) and *Poèmes antiques et modernes* (1826) . . . Guy de Maupassant (1850–93), novelist and short-story writer, born in Normandy; one of the principal figures in the realist and naturalist schools in late nineteenth-century French literature. His story collections include *Mademoiselle Fifi* (1882), and his novels *Une vie* (1883) and *Bel-Ami* (1885). De Vigny's wife was an invalid, and he had numerous mistresses, including Louise Colet, more famous as the mistress of Flaubert; de Maupassant's energetic love-life led to his contracting syphilis, which almost certainly contributed to his death at the age of forty-three.

147:16   *Tigre Reale,*   See note to 139:7.

147:21   **Matilde Serao's novels.**   See note to 103:17.

147:25   **after forty,**   Verga's home from 1872 to 1894 was Milan. He visited Sicily regularly, but did not return to live there permanently until 1894, when he was fifty-four.

147:27   **almost another forty years,**   Actually twenty-eight.

147:28   **almost forgotten.**   Verga had fallen somewhat out of fashion, and had written little of significance for over twenty years, but he was made a Life Senator of the Kingdom of Italy in 1920, and in the same year his eightieth birthday was officially celebrated, with Pirandello as the principal speaker. Verga himself, however, refused to attend.

148:1   **There are three books of Sicilian sketches and short stories,**   See note to 139:11.

148:6   *Storia di una Capinera.*   See note to 139:12.

148:10   **Jose-Maria de Heredia,**   José-Maria de Heredia (1842–1905), poet, born in Cuba but educated in France; best known for the sonnet collection *Les Trophées* (1893).

148:11   **an American lady.**   Mary A. Craig. See note to 139:18.

148:15   **Speaking, in conversation . . . in Rome,**   DHL was in Rome between 4 and 6 April 1927, and appears to have discussed Verga with the poet Lauro De Bosis (see Introduction, p. lxxv). De Bosis (1901–31), the son of an Italian father (also a poet) and an American mother, was a friend of the American author Thornton Wilder (1897–1975), and had translated Wilder's novel *The Bridge Of San Luis Rey* (1927) into Italian. By 1930 De Bosis had moved to the United States and and become a dedicated opponent of Mussolini. In October 1931 he set off from Marseilles in a small plane and flew over Rome, dropping anti-Fascist leaflets and an appeal to the King, before crashing into the Mediterranean near the coast of Corsica. Wilder, in dedicating his 1948 novel *The Ides Of March* to the memory of De Bosis, claimed that the plane had been pursued by fighters of the Italian air force, but other accounts maintain that it had simply run out of fuel.

148:19   **Pirandello,**   Luigi Pirandello (1867–1936), novelist and dramatist. His plays include *Sei personaggi in cerca d'autore* (*Six Characters in Search of an Author*, 1921), and his novels *La vita nuda* (1910).

148:21   **Tolstoi . . . George Eliot**   Count Lev Nikolaevich Tolstoy (1828–1910), Russian novelist, author of *War and Peace* (1868) and *Anna Karenina* (1877); for further comments on him by DHL, see 'Translator's Preface to *Cavalleria Rusticana*', 168:38–169:13, and note to 168:39 . . . Pen-name of Mary Anne Evans (1819–80), English novelist; her works include *The Mill on the Floss* (1860) and *Middlemarch* (1871–2). DHL said of her: 'I am very fond of her, but I wish she'd take her specs off, and come down off the public platform' (*Letters*, i. 101).

148:22   **The *Story of a Blackcap***   English translation of *Storia di una Capinera.*

148:23   *Christmas Carol*, or *Silas Marner.*   *A Christmas Carol* (1843), the best-known of the 'Christmas Books' by Charles Dickens (1812–70) . . . *Silas Marner* (1861), a novel by George Eliot.

148:32   *Les Misérables*   A novel dealing with the social conditions of the Parisian poor, by Victor Hugo (1802–85), published in 1862.

148:34   **stands at a rather low figure,**   A stock-exchange expression for commodities which have sunk in value.

149:6   **a realist, in the grim Flaubertian sense**   On account of the close and unsentimentalised observation of ordinary life in his work, Flaubert was regarded as the principal figure in the realist movement in French fiction in the 1850s and 1860s, but he himself never approved of the label.

149:21   *Madame Bovary* [149.17] . . . **Emma and Charles Bovary**   Emma Rouault, the central character of Flaubert's novel *Madame Bovary* (1857), marries the dull provincial doctor Charles Bovary.

150:17   **the appalling "flatness" of their lives.**   DHL made numerous comparable comments about the younger generation in the mid to late 1920s, e.g. of the friends of the sisters Lucille and Yvette in *The Virgin and the Gipsy* (1926): 'Their parents let them do almost entirely as they liked. There wasn't really a fetter to break, nor a prison-bar to file through, nor a bolt to shatter' (p. 38).

150:20   **stale, flat and unprofitable.**   *Hamlet*, I. ii. 133–4 ('How weary, stale, flat, and unprofitable / Seem to me all the uses of this world!').

150:23   **the long sketch or story of the little fat peasant**   Actually quite a short story, 'La roba' ('Property'), in *Novelle Rusticane*, about a peasant named Mazzaro.

151:22   **Tchekov**   Anton Chekhov (1860–1904), Russian writer and dramatist, born in Taganrog; author of many celebrated short stories, including 'The Lady with the Pet Dog', 'Gooseberries' and 'In the Ravine', and plays including *Uncle Vanya* and *The Cherry Orchard.*

151:33   **the kingdom of Dahomey.**   Dahomey was an ancient kingdom in West Africa, adjoining that of Benin (see note to 104:9). DHL tended to use the name to signify anywhere outlandish; cf. *Sketches* 178:4.

151:36   *alter ego,*   Other self (Latin).

151:38   **to pay, and get it prayed into paradise.**   Under a papal bull of Sixtus IV, in 1476, the Indulgences for the Dead formalised the common practice whereby priests were asked to intercede with prayers for the soul of one departed in return for a donation to the church treasury. The corrupt trafficking in such indulgences was a major cause of Luther's revolt against the Catholic Church in 1519 and the foundation of Protestantism.

152:2   **all he says is: I've got bitter in my mouth.**   Gesualdo is described in DHL's translation as 'ill, yellow, with his mouth always bitter' (*Mastro-don Gesualdo*, 1928, p. 395).

152:4   **he says: It is . . . swelled up inside me.**   ' "It's all the trouble I've had!—all the bitter things!—and I've had a lot!—You see, it's left the yeast here in my inside—!" ' (*Mastro-don Gesualdo*, p. 442).

152:5   **Dmitri Karamazov**   See note to 127:30.

152:23   **Once you get to Ceylon,**   DHL had sailed from Sicily to Ceylon, now Sri Lanka, in February 1922, continuing his translation of *Mastro-don Gesualdo* on board ship. He stayed on the island for six weeks before travelling on to Australia.

152:23   **Buddha**   DHL's friend Earl Brewster had gone to Ceylon to study Buddhism, and DHL had travelled with a view to discarding his prejudices and becoming interested in the religion himself, but almost as soon as he arrived his earlier hostility returned; his letters from Ceylon speak of 'hideous little Buddha temples, like decked up pigsties', and 'a rat-hole religion' (*Letters*, iv. 221, 234).

153:7   **the tall and reckless asphodel**   Cf. the sketch 'Cerveteri', written at much the same time: 'Having stood on the rocks in Sicily, with the pink asphodel proudly sticking up like clouds at sea, taller than myself . . . I confess I admire the flower . . . I believe we don't like the asphodel because we don't like anything proud and sparky' (*Sketches* 15:13–31).

153:7   **Magna Graecia**   Greater Greece: i.e. those parts of southern Italy and Sicily which were colonised by the ancient Greeks.

153:8   **"I'll learn you to be a toad!"**   Frieda Lawrence used this expression in a joint letter to Edward Garnett, 7 September 1912: 'I think L. quite missed the point in "Paul Morel" . . . he is so often beside the point "but 'I'll learn him to be a toad' as the boy said as he stamped on the toad"' (*Letters*, i. 449). See also 222:1–2 above.

153:12   *à terre,*   Down to earth (French).

153:19   **Spaniards, Bourbons,**   Sicily was officially under Spanish rule from 1412 until the treaty of Utrecht in 1713. It was subsequently claimed by Carlos of Bourbon, who proclaimed himself King of the Two Sicilies in 1738. Thereafter, apart from the period under Joseph Buonaparte, 1806–15, the Bourbons ruled Sicily until 1860.

153:20   **The Thousand and Garibaldi**   The army of a thousand volunteers which Garibaldi led to victory in Sicily in 1860; see note to 144:7.

153:26   **Palermo**   The chief city of Sicily.

153:31   **serfs**   In Russia, before emancipation in 1861, peasants, serfs, were the property of their local landowner.

153:34   **The great nobles shunned the country, as in Ireland.**   Many English owners of estates in Ireland did not live there, one of many sources of tension between Britain, as the governing power, and the native Irish population in the years prior to the forming of the Irish Free State in 1921.

154:1   **since Ulysses sailed that way.**   Many of the mythical adventures of Odysseus (Ulysses) are supposed to have occurred on and around the Sicilian coast.

154:10   **cyclamens, and sumach**   Flowers and shrubs growing wild in Sicily.

154:11   **Persephone**   In Greek mythology of the cycle of the seasons, Persephone was the daughter of Zeus and Demeter. She was abducted by Hades, god of the underworld, and only released on condition that she spend a third of the year with him. In some versions of the myth the abduction occurred in the fields around the town of Enna, in Sicily.

154:30   **Socrates.**   Athenian philosopher (470–399 BC); his teachings were preserved in the *Dialogues* of Plato.

155:1   **the tisical Bianca,**   'Tisical' is another word for consumptive; see note to 24:38. Bianca Trao, the daughter of a decayed aristocratic family, is married to Gesualdo Motta for financial reasons.

155:2   **his daughter,**   Although the narrative strongly implies it, Gesualdo himself never appears to suspect that his daughter Isabella, who eventually marries the Duca di Leyra, is in reality the child of Bianca's affair with the Baron Nini Rubiera. From one or two of DHL's own comments on the novel (e.g. 155:13–14), it would appear that this implication had not completely filtered through to him either – although, since he was writing Introductions, he may of course have been disguising the information in the interests of suspenseful reading.

155:8   **Diodata . . . one of his own hired men,**   Diodata is Gesualdo's mistress. He marries her to one of his labourers, Nanni l'Orbo, and continues his relationship with her.

155:26   **to *get on*,**   Cf. DHL's autobiographical reminiscences written in the autumn of 1926, '[Return to Bestwood]' and 'Getting On' (*Late Essays and Articles*, ed. Boulton, 15–24, 27–32).

155:28   **podesta,**   Properly, *podestà*; mayor (Italian).

156:7   **Achilles . . . Pericles . . . Alcibiades:**   In Greek mythology, the son of the goddess Thetis, the greatest Greek warrior in the Trojan War . . . Athenian statesman (490–429 BC), ruler of the city at the height of its power . . . Athenian statesman (450–404 BC), in his youth a friend of Socrates, notoriously egotistical and self-seeking. At one point he fled to Sparta and assisted the Spartans against Athens, before returning to command the Athenian fleet in 407; he was later assassinated.

156:14   **We have changed all that.**   'Nous avons changé tout cela', the words of Sganarelle in Molière's play *Le médecin malgré lui* (1666). Cf. *Letters*, iii. 395.

156:18   **Myshkin**   Prince Myshkin, hero of Dostoevsky's novel *The Idiot*. In his 1915 letter to Murry setting out his thoughts on Dostoevsky, DHL calls this his favourite among the novels (*Letters*, ii. 543).

156:23   **Hector**   In Homer's *Iliad*, the son of Priam, King of Troy; a noble warrior eventually defeated by Achilles.

156:31   **Tolstoy's Pierre,**   Pierre Bezuhov, one of the central characters in Tolstoy's novel *War and Peace* (1868).

Translator's Preface to *Cavalleria Rusticana*

163:3   **under this title**   The collection was originally published, in 1880, as *Vita dei Campi* (*Life in the Fields*).

163:5   **just "retired" from the world.**   Verga was still living in Milan at this time. See note to 147:25.

163:8   **Turiddu . . . La Lupa . . . Jeli**   Principal characters of 'Cavalleria Rusticana' ('Rustic Chivalry'), 'La Lupa' ('The She-Wolf') and 'Jeli Il Pastore' ('Jeli the Herdsman'), respectively.

163:17   **1860, the Italy of Garibaldi,**   See note to 144:7.

163:29   **the *beau monde*.**   The fashionable world (French).

163:4   **in Milan, in Florence, in Naples,**   See note to 147:8.

164:2   **love-affairs with elegant ladies:**   Verga had two principal affairs. In 1869 he fell in love with Giselda Fojanesi, who three years later married a poet from Catania, Mario Rapisardi. In 1881 Verga began a relationship with the Countess Dina Castelazzi di Sordevolo, while continuing to see Giselda. Eventually, in 1884, Rapisardi discovered his wife's affair and forced her to leave Catania and move back to Florence. In 1893 Verga resumed his affair with the Countess Dina, now a widow, and the relationship continued on and off, largely off, for the rest of his life. He appears to have been extremely circumspect during these relationships, careful not to be seen with either lady in places where he was known, and refusing ever to consider marriage.

164:5   **the Goncourts,**   Edmond (1822–96) and Jules (1830–70), the Goncourt brothers, were born in Paris. They collaborated on many novels, including *Germinie Lacerteux* (1864), and their *Journal* (1851–70). With their call for a literature of fidelity to fact, they were prominent figures in the development of realism and naturalism in French literature.

164:13   **with his sister.**   Verga's sister died in 1877, and his mother in 1878. He visited them often, but did not live with them on a permanent basis.

164:16   **responsibility for the family estate**   Verga was involved in a certain amount of business and estate management in the late 1870s, but he did not have to take full charge of his ill brother's children and the family holdings until around 1896; his brother eventually died in 1903.

164:27   **The sketch he calls** *Fantasticheria* **(Caprice)**   'Fantasticheria' was the first of the stories to be written, and in many ways is a preliminary sketch for the novel *I Malavoglia*.

164:29   *Il Come, il Quando, et il Perché* **(The How, When, and Wherefore)**   This story, of a quite different character from the others, did not appear in the original collection, but was added to the second edition, in 1881.

164:33   **Polidori,**   The main character of 'The How, When, and Wherefore'.

165:10   **jingling her scent-bottle**   In the opening scene of 'Caprice'.

165:11   **Aci-Trezza**   A fishing village near Catania, setting for *I Malavoglia*.

165:32   **Brothpot, Rosso Malpelo,**   The name 'Pentolaccia', very difficult to translate, would probably be better rendered 'Stinkpot'; at any rate, it carries a crude sexual innuendo which is rather lost in DHL's version . . . 'The Red-Headed Brat'. In his footnote to the story DHL writes: 'Red hair was very unpopular in Southern Italy, Judas having been red-haired, according to tradition. *Malpelo*, evil-haired, has something of the same force as "misbegotten"' (*Cavalleria Rusticana*, p. 119).

165:36   **Alfio.**   In 'Cavalleria Rusticana', the jealous husband who kills Turiddu.

165:39   **Maria and her Erminia**   In 'The How, When, and Wherefore', two married ladies, best friends, who both fall rather shallowly for the charms of Polidori.

166:1   **Nanni?**   The male character in 'La Lupa', seduced by Mrs Pina, the she-wolf of the title, who marries him to her daughter Maricchia so she can continue the affair.

166:6   **a realist of the Zola school.** Emile Zola (1840–1902), born in Paris, was the most celebrated novelist of the naturalist movement in France. His 20-volume sequence *Les Rougon-Macquart*, appearing between 1871 and 1893, was a series of unvarnished and deterministic novels of mostly lower-class life, including *L'Assommoir* (1877), *Germinal* (1885), and *La Bête Humaine* (1890).

166:10   **the earlier D'Annunzio.** D'Annunzio's early stories, collected in *Terra Vergine* (1884), were naturalistic accounts of peasant life.

166:14   **neurotic Virgins of the Rocks** See note to 105:30.

166:28   **Theocritus . . . an Alexandrine courtier,** Theocritus was a Greek poet (285–247 BC), author of the *Idylls*, many set in the Sicilian landscape. He is thought to have spent much of his life at the Egyptian Court in Alexandria.

166:29   **"musk and insolence"** *Maud* (1855), by Alfred, Lord Tennyson (1809–92), VI. 44–6: 'That oil'd and curl'd Assyrian Bull / Smelling of musk and of insolence, / Her brother, from whom I keep aloof'.

166:34   **the rocks that the Cyclops flung at Ulysses;** In Homer's *Odyssey*, the giant Polyphemus, the Cyclops ('one-eyed'), who lives in a cave on the coast of Sicily, imprisons Odysseus (Latin, 'Ulysses') and his companions, but Odysseus makes him drunk and blinds him, escaping with his surviving men by clinging to the bodies of sheep. The Cyclops hurls rocks in their direction as they sail away.

166:36   **Girgenti.** Old name of Agrigento, s.w. Sicily; see note to 36:27. Girgenti is famous for its temples, and was the birthplace (500 BC) of the philosopher Empedocles.

167:1   **Gramigna** In the story 'Gramigna's Lover' ('L'Amante di Gramigna'), the second story to be written. Gramigna ends up in prison for brigandage, not for killing a love rival.

167:19   *Nous avons changé tout cela.* See note to 156:14.

167:33   **the Word.** Cf. John i. 1.

168:39   **the Tolstoyan fallacy . . . exalting the peasant.** In the latter part of his life, from about 1880, Tolstoy converted to a personal and ascetic form of Christianity, involving semi-communistic doctrines, a repudiation of material wealth, and an admiration for the virtues of the peasantry, in particular the simplicity of their songs and stories (cf. his essay of 1896, 'What Is Art?').

169:5   **the later Vronsky** Count Vronsky is Anna's lover in Tolstoy's *Anna Karenina*. Cf. DHL's comment in 'The Novel' (1925): 'Nobody in the world is anything but delighted when Vronsky gets Anna Karenin' (*Hardy* 180:2–3).

169:7   **cut off his own nose to spite his face.** Proverbial; to injure oneself through one's own vindictive or resentful conduct.

169:19   **leaning down from the gold bar of heaven,** Allusion to the opening of the poem 'The Blessed Damozel', by Dante Gabriel Rossetti (1828–82): 'The blessed damozel leaned out / From the gold bar of Heaven'.

170:1   **an aureole** A halo or ring of light around a holy figure in religious painting.

170:21   **after-influenza . . . all over Europe.** DHL may have been alluding to the devastating epidemic of Spanish influenza which struck Europe in 1919, soon after the end of the First World War, and caused an almost equally large number of fatalities.

170:30 **the enormous diffusiveness of Victor Hugo,** See note to 148:32. Hugo's novels, such as *Notre-Dame de Paris* (1831), *Les Misérables* (1862) and *Les travailleurs de la mer* (1866), were massively prolix.

170:36 **Maupassant's self-effacement** See note to 147:15.

170:39 **Merimée ... *Mateo Falcone* ... *L'Enlèvement de la Redoute.*** Prosper Mérimée (1803–70), French novelist, born in Paris. *Mateo Falcone* and *L'Enlèvement de la redoute* were short novels, both published in 1833; his later works included *Carmen* (1852).

171:5 **the grand idea of self-effacement in art . . . the excellent story *Gramigna's Lover,*** The story is prefaced by an aesthetic testament, in the form of a letter to Verga's friend Farina, the central part of which DHL translated thus: 'I believe that the triumph of the novel ... will be reached when the affinity and the cohesion of all its parts will be so complete that the process of the creation will remain a mystery ... and that the harmony of its form will be so perfect, the sincerity of its content so evident, its method and its *raison d'être* so necessary, that the hand of the artist will remain absolutely invisible ... the work of art ... may ... stand by itself ... immutable as a bronze statue, whose creator has had the divine courage to eclipse himself and to disappear in his immortal work' (*Cavalleria Rusticana*, pp. 146–7).

171:28 **Maricchia** see note to 166:1.

172:12 **He tells us himself** See note to 140:14.

173:15 **men like James Joyce** See note to 122:10.

173:23 **Mascagni's rather feeble music** See note to 139:15. Verga sued Mascagni over the profits from the opera, and in 1893 was awarded 143,000 lire, a very substantial sum, but he was not satisfied with the judgement and continued the suit, losing a good deal of the original settlement in legal costs.

Foreword to *The Story of Doctor Manente*

177:2 **the *Story of Doctor Manente*** A novella by A. F. Grazzini (1503–84), known as 'Il Lasca' ('The Roach'), Florentine poet and playwright, founder in 1540 of the first Academy in Florence.

177:3 **Lungarno Series.** See Introduction, p. lxxxiii, and note to 11:17. 'Lungarno' is the name given to a series of boulevards flanking both sides of the river Arno in the centre of Florence.

177:6 **Boccaccio:** Giovanni Boccaccio (1313–75), probably born in Florence, one of the most important and influential figures in late medieval literature; author of the *Decameron*, *Teseida*, *Filostrato* and many other works.

177:11 ***beffa*, or *burla*** Comic skit or satire, burlesque (Italian). The galley proofs of the Foreword at this point printed *buffa* instead of *burla*. DHL corrected this and noted in the margin: 'for *buffa* I had *burla*. Did you change it on purpose?' In his manuscript, however, he had indeed written *buffa*. He may have forgotten, or, as seems likely given the discrepancy between the manuscript and the proofs, there may have been an intermediate version of the text, probably a revised typescript, now lost. See 'Texts', p. xcix.

177:17 *palazzi* Palaces (Italian). In England the term 'palace' implies a royal residence, but in Europe it is also used to signify a large town house or mansion, or a civic building.

177:24 **Lorenzo** Lorenzo de' Medici, called the Magnificent (1449–92), a member of the Florentine ruling family, ruled from 1469, surviving an assassination attempt by the Pazzi conspirators in 1478. He was regarded as the archetypal Renaissance prince, being both a competent ruler and an enthusiastic patron of the arts, and himself wrote much poetry and at least one novella similar to Grazzini's.

177:27 **The Grand Vicar . . . the Spanish type!** The Vicar General in the story conducts an enquiry into whether Doctor Manente had truly died, or had merely been bewitched by one Nepo de Galatrona. But the Vicar's eagerness to send Nepo to the stake for sorcery evaporates when Lorenzo the Magnificent has a quiet word with him: 'Hearing this the Vicar, who as you know was good-natured and timid in his feelings, agreed at once with Lorenzo, excusing himself by saying he did not know enough about it, and finally it was a thing they should say no more about. With this resolution he took leave of the Magnificent, not without dread of some strange malady, and so he went home, and never again in his life was he heard to speak of Nepo, neither for good or ill' (*The Story of Doctor Manente*, Florence, 1929, p. 102). DHL included a footnote, remarking that 'Nepo da Galatrona was a famous wizard and quack from the upper Arno Valley, who performed cures by reciting exorcisms and conjuration over bits of cloth dipped in the blood of the sick man, or over an apple which he had touched' (p. 117).

177:31 **Tuscan.** From Tuscany, the region of central Italy whose capital is Florence.

177:32 *terre à terre,* Down to earth (French; see note to 153:12). DHL uses the construction *à terre à terre* later in the Foreword (179:23).

177:34 **angels or winged lions or soaring eagles,** Alluding to the symbols of the Evangelists, which derived from Ezekiel i. 5–13: St Mark was represented as a lion, St John as an eagle, St Matthew as a man and St Luke as an ox; all four creatures were winged.

178:6 **Piazza della Signoria,** The main square or market-place of Florence, flanked by the Palazzo Vecchio and the Loggia dei Lanzi. A copy of Michelangelo's *David* stands in the square (the original sculpture was moved to the Accademia in 1882), along with statues by Donatello (*Judith and Holofernes*) and Giovanni da Bologna (*Cosimo the Younger*).

178:7 **Michelangelo's *David* stands livid,** Cf. DHL's essay 'David', in *Sketches* 185–9, and Explanatory notes.

178:33 **the sombre curses of Dante . . . Fra Angelico and Botticelli,** In the *Inferno*, Dante imagines in great detail the torments of the damned, torments usually reflecting the nature of the sin, so that, for example, those guilty of gluttony are eternally gnawed, the angry tear themselves and each other with their teeth, murderers are immersed up to their eyebrows in a river of blood, etc. DHL may also have had in mind the brooding, distorted figures in Leonardo's *Adoration of the Magi* or Michelangelo's *Last Judgement* . . . Fra Angelico (1387, or possibly 1400–55) and Sandro Botticelli (1445–1510) were leading painters of the early Italian Renaissance. In his 'Study of

Thomas Hardy', DHL had written that Fra Angelico's paintings 'frighten us or bore us with their final annunciations of centrality and stability. We want to escape' (*Hardy* 69:13–4 and Explanatory note). In the same work he remarked of Botticelli's *Nativity of the Saviour*: 'Perhaps there is a melancholy in Botticelli, a pain of Woman mated to the Spirit . . . But still it is joy transparent over pain. It is the utterance of complete, perfect religious art' (*Hardy* 67:4–8).

179:13   **Filippo Lippi,**   Fra Filippo Lippi (1406–69), Florentine painter, a pupil of Masaccio.

179:14   **Piero della Francesca,**   Italian Renaissance painter (1420–92), born in Umbria.

179:18   **the Uffizi Gallery.**   The principal art gallery and museum of Florence, containing among other paintings Botticelli's *Birth of Venus* and Fra Angelico's *Coronation of the Virgin.*

179:25   **D'Annunzio's peasant stories.**   See note to 166:10.

179:26   **Gonzaga of Mantua**   Mantua, the birthplace of Virgil, was ruled by the Gonzaga family from 1328 to 1708. The story to which DHL alludes here has not been identified.

180:23   **Brunelleschi . . . the Cathedral dome in Florence**   Filippo Brunelleschi (1377–1446), architect, designed the dome of the Duomo in Florence, and many other churches and buildings in the city, including the Pitti Palace.

180:23   **the *Fat Carpenter,***   The *Novella del Grasso Legnaiuolo* (*Story of the Fat Woodcarver*) (DHL originally wrote 'Woodcarver' in his manuscript but changed it to 'Carpenter'): a story circulating in Florence for many years before being written down by Antonio di Tuccio Manetti (1423–97), author of the *Life of Filippo Brunelleschi.* By an elaborate plot involving his entire acquaintance, the woodcarver Manetto was persuaded that he had turned into somebody else, a debtor named Matteo. On discovering that he had been fooled, Manetto's humiliation was such that he left Florence for Hungary, although he did return years later and resumed his friendship with those who had mocked him. According to Manetti, the plot was instigated by Brunelleschi, and the sculptor Donatello (1386–1466) was also party to it. For a recent translation of the story, see Lauro Martines, *An Italian Renaissance Sextet*, tr. Murtha Baca (New York, 1994).

180:35   **Botticelli's *Spring*:**   The *Primavera*, by Botticelli, hangs in the Uffizi in Florence; it is a complex allegorical painting, in which Flora is taken unawares by Zephyr behind her and metamorphosed into Spring, and Cupid shoots an arrow at one of the three Graces. DHL discusses the painting briefly in 'Study of Thomas Hardy'; see *Hardy* 69:19 and Explanatory note.

180:36   **Michelangelo stuck . . . the Sistine ceiling**   Michelangelo painted the ceiling of the Sistine Chapel in the Vatican between 1508 and 1512. The paintings represent the history of Creation up to the time of Moses.

181:12   **in three Suppers,**   The stories in Lasca's work were supposed to be recounted after supper. In Boccaccio's *Decameron*, the stories are recounted over a period of ten days in the mid and late afternoons.

181:15   **two volumes following on this one,**   See Introduction, p. lxxxiii.

Review of *Contemporary German Poetry*

187:1 *Contemporary German Poetry* A volume in a series of contemporary European poetry anthologies produced by the Walter Scott Publishing Co., this one in 1909. Jethro Bithell (1878–1962), whose *The Minnesingers* was also reviewed by DHL, was at this time a lecturer at Manchester University and later became Reader in German at the University of London.

187:2 *Contemporary Belgian Poetry.* Bithell also translated and edited this volume for the same series, in 1911. It had been reviewed anonymously in the *English Review* (see Introduction, pp. xxvii–xxviii, and n. 14).

187:4 **His own poem,** Bithell prefaced his volume with a sonnet, addressed to Richard Dehmel, which does not inspire great confidence in his sensitivity as a translator:

> Soul of the clashing clouds that terrorize
> > The Fathers until they a refuge take
> > In temples that thy winds of wings shall break
> Above the god who knows not that he dies:
>
> Soon as thy wrath sets free the writhen skies
> > Thy rain of rimes is a deep sun-washed lake,
> > Cooling the feverous sands of modern ache,
> And over it enchanted butterflies.
>
> And plaintive swallows like a shuttle flit
> > From thought to thought, even as the stars are knit,
> > Till, weary of wrestling with the bulk of Wrong,
> Thou liest in the arms of Midnight, who
> > Listens with bated breath and rapt ears to
> > The beating of the tender heart of Song.

187:4 **Richard Dehmel,** German poet (1863–1920), born in Brandenburg; his writings were greatly influenced by Nietzsche.

187:7 **Verhaeren and Iwan Gilkin,** Emile Verhaeren (1855–1916), Belgian Symbolist poet, author of *Les Flambeaux noirs* (1890) and *Les Campagnes hallucinées* (1893). Bithell described him as a Belgian Whitman, who 'has smitten poetry out of workshops, anvils, locomotives, girders, braziers, pavements, gin-shops, brothels, the Stock Exchange' (*Contemporary Belgian Poetry*, 1911, p. xxii). Iwan Gilkin, Belgian poet and dramatist (1858–1924), was the editor of *La Jeune Belgique* from 1882. His poems include *La Nuit*, written in imitation of Baudelaire, and his plays include *Savonarole* (1906).

187:11 **wearing the same favour.** A favour is a ribbon or other ornament worn on a ceremonial occasion, e.g. by a bride at her wedding, or given by a lady to her champion at a tournament.

187:12 **Albert Mockel** Belgian Symbolist poet and critic (1866–1945), author of a pioneering study of Stephane Mallarmé (1899).

187:13 **Baudelaire,** Charles Baudelaire (1821–67), poet, essayist and critic, one of the founding figures of modern literature; his poems *Les Fleurs du Mal* were published in 1857, his novel *La Fanfarlo* in 1847, and his essay on contemporary art, *Le Peintre de la vie moderne*, in 1863. In a letter to Louie Burrows of 18 September 1910, DHL records how he snapped up a copy of *Les Fleurs du Mal* for 9d in a bookshop in the Charing Cross Road (*Letters*, i. 179).

187:19 **makes a hollow of his hand,** Cf. Isaiah xl. 12, 'measured the waters in the hollow of his hand'.

187:25 **the poem 'Grey,'** A poem by Irene Forbes-Mosse, the German-born widow of a major in the Royal Irish Regiment; translated for Bithell's anthology by Miss H. Friederichs.

188:19 **Verlaine's "Green."** Paul Verlaine (1844–96), French lyric poet, wrote 'Green', one of his *Aquarelles*, in London in 1872; it was set to music by both Fauré and Debussy. In 1914 DHL also published a poem called 'Green' (*Poems* 216). Forbes-Mosse's poem seems to have a closer affinity with some of the lyrics in the sequence *Die Schöne Müllerin* ('The Fair Maid of the Mill'), by Wilhelm Müller (1794–1827), set to music in 1823 by Franz Schubert: in particular, 'Mit dem grünen Lautenbande' ('With the green lute-ribbon') and 'Die liebe Farbe' ('The Beloved Colour') with its refrain 'Mein Schatz hat's Grün so gern' ('My love is so fond of green').

188:23 **Synge** John Millington Synge (1871–1909), Irish dramatist, who studied and wrote of peasant life in the Aran Islands off Ireland's west coast; author of *The Playboy of the Western World* (1907).

188:24 **Thomas Hardy and George Meredith** Thomas Hardy wrote poetry throughout his career; George Meredith (1828–1909), novelist and poet, author of *Modern Love* (1862), a verse-novel of fifty sixteen-line sonnets.

189:8 **Agamemnon and Oedipus [189:2]** . . . **the Greek dramatists** Oedipus, Agamemnon and Medea are the protagonists of plays by the three great Greek tragedians, Sophocles (*Oedipus Tyrannos*), Aeschylus (*Agamemnon*) and Euripides (*Medea*), respectively. As Carl Baron pointed out in the article announcing his rediscovery of this review in 1969, it reflects DHL's 'recent reading of Greek tragedies in Gilbert Murray's translations' (*Encounter*, xxxiii, August 1969, 3).

189:8 **Swinburne.** Algernon Charles Swinburne (1837–1909), most celebrated poet of the third quarter of the nineteenth century, author of *Atalanta in Calydon* (1865) and *Poems and Ballads* (1866).

189:11 **"Venus Pandemos."** A poem by Richard Dehmel, describing a vision of Syphilis and Death sitting together in the corner of a café-brothel (*Contemporary German Poetry*, 1911, pp. 34–6).

189:13 **Peter Hille's "Morn of a Marriage Night."** Peter Hille (1854–1904), born in Berlin, was famous in his day as a kind of vagabond-poet of no fixed abode; he spent some time lodging in doss-houses in the East End of London. 'The Morn of the Marriage Night' makes some coy references to sexual intercourse (*Contemporary German Poetry*, pp. 88–92).

189:16 **jerry work** Shoddy or flimsy manufacture.

Review of *The Oxford Book of German Verse*

193:1 **THE OXFORD BOOK OF GERMAN VERSE** Edited by Hermann Georg Fiedler (1862–1945), the Oxford Professor of German, the anthology, published by The Clarendon Press in 1911, had a preface by Gerhart Hauptmann (see note to 194:31). New editions, with greatly altered selections, were published in 1927 and 1967 (the latter edited by E. L. Stahl).

193:3 **Walther von der Vogelweide** (1170?–1230), German lyric poet, born in the Tyrol; most celebrated of the Minnesingers.

193:4 **School days.** DHL studied German throughout his time at Nottingham High School, excelling at first but performing less successfully as he grew older; see *Early Years* 86–7.

193:5 **a breviary.** A book containing the service for each day, to be recited by priests.

193:10 **"Geh aus, mein Herz ... Gottes Gaben ..."** The opening lines of 'Zur Sommerzeit', by Paul Gerhardt (1607–76) (*The Oxford Book of German Verse*, p. 34) ['Freud', ...']. Oddly enough, this famous poem was omitted from later editions of the anthology.

193:12 **Beethoven, Schubert, Schumann, Brahms and Wolf,** Ludwig van Beethoven (1770–1827), Franz Schubert (1797–1828), Robert Schumann (1810–56), Johannes Brahms (1833–97), Hugo Wolf (1860–1903); German composers noted for *lieder*, musical settings of lyric poems.

193:15 **Heine's "Thalatta"** Heinrich Heine (1797–1856), German lyric poet. 'Thalatta! Thalatta!' ('The Sea! The Sea!') first appeared in his *Buch der Lieder* (1827).

193:17 **Mörike** Eduard Mörike (1804–75), poet, born in Swabia; for nine years a country parson, later a schoolteacher.

193:19 **Schaukal,** Richard von Schaukal (1874–1942), Austrian poet.

193:23 **Lenau, Keller, Meyer, Storm,** Nineteenth-century lyric poets, none of them actually born in Germany. Nikolaus Franz Nimbsch, Edler von Strehlenau, who wrote as Nikolaus Lenau (1802–50), came from Hungary; Gottfried Keller (1819–90) and Conrad Ferdinand Meyer (1825–98) were Swiss; and Theodor Storm (1817–88) was born in Schleswig-Holstein when it was still under Danish jurisdiction.

193:24 **Paul Heyse** Paul Johann Ludwig von Heyse (1830–1914), poet and translator, winner of Nobel Prize for Literature, 1910. His poems were omitted from later editions of the anthology.

193:25 **Liliencron** Detlev, Freiherr von Liliencron (1844–1909), of mixed German and American parentage, served in Prussian army during the Franco–Prussian War, 1870. DHL would have read several of Liliencron's poems in translations by Jethro Bithell in *Contemporary German Poetry*, which also included translations of poems by many of the other poets mentioned in this review: Dehmel, Hauptmann, Bierbaum, Dauthendey, Hoffmansthal, Geiger, Baum and Lasker-Schüler.

194:10 **TOD IN ÄHREN** [193:30] **... und ist verschieden.** Dehmel's poem appeared on p. 478 of *The Oxford Book of German Verse* ['Mohn, ... unverbunden,']. Bithell had translated it for his *Contemporary German Poetry*, p. 115:

'Death in the Cornfield'

In poppies and in ripening corn
 A soldier, not yet found, is lying,
Already twice through night to morn
 With festering wounds unbandaged dying.

With fever wild his pulse beats fast,
 In the death-throes his head he raises.
He sees in dream the distant past,
 With glazing eye that upwards gazes.

He hears the scythe whir through the rye,
 He smells the meadows sweet with clover;
'Good-bye, old place, old folks, good-bye' –
 And bows his head, and all is over.

194:11 **Dehmel** See note to 187:4. Dehmel's collection *Aber die Liebe* (*But what of Love?*) was published in 1893, containing the sequence 'Verwandlungen der Venus' ('The Transformations of Venus'), which was prosecuted for obscenity, but acquitted on the grounds that it was insufficiently intelligible to be threatening. It was published separately in 1907.

194:30 **NACH EINEM REGEN** [194:18] . . . **Und du lächelst.**

'After Rain'

 Look, the skies are clearing;
 The swallows are chasing themselves
 Like fish over the wet birches.
 And you want to cry?

 The bright trees and blue birds
 Will soon be a golden picture
 In your soul.
 And you weep?

 With my eyes
 I see in yours
 Two little suns,
 And you smile.

194:31 **Hauptmann** Gerhart Hauptmann (1862–1946), dramatist and poet, winner of Nobel Prize for Literature, 1912.

194:31 **Bierbaum** Otto Julius von Bierbaum (1865–1910), poet and novelist.

194:32 **Max Dauthendey's brief, impersonal sketches** Max Dauthendey (1867–1918) was a painter as well as a poet; he spent many years in the Far East and died in Java.

194:34 **Hofmannsthal, the symbolist,** Hugo von Hofmannsthal (1874–1929), Austrian poet, dramatist, librettist for several of Richard Strauss's operas. His early work is in the Symbolist tradition.

194:37   **Geiger and Peter Baum and Elsa Lasker-Schüle**   Albert Geiger (1866–1915), Johann Peter Baum (1869–1916) and Elsa Lasker-Schüler (1869–1945). The collection *Contemporary German Poetry*, which DHL had reviewed (pp. 187–9 above) was apparently the only volume published in England at that date to contain poems by any of these writers (see Armin Arnold, *D. H. Lawrence and German Literature*, Montreal, 1963, pp. 24–5). A selection of Lasker-Schüler's poems was included in later editions of *The Oxford Book of German Verse*.

Review of *The Minnesingers*

197:2   **THE MINNESINGERS . . . Translations.**   Jethro Bithell's translations from the Minnesingers, the medieval German composers of love-poetry ('Minnesang'), was published by Longmans Green in 1909. For Bithell, see note to 187:1.

197:7   **the old lyrical poetry of Provence,**   The early Troubadours of the twelfth and thirteenth centuries, including Bernart de Ventadorn and Arnaut Daniel, composed their verses in the Provençal language.

197:9   **"pièce de résistance."**   'The principal offering'; 'the finest dish' (French). Bithell's promised second volume never appeared.

197:13   **"These translations . . . finished first."**   From Bithell's rather apologetic preface to *The Minnesingers* (pp. v–vi), in which he makes clear that the scholarly part of his enterprise is more important to him than translating the actual poems.

197:26   **the author has striven . . . rather than "Wortgetreu;"**   'rather to be "sinngetreu" than "wortgetreu"' (*The Minnesingers*, p. vii); i.e. true to the thought rather than to the word.

198:6   **the very first verse [197:30] . . . is lost, sweetheart.**   This anonymous lyric from the twelfth century was also the first item in *The Oxford Book of German Verse*, where DHL would have found the original spelling and punctuation which he reproduces here; as he points out, *The Minnesingers* does not include the German originals of the translated poems.

198:18   **Walther von der Vogelweide's [198:8] . . . sang the nightingale."**   *The Minnesingers*, pp. 68–9. For Walther von der Vogelweide, see note to 193:3. The poem also appeared in *The Oxford Book of German Verse*, p. 534.

198:28   **Volkslied.**   Folk song.

198:29   **Marie de France**   French court poet, fl. 1160–90, author of the *Lays* and the *Fables*.

'The Georgian Renaissance': review of *Georgian Poetry, 1911–12*

201:2   **"Georgian Poetry"**   *Georgian Poetry, 1911–12*, was edited by Edward (later Sir Edward) Marsh (1872–1953), classicist and scholar, and published by Harold Monro (1879–1932) of The Poetry Bookshop, in December 1912. It was the first of five such anthologies, the last of which appeared in 1922. Some of the later issues included writers who became famous for their First World War poetry, such as Robert Graves, Isaac Rosenberg and Siegfried Sassoon. By the 1920s, the term 'Georgian poet' had acquired a strongly pejorative sense among Modernists such as T. S. Eliot and Ezra Pound, and champions of individual 'Georgians' took pains to dissociate their favourites from the group. Many of the poets who appeared in the anthologies are, however, still highly regarded.

201:3   **George V.**   Second son of Edward VII; reigned 1910–36.

201:4   **one poem of my own,**   'Snap-Dragon', called 'The Snapdragon' in the anthology (pp. 113–16) (*Poems* 122–6).

201:8   **Ibsen,**   Henrik Ibsen (1828–1906), Norwegian dramatist and poet, author of *Peer Gynt* (1867), *A Doll's House* (1879) and *Ghosts* (1881). DHL had read several of Ibsen's plays, and in 1909 sent Louie Burrows copies of two volumes, commending *Hedda Gabler* and *The Pretenders* in particular (*Letters*, i. 112–14). He also saw a memorable production of *Ghosts* while living at Lake Garda in December 1912; see *Twilight In Italy and Other Essays*, ed. Paul Eggert (Cambridge, 1994), 133:14 and Explanatory note.

201:18   **getting pot-bound,**   A pot-grown plant whose roots have filled the available space and have no further room to expand is called 'pot-bound'. DHL used the expression more than once; cf. 'The Crown': 'It may be that the flower is held from the search of the light, and the roots from the dark, like a plant that is pot-bound' (*Reflections* 272:20–1).

201:19   **the Temple was made a place to barter sacrifices,**   Cf. Matthew xxi. 12.

201:21   **Nietzsche the Christian Religion as it stood,**   The German philosopher Friedrich Nietzsche (1844–1900) made his most concentrated attack on Christianity in *The Anti-Christ* (1888).

201:25   **The great prisoners . . . for lying to us.**   Cf. similar imagery in 'Chaos in Poetry', 109:31–111:11 above.

202:1   **"But send [201:32] . . . Mr. Abercrombie.**   'The Sale of Saint Thomas', ll. 543–4 (Act I of a verse-play published in full in 1931), by Lascelles Abercrombie (1881–1938) (*Georgian Poetry* 21) [' . . . which is . . .']. For DHL on Abercrombie and his poetry, see *Letters*, ii. 119–20 and 176–7.

202:1   **deadly sin is Prudence,**   At the beginning of Abercrombie's play, Thomas claims that 'prudence is an admirable thing', but at the end the Stranger tells him 'prudence, prudence is the deadly sin' ('The Sale of Saint Thomas', ll. 74, 521).

202:5   **Mr. Bottomley . . . there discovered."**   'Babel: The Gate of the God', ll. 88–9, by Gordon Bottomley (1874–1948), whose *Poems of Thirty Years* were published in 1925 (*Georgian Poetry* 29) [' . . . sky, . . . vacancy, . . . discovered—'].

202:12   **Mr. Rupert Brooke [202:6] . . . Afternoon Tea.**   'Dining-room Tea', ll. 40–4, by Rupert Brooke (1887–1915), the most celebrated of the Georgian poets, who became even more famous for the sonnets he composed at the beginning of the First World War, in which he died of blood-poisoning (*Georgian Poetry* 46). For DHL's further comments on Brooke, see *Letters*, ii. 330–1.

202:17   **Mr. John Drinkwater . . . the rose—"**   'The Fires of God', ll. 221–4, by John Drinkwater (1882–1937), poet, dramatist and actor, whose work appeared in all five Georgian anthologies (*Georgian Poetry* 81–2) ['*We cherish . . . the days. / . . . clear untroubled . . . rose,*'].

202:21   **Mr. Wilfrid Wilson Gibson . . . "terror turned to tenderness" . . . her breast."** 'Devil's Edge', ll. 113, 117–18, by W. W. Gibson (1878–1962), a prolific composer of narrative verse (*Georgian Poetry* 110) [' . . . to her . . .']. For DHL's comments on Gibson, see *Letters*, ii. 85, 92, 116, 118, 119–20.

202:27   **Mr. Masefield [202:22] . . . golden moments."** 'Biography', ll. 257–61, by John Masefield (1878–1967), poet, playwright and novelist, Poet Laureate 1930–67; (*Georgian Poetry* 126) ['when . . . moments,'].

202:33   **joie d'être, joie de vivre.**   Joy of being, joy of life (French).

203:1   **"Best trust the happy moments,"**   'Biography', l. 269 (*Georgian Poetry* 127).

203:3   **Mr. W. H. Davies' lovely joy,**   Five poems by William Henry Davies (1871–1940) appeared in the anthology. He was born in Newport, South Wales, had lived as a vagrant in America, and at the time of DHL's review was best known for *The Autobiography of a Super-Tramp* (1908).

203:3   **Mr. De La Mare's . . . still moments,**   Five poems by Walter de la Mare (1873–1956) appeared in the anthology. De la Mare was already well known as a lyric poet, having published *Songs of Childhood* (1902) and *The Listeners* (1912), and later became a successful novelist and short-story writer (*Memoirs of a Midget*, 1921; *The Riddle*, 1923). DHL had numerous dealings with him in 1912 and 1913. De la Mare helped with the publication of some of DHL's poems and articles, and as reader for Heinemann made some cautious but not imperceptive comments on *Paul Morel*: 'I . . . thought – apart from the fineness of individual passages – that it was badly put together and a bit too violent here and there' (letter to Edward Garnett, 27 May 1913; see *Letters*, i. 423n.) He also reviewed *Love Poems and Others* for *The Times Literary Supplement*, 13 March 1913 ('There are poems of sheer brutality, and passages almost without a vestige of restraint or reticence. But imagination . . . and often a delicate, ecstatic beauty'). His review for the same periodical of *The Rainbow* was suppressed, but according to Catherine Carswell it was to have been largely favourable (*The Savage Pilgrimage*, Martin Secker, 1932, p. 35). De la Mare seems to have wanted to keep his distance from DHL, despite remaining on friendly terms, and he found an excuse not to accept the latter's invitation to visit while in Cornwall in 1916.

203:5   **when he "lived from laugh to laugh,"**   Another quotation from Rupert Brooke's 'Dining-room Tea': 'I sang at heart, and talked, and eat, / And lived from laugh to laugh, I too / When you were there, and you, and you.'

203:6   **Mr. Edmund Beale Sargant's . . . in the woodland**   Sargant (1855–1938), director of education for the Transvaal, contributed one poem to the anthology, 'The Cuckoo Wood' (*Georgian Poetry* 169–77).

203:8   **Mr. Bottomley . . . long snows.**   'Little men hurrying, running here and there . . . Man with his bricks was building, building yet' ('Babel: The Gate of the God', ll. 56, 81); 'The snow had fallen many nights and days; / The sky was come upon the earth at last' ('The End of the World', ll. 1–2, *Georgian Poetry* 28–9, 25).

203:10 **"Carpe diem"** 'Seize the day' (Latin), enjoy the fleeting moment. DHL used the phrase in a letter of 24 February 1913, shortly after writing this review (*Letters*, i. 518).

203:17 **Swinburne** See note to 189:8. DHL wrote of Swinburne in 1916: 'I put him with Shelley as our greatest poet. He is the last fiery spirit among us' (*Letters*, ii. 654).

203:38 **Rupert Brooke's moment triumphant in its eternality;**

> Under a vast and starless sky
> I saw the immortal moment lie.
> One instant I, an instant, knew
> As God knows all.
> ('Dining-room Tea', ll. 19–22).

203:40 **Michael Angelo . . . Corot,** The distinction between Michelangelo Buonarotti (1475–1564), Italian Renaissance painter and sculptor, and Jean Baptiste Camille Corot (1796–1875), French painter, is similar to that in DHL's two poems 'Corot' and 'Michael Angelo' (*Poems* 68–9, 920–2), originally written in 1911, which DHL had recently been revising for their appearance in *Love Poems* (February 1913; advertised, as 'Poems of Love', at the end of *Georgian Poetry*).

204:5 **"The Hare"** By W. W. Gibson (*Georgian Poetry* 93–105).

204:6 **"But a bitter blossom was born"** Imperfect recollection of Swinburne's *Atalanta in Calydon* (1865), ll. 729–31: 'For an evil blossom was born / Of sea-foam and the frothing of blood, / Blood-red and bitter of fruit'.

204:7 **Yeats, "Never give all the heart."** Title and first line of a poem from *In The Seven Woods* (1904), by William Butler Yeats (1865–1939), Irish poet and dramatist.

204:9 **"Carmen" and "Tosca"** Eponymous tragic heroines of the operas *Carmen* (1875) by Georges Bizet (1838–1875) and *Tosca* (1900) by Giacomo Puccini (1858–1924).

204:13 **Tristans and what-not** Like the hero of the opera *Tristan and Isolde* (1865) by Richard Wagner (1813–83).

204:16 **Jehovah . . . Pan . . . Aphrodite.** Medieval Latin version of the Hebrew name of God (YHVH), too sacred to be pronounced . . . Greek god of fields, woods and shepherds . . . Greek goddess of love and beauty.

'German Books': review of *Der Tod in Venedig*

207:3 **Thomas Mann** German novelist (1875–1955), born in Lübeck. *Der Tod in Venedig* appeared in 1912. After the period of his career described by DHL, Mann wrote some of his best-known works, including *Der Zauberberg* (*The Magic Mountain*, 1924) and *Doktor Faustus* (1947). He left Germany during the Nazi period and eventually settled in the USA; during and after the war he had immense prestige there.

207:5 **Heinrich Mann, with Jakob Wassermann,** Heinrich Mann (1871–1950), German novelist. His best-known works at the time of DHL's review were *Professor Unrat oder das Ende eines Tyrannen* (*Professor Unrat or the End of a Tyranny*, 1905, later re-issued as *The Blue Angel*) and *Die kleine Stadt* (*The Little Town*, 1909) . . .

Jakob Wassermann, German-Jewish novelist (1873–1934), born in Nuremberg; his best-known works at the time of DHL's review were *Der Moloch* (1902) and *Caspar Hauser* (1908).

207:11 **over middle age,** Mann was actually thirty-seven at the time of DHL's review. DHL appears to have made the error in consequence of having mistranslated 'fünfunddreißig' (thirty-five), the age when Aschenbach falls ill in Vienna, as 'fifty-three', and having associated Aschenbach with Mann throughout. See Introduction, pp. xxx–xxxi, and n. 23.

207:13 **"Buddenbrooks,"** . . . **"Tristan,"** . . . **"Königliche Hoheit,"** *Buddenbrooks* (*The Buddenbrooks*), subtitled 'Decline of a Family', was Mann's first novel, published 1901; *Tristan* a collection of stories, all published by 1903; *Königliche Hoheit* (*Royal Highness*), a short novel, appeared in 1909.

207:15 **a Lübeck "Patrizier."** The father of the Mann brothers was a corn-factor and patrician of Lübeck, a member of the city Senate.

207:20 **Alexander Pope** English poet (1688–1744); his works include *The Rape of the Lock* (1712) and *The Dunciad* (1743). DHL is generalising rather about the style and nature of English 'Augustan' poetry, and there was no real 'school' of Pope.

207:22 **"Nothing outside . . . the book,"** This would seem to be a version of an idea associated with Flaubert, rather than a direct quotation from him. Probably the nearest equivalent would be the following, from Flaubert's letter to Louise Colet, 31 January 1852, about the composition of *Madame Bovary*: 'Je tâche d'être boutonné et de suivre une ligne droite géométrique. Nul lyrisme, pas de réflexions, personnalité de l'auteur absente' ('I am trying to be buttoned up and to follow a geometrically straight line. No lyricism, no reflections, author's personality absent').

207:29 **"Literature is not . . . a curse."** DHL's translation of Tonio Kröger's comment, 'Die Literatur ist überhaupt kein Beruf, sondern ein Fluch.'

207:31 **"There is no artist . . . common life."** DHL has compressed a long sentence in 'Tonio Kröger': 'Der ist noch lange kein Künstler, meine Liebe, dessen letzte und tiefste Schwärmerei das Raffinierte, Exzentrische und Satanische ist, der die Sehnsucht nicht kennt nach dem Harmlosen, Einfachen und Lebendigen, nach ein wenig Freundschaft, Hingebung, Vertraulichkeit und menschlichem Glück,—die verstohlene und zehrende Sehnsucht, Lisaweta, nach den Wonnen der Gewöhnlichkeit!' ('No one, my dear, has a right to call himself an artist if his profoundest craving is for the refined, the eccentric and the satanic—if his heart knows no longing for innocence, simplicity and living warmth, for a little friendship and self-surrender and familiarity and human happiness—if he is not secretly devoured, Lisaveta, by this longing for the bliss of the commonplace!') (Thomas Mann, *Death in Venice and Other Stories*, tr. David Luke, 1998, p. 164).

207:34 **"Sturm und Drang."** 'Storm and Stress', the name, taken from the title of a play of 1777 by F. M. Klinger, given to a short-lived literary movement in Germany in the 1770s. It was mainly inspired by the early works of Goethe (see note to 208:6), including the play *Götz von Berlichingen* (1773) and the novel *Die Leiden des jungen Werthers* (*The Sorrows of Young Werther*, 1774). Other writers in the movement included Friedrich Müller, Heinrich Wagner and J. M. M. Lenz. The name was subsequently used to characterise various examples of art, literature and music of a romantically rebellious and agitated nature.

208:1   **fifty-three.**   See note to 207:11.

208:4   **Corot.**   See note to 203:40.

208:6   **Goethe,**   Johann Wolfgang Goethe (1749–1832), German poet, dramatist and novelist, the most important figure in German literature. His plays include *Egmont* (1788) and *Faust* (Part One, 1808, Part Two, 1832), and his novels, *Die Wahlverwandtschaften* (*Elective Affinities*, 1809) and *Wilhelm Meisters Wanderjahre* (*Wilhelm Meister's Years of Wandering*, 1821–3).

208:14   **"Wählerisch, erlesen . . . und Geschmacks."**   "Fastidious, exquisite, rich, subtle, intolerant of banality and hypersensitive in matters of tact and taste" (*Death in Venice and Other Stories*, tr. Luke, p. 154.)

208:16   **"I worked . . . one page."**   A slightly misleading translation of an extract from Flaubert's letter to Madame Edma Roger des Genettes, 13–18 March 1876, which described the birth-pangs of the story *Un Coeur simple*: 'J'ai travaillé hier pendant seize heures, aujourd'hui toute la journée et, ce soir enfin, j'ai terminé la première page' ('Yesterday I worked for sixteen hours, today the whole day and at last, this evening, I have finished the first page').

208:16   **Leitmotiv**   A term used to describe a musical motto or theme which recurs throughout a piece of music to portray a person, object or emotion. In the operas or music-dramas of Richard Wagner (1813–83), the *Leitmotiv* becomes a principle of composition. It is analogous to a structural system of metaphor or theme in a play or novel.

208:30   **"Now this method [208:17] . . . off-hand."**   This appears to be DHL's own, fairly accurate translation of part of an address by Mann to the Literary Historical Society of Bonn, given in 1906:

> Nun, diese Machart allein würde genügen, meine Langsamkeit zu erklären. Es handelt sich dabei weder un Ängstlichkeit noch um Trägheit, sondern um ein außerordentlich lebhaftes Verantwortlichkeitsgefühl, das nach vollkommener Frische verlangt und mit dem man nach der zweiten Arbeitsstunde lieber keinen irgend wichtigen Satz mehr unternimmt. Aber welcher Satz ist 'wichtig' und welcher nicht? Weiß man es denn zuvor, ob ein Satz, ein Satzteil nicht vielleicht berufen ist, wiederzukehren, als Motiv, Klammer, Symbol, Zitat, Beziehung zu dienen? Und ein Satz, der zweimal gehört werden soll, muß danach sein. Er muß – ich rede nicht von 'Schönheit' – eine gewisse Höhe und symbolische Stimmung besitzen, die ihn würdig macht, in irgendeiner epischen Zukunft wiederzuerklingen. So wird jede Stelle zur 'Stelle', jedes Adjektiv zur Entscheidung, und es ist klar, daß man auf diese Weise nicht aus dem Handgelenk produziert.
>
> (Thomas Mann, in 'Ziele und Wege Deutscher Dichtung nach Äußerungen ihrer Schöpfer', *Mitteilungen der Literaturhistorischen Gesellschaft Bonn*, 1907, Jg. 2, H.7., collected in *Reden und Aufsätze*, vol. II, Oldenburg: S. Fischer Verlag, 1965, pp. 676–7.)

There is no equivalent in the extant German text for DHL's wording 'responsibility for the choice of every word, the coining of every phrase'.

208:33   "The doctors . . . at home."   'Ärztliche Fürsorge hatte den Knaben vom Schulbesuch ausgeschlossen und auf häuslichen Unterricht gedrungen' (*Der Tod in Venedig*, Berlin, Fischer Verlag, 1913, p. 21). In commenting on his quotations DHL gives the false impression that Aschenbach is the narrator.

208:37   "When he . . . the chair."   'Als er um sein fünfunddreißigstes Jahr in Wien erkrankte, äußerte ein feiner Beobachter über ihn in Gesellschaft: "Sehen Sie, Aschenbach hat von jeher nur so gelebt" – und die Sprecher schloß die Finger seiner Linken fest zur Faust – "niemals so" – und er ließ die geöffnete Hand bequem von der Lehne des Sessels hängen' (*Der Tod in Venedig*, p. 21) ('When in his thirty-fifth year he fell ill in Vienna, a subtle observer remarked of him on a social occasion: "You see, Aschenbach has always only lived like *this*" – and the speaker closed the fingers of his left hand tightly into a fist – "and never like *this*" – and he let his open hand hang comfortably down along the back of the chair')   tr. Luke, p. 203.

209:2   "It was pardonable [208:39] . . . single inspirations."   DHL again compresses a long sentence: 'Es war verzeihlich, ja, es bedeutete recht eigentlich den Sieg seiner Moralität, wenn Unkundige die Maja-Welt oder die epischen Massen, in denen sich Friedrichs Heldenleben entrollte, für das Erzeugnis gedrungener Kraft und eines langen Atems hielten, während sie vielmehr in kleinen Tagewerken aus aberhundert Einzelinspirationen zur Größe emporgeschichtet' (*Der Tod in Venedig*, pp. 22–3). ('It was a pardonable error, indeed it was one that betokened as nothing else could the triumph of his moral will, that uninformed critics should mistake the great world of *Maja*, or the massive epic unfolding of Frederick's life, for the product of solid strength and long stamina, whereas in fact they had been built up to their impressive size from layer upon layer of daily opuscula, from a hundred or a thousand separate inspirations') – tr. Luke, p. 204.

209:6   "dass beinahe alles . . . gekommen sei."   *Der Tod in Venedig*, p. 24 [' . . . Hemmnissen zustande . . .']. David Luke renders the passage as follows: 'that nearly all the great things that exist owe their existence to a defiant despite: it is despite grief and anguish, despite poverty, loneliness, bodily weakness, vice and passion and a thousand inhibitions, that they have come into being at all' (*Death in Venice and Other Stories*, p. 205).

209:24   "For endurance of one's fate [209:9] . . . than this?"

> Denn Haltung im Schicksal, Anmut in der Qual bedeutet nicht nur ein Dulden; sie ist eine active Leistung, ein positiver Triumph, und die Sebastian-Gestalt ist das schönste Sinnbild, wenn nicht der Kunst überhaupt, so doch gewiss der in Redestehenden Kunst. Blickte man hinein in diese erzählte Welt, sah man: die elegante Selbstbeherrschung, die bis zum letzten Augenblick eine innere Unterhöhlung, den biologischen Verfall vor den Augen der Welt verbirgt; die gelbe, sinnlich benachteiligte Hässlichkeit, die es vermag, ihre schwelende Brunst zur reinen Flamme zu entfachen, ja, sich zur Herrschaft im Reiche der Schönheit aufzuschwingen; die bleiche Ohnmacht, welche aus den glühenden Tiefen des Geistes die Kraft holt, ein ganzes übermütiges Volk zu Füßen des Kreuzes, zu *ihren* Füßen niederzuwerfen; die liebenswürdige Haltung im leeren und strengen Dienste der Form; das falsche, gefährliche Leben, die rasch entnervende Sehnsucht und Kunst des geborenen Betrügers: betrachtete man all dies Schicksal und wieviel

Gleichartiges noch, so konnte man zweifeln, ob es überhaupt einen anderen Hero-
ismus gäbe als denjenigen der Schwäche. Welches Heldentum aber jedenfalls wäre
zeitgemäßer als dieses?

(*Der Tod in Venedig*, p. 25)

David Luke translates this passage as follows:

For composure under the blows of fate, grace in the midst of torment – this is not
only endurance: it is an active achievement, a positive triumph, and the figure of
Saint Sebastian is the most perfect symbol if not of art in general, then certainly of
the kind of art here in question. What did one see if one looked in any depth into
the world of this writer's fiction? Elegant self-control concealing from the world's
eyes until the very last moment a state of inner disintegration and biological decay;
sallow ugliness, sensuously marred and worsted, which nevertheless is able to fan
its smouldering concupiscence to a pure flame, and even to exalt itself to mastery in
the realm of beauty; pallid impotence which from the glowing depths of the spirit
draws strength to cast down a whole proud people at the foot of the Cross and set
its own foot upon them as well; gracious poise and composure in the empty austere
service of form; the false, dangerous life of the born deceiver, his ambition and
his art which lead so soon to exhaustion—to contemplate all these destinies, and
many others like them, was to doubt if there is any heroism at all but the heroism of
weakness. In any case, what other heroism could be more in keeping with the times?

(*Death in Venice and Other Stories*, p. 205)

209:36 **a kind of Holbein "Totentanz."** *The Dance of Death* was the title of a
series of woodcuts by Hans Holbein the Younger (1497–1543), German painter, born
in Augsburg. Cf. *Letters*, v. 496: 'Baden Baden is a sort of Holbein *Totentanz*: old, old
people tottering their cautious dance of triumph: "wir sind noch hier: hupf! hupf!
hupf!"'

209:40 **the Austrian coast of the Adriatic,** The Dalmatian coast of Croatia and
Slovenia, including Trieste, was part of the Austro-Hungarian empire until 1918.

210:11 **"dem allerliebsten, dem schönsten Liebchen."** *Der Tod in Venedig*,
p. 42: '"To your most charming, beautiful sweetheart."'

210:13 **the Lido,** A fashionable resort just outside Venice.

210:16 **St. Mark's,** The basilica of St Mark's, the state church of the Venetian
Republic, a mixture of Byzantine and Western European architecture, was founded in
1063.

210:24 **Hyacinth in the Greek myth.** Hyacinthus of Sparta was the lover of the
god Apollo, and was accidentally killed in a game of discus-throwing. Purple flowers
sprang up from the ground where his blood had spilt.

210:28 **Künstler** Artist (German).

210:37 **the Sirocco,** A warm sultry wind blowing from the Sahara Desert to southern Europe.

211:1 **Tadzio** The boy's name, the diminutive form of Tadeusz, appeared as
'Tadzin' when DHL's piece was printed in *The Blue Review*; see Textual apparatus.

212:2 **the rise of a poppy,** Cf. 'Study of Thomas Hardy', chaps. I and II; *Hardy*
7–19.

Review of *Fantazius Mallare*

215:2   **Chère Jeunesse**   Dear young people (French).

215:5   **Ben Hecht book . . . pictures . . . text.**   DHL was reviewing *Fantazius Mallare: A Mysterious Oath* (Chicago: Covici-McGee, 1922), by the journalist and screen-writer Ben Hecht (1894–1964), drawings by Wallace Smith; a copy had been sent to him by Willard ('Spud') Johnson (1897–1968). The book (a limited edition of 2,025 copies) had been the subject of a Federal obscenity suit in 1922, to which both Hecht and Smith had pleaded guilty, and were fined $1,000 each. There is no evidence that either spent any time in prison. They had gone to some trouble to be charged with the crime in order to force a trial on the issue of federal obscenity laws, but only the critic H. L. Mencken (see note on 221:7) had agreed to appear as an expert witness for the defence. Hecht did, however, lose his job on the *Chicago Daily News*. The book contained ten numbered full-page drawings; each chapter began with an initial letter in the form of a grotesque human figure, and another (extremely phallic) drawing was reproduced at the head of each of the eight pages of the 'Dedication': perhaps DHL's 'shocking little drawings' (215:29). Hecht later became a very successful dramatist and Hollywood scriptwriter, providing the screenplays for films such as Howard Hawks's *His Girl Friday* (1940), Alfred Hitchcock's *Notorious* (1946) and Henry Hathaway's *Kiss of Death* (1946).

215:6   **a Beardsley drawing,**   Aubrey Vincent Beardsley (1872–98), painter and illustrator. DHL had commented on his drawings for *Atalanta* and the tail-piece to *Salomé* in *The White Peacock*, ed. Andrew Robertson (Cambridge, 1982), 159:4–9, and one of the characters in that novel, George Saxton, had responded strongly to the 'naked lines . . . a sort of fine sharp feeling, like these curved lines' (160:25–6).

215:11   **man's coition with a tree . . . own daimon,**   Wallace Smith's First Drawing, between pages 20 and 21. The tree is distinctly (if angularly) female; the grass growing around the man's buttocks suggests that he has occupied the position for some time . . . a direct transliteration of the Greek 'daimon': genius or demon. Less than a week after writing this review, DHL would ask his American agent Robert Mountsier, about *Studies in Classic American Literature*, 'shall we call this Studies of the American Daimon, Demon?' (*Letters*, iv. 324; see also viii. 57). In 1928 he would distinguish his own 'demon' from his 'other, milder and nicer self' (*Poems* 850).

215:14   **Fantasius Malare**   DHL's spelling, in spite of reading the book 'through' (215:3). The correct title appeared in the book's running head throughout.

215:18   **penis or testicle or vagina**   Words used regularly in the text. Hecht refers, for example, to the 'national vagina' (p. 13), to the vagina as 'a door' at which men 'deliver regularly like industrious milkmen' (p. 56), and to a woman who 'does not burn incense before her vagina' (p. 124). He also referred to the 'vulva as an orifice to be approached with Gregorian chants' (p. 125). A sculpture in the novel has 'a huge phallus' and testicles 'fashioned in the form of a short-necked pendulum arrested at the height of its swing' (p. 39); men's imagination 'discharges itself through their penis' (p. 55), while the penis of a masturbating man 'is beating a ludicrous tattoo on the sofa cushion' (p. 81). See, too, pp. 157–8. Smith's drawings regularly featured erect penises, but always in the form of other things (tree stumps, candle sconces, sword-hilts).

216:3   **spunkless . . . masturbater,**   Destitute of courage, spiritless: but 'spunk' also with the slang meaning of seminal fluid. Cf. DHL's comment in a letter to Edward

Garnett on 'the lot that make up England today. They've got white of egg in their veins, and their spunk is that watery its a marvel they can breed' (*Letters*, i. 422). 'Masturbator' is not a word DHL would have seen often in print, hence perhaps the eccentric spelling (cf. 'to masterbate himself', *Letters*, ii. 285), although he did spell 'masturbation' correctly in his review of *Solitaria* (315:24) five years later. Because Mallare mistakenly thinks that he has killed the woman (Rita) he has taken to live with him, he accounts for her continuing presence by believing that he is imagining her. 'I lie and masturbate with a phantom' (p. 90) – '"I am the victim of an overwhelming desire to masturbate", I said to her' (p. 81) – and when he finally sees his servant Goliath with her, imagines that he is 'masturbating with a phantom' (p. 159). See, too, pp. 13, 15, 80, 122 and 125. For DHL on the topic of masturbation, see also 'Pornography and Obscenity' (*Phoenix* 170–87).

216:5 **rencontre,** Encounter (French).

216:9 **posing as mad . . . wet-leg,** E.g. the first words of chap. 1: 'Fantazius Mallare considered himself mad' (p. 21); cf. also 'I am too clever to go mad', 'I can prove to my satisfaction tonight that I am mad' (p. 41) . . . this passage is the earliest citation in *OED2*, where the word is defined as 'a self-pitying person'. Cf. DHL's poem 'Willy Wet-leg':

> I can't stand Willy wet-leg,
> can't stand him at any price.
> He's resigned, and when you hit him
> he lets you hit him twice.
>
> (*Poems* 559)

216:20 *machine à plaisir,* The description of women in chap. ix of *Mademoiselle de Maupin* (1835) by Théophile Gautier: 'Ce sont des machines à plaisir' ('They are pleasure-machines'). DHL cited the same phrase in *Studies* 69:39, which he revised in the winter of 1922–3. He also referred to Gautier's novel in *St. Mawr*, ed. Finney, 113:35, and repeated the phrase in February 1929 (*Letters*, vii. 179).

216:31 **Hermes Ithyphallos** Hermes (son of Zeus by the nymph Maia: see next note) with the erect penis: such sculptures were carried in the ancient festivals of Bacchus, the Roman god of wine and fruitfulness (counterpart of the Greek god Dionysus).

216:34 **Thoth . . . Horus or Apollo:** In Egyptian mythology, Thoth was a moon deity, scribe of the gods and protector of learning and the arts, associated by the Greeks with Hermes Trismegistus. The Egyptian God Horus (often pictured as a falcon) was identified with the living Pharaoh; Apollo (son of Zeus and Leda), was the Greek god of light, poetry and music.

216:38 **a night** In Aldous Huxley's 1932 edition of the *Letters*, 'night' appears as 'light', giving the sentence a meaning almost exactly opposed to the one DHL had intended (p. 558).

Review of *Americans*

221:2 **Professor Sherman** Stuart Pratt Sherman (1881–1926), born in Iowa, was a professor of literature at the University of Illinois, and literary editor of the *New York Herald Tribune*, 1924–6. He died following a canoeing accident while on holiday.

He wrote two broadly favourable articles on DHL's work: 'America is Rediscovered', a review of *Studies in Classic American Literature*, in the *New York Evening Post Literary Review*, 20 October 1923, and 'Lawrence Cultivates His Beard', a general survey of DHL's writings, in the *New York Herald Tribune Books*, 14 June 1925. See also DHL's letter to Sherman, *Letters*, v. 275–6.

221:6 **Benjamin Franklin . . . "satisfy the professors . . . offend none."** Benjamin Franklin (1706–90), American writer, scientist and statesman, was born in Boston. *Poor Richard's Almanack* (1732–57) was a widely popular collection of proverbs, mottoes and epigrams. For DHL on Franklin, see *Studies* 20–31 and Explanatory notes . . . Alluding to a passage in Franklin's *Autobiography*, where Franklin describes his 'intended creed . . . being free of every thing that might shock the professors of any religion' (*Benjamin Franklin's Autobiography*, Everyman edition of 1908, p. 112; see *Studies* 20:32n.).

221:7 **Mr. Mencken** Henry Louis Mencken (1880–1956), critic and journalist, born in Baltimore. As literary editor of *Smart Set*, and author of the six volumes of *Prejudices* (1919–27), he was a celebrated iconoclast. He refused, when invited, to be introduced to Sherman, allegedly saying 'I'd rather pass into heaven without the pleasure of his acquaintance'.

221:8 **Mr. More** Paul Elmer More (1864–1937), critic and writer of pronounced conservative inclinations, born in St Louis; editor of the *Nation* from 1909 to 1914. His critical articles were collected in the series *Shelburne Essays* (1904–21), named after Shelburne Falls, New Hampshire, where More had lived for two years in solitude as a young man.

221:11 **buns to his grizzlies.** Colloquialism for a propitiatory gesture.

221:16 **men *are* but children of a later growth.** *All for Love*, by John Dryden (1631–1700), Act IV, l. 43: 'Men are but children of a larger growth'.

221:19 **Scylla . . . Charybdis** In Greek mythology, two rocks between Italy and Sicily. In a cave in one dwelt Scylla, a monster with six barking heads and twelve feet, and under the other Charybdis, who thrice daily swallowed and then regurgitated the waters of the sea. Odysseus successfully negotiated his way between them in Homer's *Odyssey*.

221:30 **nouveau riche jeune fille of the bourgeoise,** Newly rich young lady (French). Sherman talks of the *jeune fille* in his first chapter, 'Mr. Mencken, the Jeune Fille, and the New Spirit in Letters', and the spelling 'bourgeoise' (for 'bourgeoisie') appears in the chapter on Whitman (*Americans* 1–13, 176–7).

221:31 **flappers,** 1920s slang for flighty young women.

222:3 **in Germany, where all stink-gas comes and came from,** The Germans were the first to use poison gas on the battlefield, at Ypres, in April 1915. Sherman, in his opening chapter, makes pointed reference to Mencken's German origins and alleged anti-English prejudices.

222:10 **the "Shelbourne Essays,"** *Shelburne Essays*. See note to 221:8.

222:14 **Restoration wits** More's *The Wits* (1921) was the most recent of his *Shelburne Essays*. Sherman remarks that 'Mr More values the writers of the Restoration chiefly for their wickedness' (*Americans* 325).

222:14   **high Parnassus;**   In Greek mythology, Mount Parnassus was one of the seats of Apollo and the Muses, and also sacred to Dionysus, god of wine; hence, an artists' heaven.

222:14   **Wycherley,**   William   Wycherley   (1641–1715),   Restoration   dramatist, author of *The Country Wife* (1675) and *The Plain-Dealer* (1677).

222:16   **Aphra Behn**   Restoration writer (1640–89), acclaimed by Virginia Woolf in *A Room of One's Own* (1928) as the first Englishwoman to earn her living from literature; her works include the play *The Rover* (1681) and the novel *Oroonoko* (1688).

222:20   **the hero from the Marne who mends the gas-bracket:**   For Sherman, 'the young carpenter, cited for gallantry in the Argonne, who is repairing my roof' (*Americans* 334), was the kind of reader American critics such as P. E. More were failing to address. The Marne is a river north-east of Paris, scene of two great battles of the First World War; the first in September 1914, which saved Paris from falling to the Germans, the second in July and August 1918, when French and American troops broke through the German lines.

222:23   **an addled egg**   An egg which is addled is rotten and produces no chick.

222:25   *mobile vulgus.*   The fickle crowd (Latin); hence English 'mob'.

222:33   **splashed like a futurist picture with the rotten eggs of menckenism.** The Futurists were a group of Italian artists associated with Filippo Marinetti (1876–1944), who aimed to celebrate technology and the dynamism of the new age; chief among them were Umberto Boccioni (1882–1916) and Carlo Carrà (1881–1966). Their work and their supporting publicity stunts were often highly controversial. DHL discussed Boccioni's painting 'Development of a Bottle through Space' (mistakenly calling it a sculpture) in 'Study of Thomas Hardy' (*Hardy* 75:22–76:17). It is not wholly clear whether the implication here is that Futurist paintings were made from rotten eggs, or pelted with them by disgruntled spectators. By the 1920s, when the movement itself had largely collapsed, the term 'futurist' was used more generally to mean any assertively modern art, and DHL followed this trend.

222:35   **horny hand of noble toil;**   From 'A Glance Behind The Curtain', by James Russell Lowell (1819–91), American poet and essayist: 'And blessèd are the horny hands of toil' (l. 204).

223:3   **Yahooism**   The Yahoos were the bestial, human-like creatures in Swift's *Gulliver's Travels*, book IV. See note to 84:22.

223:10   **"—the average man is [222:35] . . . negligible and transitory."**   *Americans* 335–6 ['. . . *religion of democracy* . . .'].

223:15   **The Babbitts,**   *Babbitt*, by Sinclair Lewis (1885–1951), published in the same year as *Americans*, 1922, satirised the complacency of small-town America. The name B. T. BABBITT, painted across the top of a large quayside warehouse, would have been one of the first English words seen by immigrants as they came into New York Harbour in the early years of the twentieth century.

223:28   **a sort of superlative Mr. Wanamaker,**   John Wanamaker (1838–1922), American department-store tycoon.

223:34   **Quaker Oats**   A breakfast porridge sold at this period in boxes with a picture of Franklin on them. Franklin, although not himself a Quaker, had many

Quaker associates in Philadelphia, and copied the Quaker style of dress, black with no frills. The porridge boxes still carry a small picture of a middle-aged man dressed as an eighteenth-century Quaker.

223:36   *Religion civile,*   In the closing chapter of his *Social Contract* (*Du Contrat social*, 1762), Jean-Jacques Rousseau sets out his proposal for a 'civil religion', shorn of theological and spiritual dogma, which would act as a unifying force in an ideal society; his theories had a considerable vogue in America.

223:38   **Emerson**   Ralph Waldo Emerson (1803–82), poet and essayist, born Boston, lived at Concord, Massachusetts, from 1835; the leading figure among the Transcendentalists.

224:2   **lilies may fester . . . smelling far worse than weeds**   Shakespeare's Sonnet xciv, l. 14: 'Lilies that fester smell far worse than weeds'.

224:5   **why so sad, fond lover, prithee why so sad?**   'Why so pale and wan, fond lover? / Prithee, why so pale?' Opening lines of 'Song', from *Aglaura* (1638), a play by the Cavalier poet Sir John Suckling (1609–42).

224:8   **sweals**   Burns slowly away. DHL's typist apparently did not recognise this word, and gave it as 'sweats' (see Textual apparatus).

224:16   **Sic transit veritas mundi.**   So passes the truth of the world (Latin); DHL's adaptation of the tag 'sic transit gloria mundi' (so passes the glory of the world).

224:18   **inrushes of inspirational energy from the Over-soul.**   'filled to the brim by an inrush of energy from the Over-soul' (*Americans* 82). The 'Over-Soul' was Emerson's term for the animating spirit of the universe. See his essay 'The Over-Soul', in *Essays*, First Series (1841).

224:21   **Professor Sherman says . . . passion of life.'''** *Americans* 78–9.

224:23   **"I am surrounded . . . day by day,"**   An entry in Emerson's *Journal* for 23 April 1838 (*Americans* 82) [' . . . show me credentials . . .'].

224:25   **Gabriel . . . Michael**   Two of the four Archangels; Gabriel was the messenger sent from God to announce the birth of Jesus to Mary; Michael was a warrior-angel who led the heavenly forces against Satan (Revelation xii. 7).

224:29   **cherubim . . . Israfel . . . Mormon.**   The cherubim were the second of the nine orders of angelic beings, after the seraphim . . . Israfel is named as an angel in the Koran; cf. Edgar Allan Poe's poem 'Israfel' (1831):

> In Heaven a spirit doth dwell
> 'Whose heart-strings are a lute';
> None sing so wildly well
> As the angel Israfel . . .

. . . *The Book of Mormon*, whose miraculous discovery was claimed by Joseph Smith (1805–44) and led to the founding of the Mormon Church, or Church of the Latter-Day Saints, in America, purported to be the history of the Hebrew tribes who had journeyed to America and whose descendants were the Red Indians.

224:31   *qui n'avait pas de quoi.*   Who didn't matter, didn't count (French). Colloquially, who didn't have the wherewithal, i.e. was impotent.

224:33 **Ashtaroth and Ammon are gods as well,** Ashtaroth, also called Astarte, the Phoenician goddess of fertility (see note to 65:23); Ammon, the Egyptian god-king.

224:38 **"We are all . . . the ideal painter."** An entry in Emerson's *Journal* for 24 February 1836 (*Americans* 88).

225:4 **Dostoevsky's Idiot, . . . President Wilson** Prince Myshkin, the hero of Dostoevsky's novel *The Idiot* (1868); see note to 156:18 . . . Woodrow Wilson; see note to 88:8.

225:7 **"Shall I not treat all men as gods?"** From Emerson's 'Introductory Lecture on the Times', read at the Masonic Temple, Boston, 2 December 1841: 'For if I treat all men as gods, how to me can there be such a thing as a slave?' Misquoted in *Americans* 95.

225:16 **the mills of God a-grinding.** A passage from the *Adages* of Erasmus, which DHL often quoted in its later incarnation in the *Sinnegedichte* of Friedrich von Logau (1604–55), translated by Henry Wadsworth Longfellow: 'Though the mills of God grind slowly, yet they grind exceeding small.'

225:24 **Sic transeunt Dei hominorum.** So pass the gods of men (Latin); see note to 224:16.

225:28 *The Scarlet Letter.* A novel, published 1850, by Nathaniel Hawthorne (1804–64). DHL discussed Hawthorne at length in his essays 'Nathaniel Hawthorne and *The Scarlet Letter*' and 'Hawthorne's *Blithedale Romance*' (*Studies* 81–95, 96–104).

225:31 **Professor Sherman says there is nothing erotic about *The Scarlet Letter*.** 'It is obvious that [Hawthorne] has striven sedulously to avoid all occasion for exhibiting an aberrant passion in its possible aspects of alluring and romantic glamour' (*Americans* 146).

225:35 **Hester and Dimmesdale** In *The Scarlet Letter*, Hester Prynne and Arthur Dimmesdale, the minister and father of her child, Pearl.

225:39 **serpent . . . fig-leaf.** Cf. Genesis iii. 7, and the practice of covering the genitalia of statues.

226:3 *The Marble Faun,* A novel by Hawthorne, published in 1860.

226:9 *Walt Whitman.* See note to 110:18.

226:11 **"at the first . . . lewdness or divinity,"** *Americans* 153 [' . . . one questions whether . . .'].

226:12 **"All I have said concerns you."** *Americans* 159 ['All that I have . . .']. This exact form of words does not appear to have occurred in Whitman's writings, but the sentiment is ubiquitous.

226:18 **"Whatever else it involves . . . individuals in it."** *Americans* 159.

226:26 *Noli me tangere,* Christ's words to Mary Magdalene when she sees him after his resurrection: 'Touch me not; for I am not yet ascended to my Father' (John xx. 17 – Vulgate). DHL frequently refers to these words. Cf. *The Fox, The Captain's Doll, The Ladybird*, ed. Dieter Mehl (Cambridge, 1992), 192:17–18 and Explanatory note; *The Rainbow*, ed. Kinkead-Weekes, 261:31–4; *Reflections* 150:20 and Explanatory note, 233:2 and Explanatory note; *The First and Second Lady Chatterley Novels*, ed. Dieter Mehl and Christa Jansohn (Cambridge, 1999), 277:32 and Explanatory note.

226:30   *Merci, monsieur*!   'No thank you, sir! (French).

226:34   **Professor Sherman says . . . the *bourgeoise*."**   *Americans* 176–7 [' . . . the Proletarian . . .']. See note to 221:30.

227:1   **"The true gravitation [226:35] . . . literature too"**   From Whitman's *Democratic Vistas* (1870), quoted in *Americans* 177–8 [' . . . general comfort . . . some cravings for literature, too . . .'].

227:4   **Allons! . . . before us.**   From Whitman's 'Song of the Open Road' (1856), l. 214 ['us!'].

227:6   **Miller**   Joaquin Miller (1837–1913), American poet, born in Indiana. His family joined a wagon train to Oregon in 1852 and he moved from there to California in 1854, living for some time with Native American tribespeople. His earliest poems appeared in the 1860s. He caused a stir in literary London in the 1870s with his rough and eccentric behaviour, and was much sought after as an archetypal Man of the Wild West, inventing and embellishing many stories about himself. His most famous poem was *Kit Carson's Ride* (1871); he also wrote *Life Amongst the Modocs* (1873).

227:8   **(note the Swinburnian bit)**   Sherman remarks of Miller's poem-sequence 'Olive Leaves', from *Songs of the Sun-Lands* (1873), that 'the influence of Swinburne has quite transformed and disguised the sound of his voice' (*Americans* 225). For Swinburne, see note to 189:8.

227:11   **Zane Grey . . . Bret Harte . . . Buffalo Bill.**   Zane Grey (1875–1939), writer of Westerns, notably *Riders of the Purple Sage* (1912) . . . Francis Brett Harte (1836–1902), poet and novelist, wrote of the Californian goldfields in *The Luck of Roaring Camp* (1868) . . . William Frederick Cody (1846–1917), scout and circus showman, hero of more than 200 novels, himself wrote *True Tales of the Plains* (1908).

227:12   **Carl Sandburg.**   American poet (1878–1967), born in Illinois to Swedish parents; his style of vernacular free verse (*Chicago Poems*, 1916; *Snake and Steel*, 1920) was very popular in the 1910s and 1920s. Sherman remarks of Sandburg: 'When he has me all but persuaded that he himself is at heart a barbarian . . . then he brings me to a pause by his sympathy for the "insignificant" private life, by the choking pathos of his epigram on "the boy nobody knows the name of"' (*Americans* 244–5). DHL had been dismissive of Sandburg in a letter of 27 July 1917: 'Your Sandburgs and Untermeyers, even your Edgar Lee Masters or Robert Frosts – the vanity ticklers – no, they are not to be borne' (*Letters*, iii. 141).

227:16   **Andrew Carnegie.**   Industrialist and philanthropist (1835–1919), born Dunfermline, Scotland. His family emigrated to the United States 1848; he worked from the age of thirteen in cotton factories and telegraph offices, becoming manager of a railroad company and subsequently a builder of steel mills and other industrial projects. He used around nine-tenths of his enormous fortune to found libraries (nearly 3,000 worldwide) and many institutes for science, technology, and the arts.

227:19   **Roosevelt**   Theodore Roosevelt (1858–1919), twenty-sixth President of the United States, 1901–9.

227:22   **play at being pro-German.**   In the chapter 'Roosevelt and the National Psychology', Sherman attacks what he describes as 'the Bismarckian characteristics' of Theodore Roosevelt, and in particular Roosevelt's pre-First World War admiration of the size and power of the German army. Prior to America's entering the war on the Allied side in 1917, Roosevelt was thought to have adopted a somewhat equivocal position, but other historians would interpret this as evidence of his implacable opposition to the policies of President Wilson, rather than of pro-German sympathies. Once America joined the war, Roosevelt was wholly enthusiastic in his support.

227:23 *Evolution of the Adams Family.* 'Evolution in the Adams Family', chap. XI of *Americans*. Sherman discusses the lives and works of the three brothers Charles Francis Adams II (1835–1915), historian; Henry Adams (1838–1918), also a historian, author of *The Education of Henry Adams* (1907); and Brooks Adams (1848–1927), lawyer and writer. They were the great-grandsons and grandsons respectively of two former US Presidents, John Adams (1735–1826) and his son John Quincy Adams (1767–1848).

227:28 **"Man is the animal that destiny cannot break."** *Americans* 315. Cf. DHL's Introduction to *Bottom Dogs* (120:19–20): 'the human will is indomitable, it cannot be broken, it will succeed against all odds.'

227:39 **having your cookies and eating 'em.** 'You cannot have your cake and eat it too' (proverbial).

228:1 **$350,000,000** The accredited fortune of Andrew Carnegie (see note to 227:16).

Review of *A Second Contemporary Verse Anthology*

231:2 **"It is not merely . . . entire people."** From the Editor's 'Introduction', *Anthology* xxii ['I wish that readers of this book might see in it not merely . . .'].

231:3 **"A Second Contemporary Verse Anthology."** *Contemporary Verse* was a poetry magazine, founded in 1916, which, according to its editor, Charles Wharton Stork, attempted 'to give the public the best of what is sane and vital in American poetry today'. Prizes were offered annually, and anthologies issued in book form, of which this was the second. DHL's quotations give a fair impression of the book's contents. Apart from editing the magazine, Stork (1881–1971) was himself a poet, and was well known in the 1920s for his translations from Scandinavian literature. It may have been one of his collections of 'Swedish stories' that DHL offered to review (see Introduction, p. xxvii n. 9).

231:7 **Horace,** Flaccus Quintus Horatius (65–8 BC), Roman poet, author of the *Odes* and the *Satires*.

231:14 **horn of a gramophone.** Early gramophones, or phonographs, had megaphone-like horns attached to the box, which were used both as loudspeakers and as recording instruments. Performers would crowd around the horn opening and sing or speak into it.

231:23 **footprints on the . . . dust it isn't nor to dust returneth.** Lines from 'Psalm of Life', by Henry Wadsworth Longfellow (1807–82), American poet:

> Life is real! Life is earnest!
> And the grave is not its goal;
> 'Dust thou art, to dust returnest,'
> Was not spoken of the soul.

> (ll. 5–8)

'Footprints on the sands of time', l. 28. Cf. also Genesis iii. 19: 'for dust thou art, and unto dust shalt thou return'.

231:28   **My face is wet with the rain / But my heart is warm to the core—** Opening lines of 'Walking At Night', by Amory Hare (*Anthology* 73).

232:4   **There be none of beauty's daughters . . . voice to me.**   Opening lines of 'Stanzas for Music', by George Gordon, Lord Byron (1788–1824).

232:9   **But you are a girl and run . . . On little, sandalled feet.**   Second stanza of 'Nausikaa', by Louise Driscoll (*Anthology* 41) ['. . . sandaled . . .'].

232:14   **The river boat had loitered . . . Was done—** Opening lines of 'Gamesters All', by Du Bose Heywood (*Anthology* 77).

232:17   **Now fades the glimmering landscape . . . Save where—**   Lines 5–7 of 'Elegy Written in a Country Churchyard', by Thomas Gray (1716–71).

232:22   **When lilacs last in the dooryard bloomed—**   Title and first line of poem by Walt Whitman, written immediately after the assassination of President Abraham Lincoln in 1865 ['. . . bloom'd . . .'].

232:25   **"Fly low, vermilion dragon . . . With the moon horns,"**   Opening lines of 'Fly Low, Vermilion Dragon', by Elizabeth J. Coatsworth (*Anthology* 26).

232:31   **crochet pattern.**   Crochet is a form of knitting done with a hooked needle.

232:32   **"Christ, what are patterns for?"**   The last line of the poem 'Patterns', by Amy Lowell (1874–1925) ['Christ! What . . .']. This poem, much anthologised after its first appearance in *Men, Women and Ghosts* (1916), takes the form of the interior monologue of an eighteenth-century woman confronting the conflict between convention and desire; DHL's allusion is more subtly chosen than might at first appear.

232:33   *Ladies' Home Journal.*   A best-selling American magazine, founded in 1883 and still active, aimed at middle-aged women of largely conservative tastes.

232:34   **"My heart aches," says Keats,**   Opening words of 'To A Nightingale', by John Keats (1795–1821).

232:36   **Why do I think of stairways / With a rush of hurt surprise?**   Opening lines of 'Stairways', by Hazel Hall (*Anthology* 70).

233:21   **the heavens of Ezekiel.**   Ezekiel i. 1: 'Now it came to pass . . . that the heavens were opened, and I saw visions of God'; cf. also i. 15–23, 26–8.

233:26   **Or hack a slow way through the dome of crystal.**   Cf. similar imagery in 'Chaos in Poetry', 109:31–111:11 above.

233:28   **playboys and playgirls of the Western world,**   Allusion to *The Playboy of the Western World* (1907), a play by J. M. Synge; see note to 188:24.

234:3   **gorgons and chimeras,**   In Greek mythology, the Gorgons were three sisters, Stheno, Euryale and Medusa, whose hair writhed with snakes, and who turned to stone any who looked them in the face. The Chimera was a fire-breathing monster with a lion's head, a goat's body, and a snake's tail. Colloquially, a chimera can also mean a mirage or hallucination.

234:8   **pot-bound**   See note to 201:18.

234:16   **nothing new under the sun.**   Ecclesiastes i. 9 ['. . . no new thing . . .'].

235:3   *Vive la vie!*   Long live life! (French).

235:10 *réchauffés.* Re-heated, warmed up (French).

235:12 *printanière.* Spring-like (French).

235:13 **I know a forest, stilly-deep—** First line of 'Idyl', by Amanda B. Hall (*Anthology* 59).

235:16 **My soul-harp never thrills to peaceful tunes;** First line of 'Wildness', by Stephen Moylan Bird (1897–1919) (*Anthology* 13).

235:19 **For after all, the thing to do / Is just to put your heart in song—** Opening lines of 'The Thing To Do', by Gamaliel Bradford (*Anthology* 17).

235:24 **I sometimes wish . . . his pleasant side.** Final stanza of 'Exit God', by Gamaliel Bradford (*Anthology* 16).

235:32 **Oh, ho! Now I . . . scarred dumb rocks standing;** Opening of 'Recuperated', by Robert J. Roe (*Anthology* 145).

Review of *Hadrian the Seventh*

239:1 **Baron Corvo** One of the numerous pseudonyms used by Frederick William Serafino Austin Lewis Mary Rolfe (1860–1913), novelist. Apart from *Hadrian The Seventh* (1904, reprinted by Knopf, 1925), his works include *Don Tarquinio* (1905) and *The Desire and Pursuit of the Whole* (1909). Some of his early short stories were published in *The Yellow Book* (see note to 239:11) as 'Stories Toto Told Me', in 1895 and 1896. As DHL implies, Rolfe alienated most of his friends, largely by demanding financial support from them and then abusing them in his writings. See A. J. A. Symons, *The Quest For Corvo: An Experiment in Biography* (1934).

239:8 **Huysmans's books,** Joris-Karl Huysmans (1848–1907), Belgian novelist. His most celebrated 'Decadent' works were *À rebours* (translated as *Against Nature*, 1884), and *Là-bas* (1891).

239:8 **Wilde's,** Oscar Wilde, author of *The Picture of Dorian Gray* (1891), *The Soul of Man Under Socialism* (1891), *Salomé* (1894) and *The Importance of Being Earnest* (1895). See note to 89:22.

239:11 **the Yellow Book,** An illustrated quarterly of literature and the arts, edited by Henry Harland, which ran from 1894 to 1897. It was the principal journal of the so-called 'Decadent' movement of the *fin-de-siècle*, but it also published work by writers as diverse as Henry James, Kenneth Grahame and E. Nesbit.

239:11 **Aubrey Beardsley,** See note to 215:6. As the leading artist among the Decadents, Beardsley illustrated many contemporary literary works, including Wilde's play *Salomé* (1894). He was the arts editor of *The Yellow Book*.

239:11 **Simeon Solomon,** Simeon Solomon (1840–1905), painter, began his career under the influence of the Pre-Raphaelites. He was a friend of Swinburne (see note to 189:8) and became a leading figure in the Aestheticist movement of the 1860s and 1870s. His ostentatious homosexuality and the increasingly explicit nature of his work led to his being shunned by his family, and he subsequently became an alcoholic, scraping out a living in his later years as a pavement artist in London. He was never formally associated with the *Yellow Book* circle.

239:15 **gollywog,** A black-faced, fuzzy-haired doll, popular in nineteenth- and early-twentieth-century Britain.

239:19 **like a crazy serpent, into the bosom** 'Put a snake in your bosom, and it will sting when it is warm'; John Kelly's *Scottish Proverbs* (1721): i.e. someone who repays friendship with ingratitude.

239:24 **He died about 1912,** Rolfe actually died in 1913, in Venice, having spent the last five years of his life there, refusing to leave the city even when in the direst poverty.

240:3 **Lord Rook, Lord Raven,** Translations of the Italian 'Corvo' (a crow).

240:30 **the Way of Scrutiny . . . the Way of Access . . . the Way of Compromise,** Chapter II of *Hadrian The Seventh* gives an elaborate description of the election of a new Pope. The 'Way of Access', or 'Inspiration', allows a candidate to be unanimously acclaimed by the conclave of cardinals. If this fails, the next resort is usually the 'Way of Compromise', whereby nine delegates, called compromissaries, are appointed from the full conclave to make the decision. The 'Way of Scrutiny' involves a ballot of the entire assembly. After the ballots are cast, the papers are immediately burnt, and smoke is sent up from the Vatican chimneys. Unusually, in the novel, the Way of Scrutiny is tried first, and Compromise only after Scrutiny fails to produce the necessary two-thirds majority.

240:37 **the chair of Peter,** The seat of the Papacy.

241:15 *raison d'être* Reason for existence (French).

241:28 **oubliette,** An opening or trap-door in a dungeon, through which the bodies of prisoners were dropped into another, hidden dungeon, or a moat below. From the French 'oublier' (to forget).

241:29 **the Vatican.** The palace of the Popes in the Vatican City, Rome.

241:35 **a politician of the League of Nations sort,** The League of Nations was founded after the First World War, at the instigation of US President Woodrow Wilson; its declared aim was 'to promote international co-operation and to achieve international peace and security'. See note to 88:8.

241:38 **unwinding the antimacassar** An antimacassar is a protective cloth covering placed over the back of a chair to prevent it from becoming greasy; named after Macassar, a type of hair oil popular in the nineteenth century. In *Hadrian The Seventh*, George Arthur Rose, now Pope, is presented with an antimacassar by a woman who used to cook for him when he lived in poverty, and he carefully unravels it into balls of wool to give away to children.

241:39 **a blowsy lodging-house keeper** Mrs Crowe, obsessed with Rose.

241:40 **Socialist "with gorgonzola teeth"** Jeremiah (Jerry) Sant, who from jealousy joins forces with Mrs Crowe to hound Rose after he becomes Pope.

242:7 **probably meant for Rampolla** Cardinal Rampolla (1843–1913) became papal secretary of state in 1887 during the reign of Pope Leo XIII; the Austrians, who disapproved of Rampolla's pro-French policy, vetoed his election on Leo's death in 1903, and the papacy passed instead to Pius X.

242:9   the late President Wilson . . . Hernan Cortes . . . Theodore Roosevelt, Woodrow Wilson had died in 1924 . . . Spanish conquistador (1485–1547), conqueror of Mexico, 1519–21 . . . see note to 227:19. Roosevelt was an implacable opponent of Wilson's administration. Cf. the anecdote told by Stuart Sherman, of a visitor to America who said: 'It may be . . . that Mr Wilson possesses all the virtues in the calendar; but for my part I would rather go to hell with Theodore Roosevelt' (*Americans* 257).

242:10   *The time has come for stripping*: In chap. VIII of *Hadrian The Seventh*, Hadrian, addressing the assembled cardinals, says 'Try, Venerable Fathers, to believe that the time has come for stripping. We have added and added; and yet we have not converted the world.'

242:13   peeling the onion . . . at last.   DHL is probably alluding here to Act V of Ibsen's *Peer Gynt* (see note to 201:8), where the hero compares peeling an onion with stripping the layers of the self, to find nothing at the centre.

242:18   *Lord! be to me a Saviour, not a judge!*   Hadrian's dying words when he is assassinated by Jerry Sant: 'Dear Jesus, be not to me a Judge but a Saviour.'

242:24   *The brave man* . . . says some old writer.   This quotation has not been located. It may be a translation of an unidentified classical source. In the short story 'Glad Ghosts', written soon after this review, the conspiracy of Catiline is mentioned; it seems possible that, during his time in England in September and October 1925, DHL read or re-read some Latin authors, although this particular quotation does not occur in Sallust's *Catilinian Wars*. In Dryden's *All For Love*, Cleopatra cries: 'Oh hear me; hear me, / With strictest Justice: for I beg no favour' (IV. i. 557–8); DHL had misquoted Dryden's play in his review of *Americans* (see note to 221:16).

242:29   caviare,   Sturgeon's roe; proverbially, a dish too costly, delicate and refined for popular taste. Cf. *Hamlet*, II. ii. 435, 'caviary to the general', i.e. too sophisticated for ordinary people to appreciate.

Review of *Saïd the Fisherman*

245:1   Lady Hester Stanhope   Hester Stanhope (1776–1839) was a daughter of the 3rd Earl of that title, and a niece of the Prime Minister, William Pitt, whose secretary she became in 1803. In 1810 she began travelling in the Middle East, and from 1814 settled in an abandoned convent in Syria, where she became a celebrated eccentric, wearing the costume of an Arab chieftain, surrounding herself with a sizeable retinue, and reluctantly receiving visits from many literary Westerners. She kept two horses in permanent readiness for the return of the Messiah, whom she intended to accompany in triumph to Jerusalem. DHL may well have read as a boy A. W. Kinglake's account, in *Eothen* (1844), of a meeting with her, as the extract was given in the *International Library of Famous Literature* (see note to 83:37), xi. 5125–35.

245:2   Colonel T. E. Lawrence   Thomas Edward Lawrence (1888–1935), 'Lawrence of Arabia', was born in Caernarvonshire, Wales. He did archaeological work in the Middle East before the war, becoming familiar with Arab culture, and in 1917–18 he organised and led Arab forces against the Turks. *The Seven Pillars of Wisdom*, his account of these exploits, was published in full in 1935. He became famous after the war for abandoning his rank and identity and joining the RAF as a private soldier, firstly as 'Aircraftman Ross', and again, after this ruse was discovered, as 'Private Shaw'. He was killed in a motorcycle accident. He is referred to as 'Colonel C. E. Florence' in *Lady Chatterley's Lover*, ed. Michael Squires (Cambridge, 1993), 281:12.

245:5 Bedouin Largely nomadic Arab inhabitants of the deserts and steppes of North Africa and the Middle East.

245:6 Semite Arab Arab inhabitants of the Middle East who speak Semitic languages, so named after their supposed derivation from Shem, one of the sons of Noah.

245:13 T. E. Lawrence distinguishes two kinds of Englishmen In his introduction to Doughty's *Arabia Deserta* (see note to 245:16 below): 'We export two chief kinds of Englishmen, who in foreign parts divide themselves into two opposed classes. Some feel deeply the influence of the native people, and try to adjust themselves to its atmosphere and spirit . . . However, they cannot avoid the consequences of imitation, a hollow, worthless thing . . . The other class of Englishmen . . . take refuge in the England that was theirs. They assert their aloofness, their immunity . . . They impress the peoples among whom they live by reaction, by giving them an ensample of the complete Englishman, the foreigner intact' (*Travels in Arabia Deserta*, vol. I, Lee Warner and Jonathan Cape, 1921, p. xxx).

245:14 Sir Richard Burton, English writer and adventurer (1821–90), travelled in Africa and the Middle East; author of *The Lake Regions of Central Africa* (1860) and translator of *The Arabian Nights* (1885–8) and *The Kama Sutra* (1883).

245:16 Charles M. Doughty, Charles Montague Doughty (1843–1926), traveller, writer, poet, author of *Travels in Arabia Deserta* (1888; republished with an introduction by T. E. Lawrence in 1921) and *The Dawn In Britain* (1906). In a letter to Mabel Luhan, of 19 February 1924, DHL wrote: 'I read *Arabia Deserta* long ago – but shall like to read it again' (*Letters*, iv. 586).

245:21 Marmaduke Pickthall, Orientalist, novelist and journalist (1875–1936), born in Suffolk. He travelled widely in the Near East from the mid 1890s, especially in Egypt and Turkey. *Said the Fisherman*, his most successful novel, was published in 1903, and reprinted by Knopf in 1925. He was a regular contributor to *The New Age*, 1912–20, writing in support of Turkey during the Balkan wars of 1912 and during the First World War, criticising British attitudes towards the Muslim world. He converted to Islam in 1919, and went to India in 1920, where as editor of the *Bombay Chronicle* he worked for Indian independence in support of Gandhi. In 1930 he translated the Koran, under the name Mohammad Marmaduke Pickthall.

246:5 evil genii, In Arabic folklore, a genie or djinn was a human-like creature with magical powers.

246:7 Damascus. The capital city of Syria.

246:9 Scheherazade's influence Sheherazade, or Sharzad, was the narrator of *The Arabian Nights*. The daughter of King Shahriyar's vizier, she married the King, who had had all his previous wives executed. Sheherazade successfully postponed her fate by breaking off her tales each night and keeping her husband in suspense as to the outcome.

246:10 Sinbad Sindbad the Sailor, a character in *The Arabian Nights*; a pampered wastrel who meets with marvellous adventures on his many voyages.

246:14   **a hit below the belt.**   Under the rules of boxing as laid down in 1866 by the 8th Marquess of Queensberry, hitting an opponent below the belt is illegal; hence, a foul and unexpected blow.

246:19   **incident . . . of the missionary's dressing-gown,**   In chaps. 11–12 of *Saïd The Fisherman*, Saïd steals a dressing-gown from a French missionary, thinking it a fashionable and dignified garment. While wearing it, he is taken for a grandee by villagers, but laughed at by Europeans in the city, whereupon he pretends that he was tricked into buying it, and hands it over to his servant Selim.

246:22   **picaresque novel**   A fictional form originating in sixteenth-century Spain, usually the loosely connected adventures of a rogue or *picaro*, who satirises the societies he moves through. DHL thought of his novel *Aaron's Rod* in this way, writing to Jessica Brett Young on 26 September 1920 that the stop–start composition of *Aaron* was not a serious problem, because 'I can sort of jump him picaresque' (*Letters*, iii. 602).

246:35   **gutter-snipe**   Street urchin.

247:12   **the Fates and the Furies**   In Greek mythology, the Fates, or Moirai, were three old women responsible for the destiny of every individual; Clotho spun the thread of life, Lachesis measured it, and Atropos cut it. The Furies, or Erinyes, were avenging goddesses, daughters of the Earth, who pursued wrongdoers implacably through life and into the underworld.

247:21   **Ca-Ca-Caliban. Get a new mistress, be a new man!**   Caliban's song in Shakespeare's *The Tempest*, II. ii. 180–1: "Ban, 'Ban, Ca-Caliban / Has a new master. Get a new man!'

247:36   **mind the bit,**   The bit is the mouthpiece of the bridle; hence, to 'mind the bit' is to take firm control of the reins.

248:8   **Beirut.**   The capital city of Lebanon.

248:10   **Alexandria.**   Port city in Egypt, founded in 332 BC by Alexander the Great. In the novel, Saïd is killed during the riots and looting that followed the British bombardment of Alexandria in 1882.

248:13   **leaping before he'd looked.**   Proverbial: 'look before you leap'; i.e. act prudently.

248:17   **the mills of God.**   See note to 225:16.

248:19   **When one . . . dark autumn of London,**   See Introduction, p. lxii.

Review of *The Origins of Prohibition*

251:1   **The Origins of Prohibition**   The first of many books on American social history by John Allen Krout (1896–1979), for forty years a teacher and professor at Columbia University. *The Origins of Prohibition* began life as his Ph.D. thesis.

251:8   **Rhode Island**   Island state of USA, off the coasts of Massachusetts and Connecticut.

251:22   **malmsey, and sack,**   Malmsey is a sweet red wine from the island of Madeira, although it originates from Greece, and is named from the Malvasia grape. In Shakespeare's *Richard III*, the Duke of Clarence was famously drowned in a butt of malmsey. In the 1660s, unsuccessful attempts were made to grow Malvasia vines in

Georgia, and subsequently large quantities of sack, sherry and Madeira were imported into the American colonies. Madeira was for many years the most popular of these drinks, partly because the voyage was found to improve the wine, and partly because the colonists exploited Madeira's exemption from Charles II's decree of 1663, that all exports to America had to be carried in English ships . . . 'Sack' is an old name for sherry, but also for any Spanish or Canary Island white wine imported into Britain; the name is derived from the Spanish *sacar* (to draw out).

251:23 the famous cycle From the early part of the eighteenth century, molasses, a dark syrup drained from sugar during the refining process, was shipped from plantations in the West Indies to New England, where it was used to make rum. The rum was then shipped across the Atlantic and traded on the western coast of Africa for slaves, who were shipped in their turn to the West Indies.

251:25 Washington's army getting its whiskey rations. George Washington (1732–99), 1st President of the United States, commanded the American forces during the War of Independence, 1775–81. During the war the whisky allowance for Washington's Continental troops was half a pint a day, and the local militia threatened mutiny unless they were accorded similar rights. The workers in the Trenton naval dockyard during the war were drinking between 200 and 300 gallons of whisky a week.

251:26 Dr Rush, Benjamin Rush (1745–1813), professor of medicine at the University of Pennsylvania; one of the signatories of the Declaration of Independence. As physician-general to the Middle Department of the Continental Army, 1778, he was the first army doctor to suggest that drinking spirits was deleterious to the soldiers' health. In 1784 he published *An Inquiry into the Effects of Spiritous Liquors on the Human Body and Mind*, and became an indefatigable campaigner for the temperance cause.

251:27 The Washingtonians, The Washington Temperance Society, founded in Baltimore, Maryland, in 1840, was the first temperance group to be set up by self-styled reformed drunkards. The original society was quickly followed by many other 'Washington' societies.

251:27 the Cold Water Army, A children's temperance movement founded in 1836 by Thomas P. Hunt. The movement soon had several thousand adherents. At temperance parades, wearing their distinctive blue and white uniforms, the children would recite their pledge: 'We do not think we'll ever drink / Whisky or gin, brandy or rum, / Or anything that'll make drunk come.' As a child, DHL was enlisted by his mother into the 'Band of Hope', a rather less demonstrative British children's temperance movement; see *Early Years* 66–8. Paul Morel, in *Sons and Lovers*, attends meetings of the Band of Hope, returning from one to find his mother has been attacked by her husband (*Sons and Lovers* 83:15).

251:28 Hawkins and Gough, John H. W. Hawkins, a Baltimore hatter, born 1797, became one of the most celebrated Washingtonian orators, sent by the society to make converts in New York, in 1841. Krout records that Hawkins's 'dramatic recital of the sordid incidents in his life deeply moved his audience. Several interrupted with the plea that they desired to sign the pledge at once and be saved' (*The Origins of Prohibition*, New York, 1925, p. 185). Hawkins's great rival as a temperance orator was John Bartholomew Gough, a New York bookbinder and vaudeville actor, born in Kent, England, in 1817. When Gough signed the pledge in 1842 he was regarded by the Washingtonians as their greatest prize yet, as he had been so notorious a drunkard hitherto. He toured all over the eastern States and made many converts, but frequently lapsed into his former habits. His serial re-conversions to teetotalism were much satirised in the press, but the Washingtonians regarded his unrelenting struggle with his demons as an inspiration.

252:2   **"matters indifferent," where John Knox put it**   The quotation is actually from John Calvin (1509–64), Protestant reformer. 'Calvin, himself, classed the question of the proper use of alcoholic beverages among "matters indifferent"' (*The Origins of Prohibition*, p. 300). John Knox (1515–72), who met Calvin in Geneva, was the leader of the Protestant Reformation in Scotland.

252:6   **ardent spirits**   When Benjamin Rush's book (see note to 251:26) was reissued in the early nineteenth century, the phrase 'spiritous liquors' in the title was altered to 'ardent spirits'.

252:12   **Columbus.**   Christopher Columbus (1451–1506), explorer and navigator, born at Genoa, discovered the West Indies in 1492.

252:21   **Prohibition**   A ban on the manufacture and sale of alcoholic drink in the USA, established by the 18th Amendment to the Constitution, 1919; repealed by the 21st Amendment, 1933.

252:26   **"Intemperance might . . . path of sobriety."**   *The Origins of Prohibition*, p. 300.

252:28   **"It was ridiculous . . . to the polls—"**   *The Origins of Prohibition*, p. 299 [' . . . "will of the sovereign people" . . .'].

252:29   **This is confused thinking.**   DHL seems to be attributing the preceding views to the author, but Krout, true to his 'attitude . . . of impartiality' (251:31–2), was merely reporting them.

Review of *In The American Grain*

257:2   **Mr. Williams**   William Carlos Williams (1883–1963), American poet and writer, born in Rutherford, New Jersey, of mixed English and Puerto Rican parentage. He worked as a paediatrician in his home town for most of his life. With his slogan 'no ideas but in things', he was one of the first American writers to call for a distinctively American art, arising from the materials of the place itself. His early poetry was influenced by Ezra Pound (1885–1972) and the Imagists, but in his later work he called himself an Objectivist. His late, five-volume poem *Paterson* (1946–58) recounts and re-creates the history of his home regions.

257:3   **Poe's distinction . . . the *local* in literature.**   Edgar Allan Poe (1809–49), American poet and writer, born in Boston but brought up in Richmond, Virginia. His *Tales*, including 'Ligeia', 'The Purloined Letter' and 'The Fall of the House of Usher', began appearing in journals in the 1840s, and had great influence on European literature. Williams remarks of one of Poe's essays that 'the distinction between "nationality in letters", which Poe carefully slights, and the pre-eminent importance, in letters as in all other branches of imaginative creation, of the *local*, which is his constant focus of attention, is to be noted' (*In The American Grain*, New York, 1925, p. 218). For DHL on Poe, see *Studies* 66–80 and Explanatory notes.

257:8   **Salem**   A town in Massachusetts, one of the earliest settlements in New England.

257:11 **Red Eric of Greenland,** A Norwegian-born navigator of the tenth century, whose story is re-imagined in the opening chapter of *In The American Grain*. Eric was banished from Norway and Iceland for acts of violence, and explored the s.w. coast of Greenland (so named by him in an attempt to attract further settlers), between AD 982 and 986. According to later sagas, his son Leif Ericson sailed from Greenland and landed either in Newfoundland or on what is now the n.e. coast of the United States, around AD 1000.

257:12 **Montezuma . . . Abraham Lincoln,** Montezuma, or Moctezuma, was the last ruler of the Aztecs of Tenochtitlan, now Mexico City (see note to 259:10) . . . Abraham Lincoln (1809–65), born in Kentucky, became President in 1861 and led the Union of mainly Northern states to victory in the American Civil War against the slave-holding Southern states of the Confederacy. He was assassinated in 1865.

258:3 **"Ulysses" and Marcel Proust** For DHL on James Joyce's *Ulysses*, see note to 122:10. Marcel Proust (1871–1922), French novelist, was the author of *A la recherche du temps perdu* (*In Search of Lost Time*). DHL seems to have read a certain amount of Proust on various occasions in the 1920s, but did not enjoy it; in a letter to the Huxleys of 15 July 1927, he writes 'Proust too much water-jelly – I can't read him' (*Letters*, vi. 100).

258:4 **modernist** The text as printed in the *Nation*, 122 (April 1926), gave 'modernest'; that in *Phoenix* gave 'modernist'. There is no evidence as to DHL's preference. 'Modernist' has been adopted here, given the proximity of references to Joyce and Proust, and because the same word recurs less ambiguously later in the review (259:9). In context, however, there is also a strong argument for 'modernest', as a colloquial coinage for 'most modern'.

258:7 **still-unravished bride of silences.** DHL's misremembering, or perhaps adaptation, of the opening lines of 'Ode on a Grecian Urn', by John Keats (1795–1821): ''Thou still unravished bride of quietness, / Thou foster-child of silence and slow time'.

258:11 **Conquistadores** Or Conquistadors; the Spanish invaders and conquerors of the Americas in the sixteenth century.

258:15 **The author sees . . . recoiling cruelty.** In the chapter 'De Soto and the New World', a dream-conversation between the conquistador Hernando de Soto (see note to 259:5) and the spirit of America.

259:3 **the strength of insulated smallness in the New Englanders,** Williams discusses the Puritan mentality in the chapters 'Voyage of the Mayflower' and 'Cotton Mather's Wonders of the Invisible World'.

259:4 **"being nothing" in the Negroes,** 'When they [the Negroes] try to make their race an issue – it is nothing. In a chorus singing *Trovatore*, they are nothing. But saying *nothing*, dancing *nothing*, "*NOBODY*," it is a quality – . . . bein' nothin' – with gravity, with tenderness – they arrive and "walk all over God's heaven –"' (*In The American Grain*, p. 209).

259:5 **De Soto, Boone.** Ferdinando or Hernando de Soto (1496–1542), Spanish conquistador, a companion of Francisco Pizarro in the conquest of Peru, subsequently journeyed north and discovered the Mississippi . . . Daniel Boone (1734–1820), American frontiersman, born in Tredegar, Wales; famous for his exploits among Native

American tribes in the 1760s and 1770s, while exploring the then little-known region of Kentucky.

259:10   **Tenochtitlan**   The Aztec city on the site of what is now Mexico City, destroyed by Cortes.

259:11   **(See Adolf Bandelier's "The Golden Man.")**   Adolph Francis Bandelier (1840–1914), American historian and ethnologist, born Bern, Switzerland. He wrote many studies of the life and culture of the native inhabitants of Mexico and the South-West of the USA. *The Gilded Man* (1893) argued that the legend of El Dorado, as told by the natives to the conquistadors, referred not to a place but to a person, a native deity.

259:12   **Poe's agony of** *destructive penetration,*   Williams writes of Poe's 'power of penetration . . . acid power to break down truth', of his 'monomaniacal driving to destroy, to annihilate the copied, the slavish, the FALSE literature about him', and comments on 'a population puffed with braggadocio, whom Poe so beautifully summarizes in many of his prose tales . . . It was a gesture to BE CLEAN . . . It was the truest instinct in America demanding to be satisfied' (*In The American Grain*, pp. 232, 223, 220).

Review (manuscript version) of *Heat*

263:2   **Isa Glenn,**   Isa Glenn (b. 1874), American novelist, was the daughter of a mayor of Atlanta. She studied art in Paris under Whistler, before marrying a US Army colonel, later general, Bayard Schindel, and accompanying him on various postings in the Philippines and South America. Schindel died in 1921, and Isa Glenn settled in New York, where she became prominent in the literary and philosophical circle around A. R. Orage (1873–1934), the former editor of *The New Age*, who was visiting America to promote Gurdjieff's teachings. *Heat*, dedicated to Carl Van Vechten, was her first novel, and became a best-seller; she wrote several others based on her experiences as an army wife, including *Transport* (1929), which she dedicated to Orage.

263:6   **Jane Eyre, . . . The Constant Nymph.**   A novel, published in 1847, by Charlotte Brontë (1816–55) . . . A novel, published in 1924, by Margaret Kennedy (1896–1967); the best-selling romance of the day. DHL was introduced to Margaret Kennedy in London in October 1925, reporting the encounter to Murry: 'I met The Constant Nymph . . . on Friday!!' (*Letters*, v. 322).

263:11   **the American army out there in the Philippines,**   The United States took over the Philippines after the Spanish-American War of 1898, and installed a permanent garrison in Manila.

263:24   **Manila.**   The capital of the Philippines, rebuilt after being captured by the Spanish from its Muslim rulers in 1571. The greater part of the old Walled City, the *Intramuros*, where the novel is set, was destroyed in February 1945 after the defending Japanese refused to surrender it.

264:3   **islands bought from Spain with good American dollars.**   The United States under President William McKinley paid Spain $20 million for the Philippines in 1898.

264:5   **ichthyosaurus,**   Extinct marine animal from the Mesozoic period.

264:9   **West Point**   Site of the United States Military Academy, in Orange County, New York.

264:13   **written with the pre-war outlook**   The whole of the novel is actually set immediately following the military takeover of the Philippines by the USA in 1899, and has as its background the continuing guerilla resistance to American rule, led by Emilio Aguinaldo, which was not finally suppressed until 1903.

265:4   **Dama de la Noche,**   Lady of the Night (Spanish), the name of 'the secret flowers which smelt of the honey of Paradise – the odd tiny greenish-white sweetnesses whose name meant the quality that [Tom] groped for, being called the *Dama de la Noche* – were always in hidden gardens, and always sending forth their little, dainty, insinuating whispers of delights' (*Heat* 23).

265:20   **indescribable sexual derision**   The editor of *Phoenix*, Edward McDonald, when printing the review, inadvertently or deliberately omitted the word 'sexual' from this sentence. In the novel, after visiting a native Filipino household where the men are naked except for loose loin-cloths, Charlotte 'carried off an impression that the Filipino family had been laughing at her ... They were polite; but always the laugh was underneath' (*Heat* 158–9). One of her fellow-teachers tells her about Filipino boys who have been spying on her in her bath (160–1).

265:34   **The oldest, haughtiest family on the island,**   The Ayalas, Don Sebastian and Doña Adelina, daughter Dolores and son Paraiso.

265:37   **Castilian**   Castile is the central region of Spain and the seat of its monarchy and aristocracy; the Castilian language came to be the dominant and official language of the country. Castilian is to Spanish rather what 'received pronunciation' is to English.

265:38   **mantilla!**   A scarf made of lace, worn over the hair and shoulders.

266:7   **a little brother,**   Paraiso, the boy who befriends Vernay and shares his disapproval of the native Filipinos.

266:9   **a Don**   In Spain, a gentleman of property and standing.

266:18   **resign his commission in the army first,**   Vernay does so not simply to avoid scandal, as DHL suggests, but in an attempt to placate Dolores's father and mother, who are unremittingly hostile to the American army.

266:39   **"Listen dear! ... a good girl."**   '"Listen, dear – " he was urging tenderly, "you must go home with Miss Carson. You must stay with her to-night; and tomorrow we can get the Chaplain to marry us!" ... "Why – " she cried – "I can never, never marry you! Did you not understand?" ... "Shan't we talk about that in the morning?" said Vernay gently' (*Heat* 257–8).

267:4   **"I got here . . . are so blue!"**   *Heat* 257 ['"It was so easy . . . until we sail . . . I shall, undoubtedly, have to crawl . . . to do the Stations . . . worth it, my own? Your . . ."'].

267:14   **Adios!**   So long! (Spanish).

267:25   **little native wife**   Josefa, a *mestiza* (mixed-race) woman who earlier had been Saulsbury's mistress (see 264:10).

Review (typescript version) of *Heat*

271:32   **Babbitts...Main Street.**   Alluding to two novels by Sinclair Lewis (1885–1951), American writer; *Babbitt* (1922; see note to 223:15), and *Main Street* (1920), both satirical portraits of small-town America.

272:2   **Neither does he want to change the world, or to teach it anything whatsoever,**   'Charlotte considered history as a study of conditions that she could better; while to Vernay it was the record of lives that had really been lived . . . His skin registered a vibration from the old things around him' (*Heat* 98).

273:5   **veronal or morphine or opium**   Three different kinds of sedative or narcotic drug.

273:7   **The yearning . . . America has never had,**   'Men who could sing of love and passion and heartbreak, and stop long enough to drink vino tinto – was not this the essence of life as the old races knew it and as America had not yet learned to take it?' (*Heat* 24).

273:35   **the low little brown waiter . . . without a man.**   In the novel, the waiter spills the ice-cream over both Vernay and Charlotte, and hastens to clean Vernay first. When Vernay remonstrates, the waiter says 'Ticher no matter . . . Ticher is *mujer* (woman) what iss not in the Army. Ticher is *mucho amigo* with the Filipinos' (*Heat* 71). Vernay's subsequent angry assault on the waiter earns him the approval of Paraiso, Dolores's brother, and begins the sequence of events leading to Vernay's romantic intrigue.

Review of *The World of William Clissold*

279:1   *The World of William Clissold*   A novel by H. G. Wells (1866–1946), novelist, historian and essayist, born in Bromley, Kent. He first became famous for his science fiction novels *The Time Machine* (1895) and *The War of the Worlds* (1898), before writing a series of realistic novels of lower-middle-class life, including *Kipps* (1905) and *Tono-Bungay* (1909). In a letter to Blanche Jennings, of 8 May 1909, DHL wrote: 'you've just read what's not worth reading of Wells: *War of the Worlds* and such like arrant rot—because theyre theoryish. Read *Kipps*, *Love and Mr Lewisham*, and read, *read*, *Tono Bungay*; it is a great book' (*Letters*, i. 127). He subsequently came to think less favourably of Wells, who was one of his last visitors in the sanatorium at Vence in February 1930 (*Dying Game* 529). Wells's later works include *The Shape of Things to Come* (1933) and *Mind at the End of its Tether* (1945).

279:3   **We are assured it is a novel . . . "mental autobiography" of Mr. Wells.**   In his 'Note before The Title Page', Wells writes 'This book, then, *The World of William Clissold*, is a novel. It is claimed to be a complete full-dress novel, that and nothing more . . . And it is a point worth considering in this period of successful personal memoirs that if the author had wanted to write a mental autobiography instead of a novel, there is no conceivable reason why he should not have done so' (*Clissold* i–iii).

279:5   **the two volumes yet to appear**   The volume DHL read contained only the first two 'books'; the second and third volumes of the novel appeared later the same year (1926).

279:7   *Tono-Bungay*   See note to 279:1.

279:14   **"A Note before the Title-Page"** . . . *roman à clef*: 'A Note Before The Title Page' occupies the first seven printed pages of the volume, before the author's name or the publishing details are given . . . A *roman à clef* ('novel with a key' – French) is a novel in which the characters are real people thinly disguised. 'This is not a *roman à clé*. It is a work of fiction, purely and completely' (*Clissold* iii).

279:16   **Mr. Winston Churchill . . . the Countess of Oxford and Asquith;**   Neither of these persons is actually mentioned in Wells's novel. In 1926 Winston Churchill (1874–1965) was Chancellor of the Exchequer in Stanley Baldwin's government; he had recently put the United Kingdom back on to the gold standard, one of the principal causes of the labour unrest leading to the coal strikes and the General Strike of May 1926, the after-effects of which DHL observed during his visit to England later that summer, when he wrote this review . . . Margot, Countess of Oxford and Asquith (1864–1945), wife of the former Prime Minister, Herbert Asquith, and mother-in-law of DHL's friend Lady Cynthia Asquith, was a celebrated society hostess.

279:23   **"The World . . . A Novel from a New Angle"**   The sub-title is 'A Novel at a New Angle'.

279:31   **Cannes,**   A fashionable resort on the Mediterranean coast of France.

280:13   **Mr. Gladstone**   William Ewart Gladstone (1809–98), four times Prime Minister between 1868 and 1894, the dominant political figure of the latter part of the Victorian era. 'I would invent "funny" blasphemous stories about "my friend Mr G." . . . Sometimes I would call him "the other Mr G.", because in those days British Liberalism was disastrously dominated by that astounding irrepressible person Mr Gladstone' (*Clissold* 61).

280:23   **futuristic**   See note to 222:33.

280:33   **"Oh! Oh! I cried [301:2] . . . turn on me!"**   *Clissold* 35 [' . . . day. / That . . .'].

281:6   **Bexhill**   A seaside town in Sussex.

281:9   **a mushroom city magnate,**   Figuratively, a man whose business ventures spring up from nowhere, expand rapidly, and disappear just as rapidly.

281:11   **"Hello, Sonny!"**.   The father does not actually say this, but he does say '"Which shall it be, Old Son . . . Harrow . . . or Eton . . . ?"' (*Clissold* 129), and '"Hello, you kids!"' (151).

281:12   *déjeuner*   Lunch (French); *petit déjeuner* would be breakfast.

281:18   *God the Invisible King,*   'Someone mentioned a distant relative of mine, Wells, who had employed many religious expressions in a book called "God, the Invisible King"' (*Clissold* 92). Wells's book of this title was published in 1917.

281:19   *Outline of History.*   Wells's *The Outline of History* was published in 1920.

281:28   **sweeping of the temple,**   Cf. Matthew xxi. 12–13.

281:36   **"It's no good! . . . ruffled my mind"**   *Clissold* 205 [' . . . hair. She . . .'].

282:6   **"She has a mind [281:38] . . . about the world".**   *Clissold* 209 ['Clementina has . . . water insects . . . the water-boatman knows . . .'].

282:10 "**the same lean, . . . and protecting me**", etc. *Clissold* 100 [' . . . as absurdly . . .'].

282:16 "**racial urge**",   The notion of a 'race-mind', as an account of why 'a large part of the waking hours of many people nowadays is occupied by activities that are of slight or no advantage to them whatever, although they may be of very great advantage to the race' (*Clissold* 91), is discussed at length in the chapter called 'Promethean', where it is linked with the ideas of Jung. Cf. Constance Chatterley, trying to rationalise her attraction to the gamekeeper: 'It is just race-urge which transfigures him for me, she told herself, using one of the H. G. Wells catchwords which she so despised' (*The First and Second Lady Chatterley Novels*, ed. Mehl and Jansohn, 62:34).

282:19 "**My King!**"   Clementina never actually says this in the novel. DHL remarked, of a character in John Galsworthy's *The Apple Tree*, 'She doesn't call him "My King," not being Wellsian' ('John Galsworthy', in *Hardy* 216:17–18 and Explanatory note). In Book iii, chap. iii of *Tono-Bungay*, Beatrice says to George Ponderevo: 'You are my prince, my king'.

Review (manuscript version) of *Gifts of Fortune*

287:1 "**Gifts of Fortune**"   A book of travel sketches and reminiscences by Henry Major Tomlinson (1873–1958), published by Heinemann in 1926. Tomlinson, the son of an East End dock foreman, became a journalist in 1904, writing for the *Morning Leader*, the *Daily News* and, from 1911, the *English Review*. He travelled widely, and in 1912 published his first book, *The Sea and the Jungle*. In 1914 he was appointed the official war correspondent of GHQ on the Western Front, where frequent exposure to artillery fire left his hearing severely impaired. Later books of essays included *London River* (1921) and *The Turn of the Tide* (1945); he also wrote several novels, including *Gallions Reach* (1927) and the anti-war story *All Our Yesterdays* (1930). Tomlinson was not at all warmly disposed towards DHL, and was a partisan of Norman Douglas during the Magnus affair (see Introduction, p. xlviii). In his short study *Norman Douglas* (1931), written only a few months after DHL's death, Tomlinson several times compares him unfavourably with Douglas: he claims that, beside Douglas's *Old Calabria*, 'Lawrence's *Sea and Sardinia* is mainly the captiousness of an avid adolescent with a queasy mind' (p. 3); he comments on p. 6 on the limitations of DHL's mimicry of Douglas; and on p. 35 he says, 'Compare the strident dishonouring voice in that introduction to the *Memoirs*, by Lawrence, with the defence of Magnus, by Douglas. Whose opinion would we prefer to seek?' Even then he seems unable to let the matter go, returning a few pages later to discuss Douglas's resentment at DHL's caricature of him in *Aaron's Rod* (*Norman Douglas*, pp. 39–40). For his part, DHL had described Tomlinson's review of H. G. Wells's *Men Like Gods* as 'A sort of beggar's whine . . . Mr Well's parsnips floating in warm butter' (*Letters*, iv. 462).

287:16 **Thomas Cook ones**,   Thomas Cook (1808–92), founder of the famous worldwide travel agents' company, began by organising excursions in the early days of the railways, running a trip from Leicester to Loughborough in 1841.

287:23 "**What draws us to the sea is the light over it.**" etc.   *Gifts of Fortune* 24. For the continuation of this passage, see 'Review (periodical version) of *Gifts of Fortune*', 293:23–32, and note to 293:32.

287:25 **"There are other worlds."** *Gifts of Fortune* 24.

287:28 **the gifts of fortune, "that passen as a shadow on the wall."** From Geoffrey Chaucer, *The Merchant's Tale*:

> A wyf is Goddes yifte verraily;
> Alle othere manere yiftes hardily,
> As londes, rentes, pasture, or commune,
> Or moebles, alle been yiftes of Fortune,
> That passen as a shadwe upon a wal.

This quotation forms the epigraph to Tomlinson's book.

287:30 **Lamb would never have called them that."** *Gifts of Fortune* 24. Charles Lamb (1775–1834) was an essayist and celebrated book-lover. See, for example, 'Detached Thoughts on Books and Reading' and 'Old China' in *Last Essays of Elia* (1833).

288:2 **Bates's "Amazon", Conrad's "Nigger of the Narcissus" . . . Melville's "Moby Dick"** Henry Walter Bates (1825–92), famed for his collection of tropical insects and butterflies, companion of Alfred Russel Wallace in exploring the Amazon, published *The Naturalist on the River Amazons* in 1863. On 1 January 1919, DHL asked Koteliansky to send him a copy, and in a subsequent letter, 20 March 1919, called it 'such a good book' (*Letters*, iii. 315, 340). Joseph Conrad (Konrad Korzeniowski) (1857–1924), Polish-born novelist; *The Nigger of the Narcissus* (1897) was his third novel and the first of his major sea stories . . . Herman Melville (1819–91), American novelist and poet, author of *Moby-Dick, or The Whale* (1851). DHL wrote two essays on Melville, 'Herman Melville's *Typee* and *Omoo*', and 'Herman Melville's *Moby Dick*' (*Studies* 122–32, 133–47).

288:9 **a P. & O. liner** A passenger ship operated by the Peninsular and Oriental Company.

288:15 **Hesperides,** In Greek mythology, the Fortunate Isles, the Isles of the Blessed.

288:27 **Siam . . . Kamschatka . . . Athabasca:** An alternative name for Thailand . . . A peninsula on the e. coast of Siberia . . . A lake in the Canadian Rocky Mountains. 'We . . . have never seen the smoke of a wigwam even in the distance. There remains with us a faint hope that a day will come when we shall see that smoke, for such a name as Athabasca is still in the world of the topless towers of Ilium' (*Gifts of Fortune* 40).

288:39 **England in her own wan sun . . . and self-resourceful!** See *Gifts of Fortune* 32–4. Cf. 'On Coming Home' (1923): 'Queer to hear English voices below on the tender, so curiously quiet and withheld' (*Reflections* 178:4).

289:5 **Borneo.** The largest island in the Malay archipelago.

289:11 **the mad Rajah, whom we turned out,** An English businessman whom Tomlinson met on a train in Malaya pointed out to him an elderly man covered in 'ornate decorations, brass regimental badges, and medals won by other people in the past for the most diverse things . . . central on his breast, hanging by a cord, was a conspicuous red reflector from the rear-lamp of a bicycle . . . "See his battle honours and decorations, and all that? Quite mad, you know. Used to be a rajah till we turned him out, and thinks he's one still"' (*Gifts of Fortune* 82–3).

289:14   **those realities we are supposed to accept.**   *Gifts of Fortune* 24 ['. . . we had supposed we were obliged to . . .'].

289:16   **a sketch—*Conrad is dead*.**   The subject, rather than the title, of the first part of Tomlinson's essay 'On the Chesil Bank' (*Gifts of Fortune* 84–9). Joseph Conrad died on 3 August 1924.

289:26   **Pawnees,**   A Native American tribe inhabiting the prairie area of what is now Nebraska and South Dakota. They were notorious for raiding the cattle of pioneers, and for their fearsome appearance, the warriors painting their faces and wearing their hair in a single strip shaped like a horn on the top of the head.

289:32   **"We now open a new volume [289:24] . . . its dead mother—"**   *Gifts of Fortune* 41 ['. . . with an antipathy increased to a repugnance we never felt . . . by an American writer, . . . for a museum . . . confessed that if he had not been a scientist he would have felt some remorse . . .']. This latter error of transcription by DHL left Tomlinson's sentence unintelligible.

290:8   **"It was quiet making a haze" etc.**   *Gifts of Fortune* 48. For the continuation of this passage, see 295:34–296:2 and note to 296:2.

290:11   **"A statue to St George . . . dragon to overcome."**   *Gifts of Fortune* 20.

290:15   **"And for a wolf . . . something to be said."**   *Gifts of Fortune* 137 ['. . . the wolf . . . we are beginning to feel . . .'].

290:16   **"And consider the fascination of the octopus!"**   *Gifts of Fortune* 138. Tomlinson is describing a visit to the London Zoo. The passage continues: 'And consider the fascination of the octopus! Could there be anything more sinister than the cold stare of the eyes surmounting that bulging stomach? Yet watch it shoot through the water and alight upon a rock, tentacles and all, with a flowing grace never equalled by a young lady practising a courtesy for the Court! . . . I found the largest audience of the Aquarium at the tank of the octopus, patiently waiting for what satisfaction, joy, terror, horror, consternation, or what not, it could bestow.'

290:17   **"I heard a farmer" etc.**   *Gifts of Fortune* 118. For the continuation of this passage, see 296:11–15.

290:18   **"At sunrise today"**   *Gifts of Fortune* 120. The passage continues: 'At sunrise to-day, on the high ridge of the shingle which rose between me and the sea, six herons stood motionless in a row, like immense figures of bronze. They were gigantic and ominous in that light. They stood in another world. They were like a warning of what once was, and could be again, huge and threatening, magnified out of all resemblance to birds, legendary figures which closed vast gulfs of time at a glance and put the familiar shingle in another geological epoch.'

290:19   **"Perhaps the common notion" etc.**   *Gifts of Fortune* 151. The passage continues: 'Perhaps the common notion of the tropics, a place of superb colours, with gracious palms, tree-ferns, and vines haunted by the birds of a milliner's dream, originated in the stage scenery of the *Girls from Ko-Ko* and other equatorial musical comedies, to which sailors have always given their hearty assent. That picture has seldom been denied. What traveller would have the heart to do it?'

290:22　[us]　A word is missing at this point in the manuscript, but the word 'us' appears at the equivalent point in the piece as printed in *T. P.'s and Cassell's Weekly*; see 296:18.

290:23　"But in this estuary" etc.　*Gifts of Fortune* 159. For the continuation of this passage, see 296:21–2.

Review (periodical version) of *Gifts of Fortune*

293:32　"What draws us [293:23] . . . other worlds."　*Gifts of Fortune* 24 [' . . . breaking among the reefs . . . there is wide freedom . . . And unfailingly . . . shake our old faith . . .'].

296:2　"I watched the captive [295:32] . . . was not mine."　*Gifts of Fortune* 48 ['and watched . . . conspicuous. / I took . . . the bottle . . . and the stillness . . .']. This extract begins at a point one sentence earlier than DHL's original manuscript indication (290:8).

296:4　St. Francis . . . preaching to them,　See note to 110:19.

296:9　" . . . And for a wolf . . . to be said."　*Gifts of Fortune* 137 [' . . . the wolf . . . do not . . . we are beginning to feel . . .'].

296:15　"I heard a farmer . . . ever it was."　*Gifts of Fortune* 118.

Review of *Pedro de Valdivia*

299:3　Valdivia　Pedro de Valdivia (?1498–1554), Spanish conquistador, was one of the companions of Francisco Pizarro during the invasion of Peru, and commanded the second invasion of what is now Chile, 1540–1. He founded the cities of Santiago, Valparaiso and Concepción. He was killed in an uprising of the Araucana Indians in 1554.

299:6　Mr Graham's　Robert Bontine Cunninghame Graham (1852–1936), writer, traveller, the first Socialist Member of Parliament (for North Lanarkshire, 1886–92), founder and President of the first Labour Party, and later President of the Scottish National Party. He was a friend and correspondent of Joseph Conrad, and helped him with *Nostromo* (1904). He claimed descent from the ancient Kings of Scotland. He lived for many years in South America, and died in Buenos Aires. He produced a large quantity of fiction, essays, memoirs and travel writing, including *Success* (1902), *Scottish Stories* (1914) and *The Horses of the Conquest* (1930).

299:33　Bernal Diaz,　Bernal Diaz del Castillo (?1492–1581), served under Cortés during the conquest of Mexico, 1519–21, and around 1568 wrote *The True History of the Conquest of New Spain* (published 1632). In 1923 DHL made several unavailing atttempts to obtain a copy in Mexico; see *Letters*, iv. 383, 445–6, 452.

300:1　Cortés,　See note to 242:9.

300:9　Dons in caracoling armchairs.　A caracole is a curvetting manoeuvre in horsemanship. The conquistador leaders were mounted on high, ornamented and enclosed saddles, so presumably DHL has in mind the Aztecs' and Incas' confusion as to what horses were, and whether horse and rider were one creature.

300:33   **[Flemish Charles V]**   King of Spain, 1516–66, and Holy Roman Emperor, 1519–66; born in Flanders.

300:36   **"Commentators tell us [300:15] . . . above for granted—etc."**   *Pedro de Valdivia* vii. [' . . . rather would be . . .'hands' . . . 'some slight abrasion in the process' . . . 'King and country' . . . 'amongst the Latin race . . .']

301:9   **Estremadura**   A region of s.w. Spain on the Portuguese border.

301:10   **the Italian and German wars,**   In the first decades of the sixteenth century, following the French invasion of Italy in 1494, and ending with the defeat of the French by the armies of Charles V (see above) at Pavia in 1525. The campaigns were not confined to Italy. At the same period in Germany there were numerous unrelated uprisings, inspired (although not supported) by Luther, directed against the rule of Rome; there were also several territorial incursions by princes taking advantage of Charles's involvement in wars elsewhere.

301:11   **the conquest of Venezuela,**   Venezuela ('Little Venice') was first colonised by the Spaniards in 1521. Charles V awarded most of the land to members of the Habsburg family.

301:14   **accompanied Pizarro to Peru . . . story of the Pizarros,**   Francisco Pizarro (1471–1541), Spanish conquistador, conqueror of Peru, was aided by his half-brothers Hernando (1469–1569), Gonzalo (?1505–1548) and Juan (?1506–1536).

301:16   **even Prescott has already told us.**   William Hickling Prescott (1796–1859), American historian, author of *History of the Conquest of Mexico* (1842) and *History of the Conquest of Peru* (1847). DHL probably first came across the latter book in the *International Library of Famous Literature* (see note to 83:37), which included a sizeable extract (V. 2238–56). He sent a copy of Prescott's book to Katherine Mansfield on 9 February 1919 (*Letters*, iii. 327). See also *Studies* Explanatory notes to 173:2, 197:10, and 217:10.

301:17   **Almagro crossing the Andes**   Diego de Almagro (?1468–1538), companion of Francisco Pizarro during the conquest of Peru. He commanded the first expedition to Chile in 1535, reaching as far as the Copiapó Valley before returning to Cuzco, the ancient Inca capital of Peru. He later quarrelled with the Pizarro brothers over territorial rights. He was defeated at the battle of Las Salinas, 1538, and subsequently executed.

301:25   **old Carvajal,**   Francisco de Carbajal (?1465–1548), conquistador and military commander. He supported Gonzalo Pizarro's rebellion against Spanish rule in Peru, but was defeated and captured by Pedro de la Gasca at the battle of Xaquixaguana, 1548. He was hung, drawn and quartered, at the age of eighty-three.

301:27   **Maghellan Straits;**   The Magellan Straits, connecting the Atlantic and Pacific Oceans, between the southern coast of the South American mainland and Tierra del Fuego, were discovered in 1519 by Ferdinand Magellan (1480–1521), Portuguese explorer, the commander of the first expedition to sail around the world.

301:27   **Biobio River,**   River in s. central Chile, where Valdivia established a stockade in 1550; the site of numerous attacks on his forces by the Araucanians.

301:28   **Labrador**   A largely desolate area of n.e. Canada.

301:37 **Garcilaso's book . . . Gómara.** *The General History of Peru* (published 1617), by Garcilaso Inca de la Vega (1540–1616), born in Peru of mixed Spanish and Inca stock . . . Francisco Lopez de Gómara (1511–64), chaplain and secretary to Hernán Cortés; author of *The History of the Indies*.

302:1 **"Christians seemed to have [301:38] . . . their swords."** *Pedro de Valdivia* 37 [' "Christians" seemed . . .'].

302:3 **"Cavalry in those days . . . aeroplanes,"** *Pedro de Valdivia* 42.

302:12 **the poet Ercilla,** Alonso de Ercilla y Zuniga (1533–94), Spanish poet, author of *La Araucana* (book I, 1569, books II and III, 1578), epic poem of the conquest of Chile.

302:19 **the mean La Gasca** Pedro de la Gasca (?1496–1567), an ecclesiastical lawyer, was sent by Charles V to restore order in Peru after Gonzalo Pizarro's rebellion against the rule of the Spanish crown. La Gasca defeated the rebel forces at the battle of Xaquixaguana, 1548. He was notoriously frugal and exact in his account-keeping, and his economic reforms aroused much resentment among the older settlers. Cunninghame Graham describes him as follows: 'La Gasca, who, by his execution of Gonzalo Pizarro and the other unnecessary and cruel hangings and beheadings of the prisoners after the rout of Sacsahuana [i.e. Xaquixaguana], brought odium on the name of Spain' (*Pedro de Valdivia* 73).

302:32 **he cut off . . . two hundred "rebels",** Cunninghame Graham quotes from one of Valdivia's letters after a battle at the Biobio River: 'From 200 of the prisoners I had the hands and noses cut off' (*Pedro de Valdivia* 85).

303:7 **Araucanians** The native inhabitants of what is now Chile.

303:11 **"as hard-featured a race as any upon earth."** *Pedro de Valdivia* 101.

303:14 **Columbus . . . Quesada . . . de Soto,** Christopher Columbus, see note to 252:12 . . . Gonzalo Jimenez de Quesada (?1500–79), Spanish conquistador, explored what is now Colombia in search of El Dorado, and founded the city of Bogota . . . Hernando de Soto, see note to 259:5.

303:17 **Adolf Bandelier, . . . El Dorado** See note to 259:11.

303:14 **' "God knows the trouble . . . pathetically."** *Pedro de Valdivia* 29 [' . . . the trouble that it cost . . .'].

303:29 **A Dios rogando . . . the mace.** *Pedro de Valdivia* 31 [' . . . God and . . .'].

303:31 **Philip II** King of Spain from 1555 to 1598, the son of Charles V. He sent the Armada on its disastrous voyage against England in 1588.

303:34 *Habladme por . . .* **Write to me, Don Alonso!** *Pedro de Valdivia* 91 ['Don Alonso, write to me . . . Don Alonso, hablad me por escrito'].

303:37 **The motto of the book** I.e., the motto of Ercilla's *La Araucana*.

303:39 **"El mas seguro . . . vez alguna."** *Pedro de Valdivia* 87 [' . . . la haber . . .'].

Review of *Nigger Heaven* etc.

307:1 **Harlem,** A district of upper Manhattan with a predominantly African-American population.

307:7 Mr Van Vechten's book Carl Van Vechten (1880–1964) was a writer and music critic for *The New York Times*. He was a member of Gertrude Stein's circle in Paris and a tireless advocate of her work. He was one of the first white commentators to write seriously about jazz and blues music, and, as a well-known socialite and a friend of Walter White (see note to 308:2), and Langston Hughes, he was a prominent figure in promoting the Harlem Renaissance in the 1920s. Van Vechten's best-selling novel of 1926, *Nigger Heaven* (the phrase did not only refer to Harlem, as DHL claims, but was a slang term for the segregated upper tiers of the New York theatres), was praised by some critics, white and black, but deplored by many others, who shared DHL's view that the book merely exploited black American culture for sensational purposes. Van Vechten wrote many other novels in that decade, including *The Blind Bow-Boy* (1923) and its sequel *Firecrackers* (1925), and *Parties* (1930). He was also a celebrated photographer of the Harlem scene.

307:9 Cocteau ... Morand, Jean Cocteau (1889–1963), French writer, produced poetry; plays, including *Antigone* (1922); novels, including *Thomas l'imposteur* (1923; translated as *Thomas the Impostor*, 1925); ballets; and films ... Paul Morand (1888–1976), French writer, best known at the time for the story-collection *Ouvert la nuit* (1922), translated the following year as *Open All Night*. He admired DHL's work, and in December 1928 offered him the use of one of his houses near Paris (*Letters*, vii. 42–3, 540).

307:14 Monna Lisa, DHL's spelling of the *Mona Lisa*, by Leonardo da Vinci, in the Louvre, Paris.

307:15 James Branch Cabell, Anatole France, James Branch Cabell (1879–1958), American writer, born in Virginia, produced a long series of novels of defeated idealism, set in an imaginary country called 'Poictesme', including *Jurgen* (1919) and *Something About Eve* (1927). In June 1924, Edward McDonald sent DHL a bibliography of Cabell's works, compiled by Guy Holt, as an example of what McDonald was planning; this led to the writing of 'The Bad Side Of Books' (see Introduction, pp. lvii–lviii; *Letters*, v. 63). Anatole France (1844–1924), French writer, was best known in the English-speaking world at the time for the novels *Le Crime de Sylvestre Bonnard* (1881) and *L'île des pingouins* (*Penguin Island*, 1908), a Swiftian satire on human nature. In a letter to Koteliansky of 17 April 1919, DHL described France as 'a very graceful piffler' (*Letters*, iii. 350), and in 'The Novel' he grouped *Sylvestre Bonnard* among the 'pathetic or sympathetic or antipathetic little Jesuses' (*Hardy* 182:7–9).

308:2 The author, we are told, is himself a negro. Walter White (1893–1955), writer and civil rights activist, born in Atlanta, was an African-American, but had blond hair and blue eyes, features he exploited effectively in his political work. He became a prominent member of the National Association for the Advancement of Colored People, and eventually its leader, in 1931. He had written another novel in the 1920s, *The Fire in the Flint* (1924), but no more after *Flight* (1926). He promoted the cause of black culture and self-determination both in the United States and overseas, and worked for improvements in the treatment of African-American soldiers in the US Army during the Second World War.

308:5 Creoles, People of mixed European and Negro descent in the USA and the West Indies.

308:7 **New Orleans . . . . Atlanta.** City near the mouth of the Mississippi in the state of Louisiana, founded by French settlers . . . The principal city of the state of Georgia.

308:27 **Edison gramophone** Thomas A. Edison (1847–1931), American inventor, first produced the phonograph in 1877, and oversaw its continual improvement. See also note to 231:14.

308:32 **Byron Kasson,** The central character of *Nigger Heaven.*

309:4 *ambiente,* Atmosphere, surroundings (Spanish).

309:13 **Nordic** Strictly, a person of Scandinavian or Viking descent; the term was often used for white people in general.

309:18 **the Washington Square region,** A once-fashionable area of lower Manhattan, between 4th and 6th Streets, now part of the site of New York University.

309:26 *Manhattan Transfer* By John Dos Passos (1896–1970), novelist and historian, born in Chicago. His grandfather was a Portuguese immigrant. His first two novels, *One Man's Initiation – 1917* (first published in London in 1920) and *Three Soldiers* (1921) were based on his experiences in the First World War. DHL compared *Three Soldiers* with Magnus's memoirs (see note to 69:7). *Manhattan Transfer* (the name is taken from a junction on the 'L' or 'elevated railway' that ran in New York in the early part of the century) was published in 1925, dividing the critics. Sinclair Lewis (see note to 223:15) claimed it was more important than anything by Stein, Proust or Joyce, and that 'it *may* be the foundation of a whole new school of novel-writing', while P. E. More (see note to 221:8) described it as 'an explosion in a cesspool'. Dos Passos's major trilogy, *USA* (*42nd Parallel,* 1930; *1919,* 1932; and *The Big Money,* 1936), was more overtly preoccupied with social justice and reform.

309:34 **systole-diastole** DHL used this image of the heartbeat more than once; see e.g. 'Foreword', *Sons and Lovers* 471:30 and Explanatory note, and 'Study of Thomas Hardy' (*Hardy* 7:18 and Explanatory note).

310:4 **the Lackawanna ferry-boat** Ferry across the Hudson river between Manhattan and the Hoboken terminus of the Delaware, Lackawanna and Western Railway.

310:6 **the Brevoort** A well-known New York hotel, on the corner of 5th Avenue and 8th Street.

310:7 **Central Park,** A large park of 840 acres in the centre of Manhattan.

310:8 **Hoboken . . . Greenwich Village . . . Algonquin Hotel** A town in New Jersey on the opposite bank of the Hudson river from Manhattan . . . A district of Manhattan n. and w. of Canal Street, notable for its bohemian ambience . . . A hotel on West 44th Street, well known as a meeting-place for literary celebrities, especially in the 1920s. DHL and Frieda dined there with Edward McDonald and his wife on 18 September 1925, shortly before DHL's final return to Europe. See *Letters,* v. 301.

310:10 **Broadway** A main thoroughfare running at a slight diagonal along the length of Manhattan Island from s. to n.

310:11 **Riverside Drive,** A prestigious residential area of the Upper West Side of Manhattan.

310:12   **the Palisades,**   Wooded cliffs on the New Jersey shore of the Hudson River, opposite Manhattan.

311:2   **the one character . . . "truly male."**   Stanwood Emery, admired by his mistress for being 'brown and male and lean', commits suicide at the end of the 'Roller-coaster' chapter of *Manhattan Transfer* (pp. 234–49) by setting fire to his apartment while drunk.

311:11   **the apple is a Dead Sea shiner.**   New York is popularly known as 'The Big Apple'; a 'shiner' is an apple which has been thoroughly polished. For Dead Sea fruit, see note to 114:23.

311:12   **the man who was a little boy**   The character's name is Jimmy Herf.

311:23   **Mr Hemingway**   Ernest Hemingway (1899–1961), born in Chicago, was probably the most celebrated American novelist and short-story writer of his generation. He volunteered for the ambulance service in the First World War, on the Italian front, and subsequently became a member of Gertrude Stein's circle in Paris. *In Our Time* (1925) was his first large collection of stories, all written in his early twenties. His most famous novels were *The Sun Also Rises* (1926), *A Farewell To Arms* (1929) and *For Whom The Bell Tolls* (1940). He was awarded the Nobel Prize for Literature in 1954. It is curious to note that, of the four authors DHL discusses in his review, Van Vechten and White were close friends (White named his son Carl after Van Vechten), and Hemingway and Dos Passos were also close friends, before falling out during the Spanish Civil War.

311:29   **one of the big Lakes in America—probably Superior**   Lake Superior is the largest of the Great Lakes, on the border of the USA and Canada, but Hemingway's stories were actually set around Lake Michigan.

311:39   **The "Mottoes"**   The stories in *In Our Time* are interspersed with brief italicised sketches or vignettes to create a montage of contrasted but related scenes. These vignettes, of scenes from the First World War, from the subsequent revolutions, and from bullfighting, register something of the violence lying behind the alienated or blank sensibility to which DHL was responding in the stories proper.

312:13   **"Well, boy, I guess I'll beat it."**   None of the characters in *In Our Time* actually says this, although the narrator of the story 'My Old Man' does describe how he and his father 'beat it out' from the jockeys' dressing room through the crowd of race-goers at St Cloud (*In Our Time*, 1925, p. 86).

312:13   **"It isn't fun . . . inside me."**   The character Nick Adams says this in the story 'The End Of Something' (*In Our Time*, p. 45). (' . . . everything was gone . . .').

312:26   **Krebs, in that devastating Oklahoma sketch:**   In the story 'Soldier's Home' (*In Our Time*, pp. 99–113).

Review of *Solitaria*

315:2   **Prince Mirsky**   Prince Dmitri Svyatopolk-Mirsky (1890–1939), historian and literary critic, author of *The History of Russian Literature* and *Contemporary Russian Literature* (New York, 1926). He left Russia after the revolution, living in Paris and London, but returned in 1932; he is thought to have died in prison in Siberia.

315:3   **Rozanov**   Vasily Vasilievich Rozanov (1856–1919), Russian writer, born at Kostroma. He worked as a journalist in St Petersburg and produced numerous literary and philosophical studies, including *Nature and History* (1902) and *The Family Question in Russia* (1903). *Solitaria* (*Uyedinënnoye*, or 'Solitary Thoughts') appeared in 1912, *Fallen Leaves* in 1913 and 1915, and *The Apocalypse of Our Times* in 1918.

315:7   **E. Gollerbach's long Critico-biographical Study,**   Koteliansky's translation of *Solitaria* is prefaced by his translation, in an abridged form, of E. Gollerbach's *The Life and Works of V. V. Rozanov,* published in St Petersburg in 1922. Gollerbach, a German, was a friend and enthusiastic admirer of Rozanov in the latter's last years.

315:27   *Legend of the Grand Inquisitor . . . man and life—"*   *Solitaria* 171 [' . . . which was ever . . .']. Rozanov wrote a study of Dostoevsky entitled *The Legend of the Grand Inquisitor,* published in 1894.

315:33   *mehr Schrei wie Wert.*   More shout than value (German); all show and no substance. Cf. *Sketches* 119:19 and 249:28.

316:7   **"examining my coins,"**   Rozanov describes how he relaxes late into the evenings examining his extensive coin collection, and that many of his thoughts occur at this time.

316:13   **Hamlet's: to be or not to be.**   *Hamlet,* III. i. 56 ['To be, . . .'].

316:15   **"The only *masculine* . . . your trousers:"**   *Solitaria* 56 [' . . . thing in you . . . are your trousers'].

316:23   **"Teaching is form [316:18] . . . tragic duty) . . ."**   Quoted in Gollerbach's 'Critico-Biographical Study' (*Solitaria* 9).

316:25   **Mary Mary quite contrary.**   English nursery rhyme: 'Mary, Mary, quite contrary, / How does your garden grow? / With silver bells and cockle shells, / And pretty maids all in a row.' Some commentators believe the verse originated as a satire on the licentiousness of the court of Mary, Queen of Scots, with 'cockles' standing for 'cuckolds'.

316:31   *crepitus ventris,*   Belch, breaking of wind (Latin: 'stomach crackle').

316:33   **Poor Voltaire . . . only recanted once,**   See note to 84:27. In February 1778, believing he was dying, Voltaire, the notorious anti-cleric, broke the habits of a lifetime and agreed to see a confessor, but scoffed at the incident once he had recovered. In May that year, when he really was dying, he refused to allow in the priests who had been sent for.

316:36   **"lovely faces . . . of children,**   *Solitaria* 9.

316:38   **"for two years . . . in white rayment"'**,   *Solitaria* 11 [' . . . white vestments'].

316:39   **a cold egg.**   A cold egg has been abandoned by the mother, and will not hatch.

317:2   **"I am not such a scoundrel . . . about morals."**   *Solitaria* 98.

317:3   **"Try to crucify . . . is God—"**   *Solitaria* 30.

317:11   *Apocalypse of Our Times,*   Rozanov published this work in 1918, and extracts from it are added to the end of Koteliansky's translation of *Solitaria.*

317:18 **touch of the criminal . . . in *himself.*** 'The feeling of criminality (as Dostoevsky had it) I have never had' (*Solitaria* 109).

317:30 **a kind of Rip van Winkle,** The hero of the eponymous story by Washington Irving (1783–1859), American writer, published in 1820. Rip van Winkle falls asleep for twenty years and wakes to find the world almost unrecognisable.

318:2 **Leontiev** Konstantin Nikolaevich Leontiev (1831–91), novelist and essayist, best known in the West for *A Husband's Confession* (1866), later wrote works exalting Slav consciousness and decrying the decadence of the West. Leontiev, who in his last years became a monk, is often regarded as the founder of the 'conservative tendency' in pre-revolutionary Russian thought, to which Rozanov and Shestov also belonged.

318:7 **"I speak straight out [318:2] . . . everything flows.—"** An extract from one of Rozanov's letters to Gollerbach, printed as an appendix to *Solitaria* (179).

318:21 **"The great horror [318:16] . . . without any discord."** An extract from another appendix to *Solitaria*, 'A Meeting with Rozanov', by N. N. Roussov (*Solitaria* 171). In Book III, chap. III of Dostoevsky's *The Brothers Karamazov*, Dmitri Karamazov says: 'I can't endure the thought that a man of lofty mind and heart begins with the ideal of the Madonna and ends with the ideal of Sodom. What's still more awful is that a man with the ideal of Sodom in his soul does not renounce the ideal of the Madonna . . .' (tr. Constance Garnett).

318:23 **tick-tack** In DHL's work a ticking clock often implies the mechanical, barren version of that which in its healthy, vital state takes the form of the systole-diastole rhythm (cf. note to 309:34). See especially *Women In Love*, ed. David Farmer, Lindeth Vasey and John Worthen (Cambridge, 1987), 464:31–40.

318:29 **If you're not pious [318:24] . . . Immaculate Madonna-ism** Replacing the following passage in MS: 'A healthy man is neither pious nor pornographical, lewd nor ascetic, saint nor sinner. The division itself is pernicious, and one swing causes the other. The swing towards the Madonna of immaculate conception' (p. 9).

318:31 **ad infinitum.** To infinity (Latin).

319:1 **when he says he was not "born rightly,"** A remark made in *Fallen Leaves*, quoted by Gollerbach in his 'Critico-Biographical Study' (*Solitaria* 21).

319:5 ***Oriental Motifs;*** An unfinished work by Rozanov on the origins of ancient Eastern religions. It does not appear ever to have been translated into English.

Review of *The Peep Show*

323:4 **budding author . . . Ford Hueffer . . . human document.** DHL first met the writer and editor Ford Madox Hueffer – later Ford Madox Ford – in September 1909. See Introduction, p. xxvii, and *Early Years* 214–18.

323:17 **unsophisticated author.** Walter Wilkinson (1888–1970) went on to write many books about his travels, including *Puppets in Yorkshire* (1931) and *Puppets in Wales* (1948). See Introduction, pp. lxxii–lxxiii.

323:23 **two or three years ago,** Diary entries in the book (e.g. 209) show that the year was 1923, although the book itself contains no reference to a year.

323:30 **William Morris' "News from Nowhere"** Utopian socialist romance (1891) by William Morris (1834–96), writer and artist, who began his career as a Pre-Raphaelite and subsequently pioneered the Arts and Crafts movement.

324:1 **Dostoevsky,** Dostoevsky is not mentioned in *The Peep Show*. At one point, however, the narrator 'gloomily' decides to buy a book by the artist and social theorist John Ruskin (1819–1900), but is relieved to find instead a book by R. M. Ballantyne (1825–94), the popular writer of tales for boys (154). See also 402:18 above.

324:6 **"Where's the ... one vol.?"** Not in the text of *The Peep Show*. The narrator does, however, make the book a running joke from page 31; he searches for 'the interesting works of William Shakespeare in one volume' when hunting for wool to darn his sock ('I had seen the darning wool just under the volume', 41); he and his companion consider abandoning the large volume in order to lighten their load (52); the candle goes out just when they are about to read from the book (56); they fail to read it on yet another evening (60); finally the narrator's companion takes it away (65).

324:8 **in the big sense or the little.** DHL originally wrote 'Kultur or Culture!' but failed to delete the exclamation mark when revising: *Per* incorporated it.

324:8 **simple lifer.** *OED2*'s first dated use of the phrase comes from 1927.

324:10 **not so brutal, beery and beefy, as Punch:** The traditional Punch and Judy puppet show was quite rough and violent.

324:16 **"sticks" ... bath-chair wheels.** The "sticks" were the wooden frames of the portable puppet theatre; a bath-chair was an early form of invalids' wheelchair.

324:22 *mot juste.* The right word (French).

324:25 **"It is ... lively breakers."** *Peep Show* 101.

324:35 **the old Adam** See Romans vi. 6, and the Service of Publick Baptism for Infants in *The Book of Common Prayer*: 'O Merciful God, grant that the old Adam in this child may be so buried, that the new man may be raised up in him.' It was a favourite phrase of DHL's for unregenerate man; see for example his stories 'The Old Adam' and 'New Eve and Old Adam', in *Love Among the Haystacks and Other Stories*, ed. John Worthen (Cambridge, 1987), 71–86 and 161–83.

325:6 **the very last "nobber":** A 'nobber' is the man who collects the money for a travelling entertainer (223), a role first named 'nobbler' (138). The narrator meets 'Old Professor Hill's nobber' (225) in Bath, a gipsy who is an expert in the 'pitches' where performances may be given, and who also collects the money (*Peep Show* 225–9).

325:32 **"If I were [325:7] ... will die.—"** *Peep Show* 173–4.

326:14 **when the hat comes round.** At the end of the performance the 'nobber' (see above) would use his hat to collect money from the spectators, who would pay or not as they pleased.

326:16 **cinema.** *Per* altered the word to the variant-spelling 'kinema', which became obsolete in the early 1930s.

326:20 **"nice" to him ... spit on such niceness.** Cf. 'The English Are So Nice' (*Poems* 659).

326:23 **wheer 'st keep thy ba's?"** Where do you [dost] keep your balls?' (Nottingham dialect and pronunciation).

326:33 **tight** Mean, miserly.

326:34 **chars-a-bancs** Literally, 'carriages with benches' (French): open passenger buses, normally petrol-engined. The anglicised word sometimes included an accent on the '-a-' but there was no standard plural form (see 326:38 and Textual apparatus).

326:34 **togs** Clothes (slang).

326:39 **all August:** The narrator starts his journey on 11 June (*Peep Show* 16) and ends it early in September (230), but the bulk of his book is concerned with August.

326:39 **England my England!** From 'For England's Sake' (1900) by W. E. Henley (1849–1903): 'What have I done for you, / England, my England?' Cf. DHL's story 'England, My England' (1915, rewritten 1921) in *England, My England and Other Stories*, ed. Bruce Steele (Cambridge, 1990), pp. 5–33, and *Lady Chatterley's Lover*, ed. Squires, 156:9.

327:10 **"singing songs . . . showmen lead."** *Peep Show* 230.

Review of *The Social Basis of Consciousness*

331:3 **The Social Basis of Consciousness . . . Dr Trigant Burrow** *The Social Basis of Consciousness*, subtitled 'A Study in Organic Psychology Based upon a Synthetic and Societal Concept of the Neuroses', was published by Kegan Paul, Trench, Trubner and Co. in London, and by Harcourt, Brace and Co. in New York, in 1927 . . . Trigant Burrow (1875–1950), having trained as a doctor in Virginia, studied psychoanalysis under Jung in 1910. He had met Freud in 1909 when the latter came to America to give the Clark Lectures. Burrow was the first American to set up a psychoanalytic practice, in 1911. He began to question his strictly Freudian techniques during his analysis of Clarence Shields, who in 1918 suggested that analyst and analysand should change places, an experiment which led Burrow to recognise the effect of his own authoritarian personality upon his analytic work. From this point he began to detach himself from orthodox psychoanalysis and devote himself to group analysis, eventually establishing the independent Lifwynn Foundation for Laboratory Research in Analytic and Social Psychiatry, in 1927. He was effectively expelled from the American Psychoanalytic Association in 1933. Freud himself called Burrow a 'muddled babbler'. DHL had mentioned Burrow's work favourably in *Psychoanalysis and the Unconscious*, and Burrow had sent him a number of his papers, most recently, in December 1926, 'Psychoanalysis in Theory and in Life', which formed the opening chapter of *The Social Basis of Consciousness*. DHL told Burrow that it was 'the first piece I've read for a long time that isn't out to bully somebody in some way or other'. In the same letter he commented on the exceptionally clumsy and rebarbative style of Burrow's writing: 'some times your sentences are like Laocoon snakes, one never knows where the head is, nor the tail' (*Letters*, v. 611).

331:8 **the International Library of Psychology, Philosophy and Scientific Method.** A series published by Kegan Paul, under the general editorship of C. K. Ogden, designed 'to give expression . . . to the remarkable developments which have recently occurred in Psychology and its allied sciences'. By 1927, when Burrow's book appeared, the series included such works as Wittgenstein's *Tractatus Logico-Philosophicus*, Piaget's *Language and Thought of the Child*, Richards's *Principles of Literary Criticism*, Jung's *Psychological Types*, and T. E. Hulme's *Speculations*.

331:28 **always applying a *theory*.** Burrow writes: 'For a system of psychoanalysis is itself but a substitution for life, a theory of life in place of life itself. The theory of psychoanalysis sets out with a premise; life does not. Psychoanalysis offers a solution; life is its own solution' (*Social Basis* 17).

331:32 **the inevitable incest-motive.** Burrow actually says very little in his book about this aspect of Freudian theory.

332:31 **he bit the apple:** Cf. Genesis iii. 6–7.

333:8 —**"It would appear that** [332:34] . . . ***aware."**— *Social Basis* 118 [' . . . this first moment . . . *aware!*'].

333:10 —**"That is, consciousness** . . . ***against other selves."**— *Social Basis* 119.

333:16 **the preconscious state.** The 'organic unity of personality arising naturally from the harmony of function that pertains biologically to the primary infant psyche. This original mode I have referred to in a previous work as the preconscious, and this preconscious mode I regard as the matrix of the mental life' (*Social Basis* 10).

334:24 **the neurotics, who show some sign of health.** A terse paraphrase of Burrow: 'For an analysis of the social unconscious shows that the collective reaction embodied in the adaptations commonly accepted as normal betrays a tendency to repression and replacement that is no less an indication of disease-process than is the reaction presented in the individual neurosis. Indeed, from the point of view of constructive consciousness and health, our so-called normality is, of the two, the less progressive type of reaction. In truth, normality, in evading the issues of the unconscious, envisages less the processes of growth and a larger consciousness than the neurotic type of reaction, which, however blind its motivation, at least comes to grips with the actualities of the unconscious' (*Social Basis* 11–12).

334:35 **to get on,** See note to 155:26.

335:2 **the normals betray . . . the late war.** 'Normality too, then, is neurotic . . . Could there be anywhere imagined an unconscious reaction more wasteful and destructive or one of wider scope or severer intensity than the symptom-reaction represented by the war that has recently convulsed the world?' (*Social Basis* 13–14).

335:4 **the bolshevist hysteria of today:** The Bolshevik party, in the early period of the Russian Revolution (1917–22), incited violent outbursts of vengeance and reprisal against anyone, from the aristocracy down to small-scale local traders, deemed to have oppressed or exploited the masses. See note to 90:28.

335:20 **And if he . . . very female.** Burrow comments on woman's 'social adoption of the role corresponding to the *mental image* female', and man's 'to the *mental image* male . . . This arbitrary, unbiological dictum necessitates that a "man" shall repress the female component within him . . . Conversely it makes obligatory upon the woman that she repress the male element within her' (*Social Basis* 216–17).

335:30 **The man "seeketh his own"** [335:23] **. . . St Paul . . . is not puffed up."** Paul's first epistle to the Corinthians, xiii. 4–5: 'Charity vaunteth not itself, is not puffed up / Doth not behave itself unseemly, seeketh not her own.'

335:32 **what Dr Burrow calls the "societal consciousness,"** Burrow's stress is on 'the societal instinct of our common consciousness in which is found the natural medium for the growth and activity of man' (*Social Basis* 45–6).

335:36   **Sex does not . . . only sexuality.**   Burrow draws the distinction in terms that must have particularly appealed to DHL: 'Sexuality, as it now exists, is not only utterly unrelated to sex but it is intrinsically exclusive of sex. Sex . . . is life in its deepest significance . . . By sexuality, then, I mean . . . the restless, obsessive, over-stimulated quest for temporary self-gratification that everywhere masquerades as sex and is everywhere substituted for the strong, simple, quiet flow of feeling . . . Sexuality, then, is but a larger word for self. Sexuality is the effort to limit life to the ends of personal aggrandizement' (*Social Basis* 11–15).

336:1   **Heterosexual, homosexual, narcistic [335:39] . . . self-seeking.**   The word 'narcistic' appears in Burrow's text. 'In the beginning of my analytic work . . . I was too theoretical . . . to recognize that sexuality, as it now exists socially, is everywhere of one cloth . . . all sexuality being narcistic is "homosexuality," that it is of its nature an expression of the infantile desire of self-supremacy, of self-seeking' (*Social Basis* 210).

336:21   *noli me tangere*   See note to 226:26.

Review of *The Station*, etc

339:2   **Athos**   Mount Athos, on a peninsula on the coast of northern Greece, had been the site of many monasteries since the tenth century. By 1927, twenty of these still survived, having organised a ruling council with a representative from each. Women were not allowed to visit Mount Athos; in Dostoevsky's *The Brothers Karamazov*, a character voices the popular belief that no females of any species, human or otherwise, were allowed on to the peninsula.

339:2   **Mr Byron**   Robert Byron (1905–41), historian and traveller, was born at Wembley and educated at Eton and Merton College, Oxford. He was a friend of Evelyn Waugh, Harold Acton, the Mitfords and the Sitwells (see below), and contributed occasional articles to *Vogue*. *The Station: Athos, Treasures and Men* was published by Duckworth in 1928. Byron first travelled to study Byzantine history and artefacts in 1925, and also wrote *The Byzantine Achievement* (1929) and *The Road to Oxiana* (1937), an account of the origins of Islamic art. In February 1941 he was on his way to report for the British Government on Russian activities in Persia, when his ship was torpedoed and he was drowned.

339:6   **the Sitwells,**   Edith Sitwell (1887–1964), poet, and her brothers Osbert (1892–1969) and Sacheverell (1897–1988) were the most celebrated literary family of the 1920s. DHL dined with their parents, Sir George and Lady Ida Sitwell, at their country seat, Renishaw Hall in Derbyshire, in June 1926, and was bemused by Sir George's collection of beds; he visited them again in Italy, and drew on his impressions of the family in the *Lady Chatterley* novels.

339:22   **some heavy Gregorovius.**   Ferdinand Gregorovius (1821–91), German historian. His thirteen-volume *History of Rome in the Middle Ages* appeared between 1859 and 1872.

339:29   **David . . . Mark . . . Reinecker . . . old pots.**   Byron's companions were David Talbot Rice (1903–72), who became an art historian and expert on Byzantium (*Byzantine Art*, 1954; *The Byzantines*, 1962), and Mark Ogilvie-Grant (1906–69), an artist and botanist who, in the mid and late 1920s, drew occasional cartoons of life about town for *Vogue*. He subsequently lived in Athens. The third companion, named in *The Station* as 'Reinecker', was actually the historian Gerald Reitlinger (1900–78), who had studied art at the Slade; he later wrote *A Tower Of Skulls* (1932), an account of his travels in Persia and Turkish Armenia, and several books on the Second World War. He and Byron fell out badly during their time at Athos, and Reitlinger left the expedition early. See James Knox, *Robert Byron* (2003), pp. 131–2.

340:7 **The food . . . are lurid.** Byron records, among other items, 'unmentionable vegetables, resembling large cut nails and filled with pips tasting of pharmaceutical peppermint . . . an omelette of whipped oil . . . cold octopus in oily salad . . . disintegrated and nameless fish . . . cod salted after it had rotted . . . macaroni, embalmed in the juice of goats' udders'. As for the beds, 'flocks of red bugs might be seen frolicking over the striped holland of cement mattresses. Fountains of blood – we wondered whose – squirted from their bodies as we pressed them flat like gooseberry skins' (*The Station*, p. 74).

340:26 **what Baroque is to the Sitwells.** Sacheverell Sitwell's enthusiasm for the Baroque, first expressed in his *Southern Baroque Art* of 1924, was much imitated in the artistic salons of the day.

340:29 **stone to sling at the philistine world.** One of DHL's many references to the story of the killing of Goliath by David (1 Samuel xviii. 40–51).

340:36 **Mr Williams-Ellis** Clough Williams-Ellis (1883–1978), architect and writer, was born in Northamptonshire. He campaigned on behalf of the National Trust, and was one of the founders of the Council for the Preservation of Rural England. *England and the Octopus* (Geoffrey Bles, 1928), and its similar successor *Britain and the Beast* (1937), were largely co-written with his wife. He designed many buildings, but is best known as the architect of the holiday village of Portmeirion, in Wales, which he began in 1925 to demonstrate the possibilities of harmoniously blending architecture and landscape.

341:16 **As he says . . . called a public benefactor.** 'If we technically blaspheme – mere perishable words – we are threatened with hell-fire and/or six months' hard labour . . . Yet for a deliberate act, brutally disregardful of natural beauty, essentially anti-social, sacrilegious and blasphemous, we receive the protection of the State, the accommodation of the banks, the approbation of our fellows, and the toleration of the Churches' (*England and the Octopus*, p. 20).

341:22 **the utter and hopeless . . . industrial encroachment,** Cf. DHL's essay 'Nottingham and the Mining Countryside' (*Late Essays and Articles*, ed. Boulton, pp. 287–94). The editor of the *Architectural Review*, Hubert de Cronin Hastings, was planning an issue exploring the deleterious effects of industrialisation on the face of England, and invited DHL to contribute. His essay appeared there in August 1930 under the title 'Disaster Looms Ahead'. It is interesting to note that later in the 1930s Robert Byron also wrote polemically on the same topic, in *How We Celebrate the Coronation* (1937).

341:33 **Mr Williams-Ellis' six questions** *England and the Octopus*, pp. 94–5. See Appendix VII, 'Two incomplete early versions of "Review of *The Station*, etc.", where DHL lists the six questions in full; 408:1–14 and notes.

342:8   **Mr Baring's book**   *Comfortless Memory* (Heinemann, 1928) was one of many novels by the Hon. Maurice Baring (1874–1945), novelist and journalist, a member of the Barings banking family. He worked in Russia for several years as a journalist and translator. He later became a Roman Catholic, and formed a well-known Catholic literary trio with his friends G. K. Chesterton (1874–1936) and Hilaire Belloc (1870–1953). His other novels of the 1920s included *C* (1924), *Cat's Cradle* (1925) and *Daphne Adeane* (1926).

342:16   **Goethe, Dante, Heine,**   See notes to 208:6, 110:18, 193:15.

342:27   **Mr Somerset Maugham**   William Somerset Maugham (1874–1965), novelist and short-story writer. He travelled widely and produced many books in a long career, including the novels *Of Human Bondage* (1915) and *The Razor's Edge* (1944). *Ashenden, or The British Agent* was published by Heinemann in 1928. DHL had met Maugham in Mexico City in November 1924, but they did not take to each other. DHL wrote to Murry: 'lunched with Somerset Maugham yesterday – sehr unsympatisch. He doesn't like Mexico – says the people are unfriendly. One gets what one gives' (*Letters*, v. 162).

343:1   **déclassé,**   One who has fallen in social status.

343:10   **the American dies . . . murdered by mistake,**   The American is a character called John Quincy Harrington, who in the final chapter of *Ashenden* is caught up in the Russian Revolution, but insists on going back to his hotel to collect his laundry, subsequently being killed in a riot. The Hindu is Chandra Lal, who sacrifices himself for an Italian woman, Giulia Lazzari. After his death she asks that the wrist-watch she gave him be recovered for her from his body. The Greek merchant is murdered by mistake in an episode involving the Hairless Mexican (see note to 409:22).

343:11   **It is better to be a live dirty dog than a dead lion,**   Ecclesiastes ix. 4: 'a living dog is better than a dead lion'.

Review of *Fallen Leaves*

347:5   *Fallen Leaves:*   Koteliansky's translation of Rozanov's *Fallen Leaves*, with a foreword by the Irish poet and novelist James Stephens (1882–1950), was published in an edition of 750 copies by the Mandrake Press. See Introduction, pp. lxxxv–lxxxvi.

347:9   **The book was written . . . died a few years later**   Two volumes of *Fallen Leaves* were published in Russia, the first in 1913, the second in 1915 . . . Rozanov died in 1919.

347:13   **Artzybashev, Gorki, Merejkovsky**   Mikhail Petrovich Artzybashev (1878–1927), novelist, a member of the 'Decadent' and Symbolist movements in Russia in the 1900s. DHL had borrowed Artzybashev's *Sanine* from David Garnett in July 1913, and on 4 September of that year wrote of it: 'a bit too much of an illustrated idea of how one should behave' (*Letters*, ii. 70). Maxim Gorky (Alexey Maximovich Peshkov, 1868–1936), novelist and playwright, was the leading figure in Russian literature at the time of the Revolution and for some years afterwards. DHL read his *Reminiscences of Leo Tolstoy* in the translation by Koteliansky and Leonard Woolf in 1920 (see *Letters*, iii. 640). Dmitri Sergeyevich Merezhkovsky (1865–1941), poet and essayist, with his wife Zinaida Hippius (1869–1945), poet and dramatist, led a circle of

Symbolists and occultists in pre-revolutionary Russia, and of literary émigrés in Paris after 1920. Hippius's play *The Green Ring* had been translated by Koteliansky in 1919 with assistance and advice from DHL (see Introduction, p. xxxviii n. 40).

347:15 His first wife had been Dostoevsky's mistress: In 1882 Rozanov had married Apollinaria Suslova, a former mistress of Dostoevsky; she left her husband after a few years, but refused to grant him a divorce. The bitterness caused by this refusal, and by the Russian Church's support for Apollinaria, had some influence upon Rozanov's subsequent attacks on orthodox Christianity.

348:2 "the secret [347:34] . . . practically hear nothing" *Fallen Leaves* 83.

348:9 "Lord. preserve in me . . . the glass." *Fallen Leaves* 59 [' . . . into the glass'].

348:12 "I am coquetting . . . literariness)." *Fallen Leaves* 59 [' . . . world. . . . "authorship" . . .']

348:19 "The *most happy* [348:14] . . . not to *accomplish.*" *Fallen Leaves* 3–4 [' . . . contemplator . . . actor. / I . . .'].

348:28 Stavrogins Stavrogin is a character in Dostoevsky's *The Possessed*. For DHL's comments on Stavrogin, see *Letters*, ii. 537, 542–3.

348:39 his second wife, "My Friend." Rozanov's name for his mistress Varvara Rudneva, who lived with him from 1891 and bore him five children. She was never actually Rozanov's wife (see note to 347:15). She died in extreme poverty shortly after his own death.

349:3 "European civilisation will perish through compassion," *Fallen Leaves* 116.

349:10 "'Today' was completely absent in Dostoevsky," *Fallen Leaves* 114.

349:28 Peter the Great's time. See note to 5:23.

349:32 Pushkin Alexander Pushkin (1799–1837), poet and novelist, the first major Russian writer to blend Russian and Western outlooks in his work.

349:38 the South Sea Islanders: DHL visited the South Sea Islands en route from Australia to California in 1922, but only the beauty of their vegetation impressed him: 'These are supposed to be the earthly paradises . . . You can have 'em' (*Letters*, iv. 286).

350:8 His attitude to the Jews is extraordinary. There are several comments about the Jews scattered through *Fallen Leaves* that might have caught DHL's attention, for example 'The feminine nature of Jews is my *idée fixe*' (14); the Jews 'all "walk on a little chain" before God. And that little chain preserves them, but it also limits them' (34); 'In sex is power; sex is power. And Jews are *united* with that power, Christians are *separated* from it' (56).

350:25 "At times I am aware [350:12] . . . everything round me."— *Fallen Leaves* 128–9 [' . . . also my "sins" . . . around me'].

351:3 strange and self-revealing statements concerning Weininger. Otto Weininger (1880–1903), born in Vienna, produced in 1903 *Sex and Character*, a thesis arguing the innate superiority of men over women, and the fundamentally mixed sexuality of every individual. A few months later he shot himself in Beethoven's house in Vienna. His work and his suicide caused a sensation. Rozanov comments that Weininger 'speaks of *all women*, as if they all were his rivals, just with the same irritation. But women are more generous. Each one of them having her true husband, makes no claim whatever to the street males, but leaves to Weininger's share quite a large number of trousers' (*Fallen Leaves* 13).

351:6 **"civilisation" . . . education."** Cf. DHL's article of November 1928, 'Enslaved by Civilisation', an attack on the regimenting effect of the educational system (*Late Essays and Articles*, ed. Boulton, 156–9).

Review of *Art-Nonsense and Other Essays*

355:2 **"Art Nonsense and other Essays,"** The correct title is *Art-Nonsense and Other Essays*. Eric Gill (1882–1940), sculptor and designer, established an artistic community drawing on the ideas of William Morris (see note to 323:30), and eventually called The Guild of St Joseph and St Dominic. Its first home was at Ditchling, Sussex, from 1907 to 1924, and then for four years at Capel-y-Ffin, in the Black Mountains on the Welsh border. Gill made many figures, carvings and engravings, both religious and secular.

355:4 **Mr Gill's type** *Art-Nonsense and Other Essays* was printed at Cambridge University Press in 1929, the first use of Gill's type Perpetua, which had just been realised from his design by the Monotype Corporation. The corresponding italic, called Felicity, had not yet been completed, and so could not be used until 1931. 'As the italic had not then been completed, the author's emphasis is expressed by underlining, a desperate (and unique) device which is at least preferable to the German habit of spacing lower-case letters' (Stanley Morison, *A Tally of Types*, Cambridge, 1953, pp. 101–2). Cf. 377:23–378:1.

355:13 *argefying* Slang for 'arguing', usually indicating bombastic assertiveness.

355:18 *au fond*, At bottom (French).

356:2 **"Two primary ideas [355:33] . . . in creating.'—"** *Art-Nonsense* v.

356:5 *Sally in our Alley* A verse by Henry Carey (1687–1743), set to music by numerous composers.

> Of all the girls that are so smart,
> There's none like pretty Sally.
> She is the darling of my heart,
> And she lives in our alley.

Carey also wrote the words to 'God Save The King', in 1740.

356:9 **giving Him the go-by.** Slang; to give others the go-by is to slight or disregard them.

356:18 **"God is Love [356:13] . . . Charity—"** *Art-Nonsense* 3 [' . . . lovable but . . .'].

356:21 **in the continental fashion;** See note to 355:4.

357:14 **"That state is [357:7]. . to please God."—** *Art-Nonsense* 1.

357:16   **Karl Marx ... Professor Whitehead**   Karl Marx (1818–83), the founder
of Communism, author of *The Communist Manifesto* and *Das Kapital* ... Alfred North
Whitehead (1861–1947), philosopher, collaborated with Bertrand Russell on *Principia
Mathematica*, 1910–13. A sizeable extract from Whitehead's *Religion In The Making*
(1926) is derisively quoted in the second and third versions of *Lady Chatterley's Lover*;
see *The First and Second Lady Chatterley Novels*, ed. Mehl and Jansohn, 465:40 and
note; *Lady Chatterley's Lover*, ed. Squires, 233:19–20, 36–40; 234:8–12.

357:19   **only soldering a kettle,**   Cf. the scene in *Sons and Lovers*, where Walter
Morel 'sat absorbed for a moment, soldering. Then the children watched with joy as
the metal sank suddenly molten, and was shoved about against the nose of the soldering
iron, while the room was full of a scent of burnt resin and hot tin' (*Sons and Lovers*
88:23–7).

357:37   **"The test of a [357:31] ... perfect freedom."**   *Art-Nonsense* 1–2. [' ... it
is the will ... The service ... perfect Freedom']. The phrase 'Whose service is perfect
freedom' is derived from *The Book of Common Prayer*, the Second Collect, for Peace,
in Morning Prayer.

358:17   **Happy, intense absorption ... life itself.**   Cf, for example, DHL's poems
'Things Men Have Made', 'We Are Transmitters' and 'Work' (*Poems* 448–50).

358:25   **Naples ... Barcelona ... Liverpool ... Leeds.**   Naples, in the s. of
Italy, and Barcelona, the capital of Catalonia in n. Spain, are important centres of
Catholicism; Leeds, an industrial city in the n. of England, has a strong Protestant and
Methodist tradition, but Liverpool, a port city in n.w. England, actually has a large
Catholic as well as Protestant population.

359:1   **"Beauty is absolute, loveliness is relative,"**   *Art-Nonsense* 3.

Introductory note (version 1) to *Mastro-don Gesualdo*

366:24   **the English interference under Nelson.**   Horatio Nelson (1758–1805),
English admiral, landed at Naples in 1798 to recover from injuries received at the Battle
of the Nile. He began an affair there with Emma Hamilton, a close friend of the Queen
of Naples and the Two Sicilies. The Queen made Nelson a Duke and offered him an
estate in Sicily. He began to use his forces to further factional Neapolitan interests
rather than fighting the French, going so far as to have one of his local opponents
executed, and he was eventually recalled to London under something of a cloud in
1800.

366:31   **sedan-chair**   An enclosed seat with poles projecting at either end, so that
one person could be carried by two servants.

367:4   **"I had published [366:36] ... a revelation—"**   See note to 140:14.

367:27   **"Listen to this.— [367:18] ... always the same—"**   DHL's translation
of another part of the *La Tribuna* interview with Verga; see note to 140:14.

Introduction (version 1) to *Mastro-don Gesualdo*

371:4   **Along with Sir Walter Scott and Byron,**   Sir Walter Scott (1771–1832),
Scottish novelist and poet, and the poet Byron (see note to 232:4), were by far the

most famous and influential British authors on the Continent in the first half of the nineteenth century.

371:10   *Ivanhoe . . . Paul et Virginie . . . Werther.*   A novel (1819) by Scott . . . A famous Rousseau-esque romance, published in 1787, by Bernardin de Saint-Pierre (1737–1814). DHL ordered a copy in December 1910 for the school library in Croydon (*Letters*, i. 205) . . . *The Sorrows of Young Werther*, a novel by Goethe (see notes to 207:34 and 208:6).

371:12   **the late Katharine Mansfield,**   Katherine Mansfield, b. Beauchamp (1888–1923), New Zealand-born short-story writer, wife of Middleton Murry and at one time a close friend of DHL, died of tuberculosis in January 1923. DHL sent her a copy of *I Promessi Sposi* on 9 February 1919 (*Letters*, iii. 327).

371:18   **Leoncavallo's**   See note to 139:15. DHL mistook Leoncavallo for Mascagni; when the piece was reprinted in *Phoenix*, the editor, Edward McDonald, silently corrected him (*Phoenix* 223).

371:1   **Octave Feuillet, with a touch of Gyp.**   Octave Feuillet (1821–90) was a best-selling sentimental novelist, author of *Roman d'un jeune homme pauvre* (1858). 'Gyp' was the pen-name of Marie-Antoinette de Riquetti de Mirabeau, Comtesse de Martel de Janville (1850–1932), who wrote many light and witty society novels including *Mademoiselle Loulou* (1888). 'A touch of the gyp' is slang for having a slight fever, or otherwise feeling out of sorts; e.g. 'this rheumatism is giving me gyp'.

371:33   **the depressing story . . . slap across the face.**   DHL is thinking of the novel *Il marito di Elena* (1882), which actually ends with the wife being murdered by her husband, rather than merely 'slapped'.

372:5   *Tigre Reale,* [372:1] . . . **South-Italian fashion.**   The consumptive heroine of *Tigre reale* is a Russian countess called Nata; the hero, a wealthy Sicilian diplomat called Giorgio La Ferlita. Unlike one of Nata's previous lovers, however, La Ferlita does not commit suicide as a result of his infatuation; he returns instead to his wife, who was herself tempted to commit adultery but resisted.

372:21   *Tess.*   *Tess of the D'Urbervilles* (1891), a novel by Thomas Hardy.

372:39   **Paul Bourget,**   French novelist (1852–1935), born at Amiens; his novels include *André Cornélis* (1887) and *L'Etape* (1903).

373:18   *parti pris.*   Biased, taking a preconceived view (French).

373:28   **Bastien Lepage!**   Jules Bastien-Lepage (1848–84), French painter, celebrated at the time for the naturalistic, almost photographic detail of his mainly rustic scenes. While living in Croydon, DHL had seen some of Bastien-Lepage's pictures at the Royal Academy: 'Bastien Lepage, the French peasant painter, had three terrible pictures – ah yes, haunting. Life must be dreadful for some people. Grey pictures of French peasant life – not one gleam, not one glimmer of sunshine – that is speaking literally – the paint is grey, grey-green, and brown' (*Letters*, i. 120).

373:31   *Lys dans la Vallée*   *Le lys dans la vallée* (*The Lily of the Valley*), a novel of repressed passion by Balzac (see note to 139:17), published in 1836.

374:22   **treasure of the humble.**   DHL is alluding here to a book of essays by the Belgian dramatist Maurice Maeterlinck, *Le Trésor des humbles* (1896), which extolled the mystery of silence and the unfathomable potential of humanity. DHL commended the book to Louie Burrows in a letter of 13 March 1911: 'I will borrow a translation of *Trésor des Humbles* for you, because I want you to understand it thoroughly. It will help you to understand yourself and me' (*Letters*, i. 237–8). Maeterlinck (1862–1949) was a central figure in the Symbolist movement in Europe; his best-known plays were *Pelléas et Mélisande* (1893; the basis of Debussy's only opera), *Les Aveugles* (1890) and *L'Oiseau Bleu* (*The Blue Bird*, 1908).

374:31   **Richardson**   Samuel Richardson (1689–1761), English novelist, author of *Pamela* (1741) and *Clarissa* (1747–9).

374:41   **in Cavalleria Rusticana,**   Actually in *Novelle Rusticane*; see note to 150:23.

375:10   **Paladin heroes**   See note to 110:38.

375:12   **"O cursèd spite that ever I was born to set it right."**   *Hamlet*, I. v. 188–9 [' . . . spite, / That . . .'].

375:14   **Jude,**   See note to 381:13.

376:39   **Peak and pine**   Cf. *Macbeth*, I. iii. 22–3: 'Weary sev'n-nights nine times nine / Shall he dwindle, peak, and pine.'

376:40   **some Fury**   See note to 247:12.

377:3   **solitaire**   A card game or board game played by one person; a game of 'patience'.

378:20   **Rachel or Rebecca.**   Rachel was the daughter of Laban, and one of the two wives of Jacob (see Genesis xxix); Rebecca was her mother-in-law, the wife of Isaac and mother of Jacob and Esau (Genesis xxii).

Introduction (version 2) to *Mastro-don Gesualdo*

381:7   **Hardy's "A Pair of Blue Eyes" or "Desperate Remedies".**   Two early novels by Thomas Hardy. *A Pair of Blue Eyes* appeared in 1873, and *Desperate Remedies*, the first of his novels to be published, in 1871. DHL discussed both novels briefly in 'Study of Thomas Hardy' (*Hardy* 22).

381:13   ***Jude* (really the last)**   *Jude The Obscure* (1895) was the last of Hardy's novels to be written, although *The Well-Beloved* was published after it, in 1897.

382:9   **Oh Cromwell! Why he had a wart on his face!**   Oliver Cromwell (1599–1658), leader of the Parliamentary forces in the English Civil War and later Lord Protector of the Commonwealth, was famously disfigured.

382:14   **quoted at a very low figure.**   Difficult to sell; a stock-market valuation.

388:38   **Helen was fetched back . . . "King" Menelaus.**   In Greek mythology, the abduction of Helen, wife of Menelaus, King of Sparta, by Paris, the son of Priam, King of Troy, was the cause of the Trojan War.

Prospectus for *The Story of Doctor Manente*

397:7   **Macchiavelli, Piovano Arlotta, Sirmini, Fortini, Sachetti, Poggio, Piccolomini, Alberti, Puliziani, Michelangelo, Gelli, Doni**   All these were Renaissance authors from Florence or the surrounding area. Niccolò Machiavelli (1469–1527) was most famous for *Il Principe* (*The Prince*), which he wrote in 1512 after lengthy reflection on the time he had spent in the company and service of Cesare Borgia. 'Piovano Arlotto' derives from the *Motti e facezie del piovano Arlotto*, a collection of quips, aphorisms and anecdotes dating from the 1460s, and supposedly based on the life of Arlotto de' Mainardi (1396–1484). Gentile Sermini (early fifteenth century) published a collection of bawdy *Novelle* in 1424. Matteo Fortini (1444–1528) wrote, among other things, about the voyages of Amerigo Vespucci to the New World. Franco Sacchetti (1330–1400) was a poet and writer of *Novelle*. Poggio Bracciolini (1380–1459), humanist and scholar, composed his *Facetiae* (comic and bawdy anecdotes) in Latin. Alessandro Piccolomini (1508–79) wrote comedies, including *L'amor costante* (1540). Leon Battista Alberti (1404–72), one of the great Renaissance humanists, wrote in both Latin and the vernacular. Angelo Poliziano, known as Politian (1454–94), humanist and poet, was one of the leading classical scholars of the time. Michelangelo Buonarotti (see note to 203:40) was a poet as well as a painter and sculptor. Giovan Battista Gelli (1498–1563) wrote the satirical *Capricci del bottaio* (1546), and translated many works from Latin into the vernacular. Anton Francesco Doni (1513–74) composed anthologies of comic sketches such as *La zucca* (1551).

397:9   **Edward Hutton,**   Edward Hutton (1875–1969), diplomat and man of letters, grew up in Yorkshire and spent much of his life in Florence; he founded the *Anglo-Italian Review*, and, in 1917, co-founded the British Institute in Florence. He wrote many books on Italy and Italian art and artists.

397:10   **R. Scott Moncrieff,**   Actually C. K. Scott Moncrieff; see note to 95:7.

397:15   **The Second Volume**   No further volumes appeared; see Introduction, p. lxxxiii.

Incomplete early version of 'Review of *The Peep Show*'

401:9   **W. H. Davies.**   See note to 203:3.

401:22   **four-by-six tent,**   I.e. 4 feet wide by 6 feet long, just big enough for one man to sleep in, or two if crowded.

401:28   **roundabouts-men,**   The attendants at funfair roundabout rides.

402:12   **high-falute.**   Usually 'highfalutin' or 'highfaluting', a pretentious and bombastic style of speaking or writing.

403:6   **a sort of Ishmael,**   Figuratively, a homeless wanderer; the narrator of Melville's *Moby-Dick* begins his story with the words 'Call me Ishmael.' Ishmael was the illegitimate son of Abraham and Hagar, the maidservant of Abraham's wife Sarah. When Sarah gave birth to Isaac, she commanded her husband to drive Ishmael and Hagar out into the wilderness of Beer-sheba (Genesis xvi. 1–4, 15, and xxi. 9–20).

Two incomplete early versions of 'Review of *The Station*, etc.'

407:16   **cardinal sin,**   A principal or important sin. According to St Thomas Aquinas, despair, the wilful turning away from the divine good and the hope of salvation, is one of the most grievous of sins. It would be more usual, however, to talk of the 'cardinal virtues', justice, prudence, temperance, fortitude, which, together with the three 'heavenly graces' (faith, hope, charity), are set against the seven 'deadly' or 'mortal' sins (pride, covetousness, lust, anger, gluttony, envy, sloth), which place the sinner in danger of damnation.

408:12 **pollarded** A tree that has had its trunk cut through low down, so that smaller stems sprout up to form a rounded head.

408:14 **The six questions** [407:27] . . . **do-as-you-would-be-done-by?**—etc. See note to 364:17. Of Williams-Ellis's six questions, no. 1, 'Are you practical—' continues: 'that is, are you an efficient house, shop, school, factory or church? Can a family be brought up in you, or cheese be sold, or children taught, or boots made, or services be conducted in you with convenience?' No. 2 asks 'Are you soundly and honestly built and lastingly weatherproof?' No. 3 continues, after 'ten years' time', 'or have your materials been so wisely chosen and employed that the years will pleasantly mature and mellow you?' Nos. 4 and 5 are given in full by DIIL, although he wrote 'In short' (408:9) for Williams-Ellis's 'Generally'. No. 6 continues, after 'do-as-you-would-be-done-by?' (408:14), 'Do the other buildings and the hills and trees and your surroundings near you generally gain or lose by your presence? In short, have you civilised manners?

'Those are the sort of questions that a building should be expected to answer—and *will* answer, readily and volubly, to a reasonably skilful examiner' (*England and the Octopus*, pp. 94–5).

408:31 **demi-monde** Half world (French); hence, a woman of dubious reputation.

408:33 **elusive-pimpernel** An allusion to *The Scarlet Pimpernel*, a play (1903) and novel (1905) about the French Revolution, by Baroness Orczy (1865–1947), whose hero, Sir Percy Blakeney, disguises himself in order to rescue French aristocrats from the guillotine. The stage version included the famous verse:

> They seek him here, they seek him there,
> Those Frenchies seek him everywhere!
> Is he in heaven, or is he in hell?
> That damned, elusive Pimpernel!

409:1 **Orpheus and Eurydice** In the Greek myth as retold by Ovid (*Metamorphoses* x. 1–85, xi. 1–66), when Eurydice, Orpheus's wife, dies from a snake bite, the great musician Orpheus's lament for her so moves the god Hades, lord of the underworld, that he gives permission for Eurydice to be led back to the world of the living, on condition that her husband does not turn to look at her. Unable to resist, he does turn, and she sinks back among the shades for ever.

409:9 **Geneva,** A city in Switzerland, on the lake of the same name. Switzerland, being a neutral country during the First World War, was a centre of espionage for both sides in the conflict.

409:21 **the little painted old lady** In chap. 3 of *Ashenden*, a Miss King, the elderly governess in the family of an Egyptian prince, aware that she is dying, calls for Ashenden, the only other English person in the hotel, who sits by her most of the night; she utters only one word, 'England'.

409:22 **the Hairless Mexican** This character, a General Manuel Carmona, has chap. 4 named after him. He appears at first to be a posturing, boastful mountebank, regularly changing wigs, and then turns out to be a rather inefficient professional assassin.

409:23   **the fat Englishman in Lucerne**   Grantley Caypor, an enemy spy, who is tricked by Ashenden's superiors into betraying himself, and is executed.

409:26   **the dog . . . the Hindoo . . . the woman . . . the American**   The dog is Fritzi, the improbably transparent name of a bull terrier belonging to the spy Grantley Caypor. For the others, see note to 343:10.

409:27   **Queen Victoria was not amused,**   Queen Victoria reigned 1837–1901. When efforts to entertain her failed, she famously expressed her disapproval with the words 'We are not amused.'

Notes for *The Hand of Man*

415:9   **the champak flower.**   The champak tree, which grows in India and s.e. Asia, is noted for its luxurious flowers.

415:23   **whoever makes anything . . . puts life into it,**   Cf. DHL's poem 'Things Men Have Made' (*Poems* 448).

415:24   **ghandi weaver**   Mohandas Karamchand (Mahatma) Gandhi (1869–1948), leader of the movement for Indian independence from British rule, encouraged the redevelopment of native crafts. He did actually weave in public, on a tiny handloom, to make his point. DHL wrote to Brewster, on 13 August 1929, 'Ghandi is right for India – and I'm sure every race and nation will have to fight, and fight hard, to survive the machine' (*Letters*, vii. 424).

TEXTUAL APPARATUS

TEXTUAL APPARATUS

In the apparatus, whenever the reading of the base-text is adopted (see Introduction: 'Texts'), it appears within the square bracket with no symbol. When a reading from a source later than the base-text has been preferred, it appears with its source-symbol within the square bracket; this is always followed by the reading of the base-text. Rejected readings follow the square bracket, in the sequence indicated for each text, with their first source denoted. In the absence of information to the contrary, the reader should assume that a variant recurs in all subsequent states. The following symbols are used editorially:

Ed. = Editor
~ = Substitution for a word in recording a punctuation variant
Om. = Omitted
/ = Line or page break
P = New paragraph
C = Corrections made by someone other than DHL (e.g. *TSC*)
R = Autograph corrections by DHL to a state of the text (e.g. *TSR*)
= Space
[ ] = Editorial emendation or addition
{ } = Partial variant reading

Silent emendations

The apparatus records all variants except for the two categories of silent emendation listed below. Some individual texts have additional silent emendations which are listed at the beginning of the relevant Textual apparatus. If, however, what would normally be a silent emendation occurs in the process of recording another variant, it is recorded exactly, so that the apparatus always records the states of the text accurately.

1. DHL habitually wrote dates 4th, 23rd, etc.: typists and compositors often produced 4th, 23rd, etc. DHL's practice has been preserved where appropriate manuscripts survive, but the habits of typists and compositors have not been recorded unless they form part of another variant.
2. Variations in the conventions of printed texts, such as the size of typeface, the depth of indentation, or the compression of the diphthongs 'æ' and 'œ', have not been recorded.

Foreword to *All Things Are Possible*

MS = Roberts E11a
E1 = *All Things Are Possible*, by Leo Shestov, authorised translation by S. S. Koteliansky (Martin Secker, 1920)

Silent emendation

The text of *E1* is printed in italics throughout; this has not been recorded except in
the course of recording another variant.

5:1	Foreword.] FOREWORD *E1*	5:29	reproduction *Ed.*] repetition *MS* *reproduction E1*
5:2	Spirit, *Ed.*] Spirit *MS Spirit, E1*	5:31	inherit the future *Ed.*] be very great *MS inherit the future E1*
5:7	are *Ed.*] is *MS are E1*	6:20	language] *language, E1*
5:8	different *Ed.*] quite different *MS different E1*	6:24	sluice gates] *sluice-gates E1*
5:9	culture and ethic *Ed.*] culture *MS culture and ethic E1*	6:27	forever incalculable] *forever-incalculable E1*
		6:35	servants *Ed.*] assistants *MS servants E1*
5:19	first:] *first; E1*		
5:20	ultimate;] *ultimate, E1*	7:5	logic. *Ed.*] logic. / D. H. Lawrence *MS logic.* / D. H. LAWRENCE. *E1*
5:27	christianity] *Christianity E1*		

Memoir of Maurice Magnus

MS = Manuscript (La L 11/1, UN)
MSC = Robert Mountsier's changes in *MS*
E1 = First English edition, Secker, 1924
A3 = Third American edition, ed. Keith Cushman (Black Sparrow Press, 1987)
SL = Salomone Letter (UT: for 59:18–62:28 only)

The sequence is *MS, MSC, E1, A3, SL*

Silent emendation

DHL wrote Martino, Norman Douglas, Norman, Douglas, Maurice Magnus,
Magnus, Maurice and (for the possessives) Douglas' and Magnus'. The compo-
sitors – following the publisher's instructions – produced Bernardo, N―― D――,
N――, D――, M―― M――, M――, M――, D――'s and M――'s throughout.
These substitutions are only recorded where another variant is being recorded.

11:1	*Memoir of Maurice Magnus Ed.*] Memoir of Maurice Magnus / by D. H. Lawrence *MS Introduction E1* Om. *A3*	11:5	poor― *MS, A3*] ~; *E1*
		11:8	hoped *MS, A3*] ~, *E1*
		11:13	Cooks *MS, A3*] Cook's *E1*
		11:14	Cooks *MS, A3*] Cook's *E1*
11:2	November 1919 *MS, A3*] ~, ~, *E1*	11:17	Lungarno *MS, A3*] Lung' Arno *E1*

11:23 Well *MS, A3*] ~, *E1*
11:26 Magnus—" *MS, A3*] M——" *E1*
12:2 patronisingly *MS, A3*]
      patronizingly *E1*
12:3 handbag *A3*] hand-/bag *MS*
      hand-bag *E1*
12:3 realised *MS, A3*] realized *E1*
12:10 natty *E1*] spruce *MS, A3*
12:14 room *E1*] rooms *MS, A3*
12:15 Oh *MS, A3*] ~, *E1*
12:19 —His *MS, A3*] ~ *E1*
12:20 mincing— *MS, A3*] ~, *E1*
12:22 here— *MS, A3*] ~—— *E1*
12:28 Cavalotti— *MS, A3*] Cavelotti *E1*
12:29 drawing-room— *MS, A3*] ~, *E1*
12:30 tea *MS, A3*] ~, *E1*
12:34 inside— *MS, A3*] ~, *E1*
13:4 explanations] explanation *A3*
13:7 it— *MS, A3*] ~. *E1*
13:10 *They Went MS, A3*] Om. *E1 see*
      notes
13:12 light-blue *MS, A3*] light blue *E1*
13:13 dark-brown *MS, A3*] dark brown
      E1
13:19 —I *MS, A3*] ~ *E1*
13:19 forty five *MS, A3*] forty-five *E1*
13:19 Liras *MS, A3*] lire *E1*
13:22 twenty eight *MS, A3*]
      twenty-eight *E1*
13:22 Lire *MS, A3*] lire *E1*
13:29 here.— *MS, A3*] ~. *E1*
13:30 chap—Can't] chap—can't *E1*
      chap. Can't *A3*
13:33 was. *MS, A3*] ~, *E1*
13:34 *contraire— MS, A3*] ~ *E1*
13:35 pale-blue, smallish, *MS, A3*]
      pale-blue smallish *E1*
14:4 irritable: *MS, A3*] ~; *E1*
14:11 it.— *MS, A3*] ~. *E1*
14:12 don't.— *MS, A3*] ~. *E1*
14:13 to?] ~. *E1*
14:13 irresistible *E1*] irresistable *MS,*
      A3
14:23 *are MS, A3*] are *E1*
14:24 absolute ——] ~—— *E1*
      ~ —— *A3*
14:26 trouble.— Of *MS, A3*] ~. *E1*

14:27 whiskey *MS, A3*] whisky *E1*
14:29 *always MS, A3*] always *E1*
14:31 Douglas— *MS, A3*] D——, *E1*
14:33 Beppe *MS, A3*] Beppo *E1*
14:36 good— *MS, A3*] ~, *E1*
14:37 Cos'è *MS, A3*] Cos' è *E1*
14:38 No—*No!*—] *No—No!*— *E1*
      No—*No!* *A3*
14:38 Quest'acqua *MS, A3*] Quest'
      acqua *E1*
14:39 What— *MS, A3*] ~—— *E1*
14:39 what's] What's *E1, A3*
14:39 Dio *MS, A3*] ~ ·, *E1*
14:40 evening— *MS, A3*] ~—— *E1*
15:3 piece— *MS, A3*] ~, *E1*
15:4 dark-red *MS, A3*] dark red *E1*
15:5 two thirds *MS, A3*] two-thirds *E1*
15:13 one more—perhaps *MS, A3*] one
      more perhaps— *E1*
15:16 dressing gown] dressing-gown *E1*
15:17 reddish-purple] reddish purple
      E1
15:20 cut glass] cut-glass *E1*
15:22 St] St *E1*
15:23 Convert] convert *E1*
15:24 thick-leather *MS, A3*] thick
      leather *E1*
15:25 hair brushes *MS, A3*]
      hair-brushes *E1*
15:30 D. *MS, A3*] D—— *E1*
15:33 paid *MS, A3*] paid for *E1*
15:34 whiskey *MS, A3*] whisky *E1*
15:37 Magnus, "why *MS, A3*] M——.
      "Why, *E1*
15:39 life: *MS, A3*] ~; *E1*
16:1 squeaky.— *MS, A3*] ~. *E1*
16:6 live—] ~. *E1*
16:8 all. *MS, A3*] ~? *E1*
16:13 war-famine *MS, A3*] war famine
      E1
16:16 evening: *MS, A3*] ~; *E1*
16:19 Isadora] Isidora *A3 see notes*
16:20 St *MS, A3*] St. *E1*
16:22 Roman Review *MS, A3*] *Roman
      Review E1*
16:27 —*I MS, A3*] I *E1*
16:29 ha-ha *MS, A3*] ~! *E1*

16:30 me.— *MS, A3*] ~. *E1*
16:30 him—Not *MS, A3*] ~. ~ *E1*
16:31 worlds— *MS, A3*] ~. *E1*
16:36 thing wait, *E1*] damned thing wait. *MS, A3 see notes*
16:37 yes now *MS, A3*] Yes. Now *E1*
16:39 oclock— *MS, A3*] o'clock—— *E1*
17:2 fussy —— —— *MS, A3*] ~—— *E1*
17:2 And] and *A3*
17:5 got *MS, A3*] so *E1*
17:7 busybody] ~, *A3*
17:10 eyes, *MS, A3*] ~ *E1*
17:13 oclock *MS, A3*] o'clock *E1*
17:20 it *MS, A3*] ~, *E1*
17:21 it.— *MS, A3*] ~. *E1*
17:25 champignons,— *MS, A3*] ~, *E1*
17:25 cauliflower— *MS, A3*] ~, *E1*
17:29 himself— *MS, A3*] ~ *E1*
17:30 a] the *A3*
17:33 to—" *MS, A3*] ~——" *E1*
17:34 wanted *Ed.*] only wanted *MS*
17:34 spend only *MS, A3*] spend *E1*
17:36 and *E1*] & *MS, A3*
17:39 going *MS, A3*] coming *E1*
18:5 times *MS, A3*] ~, *E1*
18:15 suitcases *MS, A3*] suit-cases *E1*
18:21 fellow *MS, A3*] ~, *E1*
18:24 had *MS, A3*] *Om. E1*
18:28 that. *MS, A3*] ~! *E1*
18:35 church *MS, A3*] Church *E1*
18:39 monk: *MS, A3*] ~; *E1*
19:3 Magnus *MS, A3*] M——, *E1*
19:3 came, *MS, A3*] ~ *E1*
19:6 *wonderful MS, A3*] wonderful *E1*
19:7 ah *MS, A3*] oh *E1*
19:17 world-famous. But *MS, A3*] ~, but *E1*
19:33 strongly.— *MS, A3*] ~. *E1*
19:36 alone."— *MS, A3*] ~." *E1*
19:37 woman-hater.—This *MS, A3*] ~. P This *E1*
19:39 *very, very—MS, A3*] very, very——. *E1*
19:40 he *MS, A3*] that he *E1*
20:1 buoyant *E1*] bouncy *MS, A3*

20:10 *right MS, A3*] right *E1*
20:14 nothingness, *MS, A3*] ~. *E1*
20:16 I did] So I did *A3*
20:19 spirit lamp *MS, A3*] spirit-/lamp *E1*
20:21 then] there *A3*
20:32 The long three *MS, A3*] It was three long *E1 see notes*
20:37 *movement MS, A3*] movement *E1*
20:37 peoples *MS, A3*] people *E1*
20:38 naïve] naive *A3*
21:2 oclock *MS, A3*] o'clock *E1*
21:4 oclock *MS, A3*] o'clock *E1*
21:18 là *MS, A3*] la *E1*
21:22 different.— *MS, A3*] ~. *E1*
21:27 maccheroni *MS, A3*] maccaroni *E1*
21:34 oak-wood *MS, A3*] oak wood *E1*
22:3 manner; *E1*] ~, *MS, A3*
22:3 an *E1*] a certain *MS, A3*
22:3 with it *E1*] *Om. MS, A3*
22:3 which *MS, A3*] *Om. E1 see notes*
22:6 pale-blue *MS, A3*] pale blue *E1*
22:9 evensong *MS, A3*] Evensong *E1*
22:9 while.— *MS, A3*] ~. *E1*
22:13 Certainly. Certainly! *MS, A3*] ~, certainly, *E1*
22:24 recognised *MS, A3*] recognized *E1*
22:28 young, *E1*] ~ *MS, A3*
22:29 and he wore spectacles, *MS, A3*] *Om. MSC see notes*
22:39 worlds *MS, A3*] world's *E1*
23:11 you Don Martino. *MS, A3*] you, Don Bernardo? *E1*
23:13 studies — —" *MS, A3*] ~. *E1*
23:15 fees— —— *MS, A3*] ~—— *E1*
23:16 a new *E1*] himself a new *MS, A3*
23:18 He, by . . . native languages *MS, A3*] He spoke English as if it were his native language *E1 see notes*
23:20 room. *MS, A3*] ~? *E1*
23:22 on *E1*] and *MS*

23:25 spirit lamp *MS, A3*] spirit-lamp *E1*
23:26 high white *MS, A3*] ~, ~, *E1*
23:27 quite a *MS, A3*] a quite *E1*
23:28 writing desk *MS, A3*] writing-desk *E1*
23:29 sitting room *MS, A3*] sitting-room *E1*
23:39 Now, *MS, A3*] ~ *E1*
24:17 *die MS, A3*] die *E1*
24:19 —Yes *MS, A3*] die *E1*
24:20 Italy— *MS, A3*] ~—— *E1*
24:22 tailor," he *MS, A3*] ~." He *E1*
24:33 picture: one *MS, A3*] ~. One *E1*
25:6 thieves *E1*] theives *MS, A3*
25:8 term.— *MS, A3*] ~. *E1*
25:8 complines *MS, A3*] Compline *E1 see notes*
25:12 electric-light *MS, A3*] electric light *E1*
25:12 church *MS, A3*] ~, *E1*
25:16 lily-white *MS, A3*] lily white *E1*
25:17 stones— *MS*] ~—— *E1* ~. *A3*
25:18 Yes *MS, A3*] ~, *E1*
25:27 choir-stalls *MS, A3*] choir stalls *E1*
25:30 dark-brown *MS, A3*] dark brown *E1*
25:40 us. *P* To *MS, A3*] ~. ~ *E1*
26:11 realised *MS, A3*] realized *E1*
26:15 cheap.— *MS, A3*] ~. *E1*
26:28 Overcoat *MS, A3*] overcoat *E1*
26:31 oak-woods *MS, A3*] oak woods *E1*
26:32 bushes *E1*] heathy bushes *MS, A3*
26:33 and seemed *E1*] *Om. MS, A3*
26:40 in the *E1*] in the the *MS*
27:1 white-bunched *MS, A3*] white bunched *E1*
27:15 mass *MS, A3*] Mass *E1*
27:23 Dons *MS, A3*] dons *E1*
27:23 dons *MS, A3*] dons' *E1*
27:24 they of course *MS, A3*] ~, ~ ~, *E1*
27:26 Don *MS, A3*] don *E1*
27:29 mass *MS, A3*] Mass *E1*

27:30 evensong *MS, A3*] Evensong *E1*
27:31 every stone] everything *E1*
27:32 courtyard *MS, A3*] Courtyard *E1*
27:36 flights] flight *E1*
27:39 courtyard *MS, A3*] Courtyard *E1*
27:40 forever.— *MS, A3*] ~. *E1*
28:3 watch tower *MS, A3*] watchtower *E1*
28:4 Benedetto *MS, A3*] Giovanni *E1*
28:8 patronising. *MS, A3*] patronizing *E1*
28:8 and patronising *MS, A3*] and patronizing *E1*
28:15 towards *MS, A3*] toward *E1*
28:29 *should MS, A3*] should *E1*
28:39 Lire *MS, A3*] lire *E1*
29:1 left — *MS, A3*] ~ *E1*
29:1 twenty five *MS, A3*] twenty-five *E1*
29:2 twenty five *MS, A3*] twenty-five *E1*
29:5 plans — *MS, A3*] ~: *E1*
29:6 mind, *MS, A3*] ~ *E1*
30:21 him, *MS, A3*] ~ *E1*
30:25 *should MS, A3*] should *E1*
30:25 turkey cock *MS, A3*] turkey-cock *E1*
30:28 *is MS, A3*] is *E1*
30:34 it is *E1*] it lies *MS, A3*
31:5 absolutely. — *MS, A3*] ~. *E1*
31:15 *yourself MS, A3*] yourself *E1*
31:19 *hypocrisy — MS, A3*] ~—— *E1*
31:25 Why *MS, A3*] ~, *E1*
31:31 today *MS, A3*] to-day, *E1*
31:34 today *MS, A3*] to-day *E1*
32:1 *ever MS, A3*] ever *E1*
32:3 just *MS, A3*] *Om. E1*
32:5 course! Of *MS, A3*] ~! of *E1*
32:7 church *MS, A3*] Church *E1*
32:8 here. — *MS, A3*] ~. *E1*
32:11 done — — *MS, A3*] ~—— *E1*
32:21 doing. — *MS, A3*] ~. *E1*
32:22 Physical relationships *E1*] The physical friendships *MS, A3*
32:23 course, and *E1*] ~. And *MS, A3*

32:33 cold.— *MS, A3*] ~. *E1*

33:5 slowly *MS, A3*] stoutly *E1*
see notes

33:5 that? — *MS, A3*] ~? *E1*

33:6 there. *MS, A3*] ~? *E1*

33:6 Don't *E1*] Dont *MS*

33:7 socialismo *MS, A3*] *socialismo E1*

33:8 communisti *Ed.*] comunisti *MS*,
A3 communisti E1

33:11 rocks, *MS, A3*] ~ *E1*

33:14 foot-hold *MS, A3*] foothold *E1*

33:14 world.— *MS, A3*] ~. *E1*

33:15 road *MS, A3*] ~, *E1*

33:16 ferrovieri *MS, A3*] *ferrovieri E1*

33:18 red white *MS, A3*] ~, ~ *E1*

33:22 middle ages *MS, A3*] Middle
Ages *E1*

33:23 worst. *MS, A3*] ~: *E1*

33:37 maybe— *MS, A3*] ~—— *E1*

34:25 very, very *MS, A3*] very *E1*

34:37 America,— *MS, A3*] ~, *E1*

35:21 sniff at *MS, A3*] smell of *MSC*
see notes on 22:29, 35:21 *and*
58:11

35:23 her eye . . . her eyes *MS, A3*] her
eyes *E1 see notes*

35:25 realise *MS, A3*] realize *E1*

35:27 We *MS, E1*] He *A3*

35:28 high-road *MS, A3*] highroad *E1*

35:33 on to *MS, A3*] on *E1*

35:34 Liras *MS, A3*] lire *E1*

35:35 journey— *MS, A3*] ~—— *E1*

35:39 brasier *MS, A3*] brazier *E1*

35:39 floor, *MS, A3*] ~ *E1*

36:2 world.— *MS, A3*] ~. *E1*

36:2 then *MS*] there *E1* this *A3*

36:6 full, *MS, A3*] ~. *E1*

36:9 maccheroni *MS, A3*] macaroni
E1

36:23 amethystine glamorous *MS, A3*]
amethystine-glamorous *E1*

36:32 it was *MS, E1*] it *A3*

36:34 wife down *Ed.*] wife went down
MS wife, went down *MSC, A3*
wife *E1 see notes*

36:37 floating *MS, A3*] flowing *E1*

36:38 to *MS, A3*] to the *E1 see notes*

37:6 below, *MS, A3*] ~. *E1*

37:20 creeper covered *MS, A3*]
creeper-covered *E1*

37:21 pale-blue *MS, A3*] pale blue *E1*

37:22 thing? *MS, A3*] ~! *E1*

37:28 San *MS, A3*] the San *E1*

37:29 San *MS, A3*] The San *E1*

37:34 Yes *MS, A3*] ~, *E1*

37:38 stammering, "let *MS, A3*] ~.
"Let *E1*

37:39 monastery.— *MS, A3*] ~. *E1*

38:1 name— *MS, A3*] ~—— *E1*

38:1 course, *MS, A3*] ~ *E1*

38:2 Awful!— *MS, A3*] ~! *E1*

38:2 Well— *MS, A3*] ~—— *E1*

38:7 that *MS, A3*] the *E1*

38:8 Well *MS, A3*] ~, *E1*

38:8 Anyhow— *MS, A3*] ~, *E1*

38:9 hastily— *MS, A3*] ~, *E1*

38:12 course, *MS, A3*] ~ *E1*

38:13 But *MS, A3*] ~, *E1*

38:14 —He *MS, A3*] ~ *E1*

38:19 nice and—well, *MS, A3*]
~ ~—, ~ *E1*

38:24 Lire *MS, A3*] lire *E1*

38:26 hill. *MS, A3*] ~, *E1*

38:28 you—. *MS, A3*] ~—— *E1*

38:29 *agony*: *MS, A3*] ~: *E1*

38:30 laugh—] ~. *E1*

39:3 San *MS, A3*] the San *E1*

39:5 Lire *MS, A3*] lire *E1*

39:5 *ruinous*—*MS, A3*] ~—— *E1*

39:11 San *MS, A3*] the San *E1*

39:12 said— "You] ~, "you *E1* ~—
"you *A3*]

39:14 them, *MS, A3*] ~ *E1*

39:15 away— *MS, A3*] ~—— *E1*

39:18 the] *Om. MSC*

39:20 Taylor *MS, A3*] —— *E1*

39:21 something— *MS, A3*] ~——
E1

39:22 expect—? *MS, A3*] ~? *E1*

39:23 Land and Water *MS, A3*] *Land
and Water E1*

39:26 Egypt—.] ~—— *E1* ~— *A3*

39:29 *I MS, A3*] I *E1*

39:29 borne *MS, A3*] done *E1*

39:31   *had MS, A3*] had *E1*
39:38   salotta *MS, A3*] salotto *E1 see notes*
39:39   Oh] ~, *E1*
40:2   situation.— *MS, A3*] ~. *E1*
40:13   suppose.— *MS, A3*] ~. *E1*
40:13   him. *MS, A3*] ~? *E1*
40:24   Americano— Dreadful]
        ~—— ~ *E1* ~——~ *A3*
40:29   come and] come *A3*
40:29   evening. *MS, A3*] ~? *E1*
40:34   pick such *MS, A3*] pick up such *E1*
40:35   people up *MS, A3*] people *E1*
40:40   oclock *MS, A3*] o'clock *E1*
40:41   on to *MS, A3*] on *E1*
41:1   Oh *MS, A3*] ~, *E1*
41:8   San *MS, A3*] the San *E1*
41:10   San *MS, A3*] the San *E1*
41:18   out.—] ~. *E1*
41:19   yesterday.—Disgusting *MS, A3*] ~; disgusting *E1*
41:24   realised *MS, A3*] realized *E1*
41:27   *well MS, A3*] well *E1*
41:28   moments. Now *MS, A3*] ~; now *E1*
41:30   San *MS, A3*] the San *E1*
41:33   it *MS, A3*] it to *E1*
41:34   Lire *MS, A3*] lire *E1*
41:36   San *MS, A3*] the San *E1*
41:40   Taylor *MS, A3*] —— *E1*
42:2   you— *MS, A3*] ~—— *E1*
42:4   San *MS, A3*] the San *E1*
42:6   Melenda *A3*] Melenga *MS see notes*
42:11   cook—splendid *MS, A3*] ~—— splendid *E1*
42:13   Melenda *A3*] Melenga *MS*
42:13   San *MS, A3*] the San *E1*
42:14   can't. *E1*] cant *MS, A3*
42:14   can't. *E1*] cant. *MS, A3*
42:18   won't. *MS, A3*] ~? *E1*
42:18   you.— *MS, A3*] ~. *E1*
42:19   me—" *MS, A3*] ~——" *E1*
42:22   loathed *MS, A3*] loathe *E1*
42:24   Taylor *MS, A3*] —— *E1*
42:31   questura *MS, A3*] Questura *E1*

42:32   Americano] American *A3*
42:37   *here—MS, A3*] ~—— *E1*
43:1   Melenda *A3*] Melenga *MS*
43:14   Melenda's *A3*] Melenga's *MS*
43:19   Lire *MS, A3*] lire *E1*
43:32   ever.— *MS, A3*] ~. *E1*
43:32   it is *E1*] it it *MS*
43:32   world, *MS, A3*] ~ *E1*
43:33   friend— *MS, A3*] ~, *E1*
43:34   —Well *MS, A3*] ~ *E1*
43:35   goes.— *MS, A3*] ~. *E1*
43:38   train,] ~ *E1*
43:38   way,— *MS, A3*] ~, *E1*
44:1   the *MS, A3*] this *E1*
44:4   him—] ~. *E1*
44:5   dislike.— *MS, A3*] ~—— *E1*
44:11   Oh *MS, A3*] ~, *E1*
44:12   do? What can I do? *MS, E1*] do? *A3*
44:13   you. If *MS, A3*] ~, if *E1*
44:14   you— — *MS, A3*] ~—— *E1*
44:15   things?— *MS, A3*] ~? *E1*
44:25   papers.— *MS, A3*] ~. *E1*
44:25   me?] ~! *E1*
44:26   —And *MS, A3*] ~ *E1*
44:32   said: *E1*] ~. *MS*
44:34   tomorrow *MS, A3*] to-morrow *E1*
44:34   Tomorrow *MS, A3*] To-morrow *E1*
44:35   oclock *MS, A3*] o'clock *E1*
44:37   —As *MS, A3*] ~ *E1*
44:38   Taormina: *MS, A3*] ~; *E1*
44:38   *I MS, A3*] I *E1*
45:2   *mistake! MS, A3*] ~ ! *E1*
45:3   So] ~, *A3*
45:5   today *MS, A3*] to-day *E1*
45:7   will.— *MS, A3*] ~. *E1*
45:10   to go: *MS, A3*] ~ ~. *E1*
45:15   bill.— *MS, A3*] ~. *E1*
45:22   lovely, lovely] lovely, lonely *A3*
45:33   there *MS, A3*] then *E1*
45:39   Cheque] cheque *E1*
45:40   Lire *MS, A3*] lire *E1*
46:4   promise.— *MS, A3*] ~. *E1*
46:5   was *E1*] was again, *MS* was again *A3*

46:6 him. *MS, A3*] ~? *E1*
46:7 Lire *MS, A3*] lire *E1*
46:7 realised *MS, A3*] realized *E1*
46:7 *not MS, A3*] not *E1*
46:9 thirty five *MS, A3*] thirty-five *E1*
46:9 thirty five *MS, A3*] thirty-five *E1*
46:15 *couldn't MS, A3*] couldn't *E1*
46:22 sympathised *MS, A3*] sympathized *E1*
46:24 well dressed *MS, A3*] well-dressed *E1*
46:25 honorable *MS, A3*] honourable *E1*
46:26 sympathised *MS, A3*] sympathized *E1*
46:27 him, *MS, A3*] ~ *E1*
46:29 hot, *MS, A3*] ~ *E1*
46:34 Salotta *MS, A3*] salotto *E1*
46:35 dato] data *A3*
46:35 Lei!— *MS, A3*] ~! *E1*
46:36 Melenda *MS, A3*] Melenga *E1*
46:39 Magnus' *A3*] Magnus *MS* M——'s *E1*
46:40 Land and Water *MS, A3*] *Land and Water E1*
46:41 Monastery *MS, A3*] monastery *E1*
47:1 Melenda's *MS, A3*] Melenga's *E1*
47:3 monastery.— *MS, A3*] ~. *E1*
47:3 Melenda *MS, A3*] Melenga *E1*
47:6 Malta . . . *Ed.*] ~. . *MS* ~. *E1*
47:7 Melenda *MS, A3*] Melenga *E1*
47:9 signore *MS, A3*] Signore *E1*
47:13 everything *MS, A3*] everything is *E1*
47:17 Lire *MS, A3*] lire *E1*
47:19 coming—] ~—— *E1* ~. *A3*
47:19 But how? *MS, A3*] Om. *E1*
47:20 Tomorrow . . . tomorrow . . . tonight . . . tomorrow *MS, A3*] To-morrow . . . to-morrow . . . to-night . . . to-morrow *E1*
47:24 signore *MS, A3*] Signore *E1*

47:28 *say MS, A3*] say *E1*
47:29 today, tomorrow, today, tomorrow *MS, A3*] to-day, to-morrow, to-day, to-morrow *E1*
47:30 signore *MS, A3*] Signore *E1*
47:33 come è!" Between] come!" *P* Between *E1* come è! *P* Between *A3*
47:38 è *MS, A3*] e *E1*
47:39 name. *MS, A3*] ~? *E1*
47:40 something— *MS, A3*] ~—— *E1*
48:4 Già! Già *MS, A3*] Gia! Gia *E1*
48:7 He looked . . . cheque story. *MS, A3*] Om. *E1*
48:14 name?— *MS, A3*] ~? *E1*
48:26 since *MS, A3*] that *E1*
48:30 then, *MS, A3*] ~ *E1*
48:33 Then *MS, A3*] then *E1*
48:33 before. *MS, A3*] ~? *E1*
48:34 San *MS, A3*] the San *E1*
48:38 Lire *MS, A3*] lire *E1*
49:1 Siccuro *MS, A3*] Sicuro *E1*
49:5 got *MS, A3*] Om. *E1*
49:7 Lire *MS, A3*] lire *E1*
49:9 questura *MS, A3*] Questura *E1*
49:9 mezzo signore *MS, A3*] mezzo-signore *E1*
49:14 mezzo signore *MS, A3*] mezzo-signore *E1*
49:15 Melenda *MS, A3*] Melenga *E1*
49:16 mezzo signore *MS, A3*] mezzo-signore *E1*
49:22 Lire *MS, A3*] lire *E1*
49:24 Cheque] cheque *E1*
49:25 Melenda *MS, A3*] Melenga *E1*
49:26 Lire— *MS, A3*] lire—— *E1*
49:28 *pays me,*] pays me, *E1 pays* me *A3*
49:28 stay— *MS, A3*] ~—— *E1*
49:28 said: *MS, A3*] ~; *E1*
49:36 Melenda *MS, A3*] Melenga *E1*
49:39 Land and Water *MS, A3*] *Land and Water E1*
50:1 Melenda *MS, A3*] Melenga *E1*

50:1 half hour *MS, A3*] half-hour *E1*

50:4 Melenda *MS, A3*] Melenga *E1*

50:4 you— *MS, A3*] ~—— *E1*

50:8 Melenda's *MS, A3*] Melenga's *E1*

50:11 *third class!* *MS, A3*] ~ ~ ! *E1*

50:16 Lire *MS, A3*] lire *E1*

50:16 Melenda *MS, A3*] Melenga *E1*

50:18 Lire *MS, A3*] lire *E1*

50:18 on *MS, A3*] *Om. E1*

50:19 Lire *MS, A3*] lire *E1*

50:23 Lire *MS, A3*] lire *E1*

50:23 day— *MS, A3*] ~—— *E1*

50:28 always *MS, A3*] *Om. E1*

50:32 paper, *MS, A3*] ~ *E1*

50:34 Lire *MS, A3*] lire *E1*

50:34 Lire, *MS, A3*] lire, *E1*

50:35 Signor *MS, A3*] Signore *E1*

50:36 paper—] ~. *E1*

50:38 me, *MS, A3*] ~ *E1*

50:38 left.— *MS, A3*] ~. *E1*

51:4 swindling— *MS, A3*] ~. *E1*

51.6 saying *MS, A3*] stating *E1*

51:10 regretted *MS, A3*] ~, *E1*

51:10 —I *MS, A3*] ~ *E1*

51:13 hours *MS, A3*] hours' *E1*

51:17 forwarded *MS, A3*] had forwarded *E1*

51:18 I O U *MS, A3*] I.O.U. *E1*

51:18 had—] ~. *E1*

51:20 four-and-a-half *MS, A3*] four and a half *E1*

51:26 Malta?— *MS, A3*] ~? *E1*

51:27 go?— *MS, A3*] ~? *E1*

51:27 knows! *MS, A3*] ~! *E1*

51:28 tomorrow *MS, A3*] to-morrow *E1*

51:29 do. *MS, A3*] ~? *E1*

51:34 Ah *MS, A3*] ~, *E1*

52:4 north] North *A3*

52:5 harbour-water *MS, A3*] harbour water *E1*

52:7 trees, *MS, A3*] ~. *E1*

52:7 burnooses *MS, A3*] burnouses *E1 see notes*

52:8 long-coats *MS, A3*] long coats *E1*

52:18 morning *MS, A3*] ~, *E1*

52:20 steam-boats *MS, A3*] steamboats *E1*

52:22 Lire *MS, A3*] lire *E1*

52:22 bill. *MS, A3*] ~? *E1*

52:24 half hour *MS, A3*] half-hour *E1*

52:27 Malta—. *MS, A3*] ~—— *E1*

52:28 Well *MS, A3*] ~, *E1*

52:31 recognised *MS, A3*] recognized *E1*

52:33 oclock *MS, A3*] o'clock *E1*

52:37 in at *MS, A3*] in *E1*

52:40 on *MS, A3*] *Om. E1*

53:2 Lire *MS, A3*] lire *E1*

53:4 today *MS, A3*] to-day *E1*

53:5 Lire *MS, A3*] lire *E1*

53:9 class: and *MS, A3*] ~. And *E1*

53:10 hours *MS, A3*] hours' *E1*

53:15 ticket; if you have a third *E1*] ticket, a second-class gentleman with a second-class ticket, and with a third-class ticket *MS, A3*

53:22 woolen *MS, A3*] woollen *E1*

53:31 course *MS, A3*] ~, *E1*

54:21 hotel-people *MS, A3*] hotel people *E1*

54:21 on-lookers *MS, A3*] onlookers *E1*

54:32 hankies *MS, A3*] handkerchiefs *E1*

54:33 flower pots *MS, A3*] flower-pots *E1*

55:4 Goodbye] Good-bye *E1*

55:6 No *MS, A3*] ~, *E1*

55:7 starting!] ~. *A3*

55:11 me . . . *MS, A3*] ~. *E1*

55:16 him.— — — *MS, A3*] ~. *E1*

55:17 tomorrow *MS, A3*] to-morrow *E1*

55:18 Empire— *MS, A3*] ~—— *E1*

55:21 first class *MS, A3*] first-class *E1*

55:22 in *E1*] with *MS, A3*

55:23 above-mentioned *MS, A3*] above mentioned *E1*

55:26 laugh,] ~. *A3*

55:28 dégagé *MS, A3*] *degagé E1*
55:31 first class *MS, A3*] first-class
E1
55:35 pale-yellow *MS, A3*] pale yellow
E1
55:36 swift, *MS, A3*] ~ *E1*
56:2 —He *MS, A3*] ~ *E1*
56:3 patronising *MS, A3*]
patronizing *E1*
56:4 —I *MS, A3*] ~ *E1*
56:12 St] St. *E1*
56:18 first- *MS, A3*] first *E1*
56:22 Commander] commander *A3*
56:34 aimiable . . . aimiable . . .
aimiability *MS, A3*] amiable . . .
amiable . . . amiability *E1*
56:36 Hôtel *MS, A3*] Hotel *E1*
57:6 oh *MS, A3*] ~, *E1*
57:6 whiskey *MS, A3*] whisky *E1*
57:12 whiskey *MS, A3*] whisky *E1*
57:17 weigh *MS, A3*] way *E1*
57:26 Mazzaiba *E1*] Mazzaibba *MS*
see notes
57:28 go for *E1*] go *MS*
57:30 island: *MS, A3*] ~, *E1*
58:2 cathedral *MS, A3*] ~, *E1*
58:8 Pauls *MS, A3*] Paul's *E1*
58:9 I forgot . . . summer villa. *MS,*
A3] leave out *MSC Om. E1 see*
note on 58:11
58:13 catholic *MS, A3*] Catholic *E1*
58:14 patronising *MS, A3*]
patronizing *E1*
58:22 Mazzaiba *E1*] Mazzaibba *MS*
58:23 forlorn little,] ~ ~ *E1* ~, ~ *A3*
58:24 him *MS, A3*] *Om. E1*
58:25 Mazzaiba *E1*] Mazzaibba *MS*
58:26 left *MS, A3*] ~, *E1*
58:27 home] house *A3*
58:29 empire *MS, A3*] Empire *E1*
58:30 *American MS, A3*] American
E1
58:33 miles *MS, A3*] miles' *E1*
58:37 fellows *MS, A3*] ~, *E1*
58:41 write. *P* During *MS, A3*] ~. *P #*
During *E1*
59:3 lurking *MS, A3*] sinking *E1*

59:4 Martino: *MS, A3*] Bernardo—
E1
59:7 Gentleman] gentleman *E1*
59:7 Rabato.— *MS, A3*] ~. *E1*
59:11 Mr *MS, A3*] Mr. *E1*
59:14 event—] ~. *E1*
59:15 and saying *E1*] as *MS, A3*
59:18 Valletta. 20 *MS, A3*] ~, 20 *E1*
22nd. *SL*
59:18 November *MS, A3*] ~, *E1*
Novbr. *SL*
59:18 Mr *MS, A3*] Mr. *E1*
59:18 Some *MS, A3, SL*] some *E1*
59:19 Daily Malta Chronicle *MS, A3*]
Daily Malta Chronicle E1
59:23 The *MS, A3*] "~ *MSC*
59:23 Mazzaiba] Michael *SL*
59:25 Mazzaiba] Borg *SL*
59:26 details] deta- *SL*
59:26 for] for whilst he is seeing to
your order *SL*
59:27 Mazzaiba *MS, A3*] "~ *MSC, E1*
Michael *SL*
59:29 (This *MS, A3*] [~ *E1 Om. SL*
59:29 is not ... the first] *Om. SL*
59:31 time.) # — *Ed.*] ~). — *MS*~.]
E1 ~.)— *A3 Om. SL*
59:31 embarassed *MS, A3*]
embarrassed *E1*
59:32 then *MS, A3, SL*] ~, *E1*
59:33 financially] ~, *SL*
59:34 upon *MS, A3*] on *E1*
59:34 as *MS, A3*] and *E1*
59:39 Mazzaiba *MS, A3*] "~ *MSC, E1*
Borg *SL*
59:41 merely] simply *SL*
60:1 rightly *MS, A3, SL*] ~, *E1*
60:2 Mazzaiba *E1*] Borg *MS, A3, SL*
see note on 57:26
60:2 could *MS, A3, SL*] would *E1*
60:5 directly,] ~ *SL*
60:6 Mazzaiba] Borg *SL*
60:8 At *MS, A3*] "~ *MSC*
60:9 exploit] form a company to
exploit *SL*
60:10 materialised *MS, A3*]
materialized *E1*

60:11 Mazzaiba *Ed.*] Borg *MS*, *A3*, *SL*
Mazzaiba was *E1 see note on* 57:26

60:12 Fortunately *MS*, *A3*] ~, *E1*, *SL*

60:13 dropped,] ~ *SL*

60:15 Last *MS*, *A3*] "~ *MSC*

60:17 months *MS*, *A3*,*SL*] months' *E1*

60:18 none *MS*, *A3*,*SL*] ~, *E1*

60:18 Mazzaiba to] Borg to *SL*

60:19 Mazzaiba could] Borg could *SL*

60:20 Mazzaiba] Borg *SL*

60:23 When *MS*, *A3*] "~ *MSC*

60:23 Mazzaiba] Borg *SL*

60:24 (the old . . . the suburb)] *Om. SL*

60:29 etc. *MS*, *A3*,*SL*] ~., *E1*

60:31 Ult *MS*, *A3*] ult *E1*, *SL*

60:31 police] Police *SL*

60:35 was *MS*, *A3*, *SL*] *Om. E1*

60:35 no] in no *SL*

60:36 Magnus *MS*, *A3*] "~ *MSC*
"M—— *E1*

60:38 Mr Salonia] Mr. Salomone *SL*
Mr. Salonia *E1*

60:39 Isld. *MS*, *A3*, *SL*] island *E1*

60:39 weeks *MS*, *A3*] weeks' *E1*

60:40 Commissioner *MS*, *SL*]
commissioner *A3*

61:1 grace,] ~ *SL*

61:2 asked] had asked *SL*

61:3 Police *MS*, *A3*] police *E1*

61:6 police *MS*, *A3*] ~, *E1* Police *SL*

61:8 We *MS*, *A3*] "~ *MSC*

61:9 Mazzaiba's office] Borg's Office *SL*

61:9 Wednesday *MS*, *A3*] ~, *E1*

61:9 3rd] 3rd. *SL*

61:9 inst. *MS*, *A3*] ~., *E1*

61:10 time] ~, *SL*

61:11 alone at noon] at noon alone *SL*

61:11 Mazzaiba] Borg *SL*

61:12 Senglea *MS*, *SL*] Singlea *E1 see notes*

61:13 4.30 *MS*, *A3*] 4.30, *E1*

61:13 Mazzaiba] Borg *SL*

61:15 up *MS*, *A3*] ~, *E1*

61:15 us *MS*, *A3*] ~, *E1*

61:15 town *MS*, *A3*] ~, *E1*

61:16 friend.] friend (Mr. Mamo). *SL*

61:17 On *MS*, *A3*] "~ *MSC*

61:17 morning *MS*, *A3*] ~, *E1*

61:17 4th] 4th. *SL*

61:17 inst. *MS*, *A3*] ~., *E1*

61:17 a.m. *A3*] a.m *MS* a.m., *E1*

61:19 Police *MS*, *A3*] police *E1*

61:20 re *MS*, *A3*] *re E1*

61:21 police] Police *SL*

61:21 excuse] ~, *SL*

61:22 Rome,] ~ *SL*

61:23 extradicted *MS*, *A3*] extradited *E1 see notes*

61:23 Authorities *MS*, *A3*] authorities *E1*

61:24 with *MS*, *A3*] in *E1*

61:25 1. Strada *MS*, *A3*] 1 Strada *E1*
1, Sda. *SL*

61:26 Pietro *MS*, *A3*] ~, *E1*

61:26 behind him *MS*, *A3*] ~ ~, *E1*

61:28 A *MS*, *A3*] "~ *MSC*

61:29 Martino] Mauro *SL*

61:30 One] one *SL*

61:33 Police *MS*, *A3*] police *E1*

61:35 roof *MS*, *A3*] ~, *E1*

61:39 At *MS*, *A3*] "~ *MSC*

61:39 8.0] 8.0. *SL*

62:2 birthday, *MS*, *A3*] ~ *E1*

62:2 7th] 7th. *SL*

62:2 Novr.) *MS*, *A3*] ~,), *E1*

62:4 Addenda:— *MS*, *A3*] "~:— *MSC* "~: *E1* ADDENDA:– *SL*

62:4 Don Martino's] Dom Mauro's *SL*

62:5 "I *MS*, *A3*] "'~ *MSC* ~ *SL*

62:5 Gabriel Mazzaiba] Michael Borg *SL*

62:6 me." *MS*, *A3*] ~.' *E1* ~. *SL*

62:7 Document] "Document *MSC*

62:7 writing table: *MS*, *A3*]
writing-table: *E1* writing table:– *SL*

62:8 "In *MS*, *A3*] ' ~ *E1* ~ *SL*

62:8 consul] Consul *SL*

62:10 wife *MS*, *A3*] ~. *E1* wife:– /
Mrs. Lucy Magnus, / c/o Mrs. Vernon, *SL*

62:10 (Address—) *MS*, *A3*] (~.) *E1*
(address) *SL*

62:11 Gabriel Mazzaiba, inform]
Michael Borg (address) advise
SL

62:11 him (Address) *MS*, *A3*] ~. (~.)
E1 ~. *SL*

62:12 Douglas (address) *MS*, *A3*] ~.
(Address.) *E1* ~ Chez Mmme.
Rola 4 Rue St. Charles Mentone
alps Maritimes France. *SL*

62:14 accrue. The] ~ – the *SL*

62:15 with. *MS*, *A3*] ~: *E1*

62:16 etc *MS*, *A3*] ~. *E1*

62:17 spoons] ~, *SL*

62:17 Gabriel Mazzaiba (address)"
MS, *A3*] ~ ~. (Address.).' *E1*
Michael Borg, (address). *SL*

62:18 The *MS*, *A3*] "~ *MSC*

62:20 expenses *MS*, *A3*] ~, *E1*

62:22 Consul *MS*, *SL*] consul *E1*

62:22 Vice consul] vice-consul *E1*, *SL*
vice consul *A3*

62:22 Mr M., *MS*, *A3*] Mr. A., *E1* Mr
Mamo *SL*

62:23 citizen] citezen *SL*

62:23 Gabriel Mazzaiba] Michael Borg
SL

62:24 Please *MS*, *A3*] "~ *MSC*

62:25 you *MS*, *A3*] you will *E1*

62:27 Magnus. Believe] ~, believe *SL*

62:27 me, / My *MS*, *A3*] ~, ~ *E1*

62:28 Mr *MS*, *A3*] Mr. *E1*

62:28 Lawrence etc.—" *MS*, *A3*] ~,
~." *E1* ~, / very respectfully
yours, / sd. Walter Salomone.
SL

62:29 (Mrs *MS*, *A3*] [Mrs. *E1* P.S.
Mrs *SL*

62:30 her husband's] M's *SL*

62:30 death.) *MS*, *A3*] ~.] *E1* ~. <u>WS.</u>
SL

62:32 said *MS*, *A3*] ~, *E1*

62:33 *realised MS*, *A3*] realized *E1*

62:34 to *MS*, *A3*] to be *E1*

62:39 still feel *MS*, *A3*] feel still *E1*

63:7 *strangers MS*, *A3*] strangers *E1*

63:8 Magnus?— *MS*, *A3*] ~? *E1*

63:8 the *MS*, *A3*] this *E1*

63:8 treachery, *MS*, *A3*] ~ *E1*

63:9 sorry *MS*, *A3*] Sorry *E1*

63:11 sooner."— *MS*, *A3*] ~." *E1*

63:15 well-intentioned *MS*, *A3*] well
intentioned *E1*

63:18 ———] *Om. E1*

63:23 surging *MS*, *A3*] swinging *E1*

63:24 drill-yards *MS*, *A3*] drill yards
E1

63:26 before his *MS*, *A3*] before the
E1

63:26 little,] ~ *A3*

63:27 *De mortui . . .* [66:18] has
courage. *MS*, *A3*] *Om. E1 see
also following entries up to* 66:12

64:2 plane—,"] ~," — *A3*

64:9 *But!*] ~. *A3*

64:23 affection,] ~ *A3*

65:20 baseness,] ~ *A3*

66:11 prostitution *A3*] prostition
MS

66:12 But] And *A3*

66:19 Oh *MS*, *A3*] ~, *E1*

66:20 *Boches! MS*, *A3*] ~ ! *E1*

66:23 towards] toward *A3*

66:23 our hero *E1*] Maurice *MS*, *A3*

66:27 mongrel— *MS*, *A3*] ~——— *E1*

66:31 Cause] cause *A3*

66:31 our hero's *E1*] Maurice's *MS*,
A3

66:32 Bel-Abbès *E1*] Bel-Abbes *MS*,
A3

66:32 Yes *MS*, *A3*] ~, *E1*

66:32 cold. One] cold. *P* One *A3*

66:35 *gentleman! MS*, *A3*] ~ ! *E1*

66:39 littérateur *MS*, *A3*] *littérateur*
E1

66:40 colonel *MS*, *A3*] Colonel *E1*

67:2 *littérateur! MS*, *A3*] *littérateur!*
E1

67:5 *littérateur! MS*, *A3*] *littérateur!*
E1

67:5 pigeon!] ~. *A3*

67:6 Bel-Abbès *E1*] Bel-Abbes *MS*,
A3

67:9   etc etc *MS, A3*] etc., etc. *E1*
67:15   dove.— *MS, A3*] ~. *E1*
67:16   did *he MS, A3*] he did *E1*
67:16   Bel-Abbès? *Ed.*] Bel-Abbes?
         MS, A3 Bel-Abbès, *E1*
67:18   Yes *MS, A3*] ~, *E1*
67:25   War—] ~. *E1*
67:27   Bel-Abbès *E1*] Bel-Abbes *MS,*
         A3
67:28   emptiness,] ~ *A3*
67:40   better.— *MS, A3*] ~. *E1*
68:1   if *E1*] *Om. MS*
68:2   friendships"— *MS, A3*]
         ~——" *E1*
68:4   grave. *MS, A3*] ~? *E1*
68:5   that *MS, A3*] there *E1*
68:11   buona sera! *MS, A3*] *buona sera!*
         E1
68:13   see!— *MS, A3*] ~! *E1*
68:14   fisacal, *MS, A3*] ~ *E1*
68:18   *Ecco!*—and *MS, A3*] ~ ! And *E1*
68:21   advantage—] ~. *E1*
69:3   humiliated,] ~ *A3*
69:4   men I know *MS, A3*] ~, ~ ~,
         E1
69:4   things, *MS, A3*] ~ *E1*
69:5   then *MS, A3*] ~, *E1*
69:7   Dos *E1*] Los *MS*
69:8   true. — *MS, A3*] ~. *E1*
69:10   them.— *MS, A3*] ~. *E1*
69:12   realise *MS, A3*] realize *E1*
69:14   *realising MS, A3*] realizing *E1*
69:16   realisation . . . realisation *MS,*
         A3] realization . . . realization *E1*
69:22   wriggle *MS, A3*] wiggle *E1*
69:26   horrible] terrible *A3*
69:29   knowledge, *MS, A3*] ~ *E1*
70:3   realisation *MS, A3*] realization
         E1
70:4   *realise MS, A3*] realize *E1*
70:9   today *MS, A3*] to-day *E1*
70:9   Dos Passos' *E1*] Los Passo's *MS*
70:12   through it . . . through: they
         MS, A3] through. They *E1*
70:14   war-medals *MS, A3*] war medals
         E1
70:15   lonely] lovely *A3*

70:19   Dos *E1*] Los *MS*
70:26   quaking, *MS, A3*] ~ *E1*
70:29   living?— *MS, A3*] ~. *E1*
71:1   realise *MS, A3*] realize *E1*
71:2   it, And] ~, and *E1*
71:5   machines. Modern militarism is
         MS, A3] *Om. E1*
71:6   for ever *MS, A3*] forever *E1*
71:7   go, guns shall go, submarines
         and warships shall *MS, A3*] *Om.*
         E1
71:13   but *MS, A3*] and *E1*
71:14   Romans *MS, A3*] Roman *E1*
71:16   war-paint *MS, A3*] war paint
         E1
71:24   many. *MS, A3*] ~, *E1*
71:25   manuscript!] ~. *E1*
71:26   *this MS, A3*] this *E1*
71:27   bitterness, *MS, A3*] ~ *E1*
71:33   —And *MS, A3*] ~ *E1*
71:34   back, *MS, A3*] ~ *E1*
71:35   gentleman's *E1*] gentlemans *MS*
71:35   *last MS, A3*] last *E1*
71:36   realise *MS, A3*] realize *E1*
72:2   October *MS, A3*] ~, *E1*
72:4   highest] higher *A3*
72:6   Magnus' *MS, A3*] M——s *E1*
72:7   Cemetery] Cemetary *A3*
72:12   just, *MS, A3*] ~ *E1*
72:12   Lethe *E1*] peace *MS, A3*
72:13   York on *MS, A3*] York, *E1*
72:13   November *MS, A3*] ~, *E1*
72:13   1876: *MS, A3*] ~; *E1*
72:14   England, *MS, A3*] ~ *E1*
72:15   Mr Liebetrau] Mr. L—— *E1*
         Mr Liebetran *A3 see note on 26:9*
72:19   importance *E1*] importance,
         royal importance *MS, A3*
72:19   manqué *MS, A3*] *manqué E1*
72:20   him.— *MS, A3*] ~. *E1*
72:20   apparently *E1*] *Om. MS, A3*
72:23   true.— *MS, A3*] ~. *E1*
72:26   alas *MS, A3*] ~, *E1*
72:29   charity. A *MS, A3*] ~—a *E1*
72:31   Also—Maurice . . . Leid
         nachgelassen *MS, A3*] *Also,*
         M—— . . . *Leid nachgelassen E1*

72:33   language. *Ed.*] language. /   LAWRENCE / TAORMINA
Taormina, January 1922. D. H.   *E1* language. / Taormina,
Lawrence *MS* language. / D. H.   January 1922 *A3*

'The Bad Side of Books': introduction to *A Bibliography of the Writings of D. H. Lawrence*

MS = Roberts E36a
TS = Roberts E36b
TSR = Autograph revisions in *TS*
A1 = *A Bibliography of the Writings of D. H. Lawrence*, edited by Edward D. McDonald (Philadelphia: The Centaur Book Shop, 1925)

75:1   There doesn't *Ed.*] Introduction to Bibliography / There doesn't *MS* THE BAD SIDE OF BOOKS / BY D. H. LAWRENCE / There doesn't *A1*
75:15   ever was] was ever *TS*
75:15   it] *Om. TS*
75:17   title page] title-page *A1*
75:19   much of a *TSR*] a real *MS*
76:1   think,] ~ *TS*
76:1   on] upon *TS*
76:10   Heinemann *A1*] Heineman *MS*
76:10   once:] ~; *A1*
76:11   he knew] *Om. TS*
76:16   objectionable",] ~," *TS*
76:20   one] *Om. TS*
76:21   Heinemann's *A1*] Heineman's *MS*
76:25   Heinemann *A1*] Heineman *MS*
76:30   and of] and *TS*
76:32   as at] at *TS*
76:36   play] ~, *A1*
76:36   *Mrs*] ~. *A1*

76:37   Mitchell *MS, A1*] Mitchel *TS*
77:3   date on] date of *TS*
77:4   Kennerley:] ~, *A1*
77:5   made it] made *TS*
77:14   *Peccavi! Peccavi! TSR*] Peccavi! Peccavi! *MS Peccavi! Peccavi! A1*
77:15   rose] arose *TS*
77:17   print,] ~ *TS*
77:18   Later,] ~ *TS*
77:20   *ex cathedra TSR*] ex cathedra *MS, A1*
77:24   takes *TSR*] receives *MS*
77:31   favorite] favourite *TS*
77:38   believe,] ~ *A1*
77:39   thistles] thistle *A1*
78:2   best] *Om. TS*
78:7   seed] ~, *TS*
78:7   whither? who] Whither? Who *TS*
78:16   bygone] by-gone *A1*
78:17   inertia. *Ed.*] inertia. / Lobo. 1st September 1924 *MS* Lobo. 1st, September 1924 *TS Lobo.* / *September 1st, 1924 A1*

Introduction (version 1) to *The Memoirs of the Duc de Lauzun*

MS = Roberts E106d
TCC = Roberts E106e
A1 = *Phoenix* (Viking)

87:1   There is] [THE GOOD MAN] / There is *A1*
87:12   hind legs] hind-legs *TCC*

87:13   "superior," *MS, A1*] "~", *TCC*
87:13   east-end] East End *A1*

87:14	amazement,] ~ *TCC*	90:3	recognised] recognized *A1*
87:27	man",] ~," *A1*	90:3	"irritability." *MS, A1*] "~".
87:27	feeling," *MS, A1*] ~", *TCC*		*TCC*
87:28	"goodness",] "~," *A1*	90:4	recognise. And] recognise, but
87:32	man",] ~," *A1*		*TCC* recognize, but *A1*
88:2	Robot] robot *A1*	90:5	recognised] recognized *A1*
88:4	man," *MS, A1*] ~", *TCC*	90:5	feeling patterns]
88:11	man"] ~," *A1*		feeling-patterns *A1*
88:11	reasonable,] ~ *TCC*	90:6	"nervousness." *MS, A1*] "~".
88:13	Robot] robot *A1*		*TCC*
88:17	nature:] ~. *TCC*	90:7	existence:] ~, *TCC*
88:21	"free",] "~," *A1*	90:16	eighteenth-century] eighteenth
88:21	"free",] "~," *A1*		century *TCC*
88:22	"good." *MS, A1*] "~". *TCC*	90:19	unbearable: *MS, A1*] ~;
88:23	"free",] "~," *A1*		*TCC*
88:24	man",] ~," *A1*	90:22	true,] ~ *TCC*
88:28	civilisation] civilization *A1*	90:28	feels and] ~, ~ *TCC*
88:30	"good." *MS, A1*] "~". *TCC*	90:36	art-forms] art forms *TCC*
88:30	"free." *MS, A1*] "~". *TCC*	90:37	life-less] lifeless *A1*
89:8	not-good] not good *TCC*	90:38	revolution.] ~? *TCC*
89:9	"good man." *MS, A1*] "~ ~".	91:1	socialists] Socialists *A1*
	TCC	91:1	bolshevists] Bolshevists *A1*
89:18	bound-up] bound up *TCC*	91:2	Buddhists] ~, *A1*
89:19	"lily." *MS, A1*] "~". *TCC*	91:2	Scientists] ~, *A1*
89:19	tight bound up] bound up tight	91:5	feeling pattern] feeling-pattern
	A1		*TCC*
89:21	is] was *TCC*	91:11	Robot] robot *A1*
89:22	is] was *A1*	91:12	realise] realize *A1*
89:27	bandage] bondage *TCC*	91:16	débâcle] *débâcleTCC*
89:36	recognise] recognize *A1*	91:16	*Déluge* was] *Déluge*, was *TCC*
89:36	own." *MS, A1*] ~". *TCC*		*déluge* was *A1*
89:37	civilised] civilized *A1*	91:20	homunculus-Robot]
89:39	don't know *TCC*] dont know		homunculus robot *A1*
	MS	91:20	man",] ~," *A1*
90:1	unrecognised] unrecognized *A1*	91:23	can not] cannot *TCC*
90:2	unrecognised] unrecognized *A1*	91:26	lowering] louring *A1*

Introduction (version 2) to *The Memoirs of the Duc de Lauzun*

MS = Roberts E106a
TCC = Roberts E106b
A1 = *Phoenix* (Viking)

95:1	The Duc de Lauzun] THE	95:5	focussed] focused *A1*
	DUC DE LAUZUN. *TCC*	95:6	fashions] fashion *TCC*
	THE DUC DE LAUZUN	95:30	half-naked] half naked *TCC*
	A1	95:31	Dauphin] dauphin *TCC*
95:2	Lauzun] Lauzun [Duc de	96:2	Count] count *TCC*
	Biron] *A1*	96:2	lacqueys] lackeys *A1*

96:3   lacquey] lackey *A1*

96:7   there] There *A1*

96:8   aloud."—] ∼." *A1*

96:10 king] King *TCC*

96:12 neglected. . . . *MS, A1*] ∼. . . . . *TCC*

96:13 regiment . . .] ∼. . . . *TCC*

96:15 Duke] Duc *A1*

96:17 fal-de-lal] falderal *A1*

96:19 love affairs *MS, A1*] love-affairs *TCC*

96:23 naïve *MS, A1*] naive *TCC*

96:24 suffocated] *Om. TCC*

96:27 fourteen *TCC*] 14 *MS*

96:28 showed] showed a *TCC*

96:29 gradually forming] forming, gradually, *TCC*

96:34 ahead."—] ∼." *A1*

96:35 honor] honour *A1*

96:36 world,"*MS, A1*] ∼", *TCC*

97:2   mistress] ∼, *TCC*

97:4   rendez-vous] rendezvous *A1*

97:9   love-affairs] love affairs *A1*

97:13 d'Esparbes] d'Espartes *TCC*

97:14 world."*MS, A1*] ∼". *TCC*

97:17 Countess] Comtesse *A1*

97:19 all] All *A1*

97:23 treacheries] treacherous *TCC*

97:24 women,] ∼ *TCC*

97:29 Mlle.] Mademoiselle *A1*

97:31 child."*MS, A1*] ∼". *TCC*

97:40 selfishnesses] selfishness *TCC*

98:2   day.—] ∼: *TCC*

98:5   say,] ∼ *TCC*

98:5   Go] '∼ *A1*

98:6   gentleman.—] ∼. *TCC* ∼.' *A1*

98:13 love?—] ∼? *TCC*

98:17 child."*MS, A1*] ∼". *TCC*

98:19 child,"*MS, A1*] ∼", *TCC*

98:20 Anyhow] ∼, *A1*

98:25 "romantic," *MS, A1*] "∼", *TCC*

98:31 decent] ∼, *TCC*

98:35 pietism] fiction *TCC*

98:38 feeling] feelings *TCC*

99:1   "wit",] "∼," *A1*

99:12 reign. *P* She] reign. She *TCC*

Introduction to *The Mother*

MS = Roberts E249.5a

E1 = *The Mother*, by Grazia Deledda, tr. Mary G. Steegman, Jonathan Cape, 1928

TCC = Roberts E249.5b

103:1   Introduction to *The Mother*] INTRODUCTION *E1* INTRODUCTION To "The Mother". *TCC*

103:8   towards *MS, TCC*] toward *E1*

103:17 Matilde] Matilda *E1*

103:18 Deledda,] ∼ *TCC*

103:29 Sardinia. *P* Still *MS, TCC*] Sardinia. Still *E1*

104:3   barbarism *MS, TCC*] barbarians *E1*

104:4   time,] ∼ *TCC*

104:8   awakening *MS, TCC*] understanding *E1*

104:11 money-sway *MS, TCC*] money sway *E1*

104:13 Instead] ∼, *TCC*

104:15 aboriginal *MS, TCC*] *Om. E1*

104:16 determined] ∼, *TCC*

104:23 "continental."] '∼.' *E1* "∼". *TCC*

104:26 exorcising *MS, TCC*] exorcizing *E1*

104:30 touched, *MS, TCC*] ∼ *E1*

104:30 annoyed] ∼, *TCC*

104:32 exposure;] ∼: *E1*

104:34 spirit solve *E1*] spirit will solve *MS see notes*

104:36 sympathising *MS, TCC*] sympathizing *E1*

104:37 sympathise *MS, TCC*] sympathize *E1*

105:2 authoress'] author's *E1*
authoress's *TCC*
105:2 *would*] would *E1*
105:4 *not*] not *TCC*
105:5 characterisation *MS, TCC*]
characterization *E1*
105:12 christianity *MS, TCC*]
Christianity *E1*
105:15 half-civilisations]
half-civilization *E1*
half-civilisation *TCC*
105:16 life; she] life—she *E1*
105:17 sex life] sex-life *TCC*
105:18 dimly-comprehended *MS,*
TCC] dimly comprehended
E1

105:19 falsely-conceived *MS, TCC*]
falsely conceived *E1*
105:27 Bronte *MS, TCC*] Brontë *E1*
105:29 "dating" *MS, TCC*] '~' *E1*
105:30 rather a] rather the *E1*
105:37 realised] realized *E1* realised,
TCC
106:1 meaning] ~, *TCC*
106:6 Sardinia] ~, *TCC*
106:7 enduring. *TCC*] enduring. /
D. H. Lawrence / for Jonathan
Cape, as by direct
arrangement—he to pay six
guineas, & anything American
extra. *MS* enduring. / D. H.
LAWRENCE *E1*

'Chaos in Poetry': introduction to *Chariot of the Sun*

MS = Roberts E65a
TS = Roberts E65b
TCCI = 'A Book Of Modern Poems', gift of Majl Ewing to UCLA
TSR = Autograph revisions in *TS*
Per = *Échanges* (December 1929), 54–62
F1 = *Chariot of the Sun* (Paris: Black Sun Press, 1931), pp. I–XVIII
TCCII = Roberts E65c
A1 = *Phoenix* (Viking)

109:1 Chaos in Poetry *Ed.*]
Introduction to Chariot of the
Sun *MS* A BOOK OF
MODERN POEMS* [at foot
of page] Introduction to:
Chariot of the Sun, by Harry
Crosby. *TS* A BOOK OF
MODERN POEMS* [at foot
of page] Introduction to:
Chariot of the Sun, by Harry
Crosby *TCCI* Chaos in
Poetry / by D. H. Lawrence [at
foot of page] Introduction to:
Chariot of the Sun, Poems, by
Harry Crosby. To be published
in the autumn in Boston
U. S. A. *TSR* CHAOS IN
POETRY. / by / D. H.
LAWRENCE *Per*
INTRODUCTION *F1*

CHAOS IN POETRY.* [at foot
of page] Introduction to:
Chariot of the Sun, Poems, by
Harry Crosby. To be published
in the autumn in Boston
U. S. A. *TCCII Chariot of the
Sun*, by Harry Crosby* [at foot
of page] The text of this
preface is taken from
Lawrence's typescript, not
from *Chariot of the Sun*. *A1*

109:2 just *TSR, TCCII*] true, just
MS, F1
109:2 much true as that *TSR,*
TCCII] *Om. MS* much as *TS,*
F1
109:4 It *TSR, TCCII*] But it *MS,*
F1
109:4 truth,] ~ *TCCII*
109:7 jingle *TS*] a jingle *MS*

109:9   things, *TS*] ∼: *MS*
109:14 known *TS*] *Om. MS*
109:15 forever-surging *MS*,
      TSR,TCCII] forever surging
      TCCI, F1 for ever surging *A1*
109:16 which *TCCI*] *Om. MS*
109:16 to, *TS*] ∼ *MS, TCCII*
109:17 consciousness, *TS*] ∼ *MS*
109:18 mind *TS*] awareness *MS*
109:18 civilisation *MS, TCCII*]
      civilization *F1, A1*
109:18 is, ultimately, *TS*] is *MS*
109:19 visions, *MS, TCCII*] ∼. *F1*
109:19 or not . . . visions. *MS, TCCII*]
      Om. F1
109:20 And] ∼, *F1*
109:21 animal, *MS, F1*] ∼ *Per, TCCII*
109:23 wrap himself in *TS*] have *MS*
109:24 make a house of apparent *TS*] a
      vision of *MS*
109:25 chaos, *MS, F1*] ∼ *Per,*
      TCCII
109:25 begins by putting *TS*] goes so
      far as to put *MS*
109:26 everlasting *TS*] eternal *MS*
109:26 whirl *TSR, TCCII*] chaos *MS,*
      F1
109:26 Then he *TS*] He *MS*
109:26 under-side *MS, TCCII*]
      underside *Per*
109:27 lives *MS, TCCII*] ∼, *F1*
109:28 umbrella. *TS*] ∼, and at last
      begins to feel something is
      wrong. *MS*
109:28 Bequeathed to . . . [109:29] is
      wrong. *TS*] *Om. MS*
109:31 Man fixes *TS*] That is what
      man is always doing: fixing
      MS
109:31 erection of his own *TS*]
      umbrella *MS*
109:32 the wild *TS*] *Om. MS*
109:32 goes *TS*] going *MS*
109:33 enemy of convention, *TS*]
      Om. MS
109:34 umbrella; *TS*] ∼, *MS*
109:34 of *MS, F1*] uf *Per*

110:1 But *TS*] And then *MS*
110:1 while, *MS, F1*] ∼ *Per*
110:1 vision *TS*] glimpse *MS*
110:1 and not liking . . . from chaos
      TS] *Om. MS*
110:2 commonplace man daubs *TS*]
      man paints *MS*
110:3 that opens *TS*] opening *MS*
110:3 on to *MS, TCCII*] on the *Per*
      onto *F1*
110:4 has got *TS*] merely gets *MS*
110:4 vision, *TS*] ∼. *MS* ∼; *TCCII*
110:5 it is . . . house-decoration. *TS*]
      Om. MS
110:5 So that *TS*] Till *MS*
110:5 at last *TS*] *Om. MS*
110:6 aspects *TS*] patches *MS*
110:6 alas] ∼! *TCCII*
110:6 all *TS*] only *MS*
110:6 simulacrum, *TS*] ∼. *MS*
110:7 in innumerable . . . glossary.
      TS] *Om. MS*
110:9 poetry *TS*] ∼, *MS*
110:9 in *TS*] poetry in *MS*
110:9 Some-one *TS, TSR*] Man *MS*
      Someone *TCCI, Per*
110:9 Titans in the . . . [110:15]
      windy chaos. *TS*] an epic in the
      clouds of March, and the epic
      is established. Gradually, it
      becomes a painted umbrella,
      and then becomes the
      decoration of our vault. It was a
      marvellous glimpse of the open
      windy chaos. It becomes a
      fresco on a vaulted roof. We go
      bleached and dissatisfied under
      the roof. Another poet makes a
      slit. *MS*
110:13 sky *TCCI*] wild sky *TS*
110:14 vaulted *TS, TCCII*] vault *F1*
110:15 on to *TS, TCCII*] onto *F1*
110:16 last *TS*] ∼, *MS*
110:17 or Leonardo, Beethoven or *TS*]
      Shakspeare, Goethe,
      Wordsworth, Keats, *MS*
110:19 in *MS, TCCII*] of *F1*

110:20 things— *TS*] ~. — *MS*

110:20 partly because . . . faded. *TS*] *Om. MS*

110:21 even so . . . natural *TS*] we have to get out of that church after a while. It is a prison. We have to get back to *MS*

110:23 crisis *TCCI*] moment *MS*

110:25 people *TS*] the people *MS*

110:26 slit: *MS, TCCII*] ~; *TCCI*

110:27 and mankind . . . [110:29] painted prison. *TS*] a civilisation goes on, more or less happily. *MS*

110:28 civilisation *TS, TCCII*] civilization *FI*

110:29 called completing the *TS*] called, the completing of *MS*

110:30 consciousness. / The *TS*] consciousness. The *MS*

110:32 Till . . . [110:35] over the slit. *TS*] Under the umbrella, shut in from the chaos of Spring, men had never seen a primrose, till then. After that, gradually, they came to see nothing primaveral but primrose. So the slit was patched over. *MS*

110:32 then, *TS, TCCII*] ~ *FI*

110:35 means, *TSR, TCCII*] ~ *TCCI, FI*

110:36 greater *TS*] still greater *MS*

110:36 Shakspeare] Shakespeare *Per*

110:36 rent, *MS, TCCII*] ~ *FI*

110:37 emotional] ~, *TCCII*

110:37 outside in the chaos *TS*] in the chaos outside *MS*

110:37 conventional idea and *TS*] *Om. MS*

110:38 paladins, *TS*] ~. *MS*

110:39 which had . . . Middle Ages. *TS*] *Om. MS*

110:40 the side walls too, *TS*] *Om. MS*

111:1 fixed and complete *TS*] complete and fixed *MS*

111:1 Man can't . . . his image. *TS*] *Om. MS*

111:3 the patches . . . and hard, *TS*] and so thick with patches and layers of plaster, that *MS*

111:4 If *TS*] Even if *MS*

111:4 slit, *MS, TCCII*] ~ *FI*

111:4 the rent . . . an outrage. *TS*] we should see no vision through the gap. The slit would not be a window into the deeps of chaos, it would only be a rent in a Puvis de Chavannes picture. *MS*

111:5 once, to match the rest. *TS*] once. *MS*

111:7 So *TS*] ~, *MS*

111:7 so, *TS*] then *MS* so *FI*

111:7 a nostalgia *TS*] also absolute *MS*

111:8 some terrific *TS*] a strong *MS*

111:9 much of . . . rest will *TS*] we shall *MS*

111:11 put *TS*] visionalise it, or put *MS*

111:11 visions *MS, TCCII*] vision *FI*

111:13 reveal?—] ~? *AI*

111:15 The fear *MS, FI*] To fear *Per*

111:15 in *TS*] *Om. MS*

111:15 forms and *TS*] form or *MS*

111:16 words!] ~, *TCCII*

111:17 image, *MS, TCCII*] ~ *FI*

111:17 which soon *TS*] which, if there is any poetry in them, soon *MS*

111:18 But the poetasters . . . [111:20] they remain *TS*] If there is no breath of poetry in them, they remain like shiny ornaments for a Christmas tree, *MS*

111:19 christmas tree *TS, FI*] Christmas tree *Per* christmas-tree *TCCII* Christmas-tree *AI*

111:21 bronzey *MS, TCCII*] bronzy *Per, AI*

111:21 title,] ~ *TCCII*

111:22 sheaf *MS, TCCII*] sheet *FI*

111:22 almost too flimsy for real bubbles *TS*] flimsy as a

breathless panting or a touch of light *MS*

111:25 Valérie *MS, TCCII*] Valéry *F1, A1*

111:25 for example, *TS*] *Om. MS*

111:26 obvious *TS*] *Om. MS*

111:26 sweet noise; *TS*] sound and rhythm, at least, none very obvious. *MS*

111:26 only too . . . breathlessly staccato *TS*] For the music of one line is almost invariably knocked out by the next *MS*

111:26 often, *TS*] ~ *TCCII*

111:27 There is *TS*] And *MS*

111:29 Where deliberate . . . clumsy *TS*] And no real pattern of symbols *MS*

111:29 There is *TS*] And *MS*

111:30 idea; *TS*] ~. *MS*

111:30 and no subtle . . . [111:32] world of *TS*] There is no safe and humanised vision, a new gleam of chaos brought into *MS*

111:31 recognisable *TS*] recognizable *A1*

111:32 There is only . . . [112:6] forest of the sun." *TS*] *Om. MS*

111:34 *Sun Rhapsody TS, F1*] Sun Rhapsody *Per* "Sun Rhapsody" *A1*

111:34 sun, *TS, F1*] ~ *Per*

111:35 "it *TS, TCCII*] ~ *F1*

111:35 it is . . . [111:40] soliloquies *TS, TCCII*] [*in italic in F1*]

111:40 soliloquies" *TS*] *soliloquies F1* ~." *TCCII*

112:1 deal.— *TS, F1*] ~. *Per, A1*

112:2 confusing: *TS, A1*] ~; *TCCII*

112:2 naiaids *TS*] naiads *Per*

112:4 "I *TS, TCCII*] I *F1* I *A1*

112:4 am . . . [112:6] the *TS, TCCII*] [*in italic in F1*]

112:6 sun."*TS, TSR, Per, TCCII*] ~" *TCC1 sun F1* sun. *A1*

112:7 What *TS*] Then what *MS*

112:7 there then, *TS, F1*] there? *MS* there, then, *Per, TCCII*

112:7 in this poetry, where there seems to be nothing? *TS*] It seems there is nothing. *MS*

112:8 For *TS, TCCII*] And *MS* For, *F1*

112:8 merely *TS*] *Om. MS*

112:9 And *MS, F1*] ~, *Per, TCCII*

112:10 "Sthhe *TS, TCCII*] *Sthhe MS* "Sthee *Per* "*sthhe F1*

112:10 fous on ssu *TS, Per, TCCII*] *fous on ssu MS, F1*

112:10 eod", *TS*] *eod, MS eod*," *F1* eod," *A1*

112:11 look of it is not inspiring *TS*] sight of the letters isn't particularly pretty *MS*

112:13 "sense",] "~," *A1*

112:13 I *TS*] we *MS*

112:13 a page *TS*] just one page *MS*

112:13 just *TS*] *Om. MS*

112:14 For *TS*] And for *MS*

112:14 there? *TS*] it? *MS*

112:14 Take, at . . . *Néant TS*] It lacks the qualities of poesy *MS*

112:14 *Néant. TS, Per*] ~: *TCC1, F1* "Néant:" *A1*

112:15 "Red *MS, TCCII*] *Red F1* Red *A1*

112:15 sunbeams from . . . [112:23] kill the *MS, TCCII*] [*in italic in F1*]

112:18 inimical. *P* Yet *MS, F1*] inimical. / Yet *Per*

112:20 sunflakes *MS, F1*] snowflakes *Per*

112:23 conqueror." *MS, TCCII*] ~," *Per conqueror. F1* conqueror. *A1*

112:24 It is . . . [112:26] be said. *TS*] It means nothing in particular. Even accepting a particular code of symbols from the author, the meaning doesn't fall into wholeness, it is fragments. As for sound, the last two lines sound unpleasantly. As for images, they are incongruous, each line knocks the next line to pieces, as far as image goes.

What is there then?—The poem is like an uneasy bubble with certain shifty colours, which gleams a moment and bursts into nothingness on the last word. The coloury bubble of nothingness. *MS*

112:27 And therein lies *TS*] But that is *MS*

112:27 charm. It *TS*] charm, because it *MS*

112:27 chaos not reduced to order *TS*] an experienced chaos, and an acceptance of the living chaos *MS*

112:28 But the chaos . . . [112:29] everlasting *TS*] The chaos is really alive, and is eternal, and *MS*

112:29 alive, and *TS, Per, TCCII*] alive. And *TCCI, F1*

112:30 From *TS*] from *MS*
112:30 our *TS*] the *MS*
112:31 stifle.— *MS, Per, TCCII*] ~. *TCCI, F1*
112:31 grace *MS, F1*] a grave *Per*

112:32 and aware . . . [112:34] own image *TS*] he conceived an almighty terror of the grand chaos which is really god, called by us chaos because we are tight in our little consciousness and horrified by our own smallness and limitation *MS*

112:33 god . . . god *TS, TCCII*] God . . . God *F1, A1*

112:35 terrified but inordinately *TS*] *Om. MS*

112:36 itself part of *TS*] *Om. MS*

112:37 living chaos *TS*] chaos of which it is a part *MS*

112:37 We must keep . . . [113:12] a "serious" mood. *TS*] That does not mean we shall not put up more umbrellas. We certainly shall. But taking the breath of chaos in our nostrils, we shall no longer be able to put up any *absolute* umbrella, neither moral absolute, or scientific absolute, or logical absolute. Each little umbrella will be able to be shut up when not needed. Even the vast parasol of the conception of the universe, the cosmos, the firmament of stars and suns, we shall be able to shut it up like any other little green sunshade: for it is no more than that. It is no more "absolutely" true than a green sunshade is absolutely true. And the conception of god already shuts up like a Japanese parasol, rather clumsily. *MS*

113:2 The *TS, Per, TCCII*] the *TCCI, F1*

113:5 sunshade, *TS, Per, TCCII*] ~ *TCCI, F1*

113:7 spread *TS, TCCII*] spreads *F1*

113:8 there, only; *TCCI*] there; only, *TS*

113:10 is.— *TS*] ~. *A1*

113:10 god: *TS, Per, TCCII*] ~; *TCCI* God; *F1* God: *A1*

113:13 *Chariot of the Sun MS, F1*] Chariot of the Sun *Per*

113:14 and big *TS*] *Om. MS*

113:14 of poesy and importance *TS*] and sunshades of poesy *MS*

113:14 has *TS*] it has *MS*

113:14 melody *TS*] rhythm *MS*

113:15 rhythm *TS*] melody *MS*

113:15 or image *TS*] or idea, *MS Om. TCCII*

113:15 sense *TS*] symbol *MS*

113:16 very much in evidence *TS*]
always there *MS*

113:16 it is ... [113:18] its
disappearing *TS*] rather as a
little explosion of gold to
explode the fixed forms of all
the other little images, than as a
positive symbol. In fact, there
is no poesy, really. So what is
there? *MS*

113:19 Hence the ... [113:22]
different *TS*] To me, at least,
there is the touch of true
poetry. There is a glimpse of
the everlasting chaos of
unknown air and countless
suns and inter-ambulating
MS

113:19 in *TS*, *F1*] is *Per*

113:23 of reality *TS*] *Om. MS*

113:23 liberation into the roving,
uncaring *TS*] resurrection into
the insouciant, sun-starred
MS

113:25 me, *MS*, *F1*] ~ *Per*, *TCCII*

113:26 an acceptance ... [113:27]
sun-imbued world *TS*] a
nothingness which accepts the
limitation of consciousness,
and lies up against the
sun-inhabited space *MS*

113:27 leaning up *TS*] leaning-up
TCCII

113:27 sun-imbued *TS*, *F1*] sun
imbued *Per*

113:30 And therefore ... [113:31] real
poetry *TS*] *Om. MS*

113:31 *not there TS*, *F1*] not there *Per*

113:32 the essential *TS*] But it has the
essential *MS*

113:33 wakes us to ... the poetic *TS*]
perceives a new world within
the world. It sees chaos, and
has *MS*

113:35 poetry of suns which are *TS*]
the poetry of the sun which is
MS

113:35 chaos, suns which are ...
[113:39] more chaotic *TS*]
chaos, the sun which changes
and is gone and is something
else; since chaos has a core that
also is chaos, and the sun itself
is a chaos. That it has a chariot
only makes it more chaotic
MS

113:37 quintessentially *TS*, *F1*]
quint-essentially *Per*

113:39 it *TS*, *F1*] in *Per*

114:1 And in the chaotic *TCCI*] But
it would manage very well
without an engraved
"portrait." That carries the
contradiction into nonsense
again. / And in the *MS* But an
engraved portrait touches
nonsense again. / And in the
chaotic *TS*

114:1 re-echoing *TS*] echoing *MS*

114:1 soul *TS*] inner ear *MS*

114:1 wisps *TS*] stray wisps *MS*

114:1 curl round *TS*, *F1*] linger *MS*
curd round *Per*

114:2 curious *TS*] a curious *MS*

114:2 soothing.—"likewise *TS*]
soothing —"—Likewise *MS*
soothing, — "like *Per*
soothing—likewise *F1*
soothing. — /"likewise *TCCII*
soothing— / Likewise *A1*

114:3 Drink fire ... sun-consoled."
MS, *TCCII*] *Drink fire, and all
my heart is sun-consoled. F1*
Drink fire ... sun-consoled. *A1*

114:4 *Water Lilies TS*, *F1*]
Water-Lilies MS, *TCCII* Water
Lilies *Per* "Water-Lilies" *A1*

114:4 suffusion in which ... [114:18]
never will cease *TS*] softness of
naiads who are also sunbeams,
sun-girls, "curving of a
darkness into light," limpid
with a tenderness which stirs
again a tenderness of true

desire in the heart, desire
which is a soft sunshine of life.
     And fragments are lovely,
with the sun in them: the inner
sun, the outer sun, the only
sun, one of the many suns: but
always sun, the gleam of the
soft unsubstantial gold of life,
soft as a lion, the livingness
that never ceases and will never
cease *MS*

114:5   touch, *TS, Per, TCCII*] ∼
          TCCI, FI
114:6   sense impression *TS*]
          sense-impression *TCCII*
114:7   in to *TS*] into *Per*
114:12   vision *TS*] visions *TCCII*
114:13   touch, *TS, FI*] ∼ *Per*
114:16   loose *TCCI*] looses *TS*
114:18   lion's *TS, FI*] lions *Per*
114:19   soft, intangible suffused
          faith . . . [114:22] purified
          receptiveness *TS*] soft,
          intangible faith that is
          sun substance itself.
          It is such faith that really
          makes poetry out of words
          MS
114:19   intangible *TS, FI*] ∼, *Per,*
          TCCII
114:23   is no *TS*] will be no more
          MS
114:23   There is . . . life *TS*] *Om. MS*
114:24   The poetry . . . dead-sea fruit.
          TS, TCCII] *Om. MS, FI*
114:24   sunless chaos *TS*] an orderly
          cosmos, or of a sunless chaos
          MS
114:25   already a bore, *TS*] now ashes.
          MS already a bore. *TCCII*
114:25   the *TS*] The *MS, TCCII*
114:25   poetry of a . . . [114:29] chaos,
          not conceit *TS*] chaos that is
          living poetry is sun-imbued,
          and sun-impulsive *MS*
114:26   bird-cage *TS, TCCII*] birdcage
          FI

114:30   "the Sun in *TS, TCCII*]
          "—the Sun in *MS The Sun in*
          FI The Sun in *AI*
114:30   unconcealèd *MS, TCCII*]
          unconcealed *Per unconcealèd FI*
114:30   rage . . . [114:31] of the *MS,*
          TCCII] [*in italic in FI*]
114:31   world" *TS*] ∼ —" *MS* world."
          Per, TCCII world FI world. *AI*
114:32   The sun . . . incalculably *TS*]
          But the sun is within us *MS*
114:33   "At *TS, TCCII*] ∼ *MS, AI*
          At FI
114:33   night . . . [114:37] To *MS,*
          TCCII] [*in italic in FI*]
114:37   cross" *TS*] ∼ *MS, AI* cross *FI*
          cross   " *TCCII*
115:1   in *TS*] to *MS*
115:1   incalculable *TS*] inner *MS*
115:1   sun, *TS*] ∼ *MS*
115:1   inner and outer *TS*] and its
          sunniness *MS*
115:3   "Sunmaid *TS, TCCII*] ∼ *MS,*
          AI Sunmaid FI
115:4   Left by . . . [115:6] you may
          MS, TCCII] [*in italic in FI*]
115:6   Sun *MS, FI*] sun *Per*
115:7   Revive" *TS*] ∼. *MS Revive EI*
          Revive." *TCCII* ∼ *AI*
115:8   And there . . . of the world *TS*]
          It is the breath of real poetry,
          fleeting as a breath in chaos,
          but like the breath, always
          renewed *MS*
115:8   corrosive, *TS*] ∼ *Per*
115:11   "Dark *TS, TCCII*] ∼ *MS, AI*
          Dark FI
115:11   clouds . . . [115:15] The *MS,*
          TCCII] [*in italic in FI*]
115:15   Sun" *TS*] ∼. *MS* Sun." *Per,*
          TCCII Sun FI Sun *AI*
115:16   may *TS*] will *MS*
115:16   perhaps *TS*] *Om. MS*
115:17   well, to . . . outside. *TS*] well.
          MS
115:18   breath, with . . . [115:21]
          human consciousness *TS*]

breath. It is the diastole to the
systole. It is the dark pulse of
the sun, and saves us from the
strain of homogeneity and
exaltation and forcedness,
which has been the curse of our
consciousness *MS*

115:19 monos, *TS, F1*] ~. *Per*

115:19 homogeneity *TS, Per,
TCCII*] ~, *TCCI, F1*

115:20 forcedness *TS, TCCII*] ~. *F1*

115:21 and all-of-a-pieceness . . .
[115:22] human consciousness.
TS, TCCII] *Om. F1*

115:21 half the time a poet *TS*] a man
half the time *MS*

115:22 effort at *TS*] epithets and
efforts of *MS*

115:22 expression! *TS, F1* ~. *MS* ~?
Per

115:22 The act . . . [115:25] pure
expression *TS*] So long as he is
making the act of real attention.
That is all that matters. The
fumbling reveals the act, as well
as the pure lit-up gesture
MS

115:26 "But *TS*] ~ *MS, A1* But *F1*

115:26 I shall . . . [115:27] cautiously
TS, TCCII] [*in italic in F1*]

115:27 around." *TS*] ~. *MS, A1*
around. F1

115:28 Whims, and . . . [115:29] of real
TS] *Om. MS*

115:30 poetry, *TS, F1*] *Om. MS* ~. *Per*

115:30 as well as pure little poems like
TS, F1] There are, however,
beautiful little poems that are
whole in sound and sense, like
MS Om. Per

115:30 *Sun-Ghost, MS, F1*] *Om. Per*
"Sun-Ghost," *A1*

115:30 *To Those Who Return, MS, F1*]
Om. Per "To Those Who
Return," *A1*

115:31 *Torse de Jeune Femme au Soleil
TS, F1*] *Torse de Jeune Femme*

MS Om. Per "Torse de Jeune
Femme au Soleil," *A1*

115:31 *Poem for the Feet of Polia.MS,
F1*] *Om. Per* "Poem for the
Feet of Polia." *A1*

115:31 Through it all runs *TS*] And
there is all through *MS*

115:32 poetry can exist, not even the
most sophisticated *TCCI*]
poetry, not even the most
sophisticated, can exist *MS*
poetry can exist, not even the
most raffiné *TS*

115:33 to the sun of chaos *TS*] like a
rose *MS*

115:34 and the soul may . . . [115:36]
open it must *TS*] like a
dandelion, like a thistle or a
hellebore or an evening
primrose, to the inward sun of
tender livingness, or the inward
moon *MS*

115:34 or a tiger-lily *TSR, TCCII*]
Om. TS, F1

115:36 opening *TS*] *Om. MS*

115:37 alone, *TS*] ~ *MS*

115:37 act of attention *TS*] religious
act *MS*

115:37 essential poetic and vital act
TSR, TCCII] act of attention
MS essential religious act *TS*
essential poetic and religious
act *TCCI, F1*

115:38 and . . . hit us *TS*] but it does
not matter *MS*

115:38 hail-stone *TS, F1*] hailstone
Per, TCCII

115:38 But it is in the course of things
TS] *Om. MS*

116:1 *liveMS, F1*] live *Per*

116:1 that *TS*] the *MS*

116:2 soul, *TS*] ~ *MS*

116:2 like a flower, like an animal, like
a coloured snake, *TSR,
TCCII*] like a flower, sweet or
poisonous, *MS, TCCI* sweet or
poisonous, *TS* like a sweet

flower, sweet or poisonous,
F1

116:3 it *TS*] that *MS*

116:3 chaotic *TSR, TCCII*] tender
       MS, TCCI, F1

116:3 livingness. *TS*] ~, or to the
       moon. *MS*

116:4 Now, after ... [116:6] sheer
       starvedness {stravedness *Per*},
       TS] At last, after long
       sophistication and flippancy
       and self-assurance, we are so
       starved of life and essential
       sun that at last we are driven
       MS

116:8 naïveté, *TS*] ~ *MS*

116:8 deliberately, and dauntlessly,
       TS] and *MS* deliberately and
       dauntlessly, *F1*

116:9 re-gained *MS, F1*] regained
       Per, A1

116:9 Round it range ... [116:36]
       black suns on gold. *TSR*]
       Round it range the red and the
       white lions of the sun, and the
       deadly ivory-gold horn of the
       unicorn defends it ruthlessly. It
       will no longer be a victim, put
       on a cross, or a beggar, scorned
       and given a pittance. It will be a
       bright lord, with an open heart
       like a rose, but with yellow
       lions in the eyes.
           It is the new naïveté, chosen,
       open-eyed, and aware. It may
       be clumsy, and make gestures
       of self-conscious crudity. But it
       is real, and for us, the essential
       reality. It is our liberation into
       the fresh air of chaos, into the
       sun of effortless being. It is our
       livingness and our poetry. And
       because it is present all through
       in *Chariot of the Sun*, this is a
       book of poetry, and the defects
       and the nonsense are the
       hither and thither of the breeze

which blows us sun-wards. /
Villa Mirenda. Scandicci.
29 April 1928. D. H. Lawrence
MS

116:12 ruthless, *TS, TCCII*] ~ *TCCI,*
        F1

116:12 defense *TS*] defence *Per*

116:12 naïve *TS, F1*] naive *Per*

116:17 and ready, sufficiently ... of
        sophistication, *TSR, TCCII*]
        chosen, open-eyed, aware, and
        dauntless *TS* chosen,
        open-eyed, aware and
        dauntless, *F1*

116:19 purring like a leopard that may
        snarl *TSR, TCCII*] fiercely
        defended *TS, F1*

116:21 the real creature of the *TSR,*
        TCCII] welling up from *TS,*
        F1

116:21 of the soul *TSR, TCCII*] the
        soul *TS, F1*

116:22 young, *TS, F1*] ~ *Per, TCCII*

116:22 the real self *TSR, TCCII*] life
        TS, F1

116:23 wild *TSR, TCCII*] fresh *TS,*
        F1

116:24 both *TS, TCCII*] Om. *TCCI,*
        E1

116:27 "opportunity", *TS*] "~," *A1*

116:30 them silly *TSR, TCCII, A1*] to
        madness *TS, F1*

116:31 speckled leopard ... [116:36]
        black suns on gold *TSR,*
        TCCII] chaos of suns. Back to
        the pool of renewal, where we
        dip ourselves in life again, and
        let the old case-hardened
        self-conceit wash off us, and let
        the body unfurl in all its
        sensitiveness and naiveté again,
        like a magnolia, to the suns.
        And this is not so easy. You
        can't do it by just saying you
        will do it. It is a slow, blind
        process, a painful discarding of
        shells and defences that are

only obstructions, and a taking
on of a new sensitiveness,
awareness, and a new faith in
the sun.

And because this little book
of poems seems to me to be a
pool of sun, in which conceited
man is washing himself new
again, it is to me a book of
poetry, and the defects and
nonsense are only the
staggering in the pool. / D. H.
Lawrence / Scandicci
{, *TCCI*} May 1st 1928
TS chaos of suns. Back to the
pool of renewal, where we dip
ourselves in life again, and let
the old case-hardened
self-conceit wash off us, and let
the body unfurl in all its
sensitiveness and naiveté again,
like a magnolia, to the suns.

And this is not so easy. You
can't do it by just saying you
will do it. It is a slow, blind
process, a painful discarding of
shells and defences that are
only obstructions, and a taking
on of a new sensitiveness,
awareness, and a new faith in
the sun.

And because this new
awareness and new faith are
present all through in *Chariot
of the Sun* this is a book of
poetry, and the defects and
the nonsense are the hither
and thither of the breeze
which blows us sunwards.
/ D. H. LAWRENCE
/ Scandicci, May 1, 1928
F1

116:33   shade! *TSR*] ~? *TCCII*
116:36   on *TSR*] in *TCCII*

Introduction to *Bottom Dogs*

MS = Roberts E54a
TCCIR = Roberts E54c
E1 = *Bottom Dogs*, by Edward Dahlberg (G. P. Putnam's Sons, 1929)
TCCII = Roberts E54b and E54d

119:1   Introd. to Edward Dahlberg's
novel, for Putnams / Bottom
Dogs] INTRODUCTION TO
EDWARD DAHLBERG'S
NOVEL, / for PUTNAMS.
TCCIR [*see 'Texts'*]
INTRODUCTION *E1*
INTRODUCTION to Edward
Dahlberg's novel, / for
Putnams. *TCCII*

119:3   realise *MS, TCCIR, TCCII*]
realize *E1*
119:4   still go] ~ ~, *TCCII*
119:13 first-comers *MS, TCCII*]
first-comer *TCCIR*
119:15 hard work *MS, E1*] hard-work
TCCIR

119:25 sentimentalised]
sentimentalized *E1* sentimental
TCCII
119:31 obdurate? *MS, TCCII*] ~!
TCCIR
120:2   genuine] ~, *TCCII*
120:6   colonised *MS, TCCIR,
TCCII*] colonized *E1*
120:6   civilised *MS, TCCIR, TCCII*]
civilized *E1*
120:7   pioneers] pioneer *TCCII*
120:12 heart,] ~ *TCCII*
120:12 belief *MS, E1*] ~, *TCCIR*
120:14 fundamental,] ~ *TCCII*
120:15 good.— *MS, TCCII*] ~.
TCCIR
120:15 Now] ~, *TCCII*
120:18 cynicism:] ~, *TCCII*

120:22 same.— *MS, TCCII*] ~.
TCCIR

120:24 Indian, *MS, TCCIR, TCCII*]
~ *E1*

120:25 As *MS, TCCII*] So *TCCIR*

120:28 today *MS, TCCIR, TCCII*]
to-day *E1*

120:34 conflicting, *MS, E1*] ~ *TCCIR*

120:34 Instead, *MS, TCCII*] ~
TCCIR

121:8 private, *MS, TCCII*] ~
TCCIR

121:12 flow *MS, TCCII*] glow *TCCIR*

121:14 another, *MS, TCCII*] an other
TCCIR another *E1*

121:21 civilisations *MS, TCCIR,*
TCCII] civilizations *E1*

121:22 kitchens.— *MS, TCCII*] ~.
TCCIR

121:27 "plumbing", *MS, TCCIR,*
TCCII] "~," *E1*

121:30 "halitosis", *MS, TCCIR,*
TCCII] "~," *E1*

122:10 André *MS, TCCII*] Andre
TCCIR

122:19 fell, *MS, TCCII*] ~ *TCCIR*

122:21 cess-pools] cesspools *TCCII*

122:25 exacerbation, *MS, TCCIR,*
TCCII] ~ *E1*

122:29 stink! *MS, TCCII*] ~.
TCCIR

122:32 *social*] social *TCCII*

123:6 stink!— *MS, TCCII*] ~!
TCCIR

123:9 orphanage *MS, TCCII*]
Orphanage *TCCIR*

123:9 realised *MS, TCCIR, TCCII*]
realized *E1*

123:16 *unaware MS, TCCII*] unaware
TCCIR

123:21 always *MS, TCCII*] Always
TCCIR

123:23 Mr . . . Mr] ~. . . . ~.
TCCII

123:39 sympathy *MS, TCCII*] ~,
TCCIR

123:39 His mother? . . . [124:2] a
certain disgust. *MS, TCCIR,*
TCCII] *Om. E1*

123:39 mother?—we *MS, TCCII*]
mother? We *TCCIR*

124:4 dramatises *MS, TCCIR,*
TCCII] dramatizes *E1*

124:4 rôle *MS, E1*] role *TCCIR*

124:5 dramatise *MS, TCCIR,*
TCCII] dramatize *E1*

124:10 Beatrice,] ~ *TCCIR*

124:10 -Oregon,] Oregon, *TCCIR* —
Oregon — *TCCII*

124:11 nothing,] ~ *TCCII*

124:20 Spinosa *MS, TCCIR, TCCII*]
Spinoza *E1*

124:20 strange *MS, TCCII*] ~,
TCCIR

124:21 external, *MS, TCCII*] ~·
TCCIR

124:30 strides, *MS, TCCII*] ~
TCCIR

124:33 non-dramatised *MS, TCCIR,*
TCCII] non-dramatized
E1

124:39 being. *Ed.*] being. / D. H.
Lawrence / Bandol. 1929 *MS*
being. / D. H. Lawrence. /
Bandol 1929 *TCCIR* being. /
D. H. LAWRENCE. /
BANDOL, 1929. *E1* being. /
Bandol, 1929 *TCCII*

Introduction to *The Grand Inquisitor*

MS = Roberts E151a
TCCI = Roberts E151b
E1 = *The Grand Inquisitor*, by F. M. Dostoevsky, tr. S. S. Koteliansky (Elkin Mathews
and Marrot, 1930.)
TCCII = Roberts E151c

Silent emendation

The text of *E1* is printed in italics throughout, with roman used for emphasis. This has not been recorded, except in the course of recording another variant.

127:1 Introd. to The Grand
Inquisitor]
INTRODUCTION TO
"THE GRAND
INQUISITOR" / by /
D. H. Lawrence *TCCI*
INTRODUCTION E1
INTRODUCTION to "The
Grand Inquisitor". *TCCII*

127:2 experience, *MS, TCCII*]
experience E1

127:3 *The Brothers Karamazov, MS,
TCCII*] The Brothers
*Karamazoi, TCCI "The
Brothers Karamasov," E1*

127:5 Middleton Murry *MS,
TCCII*] *Katherine Mansfield E1*
see Introduction, footnote 135

127:6 that *MS, TCCII*] the *TCCI,
the E1*

127:6 story."] ~". *TCCI, TCCII
story." E1*

127:7 rubbish."— *MS, TCCII*] ~."
TCCI rubbish." E1

127:8 showing-off] *showing-off E1*
showing off *TCCII*

127:11 black-a-vised] *black-a-vised E1*
blackavised *TCCII*

127:12 pose,] ~; *TCCI,TCCII pose;
E1*

127:13 showing-off] *showing-off E1*
showing off *TCCII*

127:14 the *Brothers Karamazov*] The
Brothers Karamazoi *TCCI*
"The Brothers Karamasov" E1
The Brothers
Karamazov*TCCII*

127:16 Inquisitor*MS, TCCII*]
"Inquisitor" E1

127:19 devastating *TCCI*] devasting
MS devastating E1

127:19 summing-up, *MS, TCCII*] ~.
TCCI summing-up. E1

127:19 unanswerable because . . .
humanity. *MS, TCCII*] *Om.
TCCI*

127:21 Jesus'] *Jesus' E1* Jesus *TCCII*

127:23 then *MS, TCCII*] *Om.TCCI*

127:26 revolutionary *MS, TCCII*]
Revolutionary *TCCI*
Revolutionary E1

127:27 himself, *MS, TCCII*] ~ *TCCI
himself E1*

127:28 half hated *MS, TCCII*]
half-hated E1

127:32 Inquisitor *MS, TCCII*] Grand
Inquisitor E1

127:34 you.—] *you. E1* you. *TCCII*

128:15 "free,"] "~", *TCCI, TCCII
"free," E1*

128:17 bread:] *bread: E1* bread,
TCCII

128:21 down. *TCCII*] down to. *MS
down. E1*

128:22 mystery *MS, TCCII*] *mystery,
E1*

128:22 authority] *authority, E1*
authority, *TCCII*

128:23 "free." *MS, TCCII*] "~".
TCCI "free." E1

128:23 "weakness." *MS, TCCII*] "~".
TCCI "weakness." E1

128:25 mystery, *MS, TCCII*] ~ *TCCI
mystery E1*

128:26 gods *MS, TCCII*] Gods *TCCI
Gods E1*

128:31 summing up] summing-up
TCCI, TCCII summing-up E1

128:35 Thou *MS, TCCII*] thou *TCCI
thou E1*

128:35 respectedest] respected *TCCI,
TCCII respected E1*

128:37 lighter. " *MS, TCCII*] ~".
TCCI lighter." E1

129:2 "him", *MS, TCCII*] "~".
TCCI "him." E1

129:2   that other . . . on *MS, TCCII*]
      Om. TCCI

129:3   "him."] *Om. TCCI* "him".
      TCCII

129:10   annihilation] *annihilation E1*
      annihilation, *TCCII*

129:17   demand] *demand E1* demand,
      TCCII

129:18   Today *MS, TCCII*] *To-day E1*

129:19   aeroplanes] *aeroplanes E1*
      aeroplane *TCCII*

129:21   did *MS, TCCII*] did it *TCCI*
      did it E1

129:22   medicine *MS, TCCII*]
      medecin *TCCI medicine E1*

129:23   spiritualists *MS, TCCII*]
      Spiritualists *TCCI Spiritualists*
      E1

129:24   scientists *MS, TCCII*]
      Scientists *TCCI Scientists E1*

129:25   despotism, *MS, TCCII*]
      despotism. *E1*

129:26   rationalised *MS, TCCII*]
      rational *TCCI rational E1*

129:31   vicious] *vicious E1* vicious,
      TCCII

129:35   bread". *MS, TCCII*] *bread."*
      E1

129:36   men] *men, E1* men, *TCCII*

129:37   bread,"] ~", *TCCI, TCCII*
      bread," E1

130:2   "elect,"] "Elect", *TCCI*
      "elect," E1 "elect", *TCCII*

130:5   none the *MS, TCCII*] more or
      TCCI more or E1

130:10   terrible *MS, TCCII*] *terrible,*
      E1

130:10   that therefore *MS, TCCII*]
      that, therefore, E1

130:11   no-one] *no one E1* no one
      TCCII

130:24   devil:] *devil: E1* devil,
      TCCII

130:32   men *MS, TCCII*] menkind
      TCCI mankind E1

130:35   mankind] *mankind E1*
      mankind, *TCCII*

130:37   degrees *MS, TCCII*] degree
      TCCI degree E1

131:3   Anyhow] *Anyhow, E1* Anyhow,
      TCCII

131:5   the *MS, TCCII*] of the *TCCI*
      of the E1

131:5   old wise *MS, TCCII*] *old, wise*
      E1

131:8   great *MS, TCCII*] *great,*
      E1

131:13   with her *MS, TCCII*] the
      TCCI the E1

131:13   bullying;] *bullying; E1*
      bullying, *TCCII*

131:14   Catholic] *Catholic E1* catholic
      TCCII

131:19   *auto da fé*] auto-da-fé *E1* auto
      da fé *TCCII*

131:21   that] *that E1* that, *TCCII*

131:21   slightly-criminal *MS, TCCII*]
      slightly criminal *TCCI slightly*
      criminal E1

131:23   diabolic *MS, TCCII*]
      diabolical *TCCI diabolical E1*

131:35   Socialists] *Socialists E1*
      socialists *TCCII*

131:35   today, what *MS, TCCII*] today.
      What *TCCI to-day.*
      What E1

131:37   Christians] *Christians E1*
      Christianity *TCCII*

131:39   bread:] *bread: E1* bread,
      TCCII

132:1   today *MS, TCCI*] *to-day E1*

132:3   sanitation] ~, *TCCI, TCCII*
      sanitation, E1

132:3   etc] ~. *TCCI, TCCII etc.*
      E1

132:5   And *MS, TCCII*] But *TCCI*
      But E1

132:6   today *MS, TCCII*] *to-day E1*

132:10   is the *MS, TCCII*] is *TCCI is*
      E1

132:12   Christianity] *Christianity E1*
      Christianity, *TCCII*

132:17   authority] *authority E1*
      authority? *TCCII*

132:19 Father's *MS, TCCII*] father's
TCCI father's E1

132:19 mansions." *MS, TCCII*] ~".
TCCI mansions." E1

132:22 emotions] *emotions E1* emotion
TCCII

132:23 emotions] *emotions E1* emotion
TCCII

132:24 today *MS, TCCII*] *to-day E1*

132:32 religions] *religions E1* religious
TCCII

132:37 bolshevist *MS, TCCII*]
Bolshevist *TCCI Bolshevist*
E1

133:1 *he must* not] he must not *E1* he
must not TCCII

133:4 procreation *MS, TCCII*]
pro-creation *TCCI pro-creation*
E1

133:4 recreation *MS, TCCII*] recreation *TCCI re-creation E1*

133:7 Again] *Again E1* Again, *TCCII*

133:10 harvest home] harvest-home
TCCI, TCCII
harvest-home *E1*

133:11 our] the *TCCI, TCCIIthe E1*

133:12 activity, contact *MS, TCCII*]
activity. Contact *TCCI activity.*
Contact E1

133:14 hard,] ~; *TCCII*

133:23 to."] ~". *TCCI, TCCII to."*
E1

133:24 first, *MS, TCCII*] just *TCCI*
just E1

133:29 work:] ~; *TCCII*

133:32 men who] ~, who *TCCI,*
TCCII men, who E1

134:9 life,] ~ *TCCII*

134:10 the common *MS, TCCII*] this
common *TCCI this common*
E1

134:13 nature-hero *MS, TCCII*]
nature-hero, E1

134:21 re-discovery *MS, TCCII*]
re-discovering *TCCI*
re-discovering E1

134:28 money-values,] ~; *TCCII*

134:29 nice *MS, TCCII*] *nice, E1*

134:35 Thank *MS, TCCII*] "Thank
E1

134:35 man!— *MS*] *man!"— E1* ~!
TCCII

134:36 Thank *MS, TCCII*] "Thank
E1

134:36 me!— *MS, TCCII*] *me!"*
E1

134:37 Inquisition] *Inquisition E1*
Inquisitors *TCCII*

134:37 *autos da fé*] autos-da-fé *E1*
autos-da-fé TCCII

Introductory Note to *Mastro-don Gesualdo*

MS = Roberts E231c
TCC = Roberts E231d
A1 = *Mastro-don Gesualdo*, by Giovanni Verga (New York: Seltzer, 1923)

139:1 Introductory Note] Preface
TCC BIOGRAPHICAL
NOTE *A1*

139:3 January] ~, *A1*

139:11 *Una MS, A1*] una *TCC*

139:16 *Comédie Humaine;*] *Comédie*
Humaine; A1

139:17 *Vinti:*] ~: *TCC*

139:19 sea-coast] seacoast *A1*

139:19 the struggle] their struggle
TCC

139:22 *Gesualdo, MS, A1*] ~, *TCC*

139:25 *Leyra:*] ~: *A1*

139:29 *Gesualdo,*] ~: *A1*

140:1 *P* But] / But *TCC*

140:10 sailing-ship] sailing ship
TCC

140:17 *Rusticane,*] ~, *A1*

140:18 *Rusticana,*] ~, *A1*

140:24 *maestro*] *Maestro TCC*

140:26 *compère*] *compere TCC*

140:27 —But] ~ *A1*

Note on Giovanni Verga, in *Little Novels of Sicily*

A1 = *Little Novels Of Sicily* (Seltzer, 1925)
E1 = *Little Novels Of Sicily* (Blackwell, 1925)

143:2	surely the . . . fiction] by many Italian critics esteemed the best writer of fiction Italy has produced *E1*	143:15	*Malavoglia*] *Malaroglia E1*
		143:19	school-girls] schoolgirls *E1*
		143:21	the first] one *E1*
		143:29	no doubt] probably largely *E1*
143:4	Sicily] in Sicily *E1*	143:31	these] the *E1*
143:5	January,] ~ *E1*	143:33	any one] anyone *E1*
143:6	society] Society *E1*	144:1	Biviere] *Riviere E1 see notes*
143:9	bc] bccome *E1*	144:4	other. / The stories
143:12	*Eva,] Om. E1*		belong . . . [144:24] in 1883.
143:13	"elegance":] "~." *E1*		*Ed.*] in 1883. / D. H.
143:13	a little . . . own depth.] *Om. E1*		LAWRENCE *A1* other. /
143:15	novels:] ~, *EI*		D. H. LAWRENCE *E1*

Biographical Note to *Mastro-don Gesualdo*

E1 = *Mastro-don Gesualdo*, by Giovanni Verga, translated by D. H. Lawrence (Jonathan Cape, 1928) (Roberts A28b), pp. xxi–xxii.

159:23 Manzoni *Ed.*] *Manzoni E1*

Translator's Preface to *Cavalleria Rusticana*

TCC1 = Roberts E63c pp. 1–11
TCC1R = Autograph revisions in *TCC1* + Roberts E63a
TCC1C = Compositor's revisions in *TCC1*
TCC1I = Roberts E63c pp. 14–22
E1 = *Cavalleria Rusticana* (Jonathan Cape, 1928)
Base-text is *TCC1R*.

163:2	*Cavalleria Rusticana*] *CAVALLERIA RUSTICANA TCC1C*	167:23	they] things *TCC1*
		167:26	earth,] ~ *E1*
		167:28	always] *Om. TCC1*
163:12	lived] lived, apparently, *TCC1*	167:32	phcnomcnon] Phenomenon *E1*
163:12	sea-port] seaport *TCC1C*	168:22	in check] nourished *E1*
163:16	Continent",] ~," *TCC1C*	168:22	or modified] *Om. TCC1*
164:5	seventies]' seventies *E1*	168:27	only] *Om. TCC1*
164:11	"Continent",] "~," *TCC1C*	168:40	was] is *TCC1I*
164:25	in *TCC1C*] im *TCC1*	169:7	Tolstoi *TCC1I*] Tolstoy *TCC1*
165:4	safe-guards] safeguards *E1*	169:12	the malice] malice *TCC1I*
165:10	scent-bottle] scent-bottles *TCC1*	169:14	else,] ~; *TCC1I*
		169:20	the middle class] middle-class *TCC1I*
165:22	not;—] ~ — *E1*		
166:1	or Nanni?] Or Nanni? *E1*	169:23	their humility] humility *TCC1I*
167:9	prison,] ~ *E1*	169:36	today] to-day *TCC1I*
167:17	"honour".] "~." *TCC1C*	170:4	saint-like] ~, *TCC1I*

170:6	defeat,] ~; *TCCII*		172:1	sliding over] sliding-over
170:16	out-of-date] out of date *E1*			*TCCII*
170:18	Americanised] Americanized		172:5	southerner] Southerner *TCCII*
	E1		172:7	Instinctively,] ~ *E1*
170:21	realise] realize *E1*		172:12	style. "I] ~: *P* "~ *TCCII* ~: *P*
170:23	faintly wriggling]			'I *E1*
	faintly-wriggling *TCCII*		172:15	sheet] ~, *TCCII*
170:38	Merimée] Mérimée *E1*		172:20	revelation—] ~ . . ." *TCCII*
170:39	*L'Enlêvement*] *L'Enlèvement*		172:30	round,] ~ *TCCII*
	TCCII		172:31	pain *TCCIR, E1*] view *TCCII*
171:5	*Lover,*] ~ *TCCII*		172:32	interest] concern *E1*
171:11	is] ~, *TCCII*		172:33	time sequence] time-sequence
171:12	course] ~, *TCCII*			*TCCII*
171:17	*La Lupa TCCIR, E1*] La Lupa		172:38	closing in] closing-in *TCCII*
	TCCII		173:1	against time] illogical *E1*
171:18	fact] ~, *TCCII*		173:1	Afterwards,] ~ *E1*
171:25	reason,] ~ *TCCII*		173:6	"Brothpot"] *Brothpot TCCII*
171:31	*Rosso Malpelo*] Rosso Malpelo		173:10	annoying.—] ~. *TCCII*
	E1		173:20	dramatised] dramatized *E1*
171:33	time,] ~ *E1*		173:21	dramatised] dramatized *E1*
171:33	vapour] vapours *TCCII*		173:23	immortalise] immortalize *E1*

Foreword to *The Story of Doctor Manente*

MS = Roberts E380a; La Z 2/8/4/1 (UN)
GR = Corrected galley sheets for Orioli (Roberts E380b)
O1 = *The Story of Doctor Manente* (Florence: G. Orioli, 1929)

177:1	FOREWORD *GR*] Foreword		177:22	setting a . . . works. *GR*] *Om.*
	to *The Story of Doctor Manente*			*MS*
	MS		177:23	In *GR*] The characters are full
177:2	the *Story GR*] *The Story*			*MS*
	MS		177:25	through and *GR*] wandering,
177:3	Series *GR*] series *MS*			trying to get someone to
177:5	sensitive genius *GR*] pure			recognise him—he is Doctor
	genius *MS*			Manente through and *MS*
177:6	a sensitive *GR*] a pure or		177:26	easily *GR*] so easily *MS*
	delicate *MS*		177:26	an *GR*] the *MS*
177:7	ordinary, *GR*] ~ *MS*		177:27	Spanish type! *GR*] Spanish. *MS*
177:9	typical Florentine *GR*] master		177:31	Tuscan *GR*] Italian *MS*
	MS		178:9	name. *GR*] ~, any more than
177:11	*burla GR*] *buffa MS see notes*			Quetzalcoatl would be. *MS*
177:11	Joke *GR*] joke *MS*		178:9	Their outward-roaming
177:13	the story *GR*] it *MS*			. . . [178:11] are centripetal.
177:14	*novelle GR*] stories *MS*			*GR*] *Om. MS*
177:15	sharp *GR*] *Om. MS*		178:13	mad; *GR*] ~: *MS*
177:17	thing perfectly, *GR*] ~, ~: *MS*		178:15	The bulk of . . . [178:16] them
177:22	bettered, *GR*] ~. *MS*			matter. *GR*] *Om. MS*

178:18   trial are *GR*] trials is *MS*
178:20   take an objective *GR*] dwell on *MS*
178:20   view of *Ed.*] *Om. MS* wiew of *GR*
178:21   he refuses to *think*, *GR*] *Om. MS*
178:23   and *GR*] & *MS*
178:23   Mental torture has . . . [178:25] suffering. *GR*] *Om. MS*
178:26   reveals! *GR*] ~. *MS*
178:27   earth, and centripetal. *GR*] earth. *MS*
178:28   really, *GR*] ~ *MS*
178:28   ideals, *GR*] ~. *MS*
178:29   but *physically* . . . a tree. *GR*] *Om. MS*
178:30   gets stuck sometimes, in this self-centred physicality *GR*] knows this essentially *substantial* quality *MS*
178:36   famous *GR*] ~, *MS*
179:1   and *GR*] & *MS*
179:3   pranks *GR*] jokes *MS*
179:7   truth; *GR*] ~ — *MS*
179:8   *beffa GR*] *Beffa MS*
179:9   trick". *GR*] ~." *MS*
179:10   *beffa GR*] beffa *MS*
179:22   substantial] sustantial *GR*
179:23   This self-centred physical nature . . .[180:16] Florence and Rome. *GR*] This *terre à terre* quality sometimes becomes a little gross, crude, perhaps bestial, and the Italian has periods when he is acutely sensitive to the fact. The present day is one of them, so the government and the municipality suppress every possible sign of the physical Adam. The squeamishness becomes ridiculous, but it is a sort of recoil.

In the Renaissance it was something the same, without our squeamish priggishness.

The Renaissance was brutal about it. If a man was a bit fat and simple, but especially if he overflowed a little in physical self-assertion, rather natural to these people, the naïve loudness of the Italian in the street or café, then the wits marked him down as a prey.

We have to remember the extraordinary brutality and mindless self-assertion of the 13th, & 14th centuries to understand the extraordinary brutality of the *beffe*, the jokes which were practised on self-assertive people in the 15th and 16th centuries. It was wit taking its revenge on brute force and on showy animal spirits. Any man who overflowed and showed insolence in his animal spirits, was marked down. It was, in a sense, a corrective measure, a chastening and a disciplining of the natural animal assertion of the Italian. In a sense, it was necessary, no doubt. *MS*

179:31   egoistic *Ed.*] *Om. MS* egoistie *GR*
179:34   silliness. *P* Indeed *GR*] *Om. MS* silliness. Indeed *O1*
180:5   overflowed *Ed.*] *Om. MS* owerflowed *GR*
180:10   hypocrisy *GR*] *Om. MS* hypocrisy, *O1*
180:17   Like *GR*] But like *MS*
180:17   the *beffa GR*] it *MS*
180:17   often *GR*] *Om. MS*
180:18   unjust *GR*] ~, *MS*
180:19   wits *GR*] Wits *MS*
180:20   to] *Om. GR*
180:21   slower-witted citizen. *P* It *GR*] witless—or slower-witted— animal Italians of the Renaissance. Wit, intelligence

had been cruelly trampled on   180:36   for safety *GR*] *Om. MS*
by the brutal feudal ages. They   181:1   who *GR*] who among us *MS*
came into their own, and   181:9   Grazzini *GR*] Grassini *MS*
proceeded to take their   181:12   the *Story GR*] *The Story MS*
revenge. It *MS*   181:13   Third] third *GR*
180:23   the *Fat GR*] *The Fat MS*   181:14   Supper and *GR*] ~, ~ *MS*
180:24   the *GR*] The *MS*   181:14   First Supper,] First supper, *GR*
180:28   himself; *GR*] ~, *MS*   181:16   work. *Ed.*] work. / D. H.
180:31   splendid *GR*] ~, *MS*   Lawrence. Florence 1929 *MS*
180:33   that *GR*] *Om. MS*   work. / D. H. LAWRENCE. /
180:36   Sistine] Sistina *GR*   *Florence, 1929. GR*

Review of *Contemporary German Poetry*

Per 1 = *English Review*, ix (November 1911)
Per 2 = *Encounter*, xxxiii (August 1969)

187:1   This *Per 2*]   187:25   'Grey,'] "~," *Per 2*
         CONTEMPORARY   187:26   Friederichs":—] ~ *Per 2*
         GERMAN POETRY. Selected   187:28   Gowns of . . . [188:20] Milky
         and translated by JETHRO   Way.] [*in italics in Per 2*]
         BITHELL, M.A. Walter Scott   189:16   it [is] *Per 2*] it *Per 1*
         Publishing Co. 1s. / This *Per 1* 189:25   good:] ~; *Per 2*

Review of *The Oxford Book of German Verse*

Per = *The English Review*, x (January, 1912)
C1 = *D. H. Lawrence and German Literature*, by Armin Arnold (Montreal: Mansfield
        Book Mart: H. Heinemann, 1963)

Silent emendation

The text of *C1* is printed in italics with quotations in roman; this has only been recorded
in the course of listing another variant.

193:1   THE OXFORD BOOK OF   Gerhart Hauptmann, [Oxford,
         GERMAN VERSE *Ed.*] THE   The Clarendon Press, 1911]
         OXFORD BOOK OF   appears on pp. 373–74 of
         GERMAN VERSE—FROM   Vol. X of the *English Review*).
         THE 12TH TO THE 20TH   *C1*
         CENTURY. Edited by H. G.   193:30   TOD IN ÄHREN] Tod in
         FIEDLER, with a preface by   Aehren *C1*
         GERHART HAUPTMANN.   194:9   Ährenfeld] Aehrenfeld *C1*
         The Clarendon Press, Oxford. 194:12 das] sein *C1*
         6s. net. *Per* (The Review of   194:20   NACH EINEM REGEN]
         The Oxford Book of German   Nach einem Regen *C1*
         Verse—From the 12th to the   194:25   deiner] Deiner *C1*
         20th Century, ed. by H. G.   194:39   Lasker-Schüle] *Lasker-Schüle*
         Fiedler, with a Preface by   *[sic] C1*

Review of *The Minnesingers*

Per = The English Review, x (January, 1912)
C1 = D. H. Lawrence and German Literature, by Armin Arnold (Montreal: Mansfield Book Mart, H. Heinemann, 1963)

Silent emendation

The text of *C1* is printed in italics with quotations in roman; this has only been recorded in the course of listing another variant.

197:1	THE MINNESINGERS ... Translations. *Ed.*] THE MINNESINGERS. By JETHRO BITHELL, M.A. Vol I.—Translations. Longmans Green & Co. 5s net. *Per* (The Review of Jethro Bithell's *The Minnesingers* [London, Longmans Green, 1909] appears on pp. 374–76 of volume X of the *English Review*). *C1*	197:10 197:10 197:13 197:14 197:14 197:20 197:20 197:27 198:4 198:24	"These translations,"] ~ ~, *C1* "may] ~ *C1* first."] ~. *C1* "The] ~ *C1* easier."] ~. *C1* "The] ~ *C1* easier ..."] ~ ... *C1* so easy] *easy C1* herzen:] ~ *C1* ballad-like *Ed.*] ballad-/like *Per balladlike C1*

'The Georgian Renaissance': review of *Georgian Poetry, 1911–12*

Per = Rhythm (March 1913), pp. xvii–xx
A1 = Phoenix (Viking)

201:1	THE GEORGIAN RENAISSANCE] *Georgian Poetry: 1911–1912 A1*	202:9 202:11	transiency,] ~ *A1* immortal"] ~ *A1*
201:2	"Georgian Poetry"] *Georgian Poetry A1*	202:12 202:14	Tea. / Mr.] Tea. Mr *A1* "We] ~ *A1*
201:20	Art] art *A1*	202:17	rose—"] ~ — *A1*
201:20	Science] science *A1*	202:18	tenderness] ~, *A1*
201:21	Art] art *A1*	202:20	"I] ~ *A1*
201:21	Nietzsche] ~, *A1*	202:21	breast."] ~. *A1*
201:22	stood,] ~; *A1*	202:23	"When] ~ *A1*
201:22	Hardy] ~, *A1*	202:27	moments."] ~. *A1*
201:22	endeavour,] ~: *A1*	202:32	joie d'être, joie de vivre] *joie d'être, joie de vivre A1*
201:22	Flaubert] ~, *A1*		
201:32	"But] ~ *A1*	203:2	Davies'] Davies's *A1*
201:33	soul,"] ~, *A1*	203:7	Mr.] Mr. Gordon *A1*
202:4	"Yet] ~ *A1*	203:10	"Carpe diem"] *carpe diem A1*
202:5	discovered."] ~. *A1*	203:17	Poets] poets *A1*
202:7	"every] ~ *A1*	203:17	Love Poets] love poets *A1*
		203:18	Poets] poets *A1*

203:19	love-poets] love poets *A1*
203:19	love-poet] love poet *A1*
203:20	being.] ∼? *A1*
203:33	mine.] ∼? *A1*
203:39	Michael Angelo] Michelangelo *A1*
204:3	love-poets . . . love-poets] love poets . . . love poets *A1*

204:5	love-poem] love poem *A1*
204:7	bitter-blossom] bitter blossom *A1*
204:8	such like] such-like *A1*
204:9	"Carmen"] *Carmen A1*
204:9	"Tosca"] *Tosca A1*
204:21	Anthology] anthology *A1*
204:21	Georgian Poetry] *Georgian Poetry A1*

'German Books': review of *Der Tod in Venedig*

Per = *Blue Review* (July 1913), no. III
A1 = *Phoenix* (Viking)

207:1	GERMAN BOOKS By D. H. LAWRENCE / Thomas Mann] German Books: Thomas Mann *A1*
207:12	"Buddenbrooks,"] *Buddenbrooks, A1*
207:13	"Tristan,"] *Tristan, A1*
207:13	"Novellen"] *Novellen A1*
207:13	"Königliche Hoheit" *Ed.*] "Konigliche Hoheit," *Per* *Königliche Hoheit A1*
207:14	"Der Tod in Venedig."] *Der Tod in Venedig. A1*
207:26	"Novelle"] *Novelle A1*
207:27	"Tristan"] *Tristan A1*
207:34	"Sturm und Drang."] *Sturm und Drang. A1*
208:12	"Tonio Kröger," *A1*] ∼ ∼, *Per*
208:12	"Wählerisch, erlesen . . . [208:14] Geschmacks."] [*in italics in A1*]
208:15	to-day] today *A1*
208:16	Leitmotiv] *Leitmotiv A1*
208:23	beforehand] before hand *A1*

208:24	motiv] *Motiv A1*
208:25	connection] connexion *A1*
208:33	"Der Tod in Venedig."] *Der Tod in Venedig. A1*
209:3	belief—] ∼: *A1*
209:3	"dass beinahe . . . [209:6] sei."] [*in italics in A1*]
209:6	Zustande] *Züstande A1*
209:25	"Der Tod in Venedig,"] *Der Tod in Venedig, A1*
209:31	motive] *Motiv A1*
209:36	"Totentanz."] *Totentanz A1*
210:6	connection] connexion *A1*
210:10	"dem allerliebsten . . . Liebchen."] [*in italics in A1*]
210:28	Künstler] *Künstler A1*
210:32	folk] folks *A1*
210:37	Sirocco] *sirocco A1*
211:7	verandah] veranda *A1*
211:18	art] ∼, *A1*
211:37	banal *A1*] banale *Per*
211:37	banal *A1*] banale *Per*
212:6	"Madame Bovary"] *Madame Bovary A1*
212:7	"Macbeth"] *Macbeth A1*

Review of *Fantazius Mallare*

MS = Roberts E199.5a
Per = *Laughing Horse*, issue 4 (1922)
E1 = *The Letters of D. H. Lawrence*, ed. Aldous Huxley (1932)

215:1 Taos 12 October 1922] *D. H. Lawrence /* The famous English novelist, writes a letter to the readers of The Laughing Horse, reviewing Ben Hecht's new privately printed novel, "Fantazius Mallare"; and takes the opportunity to give them some sound advice. / (Note: We were advised at the last moment to leave out words in this letter which might be considered objectionable. We hope that this censorship will in no way destroy the sense of the text.) / Taos. 12 October, 1922. *Per* To Willard Johnson. *Taos, New Mexico. / Early Autumn,* 1922. *E1*

215:2 Chère Jeunesse] Chere Jeunesse: *Per* CHÈRE JEUNESSE,– *E1*

215:3 sending me] *Om. E1*

215:3 Ben Hecht] —— *E1*

215:5 to me] *Om. E1*

215:6 wit,] ~ *E1*

215:7 so completely *MS, E1*] completely *Per*

215:7 crass, *MS, E1*] ~ *Per*

215:7 so strained,] and so strained. *Per* so strained *E1*

215:8 and so would-be *MS, E1*] *Om. Per*

215:8 reveal,] ~ *E1*

215:9 coition *MS, E1*] (——) *Per*

215:11 wicked] ~, *E1*

215:12 lie *MS, E1*] (——) *Per*

215:12 these *MS, E1*] those *Per*

215:14 Fantasius Malare] Fantazius Mallare *Per* —— *E1*

215:15 a *MS, E1*] the *Per*

215:16 penis *MS, E1*] (——) *Per*

215:16 testicle under *MS, E1*] (——) on *Per*

215:18 penis or testicle or vagina *MS, E1*] (——) or (——) or (——) *Per*

215:19 enough a man] enough of a man *Per* man enough *E1*

215:19 organs *MS, E1*] (——) *Per*

215:20 names] **names** *Per* names *E1*

215:21 me:] ~; *Per*

215:21 even *MS, E1*] the *Per*

215:21 reactions,] ~ *E1*

215:22 sensations,] ~ *E1*

215:22 in my head *MS, E1*] **in my head** *Per* in my head *E1*

215:23 Fantasius,] Fantazius, *Per* —— *E1*

215:23 copulation *MS, E1*] (——) *Per*

215:24 mental *MS, E1*] mental *Per*

215:24 fornication and sodomy *MS, E1*] (——) and (——) *Per*

215:25 modern] *Om. Per*

215:25 wants to *MS, E1*] might *Per*

215:28 sexual *MS, E1*] (——) *Per*

215:30 never *MS, E1*] **never** *Per* never *E1*

215:30 sex *MS, E1*] (——) *Per*

215:31 and so] so *E1*

216:1 tedious,] ~ *Per*

216:3 Fantasius] —— *E1*

216:3 masturbater] (——) *Per* masturbator *E1 see notes*

216:3 sex-contact *MS, E1*] (——) *Per*

216:5 rencontre] rencontre *E1*

216:5 delight,] ~ *E1*

216:6 Fantasius] Fantazius *Per* —— *E1*

216:9 wet-leg *MS, E1*] (——) *Per*

216:9 to *Per*] *Om. MS*

216:10 embrace with a woman] (—— —— ——) *Per* embrace with woman *E1*

216:11 sex *MS, E1*] (——) *Per*

216:11 head, *MS, E1*] heads *Per*

216:11 instead of *MS, E1*] and not *Per*

216:12 below] below a *Per Om. E1*

216:12 feebly] *Om. E1*

216:12 copulating *MS, E1*] (——) *Per*

216:13 through] with *E1*

216:13 such *MS, E1*] *Om. Per*
216:14 Fantasius] Fantazius *Per* ——
E1
216:15 for sub-title] for a sub-title *Per*
for its sub-title *E1*
216:15 "Relaxations for the
Impotent."] *Relaxations for the
Impotent. E1*
216:16 trouble:] ~; *E1*
216:16 sex *MS, E1*] (——) *Per*
216:17 heads] head *E1*
216:17 start all *MS, E1*] all start *Per*
216:18 downwards. Which] ~, which
E1
216:19 time. No] ~, no *E1*
216:20 *machine à plaisir*] (—— ——)
Per machine-à-plaisir E1
216:22 can't] can *Per* don't *E1*
216:22 *jeunesse MS, E1*] **jeunesse**
Per
216:22 sex *MS, E1*] (——) *Per*
216:23 centres *MS, E1*] centers *Per*
216:24 understood. *MS, E1*] ~: *Per*
216:24 God *MS, E1*] Good *Per*
216:24 Egyptians. And] ~, and *E1*
216:26 darkness,] ~ *E1*
216:28 our great] your *E1*
216:29 blood-vessels] blood vessels
E1

216:29 phallos *MS, E1*] (——) *Per*
216:29 vagina *MS, E1*] (——) *Per*
216:30 passions;] ~. *E1*
216:31 Ithyphallos *MS, E1*] Ithypallos
Per
216:32 terrible: *MS, E1*] ~; *Per*
216:33 promptings,] prompting *E1*
216:33 different] different mysterious
E1
216:34 Thoth] ~, *E1*
216:34 Bacchus or Horus] ~ ~ ~, *Per*
~, ~ ~, *E1*
216:34 Apollo: *MS, E1*] ~; *Per*
216:36 the head . . . [216:38] patient
in] *Om. Per*
216:38 night] light *E1*
216:38 you.] ~? *Per*
216:39 then] *Om. E1*
216:39 and *MS, E1*] and the *Per*
217:1 reverence] a reverence *E1*
217:1 again, and be grateful] *Om. E1*
217:3 Fantasius Malare] Fantazius
Mallare *Per* —— *E1*
217:3 impoverished, *MS, E1*] ~ *Per*
217:5 gate] gates *E1*
217:6 affair. *Ed.*] affair, / D. H.
Lawrence *MS* affair. / —D. H.
Lawrence. *Per* affair. / D. H.
LAWRENCE. *E1*

Review of *Americans*

TS = Ribbon-copy typescript (Roberts E14.3b)
TSR = DHL's revisions in *TS*
TSC = Copy-editor's revisions in *TS*
GP = Galley proofs for *The Dial* (Roberts E14.3a)
GR = DHL's revisions in *GP*
Per = *The Dial*, lxxiv (May 1923)
A1 = *Phoenix* (Viking)
TSR is base-text.

221:1 MODEL AMERICANS *Ed.*]
MODEL AMERICANS /
"Americans." By Stuart P.
Sherman. Charles Scribner's
Sons. *TSR* MODEL
AMERICANS /

AMERICANS. *By Stuart P.
Sherman. 12mo. 336 pages.
Charles Scribner's Sons. $2.
TSC Americans, by Stuart P.
Sherman A1*
221:2 coaxing *TSR*] persuades *TS*

221:7   Mr. *TSR, A1*] ~ *TSC*
221:8   Mr. *TSR, A1*] ~ *TSC*
221:10 treats *TSR, A1*] treates *GP*
221:14 sweets. *TSR*] sweets to the sweet. *TS* sweets? *A1*
221:15 but *TSR*] *Om. TS*
221:17 As *TSR*] Now *TS*
221:19 Mr. *TSR, A1*] ~ *TSC*
221:19 Mr. *TSR, A1*] ~ *TSC*
221:21 Mr. *TSR, A1*] ~ *TSC*
221:24 Mr. *TSR, A1*] ~ *TSC*
221:25 Democracy] democracy *A1*
221:25 menckenise] menckenize *A1*
221:26 *to*] to *A1*
221:30 nouveau riche jeune fille] *nouveau riche jeune fille TSC*
221:30 bourgeoise] *bourgeoisie Per see notes*
221:31 flappers,] ~ *A1*
221:31 Mr. *TSR, A1*] ~ *TSC*
221:33 GREAT MAN] Great Man *TSC*
221:33 GREAT MEN] Great Men *TSC*
221:34 swindle *TSR*] fraud *TS*
221:34 "nouveau riche jeune fille,"] "*nouveau riche jeune fille,*" *TSC nouveau riche jeune fille, Per*
222:1   Mr. *TSR, A1*] ~ *TSC*
222:2   Mr. *TSR, A1*] ~ *TSC*
222:3   and came] *Om. A1*
222:3   from, according to Professor Sherman. *GR*] from. *TS*
222:3   Mr. *TSR, A1*] ~ *TSC*
222:4   Democracy] democracy *A1*
222:5   AMERICAN] American *A1*
222:7   Mr. *TSR, A1*] ~ *TSC*
222:8   Mr. *TSR, A1*] ~ *TSC*
222:9   Mr. *TSR, A1*] ~ *TSC*
222:9   "Shelbourne Essays,"] ~ ~, *TSC Shelburne Essays, A1*
222:11 Mr. *TSR, A1*] ~ *TSC*
222:11 Mr. *TSR, A1*] ~ *TSC*
222:13 even alasser,] ~, ~! *TSC*
222:18 Mr. *TSR, A1*] ~ *TSC*

222:20 gas-bracket] gas bracket *GP*
222:21 odour *TS, Per*] odor *GP*
222:21 malodorous, says the professor. *TSR*] malodorous. *TS*
222:22 Mr. *TSR, A1*] ~ *TSC*
222:22 GREAT MEN] Great Men *TSC*
222:22 GREAT PAST] Great Past *TSC*
222:24 Mr. *TSR, A1*] ~ *TSC*
222:24 GREAT MEN] Great Men *TSC*
222:24 GREAT PAST] Great Past *TSC*
222:27 GREAT PAST] Great Past *TSC*
222:28 Jeer *TSR*] Scoff *TS*
222:28 GREAT PAST] Great Past *TSC*
222:29 GREAT DEAD] Great Dead *TSC*
222:31 TRADITION] Tradition *TSC*
222:31 honorable] honourable *Per*
222:31 honorable] honourable *Per*
222:32 futurist] futurist's *A1*
222:35 toil;] ~: *A1*
222:35 Mr. *TSR, A1*] ~ *TSC*
222:37 transitory;] ~: *A1*
223:3   to-day] today *A1*
223:5   neighbor] neighbour *Per*
223:16 mighty] the mighty *GP*
223:22 italicises] italicizes *TSC*
223:24 *Mr. Mencken*] Mr Mencken *TSC* Mr. Mencken *A1*
223:24 *Tradition*] Tradition *TSC*
223:24 *Franklin*] Franklin *TSC*
223:28 Mr. *TSR, A1*] ~ *TSC*
223:29 profit-and-loss *Per*] profit-and-lost *TS*
223:30 system:] ~; *GP*
223:32 Dr. *TSR, A1*] ~ *TSC*
223:37 *Emerson*] Emerson *TSC*
223:37 *The Emersonian Liberation.*] The Emersonian Liberation. *TSC* "The Emersonian Liberation." *A1*

224:2 VIRTUE] Virtue *TSC*
224:5 *Virtue*] Virtue *TSC*
224:7 GOODNESS] Goodness *TSC*
224:8 sweals *TSR*] sweats *TS*
224:8 GOOD] Good *TSC*
224:9 GOOD] Good *TSC*
224:10 GOOD] Good *TSC*
224:12 *Emersonian Liberation*]
Emersonian Liberation *TSC*
224:16 Sic transit veritas mundi] *Sic transit veritas mundi TSC*
224:17 Idealist] idealist *GP*
224:18 Over-soul] Over-Soul *A1*
224:20 thine own *TSR*] thin out *TS*
224:24 cosily] cozily *Per*
224:25 smooth-shaven *TSR*] fluffy *TS*
224:26 the credentials of *TSR*] *Om. TS*
224:28 messages *TSR*] credentials *TS*
224:30 nicely-aureoled] fluffily auraed *TS* nicely aureoled *Per*
224:32 message,] ~ *A1*
224:32 one only] only one *GP*
224:35 'phone *TSR*] ~ *TS, A1*
225:3 Dostoevsky's] Dostoievsky's *A1*
225:12 make *TS, Per*] makes *GP*
225:15 Professor] professor *A1*
225:18 Over-soul] Over-Soul *A1*
225:21 a different *Per*] different *TS*
225:23 Sic transeunt Dei hominorum] *Sic transeunt Dei hominorum TSC*
225:26 to follow Ralph Waldo's trail *TSR*] into Ralph Waldo's footsteps *TS*
225:27 *Hawthorne: A Puritan Critic of Puritanism*] Hawthorne: A Puritan Critic of Puritanism *TSC*
225:28 *The Scarlet Letter TSR, A1*] The Scarlet Letter *TSC*
225:30 duplicity.] ~? *A1*
225:31 *The Scarlet Letter TSR, A1*] The Scarlet Letter *TSC*

225:32 SIN] Sin *TSC*
225:33 FORBIDDEN] Forbidden *TSC*
225:35 situation] situations *GP*
225:35 SINNERS] Sinners *TSC*
225:36 SIN] Sin *TSC*
225:38 something] somewhat *A1*
226:1 *The Scarlet Letter TSR, A1*] The Scarlet Letter *TSC*
226:2 masterpiece, but *TSR*] masterpiece *TS*
226:3 *The Marble FaunTSR, A1*] The Marble Faun *TSC*
226:7 mediaeval *TSR*] mediaevalism *TS* medieval *A1*
226:8 ferret *TSR*] puppy *TS*
226:9 *Walt Whitman*] Walt Whitman *TSC*
226:12 you."—] ~." *A1*
226:18 it."—] ~." *A1*
226:18 Oh] O *Per*
226:20 Universe.] ~! *Per*
226:22 wonderful,] ~ *A1*
226:23 Slaves] slaves *A1*
226:24 whole hullabaloo *TSR*] universe *TS*
226:26 you.] "~." *TSC*
226:27 you.] "~." *TSC*
226:28 Whitman's . . . get me. *TSR*] *Om. TS*
226:29 Or to be . . . [226:30] *Merci, monsieur! TSR*] Pfui! *TS*
226:30 Walt's *TSR*] Waldo's *GP*
226:33 Millenium] Millennium *A1*
226:34 Tis n't my spelling *TSR*] *Om. TS* Tisn't my spelling *GP* 'Tisn't my spelling *Per*
226:38 wealth. . . . .] ~. . . . *GP*
227:2 certain *TSR*] my *TS*
227:2 books. *P* Oh] books. Oh *Per*
227:4 Allons!] *Allons! TSC Allons! GP*
227:5 *Joaquin Miller: Poetical Conquistador of the West*] Joaquin Miller: Poetical Conquistador of the West *TSC*

227:7 Woolly *TS, Per*] Wooly *GP*
227:7 imitator] imitation *A1*
227:10 The Wild West . . . [227:11] Buffalo Bill. *TSR*] *Om. TS*
227:11 today *TSR, A1*] to-day *Per*
227:12 *A Note on Carl Sandburg*] A Note on Carl Sandburg *TSC* A note on Carl Sandburg *A1*
227:12 literairy] literary *GP*
227:14 brow: but . . . tomato. *TSR*] brow. *TS*
227:16 *Andrew Carnegie*] Andrew Carnegie *TSC*
227:18 pays, in hard cash. *GR*] pays. *TS* pays, in cold cash. *Per*
227:19 *Roosevelt and the National Psychology*] Roosevelt and the National Psychology *TSC*
227:23 *Evolution of the Adams Family*] Evolution of the Adams Family *TSC*

227:29 Man,] ~ *A1*
227:32 Allons! en-masse] *Allons! en-masse TSC Allons! en-masse GP*
227:35 An Imaginary Conversation With Mr P. E. More *GR*] *An Imaginary Conversation with Mr. P. E. More TS* An Imaginary Conversation with Mr P. E. More *TSC* An Imaginary Conversation with Mr. P. E. More *A1*
227:37 Well,] ~ *A1*
227:39 are *TS, GR*] and *GP*
228:2 most of *GR*] *Om. TS*
228:2 back *TSR*] away *TS*
228:3 Oh] ~, *TSC*
228:5 again."/ *P* P.S. You *A1*] again." / D. H. Lawrence. {D. H. LAWRENCE *GP*} / *P* P.S. You *TS*

Review of *A Second Contemporary Verse Anthology*

Per = *New York Evening Post Literary Review*, 29 September 1923
A1 = *Phoenix* (Viking)

231:1 "It is *Ed.*] A Spiritual Record / A SECOND CONTEMPORARY VERSE ANTHOLOGY. Selected by CHARLES WHARTON STORK. New York. E. P. Dutton & Co. 1923. $3. / Reviewed by D. H. LAWRENCE / "It is *Per A Second Contemporary Verse Anthology* / "It is *A1*
231:2 "A Second Contemporary Verse Anthology."] *A Second Contemporary Verse Anthology. A1*
231:20 To-day] Today *A1*
231:28 core——] ~. . . . *A1*
232:14 done——] ~— — *A1*

232:18 where——] ~— — *A1*
232:23 bloomed——] ~— — *A1*
233:2 forever] for ever *A1*
233:12 forever] for ever *A1*
233:27 Western] western *A1*
233:29 Western] western *A1*
233:36 mediaevals] medievals *A1*
233:40 color-process] colour-process *A1*
234:7 mediaeval] medieval *A1*
234:22 noise. *P* There *A1*] noise. / * * *P* There *Per*
234:24 to-day] today *A1*
234:34 loopholes] loop-holes *A1*
235:13 stilly-deep——] ~ . . . *A1*
235:19 song——] ~ — — *A1*
235:31 to-day] today *A1*

Review of *Hadrian The Seventh*

Per = *Adelphi*, iii (December 1925)
A1 = *Phoenix* (Viking)

239:1 In *Hadrian Ed.*] BARON
CORVO.— / In *Hadrian Per*]
Hadrian the Seventh, by Baron
Corvo / In *Hadrian A1*
239:1 *Seventh A1*] ~* / [at foot of
page] *Hadrian the Seventh*. By
Frederick Baron Corvo.
(Knopf: New York.) *Per*
239:8 Huysmans's *A1*] Huysmans's
Per
239:8 Wilde's,] ~ *A1*
239:10 'nineties . . .'nineties]
nineties . . . nineties *A1*
239:11 Yellow Book] *Yellow Book*
A1
239:15 'nineties'] nineties' *A1*

239:22 'nineties'] nineties' *A1*
240:1 mediaeval] medieval *A1*
240:4 connection] connexion *A1*
240:21 affective *A1*] effective *Per*
240:26 Bishop . . . Archbishop]
bishop . . . archbishop *A1*
240:28 Pope] pope *A1*
240:40 and,] ~ *A1*
241:5 protestant] Protestant *A1*
241:24 analyze] analyse *A1*
241:33 Authority] authority *A1*
241:36 mediaevalism] medievalism *A1*
242:8 Hernan Cortes] Hernán Cortés
A1
242:29 fish. *A1*] fish.—D. H.
LAWRENCE. *Per*

Review of *Saïd The Fisherman*

Per1 = *New York Herald Tribune Books*, 27 December 1925
Per2 = *Adelphi* iv (January 1927)
A1 = *Phoenix* (Viking)

245:1 Since the days . . . [245:10] But
the *Ed.*] An Englishman's Arab
/ *SAID THE FISHERMAN.*
/ *By Marmaduke Pickthall.* /
New York: Alfred A. Knopf.
$3. / Reviewed by / D. H.
LAWRENCE. / The *Per1*
"SAÏD THE FISHERMAN"
/ *By* D. H. Lawrence / Since
the days . . . [245:10] But the
Per2 Saïd the Fisherman, by
Marmaduke Pickthall / Since
the days . . . [245:10] But the
A1
245:11 Arab, *Per2*] ~ *Per1*
245:15 morals, *Per2*] ~ *Per1*
245:19 Country *Per2*] country *Per1*
245:19 forever] for ever *A1*
245:20 hair. / Marmaduke *Per2*] hair.
Marmaduke *Per1*

245:25 suffer, *Per2*] ~ *Per1*
245:25 dare *Per2*] ~, *Per1*
245:26 eyes. / It *Per2*] eyes. It *Per1*
245:28 religion. When *Per2*] religion.
/ When *Per1*
245:30 wife Hasneh *Per2*] ~, ~,
Per1
245:30 strong-bodied, *Per2*]
strong-bodied *Per1*
245:31 fade. / The *Per2*] fade. The
Per1
246:1 called: *Per2*] ~ *Per1*
246:1 his *Per2*] His *Per1*
246:2 half: *Per2*] ~ *Per1*
246:2 his *Per2*] His *Per1*
246:3 of revenge *Per2*] revenge
Per1
246:5 and taking *Per2*] ~, ~ *Per1*
246:6 lets] and lets *Per2*
246:8 his *Per2*] His *Per1*

246:8	Arabian Nights] *Arabian Nights A1*	247:18	sea-shore, *Per2*] ~ *Per1*
246:9	Scheherazade's *Per1, A1*] Sheherazade's *Per2*	247:20	Ca-Ca-Caliban. *Per2*] Ca Ca Caliban, *Per1*
246:10	Sinbad *Per2*] Sindbad *Per1*	247:21	Get *Per2*] get *Per1*
246:11	time, *Per2*] ~ *Per1*	247:21	mistress *Per2*] master *Per1*
246:13	gaily *Per2*] gayly *Per1*	247:23	gratification; *Per2*] ~, *Per1*
246:14	straight away *Per2*] straightway *Per1*	247:25	all *Per2*] *Om. Per1*
246:16	up, *Per2*] ~ *Per1*	247:27	round *Per2*] around *Per1*
246:19	dressing-gown, *Per2*] dressing gown *Per1*	247:31	poor *Per2*] ~, *Per1*
246:23	picaro, *Per2*] ~ *Per1*	247:33	kept *Per2*] had kept *Per1*
246:23	sneak, *Per2*] ~ *Per1*	247:33	up, *Per2*] ~ *Per1*
246:25	Mr. *Per2*] *Om. Per1*	247:33	neither be *Per2*] be neither *Per1*
246:28	him, *Per2*] ~ *Per1*	247:34	was *Per2*] is *Per1*
246:28	him. / It *Per2*] him. It *Per1*	247:36	If you ride . . . [247:41] Saïd had little. *Per2*] *Om. Per1*
246:30	novelist, *Per2*] ~ *Per1*	247:40	sight *Per2*] ~, *A1*
246:30	towards *Per2*] toward *Per1*	247:40	mind *Per2*] ~, *A1*
246:31	with. / Saïd *Per2*] with. Saïd *Per1*	248:1	him *Per2*] Saïd *Per1*
246:33	indeed, *Per2*] ~ *Per1*	248:1	alert: *Per2*] ~ – *Per1*
246:34	belt, *Per2*] ~ *Per1*	248:4	cautious, *Per2*] ~ *Per1*
246:35	gutter-snipe *Per2*] guttersnipe *Per1*	248:8	Beirut *Per1, A1*] Beyrût *Per2*
246:40	Englishman, *Per2*] ~ *Per1*	248:8	London: *Per2*] ~, *Per1*
246:41	uneasy. P So *Per2*] uneasy. So, *Per1*	248:9	city: *Per2*] ~, *Per1*
247:1	over-scrupulous *Per2*] overscrupulous *Per1*	248:9	for ever *Per2*] forever *Per1*
		248:9	white-haired *Per2*] ~, *Per1*
247:4	non-moral *Per2*] ~, *Per1*	248:11	We would fain think *Per2*] And *Per1*
247:5	Saïd, *Per2*] ~ *Per1*	248:11	because *Per2*] not because *Per1*
247:6	it, *Per2*] ~ *Per1*		
247:9	rational. *Per2*] ~; *Per1*	248:12	But it didn't. *Per2*] *Om. Per1*
247:11	spell, *Per2*] ~ *Per1*	248:15	summing-up *Per2*] summing up *Per1*
247:14	Hasneh, *Per2*] ~ *Per1*	248:15	sympathetic, *Per2*] ~ *Per1*
247:15	Selim. / As *Per2*] Selim. As *Per1*	248:19	dark *Per2*] *Om. Per1*
		248:19	London, *Per2*] ~ *Per1*
		251:20	wonders: *Per2*] ~ *Per1*

Review of *The Origins of Prohibition*

MS = Roberts E297a
Per = *New York Herald Tribune Books*, 31 January 1926
TCC = Roberts E297b
A1 = *Phoenix* (Viking)

251:1 The Origins of Prohibition
Ed.] The Origins of
Prohibition—John A. Krout /
(A. A. Knopf.) *MS* D. H.
Lawrence on American
Prohibition / *THE ORIGINS
OF PROHIBITION.* / *By
John A. Krout.* / *New York:
Alfred A. Knopf. $3.50* /
Reviewed by / D. H.
LAWRENCE *Per* THE
ORIGINS OF
PROHIBITION. – John A.
Krout. / (A. A. Knopf) *TCC*
The Origins of Prohibition, by
J. A. Krout *A1*

251:2 work."*MS*, *A1*] ~". *TCC*

251:3 work, *MS*, *TCC*] ~ *Per*

251:10 book, *MS*, *TCC*] ~ *Per*

251:10 realise *MS*, *TCC*] realize *Per*,
A1

251:13 enquiry *MS*, *TCC*] inquiry
Per

251:13 that, *MS*, *TCC*] ~ *Per*

251:15 almost, *MS*, *TCC*] ~ *Per*

251:15 notes, *MS*, *TCC*] ~ *Per*

251:16 but] ~, *Per*

251:19 adding-up *MS*, *TCC*] adding
Per

251:20 laws, *MS*, *TCC*] ~ *Per*

251:23 molasses—rum—slaves—
molasses—rum— *MS*, *TCC*]
~, ~, ~, ~, ~, *Per*

251:23 slaves makes] ~, ~ *Per* ~ —
~*TCC*

251:25 whiskey] whisky *Per*

251:25 individual, *MS*, *TCC*] ~ *Per*

251:26 Dr] ~. *Per*

251:26 Rush, *MS*, *TCC*] ~ *Per*

251:26 Dr] ~. *Per*

252:2 indifferent,"*MS*, *A1*] ~",
TCC

252:2 put it. *P* We *MS*, *TCC*] put it.
We *Per*

252:3 quite:] ~, *Per*

252:4 decision. For *MS*, *TCC*]
decision. *P* For *Per*

252:6 oh] ~, *TCC*

252:7 sugar-cane *MS*, *TCC*] sugar
cane *Per*

252:8 and] And *Per*

252:9 whiskey] whisky *Per*

252:13 Get] get *TCC*

252:16 mankind, *MS*, *TCC*] ~ *Per*

252:16 few] ~, *TCC*

252:16 surely] ~, *TCC*

252:16 whiskey] whisky *TCC*

252:17 ago, *MS*, *TCC*] ~ *Per*

252:18 beer.—] ~. *Per*

252:20 View", *MS*, *TCC*] ~," *Per*, *A1*

252:21 Prohibition *MS*, *TCC*]
prohibition *Per*, *A1*

252:22 self-responsible.—] ~. *Per*

252:26 sobriety."— *MS*, *TCC*] ~."
Per

252:27 *people*, *MS*, *TCC*] ~ *Per*

252:28 polls—"] ~." *Per*

252:31 how, *MS*, *TCC*] ~ *Per*

252:31 *forced? P* The *MS*, *TCC*]
forced? The *Per*

252:33 do, is *MS*, *TCC*] ~ ~ *Per*

252:38 Republic *MS*, *TCC*] republic
Per, *A1*

252:39 honorably] honourably *TCC*

253:3 idea." *MS*, *A1*] ~". *TCC*

253:6 would not *MS*, *TCC*] ~ ~,
Per

253:7 themselves, *MS*, *TCC*] ~
Per

253:8 coerced.—] ~. *Per*

253:9 neighbour,] neighbor *Per*
neighbour *TCC*

253:10 somewhere *MS*, *TCC*]
somehow *Per*

253:11 it. Since *MS*, *TCC*] it: since *Per*

253:13 neighbour *MS*, *TCC*] neighbor
Per

253:14 pages,] ~ *Per*

253:19 And *MS*, *TCC*] ~, *Per*

253:21 bad, *MS*, *TCC*] ~ *Per*

253:24 each *MS*, *TCC*] in which each
Per

253:24 neighbour *MS*, *TCC*] neighbor
Per

253:28	honorable] honourable *TCC*	253:30	afterwards. *A1*] afterwards. / D. H. Lawrence. *MS*
253:29	voted, *MS*, *TCC*] ~ *Per*		afterward. *Per* afterwards. /
253:30	smile] smell, *TCC*		D. H. LAWRENCE. *TCC*

Review of *In The American Grain*

Per = *The Nation* (New York), 122 (April 1926)
A1 = *Phoenix* (Viking)

257:1	American Heroes *Ed.*] American Heroes / *In the American Grain*. By William Carlos Williams. Albert and Charles Boni. $3. *Per In the American Grain*, by William Carlos Williams *A1*	258:2	"Ulysses"] *Ulysses A1*
		258:4	modernist *A1*] modernest *Per see notes*
		258:8	glamor] glamour *A1*
		258:34	American;] ~: *A1*
		259:11	"The Golden Man."] *The Golden Man. A1*
257:12	Cortes] Cortés *A1*	259:12	bastard-European]
257:24	element—Oh] element, O *A1*		bastard-Europe *A1*
257:24	Americans!] ~!, *A1*	259:17	book. *A1*] book. D. H.
258:2	ninety nine] ninety-nine *A1*		LAWRENCE *Per*

Review (manuscript version) of *Heat*

MS = Roberts E158a
A1 = *Phoenix* (Viking)

263:1	Heat.] *Heat*, by Isa Glenn *A1*	265:13	cocoa-nut] coconut *A1*
263:2	"Heat"] *Heat A1*	265:18	"ticher":] "~," *A1*
263:6	*Eyre*,] *Eyre*, *A1*	265:20	sexual] *Om. A1*
263:8	"Heat"] *Heat A1*	265:21	east] East *A1*
263:10	her] the *A1*	265:26	silent,] ~ *A1*
263:18	honorable] honourable *A1*	265:32	wildly] ~, *A1*
263:22	statue] Statue *A1*	265:33	time,] ~ *A1*
263:24	repellant] repellent *A1*	265:37	speech!—] ~! *A1*
263:33	gorping fishes] groping-fishes *A1*	266:6	enamoured &] enamoured, and *A1*
264:18	"wise",] "~," *A1*	266:8	Ah] ~, *A1*
264:22	her: in] her in *A1*	266:9	Ah] ~, *A1*
264:23	also always] always *A1*	266:15	love affair] love-affair *A1*
264:27	unprotected, so] unprotected too, *A1*	266:16	parents' *A1*] parents *MS*
		266:21	officers' *A1*] officers *MS*
264:31	education.—That] education. That *A1*	266:23	dinner party] dinner-party *A1*
		266:25	her,] ~: *A1*
264:37	his] her *A1*	266:25	school-teacher] ~, *A1*
265:11	cheap] ~, *A1*	266:30	mousey] mousy *A1*
265:11	lodging house] lodging-house *A1*	266:34	honorable] honourable *A1*

266:35   "Listen dear! You] "Listen,
         dear, you *A1*
266:37   Chaplain] chaplain *A1*
266:37   Why!] ~? *A1*
266:37   never, never] never *A1*
266:39   girl."—Dolores] girl." Dolores
         A1
266:40   girl",] ~," *A1*
267:1   easily",] ~," *A1*

267:13   she!—] ~! *A1*
267:13   Ah!—But] Ah! But *A1*
267:15   club] Club *A1*
267:19   whiskey lapper] whisky-lapper
         A1
267:31   Ah] ~, *A1*
267:31   admit] admit it *A1*
267:34   school-teacher.—] ~. *A1*

Review (typescript version) of *Heat*

TS = Roberts E158b
TSR = Autograph revisions in *TS*

271:1   HEAT *Ed.*] HEAT / by /
         D. H. Lawrence *TS*
271:2   Glenn, *Ed.*] ~ *TS*
273:7   with *TSR*] wi *TS*
273:9   him *TSR*] hi *TS*
273:19   pupils *Ed.*] puplils *TS*
273:24   Glory! *TSR*] ~ *TS*
274:16   almighty *TSR*] allmighty *TS*

274:16   self-sufficient *TSR*]
         self-sufficie *TS*
274:26   has had *TSR*] had has
         TS
274:30   throw *TSR*] throww *TS*
274:32   figures *TSR*] figur *TS*
275:20   off *TSR*] of *TS*
275:21   *She TSR*] She *TS*

Review of *The World of William Clissold*

Per = *Calendar* (October 1926)
A1 = *Phoenix* (Viking)

279:1   *The World Ed.*] THE WORLD
         OF WILLIAM CLISSOLD.
         By H. G. WELLS. Books I and
         II. BENN, 7/6. / The World
         Per The World of William
         Clissold, by H. G. Wells / *The*
         World A1
279:5   the hope] hope *A1*
279:12   Title-Page",] ~," *A1*
279:14   *clef*:] ~: *A1*
279:25   *Book I: The Frame of the*
         Picture.] Book I: "The Frame
         of the Picture." *A1*
279:30   well-off] well off *A1*
280:4   animal",] ~," *A1*
280:4   "ideas",] "~," *A1*
280:6   proceed!";] Proceed!"
         A1
280:34   Forget-me-nots".] ~." *A1*

281:11   Sonny!".] ~!" *A1*
281:17   *The Frame*] "The Frame"
         A1
281:17   resumé] résumé *A1*
281:18   *The Story, Book II*] The Story,
         Book II *A1*
281:19   resumé] résumé *A1*
281:19   Cavemen] Cave-men *A1*
281:22   "systems",] "~," *A1*
281:35   to-day] today *A1*
282:4   world".] ~." *A1*
282:10   me", etc.—] me," etc.
         A1
282:12   *Clissold*:] ~: *A1*
282:16   urge",] ~," *A1*
282:18   urge".] ~." *A1*
282:30   course,] ~ *A1*
283:16   II. *A1*] II. / D. H.
         LAWRENCE. *Per*

Review (manuscript version) of *Gifts of Fortune*

MS = Roberts E145a
TCC = Roberts E145b
A1 = *Phoenix* (Viking)

287:1   "Gifts of Fortune"] *Gifts of Fortune*, by H. M. Tomlinson / *Gifts of Fortune A1*

287:1   travel book] travel-book *TCC*

287:7   Mr] Mr. *TCC*

287:7   "Gifts of Fortune . . . to] *Gifts of Fortune: With Some Hints to Those About to A1*

287:8   Travel,"] ~" *TCC* Travel *A1*

287:11   entitled:] ~, *TCC*

287:11   Hints] "Hints *A1*

287:11   Travel.] ~." *A1*

287:14   Mr] ~. *TCC*

287:19   Mr] ~. *TCC*

287:22   Mr] ~. *TCC*

287:23   it." etc. *Ed.*] it. etc. p. 24) *MS* it," etc. (p. 24). *TCC* it," etc. *A1 see notes*

287:27   illusions] illusion *TCC*

287:28   passen] passes *A1*

288:1   Bates'] Bates's *A1*

288:1   "Amazon",] *Amazon, A1*

288:1   "Nigger of the Narcissus",] *Nigger of the Narcissus, A1*

288:2   "Moby Dick"] *Moby Dick A1*

288:5   Mr] ~. *TCC*

288:9   Mr] ~. *TCC*

288:27   Kamschatka] Kamchatka *A1*

288:27   Athabasca] Athabaska *A1*

288:32   Mr] ~. *TCC*

289:8   civilisation] civilization *A1*

289:15   sketch—] ~: *TCC*

289:15   *Conrad is dead.*] "Conrad Is Dead." *A1*

289:19   Mr] ~. *TCC*

289:25   Mr] ~. *TCC*

289:32   mother—"] ~." *TCC*

289:33   Mr] ~. *TCC*

289:36   face *MS, A1*] fact *TCC*

290:4   Mr] ~. *TCC*

290:5   will] still *TCC*

290:6   Mr] ~. *TCC*

290:8   haze" etc. *Ed.*] haze etc. p. 48 *MS* haze," etc. (p. 48) *TCC* haze," etc. *A1*

290:9   St] ~. *TCC*

290:11   saint] Saint *A1*

290:12   exist.—] ~. *A1*

290:13   &] and *TCC*

290:14   do] did *TCC*

290:16   octopus!" *A1*] ~! (p. 138) *MS* ~!" (p. 138) *TCC*

290:17   farmer" etc. *Ed.*] ~ etc. p. 118 *MS* ~," etc. (p. 118) *TCC* ~," etc. *A1*

290:18   today" *Ed.*] ~ p. 120 *MS* ~," (p. 120) *TCC* ~," etc. *A1*

290:19   notion" etc. *Ed.*] ~ etc p. 151 *MS* ~," etc. (p.) *TCC* ~," etc. *A1*

290:23   estuary" etc.— *Ed.*] ~ etc. p. 159)— *MS* ~," etc. (p. 159). *TCC* ~," etc. *A1*

290:27   Mr] ~. *TCC*

Review (periodical version) of *Gifts of Fortune*

Per = *T. P.'s and Cassell's Weekly*, Vol. vii, no. 166 (1 January 1927)

293:1   "Gifts of Fortune" *Ed.*] The Coast of Illusion / *A New Face for the Old World: The Philosophy of Travel* / By D. H. LAWRENCE / "Gifts of Fortune" *Per*

Review of *Pedro de Valdivia*

TS = Roberts E306
TSR = Autograph revisions in *TS*
TSC = Printer's revisions in *TS*
Per = *Calendar*, iii (January 1927)
A1 = *Phoenix* (Viking)

299:1   PEDRO DE
         VALDIVIA—Conqueror of
         Chile. *Ed.*] PEDRO DE
         VALDIVIA—Conqueror of
         Chile. / by R. B. Cunninghame
         Graham. / Heinemann. 15/-
         net. *TS* PEDRO DE
         VALDIVIA—Conqueror
         of Chile. By R. B.
         CUNNINGHAME
         GRAHAM. Heinemann,
         15/- net. *TSC PEDRO DE
         VALDIVIA—CONQUEROR
         OF CHILE. By R. B.
         CUNNINGHAME
         GRAHAM. Heinemann, 15/-
         net. Per Pedro de Valdivia*, by
         R. B. Cunninghame Graham
         A1
299:6   Mr] ~. *Per*
299:7   title.—] ~ — *Per*
299:7   "Pedro de Valdivia, Conqueror
         of Chile.] *"Pedro de Valdivia,
         Conqueror of Chile. A1*
299:8   short] Short *Per*
299:8   together] Together *Per*
299:9   —So?] ~? *A1*
299:10   conquistador] *conquistador
         TSC* Conquistador *A1*
299:12   15/-] fifteen shillings
         TSC
299:15   Mr] ~. *Per*
299:17   "Short Account"] ~ ~ *A1*
299:18   Mr.] ~. *TSC*
299:25   Mr] ~. *Per*
299:27   conquistador] *conquistador
         TSC* Conquistador *A1*
299:28   conquistador] *conquistador
         TSC* Conquistador *A1*
299:28   Mr] ~. *Per*

299:31   conquistadores] *conquistadores
         TSC* Conquistadores *A1*
300:1   inner] living *Per*
300:2   visionless,] ~ *TSC*
300:5   colour] ~, *Per*
300:13   Mr] ~. *Per*
300:13   note, in] ~ ~ *Per*
300:17   death,] ~ *TSC*
300:19   Mr] ~. *Per*
300:20   If] "~ *TSC*
300:22   (sic)] [*sic*] *Per* [sic] *A1*
300:23   Ah] ~, *TSC*
300:26   so,] ~ *TSC*
300:26   Mr] ~. *Per*
300:26   and] ~, *Per*
300:27   !—]!!— *TSC*
300:30   fault,] ~ *TSC*
300:30   Mr] ~. *Per*
300:30   Graham]] ~], *Per*
300:32   it?]] ~?], *A1*
300:34   today *TS, A1*] to-day *Per*
300:35   dear-dear!] Dear-dear! *Per*
300:37   Mr] ~. *Per*
300:37   swash-buckling *TSC, A1*]
         swash buckling *TS*
         swashbuckling *Per*
300:39   conquistadores] *conquistadores
         TSC* Conquistadores *A1*
301:2   educational *TSR*] *Om. TS*
301:2   Spanish *TSR*] the Spanish
         TS
301:3   The conquistadores *TSR*]
         They *TS* The *conquistadores
         TSC* The Conquistadores
         A1
301:5   Yet at least] ~, ~ ~, *TSC*
301:8   Mr] ~. *Per*
301:9   cares! *TSR*] ~ *TS*
301:11   Venezuela, and] ~, ~, *TSC*
301:11   1532] ~, *TSC*

301:12 Mr] ~. *Per*
301:13 known *TSR*] know *TS*
301:20 coloniser] colonizer *TSC*
301:22 colonisation] colonization *TSC*
301:26 colonising] colonizing *TSC*
301:35 colonising] colonizing *TSC*
301:36 Mr] ~. *Per*
301:37 Mr] ~. *Per*
302:1 swords." *TS, A1*] ~". *Per*
302:1 Oh] ~, *Per*
302:2 proximity *TSR*]
   existence *TS*
302:2 usually!—] ~.— *Per* ~. *A1*
302:3 Mr] ~. *Per*
302:3 seems to *TSR*] must *TS*
302:4 by mistake *TSR*] then *TS*
302:7 Mr] ~. *Per*
302:20 overdone *TS, A1*] over done
   Per
302:20 bluff] ~, *Per*
302:25 conquistador] *conquistador*
   TSC Conquistador *A1*
302:28 he was *TSR*] they were *TS*
302:32 "rebels",] "~," *A1*
303:4 Mr] ~. *Per*
303:10 today *TS, A1*] to-day *TSC*
303:11 earth." *TS, A1*] ~". *Per*
303:12 Mr] ~. *Per*
303:14 Columbus *TSR*] Om. *TS*
303:15 conquistadores] *conquistadores*
   TSC Conquistadores *A1*
303:18 conquistadores] *conquistadores*
   TSC Conquistadores *A1*
303:19 Mr] ~. *Per*
303:20 foot-notes] footnotes *A1*
303:21 our author *TSR*] Mr Graham
   TS
303:23 unsatisfactory.—] ~: *A1*
303:24 pathetically."—] ~".— *Per*
   ~." *A1*
303:24 "pathetically".] "~." *A1*
303:25 foot-note] footnote *A1*
303:25 "Un bergantin . . . lo] [*in italics
   in TSC*]
303:26 sabe."] *sabe." TSC sabe"* Per
   sabe." A1
303:26 knows." *TS, A1*] ~". *Per*

303:27 *pathetically?*] *pathetically?*
   Per pathetically *A1*
303:27 A] "*A TSC*
303:27 Dios rogando . . . maza]
   [*in italics in TSC*]
303:28 dando,] *dando"*, TSC *dando,"*
   A1
303:28 Praying] "~ *TSC*
303:29 mace.—] ~".— *TSC* ~." *A1*
303:32 *Habladme TSR*] Habladme *TS*
   "*Habladme TSC*
303:32 *por escrito TSR*] por escrito
   TS
303:33 *Alonso! TSR*] Alonso!
   TS Alonso!" Per
303:33 is: *Say TSR*] is: Say *TS* is:
   "Say *A1*
303:33 it . . . Don *TSR*] it . . . Don *TS,*
   A1
303:33 *Alonso! TSR*] Alonso! *TS*
   Alonso!" *TSC Alonso! Per*
   Alonso!" *A1*
303:33 Mr] ~. *Per*
303:34 it: *Write TSR*] it: Write *TS* it:
   "*Write TSC* it: "Write *A1*
303:34 to me, Don *TSR*] to me, Don
   TS, A1
303:34 *Alonso!— TSR*] Alonso!— *TS*
   Alonso!"— *TSC Alonso!"* . . .
   Per Alonso!" . . . *A1*
303:37 is: *TS, A1*] ~:— *Per*
303:38 "El] *El TSC*
303:38 mas seguro . . . vez] [*in italics in
   TSC*]
303:39 alguna."] *alguna." TSC alguna.*
   Per
304:1 Mr] ~. *Per*
304:2 all."—] ~".— *Per* ~."
   A1
304:4 not to *TSR*] never to *TS*
304:4 once."—] ~".— *Per* ~."
   A1
304:5 "fortuna"] "*don de la fortuna"*
   Per "don de la fortuna" *A1*
304:5 second,] ~ *TSC*
304:6 Mr] ~. *Per*
304:7 own *TSR*] Om. *TS*

304:7   fashion. *A1*] fashion. /   Mirenda / Scandicci. /
         D. H. Lawrence. {D. H.   Florence. Italy. *TS* fashion. /
         LAWRENCE. *TSC*} / Villa   D. H. LAWRENCE. *Per*

Review of *Nigger Heaven* etc.

MS =Roberts E271a
Per = *Calendar*, iv (April 1927)
TCC = Roberts E271b
A1 = *Phoenix* (Viking)

307:1   Nigger *Ed.*] Nigger   307:14   Monna] Mona *Per*
         Heaven—Carl Van Vechten   307:15   Cocteau etc] ∼, ∼. *Per*
         (Knopf) / Flight—Walter   307:17   "idealistic" *MS*, *TCC*] ∼ *Per*
         White (Knopf) / Manhattan   307:18   golden brown] golden-brown
         Transfer—John Dos Passos   *Per*
         (Constable) / In Our   307:20   that] *Om. TCC*
         Time—Ernest Hemingway   307:22   palish brown] palish-brown *Per*
         (Cape) / Nigger *MS NIGGER*   307:23   whatsoever *MS*, *A1*] whatever
         HEAVEN. By CARL VAN   *TCC*
         VECHTEN. Knopf, 7/6. /   307:27   red peppers] red-peppers *Per*
         FLIGHT. By WALTER   307:31   fake] false *TCC*
         WHITE. Knopf, 7/6. /   308:1   respectable, *MS*, *TCC*] ∼ *Per*
         MANHATTAN TRANSFER.   308:2   negro] Negro *A1*
         By JOHN DOS PASSOS.   308:4   informed,] ∼ *Per*
         Constable, 7/6. / *IN OUR*   308:5   Creoles, *MS*, *A1*] ∼ — *Per*
         TIME. By ERNEST   creoles, *TCC*
         HEMINGWAY. Cape, 6/-. /   308:6   mixture—] ∼, *TCC*
         Nigger *Per* NIGGER   308:6   Creole *MS*, *A1*] creole *TCC*
         HEAVEN—Carl Van Vechten.   308:7   negro] Negro *A1*
         (Knopf) / FLIGHT—Walter   308:8   Creole *MS*, *A1*] creole *TCC*
         White. (Knopf) /   308:9   Jews] ∼' *Per*
         MANHATTAN   308:9   Burying Ground *MS*, *TCC*]
         TRANSFER—John Dos   burying ground *Per*, *A1*
         Passos. (Constable) / IN OUR   308:10   negro] Negro *A1*
         TIME—Ernest Hemingway.   308:11   Mr] ∼. *Per*
         (Cape) / Nigger *TCC Nigger*   308:11   Creoles *MS*, *A1*] creoles
         Heaven, by Carl Van Vechten;   *TCC*
         Flight, by Walter White;   308:12   Mr] ∼. *Per*
         Manhattan Transfer, by John 308:12   Golden-browns *MS*, *TCC*]
         Dos Passos; *In Our Time*, by   golden-browns *Per*, *A1*
         Ernest Hemingway / Nigger   308:14   negro] Negro *A1*
         A1   308:15   negro] Negro *A1*
307:2   hundred and twenty-fifth *MS*, 308:15   Creole *MS*, *A1*] creole *TCC*
         TCC] Hundred and   308:17   negro] Negro *A1*
         Twenty-Fifth *Per*, *A1*   308:18   negroes] Negroes *A1*
307:7   Mr] ∼. *Per*   308:18   negro] Negro *A1*
307:13   the *MS*, *TCC*] *Om. Per*   308:20   skin: *MS*, *TCC*] ∼, *Per*

308:24   negroid] Negroid *A1*

308:25   and with *MS, TCC*] and
Per

308:29   records. *P* New *MS, TCC*]
records. New *Per*

308:30   melting pot] melting-pot *Per*

308:31   melting pot] melting-pot *Per*

308:31   pale greyish-brown]
pale-greyish-brown *TCC*

308:32   Mr] ~. *Per*

308:36   them—Unless] ~.— ~ *Per* ~.
~ *TCC*

308:37   Apparently *MS, TCC*] ~, *Per*

308:37   *feeling*] feeling *Per*

308:37   negro] Negro *A1*

308:38   Mr] ~. *Per*

309:1   books.— *MS, TCC*] ~. *Per,*
A1

309:3   negro] Negro *A1*

309:5   negro] Negro *A1*

309:5   *knows MS, TCC*] knows *Per*

309:5   do, *MS, TCC*] ~ *Per*

309:7   There] ~, *TCC*

309:10   *Flight*] ~, *Per*

309:13   Harlem.—] ~. *Per*

309:18   extraction." *MS, A1*] ~". *Per*

309:24   heaven] Heaven *Per*

309:27   But at least *MS, TCC*] ~, ~ ~,
Per

309:28   Mr] ~ *Per*

309:29   Mr] ~. *Per*

309:33   recognise *MS, TCC*] recognize
Per, A1

309:35   another nowhere *MS, TCC*]
nowhere *Per*

309:40   Mr] ~. *Per*

310:4   Lackawanna ferry-boat *MS,*
A1] Sackawanna Ferry-boat
TCC

310:5   1900 *MS, TCC*] ~, *Per*

310:8   apartment!] ~. *TCC*

310:10   snowflakes—] ~. *Per*

310:11   gone! a] ~! — a *Per*

310:12   night,] ~ *Per*

310:12   But gradually] ~, ~, *TCC*

310:14   Mr] ~. *Per*

310:16   But] ~, *Per*

310:16   realise *MS, TCC*] realize *Per,*
A1

310:18   becomes,] ~ *Per*

310:22   realises *MS, TCC*] realizes *Per,*
A1

310:24   *all MS, TCC*] all *Per*

310:30   itself *MS, TCC*] ~, *Per*

310:31   first *MS, TCC*] ~, *Per*

310:32   York.— *MS, TCC*] ~. *Per, A1*

310:32   realise *MS, TCC*] realize *Per,*
A1

310:34   ranting,] ~ *Per*

310:35   realises *MS, TCC*] realizes *Per,*
A1

311:2   male." *MS, A1*] ~". *TCC*

311:4   haven't *Per*] havent *MS*

311:8   today *MS, TCC*] to-day *Per*

311:10   ever *MS, TCC*] even *Per*

311:14   Twenty-third street]
Twenty-Third Street *Per*
Twenty-third Street *TCC*

311:17   "'Say] "~ *Per*

311:18   wheel.] ~ *Per*

311:18   furniture van)] furniture-van).
Per

311:21   The End.'] *The End. Per, A1*
The End. *TCC*

311:22   nowhere!" *MS, TCC*] ~"! *Per*

311:23   Mr] ~. *Per*

311:28   Lakes] lakes *Per*

311:28   America *MS, A1*] ~, *TCC*

311:30   home] ~, *TCC*

311:31   way *MS, A1*] was *TCC*

311:31   west *MS, TCC*] West *Per*

311:32   Europe: *MS, TCC*] ~; *Per, A1*

311:33   Paris: *MS, TCC*] ~; *Per, A1*

311:33   region *MS, TCC*] Region *Per*

311:39   "Mottoes"] "mottoes" *TCC*

312:1   affected.)— *MS, TCC*] ~.)
Per, A1

312:5   Nowadays *MS, TCC*] ~, *Per*

312:6   *conscious MS, TCC*] conscious
Per

312:7   Mr] ~. *Per*

312:12   it!— *MS, TCC*] ~! *Per, A1*

312:13   it." *MS, TCC*] ~". *Per*

312:14   Mr] ~. *Per*

312:14 sketches, *MS, TCC*] ~ *Per*
312:14 reason,] ~ *Per*
312:16 cigarette end *MS, TCC*]
        cigarette-end *Per, A1*
312:20 Mr] ~. *Per*
312:24 Mr] ~. *Per*

312:24 good, *MS, TCC*] ~ *Per*
312:28 anywhere, *MS, TCC*] ~; *Per*
312:32 Anyhow] ~, *Per*
312:32 doesn't. *TCC*] doesn't. / D H
        Lawrence *MS* doesn't. / D. H.
        LAWRENCE. *Per*

Review of *Solitaria*

MS = Roberts E368a
TSC = Roberts E368d
Per = *Calendar*, iv (July 1927)
TCC = Roberts E368b
A1 = *Phoenix* (Viking)

315:1 *Solitaria by V. V. Rozanov. Ed.*]
       Solitaria by V. V. Rozanov /
       with an abridged Account
       of the author's Life, by
       E. Gollerbach, / and other
       biographical material, and
       matter from / The Apocalypse
       of Our Times. / Translated
       from the Russian by S. S.
       Koteliansky. / Wishart. 12/6
       net. MS SOLITARIA. / *by* /
       V. V. ROZANOV. / With
       an abridged account of
       the author's Life, / by
       E. Gollerbach, and other
       biographical / material, and
       matter from / *The Apocalypse*
       of Our Times. / Translated
       from the Russian by S. S.
       Koteliansky. / Wishart 12/6
       TSC SOLITARIA. *By V. V.*
       ROZANOV. With an abridged
       account / of the author's Life, by
       E. Gollerbach, and other
       biographical / material, and
       matter from "The Apocalypse
       of Our Times", / translated
       from the Russian by S. S.
       Koteliansky. Wishart, / 12/6.
       Per Solitaria. By V. V.
       Rozonov: with an abridged
       account of the / author's Life,
       by E. Gollerbach, and other

       biographical material, / and
       matter from *The Apocalypse of*
       Our Times. / Translated from
       the Russian by S. S.
       Koteliansky. / *Wishart.* 12/6
       net. *TCC Solitaria*, by V. V.
       Rozanov *A1*
315:3 times . . . *MS, TCC*] ~. . . . .
       TSC
315:5 West." *MS, TCC*] ~". *Per*
315:6 And *MS, TCC*] ~, *TSC*
315:7 Critico-biographical Study, 43
       pp.,] "Critico-Biographical
       Study", forty-three pages,
       TSC critico-biographical
       Study, 43 pp., *TCC*
       "Critico-Biographical Study,"
       forty-three pages, *A1*
315:10 are,] ~; *TCC*
315:12 his . . . his *MS, TCC*] His . . .
       His *TSC, A1*
315:13 Dostoevsky *MS, TCC*]
       Dostoievsky *TSC, A1*
315:13 familiarised *MS, TCC*]
       familiarized *TSC, A1*
315:14 gamin-religious *MS, TCC*]
       gamin-religious *TSC, A1*
315:14 Russians,] ~ *TCC*
315:15 pie-bald] piebald *TSC*
315:15 souls,] ~ *TCC*
315:17 or *MS, TCC*] nor *Per*
315:18 civilisation *MS, TCC*]
       civilization *TSC, A1*

315:20 recantation,] ~; *TCC*
315:22 Christlike] Christ-like *A1*
315:22 and then *MS, TCC*] ~, ~,
TSC
315:25 Dostoevsky's *MS, TCC*]
Dostoievsky's *TSC, A1*
315:26 "is *MS, TCC*] ~ *TSC*
315:27 life—"] life— *TSC* life."
TCC
315:27 As *MS, TCC*] as *TSC*
315:29 Dostoevsky *MS, TCC*]
Dostoievsky *TSC, A1*
316:1 Dostoevsky *MS, TCC*]
Dostoievsky *TSC, A1*
316:2 100 pp. *MS, TCC*] a hundred
pages *TSC, A1*
316:6 W. C.] w.c. *TCC*
316:6 bathing slipper]
bathing-slipper *TCC*
316:7 w. c. *TCC*] w. c *MS* W. C.,
TSC
316:7 coins," *MS, A1*] ~", *TSC*
316:8 odds!] ~? *TCC*
316:9 cab"] ~," *A1*
316:12 to jesus] To Jesus *TSC*
316:13 jesus!] Jesus! *TSC*
316:13 Hamlet's: to] Hamlet's: To
TSC Hamlet's To *Per*
316:13 be.—But *MS, TCC*] be;—but
TSC be; but *Per* be. But *A1*
316:14 parody.—] parody. *TSC*
316:15 you - - is] you . . is *TSC*
you—is *TCC*
316:15 trousers: " *MS, TCC*] ~",
TSC ~": *A1*
316:18 with.—] ~. *TCC*
316:22 (except *MS, TCC*] [except
TSC
316:23 duty) . . . *MS, TCC*]
duty] . . . . *TSC* duty] . . . . .
Per duty) *A1*
316:24 Dostoevsky *MS, TCC*]
Dostoievsky *TSC, A1*
316:25 Mary Mary quite contrary] ~,
~ ~ ~ *TSC* Mary-Mary-
quite-contrary *TCC*
316:27 And] ~, *TSC*

316:27 Mary Mary quite contrary] ~,
~ ~ ~ *TSC* Mary-Mary-
quite-contrary *TCC*
316:28 I want] "I want *TSC* I
want TCC I want *A1*
316:28 am good!] *am* good: *TCC*
316:29 above all, *MS, TCC*] ~ ~ *Per*
316:30 purity! *MS, TCC*] ~!" *TSC*
316:31 *ventris,*] ~ *TCC*
316:32 Dostoevsky *MS, TCC*]
Dostoievsky *TSC, A1*
316:32 hard boiled] hard-boiled
TSC
316:33 he only *MS, TCC*] only
TSC
316:35 forever] for ever *A1*
316:37 Easter',] ~,' *A1*
316:37 'in *TCC*] "~ *MS* ~ *TSC, A1*
316:37 bells,'] ~", *TSC* ~', *TCC* ~,"
A1
316:38 rayment'", *Ed.*] raymcnt', *MS*
raiment", *TSC* rayment'" *TCC*
raiment," *A1 see notes*
316:38 hard boiled] hard-boiled *TSC*
317:2 morals." *MS, TCC*] ~". *Per*
~" *A1*
317:3 God—"] ~." *TSC* ~",
Per ~"— *TCC*
317:4 gutter-snipe] gutter-/snipe
TSC, A1 guttersnipe *Per*
317:6 come *MS, TCC*] came *TSC*
317:10 Apocalypse *MS, TCC*] The
Apocalypse *Per, A1*
317:11 and *MS, TCC*] ~, *TSC*
317:11 once,] ~ *TCC*
317:12 The *Apocalypse MS, A1*] The
Apocalypse *TCC*
317:13 Now *MS, TCC*] ~, *TSC*
317:14 last *MS, TCC*] ~, *TSC*
317:15 West." *MS, A1*] ~". *TSC*
317:17 Dostoevsky *MS, TCC*]
Dostoievsky *TSC, A1*
317:18 Somewhere, *MS, TCC*] ~ *TSC*
317:19 brave] grave *A1*
317:20 Dostoevskian *MS, TCC*]
Dostoievskian *TSC, A1*
317:21 and *MS, TCC*] ~, *TSC*

317:22 or recanting *MS*, *TCC*] nor
       recanting *TSC*
317:23 jibing *MS*, *TCC*] jibbing *Per*
317:23 or criticism *MS*, *TCC*] nor
       criticism *TSC*
317:23 or pulling *MS*, *TCC*] nor
       pulling *TSC*
317:27 time,] ~ *TCC*
317:28 Tolstoy] Tolstoi *A1*
317:28 Dostoevsky *MS*, *TCC*]
       Dostoievsky, *TSC* Dostoievsky
       A1
317:29 Rozanov, *MS*, *TCC*] ~ *Per*
317:29 Van] van *TCC*
317:31 vast *MS*, *TCC*] ~, *TSC*
317:31 And *MS*, *TCC*] ~, *TSC*
317:32 civilisation *MS*, *TCC*]
       civilization *TSC*
317:32 it] ~? *Per*
317:37 him: *MS*, *TCC*] ~, *TSC*
318:1 and perhaps, *MS*, *TCC*] ~, ~,
       TSC ~, ~ *Per*
318:2 Tolstoy] Tolstoi *A1*
318:2 Dostoevsky *MS*, *TCC*]
       Dostoievsky *TSC*, *A1*
318:4 all.— *MS*, *TCC*] ~.” . . . *TSC*,
       A1 ~” . . . . *Per*
318:4 But *MS*, *TCC*] “~ *TSC*, *A1*
318:4 (in *MS*, *TCC*] [in *TSC*
318:5 Dostoevsky) *MS*, *TCC*]
       Dostoievsky] *TSC* Dostoievsky]
       Per Dostoievsky) *A1*
318:7 phallus *MS*, *TCC*] ~, *TSC*
318:7 flows.—”] ~.” *TSC*, *TCC* ~”.
       Per
318:10 is positive] are positive *A1*
318:11 Then again *MS*, *TCC*] ~, ~,
       TSC
318:11 Russianise *MS*, *TCC*]
       Russianize *TSC*, *A1*

318:12 himself, *MS*, *TCC*] ~ *TSC*
318:13 “dual.” *MS*, *A1*] “~”. *TSC*
       ‘~’. *TCC*
318:14 dual, *MS*, *TCC*] ~ *TSC*
318:14 Dostoevskian *MS*, *TCC*]
       Dostoievskian *TSC*, *A1*
318:15 pose: *MS*, *TCC*] ~; *TSC*
318:15 Mary Mary quite contrary] ~,
       ~ ~ ~ *TSC* Mary-Mary-
       quite-contrary *TCC*
318:16 business.—] ~. *A1*
318:21 discord.” *MS*, *TCC*] ~”. *Per*
318:22 that, is] ~ ~ *Per* ~ ~, *TCC*
318:25 vice versa] *vice versa TSC*
318:25 saints *MS*, *TCC*] ~, *TSC*,
       A1
318:31 *soul*] soul *TCC*
318:32 cretin *MS*, *TCC*] *crétin Per*
318:34 russianising *MS*, *TCC*]
       Russianizing *TSC*, *A1*
318:36 interesting, *MS*, *TCC*] ~ *TSC*
318:37 russianising *MS*, *TCC*]
       Russianizing *TSC*, *A1*
318:39 importance, *MS*, *TCC*] ~ *TSC*
318:40 Dostoevsky *MS*, *TCC*]
       Dostoievsky *TSC*, *A1*
319:1 and *MS*, *TCC*] ~, *TSC*
319:1 rightly”,] ~,” *A1*
319:2 Dostoevsky *MS*, *TCC*]
       Dostoievsky *TSC*, *A1*
319:3 Dostoevsky *MS*, *TCC*]
       Dostoievsky *TSC*, *A1*
319:5 Our *MS*, *TCC*] our *TSC*
319:5 *Motifs*;] ~. *TSC*
319:6 matters, *MS*, *TCC*] ~
       TSC
319:6 future. *TCC*] future. / D. H.
       Lawrence {Lawrence. *TSC*}
       MS future. / D. H.
       LAWRENCE. *Per*

Review of *The Peep Show*

MS = Roberts E307c
MSC = Typesetter's corrections to *MS*
Per = *Calendar*, iv (July 1927)
A1 = *Phoenix* (Viking)

323:1 When I *Ed.*] The Peep
Show.—By Walter Wilkinson.
/ (Bles) 10/6 net. / When I
MS The Peep Show.—by
Walter Wilkinson. / *Bles. 10/6
net.* / When I *MSC THE
PEEP SHOW. By WALTER
WILKINSON. Bles, 10/6 net.*
/ When I *Per The Peep Show,*
by Walter Wilkinson / When
I *A1*

323:7 document] documents *A1*
323:16 document," *MS, A1*] ~", *Per*
323:20 *makes*] makes *A1*
323:24 just] *Om. A1*
323:26 means,] ~ *Per*
323:29 nice, modern] ~ ~ *A1*
323:29 "News from Nowhere"] *News
from Nowhere Per*
323:32 people." *MS, A1*] ~". *Per*
324:1 Dostoevsky] Dostoievsky *Per*
324:2 works] Works *Per*
324:2 Shakspeare] Shakespeare *Per*
324:2 volume," *MS, A1*] ~", *Per*
324:3 puppet show *MS, A1*]
puppet-show *Per*
324:4 Shakspeare] Shakespeare *Per*
324:5 Shakspeare] Shakespeare *Per*
324:8 little] ~! *Per see notes*
324:10 beery] ~, *Per*
324:10 Punch:] ~; *Per*
324:12 two-months'] two months' *A1*
324:14 back,] ~ *Per*
324:17 And] ~, *Per*
324:22 *juste.*—] ~. *Per*
324:25 breakers." *MS, A1*] ~". *Per*
324:27 sea-side] seaside *A1*
324:27 night-school] night school *Per*
324:28 pleasure",] ~," *A1*
324:28 air",] ~," *A1*
324:30 wall",] ~," *A1*
324:30 (sic)] [*sic*] *Per* [sic] *A1*
324:31 shore",] ~," *A1*
324:36 nice",] ~," *A1*
324:37 you,] ~ *Per*
324:40 breakers." *MS, A1*] ~". *Per*
325:2 "nice." *MS, A1*] "~". *Per*

325:3 But, still . . . nice. *Per*] *Om. MS*
325:4 So *Per*] Yet *MS*
325:5 save] ~, *Per*
325:7 *just.*—] ~. *Per*
325:8 'ism',] '~,' *A1*
325:13 (sic)] [*sic*] *Per* [sic] *A1*
325:21 smoky] smoking *Per*
325:21 valleys;] ~, *Per*
325:29 Luckily] "~ *Per*
325:32 die.—"] ~." *A1*
325:33 "philosophy," *MS, A1*] "~",
Per
325:35 And] ~, *Per*
325:37 vivid. *P* The] vivid. The *Per*
325:39 realisation] realization *Per*
326:2 more ordinary *Per*] less vital
MS
326:5 starts out by being *Per*] is
MS
326:7 day's *Per*] days *MS*
326:10 fifteen-shillings] fifteen
shillings *Per*
326:11 pay,] ~ *Per*
326:11 And you can live on it. *Per*]
Om. MS
326:15 Even on their holidays. *Per*]
Om. MS
326:15 in] to *Per*
326:16 cinema] kinema *Per see notes*
326:21 determination —] ~ *Per*
326:23 wheer 'st] wheer'st *Per
see notes*
326:24 admirable—but—.] ~, ~ . . .
A1
326:27 puppet-showman] puppet
showman *Per*
326:30 puppet-showman] puppet
showman *Per*
326:32 "nice",] "~," *A1*
326:33 Jove] jove *Per*
326:34 chars-a-bancs] chars-à-bancs
Per
326:34 cinemas] kinemas *Per*
326:38 char-a-bancs] chars-à-bancs
Per
327:8 holidaymaking]
holiday-making *A1*

327:10   lead." *MS, A1*] ~". *Per*
327:11   nasty to you] *nasty to you Per*
327:12   Even though . . .the trip. *Per*]
         Om. *MS*
327:14   songful] ~, *Per*

327:15   nice] ~, *Per*
327:16   "nice." *A1*] "nice." / D H
         Lawrence {D H LAWRENCE
         MSC} *MS* "nice". / D. H.
         LAWRENCE. *Per*

Review of *The Social Basis of Consciousness*

MS = Roberts E366a
Per = *Bookman* (New York), 66 (November 1927)
TCC = Roberts E366b
A1 = *Phoenix* (Viking)

331:1   The Social Basis of
         Consciousness by Trigant
         Burrow *Ed.*] The Social Basis
         of Consciousness by Trigant
         Burrow / Kegan Paul. 12/6
         net *MS* A NEW THEORY
         OF NEUROSES / By
         D. H. Lawrence / THE
         SOCIAL BASIS OF
         CONSCIOUSNESS. *By
         Trigant Burrow. Harcourt,
         Brace. $3.75 Per THE SOCIAL
         BASIS OF
         CONSCIOUSNESS / by
         Trigant Burrow. / Kegan Paul.
         12/6 net. TCC The Social Basis
         of Consciousness, by Trigant
         Burrow A1*
331:2   Dr] DR. *Per* Dr. *TCC*
331:2   psychoanalyst] psychologist
         TCC
331:9   Dr] ~. *Per*
331:9   psychiatrists *MS, A1*]
         psychologists *TCC*
331:11   honest, all] honest: all *TCC*
331:14   experience] experiences *TCC*
331:17   Dr] ~. *Per*
331:17   ago, *MS, TCC*] ~ *Per*
331:18   psychoanalyst *MS, A1*]
         psycho-analyst *TCC*
331:19   gradually,] ~ *TCC*
331:20   wrong, in *MS, TCC*] wrong,
         both in *Per*
331:21   psychoanalysis *MS, A1*]
         psycho-analysis *TCC*

331:21   both *MS, A1*] Om. *Per,*
         TCC
331:23   methods, *MS, TCC*] ~ *Per*
331:23   working?] ~. *TCC*
331:25   Dr] ~. *Per*
331:25   Burrow's *Per*] Burrows *MS*
331:27   his criticism] the criticism
         TCC
331:27   Dr] ~. *Per*
331:28   experience] experiences *TCC*
331:31   experience] ~, *Per*
331:32   incest-motive *MS, A1*]
         incest-notion *TCC*
331:33   Dr] ~. *Per*
331:34   repression *MS, A1*] expression
         TCC
332:1   image substitution *MS, TCC*]
         image-substitution *Per, A1*
332:4   psychoanalyst *MS, A1*]
         psycho-analyst *TCC*
332:5   business, *MS, TCC*] ~ *Per*
332:7   motive *MS, TCC*] ~, *Per*
332:11   incest motive] incest-motive
         TCC
332:20   psychoanalytic *MS, A1*]
         psycho-/analytic *Per*
         psycho-analytic *TCC*
332:21   If] ~, *TCC*
332:21   Dr] ~. *Per*
332:24   one, *MS, TCC*] ~ *Per*
332:25   "theory." *MS, A1*] "~".
         Per
332:25   Dr] ~. *Per*
332:26   conclusion,] ~ *Per*
332:28   and also] ~, ~ *TCC*

332:29 "separateness,"] "~" *Per*
332:32 Suddenly, *MS*, *TCC*] ~ *Per*
332:34 —"It *MS*, *TCC*] "It *Per*, *A1*
332:39 spell-bound] spellbound *TCC* spell-/ bound *A1*
333:5 'created,' *MS*, *A1*] '~', *Per*
333:6 God.' *MS*, *A1*] ~'. *Per*
333:6 For] ~, *TCC*
333:7 agelong] age-long *Per*
333:8 *aware.*"—] *aware.*" *Per*, *A1* aware." *TCC*
333:9 "That *MS*, *TCC*] "~ *Per*, *A1*
333:10 *selves.*"— *MS*, *TCC*] ~." *Per*, *A1*
333:13 aloneness, *MS*, *TCC*] ~ *Per*
333:14 individuality; *MS*, *TCC*] ~: *Per*
333:16 Dr] ~. *TCC*
333:16 preconscious *MS*, *A1*] pre-conscious *TCC*
333:17 Dr] ~. *Per*
333:18 fellow men] fellowmen *TCC* fellow-men *A1*
333:22 Dr] ~. *Per*
333:26 another,] ~ *Per*
333:29 ego-centric *MS*, *TCC*] egocentric *Per*, *A1*
333:36 Dr] ~. *Per*
333:37 he made . . . himself. Then *MS*, *A1*] *Om.* *TCC*
333:40 picture,] ~: *TCC*
334:1 civilisation *MS*, *TCC*] civilization *Per*, *A1*
334:11 society"— *MS*, *A1*] ~".— *TCC*
334:13 strictly, *MS*, *A1*] ~ *TCC*
334:18 neurosis] ~, *TCC*
334:21 adding-to *MS*, *TCC*] adding to *Per*, *A1*
334:22 set *MS*, *TCC*] all *Per*
334:24 great mass *MS*, *TCC*] ~ ~, *Per*, *A1*
334:27 incest-bogey] incest bogey *TCC* incest-bogy *A1*
334:27 bogey] bogy *A1*

334:30 Dr] ~. *Per*
334:30 Burrow's *Per*] Burrows *MS*
334:33 himself,] ~; *TCC*
334:39 "normals." *MS*, *A1*] "~". *Per*
335:1 then,] ~ *Per*
335:4 bolshevist] Bolshevist *A1*
335:5 civilisation *MS*, *TCC*] civilization *Per*, *A1*
335:14 contrary, *MS*, *TCC*] ~ *Per*
335:16 society *MS*, *TCC*] ~, *Per*
335:18 absolute, *MS*, *TCC*] ~ *Per*
335:21 today *MS*, *TCC*] to-day *Per*
335:25 St] ~. *Per*
335:26 always, *MS*, *TCC*] ~ *Per*
335:30 up." *MS*, *A1*] ~". *Per*
335:32 Dr] ~. *Per*
335:32 "societal consciousness," *MS*, *A1*] "Societal consciousness" *Per* "societal consciousness", *TCC*
335:33 image consciousness *MS*, *TCC*] "image-consciousness" *Per*
335:35 exist,] ~; *TCC*
335:39 narcistic] narcissistic *A1* *see notes*
335:39 normal] ~, *A1*
336:4 idol: *MS*, *Per*] ~, *TCC*
336:4 no me! *MS*, *TCC*] norm! *Per*, *A1*
336:5 bird *MS*, *TCC*] ~, *Per*, *A1*
336:5 it sings *MS*, *TCC*] ~ ~, *Per*, *A1*
336:8 isolation *MS*, *TCC*] ~, *Per*
336:10 bogeys] bogies *A1*
336:13 Dr] ~. *Per*
336:15 possible, *MS*, *TCC*] ~ *Per*
336:17 men, *MS*, *TCC*] ~ *Per*
336:25 Dr] ~. *Per*
336:25 feel *MS*, *TCC*] feel that *Per*
336:26 résumés] *résumés* *Per*
336:27 "criticising" *MS*, *TCC*] "criticizing" *Per*, *A1*
336:29 life. *Per*] life. / D. H. Lawrence *MS*

Review of *The Station*, etc.

MS = Roberts E377.5c
Per = *Vogue* (8 August 1928)
A1 = *Phoenix* (Viking)

339:1   Review for Vogue *Ed.*] Review
for Vogue – by D. H. Lawrence
/ The Station: Athos,
Treasures and Men. by Robert
Byron / (Duckworth. 18/- net)
/ England and the Octopus –
by Clough Williams-Ellis /
(Geoffrey Bles. 5/- net) /
Comfortless Memory. by
Maurice Baring (Heinemann
6/- net) / Ashenden, or The
British Agent. by W. Somerset
Maugham / (Heinemann –
7/6) *MS* TURNING OVER
NEW LEAVES / Concerning
a Sacred Mountain, a
Threatened Island / And Two
New Works of Fiction by
Famous Novelists / By D. H.
LAWRENCE *Per The Station:
Athos, Treasures and Men*, by
Robert Byron; *England and the
Octopus*, by Clough
Williams-Ellis; *Comfortless
Memory*, by Maurice Baring;
Ashenden, by W. Somerset
Maugham *A1*

339:2   Athos is *MS, A1*] The books
reviewed below are: *The
Station: Athos, Treasures and
Men*, by Robert Byron
(Duckworth, 18s.); *England
and the Octopus*, by Clough
Williams-Ellis (Geoffrey Bles,
5s.); *Comfortless Memory*, by
Maurice Baring (Heinemann,
6s.); *Ashenden, or the British
Agent*, by W. Somerset
Maugham (Heinemann, 7s.
6d.). / Athos is *Per*

339:2   Mr] ∼. *Per*
339:5   Mr] ∼. *Per*

339:14   then, with] ∼ ∼ *A1*
339:19   utterly-learned] utterly learned
A1
339:20   Mr] ∼. *Per*
339:25   visited; *MS, A1*] ∼, *Per*
339:32   to] *to Per*
339:34   earnest,] ∼ *Per*
340:5   paradise] Paradise *Per*
340:10   boil *MS, A1*] ∼, *Per*
340:15   though *MS, A1*] ∼, *Per*
340:15   course *MS, A1*] ∼, *Per*
340:20   state *MS, A1*] a state *Per*
340:21   stomachs. *P* Then *MS, A1*]
stomachs. Then *Per*
340:24   world. *P* For *MS, A1*] world.
For *Per*
340:25   Mr] ∼. *Per*
340:33   —But] ∼ *Per*
340:34   Mr] ∼. *Per*
340:35   Mr] ∼. *Per*
340:36   elder:] ∼; *Per*
340:36   least *MS, A1*] ∼, *Per*
340:36   Mr] ∼. *Per*
340:37   Octopus *MS, A1*] octopus
Per
341:1   England.—] ∼. *Per*
341:2   Mr] ∼. *Per*
341:2   Oh] ∼, *Per*
341:5   Mr] ∼. *Per*
341:10   mark,] ∼ *Per*
341:10   —But] ∼ *Per*
341:12   Mr] ∼. *Per*
341:15   countryside] country-side *A1*
341:16   —And] ∼ *Per*
341:16   that. *P* And *MS, A1*] that. *P*
SINCERITY AND
HUMOUR *P* And *Per*
341:17   excellent: *MS, A1*] ∼, *Per*
341:18   even] and even *Per*
341:19   it, whether *MS, A1*] ∼ ∼ *Per*
341:21   countryside] country-side *A1*
341:25   this, *MS, A1*] ∼ *Per*

341:27   Mr] ~. *Per*
341:27   eye] age *Per*
341:32   picture. *P* Mr] picture. *P* SIX
         QUESTIONS *P* Mr. *Per*
         picture. *P* Mr. *A1*
341:33   Williams-Ellis']
         Williams-Ellis's *Per*
341:37   Mr] ~. *Per*
341:40   factory-chimneys *MS, A1*]
         factory chimneys *Per*
342:5   seriously, *MS, A1*] ~ *Per*
342:8   Mr] ~. *Per*
342:8   book *MS, A1*] ~, *Per*
342:8   Memory*MS, A1*] ~, *Per*
342:11   Mr] ~. *Per*
342:13   Mr] ~. *Per*
342:14   Reality *MS, A1*] reality *Per*
342:14   Mr] ~. *Per*
342:20   to!! *MS, A1*] ~! *Per*
342:21   comfortably-married]
         comfortably married *Per*
342:25   comfortably-married]
         comfortably married *Per*
342:26   funny. *P* Mr] funny. *P*
         "ASHENDEN" *P* Mr. *Per*
         funny. *P* Mr. *A1*

342:27   Mr] ~.
342:29   war] War *A1*
342:32   Mr . . . Mr . . . Mr] ~. . . .
         ~. . . . ~. *Per*
342:34   seriously, with *MS, A1*] ~ ~
         Per
342:34   out-of-date] out of date
         Per
342:36   Mr] ~. *Per*
342:39   clever women] women *Per*
342:40   tricksters,] ~ *Per*
343:1   déclassé] *déclassé Per* declassé
         A1
343:3   Colonel] colonel *A1*
343:11   Mr . . . Mr] ~. . . . ~. *Per*
343:12   Ashenden. *P* But *MS, A1*]
         Ashenden. *P* A SPLENDID
         OBSERVER *P* But *Per*
343:13   Mr] ~. *Per*
343:15   excellently-observed]
         excellently observed *Per*
343:16   Mr] ~. *Per*
343:18   humour",] ~," *Per*
343:19   stories, *MS, A1*] ~. *Per*
343:20   in which . . . rancid. *MS, A1*]
         Om. Per

Review of *Fallen Leaves*

MS = Roberts E124a
TS = Roberts E124b
Per = *Everyman*, 23 January 1930
TCC = Roberts E124c
A1 = *Phoenix* (Viking)

347:1   *Fallen Leaves.* by *V. V. Rozanov*
         Ed.] *Fallen Leaves. by V. V.*
         Rozanov / translated from the
         Russian by S. S. Koteliansky /
         Limited Edition of 750 copies.
         The Mandrake Press *MS*
         FALLEN LEAVES / by V. V.
         Rozanov / Reviewed by *D. H.*
         LAWRENCE. / Translated
         from the Russian by S. S.
         Koteliansky / (Limited Edition
         of 750 copies. / The Mandrake
         Press) *TS* A REMARKABLE

         RUSSIAN / By D. H.
         LAWRENCE *Per* FALLEN
         LEAVES. By V. V. Rozanov. /
         Translated from the Russian by
         S. S. Koteliansky. / Limited
         Edition of 750 copies. / The
         Mandrake Press. *TCC* Fallen
         Leaves, by V. V. Rozanov *A1*
347:5   Leaves *MS, TCC*] ~, which has
         now been translated from the
         Russian by S. S. Koteliansky
         (Mandrake Press, 21s.) *Per*
347:7   quiet *MS, Per*] quite *TS*

347:9   western *MS, TCC*] Western
        TS
347:10 something *MS, TCC*]
        Om. TS
347:12 Rozanov is . . . [347:21]
        esteemed books *MS, TCC*]
        Om. Per
347:12 Tchekov] Chekhov *A1*
347:13 Artzybashev, *MS, A1*]
        Artzybasher, *TS* Artzybasher
        TCC
347:13 Gorki] Gorky *A1*
347:13 Merejkovsky] Merejkovski
        A1
347:15 Dostoevsky's] Dostoievsky's
        A1
347:16 connection] connexion *A1*
347:17 Dostoevskian] Dostoievskian
        A1
347:25 the reader *MS, TCC*]
        thereafter *Per*
347:26 night *MS, TCC*] Night *TS*
347:26 work *MS, TCC*] Work *TS*
347:26 In the W.C. *MS, TCC*] etc. *Per*
        in the w.c. *A1*
347:27 systematisation *MS, TCC*]
        systematization *Per, A1*
347:29 Anyhow] ~, *TS*
347:30 himself,] ~ — *Per*
347:30 *moment MS, TCC*] *movement*
        TS
347:34 secret,] ~ *Per*
348:4   The description . . . [348:12]
        literariness)." *MS, TCC*] *Om.*
        Per
348:4   whole] ~, *TCC*
348:5   himself,] ~; *TCC*
348:8   Lord, *MS, TCC*] ~ *TS*
348:10 liar,] ~ *TCC*
348:11 world;] ~, *TCC*
348:12 literariness)." *MS, TCC*] ~)".
        TS
348:14 *literary. MS, TCC*] ~! *Per*
348:14 "The *MS, TCC*] *P* The *Per*
348:16 'My Friend's' *MS, TCC*]
        "My Friend's" *Per*
348:19 not *MS, TCC*] *Om. TS*

348:19 There *MS, TCC*] *P* There *Per*
348:22 if *MS, TCC*] far as if *TS*
348:23 "lying", *MS, TCC*] "~," *Per,*
        A1
348:28 Stavrogins] ~, *TCC*
348:28 Dostoevsky] Dostoievsky *A1*
348:30 Tchekov] Chekhov *A1*
348:34 today *MS, TCC*] to-day *Per*
348:37 "sin." *MS, Per*] "~". *TS*
348:37 a *MS, TCC*] *Om. Per*
348:38 love,] ~ *TCC*
348:39 Friend." *MS, Per*] ~". *TS*
349:3   "pity." *MS, Per*] "~". *TS*
349:3   civilisation *MS, TCC*]
        civilization *Per, A1*
349:3   compassion," *MS, Per*] ~",
        TS
349:6   Dostoevskian] Dostoievskian
        A1
349:7   wife. There *MS, TCC*] wife. *P*
        There *Per*
349:8   liked *MS, TCC*] tried *TS*
349:9   affection. *MS, TCC*] ~! *Per*
349:9   Today *MS, TCC*] To-day *Per*
349:10 Dostoevsky] Dostoievsky *A1*
349:10 writes. Which *MS, TCC*]
        writes, which *TS*
349:11 Dostoevsky] Dostoievsky *A1*
349:12 "today," *MS, A1*] "~", *TS,*
        TCC "to-day," *Per*
349:13 "today." *MS, A1*] "~". *TS,*
        TCC "to-day." *Per*
349:13 So *MS, TCC*] *P* So *Per*
349:14 paralysis,] ~ *TCC*
349:15 "today", *MS, TCC*] "to-day,"
        Per "today," *A1*
349:16 end, *MS, TCC*] ~ *TS*
349:19 all:] ~, *TCC*
349:20 seem, *MS, TCC*] ~ *TS*
349:21 very *MS, TCC*] *Om. TS*
349:23 And *MS, TCC*] ~, *TS*
349:23 After all . . . [349:26] false,
        repulsive. *MS, TCC*] *Om. Per*
349:23 Dostoevskian] Dostoievskian
        A1
349:28 régime *MS, Per*] regime *TS,*
        A1

349:29   Western] western *A1*
349:37   civilisation *MS, TCC*]
         civilization *Per, A1*
349:38   Islanders: *MS, TCC*] Islander:
         TS Islander; *Per*
349:39   Once *MS, Per*] One *TS*
349:40   civilising *MS, TCC*] civilizing
         Per, A1
350:1   civilising *MS, TCC*] civilizing
         Per, A1
350:6   today *MS, TCC*] to-day *Per*
350:7   His attitude . . . [350:10] were
         going. *MS, TCC*] *Om. Per*
350:9   "conservatism," *MS, A1*] "~",
         TS, TCC
350:11   already,] ~; *TCC*
350:12   "dreaminess." "At *MS, A1*]
         "~". "~ *TS, TCC* "~": /
         "~ *Per*
350:15   I] "~ *TCC*
350:16   And] "~ *TCC*
350:17   For] "~ *TCC*
350:18   From] "~ *TCC*
350:20   Friend—[his wife]—and]
         Friend—his wife—and
         Per Friend [his wife]—and
         TCC
350:22   P In] In *TSP* "In *TCC*

350:23   And] But *TS* "And *TCC*
350:23   ('sin'). *MS, Per*] ['~']. *A1*
350:25   me."— *MS, TCC*] ~." *Per,*
         A1
350:26   "dreaminess" *MS, TCC*] "~",
         TS "~," *Per*
350:27   nothing] ~, *TCC*
350:27   "anything." *MS, Per, A1*] "~".
         TS, TCC
350:30   So that's . . . [350:31] being
         damned. *MS, TCC*] *Om. Per*
350:32   there *MS, TCC*] then *TS*
350:32   Russian, *MS, TCC*] ~ *Per*
350:33   débâcle] debacle *Per*
         débâcle TCC
350:34   apparently] ~, *A1*
350:35   sympathise *MS, TCC*]
         sympathize *Per, A1*
350:37   "dreaminess", *MS, TCC*] "~,"
         Per, A1
351:1   little] ~, *TCC*
351:5   "civilisation" *MS, TCC*]
         "civilization" *Per, A1*
351:6   "education." *Per, A1*]
         "education." D. H. Lawrence
         MS "education". / D. H.
         Lawrence *TS* "education".
         TCC

Review of *Art-Nonsense and Other Essays*

MS = Roberts E24.5a
Per = *Book Collector's Quarterly*, xii (Oct.–Nov. 1933)
TCC = Roberts E24.5b
A1 = *Phoenix* (Viking)

355:1   Eric Gill's "Art Nonsense."
         Ed.] Eric Gill's "Art
         Nonsense." / by D H
         Lawrence. (*at bottom of page*)
         Art Nonsense and Other
         Essays by Eric Gill (Cassell
         Walterson) 21/- net one guinea
         MS D. H. LAWRENCE /
         ERIC GILL'S 'ART
         NONSENSE' / Lawrence
         wrote this unfinished review a few
         days before he died. The book

         interested him, and he agreed
         with much in it. Then he got tired
         of writing and I persuaded him
         not to go on. It is the last thing he
         wrote.—Frieda Lawrence.
         Per Eric Gill's "ART
         NONSENSE". By D. H.
         Lawrence. *TCC Art Nonsense*
         and Other Essays, by Eric Gill
         A1
355:2   "Art Nonsense and Other
         Essays,"] *Art Nonsense and*

Other Essays, Per, A1 "Art Nonsense and Other Essays", TCC

355:3 handsomely printed MS, A1] handsomely-printed Per

355:3 reads: "Art Nonsense and Other Nonsense,"] reads "Art Nonsense and Other Nonsense", Per reads: *Art Nonsense and Other Nonsense* A1

355:4 O MS, TCC] 'O' Per "O" A1

355:4 Mr] ~. Per

355:9 Mr] ~. Per

355:12 word: maddening MS, TCC] ~, ~ Per

355:13 pub.] ~ Per

355:13 *argefying MS, TCC*] 'argefying' Per

355:15 Mr] ~. Per

355:15 craftsman, MS, TCC] ~ Per

355:17 pub. MS, TCC] ~ Per, A1

355:18 *moral MS, TCC*] moral Per

355:21 Mr] ~. Per

355:21 mediaeval MS, TCC] medieval Per, A1

355:22 Apology] "~" A1

355:23 *Slavery and Freedom MS, TCC*] 'Slavery and Freedom' Per "Slavery and Freedom" A1

355:23 *Essential Perfection MS, TCC*] 'Essential Perfection' Per "Essential Perfection" A1

355:24 *A Grammar of Industry MS, TCC*] 'A Grammar of Industry' Per "A Grammar of Industry" A1

355:24 *Westminster Cathedral MS, TCC*] 'Westminster Cathedral' Per "Westminster Cathedral" A1

355:25 *Dress TCC*] Dress MS 'Dress' Per "Dress" A1

355:25 *Songs without Clothes Ed.*] Songs without Clothes MS 'Songs Without Clothes' Per

Songs Without Clothes TCC "Songs without Clothes" A1

355:25 *Of Things Necessary and UnnecessaryMS, TCC*] 'Of Things Necessary and Unnecessary' Per "Of Things Necessary and Unnecessary" A1

355:26 *Quae ex Veritate et Bono MS, TCC*] 'Quae ex Veritate et Bono' Per "Quae ex Veritate et Bono" A1

355:27 fourth] ~, Per

355:27 *Art Nonsense MS, TCC*] 'Art Nonsense' Per "Art Nonsense" A1

355:28 "Essential Perfection" MS, TCC] 'Essential Perfection' Per

355:29 "Songs without Clothes" MS, TCC] 'Songs Without Clothes' Per

355:30 *Grammar of Industry?,*] 'Grammar of Industry'? Per Grammar of Industry? TCC "Grammar of Industry," A1

355:30 has MS, TCC] is Per

355:31 words.] ~? A1

355:33 Mr] ~. Per

355:33 Gill's Per] Gills MS

355:33 *Apology MS, TCC*] 'Apology' Per "Apology" A1

355:33 "Two MS, TCC] '~ Per

356:1 'art MS, TCC] "~ Per

356:2 making' MS, TCC] ~', Per

356:2 'art MS, TCC] "~ Per

356:2 creating.'—"] ~.'" Per ~.'" TCC

356:3 'Art] "~ TCC

356:4 making.'] ~." TCC

356:5 *Sally in our Alley MS, TCC*] 'Sally in our Alley' Per "Sally in our Alley" A1

356:6 making." MS, A1] ~'. Per ~". TCC

356:7 creating." MS, A1] ~'. Per ~". TCC

356:8 hobnobbing] hob-nobbing *A1*

356:10 Mr] ~. *Per*

356:11 over: "Upon] over, 'upon *Per* over, "Upon *TCC* over, "upon *A1*

356:11 contrary," *MS, A1*] ~' *Per* ~" *TCC*

356:12 "on *MS, TCC*] '~ *Per*

356:12 contrary": his] ~', ~ *Per* ~", ~ *TCC* ~," ~ *A1*

356:12 *Essential Perfection*] 'Essential Perfection' *Per* Essential Perfection *TCC* "Essential Perfection" *A1*

356:13 "God *MS, TCC*] '~ *Per*

356:14 he] He *TCC*

356:14 absolute] ~, *Per*

356:18 Charity—"] ~'— *Per* ~"— *TCC*

356:21 continental] Continental *Per*

356:21 fashion;] ~·? *Per*

356:22 pub. *MS, TCC*] ~ *Per, A1*

356:25 Mr] ~. *Per*

356:26 words *MS, TCC*] word *Per*

356:28 Catholics. As protestants] Catholics to Protestants *Per*

356:31 and little *MS, TCC*] and the little *Per*

356:33 Catholic,] ~; *Per*

356:34 Mr] ~ *Per*

356:35 *Holy Church MS, TCC*] 'Holy Church' *Per* "Holy Church" *A1*

356:35 *a good R. C. MS, TCC*] 'a good R. C.' *Per* "a good R. C." *A1*

356:35 easily] ~, *Per*

356:38 grumble] preamble *Per*

356:38 Mr] ~. *Per*

356:39 language, *MS, TCC*] ~ *Per*

357:1 Mr] ~. *Per*

357:4 Mr] ~. *Per*

357:6 Slavery and Freedom *MS, TCC*] 'Slavery and Freedom' *Per* "Slavery and Freedom" *A1*

357:7 "That *MS, TCC*] *P* ~ *Per*

357:8 time and *MS, TCC*] ~, ~ *Per*

357:11 That] "~ *TCC*

357:14 God."—] ~. *P Per* ~." *TCC*

357:16 Whitehead *MS, TCC*] ~, *Per*

357:17 God," *MS, A1*] ~', *Per* ~", *TCC*

357:20 "To *MS, TCC*] '~ *Per*

357:20 God" *MS, TCC*] ~' *Per*

357:26 Here then *MS, TCC*] ~, ~ *Per, A1*

357:26 Mr] ~. *Per*

357:31 "The *MS, TCC*] *P* ~ *Per*

357:34 free." *MS, TCC*] ~. *Per*

357:35 "There *MS, TCC*] ~ *Per*

357:35 Will] will *Per*

357:37 The] "~ *TCC*

357:37 freedom." *MS, TCC*] ~. *P Per*

357:38 Here *MS, TCC*] ~, *Per, A1*

357:38 "service of God" *MS, TCC*] '~ ~ ~' *Per*

357:39 alive *MS, TCC*] ~, *Per*

357:39 "will of God" *MS, TCC*] '~ ~ ~' *Per*

358:1 God *MS, TCC*] '~' *Per*

358:1 today *MS, TCC*] to-day *Per*

358:2 fetish-word *MS, TCC*] fetish word *Per*

358:3 Almighty *MS, A1*] almighty *TCC*

358:4 words. And *MS, TCC*] words, and *Per*

358:6 meaning, Strength *MS, TCC*] meaning, strength *Per* meaning: strength *A1*

358:6 glory *MS, TCC*] ~, *Per*

358:6 might *MS, TCC*] ~, *Per*

358:8 today *MS, TCC*] to-day *Per*

358:9 glory *MS, TCC*] ~, *Per*

358:9 honour *MS, TCC*] ~, *Per*

358:10 worship. And *MS, TCC*] worship; and *Per*

358:18 Mr] ~. *Per*

358:19 civilisation *MS, TCC*] civilization *Per, A1*

358:20 first, *MS, TCC*] ~ *Per*

358:20 &] and *Per*

358:21 Mr] ~. *Per*

358:28 glory *MS, TCC*] ~, *Per*

358:28 wisdom: *MS, TCC*] ∼; *Per*
358:29 "good" *MS, TCC*] '∼'
   Per
358:29 God. And *MS, TCC*] God,
   and *Per*
358:30 "good" *MS, TCC*] '∼' *Per*
358:31 Protestant church] Protestant
   Church *Per*
358:33 "faith" *MS, TCC*] '∼' *Per*
358:34 life] Life *Per*
358:35 Mr] ∼. *Per*
358:35 "work done well" *MS, TCC*]
   '∼ ∼ ∼' *Per*

358:35 "beauty," or] 'beauty'—or *Per*
   "beauty"—or *TCC*
358:36 "Beauty." *MS, A1*] "∼". *Per*
358:38 Why] ∼, *Per*
358:38 why] ∼, *Per*
358:40 definition.] ∼? *Per*
359:1 "Beauty *MS, TCC*] '∼ *Per*
359:1 relative," *MS, TCC*] ∼',
   Per
359:2 Mr] ∼. *Per*
359:2 Yes yes] ∼, ∼ *Per*
359:3 Mr] ∼. *Per*
359:4 carnal] casual *Per*

Introductory Note (version 1) to *Mastro-don Gesualdo*

MS = Roberts E231a
TS = Roberts E231b
TSC = Revisions in *TS*

365:1 Introductory Note.]
   INTRODUCTORY NOTE
   TS
365:2 in] at *TSC*
365:2 in] at *TSC*
365:4 village *MS, TSC*] Village
   TS
365:4 south-east] southeast *TSC*
365:9 early] last *TS*
365:20 *Eva*, 1873] *Eva* and *TSC*
365:21 *Reale*, 1873] *Reale* in *TSC*
365:21 *Eros*] and *ErosTSC*
365:22 Milan,] ∼ *TS*
365:22 *Campi*:] ∼; *TS*
365:31 for *MS, TSC*] you *TS*
366:3 surely] *Om.TS*
366:15 *compère*] *Compère TS*
366:15 *commère*] *Commère TS*
366:16 *Don TSC*] Don *MS*
366:17 respectable] respected *TS*
366:18 *Donna TSC*] Donna *MS*
366:19 *Don TSC*] Don *MS*

366:27 48] '48 *TS*
366:30 performed] *Om. TS*
366:35 *Tigre Reale* and *Eros*,] Tigre
   Reale and Eros *TS Tigre Reale*
   and *Eros TSC*
366:38 *broadside*] broadside
   TSC
367:4 revelation—] ∼. — *TS*
367:15 *Mastro-don Gesualdo Ed.*]
   Mastro-don Gesualdo *MS*
367:18 *I Malavoglia TSC*] I
   Malavoglia *MS*
367:22 percentage . . . *Ed.*] ∼ - - *MS*
367:23 well . . . *Ed.*] ∼ - - *MS*
367:25 *Mastro-don Gesualdo TSC*]
   Mastro-don Gesualdo *MS*
367:26 *Mastro-don Gesualdo TSC*]
   Mastro-don Gesualdo *MS*
367:26 And] and *TS*
367:29 goes— *Ed.*] goes— / Kandy.
   March 1922. D. H. Lawrence
   MS

Introduction (version 1) to *Mastro-don Gesualdo*

MS = Roberts E231e
TCC = Roberts E231f
A1 = *Phoenix* (Viking)

371:1 It seems] [*Mastro-don Gesualdo*, by Giovanni Verga] / It seems *A1*
371:4 "Romance",] "~" *TCC*
371:8 courses." *MS, A1*] ~". *TCC*
371:18 Leoncavallo's] Mascagni's *A1 see notes*
371:20 volume,] ~ *A1*
371:20 *Rusticane,*] ~ *A1*
371:23 Tchekov . . . Tchekov] Chekhov . . . Chekhov *A1*
371:24 depressing." *MS, A1*] ~". *TCC*
371:24 Tchekov] Chekhov *A1*
372:5 Matilde] Matilda *A1*
372:14 *Mastro-don Gesualdo MS, A1*] Mastro-don Gesualdo *TCC*
372:16 *una*] *Una TCC*
372:16 *Capinera MS, A1*] Capinera *TCC*
372:19 *una*] *Una TCC*
372:23 Dickens'] Dickens's *A1*
372:24 "ridiculous",] "~," *A1*
372:28 "gothic",] "~" *TCC* "Gothic" *A1*
372:28 Germanic *MS, A1*] germanic *TCC*
372:30 D'Annunzio] d'Annunzio *TCC*
372:31 up." *MS, A1*] ~". *TCC*
373:9 nineteenth century] nineteenth-century *TCC*
373:9 literature] ~, *A1*
373:19 onesided] one-sided *TCC*
373:19 therefore,] ~ *TCC*
373:28 woe-begone] woebegone *A1*
373:28 Lepage!] ~. *TCC*
373:32 per-cent] per cent *A1*
373:33 with the] with all the *TCC*
373:34 per-cent] per cent *TCC*
373:37 ever] even *TCC*
374:2 *Madame Bovary,*] Madame Bovary *TCC Madame Bovary A1*

374:7 "heroes",] "~," *A1*
374:9 Madame Bovary] *Madame Bovary TCC*
374:15 Shakspeare] Shakespeare *TCC*
374:15 Kings] kings *TCC*
374:16 princes,] ~ — *TCC*
374:30 spirit,] ~ *TCC*
374:40 Cavalleria Rusticana] *Cavalleria Rusticana TCC*
375:1 laborers] labourers *TCC*
375:5 and] ~, *TCC*
375:11 exemplars, and] exemplars. And *TCC*
375:11 cursèd] cursed *TCC*
375:16 to *MS, A1*] too *TCC*
375:28 course,] ~ *TCC*
375:28 coruscate] ~, *TCC*
375:30 Dostoevsky] Dostoievsky *A1*
375:30 Tchekov etc] ~ ~. *TCC* Chekhov, etc., *A1*
375:35 else!—] ~! *TCC*
375:36 Dostoevsky . . . Tchekov] Dostoievsky . . . Chekhov *A1*
375:36 nonsuch] nonesuch *A1*
376:10 exist.—] ~. *TCC*
376:16 *Mastro-don Gesualdo MS, A1*] Mastro-don Gesualdo *TCC*
376:26 setting:] ~, *TCC*
376:26 then] this *TCC*
377:2 of soul] of souls *TCC*
377:9 realise] realize *A1*
377:9 Singhalese] Cingalese *A1*
377:11 spiritualise] spiritualize *A1*
377:13 mediaeval] medieval *A1*
377:14 mediaevalism] medievalism *A1*
377:16 Kingdom] kingdom *A1*
377:18 consequently,] ~ *TCC*
377:22 Palermo,] ~ *TCC*
377:29 other] others *TCC*
377:30 "Americans".] "~." *A1*
377:35 night] the night *TCC*
377:40 oh] ~, *TCC*
378:12 countryside] ~, *A1*
378:16 life-long] lifelong *A1*
378:30 with: To] with "To *TCC*
378:30 be,—] ~", *TCC* ~," *A1*

Introduction (version 2) to *Mastro-don Gesualdo*

TS = Roberts E231g

385:12   it *Ed.*] in *TS*

Incomplete early version of 'Review of *The Peep Show*'

MS = Roberts E307a
MSC = Revisions in *MS*
TCC = Roberts E307b

401:1] but not] Review / of Puppet Show / Pages 1 & 2 / missing / but not *MSC* REVIEW OF "The Peep Show". / *(Pages 1 and 2 are missing)* / but not *TCC*
401:1   living"] ~ *TCC*
401:1   artist] "~ *TCC*
401:1   more?] ~". *TCC*
401:3   document,"] ~", *TCC*
401:4   life,"] ~", *TCC*
401:4   realm] values *TCC*
401:4   art."] ~". *TCC*
401:6   "ordinary,"] "~", *TCC*
401:6   author"] ~", *TCC*
401:7   life:] *Om. TCC*
401:7   "Oh] "~, *TCC*
401:16 puppet shows] puppet-shows *TCC*
401:16 Punch and Judy] Punch-and-Judy, *TCC*
401:16 shows with] ~, ~ *TCC*
401:29 char-a-bancs] char-à-bancs *TCC*
401:29 motor cars] motor-cars *TCC*

401:32 experience] experiences *TCC*
402:11 simple lifer] simple-lifer *TCC*
402:11 steaks,"] ~", *TCC*
402:11 camping out] camping-out *TCC*
402:15 pig-corpse."] ~". *TCC*
402:19 Shakspeare] Shakespeare *TCC*
402:19 volume,"] ~", *TCC*
402:20 puppet show] puppet-show *TCC*
402:21 Shakspeare] Shakespeare *TCC*
402:22 Shakspeare] Shakespeare *TCC*
402:25 "nice."] "~". *TCC*
402:28 puppet showman] puppet-showman *TCC*
402:35 "extraordinary."] "~". *TCC*
402:39 it's *Ed.*] its *MS* it is *TCC*
403:9   "nice."] "~". *TCC*
403:12 *ordinary*] ordinary *TCC*
403:22 clichés] *clichés TCC*
403:23 —"It] "~ *TCC*

Two incomplete early versions of 'Review of *The Station*, etc.'
Version 1

MS = Roberts E377.5a

407:2   Review for Vogue *Ed.*] Review for Vogue / by D H Lawrence. / England and the Octopus. by Clough Williams-Ellis. / (Geoffrey Bles. 5/- net) / Comfortless Memory by Maurice Baring. / (Heinemann 6/- net) / Ashenden, or The

British Agent by W. Somerset
Maugham / (Heinemann 7/6)
/ The Station.—Athos,
Treasures and Men. by Robert
Byron / (Duckworth 18/- net)
MS

407:10   phenomenon *Ed.*] phenomen
         MS
407:32   edifice: / 1. *Ed.*] edifice: 1 *MS*
408:12   chemist's *Ed.*] chemists *MS*

Version 2

MS = Roberts E377.5b

411:2   Athos *Ed.*] The Station: Athos,
        Treasures and Men / by
        Robert Byron (Duckworth
        18/-) / England and the
        Octopus / by Clough
        Williams-Ellis (Geoffrey Bles.
        5/- net) / Comfortless

Memory / by Maurice Baring
(Heinemann 6/- net) /
Ashenden, or The British
Agent / by W. Somerset
Maugham (Heinemann 7/6). /
Athos *MS*

Line-end hyphenation

Of the compound words which are hyphenated at the end of a line in this edition, only the following hyphenated forms should be retained in quotation.

24:22	self-approving	227:21	pro-German
29:30	peasant-farmer	240:8	highly-bred
32:26	blood-sympathy	240:36	triple-crowned
52:5	harbour-water	245:30	strong-bodied
54:14	red-haired	247:20	Ca-Ca-Caliban
57:34	dust-yellow	253:23	self-responsibly
58:4	church-dome	259:12	bastard-European
63:28	morally-indignant	267:34	school-teacher
66:9	self-destroying	271:9	sisterly-motherly
66:26	*mother-tongue*	271:19	school-teacher
76:35	re-wrote	273:3	love-song
89:33	bandaged-up	275:19	citizen-of-the-United-States
105:17	semi-barbaric	281:2	elderly-gentleman
114:26	sun-suffused	288:20	money-investment
120:3	will-to-forget	300:2	His-Most-Sacred-Majesty
124:10	Portland,-Oregon	300:10	four-legged
127:8	showing-off	300:37	swash-buckling
128:26	Christ-demand	307:19	self-consciousness
131:21	slightly-criminal	308:12	skin-deep
133:2	ever-renewed	308:16	Yankee-American
139:28	*Mastro-don*	310:13	close-ups
149:34	all-is-misery	316:17	self-probing
151:19	sympathy-suffering	316:27	ever-recurrent
152:6	soul-twisters	317:3	self-conscious
153:27	pack-mules	324:12	two-months'
164:13	brother-in-law	334:33	self-interest
165:21	Aci-Trezza	335:36	Self-seeking
169:17	greedily-selfish	340:31	honest-to-God
170:4	self-sacrificial	342:21	comfortably-married
170:20	will-lessness	374:32	treasure-of-the-humble
172:3	self-effacement	375:6	head-and-shoulders
197:29	off-hand	375:21	every-man-his-own-hero
204:7	bitter-blossom	378:16	love-affair
211:12	pest-smitten	382:16	sea-coast
216:3	sex-contact	386:14	all-is-misery
217:3	self-conscious	384:8	idea-germ
222:30	stink-bombs	387:10	pack-mules
223:29	profit-and-loss	402:31	free-lifers

A note on pounds, shillings and pence

Before decimalisation in 1971, the pound sterling (£) was the equivalent of 20 shillings (20/- or 20s). The shilling was the equivalent of 12 pence (12d). A price could therefore have three elements: pounds, shillings and pence (£, s, d). (The apparently anomalous 'd' is an abbreviation of the Latin *denarius*, but the other two terms were also originally Latin: the pound was *libra*; the shilling *solidus*.) Such a price might be written as £1 2s 6d or £1/2/6; this was spoken as 'one pound, two shillings and sixpence', or 'one pound two-and-six', or 'twenty-two and six'. Prices below a pound were written (for example) as 19s 6d, or 19/6, and spoken as 'nineteen shillings and sixpence' or 'nineteen and six'.

The penny was divided into two half-pence (pronounced 'ha'pence') and further divided into four farthings, but the farthing had minimal value and was mainly a tradesman's device for indicating a price fractionally below a shilling or pound. So 19/11³/₄ ('nineteen and elevenpence three farthings') produced a farthing's change from a pound, this change sometimes given as a tiny item of trade, such as a packet of pins.

The guinea was £1 1s 0d (one pound, one shilling) and was a professional man's unit for fees. A doctor would charge in guineas (so £5 5s 0d = 5 gns.). Half a guinea was 10s 6d or 10/6 (ten and six).

The coins used were originally of silver (later cupro-nickel) and copper, though gold coins for £1 (a sovereign) and 10s (half-sovereign) were still in use in Lawrence's time. The largest 'silver' coin in common use was the half-crown (two shillings and sixpence, or 2/6). A two-shilling piece was called a florin. Shillings, sixpences and threepences were the smaller sizes. The copper coins were pennies, half-pence (ha' pennies) and farthings.

Common everyday terms for money were 'quid' for a pound, 'half a crown', 'two bob' for a florin, 'bob' for a shilling (or shilling piece), 'tanner' for a sixpence (or sixpenny piece), 'threepenny-bit', and 'coppers' for pennies, half-pence or farthings.

The pound since 1971 has had 100 pence, distinguished from the old pennies by being abbreviated to 'p' instead of 'd'.

INDEX

INDEX OF LAWRENCE'S WORKS